Instruction and Technology

Instruction and Technology

Designs for Everyday Learning

Brad Mehlenbacher

The MIT Press
Cambridge, Massachusetts
London, England

For information about special quantity discounts, please email special_sales@mitpress.mit.edu

This book was set in Stone Sans and Stone Serif by Toppan Best-set Premedia Limited. Printed and bound in the United States of America.

Library of Congress Cataloging-in-Publication Data

Mehlenbacher, Brad.
Instruction and technology : designs for everyday learning / Brad Mehlenbacher.
    p. cm.
Includes bibliographical references and index.
ISBN 978-0-262-01394-9 (hardcover : alk. paper)
1. Education—Computer network resources. I. Title.
LB1044.87.M44 2010
371.33′4—dc22

                                                                          2009036080

10 9 8 7 6 5 4 3 2 1

This book is dedicated to Eleanor Dare and Frances Elizabeth.
I never had time for it when I was with them.

Contents

Preface

Several years after copublishing a quantitative study of the differences and similarities between face-to-face and Web-based instruction (Mehlenbacher, Miller, Covington, and Larsen 2000), I was offered a position as Associate Professor of Distance Learning in a College of Education and began a long-term investigation of peer-reviewed empirical research on Web-based instruction that fell under the broad area of instruction and learning with technology. Our 2000 study had strengthened my conviction that emerging technologies were forcing us to reevaluate traditional understandings of instruction and learning, a conviction that had grown out of a decade of research on how to design online information that helped users accomplish their goals using performance-based software. The challenges faced by the designers of error messages, help systems, print versus online reference materials, tutorials, and online communication environments were rapidly coming together in the form of contemporary Learning Management Systems (LMSs) and Web-based instructional environments.

At the same time, administrators, instructors, and research colleagues from distance education, instructional and educational technology, human–computer interaction, learning assessment, information design, and technical communication were encouraging me to pursue a line of research on instruction and learning with technology and distance teaching and learning. Their reasoning was that this was a burgeoning educational topic and that limited research existed on numerous issues in the area. Because our 2000 study had drawn on Felder's (1993) research on learning styles, I began with the plan of further elaborating on the relationship between learning styles and online versus face-to-face instruction. In contrast to my colleagues' perceptions that limited research existed on the subject, I was alarmed to find, instead of a dozen studies focusing on learning styles, hundreds of peer-reviewed articles from more disciplines than I could quickly identify.

Journals publishing peer-reviewed research articles related to learning styles included, for example, *Accounting and Finance, American Journal of Distance Education, British Journal of Educational Technology, British Medical Journal, Educational and Psychological Measurement, Educational Psychology, Educational Studies, Engineering Education,*

Human Relations, IEEE Transactions on Education, Instructional Science, Interacting with Computers, Journal of Asynchronous Learning Networks, Journal of College Student Development, Journal of College Science Teaching, Journal of Natural Resources and Life Sciences, Journal of Research on Technology in Education, Journal of the American Society for Information Science and Technology, Marketing Education Review, MIS Quarterly, New Directions for Teaching and Learning, Online Journal of Distance Learning Administration, Review of Educational Research, and the *Modern Language Journal.* Not only was I surprised by the quantity of articles that existed on a single topic related to Web-based instruction, I was also frustrated by the limited number of references between articles to prior research on learning styles. Indeed, an intense discussion about the validity of the construct in general was being carried out in several articles that few of the studies of learning styles even acknowledged.

Naively, I decided that a long-term, systematic "literature review" of research related to instruction and learning with technology was in order. At the very least, I would be able to characterize the numerous cross-disciplinary discussions going on related to the important subject. Over time, I imagined I would be able to map out the articles, fields, and disciplines publishing on the topic. Ideally, I would be able to articulate the most pressing research issues, questions, and challenges facing instructors, researchers, and students new to the area of instruction and learning with technology.

This book describes that process. Beginning with an overview of the transformative influences of technology on instruction and learning, the manuscript draws on research related to learning in work, leisure, and higher educational settings, highlights important topics related to instruction and learning with technology, sets out a general guide to multidisciplinary research related to the area, proposes a unified rhetorical design perspective toward the design and evaluation of instruction and learning with technology, reviews more than a dozen models of both face-to-face and online teaching and learning, proposes a framework for everyday instructional situations, and summarizes some implications related to design and evaluation and to new understandings of space and time. Most importantly, I hope this manuscript encourages and enlivens meaningful dialogue among researchers interested in instruction and learning with technology by providing them with a common framework for characterizing, understanding, describing, and evaluating the complex relationship between technology, learning, and instruction.

Introduction

There is no going back. The traditional classroom has been transformed.
—e-Testimony to the Web-Based Education Commission (2000, p. 1)

There is so much to talk about and to build—let us begin.
—David Durlach (1997, p. 249)

The primary goal of this book is to outline the accelerated and profound influence that emerging technologies are having on the way we design and evaluate instruction and on how we understand and conceptualize learning and learning environments. Indeed, technology has already made it possible for us to inhabit multiple learning worlds as a result of what Gleick (1999) has identified as the networked "phase transition" of the new millennium, except, as Gleick extends the metaphor, "the controlling factor here is not heat or energy but pure connectivity" (1999, p. 69). This connectivity has challenged traditional notions of communication and community and offered in their place globalized knowledge-making and uncharted social and organizational dynamics. Connectivity also results in our perception that processes are accelerating or quickening and that the events in our everyday lives are separated by increasingly shortened intervals in time.

My interest in instruction and learning with technology began in 1985 when I served as a teaching assistant for an experimental course entitled "Computer-Assisted Learning" offered at the University of Waterloo. Since that time, and during my graduate studies, my research has always been intimately connected with instructional issues, focusing on the design and evaluation of online information, human–computer interaction, usability, and most recently on Web-based instruction (WBI). In 1990, while a Ph.D. candidate in Rhetoric at Carnegie Mellon University, I taught a graduate course entitled "Computers and Writing" and, in 1994, as an Assistant Professor of Rhetoric and Technical Communication at North Carolina State University, I taught a reading and writing course using multi-user domains, object-oriented (MOO). I have designed around twenty instructional Web sites since 1995 and have used enterprise-level Learning Management Systems (LMSs) to teach online courses since 2002. That same year, when I joined the College of Education at NC State University as an Associate Professor of Distance Learning, I began in earnest to master the research literatures related to instruction and learning with technology, broadly defined. I immediately found that research relevant to my object of inquiry was ubiquitous— distributed widely across numerous disciplines—and simultaneously hidden from researchers and practitioners searching within their particular disciplines.

During the same two proto-electronic decades, increased pressures on higher educational settings from corporations, the general public, governmental institutions, and funding agencies have called into question the job that higher education is doing in preparing learners for the twenty-first century. Hanna (2003) states:

Demand for learning across the globe is increasing as national economies become increasingly based on knowledge and the pace of technological change continues to be accelerated. Rapid growing and increasingly youthful populations in many areas of the world are also fueling pressures on higher education institutions to respond in new and creative ways. In all countries, continuous learning for adults is becoming essential as jobs change and entire career tracks are eliminated and new ones develop. Access to education from any location, at any time, for any age, and in many ways is critical for individual and collective well-being. (2003, pp. 67–68)

The relationship between state and federal support and calls for increased accountability have, as well, encouraged higher educational institutions to reevaluate their basic values as credentialing businesses (or "Diploma Mills," to use Noble's 1998 expression), their mission as general education providers, and their commitment to nontraditional learning populations. Ironically, the pressure to prepare learners for increasingly complex, multipurpose, global workplaces has been further heightened by the inability of most corporate and government institutions to articulate what exactly it is that they require of their employees. How, for example, can skills and knowledge be optimized for teamwork while preserving individual entrepreneurial instincts and performance flows that meet rapidly changing business demands?

Indeed, the nature of work and the role of learning within the workplace are being redefined dramatically to respond to accelerated changes brought about by technologies, collaboration, and the global competition in part made possible by them. As time-to-market cycles have narrowed, the need for training and retraining, for creative problem solving, innovative teamwork, and elegant and scalable solutions has intensified. Traditional organizational structures are being pitted against entrepreneurial, distributed, horizontal matrices, and the resulting configurations are currently unknown.

Beyond the workplace falls that much sought-after space and time reserved for our leisure or, rather, for the leisure industries that we have invented for our leisure. Having effectively transcended time and space, we must now reidentify the boundaries that once protected us from "24/7" commitments to productivity. Thus, technologies developed over the last twenty years have made it possible for us to fax a memo from the beach, whether we want or need to in the first place. We can order movie tickets, purchase season tickets for the museum, download chapter excerpts of books that we are considering reading, pause television shows on one channel while recording movies on another. We are left wondering if spaces where increased learning is not demanded still exist. And our desire for more time encourages us to develop yet more technologies that promise to save more time for us.

Responding too to the conflation of learning worlds that we inhabit and the technologies that are helping conflate them is the research-based information that we traditionally rely on to help us in our decision making and practical pursuits. Digital libraries and the paroxysmal spread of research literatures, methodologies, and peer-reviewed journal publications have generated a mass of research that promises to overwhelm us (Johnson and Magusin 2005). A mass of research on instruction and learning with technology has been published as well, yet, simultaneously, research on the practice of instruction and learning with technology is still in its infancy. The communication technologies that make it possible for the rapid expansion of efforts, institutions, and literatures connected to instruction and learning with technologies continues to infiltrate our learning spaces. For these reasons, it is all the more important that we reflect on developments in instruction and learning with technology and related disciplines to provide a historical context for current theory building and practice.

The motivation for attempting to document the vast stores of research related to instruction and learning with technology is twofold. First, with the exception of retrospective reviews of literature related to research in this area (Allen et al. 2002; Álvarez and Kilbourn 2002; Berge and Mrozowski 2001; Bernard et al. 2004a,b; Larreamendy-Joerns and Leinhardt 2006; Liao 1999), many published articles and studies quickly narrow their review of the research to immediate, pragmatic research gaps covered in two-to-three-page literature review sections (Onwuegbuzie and Leech 2005). Second, a broad review of the literatures related to instruction and learning can inform a conceptual framework for everyday instructional situations that can, in turn, help us approach the exponentially growing number of studies devoted to instruction and learning.

Therefore, rather than beginning a review of online instruction where so many others begin—by expounding on how more and more courses and programs are moving online or by concluding, as Meyer (2002) does, that "Online learning is here to stay" (p. 103)—I examine the literatures on instruction and learning with technology, broadly defined. Not only can one identify hundreds of journals that contain research germane to any systematic study of instruction and learning with technology, but, I argue, these journals can be organized around several clusters or general areas of research. Reviewing the literatures related to instruction and learning with technology thus provides us with a common database of references on historical and contemporary developments in the design and evaluation of online instruction. A comprehensive view of the literatures also gives us a language for developing a framework for everyday instructional situations.

A Note about Terminology

Obviously, clarifying terminology is critical in a comprehensive review of literatures dealing with rapidly evolving phenomena described by so many theorists and practitioners from practically every discipline in the academy. The first clarification must begin, at least for the purposes of this book, with the terms "instruction and learning with technology" and "Web-based instruction," which overlap in ways typically misunderstood. The concept of "Web" has a considerably richer etymology than its current definition as the browser-based information that we access via the Internet. This latter level of technical specificity is precisely where researchers attempting to define WBI run aground and risk anachronistic elaborations. Importantly, many of the arguments and research-based design principles that are covered in this book would have applied to the hypertext systems of the late-1980s as much as they may have applied to the designs of yesterday's paper-based correspondence courses, and as much as they apply to the mobile learning devices in use today, or to the wearable devices of tomorrow. An educational environment can be filled with technologies that support instruction and learning including computational ones that include WBI. But, for our purposes, we also want to remember that the term "Web" refers to the vast network of multimedia information that is accessible for communication beyond the educational environment and around the globe.

Instruction and learning with the more inclusive term "technology," conversely, involves any technology (e.g., telephone, audiotape, typewriter) that disturbs normative time and space, either in terms of our perception of the passage of time or our sense of what is real and what is artificial. Clearly, as technologies have evolved to include digitally enhanced information and communication technologies (ICT), distinctions between fixed and fluid and between natural and artificial have become harder to maintain. As Bird (2003), in her description of media use in our everyday lives, notes, "We cannot isolate the role of the media in culture, because media are firmly anchored into the web of culture, although articulated by individuals in different ways. . . . The 'audience' [for media] is everywhere and nowhere" (p. 3). Brown (1999) thus writes, "the Web . . . is a transformative infrastructure very much like electrification was for the United States at the turn of this century. Electrification changed nearly every aspect of how we lived, how we worked and how we learned." Webs describe the spaces that characterize the majority of my instructional and learning activities and the audience for instruction is increasingly everywhere and nowhere.

Overview of the Book

Educational researchers and educators have a historical habit of exaggerating the educational "paradigm shift" that will result from WBI. They also have a habit of ignoring the implications of design, human–computer interaction research, rhetorical theory, and usability when discussing online instructional materials, in part because usability has tended to stress "performance" rather than learning, long- and short-term, and partly because the activities that learners engage in and technologies they learn with are considered peripheral to learning content in general.

However, the most compelling rationale for a thorough investigation of instruction and learning with technology is that it artificializes our definitions of learning and the learner, instruction and its relationship to the classroom ("formal" learning settings), resources and artifacts for instruction, and the lifelong learning that pervades our professional and personal learning worlds. The technologies that distribute my classroom across time and space necessitate a rearticulation of what I value as natural about my nondistributed, "traditional" classroom. Deuze (2006), in this respect, describes what he calls "two mutually constitutive features of digital culture," that is, "remediation as in the remix of old and new media, and bricolage in terms of the highly personalized, continuous, and more or less autonomous assembly, disassembly, and reassembly of mediated reality" (p. 66). As Fry (1995) reminds us, "There is no way to find or to recognize new ways of thinking without old thought" (p. 205).

Rather than providing prescriptive recipes for creating online instruction or simply applying methods from human–computer interaction and usability research to the study and evaluation of online learning environments, a long-term, multidisciplinary research investigation is required. Such an investigation, for which I attempt to lay the groundwork in the following chapters, entails:

• tracing the transformative influence of technologies on how humans communicate, understand, and mediate our cognitive, social, and cultural realities, to help us to place discussions about instruction, learning, and technology within an appropriately rich multidisciplinary context;
• describing three primary learning worlds—work, leisure, and educational settings—to enable us to see how accelerated technological developments are rewriting the individual and social organization of learning;
• researching the literatures related to instruction and learning with technology, to enrich our understanding of the multidisciplinary nature of our inquiry and highlighting common issues across disciplines and learning worlds related to learners, tasks, and contexts for everyday instruction;

• reviewing instruction, learning, and technology within the context of numerous research-based models of teaching and learning, to allow us to identify common attributes of instructional situations;
• articulating a rhetorical design perspective that includes recent research on design, usability, and human–computer interaction, to strengthen the interaction between theory and practice related to instruction, technology, and learning;
• developing a conceptual framework of everyday instructional situations, to assist researchers and practitioners in more strategically approaching the multidisciplinary literatures related to instruction and learning with technology, as well as to provide them with a framework for describing and evaluating any instructional situation; and
• elaborating on the five dimensions of everyday instructional situations, to help researchers and practitioners begin to develop heuristics for designing, evaluating, and researching instruction and learning with technology in general, and WBI and online learning environments specifically.

My hope is that a perspective toward instruction and learning that emphasizes learners, their tasks, social dynamics, instructional activities, and the learning environments that they inhabit will provide a rich language for researchers and practitioners as they shape and extend the boundaries of this emerging discipline. Finally, I describe several avenues for future research on instruction and learning with technology that are both theoretically compelling and offer alternative perspectives on the design and evaluation of instruction and learning in artificial environments. These areas culminate around issues no less fundamental than notions of space and time.

The title of this book is influenced by three books that shaped my early thinking about the design and evaluation of instruction and learning with technology: Donald A. Norman's (1990) *The Design of Everyday Things*, Donald A. Schön's (1983) *The Reflective Practitioner*, and Herbert A. Simon's (1969, 1981) *Sciences of the Artificial*. Until I came upon these texts, I was unaware that I was caught in a state of academic awe between the works of classical rhetoric and my ongoing practical exposure to contemporary design perspectives, usability theory, and human–computer interaction. While researching this book, I encountered a term that captures the disconnect between my academic training and my daily practical experience: "neotoric," coined by Buchanan (1992), which he ambitiously defines as "the inherently rhetorical dimension of all design thinking" and which is aimed at capturing the strengths of both perspectives (Buchanan 1995, p. 24).

Norman (1990), Schön (1983), and Simon's (1969, 1981) books present brief, elegant, grand arguments and, as such, provide an apposite contrast to this project, which represents my attempt to begin integrating a vast number of research literatures in order to put forward several tentative assertions. A growing sense that numerous research conversations are going on in parallel, that these conversations need to be synthesized and shared, and my empirical faith in the relationship between research and "real-world" problems encourages overciting. I apologize for this in advance, suspecting that reading too much can deter from the production of eloquent arguments.

Audience for the Book

This book developed out of separate conversations that I have enjoyed with individuals who too infrequently interact but whose research and practical interests intersect in important ways. In many ways they helped me envision the six primary audiences for this book:

• *Educational researchers new to the multidisciplinary history and research on distance education (DE) and instruction and learning with technology.* Individuals who may be engaged in debates over the strengths and weaknesses of online courses or programs but who are unfamiliar with the rich intellectual history and research on instruction and learning with technology (especially chapter 1).

• *Researchers and students interested in the cognitive and social dimensions of instruction and learning with technology, rhetorical theories of technology, contemporary design, and usability research.* Individuals from the humanities and social sciences, education, engineering design, sociology, philosophy, psychology, and computer science interested in studying computer technology as a human and social phenomenon, focusing on the interaction between users-as-learners, technology, values, beliefs, and community formation (especially chapters 1, 2, and 3).

• *Instructors planning to create Web-based instruction (WBI) and e-learning.* Instructors, administrators, educational and instructional technologists, faculty interested in distance learning, and subject-matter experts from any discipline exploring the implications of WBI for their existing classroom-based teaching (especially chapters 6 and 7).

• *Human–computer interaction and usability specialists interested in applying effective principles for design to WBI.* Researchers and practitioners in human factors engineering (HFE), general user interface (GUI) experts, Web designers, information architects (IA) usability engineers, testing and quality assurance personnel, and instructors and administrators interested in assessment issues related to WBI (especially chapters 5, 6, and 7).

• *DE and assessment specialists evaluating online instructional materials.* Specialists in university planning and analysis offices and DE units who coordinate the evaluation of new and emerging approaches to teaching and learning, and individuals in corporate training units who evaluate the success and expense of ongoing employee training programs (especially chapters 4, 6, and 7).

• *Technical communicators and training specialists developing WBI and performance-support materials for use on the Web.*   Trainers, writers, editors, graphic designers, and illustrators who create Web-based materials that introduce, assist, support, and train users of other, primary applications (especially chapters 6 and 7).

Summary of Chapters

This book is organized around seven interconnected chapters that draw on bodies of research that offer to enrich and complicate issues related to instruction, learning, and technology. Indeed, one of the major goals of this book is to explore as yet unexamined connections between diverse research literatures and to encourage multidisciplinary dialogues that contribute to our understanding of instruction and learning with technology.

• Chapter 1: *Everyday Learning.*   Most publications focusing on instruction and learning with technology and distance education deemphasize the compelling ways that technologies are transforming not only teaching and learning, but how we understand communication and language and perceive, interact with, and interpret the world around us. Emerging technologies are rapidly forcing us to rethink and repurpose our everyday instructional needs and contexts for interacting with information, with ourselves, and with one another.

• Chapter 2: *Learning Worlds.*   Accelerated technological developments encourage a divergence of learning across traditionally separate domains: work, leisure, and higher educational spaces. Understanding these learning contexts broadens our perspective toward instruction and learning in our technology-rich lives. Researchers have noted that it is becoming increasingly difficult to identify learning spaces free of occupational commitment, efficiency management, and haste. Since distributed instruction narrows the distance between our learning worlds, balancing higher-order educational goals with personal, performance, and production goals becomes increasingly important.

• Chapter 3: *Research Conversations.*   In this chapter, I review and examine the prodigious efforts of researchers interested in instruction and learning with technology in general and distance education specifically. I present 300 peer-reviewed research journals related to instruction and learning with technology and organize them broadly according to traditional disciplinary boundaries, with the goal of positioning us for interdisciplinary conversations about the complex relationship between instruction, learning, and technology.

• Chapter 4: *Models of Instruction and Learning with Technology.*   Following operational definitions of learning, technology, and instruction, I provide in this chapter an overview and analysis of a dozen models of instruction and learning with technology derived from the peer-reviewed research. Although some distance education researchers claim that there is a paucity of theory on instruction and learning with technology, a multidisciplinary perspective toward research related to the area reveals the opposite.

• Chapter 5: *Designs for Learning.*   Given the exponential rate of publishing on instruction and learning with technology, traditional dichotomies between science and nonscience and between theory and practice become difficult to maintain. Understanding the relationship between these endeavors is critical if we hope to develop theories we can apply and to understand how our applications embody working theory. A third, integrative rhetorical design perspective is proposed.

• Chapter 6: *A Framework for Everyday Instructional Situations.*   Instruction and learning with technology can be characterized and contextualized by describing *all* learning or *everyday* instructional situations. Everyday instructional situations consist of five interdependent dimensions: learner background and knowledge, learner tasks and activities, social dynamics, instructor activities, and learning environment and artifacts.

• Chapter 7: *Futures for Instruction and Learning with Technology.*   These diverse literatures we have been discussing—of distance education; computers and the humanities; educational, communication, instructional, and information technologies; the learning sciences; psychology; computer science; design; human–computer interaction; and rhetorical theory—position researchers interested in instruction and learning with technology to contribute in novel and, as yet, only tentatively explored ways. Theoretical and empirical investigations that explore the relationship between design and evaluation, space and time, and instruction and learning with technology are but a few possible areas for future research.

1 Everyday Learning

Most publications focusing on instruction and learning with technology and distance education deemphasize the compelling ways that technologies are transforming not only teaching and learning, but how we understand communication and language and perceive, interact with, and interpret the world around us. Emerging technologies are rapidly forcing us to rethink and repurpose our everyday instructional needs and contexts for interacting with information, with ourselves, and with one another.

In a world in which the total of human knowledge is doubling about every ten years, our security can rest only on our ability to learn.
—Nathaniel Branden (1994, p. 34)

Knowledge now doubles every seven years, primed by the ten thousand scientific articles that are published every day.
—Carol Tomlinson-Keasey (2002, p. 134)

Marshall McLuhan (1964) has eloquently described that "Just before an airplane breaks the sound barrier, sound waves become visible on the wings of the plane. The sudden visibility of sound just as sound ends is an apt instance of that great pattern of being that reveals new and opposite forms just as the earlier forms reach their peak performance" (p. 27). McLuhan (1964) captures the poetic nature of change; in this case, change that results in rapid acceleration through the use of sophisticated technologies. The sudden visibility of human knowledge, doubling every decade according to Branden in 1994 and every seven years by 2002 according to Tomlinson-Keasey, is being fueled by digital technologies. The change we are focused on in this book is how these technologies are influencing instruction and learning and, specifically, on the rapid movement online of "traditional" education.

Technology, digital or otherwise, is not merely utilitarian or instrumentalist in its influence on the way we instruct and learn; nor does technology degrade or enhance instruction and learning in uniform ways. Technology use in instruction and learning is a complex domain for study, primarily because it is exceedingly difficult to define in a satisfying manner the precise natures of technology, instruction, and learning.

Although our initial tendency is to begin by describing contemporary, formal learning environments—that is, classroom-based instruction—learning in the broadest and most compelling sense plays a much more significant role in our everyday informal lives. Indeed, when technology is injected into the mix, learning can be viewed as that great pattern of being that defines humans and distinguishes us from lower-order species and artifacts.

We live in multiple learning worlds. Our connectivity and technological ability to transcend space and time has brought learning to the foreground, contextualized by our notions of whether we are at work, involved in leisure activities, or pursuing higher learning in formal educational settings. Gleick (1999) describes these "new orders of magnitude" as being pushed and pulled by the development of the modern Internet:

Roughly speaking, everybody's computers, connected. It is not just more; it is different. Chaos theorists understand such systems to undergo phase transitions, as water does when it turns coherently to ice or incoherently to steam. The controlling factor here is not heat or energy but pure connectivity. (p. 69)

Connectivity makes possible global, instantaneous communication on a level only hypothesized with historical technologies (see, e.g., Carr-Chellman 2005). Mumford (1934), for example, describes our desire to simulate face-to-face interaction with the development of the telegraph:

With the invention of the telegraph a series of inventions began to bridge the gap in time between communication and response despite the handicaps of space: first the telegraph, then the telephone, then the wireless telegraph, then the wireless telephone, and finally television. As a result, communication is now on the point of returning, with the aide of mechanical devices, to that instantaneous reaction of person to person with which it began; but the possibilities of this immediate meeting, instead of being limited by time and space, will be limited only by the amount of energy available and the mechanical perfection and accessibility of the apparatus. When the radio telephone is supplemented by television communication it will differ from direct intercourse only to the extent that immediate physical contact will be impossible. (pp. 239–240)

Although our attention is primarily on the instruction and learning that occurs in formal settings—higher educational ones—it is useful periodically to remind ourselves that learning in the most general sense is one of the most interesting subjects for study we might imagine. How we learn, under what circumstances, where, and in relation to what particular "subjects"—whether formally or informally, about work or play or relationships or ourselves and our capabilities, or about "life" in general—consumes a great many discussions and influences fictional and nonfictional explorations in every conceivable medium across cultures and history. Our attempts to anticipate the future, to construct a meaningful past, and to succeed in the present are drawn from the learning situations that make up our everyday lives.

Despite this, it is difficult to gauge when exactly traditional classroom-based instruction reached its unquestioned peak in higher education in this country, even though it is clear that we are at an exciting crossroads if the heatedness of the debate between online teaching and learning advocates and more conservative "brick-and-mortar" voices is any indication of the changes afoot. Certainly histories of formal distance education (DE) vary on their definitions of when and where DE finds its beginnings in the United States. Gunawardena and McIsaac (2004, p. 356) mark the beginning of DE as the late 1800s with the advent of the University of Chicago's first correspondence program. Penn State dates the beginning of its first correspondence program as 1892, supported by Rural Free Delivery along with the University of Wisconsin and the University of Chicago (Outreach Communication 2005). Others mark the true beginnings of DE as being less than twenty years ago, driven by a confluence of forces including the rapid development of telecommunications technologies, globalization, and emerging social perspectives toward knowledge making and learning (Hanna 1998).

I date the beginnings of an energized DE program of research and practice in this country as being November 20, 1993, when the White House announced in an official press release the creation of Mosaic. The release described Mosaic's creation as the "digital cannon felt around the world" (Andrews 1999) and, whereas prior to 1992 only four peer-reviewed journals emphasizing DE existed (the *American Journal of Distance Education*, *Distance Education*, the *Journal of Distance Education*, and *Interactive Learning Environments*), by 1998 there were ten journals and by 2005 there were 29 (see table 1.1).

Today it is difficult to imagine a computing universe without the World Wide Web and, by default, to imagine a home-based information delivery system that does not provide instant access to Public Broadcasting Corporation's educational software for elementary school children, multiplayer gaming for middle school kids interested in quest fiction, map programs for charting directions from the airport to one's destination, applications for sharing numerical data, pictures, text, and video images, or online shopping, purchasing, and shipping for last-minute gift buying.[1] And these are only the online activities that I have engaged in this evening while preparing my daughters for bedtime reading. Indeed, without the Web, it is impossible for me to imagine carrying out the bulk of the research that fed into and shaped the writing of this book.

The realization of Web-based instruction (WBI) has forced a review of traditional definitions of instruction, learning, information, knowledge, cognition, assessment, and the classroom that cannot be denied, and has accelerated the instructional

Table 1.1

Peer-reviewed distance education and e-learning journals: 1979–2006

Journal Name	URL	Publication Date
American J. of Distance Ed.	www.ajde.com	1987–present
Asian J. of Distance Ed.	www.asianjde.org	2003–present
Distance Ed.	www.tandf.co.uk/journals/carfax/01587919.html	1979–present
E-Learning	www.wwwords.co.uk/elea	2004–present
E-Learning and Education	eleed.campussource.de	2005–present
European J. of Open, Distance and e-Learning	www.eurodl.org	1997–present
Indian J. of Open Learning	www.ignou.ac.in/ijol/ijol.html	1992–present
Innovate: J. of Online Ed.	innovateonline.info/index.php	1997–2003 as *The Tech. Source*; 2003–2009
Interactive Learning Environments	www.tandf.co.uk/journals/titles/10494820.asp	1990–present
Int. J. of Distance Ed. Technologies	jdet.mine.tku.edu.tw	2003–present
Int. J. of Interactive Technology and Smart Ed.	www.troubador.co.uk/itse	2004–present
Int. J. of Learning Technology	www.inderscience.com/browse/index.php?journalID=87	2004–present
Int. J. of Web-based Learning and Teaching Technologies	www.igi-pub.com/journals/details.asp?id=4286	2006–present
Int. J. on E-Learning	www.aace.org/pubs/ijel	1995–2001 as *Int. J. of Ed. Telecom.*; 2002–present
Int. J. of Instructional Technology and Distance Learning	www.itdl.org	2004–present
Int. Review of Research in Open and Distance Learning	www.irrodl.org/index.php/irrodl	2000–present
Internet and Higher Ed.	www.elsevier.com/wps/find/journaldescription.cws_home/620187/description#description	1998–present
J. for Asynchronous Learning Networks	www.sloan-c.org/publications/jaln/index.asp	2000–present
J. of Distance Ed.	www.jofde.ca/index.php/jde	1986–present
J. of Educators Online	www.thejeo.com	2004–present

Table 1.1

(continued)

Journal Name	URL	Publication Date
J. of e-Learning and Knowledge Society	www.je-lks.it	2005–present
J. of Interactive Learning Research	www.aace.org/pubs/jilr	1999–present
J. of Online Learning and Teaching	jolt.merlot.org	2005–present
Online J. of Distance Learning Administration	www.westga.edu/~distance/ojdla	1998–present
Open Learning: The J. of Open and Distance Learning	www.tandf.co.uk/journals/carfax/02680513.html	1999–present
Quarterly Review of Distance Ed.	www.infoagepub.com/index.php?id=39	2000–present
Texas J. of Distance Learning	tjdl.uh.edu	2004–present
Turkish Online J. of Distance Ed.	tojde.anadolu.edu.tr	2000–present
USDLA Online J.	www.usdla.org/html/resources/journal.htm	1999–present

computing research and practice that began in the early 1960s (Halasz 1988; Hannafin and Peck 1988). Extending McLuhan's (1964) transonic travel metaphor to technological change and its influence on traditional notions of instruction, we cannot help noting that—as an airplane approaches the speed of sound—the drag force increases, necessitating an increase in the speed of the airplane. So too with emerging technologies and their interaction with traditional modes of instruction and spaces for learning: traditionalists are quick to point to insignificant differences between old and new learning environments (Russell 1999). And to add to the complex of fluid mechanics, approaching the sound barrier produces shock waves close to the airplane that disturb existing flow and further contribute to drag force. The transition from old to new presents itself as a theater of tension rather than as an inevitable process.

1.1 Transformational Paradigm Mediums

Exploring a considerably lengthier movement from the old to the new—the historical transformation from an oral to a literate culture—Walter Ong (1982) echoes the tension between one dominate medium and another. Ultimately, Ong (1982) distinguishes between the oral and the literate and highlights the inevitable interaction between the two cultural forces. He writes, "Once the word is technologized [through literacy], there is no effective way to criticize what technology has done with it without the aid of the highest technology available. Moreover, the new technology is not merely used to convey the critique: in fact, it brought the critique into existence" (p. 80). And so it is with all developments in human communication. As Miller (1979) argues, the historical dichotomy between a transmissional and a transformational view of language is based on "a conviction that content (that is, ideas, information, facts) is wholly separable from words" and "presupposes what has been called the 'window-pane theory of language': the notion that language provides a view out onto the real world, a view which may be clear or obfuscated" (pp. 611–612). Our existing systems for exchange undergo radical transformations as a result of the emerging system(s) and are, therefore, impossible to review without applying the beliefs, values, and cultural assumptions that were brought about as part of the transformation. Text is intertextual, discourse is contextualized by metadiscourse, and media become elements of multimedia.

In addition to constructs such as literacy significantly influencing human behavior and knowledge making, additional "paradigm mediums"—such as money and technology—serve critical roles in our sociohistorical development (Feenberg 1999). Moreover, these paradigm mediums are so central to our motivations and interactions that it is often difficult to find a language for evaluating the influence they have and have had on our lives. Table 1.2 extends Ong's (1982) analysis of the relationship between literacy and technology, drawing on Feenberg's (1999) discussion of paradigm mediums.

Table 1.2
Fundamental topoi of human civilization[a]

Activity Construct	Rationale	Benefits	Issues
Education	Enculturation	Cross-generational transfer, behavior modeling, real-world problem solving	Rote memorization, mass delivery, unidirectional transmission
Literacy	Memory	Analytic reasoning, portability, authority	Ownership, oral tradition, class systems
Money	Utility	Trading, portability, standardization, community building	Currency, exchange, greed
Power	Efficiency	Uniformity, streamlining, centralization	Inequality, compensation, accountability
Technology	Productivity	Expense, time savings, efficiency	Commodification, repetition, reductionism, decontextualization

[a]Extension of Feenberg (1999); Ong (1982).

Feenberg (1999) holds that we can begin to understand human civilization and behavior when we identify its paradigm mediums—money, power, and technology. Further, understanding the paradigm mediums that we design and that ultimately design our meanings and activities allows us to elaborate on both the benefits and the issues we face as a result of our inventions. To Feenberg's (1999) list we can add literacy and education and can equally assume that these constructs are transformative rather than transmissional. That is, a host of individual, social, institutional, and cultural factors interact with these primary developments in ways that alter human behavior, values, and beliefs. Once these developments are in place, it becomes exceedingly difficult to disentangle them from our predictions about the future. Technology certainly works that way, encouraging increasingly progressive narratives about "tomorrow" and discouraging discussions about disruptive events that might produce nontechnological futures. As well, it becomes very difficult to conceptualize our past before these developments without transposing anachronistic interpretations on unknowable perspectives. Thus, money as a constant contemporary construct interferes with our ability to imagine how immediate our perceptions of time, value, and exchange would be if experienced through the immediacy of bartering.

King and Frost (2002) refer to paradigm mediums as disambiguous technologies (in the Greek sense of *tekhnologia* or systematic treatments) and, using writing and money as examples, describe how "Both provided a fixity to meanings across space, allowing a shorthand that relieved users from having to reframe endlessly the meanings of messages and markets. Each afforded mechanisms whereby meanings separated by space become clearer and spatially separated cognitive communities could be reliably built" (p. 5).

Paradigm mediums or disambiguous technologies are not mere extensions of our capabilities or platforms on which our content is placed; paradigm mediums cannot be "served up" from a sender to a passive receiver (cf. Shannon 1949). Neither can paradigm mediums be reduced to rigid expressions such as "rich" and "lean" since, as Nardi (2005) points out, understanding "the amount and type of information flowing through 'channels' of varying 'bandwidth'" fails to capture the human activities surrounding media, activities "geared to establishing feelings of connection with others for the purpose of continued interactions over time" (pp. 91–92).

Because paradigm mediums such as education and technology form the very core of our systems for understanding, conceptualizing, and promulgating knowledge about, with, and into the world around us, they are exceedingly difficult to understand, isolate, parameterize, or control. Instead, we are tempted to either set them apart from the phenomena or phenomenon we are studying and to ignore them or, worse, to treat them as individual variables that we can either include or remove from our analyses. Inversely, we study the disambiguous technologies but we marginalize the actors, genres, actions, and contexts within which they operate, reducing them to the pieces and parts that make up their functionality.

Weinberger (2007) posits that computational connectivity has begun to operate as the ultimate disambiguous amplifier. That is,

Tags may become more useful, meaningful, relevant, and clearer the more there are. If that is the case, the blind reasoning power of computers is only part of the explanation. Algorithms can find these relationships of meaning only because, just as all the items in our drawer of kitchen miscellany share the fact they are related to food, the items in the global miscellaneous drawer share a vast set of similarities in what we humans care about and how we talk about what we care about. Computers can cluster tags only because human interests and expressions cluster. (p. 168)

To examine the historical interaction between instruction, learning, and technology, then, we must explore our relationship with both things and the things that we use to communicate our relationship to things. Beginning with "real-time" orality and culminating in contemporary multimodal communication media systems, it becomes clear that dichotomies between "traditional" modes of interaction and evolving ones are impossible to maintain. As Burbules (2004) argues,

Bifurcation of the synthetic and the real has obscured a deeper understanding of what is changing in the ways we make and explore our worlds, mediated by and through new technologies. Very rarely, if ever, is there a "direct perception" of anything; we actively observe, select, filter, and interpret our experiences in all sorts of ways that construct distinct and sometimes idiosyncratic *versions* of the world. Some of these mediations are overtly technological in nature: eyeglasses, cameras, telescopes—or, more subtly, concepts, categories, theories, and assumptions. The world we perceive is always already a world we "make" to some extent. (p. 165)

Miah (2000), in addition to reminding us that it is problematic to understand "the virtual in virtual reality" as the opposite of the real in our natural world, adds that it is also problematic to equate the mediation of reality through our senses to the mediation experienced via simulated environments. Although our temptation is to stress that we as humans (even as sensory input devices) are consciously filtering, interpreting, and understanding the environments around us, recent research in neuroscience reminds us that learners are just as frequently designed and constrained in response to the environments built for them. Bransford et al. (2006), for example, note that brain research suggests "evolution has created a neural system that 'expects' information from the environment at a particular time, allowing animals to acquire knowledge that is specific to their own environments when exposed to that information" (pp. 20–21). Just as technologies complicate our initial understandings of fundamental processes, so, too, must we challenge initial understandings of instruction and learning as standing apart from or in contrast to technology.

1.2 Artificial and Real Opportunities for Reflection

Thus, our literate "progress" from oral to textual culture undermines the dichotomy between what we understand as natural and what we understand as artificial. Paradigm mediums are not natural: they are human-made, artificial inventions, ersatz solutions. Despite our innate ability to mediate our natural experiences with artificial "improvements," we still exhibit a tendency to idealize constructs that we define as natural. Doheny-Farina (1996) thus asserts that "we do not need electronic neighborhoods; we need geophysical neighborhoods, in all their integrity. The revolution that must be joined is not one that removes us from place but one that somehow reintegrates the elements of our dissolving placed communities" (p. xi). Ong (1982), however, does not privilege the natural over the artificial:

To say that writing is artificial is not to condemn it but to praise it. Like other artificial creations and indeed more than any other, it is utterly invaluable and indeed essential for the realization of fuller, interior, human potentials. Technologies are not mere exterior aids but also interior transformations of consciousness, and never more than when they affect the word. Such transformations can be uplifting. Writing heightens consciousness. Alienation from a natural milieu can be good for us and indeed is in many ways essential for full human life. To live and to understand fully, we need not only proximity but also distance.

Technologies are artificial, but—paradox again—artificiality is natural to human beings. Technology, properly interiorized, does not degrade human life but on the contrary enhances it. (pp. 82–83)

The artificial provides us with the opportunity to review what we mean by natural and to avoid, as Bruner (1966) warns, the "failure to recognize how difficult it is for human beings to see generality in what has become familiar" (p. 93). And what could be more familiar than the technologies that surround and "warm" us. Fry (1995), in his "Sacred Design I," puts it somewhat more poetically:

"Thing," in stasis or animated (thinging) wraps a form (*morphe*) in a look (*eidos*). In being surrounded by things we are enmeshed in the web of their performative presence. We think of things relationally as how they appear and act. While we inscribe things they mark us. We/things act to reveal and conceal themselves. (p. 201)

The things we build are everywhere and, more and more, we are designing technologies for simulating things that help us understand nature itself (Heller and Parker 2005). Thus, Simon (1969, 1981), more than a quarter of a century ago, reasons that "The world we live in today is much more a man-made, or artificial, world than it is a natural world. Almost every element in our environment shows evidence of man's artifice" (pp. 4–5). This phenomenon, according to Buchanan (1992), demands a new science of the artificial and the primary challenge in pursuing this goal is that

Designers conceive their subject matter in two ways on two levels: general and particular. On a *general level*, a designer forms an idea or working hypothesis about the nature of products or the nature of the human-made world. This is the designer's view of what is meant . . . by "artificial" in relation to the "natural." In this sense, the designer holds a broad view of the nature of design and the proper scope of its application. . . . They provide an essential framework for each designer to understand and explore the materials, methods, and principles of design thinking. But such philosophies do not and cannot constitute sciences of design in the sense of any natural, social, or humanistic science. The reason for this is simple: design is fundamentally concerned with the particular, *and there is no science of the particular.* (p. 17)

Thus the advent of chess-playing computers enlivens Adrienne Rich's appreciation of what is general and what is particular about human intelligence and creativity, and prompts her (1961) poem, "Artificial Intelligence":

Still, when
they make you write your poems, later on,
who'd envy you, force-fed
on all those variorum
editions of our primitive endeavors,
those frozen pemmican language-rations
they'll cram you with? denied
our luxury of nausea, you
forget nothing, have no dreams.
(Reprinted in Ledbetter 1986, p. 39)

Rich (1961) captures our fear that blurring the line between the natural and the artificial will ultimately result in language erosion, a flattening of historical perspectives, scattering of our attentions, waning of the private self, and decentering of what is real for what is simulated (cf. Birkerts 1994; Carr 2008; Clarke 1997; Doheny-Farina 1996). Wooley (1992) speculates that "The prejudice that favours the products of nature over our own is, perhaps, understandable. Nature's approvals process is slower even than the FDA's, working at the pace of evolutionary time to separate dangerous substances from those to whom they are a danger" (p. 3).

Or, to frame the tension between the natural (human) and the artificial (computation) in the opposite direction, Peters (2001) asserts, "It is human frailty, rather than rationality, that machines have difficulty mimicking. Turing thought 'the shape of the human body' quite irrelevant to establishing communication, but disability and imperfection may be the only sources of real contact we can claim" (p. 237). The invention of a state that is *not* the current state, of a virtual classroom that we almost nostalgically refer to as "traditional," allows us to reflect on the dreams and on the vulnerability of our current condition. The drag force encouraged by emerging technologies invites the need for a reevaluation of what is defined as natural. Technologies that distribute my classroom across time and space necessitate a rearticulation of what I value as natural about my nondistributed, "traditional" classroom.

But what is experienced as natural might then be viewed as a bygone and evanescent anomaly. As Simon (1969, 1981) reminds us, "A forest may be a phenomenon of nature; a farm certainly is not" (p. 5); and we clearly require reminding, for it is easy at times to think of a farm, in contrast to our metro-urban habitat, as natural, traditional, and nonmanufactured. So, too, is it tempting to think of the contemporary face-to-face classroom (which might more accurately be described as "faces-to-face" classroom in terms of the use of space) as authentic, genuine, foundational, or "natural."

Our relationship with communication media tends to replicate this error in that we deem some literacies (textual) as primary and natural and others (computational) as artificial and simulated. But Jasinski (2001) writes that we view language and rhetoric with suspicion precisely because we connect them "with artifice, the artificial, mere appearances, or the simply decorative" (p. xiii). Thus, in the case of once elite "broadcast" production methods and processes (paper and pencil, radio, television, and film, computers and the Internet), distribution to the "masses" is inevitable. Moreover, mass distribution has always resulted—at least initially—in both liberation and chaos, ultimately returning to unhinge the very institutions that developed, housed, and protected those processes from the general population.

Indeed, transformative technologies take their most dramatic shape when the general population interacts with them. Thus, in 1987, just six years after the creation of the Xerox STAR in 1981 and three years after the release of the Macintosh Graphical User Interface (GUI), when Apple released HyperCard and announced that one of its goals was to make everyone a programmer, the response of many individuals who wrote programs for computers was "Just anyone shouldn't be able to generate computer programs." Ultimately, though, powerful technologies become deeply embedded cultural realities, taking on the appearance of being transparent, but always at their core constantly evolving symbol-making and exchanging systems that transform the way human beings carry out their tasks and activities. Pencils, writing, typewriters: all of these are technologies and, as technologies, can only ever strive for the elusive and unobtainable goal of transparency. As Kreitzberg and Shneiderman (2001) remind us, "The Web has transformed the computer into a mass medium like the television or telephone" (p. 12); and, similar to the television or telephone, rules for the everyday use of the Web are evolving in both predictable and unpredictable ways (cf. Brown and Perry 2000). As Putnam (2000) observes, "both utopianism and jeremiads are very likely misplaced" (p. 179). For this reason, Penzias's (1989) book, *Ideas and Information: Managing in a High-Tech World*, resonates as much today as it did when he wrote it:

Throughout the ages, technology has helped shape the facts we humans think about. As our knowledge has increased, so have our tools and the ways we employ them. Today, technology is so complex and pervasive that it dominates much of the environment in which human beings live and work. For this reason, . . . we need a better understanding of how technology affects the ways in which we now create and explore ideas. (p. 180)

This is not a novel perspective, either. More than sixty years ago, Vannevar Bush, the director of the Office of Scientific Research and Development under President Roosevelt, described the need for a revolutionary system entitled "memex" (for memory extender), as a response to

a growing mountain of research. But there is increased evidence that we are being bogged down today as specialization extends. The investigator is staggered by the findings and conclusions of thousands of other workers—conclusions which he cannot find time to grasp, much less to remember, as they appear. Yet specialization becomes increasingly necessary for progress, and the effort to bridge between disciplines is correspondingly superficial. (Bush 1945, p. 101)

Prevalence and pervasiveness do not equal progress or transparency: things that pervade our activities pass, extend, or flow through what we do, but they cannot do so without altering irrevocably our nature or the nature of how we do things. Being saturated by something is not a reversible state. Hence, our love relationship with digital technologies is not captured by the metaphor of a tool. Tools, strictly defined, extend our potential and capabilities in one direction. The metaphor of a hammer as tool does not account for the obvious reciprocity of our relationship with contemporary, complex artifacts such as computers or, especially, digitally enhanced technologies, because it is difficult to identify exactly what these hammers *do back to us* or to our learning ecologies. Instruction with technology does not allow us to learn faster, to learn more, or to remember it for longer periods of time. Nor, as Clark (1983) has claimed, are technologies "mere vehicles that deliver instruction but do not influence student achievement any more than the truck that delivers our groceries causes changes in our nutrition" (p. 445). Technology without instruction does not equal electricity and cannot be reduced to a container any more than brain surgery without light can continue to be viewed as unaltered brain surgery (McLuhan 1964, p. 24).

1.3   Contexts for Information and Instruction

Just as electricity cannot be reduced to mere bits and bytes without content, so too is it problematic to reduce instruction to content, modules, objects, or units. Instruction cannot occur without information, and information requires communication. To be a communication act, something must be articulated, inquiry must occur, interpretations must be organized as arguments; and these acts require community and context.

To learn is to instruct where a subject or skill must be identified and then experienced, studied, or understood. Similarly, interpretations of information that reduce it to modularized, quantifiable data ignore the complex and etymologically rich development of the word. Hobart and Schiffman (1998) provide the following, compelling history of information:

The term . . . traces back to the Latin verb *informare*, which for Romans generally meant "to shape," "to form an idea of," or "to describe." The verb, in turn, supplied action to the substantive, *forma*, which took varied, cognate meanings that depended mostly on context. The historian Livy used *forma* as a general term for "character," "form," "nature," "kind," and "manner." Horace applied it to a shoelast, Ovid to a mold or stamp for making coins, while the wily Cicero, among other uses, extended it to logic as "form" or "species," his rendering of the Greek *eidos kai morphe~*, a philosophical expression denoting the essence or form of a thing as distinguished from its matter or content. The practical notion of "form" as a last, mold, or stamp remained closely tied to its more abstract, logical meaning, which paired content and container. These connotations passed into the earliest English uses of the verb "inform" ("to give form" or "character" to, or "imbue" with), which date from the fourteenth century, and from which our noun derives.

Behind the late-twentieth-century idiom, then, are the historically grounded notions of information as something informed, shaped by a pattern, and something preserved, set aside from the immediacy of experience. Each notion requires the other. The pattern, the indwelling form, is an abstraction (from the Latin verb *abstrahere*, "to pull," "drag," or "draw away from"), the product of a reflective mental operation that fixes the flux of experience, both ordering and preserving it. This act involves two closely intertwining movements, (1) "drawing away from" experience, such that we are no longer immersed in it and can see it from a critical perspective, and (2) "pulling" or "dragging" something out of it. The twofold movement of abstraction is the sine qua non of information, without which it cannot exist. The mental act implicit in the etymology of the term has become obscured by the contemporary metaphor's imperialistic reach, which has extended beyond the human world into the natural one. Long before information became the stuff of nature, it was the stuff of mind. (pp. 3–4)

Information commingles the general and the particular, the explicit with the implicit, and the simple with the complex (cf. Weinberger 2007, which supplants information with knowledge that is derived from data and which leads to understanding). Information is both formed and forming. Information is designed. To mistake information for the stuff of nature is to mistake ideas for material that can be managed, education for "infodelivery," information for "knowledge," or learning as "infoconsumption" (Brown 2002b, p. 54; Brown and Duguid 2000, p. 211). Information, that is, language itself, is, as Bleich (2003) writes, "a feature of an interpersonal context and not merely a self-generated event influenced by social forces" (p. 41). As Miller (1979) asserts, "whatever we know of reality is created by individual action and by communal assent. Reality cannot be separated from our knowledge of it; knowledge cannot be separated from the knower; the knower cannot be separated from a community" (p. 615). And Allen (1996) collapses learning and informing into the same larger process, concluding that "The processes of knowing, learning, informing, and being informed are inextricably bound up with each other" (p. 3).

Similarly, to divide technologies from instructional content or instructional content from the learner, a significant and problematic reduction must be committed. Hamilton et al. (2004) describe this phenomenon as the industrialization of learning, stating:

The industrialisation or technologisation that suffuses the learning society and the knowledge economy is underpinned by a mythology of the *autonomous* and *disembodied* tool. A tool becomes autonomous when it can be used anywhere, anytime; and it becomes disembodied when its use does not require the mediation of a knowing user. The technologisation of the learning society assumes that learning environments are technical systems that deliver learning. By analogy with fast food, they deliver fast knowledge: McKnowledge. (p. 844)

Borgmann (2000), too, notes that technologized visions of education reduce knowledge to a commodity for efficient consumption:

The rhetoric of recasting education within the framework of information technology is well attuned to the promise of technology and, in fact, to the implementation of that promise. The disburdenment from the constraints of time, place, and the decisions of other people is the unique accomplishment of modern technology and finds its everyday realization in consumption. Supported by the machinery of technology, consumption is the unencumbered enjoyment of whatever one pleases. The pleasures of consumption require no effort and hence no discipline. Few proponents of course would claim that distance learning will be effortless. But they fail to see that the discipline needed to sustain effort in turn needs the support of the timing, spacing, and socializing that have been part of human nature ever since it has evolved in a world of natural information. (p. 207)

Thus, how we integrate information and technology into our instruction and learning spaces is connected to complex social factors, including notions of public versus private use, perceptions about work and leisure and socioeconomic status, and beliefs and values about the progressive role of technology in our lives (Haddon 2006). In addition to the (neoliberal) progressive visions of global collaboration, communication, and community promoted by our developing corporate-educational-government leaders (Drucker 1994; Gates 1995; Gee 2000; Gumport 2002), it is also important to evoke that handful of dissenting voices (e.g., Borgmann 2000; Doheny-Farina 1996; Jones 1995; Oppenheimer 1997) who question the promises of technologists and media spokespersons. As Mattelart (2000) summarizes:

As vehicles of modern behavior, the media were seen as key agents of innovation. As messengers of the "revolution of rising expectations," they propagated the models of consumption and aspirations symbolized by those societies that had already attained the higher stage of evolution.

This absolute belief in exponential progress and in the modernizing virtue of the media merely updated ethnocentric conceptions of nineteenth-century diffusionist theories. (p. 56)

Hayles (1999) traces our contemporary preoccupation with information as a "free-floating, decontextualized, quantifiable entity" (p. 74) to Shannon's (1949) mathematical theory of communication:

In information theoretic terms, no message is ever sent. What is sent is a signal. The distinction that information theory posits between signal and message is crucial. A message has an information content specified by a probability function that has no dimensions, no materiality, and no necessary connection with meaning. It is a pattern, not a presence. Only when the message is encoded in a signal for transmission through a medium—for example, when ink is printed on paper or electrical pulses are sent racing along telegraph wires—does it assume material form. (Hayles 1999, pp. 73–74)

To be information, information must have meaning. But Chomskyan or analytic linguistics, according to Fahnestock (2005), "is not rooted in a theory of language as communicative medium. It is rooted in a theory of language as a referential or representational medium or as a formal/logical or computational system" (p. 162). Similarly, early conceptions of postmodernism hold, as Lyotard (1979, 1984) predicts, that "We may . . . expect a thorough exteriorization of knowledge with respect to the 'knower'" and that "The old principle that the acquisition of knowledge is indissociable from the training (*Bildung*) of minds . . . is becoming obsolete and will become ever more so" (p. 4).

Meaningful information without context cannot exist; and context is always mediated. Thus, the fluidity of learning, information, and self and the blurring between the natural and the artificial are at the heart of our uncomfortable perception that the technologies we have created and use are, in turn, creating and using us. As Weinberger (2007) asserts, our "solution to the overabundance of information is more information" (p. 13). Thus, Hutchins (1995) captures the ironic consequences of empirical acts of imitation:

AI and information-processing psychology proposed some radical conceptual surgery for the modeled human. The brain was removed and replaced with a computer. The surgery was a success. However, there was an apparently unintended side effect: the hands, the eyes, the ears, the nose, the mouth, and the emotions all fell away when the brain was replaced by the computer.

The computer was not made in the image of the person. *The computer was made in the image of the formal manipulations of abstract systems. And the last 30 years of cognitive science can be seen as attempts to remake the person in the image of the computer.* (p. 363)

To capture the essential argument made by Weinberger in his (2007) book "*Everything Is Miscellaneous*," in the connected, digital world, *nothing* is miscellaneous, even though it might appear so at any given time to an individual viewing it: "the miscellaneous is a set of things that have nothing in common. Of course, that 'nothing' is relative since the utensils in your kitchen's miscellaneous drawer all have a use in preparing and eating food, all are physical objects, and all are smaller than the drawer itself" (p. 86).

Yet as the subtlety of our interactions with technologies increases, their sensory-perceptual, affective, and social implications are beginning to draw our attention. Technology pervades and produces us. Sherry Turkle (1999), mirroring her second self (1984), sums up our discomfort as follows:

People who grew up in the world of the mechanical are more comfortable with a definition of what is alive that excludes all but the biological and resist shifting definitions of aliveness. So, when they meet ideas of artificial life which put the processes of replication and evolution rather than biology at the center of what is alive . . . they tend to be resistant, even if intrigued. They feel as though they are being asked to make a theoretical choice against biology and for computational process. Children who have grown up with computational objects don't experience that dichotomy. They turn the dichotomy into a menu and cycle through its choices. Today's children have learned a lesson from their cyborg objects. They cycle through the cy-dough-plasm into fluid and emergent conceptions of self and life. (p. 552)

Pervasiveness undermines the dichotomy between natural and artificial, and, Turkle (1998) asserts, "With the radical change in the nature of objects, the internalized lessons of the object world have changed" (p. 328).

Contemporary technologies are extensions of man (to use McLuhan's expression) because they *mirror* us, not because they are tools that we *use* in a nondialectic relationship. And, as though to provoke Ong (1982) and his image of technologies both as methods for and instigators of critique on our traditional-natural ways of being, we feel compelled to create computer programs that mirror our future appearance or to design robots that—literally—imitate our gestures after studying *us*.[2]

Artificial learning environments, therefore, imitate and distribute our experience of learners, learning, instructors, and instructing. The simulation itself has something to teach us. As Bransford et al. (2000) argue, "Like a textbook or any other cultural object, technology resources for education . . . function in a social environment, mediated by learning conversations" (p. 230); and, currently, children have been observed to spend more time watching television than they do in school (p. 26).

When technology becomes a cultural object, we can perhaps put it into perspective in terms of its capacity to "improve learning" in and of itself. Or we run the risk of taking technology for granted, to take Turkle's (1997) position: "Simulations enable us to abdicate authority to the simulation; they give us permission to accept the opacity of the model that plays itself out on our screens." Flash representations of stars collapsing, graphical interpretations of string theory, process illustrations of complex organizational communication patterns—all suggest a certain surface believability that we demand, digest, and distribute. For good reason, then, Brown and

Duguid (2000) decenter technology momentarily, reminding us that "Circulating human knowledge . . . is not simply a matter of search and retrieval, as some views of knowledge management might have us believe. While knowledge is often not all that hard to search, it can be difficult to retrieve, if by *retrieve* people mean detach from one knower and attach to another" (p. 124).

Indeed, technological information currently demands our attention and interaction as readily as natural and cultural information, for, as Borgmann (2000) notes, technological information

introduces a new kind of information. To information *about* and *for* reality it adds *information as reality*. The paradigms of report and recipe are succeeded by the paradigm of the recording. The technological information on a compact disc is so detailed and controlled that it addresses us virtually *as* reality. What comes from a recording of a Bach cantata on a CD is not a report about the cantata nor a recipe—the score—for performing the cantata, it is in the common understanding of music itself. Information through the power of technology steps forward as a rival of reality. (p. 2)

Thus, in viewing technology as a (mere) tool, that is, as something that does not require its own series of disciplinary theories, we make the error of privileging our approaches and methods and of separating technology's inevitable and transformative influence on what we do, think, develop, analyze, and evaluate. The dichotomy between form and function—between the medium and the message, to use McLuhan's (1964) terminology—is an illusion, and it is an illusion that is unfortunately promulgated in most fields. Manzini (1995) contends that our desire to dominate nature further exemplifies our erroneous and profoundly nonecological thinking:

This way of thinking and operating, which has shown its efficacy over a long period of time, is now beginning to look simplistic and myopic. The continuous fracture of circular and cybernetic structures and their substitution by linear sequences cannot continue forever. The links that have been neglected are reappearing as problems. The grand project of the simplification of reality is showing its limitations. The systemic complexity that was thrown out the window is entering now through the front door. To confront it, to find a type of behavior that can bring up to date our Western idea of doing, we must first develop new models with which to comprehend reality. We need models that will let us understand reality without losing what we have discovered about its irreducible complexity. (p. 228)

Perhaps we do require a science of the particular, one that acknowledges that technology is never transparent. Disciplines that employ technology but that do not understand it beyond its particular utilitarian nature, that believe that technology can improve and never impede their progress, processes, products, or productivity, are clearly not familiar with Castells's (1996) conclusion that "no systematic structural relationship" exists between technology and employment levels (p. 263) or Landauer's (1997) argument that technology has improved productivity less than 1 percent since its introduction to the workplace.

Unfortunately, the tool metaphor is firmly located in educational research as well. Furr, Ragsdale, and Horton (2005), for example, argue on the one hand that we not forget "the non-neutrality of technology effects," while simultaneously asserting that "computer technology is a tool, just as is language, pencil, and paper" (p. 286). Kirkwood and Price (2006) extend the tool metaphor to all information and communication technologies (ICT), concluding "that basically ICT offers just tools" (p. 2) and reminding us that effective teaching may be improved by technology but technology will never improve ineffective teaching. Indeed, the tool metaphor has a wide appeal that crosses disciplines and derives much of its initial support from the software industries that produce computer and technological products. "Tool" suggests something that extends and augments what we are already capable of doing. "Tool" suggests that, in the fashion of a hammer, little or no human difficulty or attention is demanded *by* the tool *itself*. We do not *learn* tools; we *use* them, and we tend to use them alone rather than in groups (cf. Repenning, Ioannidou, and Ambach 1998).

I prefer Turkle's (1999) subtler and more troubling metaphor of technology as *mirror*. We create, in our technologies, images or representations of what we want to do and—by extension—what we are. Mirrors in turn reflect back on us and enable us to come to new understandings about the original knowledge and acts that we aimed to delegate to them. The mirror metaphor, unlike the tool metaphor, does not necessarily hold that technological developments result in progress—or it at least suggests that progress is a complex and long-term proposition. The cognitive amplification promised by Nickerson (2005)—in terms of information finding, real-time tutorial help, memory aids and reminders, inferencing, communication, and decision-making systems—are as much a list of potential strengths of information technologies as they are a list of human–computer interaction challenges.

Contrasting a mirroring perspective to the tool perspective that currently dominates much discourse about technology in everyday life is, thus, a provocative exercise. Nowhere is the myth of technological progress promised by the metaphor of the tool more consistently applied, embedded, and affirmed than in our contemporary learning worlds. In the workplace, technology promises the impossible: to serve as labor-reducing devices in settings where increased labor is the cost-saving goal. The promise is that, with the increased technological demands of "twenty-first-century work," employees can use technologies to learn everything they need to know about using the technologies that help them accomplish more in less time, everywhere, anytime. Simultaneously, technology advocates vow to increase and enhance the amount of leisure we are able to enjoy, to enable us to acquire more information in less time, to empower us to exercise while ordering news without ever leaving our homes. Finally, technology continues to accelerate and revise our basic assumptions about higher learning, whether based in one-room schoolhouses or via simultaneous video broadcast to rooms in two universities on opposite ends of the same state (as currently offered in my academic department).

Three major arguments have been forwarded in this chapter. First, a transformational perspective toward technology-mediated communication enriches our understanding of instruction and learning with technology. Second, dichotomies between *artificial* and *real* encourage comparison-contrast but undermine the opportunity to study how technologies mirror, enhance, and distort us as communicators and learners. Third, instruction and information cannot be decontextualized from human interaction, action, and the artifacts that communicate them. The stance being taken here is that much can be gained in terms of theory building if we resist the urge to proceduralize or draw neat causal conclusions about our relationship with technology, our learning environments, and the various instructional contexts within which we find ourselves.

The next chapter presents some of the promises and challenges introduced by current conceptions of work and of learning in the workplace, of leisure learning, and of higher-learning environments. Complex problem solving, ill-structuredness, accelerated activity and decision making, everyday media interactions, and the growing need for collaboration are common issues across these domains.

2   Learning Worlds

Accelerated technological developments encourage a divergence of learning across traditionally separate domains: work, leisure, and higher-educational spaces. Understanding these learning contexts broadens our perspective on instruction and learning in our technology-rich lives. Researchers have noted that it is becoming increasingly difficult to identify learning spaces free of occupational commitment, efficiency management, and haste. Since distributed instruction narrows the distance between our learning worlds, balancing higher-order educational goals with personal, performance, and production goals becomes increasingly important.

As an activity, learning entails working. It also transcends working. The purpose of learning is not the production of something that remains as a separate object when the learning person leaves the scene, but it is rather the production of something that goes with the learning person: An internal state has changed, a subjective product has been created, tied to the learning person.
—Gerhard Fischer, Joan Greenbaum, and Frieder Nake (2000, p. 510)

But technology frequently has effects in areas other than those intended by its creators.
—Stephen T. Kerr (2004, p. 113)

We inhabit three primary learning worlds, broadly defined: work, leisure, and educational settings (see figure 2.1):

Represented as a Venn diagram, figure 2.1 consists of eight potential worlds including the outside line as one individual's life-world. Further examination reveals the possibility of 256 Boolean combinations, and the spaces where intersections occur are where the greatest opportunities for understanding and tension among the learning worlds can be found (Barney and Gordon 2005).

Thus, in more socioeconomically developed countries, leisure learning continues to grow, in addition to access to higher learning for more diverse populations. Work learning ranges from the formal—training, workshops, and certification—to the

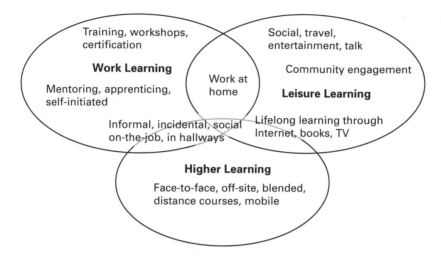

Figure 2.1
Connectivity and multiple learning worlds (adapted from Mehlenbacher 2007a, citing Gleick 1999).

informal—apprenticing, on-the-job, and learning by doing. Leisure learning, too, ranges from the formal—museums and community-based educational offerings—to the informal—television, day-to-day discourse and news, and the Internet. Higher learning continues to maintain the three-month sequestering structure but is moving from one-to-many instruction on-site to many-to-many instruction distributed across technologies and locations.

Accelerated developments in ICT, in combination with numerous social and cultural factors, are increasingly intertwined learning worlds that historically we were able to separate or set into predetermined life phases. Glastra, Hake, and Schedler (2004) elaborate:

Phases of learning, work and unemployment, caring, and resting have become spread throughout the course of life in recurrent cycles. This development has two corollaries. One is that in certain periods of life, many different tasks must be combined. . . . The second is that given the individualization of life courses, coordination of life and work on an aggregate social level becomes problematic. . . . Conflicts of interest arise continuously where these life courses intersect. (p. 295)

As our learning worlds or life courses intersect and fragment, the definition and purpose of our day-to-day activities and social interactions too will require reexamination. Similar considerations were surely required early in the Industrial Revolution as economic forces initially separated work from home. And importantly, such shifts in sociospatial patterns inevitably require dramatic reconceptualizations of education.

As Kostogriz (2006) observes, "meaning-making and learning are obviously spatial phenomena and space is implicated in pedagogical practices at all levels" (p. 176). Nippert-Eng (1995) provides a thoughtful discussion of the boundary blurring that has been playing out as our learning worlds conflate. Our work and home realms, she argues, produce different degrees of continuity and discontinuity and can be better understood by examining

• The physical environment of a realm.
• The social ambiance of realms.
• One's orientation toward time and perception of time within realms.
• An individual's sense of the rewards sought within each realm and how well rewarded one is.
• The sense of commitment to others in each realm.
• Whether or not there are good friends/confidants in each realm and whether this is important or not.
• How challenging one's efforts are in either realm.
• Whether or not one seeks and/or achieves a sense of immortality or tries to carry on important traditions through one's efforts in each realm.
• Whether or not one has the sense of making unique contributions in each realm (how "irreplaceable" one feels).
• The moral frameworks used in either realm to interpret others' actions and guide one's own.
• The amount of direction and interruptions one experiences in either realm (the ability to set an agenda of one's own and carry it out unimpeded).
• The privateness/publicness of one's activities and mindset in either realm. (Nippert-Eng 1995, pp. 227–228)

Examining the research on work, leisure, and higher learning worlds can, therefore, help us to begin viewing these spaces as interdependent continuums where learning is conceived in formal and informal ways, and where the strengths and limitations of one realm can be reviewed in the light of another.

2.1 Work Learning

At my daughter's school, the preschoolers set up an "office" play area that consists of a computer keyboard, a crayon-generated computer display terminal, a phone, stapler, notepads, envelopes, pencils and pens, and a three-hole punch. Drawn on the two desks on dark construction paper are two ink blotter pads, a crayon calendar is taped to the wall, a box of post-its sits next to a calculator (that opens automatically when one presses ON), and a cell phone rests next to the keyboard.

When I tell my daughter and two of her workmates that we have a deadline tonight, one of them instantly picks up the phone and says, "Yes, okay. We'll have it for you tonight. Yes. I'll call back. Okay." The second workmate asks for envelopes, takes a seat in front of the keyboard, and begins typing energetically. My daughter, after turning on the calculator, begins addressing an envelope using make-believe symbols and asks me for the stickers on the other desk; her workmate, still on the phone, hands the sticker box to her while continuing to pretend-interact with her imaginary client. My daughter's teacher informs me that the children had set up the space themselves, and she observes how remarkable it is how effortlessly they step into the role when asked if they would like to *play* office.

And it is remarkable, when you consider that the children are preschoolers, have not likely visited an authentic (notably white-collar) office space, and still manage to include in their make-believe "office of the future" aspects of most contemporary offices—including technologies for generating, manipulating, and distributing hard-copy and digital "paper," asynchronous and synchronous communication media and processes, and a workspace organized around teamwork, interruptions, deliverables, vicious product cycles, and accelerated deadlines (cf. Perlow 1999). Without imagining the irony, the preschoolers "play" captures, in Spinuzzi's (2003) words, "The messiness of everyday work life—the unofficial, unpredictable ways workers assert their own agency, turn to their own problem-solving skills, and individually or cooperatively design practices, tools, and texts to deal with recurrent problems" (p. 3). Indeed, the preschoolers, in deciding to "play work," have underscored the most notable feature of contemporary work: its definition as any meaningful production activity we choose to set off temporally and to label as work. Work, however, does not require a stable workplace, and, for this reason, discussions of work–life balance have become increasingly common (Fenwick 2006).

We know these things about contemporary work and yet we have an exceedingly difficult time addressing them in our educational systems and training programs. Gumport (2002) summarizes our dilemma as follows: "Keeping pace with knowledge change in the contemporary era is compounded by changes in knowledge creation and dissemination practices. Worldwide, there is an increased societal demand for specialist knowledge producers at nonuniversity sites, and a diffusion of technological applications that make possible new patterns of communication and collaboration" (p. 48). In fact, numerous business leaders have made good livings as lecturers addressing these aspects of corporate life and warning that companies that are unable to adapt to the new "global, high-tech economy of the twenty-first-century," the "postindustrial economy," the "knowledge sector," "global workplace," "consumer society," "information age," "glocalized commercialization," "flat world," "creative sector," "third-wave postcapitalism," "digitized society," or "globally competitive environment" (choose a millennial catchphrase) will suffer the same plight as turn-of-the-century agricultural and manufacturing organizations or the contemporary service sector.

Of course, this perspective toward organizations is not entirely new. March and Simon (1958) provide a typology of work that is still highly relevant today

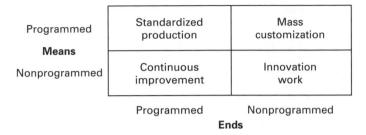

	Programmed	Nonprogrammed
Programmed	Standardized production	Mass customization
Nonprogrammed	Continuous improvement	Innovation work

Means

Programmed — Nonprogrammed

Ends

Figure 2.2
Typology of work (adapted from March and Simon 1958).

(see figure 2.2). Whereas industrialization and mass production demanded the "management" of highly programmed work, developments between the 1940s and the turn of the century have resulted in the rapid movement from automized control to computerized individualism to the digitized and extended contemporary workplace (Hollnagel 2001). In programmed work, means and ends are well defined, whereas, in nonprogrammed work, individuals and groups are required to work in ill-structured problem domains. Ill-structured domains, according to Spiro et al. (1992), exhibit the following characteristics: "(a) each case or example of knowledge application typically involves the simultaneous interactive involvement of multiple, wide-application conceptual structures (multiple schemas, perspectives, organizational principles, and so on), each of which is individually complex (i.e., the domain involves concept- and case-complexity); and (b) the pattern of conceptual incidence and interaction varies substantially across cases nominally of the same type (i.e., the domain involves across-case irregularity)" (p. 60). Ill-structured domains are *unstable*; this word captures contemporary changes in the way people work. As Spinuzzi (2007) observes, these work settings are characterized by "downsizing, automation, flattening of work hierarchies, increasing numbers of relationships between companies, continual reorganization, the breaking down of silos or stovepipes in organizations, and perhaps most importantly, the increase in telecommunications (phones, faxes, Internet connections), which has made it possible to connect any one point to any other, within and across organizations" (p. 265).

In short, ill-structured domains demand flexibility, a creative ability to organize across single data points, and to understand, argue, and evaluate categorically, that is, at the conceptual level. Moreover, ill-structured domains require strategies for carrying what has been learned into new situations and contexts, for managing trade-offs, and for turning that understanding into actions (Fischer 2006).

Within this organizational context, individuals are characterized as symbol-making, symbol-using "systems" that act primarily as problem solvers, attempting to discover—through varying combinations of trial, error, and selectivity—accurate state and process descriptions of some element of nature (Newell and Simon 1972). Problem-solving individuals must, in turn, create and maintain "intensional networks" where, according to Nardi, Whittaker, and Schwarz (2000), "Joint activity is accomplished by the assembling of sets of individuals derived from overlapping constellations of personal networks." On top of that, the relationship between individuals and their environment involves an ongoing interaction between (a) incoming information about the status of the environment (perception), (b) information processing (thinking), and (c) environmental response(s) (motor activity) (Vera and Simon 1993, p. 10). Since these individuals' problem spaces are ill-structured ones, they must constantly and creatively contend with complex and changing problems, goals, subgoals, and with their current knowledge of the solution constraints and the bounded nature of human rationality (Simon 1979; Voss et al. 1983).

In addition, contemporary problem solvers are frequently engaged in ill-structured domains, collecting, sorting, analyzing, interpreting, designing, and reporting data, and collaborating, communicating, interacting, and negotiating with other problem solvers. And none of these activities offers single-solution paths or obvious checkmate situations (Kotovsky, Hayes, and Simon 1985; Spiro et al. 1987). They are what Chi, Glaser, and Rees (1982) call "real-world problems" and, as such, present "new obstacles that were not encountered previously in puzzle-like problems" since "the exact operators to be used are usually not given, the goal state is sometimes not well defined" and "a large knowledge space" is essential (p. 7). For Jonassen (1997), ill-structured problem solving requires that learners be able to express problem spaces and contextual constraints, to manage alternative shareholder perspectives and positions, to produce potential problem solutions, to assess the viability of different possible solutions through argumentation, monitor options, and implement and adapt solutions (pp. 79–83).

Contemporary, ill-structured domains are technology rich. Asaolu (2006) provides a useful snapshot of the differences between turn-of-the-century, *Fordist* technological settings and *ICT* (emerging) technological settings (see table 2.1). Gee (2000), for this reason, places design at the center of what it means to "add value" in the new capitalism:

What it means to add value is, by and large, to bring *knowledge* to bear on some aspect of the design or redesign of work processes, or on some aspect of the relationship among workers or of workers with customers, or on some aspect of the design, production, distribution, or marketing of a product or service. . . . It is *sociotechnical design knowledge* (knowledge about how to design and transform environments, relationships, projects, and identities) that counts most in the new capitalism. Even low-level workers are expected to redesign their work groups and work processes, to represent (to be) the business to the customer, and to take on new identities, for example, to see themselves as "partners" or as "entrepreneurs" contracting out their services, not as workers hired by someone else for a permanent job. (pp. 517–518)

Table 2.1
Comparison of contemporary technology developments (adapted from Asaolu 2006, p. 337)

Fordist (Old)	ICT (New)
Energy-intensive	Information-intensive
Standardized	Customized
Rather stable product mix	Rapid changes in product mix
Dedicated plant and equipment	Flexible production systems
Automation	Systemation
Single firm	Networks
Hierarchical management structures	Flat horizontal management structures
Departmental	Integrated
Product with service	Service with products
Centralization	Distributed intelligence
Specialized skills	Multiple skills
Minimal training requirements	Continuous training and retraining
Adversarial industrial relations; collective agreements codify provisional armistices	Moves toward long-term consultative and participative industrial relations
Government control and planning and sometimes ownership	Government information, regulation, coordination, and vision
Capital intensive (funded by the government or through loans, etc.)	Phased investment (by individuals, venture capitalists, etc.)
Emphasis on full-time employment for adult (age 16–65) male workers	More flexible hours and involvement of part-time workers and postretirement people

Moving from specialists hired for life to fulfill programmed tasks (or "modular" workers, to employ Spinuzzi's 2007 term) to distributed sociotechnical designers working across boundaries on complex tasks in fast-paced contexts is a significant shift (DeSanctis and Monge 1999). Historically, Fordist approaches to product development involved bringing together specialists organized by technology to create parts of a whole that they rarely saw, and one can see how early conceptions of computing in the workplace adopted many of these same assumptions. Certainly Fordism and its Taylorist foundations that largely ignore psychological factors and assume that "soldiering" is required to achieve worker productivity (Mattelart 1996) have been adopted by early technology advocates who have emphasized efficiency and time "management" as the greatest benefits of computation. Indeed, some might argue that this emphasis on timely, effective, efficient software product-line engineering continues unquestioned today, and our faith in machine-based automation has grown considerably during the last four decades (Krueger 2006; Sugumaran, Park, and Kang 2006).

Perhaps this explains why Asaolu (2006) describes workplace developments before ICT as Fordist rather than as automationist or early computationalist. After all, our contemporary relationship with ICT in the workplace is certainly complicated by an early, adversarial relationship between human beings and organizational computing. Winner (1995) reinforces this historical tension, writing, "The linguistic root of the concept is, appropriately for our purposes, the Greek *ergon*, which means 'work.' As practiced by most engineers and industrial designers, such work is narrowly focused upon ways in which instruments do or do not offer ease of individual performance; however, the social, moral, and political dimensions of the human relation to material implements are seldom taken into account" (p. 163).

2.1.1 Adversarial Beginnings with Powerful Computing

When American corporations first began to use computers in the 1950s, the monoliths were employed to manipulate enormous amounts of numerical data that, in turn, were used to justify reductions in labor costs. These machines produced considerable heat and were housed in large, sterile, well-ventilated rooms that were unfriendly to human inhabitants. The initial industrial relationship between computers and humans in organizations, therefore, was a distinctly adversarial one where computers were used to reduce human involvement in what were initially described as low-level production activities. During this same time, funds coming from the Pentagon factored into the development of IBM's first transistor-based computers in 1959 (Mattelart 2000), and a strong military investment in computing and training continues to this day (Curda and Curda 2003). Most certainly, in those early days, computers were not viewed as something that educational researchers, humanities scholars, or social scientists might need to focus on, given that computers were solely meant to accomplish activities that did not need to be carried out by human beings.

Ultimately, computers were recognized as powerful marketing devices for forecasting sales and anticipating market trends: an industry of applications developers and computer systems analysts were born. An uneasy partnership began, between computers and expert analysts and knowledgeable users, with computers being extended to help analysts, as Moldow (1985) puts it, "better understand interrelationships between different business processes" (p. 106). And thus began the exponential growth and increased complexity of modern-day computer systems.

Moldow (1985) suggests that, in time, "user computer organizations became more highly centralized, complementing the then widely accepted Grosch's law, which postulated that every dollar spent on a computer would return doubled computer power—in essence, the bigger the better" (p. 107). Predictably, the more complex the solution, the more likely the solution brought with it an unanticipated host of new subproblems. Computer departments thus become specialized organizational units with their own sets of needs, resources, and limitations—in addition to storing, maintaining, and updating the daily data needs of the business, they become bottlenecks in the business's ability to act, to make decisions, and to manage change.

This, according to Moldow (1985), is the beginning of "the creation of a mystique associated with the computing department" (p. 107), a mystique that contains and promotes itself to this day. Such departments are commonly referred to with some reverence as the "Core Group" or the "Basement" or the "Skunkworks," and they produce the latest version for release, "million-dollar versions," or "the lines" (for lines of code). They are frequently the wealthiest departments in high-tech companies, and they tend to be populated primarily by computer scientists, engineers, and technical specialists. They report directly to upper management or the administration or the CEO of companies. And thus the user's relationship with computers has become fully alienating: groups of users depend and rely on computers to help them succeed but also depend on a buffer of technical experts to make sense of their computationally generated "solutions."

But just as computing departments and organizations were digging in for a long and prosperous organizational haul, other splinter markets were being born around Unix-based minicomputers. Ultimately, by the late 1970s, microcomputers were being purchased by computing enthusiasts and specialists with an eye toward a computer-based future.

The computing universe that Nicholas Negroponte described in his prophetic (1979, 1996) article, "Books without pages," originally published in the *Proceedings of the International Conference on Communications* (ICC), presaged both an exaggerated and an underestimated potential future for computing. Coincidentally, 1979 was the year that I graduated from high school and was introduced to my first software program, VisiCalc, and microcomputer, a TRS-80 with 64 bytes of memory. I was working in the marketing department of a large financial institution in Canada, and the vice president of marketing felt strongly that "the computer" could help us to understand our customers and competition better: my responsibility was to show him how that might work using our newly acquired TRS-80.

It is difficult to remember the radical realignment that computer users experienced at the time, moving as we were from crude input and output devices to the beginnings of direct manipulation interfaces. But this conceptual revolution was already well underway since, at the same time, Negroponte (1979, 1996) had begun to describe the MIT Media Lab's early development efforts on the Spatial Data Management System (SDMS), a design effort that is still—at least metaphorically—in progress today. Negroponte's SDMS represented a conceptual draft version of our brave new contemporary technological world, where "image processing, broadcast television, and computer graphics" or the "telephone, television, and microprocessing" have emerged as seamless "media for communication" (p. 2).

"Books without Pages" contains six provocative headings:

• *The page as a syntactic chunk*:   In this section, Negroponte problematizes the metaphor of the "page" as we move online, asking questions that contemporary researchers interested in the design of online instruction are still trying to answer—"are there similar chunks? What purposes do they serve? What use does the sense of place in text serve? Are there meaningful textual gestalts?"

• *Pages without paper*:   Here, influenced by emerging videodisc technology, the author uses the word "frame" instead of "page" to describe massive storage devices that might hold the *Encyclopedia Britannica*, for example.

• *Talking pages*:   Here, the author describes a system where "assembly instructions [are] spoken" and "where quadraphonic or octaphonic sound systems produce spatially localized sound."

• *Personalized pages*:   The author outlines the development of personalized pages that can be tailored "both to the particular subject matter and the particular user" and that employ and anticipate "a wide range of abbreviations and subtleties gained through familiarity, shared metaphors, and the complicated mechanisms of inference making" as we do in human-to-human discourse.

• *Pages with places*:   The author posits that frequently "'data' [is] accessed by where it is, versus what it is" and employs the metaphor of a computer "Dataland, upon which data are placed, in a variety of forms, sometimes in neighborhoods, frequently with landmarks"—these data, he summarizes, can come in the form of "animation, sound, movies, slides, and the like."

• *Books in which we might live*:   Negroponte imagines a "gaggle of equipment . . . assembled with the idea of going to the fullest extreme of human interfacing, leaving no channel untapped and no mode or medium of presentation unused" (Negroponte 1979, 1996, pp. 5–8).

The eight-page "Books without Pages" monograph anticipates contemporary desktop metaphors, direct-manipulation interfaces, virtual reality and simulation environments, the Internet and the Web and social networking spaces, alternative peripheral designs, computational portability, and contemporary U.S. legislation that increasingly encourages telephone, entertainment, media, and computer companies to compete openly for each other's markets.

So, in retrospect, our present-near-future is a vision that has been described by Negroponte (1979, 1996) and that has a well-funded twenty-five-year history at MIT (Brand 1987). A little more than fifteen years later, Negroponte (1995) could describe a present that contained versions of the past he had contributed to, in addition to forecasting a future where *my time*, not Prime Time (p. 172), is the norm.

Although the advent of the personal computing that Negroponte (1979, 1996) envisions has been heralded by some as a technological future that will improve productivity, researchers have observed that a relationship between computer systems and human productivity has yet to be established (Bullen and Bennett 1991; Landauer 1997; Selber 2004b). Similar claims that technological developments in the home will reduce housework have produced similar results: technologized housework requires approximately the same amount of time in the form of a whole new set of tasks, for example, operating and maintaining vacuum cleaners, repairing refrigerators, cleaning and moving appliances, and loading and unloading dishwashers (Wajcman 1991). And in the workplace, despite the ready availability of devices designed to facilitate appointment management, to-do lists, and other "notable information" (e.g., cell-phone text messaging, handheld instruments, laptops), people still tend to prefer paper notes because they are optimally "temporary, viewable, mobile, postable, transferable, short, easy to create and destroy" (Campbell and Maglio 2003, p. 902).

Interestingly, in the case of developing electronic note-taking technologies, we inadvertently learn a great deal about the nontechnical nature of notes. Again, imitating the "natural" (in this instance, the unnatural but pervasive post-it), our simulations provide us with transformative learning opportunities. Campbell and Maglio (2003) observe, for example, that notes contain an incredible range of information types, including "names, phone numbers, e-mail addresses, URLs, to-do items, references, how-to's, appointments/meetings, passwords, phone messages, procedures, policies, product specifications, server addresses, directory paths, helpdesk numbers, research paper references, install keys for software, the person's schedule, and configuration parameters" (p. 903).

And if all we do is learn more about our natural selves by generating artificial and imperfect (or flawless) versions of our selves, these are still exciting technological times. During the last sixty years of computing history, we have seen changes that stagger the imagination and defy our predictive abilities. But it also seems problematic to frame our study of instruction and learning with technology around well-worn topoi that (1) include phrases such as "in this fast-paced, knowledge-driven society," (2) recite references to the growing number of users who are connected to the Internet in their jobs and in their homes, or (3) imply in any way that technology—in and of itself—holds the promise of curing our organizational illnesses or eliminating our educational problems.

A cursory glance at the influence of technology on our lives would suggest the direct opposite: it is rewiring our traditional notions of work, confusing the relationship between our professional and personal lives, exponentially increasing the availability of practical and research-based information related to almost everything, and promising to extend our capabilities while at the same time appearing determined to frustrate even the most simple of human tasks, from voting to the making of grocery lists (cf. Lazar et al. 2006). Cooper (2005) posits that "home-workers and micro-entrepreneurs of the future" are often more vulnerable to poorly designed technologies because they lack centralized technical support and access to organized training units, and frequently work in isolation augmented only by minimal and virtual social interaction. One can argue that, given the pervasiveness of ICT in the workplace, the contemporary problem solver's large knowledge space has in effect been multiplied by three. Shneiderman's (1987) model of the knowledge types of computer users illustrates the nature of the problem. When we employ technology to accomplish our work, we must integrate our knowledge of *task semantics* (the real-world task) with *computer semantics* (task knowledge about the computer) with *syntactic knowledge* of the computer (device-specific details).

Thus we are simultaneously awed by our global reach and humbled into remembering our console-based illusions of control. Pesce (2000), twenty years after Negroponte's (1979, 1996) visionary paper, retells the story of *Encyclopaedia Britannica's* introduction to worldwide distribution:

On October 19, 1999, www.britannica.com launched on the World Wide Web. And immediately crashed.

It seems that so many people were hungry for the solid facts to *Britannica's* virtual pages that they simply overloaded the Web servers. Something like fifteen million bits—individual queries to *Britannica's* knowledge base—were recorded by the system before it overloaded and expired, leaving *Britannica* a bit red-faced with embarrassment. . . . The technical wizards at *Encyclopaedia Britannica* dusted themselves off . . . and brought the site back online in mid-November. . . . (p. 142)

Extraordinary promise, reasonable setback (in hindsight), renegotiation of the problem, tempered attempt: the ingredients of technological trial-and-error—and of contemporary knowledge making. Resnick, Lesgold, and Hall (2005) remind us that our definition of what constitutes knowledge has changed dramatically during that last several technological decades. Knowledge is no longer represented in the form of lists, *primary* sources, controlled and parameterized areas, or fixed, private states of understanding; instead, knowledge is contingent, framed by schemas and high-order structures, drawn from multiple, emergent sources, and publicly distributed (p. 79). Now, for example, in addition to having easy access to the interview manuscripts of dozens of academic and industry visionaries from computer science (Ubiquitous Conversations 2005), we can access international news stories according to the number of stories published in a given day (Westamp 2004), quickly review American baby names from 1880 to 2005 according to their popularity (babynamewizard.com, 2004–2005), or search and view over 2000 educational, amateur, advertising, and industry films created between 1927 and 1987 (Internet Archive 2001).

According to Horrigan and Rainie (2006), approximately four in ten Internet-using adults report that the Internet has played a major role in helping them to choose a college for their children or themselves, to look for a new place to live, or to make significant financial decisions. High-powered research tools have infiltrated our daily lives. Thus, methods for assessing knowledge have moved away from individualized skill-testing and question-and-answer formats to situations that encourage distributed explanation and elaboration, inquiry and argumentation (p. 80). Cognitive aptitude has become incremental, open, and learnable via well-articulated heuristics that promise progress.

2.1.2 The Organization of Learning

So, in some ways, it is naive to advise contemporary organizational leaders to capitalize on distributed and multimedia technological developments. That is, individual problem solvers and organizations bring a host of preestablished patterns for interaction and communication, and their relationship to information technologies is not easy to characterize because information technologies are not easy to define. We cannot even reach agreement on the distinction between information, instructional, communication, and educational technology as names intended to capture our interactions with computer technologies. Rice and Gattiker (2005) remind us that, in addition to traditional concepts such as structural hierarchies and information flow, organizations both limit and enhance technology integration and use, and technologies, in turn, produce organizational changes that are difficult to identify:

Typically, researchers and ordinary folk alike tend to lump communication media into familiar, binary, and mutually exclusive categories. Examples include mass media/interpersonal, objective/socially constructed, information rich/lean, organic/technological, traditional/new, democratizing/hegemonic, same/different times/places, content sources/users are institutions/individuals/computer systems, and so forth. . . .

Yet media in general and [computer information systems] in particular are inherently ambiguous (because they can be interpreted in multiple and possibly conflicting ways), can rarely be fully understood, and continue to be adapted, reinvented, and redesigned. . . . So taking a multidimensional perspective toward conceptualizing media seems necessary and appropriate. (p. 546)

Just as workplace media analysts tend to lump communication into clumsy dichotomies, so too do they tend to describe workplace learning as a freestanding entity that either does or does not occur. Of course, the dichotomy between work and learning is a dubious one. As Fischer, Greenbaum, and Nake (2000) assert:

Work at all times implies learning, hidden or overt. Learning always requires some kind of work. If it were true that work disappeared, would learning disappear also? Or, if work disappeared generally, would a conscious learning effort enable some individuals to find niches where work had not disappeared yet? (p. 509)

When we learn, we work. To learn, we must acquire knowledge, skills, or procedures. We do not necessarily learn when we are instructed because we must actively attend to the instruction, process the information, integrate it into our existing knowledge, and, in some cases, share it with others or apply it to new situations. These activities require processing, and processing is work; and, although we are rarely paid to learn, but rather are paid for labor, we work all the time. Eight million American adults used the Internet in 2005 to change jobs, while a staggering 21 million used it to get additional training for their careers (Horrigan and Rainie 2006).

Thus, perhaps reductively, learning has been explicitly connected to success in the contemporary workplace. Just as organizations are experiencing dramatic change, so too are workplace training and on-the-job education. Training in the new economy is viewed as a competitive advantage rather than as a cost. Berge (2003) argues, as well, that training in the new economy demands lifelong learning, requires that content rather than learners be flexible and mobile, capitalizes on multimodal information sharing, and provides learning environments that support distributed learning communities rather than leaving learners to work in virtual isolation (p. 603).

With this perspective toward work and learning in mind, it becomes increasingly important that we acknowledge that, in order to understand work, we must understand the learning that occurs around, within, and outside places of work. Ellström (2001) defines organizational learning as "changes in organizational practices (including routines and procedures, structures, technologies, systems, and so on) that are mediated through individual learning or problem-solving processes" (p. 422) and describes four levels of organizational learning that adhere to March and Simon's (1958) typology of work (see figure 2.2):

• *Reproductive (1)*—routinized (automated) actions performed without much conscious attention and control.
• *Productive, Type I (2)*—emphasizing results or choice and use of methods.
• *Productive, Type II (3)*—more active process of knowledge-based problem solving through experimentation (involves novel or unfamiliar situations for which no rules or procedural knowledge are available from previous experience).
• *Creative (4)*—when individuals or groups of individuals within an organization begin to question established definitions of problems or objectives and to act to transform institutionalized ideologies, routines, structures, or practices (pp. 423–424).

Ellström's (2001) work-learning types capture a movement from the programmed work described by March and Simon (1958) through to the idealized sociotechnical design knowledge that Gee (2000) anticipates. It is clear, however, that we are still aiming at that *Creative* goal. Torraco (1999), in his review of the work practices of photocopier repair, software support, and dairy delivery employees, notes that contemporary workers are frequently being challenged by *Productive, Type II* problem situations:

Employees are confronted with novel or poorly defined problems that cannot be fully anticipated in advance. Successful performances require employees to go beyond scripted procedures to resolve problems in innovative ways. To understand and respond to these ambiguous situations, they must make resourceful use of materials, local conditions, and social circumstances, thus deploying contingent work strategies that reflect the changing properties of the task environment. (p. 257)

Unfortunately, the management of workplace learning turns out to be as or more traditional in many respects as learning in institutions of higher education (McCracken and Wallace 2000). Sugrue and Rivera (2005), in their report of the 2004 survey results of 281 U.S. organizations distributed by size and industry, found that although instructor-led training continued to dominate the training efforts of the companies (at approximately 68 percent), "The downward trend in live classroom delivery from 1999 to 2003 stabilized in 2004" with "further decrease . . . projected . . . in 2005." The authors conclude that "The upward trend in delivery via learning technologies continued in 2004" and that "Technology-based learning delivery in 2004 was 28 percent" across the 281 organizations (p. 14). Indeed, Bennett (2002) describes the movement away from face-to-face training to technology-based training as inexorable and inevitable from a cost-savings perspective alone. Citing examples from Southwest Airlines, General Electric, Wal-Mart, and Cisco Systems—the latter of which estimates a 40–60 percent savings in employee travel costs for traditional training—Bennett (2002) sets the stasis point with the assumption that technology is here to stay and that employees without technology knowledge will, in effect, be unemployable in the global economy.

Additional challenges that workplace training organizations face beyond a tradition of conservative instructor-led training include (a) naive notions that providing content creates learning; (b) organizational positioning that disconnects learning, research, and development from products, processes, and profits and that, therefore, rewards reactive versus strategic training initiatives; (c) a traditional emphasis on skills versus knowledge although research suggests that the two are invariably interdependent (Ummelen 1997); and (d) a history of organizing instruction around "hard" skills that do not meet current work-learning demands versus "soft" skills that are increasingly required in ill-structured work situations. Soft skills that routinely fall under this heading include communication and writing, business ethics, and diversity issues, but the soft skills that stimulate the new capitalism actually include broader "skills" such as elemental strategies for inquiry, systematic approaches to data use, and impromptu heuristics for persuading, designing for, and collaborating with others. It is these soft skills, then, that are required to produce what Schön (1983) describes as "reflective practitioners," that is, "agents of society's reflective conversation with its situation, agents who engage in cooperative inquiry within a framework of institutionalized contention" (p. 352), agents who must contend with "problematic situations characterized by uncertainty, disorder, and indeterminacy" (pp. 15–16).

In this respect, one might argue that the technology-rich projections about the centrality of online training in industry extend past the current reality and observe as well that this pattern is similar to forecasts of technology use in higher education settings. Similar to higher education, challenges related to technology capacity and access, information literacy, trust and control, limited resources, and poorly designed learning-support materials are also issues (Sambrook 2003; Woodall 2004).

But it is also worth noting that the training market is a growing one: D'Antoni (2003) cites one industry research firm's estimation that the information technology training and education market alone will "increase at a modest compound annual rate of about 5% between 2002 and 2007. Corporate training is expected to increase at twice the rate in the United States—10.5% over the same period." Clark (2005) notes that 16 percent of business instruction is currently computer-based (p. 589). A survey of 526 North American companies reported by Bersin (2006) suggests that e-learning makes up "33 percent of all workplace training, up from 29 percent in 2004 and 24 percent in 2003" (p. 20). And Kenney, Hermens, and Clarke (2004) note that the United States is particularly well suited nationally for e-learning given its existing educational systems, free markets, and cultural faith in high technology.

Arguments for the inevitability of increased online instruction in the workplace can be found in the fundamental changes in work that have occurred over the last twenty years rather than by reviewing the current practice of many contemporary training and development units. Indeed, beyond accelerated workplace productivity demands, general expectations and projections about the new realities of lifelong learning in general have reached a critical mass. Tomlinson-Keasey (2002) asserts, "As more workers depend on knowledge throughout their careers, knowledge must necessarily be acquired past the traditional age at which schooling ends and often in educational settings outside of traditional classrooms. A conservative estimate is that meeting the needs of 'knowledge workers' in traditional settings would require the addition of 250,000 students per year to college and university campuses" (p. 135).

But exactly where (in formal educational settings, at work, in our leisure time) and when (during our K–16 years, while working, between projects, after work, in retirement) we are expected to learn remains open to debate. Fischer (2000) argues, "Learning can no longer be dichotomized into a place and time to acquire knowledge (school) and a place and time to apply knowledge (the workplace). Today's citizens are flooded with more information than they can handle, and tomorrow's workers will need to know far more than any individual can retain" (p. 265).

For certain, workers now understand that multiple communication devices and complex workplace problems demand that they learn to perform numerous tasks in minimal amounts of time and that this ability is evaluated favorably by many contemporary managers (Perlow 1999). Mulder et al. (2006), in their study of information overload, found that ill-defined tasks increase stress more than well-defined tasks, unless those tasks require elaborate communication and coordination. Ill-defined tasks most often produce feelings of information overload when they have to be performed in constrained time periods within environments that do not allow concentration, reflection, and focus (p. 249). Turner and Reinsch (2007) provide an illuminating discussion of the integral role of polychronicity, multitasking, equivocality, and multicommunicating in the workplace and conclude that successful workplace learners are "presence allocators," that is, individuals who can "survey the available communication technologies, choose a medium that provides the right cues for each interaction, and divide [their] presence among two or more interlocutors" (p. 47).

According to Bluedorn (2002), "polychronicity is the extent to which people (1) prefer to be engaged in two or more tasks or events simultaneously and are actually so engaged (the preference strongly implying the behavior and vice versa), and (2) believe their preference is the best way to do things" (p. 51). Polychronicity is about preference, whereas multitasking is about getting more things done, a goal that stresses speed (p. 107). Research on polychronicity suggests—counter to popular characterizations—that females are no more likely to be polychronous than males and that there does not appear to be a relationship between age and multitasking behaviors (up to 65 years of age). Not surprisingly, as one's level of educational attainment increases, so too does one's tendency to engage in polychronous activities (Bluedorn 2002, pp. 62–63). Finally, Bluedorn reports that more polychronic individuals tend to be more extroverted, amenable to change, flexible about ambiguity, educated, achievement oriented, impatient and irritable, and more frequently late. Stress, though, was found to differ from polychronistic job type to job type (p. 68).

Unfortunately, effective presence allocation is not necessarily a natural capability, although, at some level, all humans are able to apply different attention levels at the same time to multiple tasks. The challenge is, first, to find flexible strategies for applying rules and, second, to accept that bioperceptual capabilities are irrevocably limited (Meyer and Kieras 1997; Sweller, van Merriënboer, and Paas 1998). Maynard, Subrahmanyam, and Greenfield (2005) report a series of experiments, for example, that suggest that expert game players are significantly more successful than novice game players at dividing attention between two online targets when the targets are in high-probability or low-probability locations, although differences between the player groups diminished when targets appeared at equal rates. These findings support arguments that attentional strategies can be augmented through instruction and practice, even though at some level human-cognitive processing capabilities will always be constrained. These cognitive realities accepted, it is probably hopeful to assume that our brains will adapt in a generation or two to multitasking (Foehr 2006) and pessimistic to assume that multitasking ultimately undermines our happiness, creativity, and ability to reflect (Brooks 2001). Media multitasking is relatively new, but multitasking is not.

Hafner (2005) and Turner and Reinsch (2007) have described how "multitasking," "polychronicity," and "pseudo–attention deficit disorder" are terms that are gaining increasing attention in the research literature. Ancona, Okhuysen, and Perlow (2001) concur, noting that

Suddenly, "time" and "timing" are everywhere. Speed, acceleration, just in time, and Internet time are just a few concepts making headlines in the popular press. Academic journals also have seen a proliferation of research papers on time and timing. New terms, metaphors, and theories are emerging (e.g., time famine, entrainment, polychronicity, chronos and kairos, temporal linkages, cohort effects). . . . As the pace of research dramatically accelerates, . . . time and timing have moved from the background to the foreground. (p. 512)

Putnam (2000), as well, highlights our American perceptions of "busyness," noting that "the proportion of us who say we 'always feel rushed' jumped by more than half between the mid-1960s and the mid-1990s" (p. 189). Davenport and Beck (2001) even go as far as to argue that one of the outcomes of technological spontaneity is the symptom of organizational ADD (attention deficit disorder) . The authors define organizational ADD as encouraging

• an increased likelihood of missing key information when making decisions;
• diminished time for reflection or anything but simple information transactions such as e-mail or voice mail;
• difficulty holding others' attention (e.g., having to increase the glitziness of presentations and the number of messages to get and keep attention); and
• decreased ability to focus when necessary.

For this reason, Gray (2001) stresses that emerging entrepreneurial approaches to working life are inevitable: "It's a kind of radicalization of the notion of autonomy, in which an autonomous life is seen as a succession of different episodes, activities, or projects one after the other so that the value of that working life is not its consistency or continuity, the way it might have been in the past, but rather its variety, its spontaneity, its responsiveness to the moment" (cf. Ladner 2008). In Spinuzzi's (2007) words, "this distributed work [is] coordinative, polycontextual, cross-disciplinary work that splices together divergent work activities (separated by time, space, organizations, and objectives) and that enables the transformations of information and texts that characterize such work" (p. 266).

Given mounting time constraints and demands for multitasking abilities, contemporary workers are less likely to succeed without adequate technological training and well-established strategies for problem solving. And these activities will ultimately require that we find strategic methods of introducing distracted workers to meaningful heuristics for discovering, annotating, referring, sampling, organizing, analyzing, illustrating, representing, generalizing, inventing, arguing from, and communicating with alternative audiences, purposes, and contexts (cf. Buchanan 1995; Mayer 2001; Unsworth 2000).

Eraut (2004) describes the relationship between modes of cognition in workplace learning, performance, and time, noting that "references to the pace and pressure of the workplace . . . raise the question of when and how workers find the time to think" (p. 259). Thus, one's mode of cognition can range from reflexive cognitive processes (e.g., pattern recognition, instant response, routinized action, and situational awareness) to rapid cognitive processes (e.g., intuitive interpretation, routines with decisions, and reactive reflections) through deliberative or analytic cognitive processes (e.g., review, discussion, analysis, planning, and monitoring) (p. 260). Eraut (2004) summarizes the balance between time and action (learning plus performance) in the workplace as follows:

The relationship between time and cognition is probably interactive: shortage of time forces people to adopt a more intuitive approach, while the intuitive routines developed by experience enable people to do things more quickly. Crowded contexts also force people to be more selective with their attention and to process their incoming information more rapidly. Under conditions of rapid interpretation and decision-making, meta-processes are limited to implicit monitoring and short, reactive reflections. But as more time becomes available the role of meta-processes becomes more complex, expanding beyond self-awareness and monitoring to include the framing of problems, thinking about the deliberative process itself and how it is being handled, searching for relevant knowledge, introducing value considerations, and so on. (p. 261)

Burns and Hajdukiewicz (2004) stress the increasingly important role that situational awareness plays in user-interface and workflow design, defining situation awareness as "the experience of fully understanding what is going on in a given situation, seeing each element within the context of the overall goal, and having all the pieces fit together into a coherent picture" (p. 265). Situational awareness thus embodies perceptual, cognitive, and situational abilities, enabling people to see what is important in a given situation, to integrate the dynamics of the situation into a meaningful set of goals, and to project future states from one's current state: "Time is a critical aspect of understanding Situation Awareness. Users need to know the time-based dynamics of the situation, including how much time is required to perform tasks and how much time is left before an event occurs" (p. 266).

In a nine-month study of 17 software engineers working at one Fortune 500 Company, Perlow (1999) interviewed, followed around, and collected tracking logs of engineers to capture how they used their time and why they used their time the way they did. In general, Perlow found that the engineers cycled between time pressures and deadline crises that, in turn, limited their ability to keep to their initial time goals or to plan ahead, producing yet more time pressures and crises. In an attempt to limit these pressures and the large number of interruptions experienced on a daily basis by the engineers, Perlow collaborated with the managers and the team to institute "quiet times" in order to heighten productivity, planning, and to encourage autonomous task completion. Interestingly, returning six months later to the company, Perlow (1999) concluded that "results of the quiet-time study . . . indicate that altering the timing of work activities can enhance collective work outcomes." Unfortunately, Perlow (1999) also noted, after only a brief amount of time with no organizational incentives in place to maintain the change, the engineers quickly reverted to their "old work patterns" (p. 75).

Stinson (2004), citing Drucker (1994) and Tapscott (1997), characterizes the demanding world outside of formal education as the knowledge age, where learning and work are the same thing. It follows then that

Increasingly, employees are being called on to continually expand their capabilities, not to do *more* work, but to do *more* complex work, to make *more* decisions and make them *more* independently. This implies that people need to be continually developing competencies—not just job skills, but also intellectual skills. It implies that learning opportunities need to be available to them anytime and anywhere, and that learning needs to be available just-in-time as needed for their use. (p. 167, italics mine)

Snyder (2002) elaborates on how "the new communication order" has produced a new work order consisting of

more stressful and demanding work for those with good jobs; a proliferation of low-paying and temporary jobs and many without jobs; a widening gap between the rich and poor; a world in which national borders matter less. But the world of the new work order also includes the promise of more meaningful work, the valuing of diversity, the dispersal of centralised authority and the wider distribution of knowledge across communities. The sheer challenge of attempting to reconcile these apparently contradictory forces is sobering to say the least. (p. 5)

The sociointernational challenge, therefore, involves numerous institutions vying for a piece of "the world outside of formal education." And it is a moneyed world. Capper (2001, pp. 237–238) has described an exponentially expanding market that consists of

- approximately 700 e-learning companies in the United States,
- an estimated educational investment of more than $700 billion,
- a corporate training market of more than $100 billion,
- a lifelong learning market worth $25 billion, and
- education as the second largest industry after health care.

As Downey et al. (2005) summarize, "E-learning is one of the fastest growing and most promising markets in the education industry. The online training market is expected to nearly double in size every year, reaching approximately $11 billion by 2005" (p. 48).

2.1.3 Productive Training

Productivity is most crudely defined as labor accomplished per "person" hour and, whether distributed, creative, virtual, or global in nature, "just-in-time" productivity is the ideal that shapes many discussions of learning in the twenty-first-century technological workplace. As Rowe and Cooke (1995) state explicitly, "When incorporating high-technology equipment into a particular work setting, the goal is to increase productivity" (pp. 243–244). The marketing mantra reads, "Learn what you want, when you want, where you want" and attain "the freedom of learning across space and time." This unquestioned desire for more learning, more efficiently incorporated, and easier to apply in turn acts as one of the primary arguments for integrating technology into the business of instruction and training. Indeed, a quick review of articles describing the strengths of technology-based training turns up the phrase "anywhere, anytime use" frequently, although Shank (2004) is honest enough to add that "online learning makes little sense for learners when . . . they don't have access or time" (p. 36).

Pruitt and Barrett (1991) argue, though, that distributed workspaces are going to increasingly blur the lines between what we traditionally define as work, personal, corporate, public, and learning spaces. Thus, when Botkin and Kaipa (2004) outline their five stages of the evolution of e-learning in business, it becomes clear that the development involves a fundamental shift from an emphasis on the management of content to an emphasis on learners. This shift, which is already occurring, will involve the creation of secondary forms that organize and elaborate on primary forms and, ultimately, the development of tertiary forms that eliminate inevitable redundancies provided by both the primary and secondary forms. Learner emphases, as well, will move beyond providing procedural information to the organization of conceptual understanding and application. Botkin and Kaipa's (2004) stages thus move from a content focus (stage 1), to a portal focus (stage 2), to a module focus (stage 3), to a performance focus (stage 4), to a learner focus (stage 5) (pp. 417–418).

This shift from content to learner focus is not surprising given that, with the constraints of space and time removed from workplace collaborations, the distinction between human–human and human–content "interactions" becomes less obvious. Quan-Haase and Cothrel (2003), for example, found that employees in an "Internet-era company" tended to use information sources very differently from employees in traditional companies. Thus, although Internet-era employees perceived that access to human information sources online resulted in higher individual performance, it became clear that the distinction between human and documentary sources of information became increasingly blurred in online realms:

When an employee obtains information from an e-mail sent by a coworker, the source is obviously human. But what if the e-mail is two years old, and the employee retrieves it not from the source, but from storage on his or her own computer? Or if the employee retrieves it from a repository, where another employee has placed it as something that might benefit others? Our research indicates that employees are consciously aware that the information they share with, or receive from, coworkers may have a "second life" as a documentary source, and are adapting their behavior accordingly. (p. 157)

Ducheneaut and Bellotti (2003), similarly, found that objects in e-mail (e.g., attachments and embedded links) became increasingly contextualized by the e-mail messages that surrounded them, to the point where the content of the "e-mail conversations sometimes became objects in themselves" (p. 104). The authors conclude, "Progressively transformed into a habitat, e-mail has . . . become a powerful way to organize one's work and rapidly access work objects rather than a poor textual envelope for things better discussed face-to-face" (p. 107). *Ceci n'est pas une pipe*—or is it?

Thus it is difficult to identify exactly which stage of e-learning contemporary organizations have reached; but one undeniable workplace reality is that knowledge is power and the easier and faster it is to capture, transmit, and "utilize" information that facilitates more effective and efficient decision making (i.e., knowledge), the better. Brandt (2005) therefore concludes that "Growing knowledge is why training and learning are so important in the new economy" because, after all, "in the knowledge economy, learning is regarded as a basic task of production and part of what is created at every stage of production so that new knowledge can be cycled back into the production process" (pp. 188–189). And the only ambition greater than producing knowledge is producing knowledge quickly and inexpensively. As Gleick (1999) asserts:

The calculus of productivity, *anything* per unit time, is so deeply engrained in the post-industrial world that we can barely conceive of a workplace psychology omitting it. Yet it did not exist before "Speedy Taylor" forged his methods and ideas in the factories of the Northeast in the late 1870s, as the Industrial Revolution reached its height. Taylorism is the ideal of efficiency applied to production as a scientific method—humans and machines working together, at maximum speed, with clockwork rationality. (p. 213)

If we agree with Feenberg (1999) that one of the fundamental motivations for technological innovation is to increase productivity, then we have to acknowledge how time operates front and center in any definition of contemporary productivity. Certainly, integral to Taylor's vision of management science was a desire to capture human workflows by strict measurement of the passage of time (Mattelart 1996); and economists have built models of time allocation based on income distribution (Becker 1965). Similar to Taylor, Henry Ford's vision of automotive efficiency was equally driven by a fascination with clocks, time, watches, and precise pacing (Bluedorn 2002). Defining productivity as units produced is only possible if we deliberately refuse to carefully examine each unit produced: the moment units are scrutinized, we are forced to consider quality, errorlessness, or reduction in system stress; and, again, these constructs ultimately require measurement against the standard construct, time. Kiesler and Cummings (2002) remind us, for example, that "e-mail seems to encourage ever more communication and therefore is time-consuming," and that an increase in communication that does not encourage "backchannel feedback to promote mutual understanding" does not necessarily result in communication that is either more efficient or more effective. Yet, ironically, this very assumption that speed and novelty are of the essence, according to Johnson-Eilola, Selber, and Selfe (1999), is what disables us as critical consumers of the technologies that "accelerate" us:

Unfortunately, the more things change, the more they remain the same. Because so many corporations are scrambling to integrate new technologies into the work and lives of employees, and because technological change continues at such a rapid pace, . . . few individuals in any position . . . are encouraged, or educated, to consider in critically informed ways the complex relationships between people and machines, or the relationships between the machines and the social contexts in which they are used. And yet, these particular habits of mind are essential to the task of rethinking the relationships we have constructed with technology and realizing the possibilities of technological change within particular social, cultural, economic, and political contexts. (p. 199)

Part of the emerging interest on community, then, can be characterized as a reaction to the contemporary realization that "expertise" and by implication, experts, are increasingly difficult to locate. That is, there are few individuals we would define as experts whom we can find at any single location or in any single laboratory. Are we looking for an expert on the same statistical analysis application, a similar experimental design, a particular statistical method, or an alternative to the statistical programming language we have been using that does not apply to our particular problem? Setting aside domain expertise, notions of life experience, familiarity with similar problems or approaches, and focusing only on computer expertise, experts are still difficult to find. Although the number of software and hardware alternatives has expanded exponentially and at a rapid pace, the number of individuals able to claim total familiarity with the growing number of systems that we routinely access has decreased. The most common form of user assistance—"Excuse me, do you know how I . . . ?"—is no longer a useful strategy for approaching problems encountered during our computer interactions (Duffy, Palmer, and Mehlenbacher 1993).

In addition, most users are not developing a level of familiarity with their computers that computers once demanded. Thus, we no longer feel that our interactions with computers necessitate the in-depth, comprehensive knowledge of our personal computers that they once did. In the early days of computing, conceptions of the computer user differed significantly from today's conception. Whereas early users of computers were primarily programmers, engineers, and technical specialists, frequent users of computers today often employ computers with specific tasks in mind, infrequently, and for limited periods of time. Users present slide presentations for tasks they are given the next day, or update their bank balances occasionally, or check their e-mail for new messages daily. Our knowledge, goals, and strategies for computing do not necessarily transfer from one computing situation to another or from one application to another. When colleagues ask, "How do I . . . ?," the appropriate response is frequently, "Well, on my machine, you do the following . . . ," admitting outright to the situated nature of expertise.

Work and learning in the workplace, therefore, are as distributed as the expertise that we used to seek out in our colleagues with "a history." Our increasingly complex problem-solving contexts require on-demand instruction; and our learning is necessarily incomplete, task-oriented, nonprogrammed, and invisible (Nardi and Engeström 1999). Technologies have moved us from mechanistic specialization to information- and communication-driven cooperation. Our relationship with technology mirrors the shift from monolithic, centralized machinery that governs individual behaviors to networked teams that organize around common problems, processes, product-development efforts, and hyperaccelerated timelines.

Training in the workplace has, in some respects, followed a similar trajectory from bringing individuals together to attend to the same instructional content to interweaving content into the fabric of everyday work and building shared opportunities for learning across departmental boundaries and expertise. As Spinuzzi (2006) notes, "Too often, workers receive support for vertical learning through multiple channels—formal training, documentation, etc., to help them master their trades, fields, and disciplines. But support for horizontal learning, learning across workplace boundaries, is restricted to informal, contingency-oriented channels."

Finally, along with developing nonhierarchical strategies for training within the contemporary workplace, Angervall and Thång (2003) point out that organizations need to begin looking outside the contemporary workplace: that is, "learning most often concerns the participants' strategies for living and not their strategies for life" (p. 267). Organizations that take a transmissional, productivity-based view of work learning, according to Angervall and Thång (2003), are guilty of ignoring the symbiotic relationship between work, learning, and everyday life:

This means that learning can be misunderstood as a theoretical conception that has no relevance for real life, at least if it's understood in the sense of "developing for life". . . . Work-related learning (training) is looked upon as something very positive by the workforce as long as it is related to the actual work performed. . . . Other learning activities are sometimes experienced as pointless, expensive and time-consuming, especially in small and medium-sized enterprises. We believe that to be able to practice the concept of continuing education, companies must first of all start to develop long-term strategies for work and life. (p. 267)

2.2   Leisure Learning

Given the accelerated work worlds that we commonly inhabit, it is tempting to assume that we have worked very hard to maintain the singular, one-dimensional simplicity of our leisure spaces. Researchers interested in social and personal spaces, however, have tended to observe the exact opposite. For many Americans, leisure time looks anything but leisurely; and this is not entirely surprising since the majority of our definitions of leisure, as with our conceptions of work and learning, are intimately connected to time.

Leisure is what we do *to pass* the time, or *to fill* the time, or *to use* our personal time. Leisure is not the opposite of work, or education, formal learning, or even non-learning events, but instead enables us to treat time as a landmark that we can move beyond, as a container that we can top off, or as a currency that we can protect or spend. In addition to being characterized by frequent references to time, leisure is also described spatially, as a space that is given meaning partly metaphorically and partly in terms of what people *do* in it, where certain things happen or are remembered, in addition to being the distance between things (cf. Bachelard 1958). Hence the appropriateness of the term "leisure learning." Glastra, Hake, and Schedler (2004) write, "The application of information and knowledge in all spheres of social life has become the most dynamic feature in the transformation of late-modern societies. This, in turn, gives rise to learning as a permanent feature of social life" (p. 293). Leisure learning is not the same as *in*formal learning but, instead, ought to be viewed as an aspiration rather than as a derivative of formal learning. And similar to learning, the relationship between technology and our leisure spaces is a complex one, marked by evolutionary processes rather than revolutionary progress. Claims regarding the future of "NetGen" learners, therefore, are most likely exaggerations and part of the larger utopian, populist discourses that surround technology in general (Haddon 2006).

Wachter and Kelly (1998) reinforce the centrality of the relationship between humans, our needs and expectations, and the entertainment settings and devices available to us. In their study of 119 VCR-viewing middle-class households (mean age of 40, 90 percent white, 73 percent college graduates, 63 percent employed, and 45 percent earning more than $35,000 per year), Wachter and Kelly (1998) observed that 78 percent of the households (70 participants) used their VCR approximately eight hours per week to record and playback and to rent movies. Not only did the authors find interesting interactions between gender (women used playback more than men) and age (VCR viewing declined as age increased, perhaps supporting the adage that "youth is wasted on the young"), but VCR viewing declined also with the addition of a partner or spouse or children to the household. Participants performed various leisure activities while recording, including dining, movies, parties, bars, attending sporting events, exercising, traveling, meetings, babysitting, shopping, or sleeping

(p. 221). VCR technology, then, distributes time in two ways: first, by allowing us to perform other leisure activities while simultaneously using the technology and, second, by allowing us to watch a preprogrammed show whenever we wish rather than according to the networks' schedule (*my* time rather than *prime* time).

As with entertainment, so too with education, for, as Hendricks (2004) has stated, "Technology makes possible a reconfiguring of school; a refocusing of everyday life." Whether formal instructional contexts are spilling over into our traditionally private spaces or whether informal expectations about instruction are infiltrating our traditional conceptions of "school," it is safe to assert that notions of space and time are being revised dramatically. Before correspondence education was conceptualized, personal and business correspondence dominated the highway networks. But only proper historical context can help us adjust our expectations about the time required to communicate via traditional highway delivery. Cubitt (1998) provides just such a timeline when he writes, "a letter sent from London on Commonwealth business on 31 October 1645 arrived at Basta on 10 April 1646, finally delivered to Surat on the western coast of India on 12 October, almost a year after despatch" (p. 124). The Hudson's Bay Company, one of the oldest companies in continuous business for over three centuries, had approximately seven forts or posts that required more then ten days' travel by lake or terrain and depended on the company's London-based ships to transport its goods and all communications every fall when Hudson Bay was not frozen (O'Leary, Orlikowski, and Yates 2002).

Our expectations about "timely" information delivery have increased exponentially as has the amount of information that we now routinely sift through any given day. Hassani's (2006) data on multilocational Internet users indicates that not only do "the locations where individuals use the Internet shape their online pursuits" but also "having access at home is a key factor that is strongly associated with applying the Internet toward ends that enhance individual wellbeing" (p. 265). Kress and van Leeuwen (1996) add that the prevalence of graphical and visual representations of the information we access suggests that "Pleasure, entertainment and immediacy of apprehension determine how 'reading' is constructed here" (p. 30).

2.2.1 Accelerating Overload and Leisure Time

A brochure arrives in the mail that promises "a systematic solution for information overload." The following reassuring scenario is presented:

Suppose you had an assistant who screened all the books and selected only the quality ones for you, and who then culled the most important ideas from each one and compiled a report for you. That way, you could "read" the book—in a fraction of the time. Now you can hire that "assistant." It's called *Soundview Executive Book Summaries*. Every month you receive time-saving summaries of the best new business books. Each contains all the key points of the original book.

But instead of 200 to 500 pages, the summary is only 8 pages. Instead of taking 5, 10, or more hours to read, it takes you just 15 minutes! If you prefer, you can also receive your summaries on audiotapes or audio CDs. Each summary is no more than 20 minutes, which is easy to listen to in the car, on an airplane, or while working out.

The scenario seems too good to be true. I worry that no one can summarize the contents of 500 pages in 15 minutes. The brochure suggests otherwise:

A *Soundview Executive Book Summary* is not a review. Nor is it a digest or excerpt. It's a skillful distillation that preserves the content and spirit of the entire book. Superbly designed for maximum ease of access, it consists of short, self-contained "bite-size" passages that allow you to scan, skip, and extract exactly what you need to know—*fast*.

Finally, the brochure summarizes the "six important advantages" of *Soundview Executive Book Summaries*:

1. *Gain a competitive edge.* Learn the secrets of success of the world's leading corporations.
2. *Get ideas you can use.* Discover practical techniques you can put to work immediately.
3. *Bolster your business confidence.* You'll acquire an understanding of the key points from the newest books. When a title or author comes up in discussion, you'll respond intelligently.
4. *Learn more, remember more.* In Soundview Executive Book Summaries, each author's ideas are presented in the simplest, clearest, most logically organized way. Studies in psychology journals prove that you can retain the content of a summary better than a book.
5. *Slash hundreds of hours off your reading time.*
6. *Never waste another minute or dime on a worthless book.* We select the truly worthwhile titles—and discard the rest. With Soundview Executive Book Summaries, you can keep up with the best business books in less time than it takes to read the daily newspaper!

Thus the *Soundview* brochure evokes the issues of our anxious age: edgy competition, ideas and knowledge, expertise, learning, attention, memory, and the increasingly valuable commodity of time. Ayres and Sweller (2005) define split-attention as something that "occurs when learners are required to split their attention between and mentally integrate several sources of physically and temporally disparate information, where each source of information is essential for understanding the material" (p. 135), but it has become increasingly challenging to determine what we mean by "essential" (when we are also frequently inundated with redundant information sources), let alone what we define as "understanding" (when we are highly bound by our particular circumstances and situations) in everyday life.

It is difficult to determine where exactly our limited expectations about human attention and interest begin, with information providers or with information users. Gleick (1999) links our diminishing attention to the collapse of traditional leisure time:

We have a word for *free* time: leisure. Leisure is time off the books, off the job, off the clock. If we *save* time, we commonly believe we are saving it for our leisure. We know that leisure is really a state of mind, but no dictionary can define it without reference to passing time. It is unrestricted time, unemployed time, unoccupied time. Or is it? Unoccupied time is vanishing. The leisure-industries (an oxymoron maybe, but no contradiction) fill time, as groundwater fills a sinkhole. The very variety of experience attacks our leisure as it attempts to satiate us. We work for our amusement. (p. 10)

Although Gleick (1999) is, at times, almost enthusiastic about our insatiable desire to "leave the laws of physics behind" in our contemporary rush for information, leisure, entertainment, satisfaction, and connectivity, he is also tentative about its long- and short-term effects on our capacity for processing:

As our attention has demanded more stimulation, we have gained an ability to process rapid and discontinuous visual images. It seems that we are quicker-witted—but have we, by way of compensation, traded away our capacity for deep concentration? No one knows for sure. (p. 200)

We do know that technological developments in the home, despite early claims, have not reduced housework (Wajcman 1991) and that, although proponents of distance education have argued that it saves time, particularly for women with children (Kramarae 2003, p. 262), it is more likely that it simply supports convenience by reducing the amount of time learners spend making arrangements and traveling to and from regular teaching spaces (Peters 2003, p. 97). We also know, as Bowden and Offer (1994) observe, that television "Viewing time is inversely related to education, and to income" and "Television (with radio, video, and listening to recorded music) has come to dominate discretionary time in Britain and the US, claiming an average of 2 hours and 2 minutes per day in the US" (p. 736)—or approximately half of all the leisure time of both American men and women (U.S. Department of Labor 2006).

So although technology clearly plays an important part in our leisure lives, Haddon (2006) is correct in warning that the relationship between humans and technology is intensely reciprocal and grounded in "longer term social commitments, including commitments to other people" (p. 197). Domestic technologies have produced the equivalent of the productivity paradox by distributing increased but fragmented leisure time across time-saving and time-using devices.

So the unreality of our experiences in school may have more in common with our use of time and resources in the home than we are comfortable acknowledging. Resnick, Lesgold, and Hall (2005) characterize adult home life and schooling as follows:

Many of the skills needed to adapt to adult life outside of school are different from those needed inside the school world. In an era of information overload and continuous multitasking, people have to learn how to manage attention, choose among multiple sources of information, and query the environment productively. Too much of schooling, however, assumes that children are being motivated at home to pay attention and to persist in complex cognitive activity. It is assumed that teachers, if motivated by various accountability provisions, will become able and willing to present learning opportunities of which children, because they are motivated by standards and by their parents, will afford themselves effectively.

All parties involved in this set of assumptions still carry the historic baggage of seeing much of being a good student as following directions, obeying orders, and producing work as required. (pp. 77–78)

It is this multitasking reality into which we thrust our contemporary problem solver; and researchers are rushing to find new ways to describe emerging human behaviors and communication patterns that are developing in response to these fundamental environmental changes. Begole et al. (2002), for example, argue that "One area of interest for further exploration is the difference between being *reachable* for communication and being *available* for it. Availability depends not only on physical presence but also on mental receptivity to communication" (p. 342). E-mail alone is dramatically changing our interactions with others, taking work into our homes, heightening our dependency on regular access, forcing its way into our business meetings and social engagements (CNN.com 2005). Diminished attention, interruptability, multitasking, dual processing, polychronicity, information overload, and pseudo–attention deficit disorder are some of the terms applied to the growing demands placed on technology users (Carlson 2005; Hafner 2005; Lohr 2007; Turner and Reinsch 2007).

These issues are irrevocably fused with our relationship to technology-mediated living. That is, rather than being faced with the limits of technological possibility, it is our limited sensory-perceptual and cognitive capacity, the boundedness of our working memory, and our restrained auditory and visual processing ability to represent, integrate, and reconfigure ongoing experiences that are at the core of the attention problem (Mayer 2001; Mayer and Moreno 2003; Simon 1979; van Merriënboer and Sweller 2005). As Mayer (2005) summarizes, "These constraints on our processing capacity force us to make decisions about which pieces of incoming information to pay attention to the degree to which we should build connections among the selected pieces of information, and the degree to which we should build connections between selected pieces of information and our existing knowledge. *Metacognitive strategies* are techniques for allocating, monitoring, coordinating, and adjusting these limited cognitive resources" (p. 36).

What Mayer (2005) and others (Guri-Rozenblit 1988) tend to deemphasize about the "pieces of information" that whirl around and infiltrate our everyday lives is how our definitions of an information piece or chunk or element are changing rapidly as a result of emerging work and leisure technologies (Beale 2005). Thus, news programs combine multimedia elements and information pieces as though guided by the "more is better" and the "entertainment is engaging" principles of design; and what were once considered the rules of engagement for games, we now seriously consider for integration into training and formal educational settings. Radio, rather than following formats that alternate between news and music—punctuated by commercials—now operates as a cacophony of news "briefs," advertising "bits," information "spots," and music programmed to map onto our daily commuting patterns. No wonder average Americans aged 15 and over report spending the same amount of time per day "playing games: using computer for leisure"—19 minutes—as they do "relaxing and thinking" (U.S. Department of Labor 2006).[1]

More than technology and chronology, our setting has traditionally defined our activities, attentions, and relationship formations and maintenance. And the setting where we presume that work (and by indirect implication, learning) is not *required* is the home. But, as Krendl and Warren (2004) note, the infiltration of new media into our home settings has a considerable history in educational research:

Research on media and learning outside the classroom dates back to early studies of the introduction of mass media. As each new medium—film, radio, television, computer—was adopted into the home setting, a new generation of research investigations examined the role of the medium and its potential as a teacher. In addition to questions of how a new dominant mass medium would alter people's use of time and attention, one of the central research questions was how and to what extent audiences would learn from the new media system. (p. 59)

A great many of these media effect studies were framed by cognitive science and information-processing perspectives, and thus, they clustered around studies of attention, comprehension, retention, active versus passive processing, and higher-order cognition processing. Of course, the motivation to study informal learning environments, Kerr (2004) reminds us, is that "Social aspects of informal online learning (collaboration, competition, types of informal learning projects undertaken, settings where explored, etc.) could also be profitably explored" (p. 125).

Although I have certainly observed and even celebrated the potential for emerging technologies to transform and augment human visuospatial comprehension and reasoning elsewhere (Hill and Mehlenbacher 1998), I also privilege the transformative process, in Cubitt's (1998) words, of a "good read" which at its heart is initially a private and personal educational experience:

The good read, founded on forgetting who and where you are, is premised on the fading of experience itself, when experience was understood as a property of the self. In the place of the ideal subject of the public sphere—rational, clear-headed, sociable—there arrives a fading subject, motivated by the desire to forget, regressing into a bodily leisure . . . which runs through quasi-socialised identification with the characters or narration, towards its obverse, a descent into abjection, the horrifying yet tantalising dissolution of selfhood. A good read is the process of oscillation between self-loss and abjection, on the one hand, and, on the other, the constant resupply of ego-ideals, displaced and heroicised versions of the self, in the form of psychological-realist characters and fictions. This dialectic I take to be the heart of the predomination of narrative fiction in this mode of reading: the narrative of pursuit, of loss and recovery, of a wholeness always postponed until the moment of closure, when you must return again to the world of the self. (p. 8)

Thus, engagement in information, whatever its content and conceptual nature, is critical to learning, reflection, and maintenance of self in either formal or informal settings. The interdependent relationship between learner-viewer attention, interest, and comprehension has been studied intensely by television and film researchers as well (Seels et al. 2004). More recently, marketing researchers have begun to study perceptions of time and particular Web design features and find, for example, that Web sites that employ chroma and value levels that enhance a relaxed attitude reduce user impatience with download times (Gorn et al. 2004). Slowing down time, particularly leisure time, may be central to our preoccupation with the "management" of time.

2.2.2 Older Media Can Be Exciting Too

It is all too common for researchers to begin their studies of Web-based media use by first minimizing the relationship between previous unidirectional "viewing" technologies and emerging technologies. This habit, unfortunately, has resulted in a tendency among researchers to increasingly rely on studies *only* of media perceived to be contemporary and situated in particular contexts of use. This has, in turn, produced a multitude of studies focused on specific technologies that could have benefited from a thorough investigation of historical technologies that have clear parallels in design and use (cf. Glass 1998). Thus, several years back, I read a great number of studies on designing personal digital assistants (PDAs) that made no attempt to connect what we already know about designing for the small screen based on numerous studies of 9- and 12-inch text-based monitors common in the late 1970s and early 1980s. And it is notable that, when asked in a 1995 survey about their time spent playing video games, male American college students, on average, were three times more likely to game than females (59.5 versus 18.3 percent), six times more likely to spend a minimum of one hour per week (36 versus 6.2 percent), and 11 times more likely to engage in this activity for over six hours per week (8 versus 0.7 percent; Astin 1998, p. 122). The popularity of computer games is not a new phenomenon.

Of course it is problematic to conflate media types or instructional modes casually, for example, by defining all face-to-face instructional formats, instructor–learner e-mail exchanges, or chatroom-based instruction as equal. Different technologies support different tasks differently. Honeycutt (2001) observes that e-mail peer review tends to facilitate "deeper processing of documents under revision as reflected by greater document-related referencing" than synchronous conferencing (p. 51), and the differences between synchronous and asynchronous communication environments does not necessarily generalize across all platforms and system types. Although most chatrooms or synchronous computer-mediated communication environments operate as half-duplex systems (messages are composed and then sent), other full-duplex systems allow learners to see each message as it is being generated (Winiecki 2003), and MOO environments (multi-user domains, object-oriented) support sophisticated collaborative programming in addition to chatlike communication options (Mehlenbacher et al. 1994). As well, Foehr (2006) found that, with conventional media such as music, books, or television, people tend to multitask with non-media activities such as eating and exercise whereas, with computers, people tend to multitask with other media activities such as browsing the Web or chatting online. Foehr (2006) suggests that the computer may encourage multitasking behaviors, noting that younger users with early access to computers tend to multitask more than older users. So not all media users use media alike.

It is also risky to make strong claims that the instructional potential of blogs, discussion lists, or open source bulletin boards are necessarily dramatically different. Allen et al. (2002), in their meta-analysis of student satisfaction with distance education, found that although fax- and e-mail-based distance formats were preferred over video-based formats by higher-education learners, these differences were minimal when the *amount* of information contained in the video elements was reduced. Moreover, as Allen et al. (2002) admit, "Satisfaction with the educational process provides only one possible source of evaluation and must be compared to other evaluations of the effectiveness of any pedagogical device or procedure" (p. 92). Wisher and Curnow (2003), in their review of video-based instructional materials, note that "Students and administrators might react positively to a certain video program delivered on the Internet, but that same program might actually prove to be instructionally ineffective" (p. 327). So it is always worth reminding ourselves that comparative studies of media influence on learner satisfaction and behavior—when everything is analyzed and reported—do not necessarily allow us to conclude that students *learn* more. When we compare one medium with another, it is exceedingly difficult to control the numerous experimental variables surrounding media use; and, if we control the media too strictly (e.g., we compare a video of a traditional lecture to an *actual* traditional lecture), we surely end up comparing the same object.

In this context, then, it is critical that we review historical media use and its implications for instruction and learning as the *context* for studies of contemporary media. Figure 2.3 presents a model of developmental changes in interest and attention that,

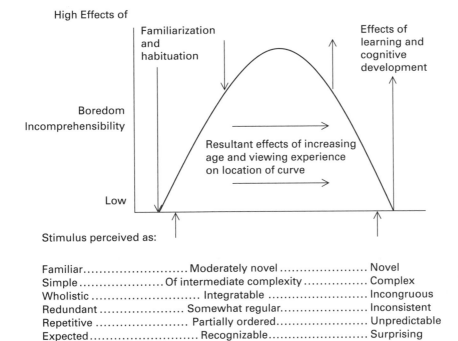

High Effects of

Familiarization and habituation

Effects of learning and cognitive development

Boredom
Incomprehensibility

Resultant effects of increasing age and viewing experience on location of curve

Low

Stimulus perceived as:

Familiar.......................... Moderately novel .... Novel
Simple .... Of intermediate complexity .... Complex
Wholistic .... Integratable .... Incongruous
Redundant .... Somewhat regular..................... Inconsistent
Repetitive .... Partially ordered..................... Unpredictable
Expected........................... Recognizable....................... Surprising

Figure 2.3
Model of developmental changes, interest, and attention regarding television (adapted from Seels et al. 2004, p. 265, citing Rice, Huston, and Wright 1982).

although applied to television, can certainly be applied meaningfully to alternative media.

Television viewers with a high degree of cognitive development and familiarization or habituation with program elements that are simple, redundant, or repetitive tend to experience boredom; inversely, viewers of novel, unpredictable, or surprising elements tend to learn more, although of course this decreases as familiarization increases. Establishing learner engagement, then, is an affective, cognitive, and contextual mix.

And taking this into account helps explain why higher learning settings, that is, formal educational spaces, can never really hope to compete with leisure learning situations or even with work learning spaces. In truth, we may not want to. Astin (1998), in his survey of American television viewers, has argued that the shift between the 1960s and the 1980s from "developing a meaningful philosophy of life" to more materialistic values "may be attributable, at least in part, to the effects of television" (p. 134). Although media developments clearly influence sociocultural orientations, a transformational perspective would probably hold that increased consumerism in America is the result of a complex of issues and developments. But it is also worth noting that a transformational perspective can account for television as both a transmitter of particular audience messages and as a reflection of audience expectations.

This noncompetitive reality, then, is only partly the fault of the higher learning institutions, which, after all, find themselves increasingly in competition with the contemporary Western desire for *more faster easier* (punctuation eliminated to save time). Barber (1995) astutely describes how higher learning requires more than ever that we aim to improve ourselves for less tangible reasons than extrinsic reward and credentialing, career development, and income improvement:

Education is unlikely ever to win an "open market" competition with entertainment because "easy" and "hard" can never compete on equal ground, and for those not yet disciplined in the rites of learning "freedom" will always mean easy. Perhaps that is why Tocqueville thought that liberty was the most "arduous of all apprenticeships." To grow into our mature better selves, we need the help of our nascent better selves, which is what common standards, authoritative education, and a sense of the public good can offer. Consumption takes us as it finds us, the more impulsive and greedy, the better. Education challenges our impulses and informs our greediness with lessons drawn from our mutuality and the higher goods we share in our communities of hope. (p. 117)

Indeed, Barber's (1995) argument finds support in early research on high-end video-based instructional environments. Wisher and Curnow (2003) summarize: "As with instructional television, training simulators, and virtual reality environments, it is not always necessary to increase the video capability of a distance learning program in order to increase training effectiveness. Too often, developers and designers become captivated with technical capabilities rather than an examination of the influence of media on the underlying learning process" (p. 327). Humans frequently, after all, learn *despite* the contextual constraints facing them.

2.2.3 Nonlearning Spaces

One way of defining a thing is to identify its opposites, and to proceed in reverse until one comes upon the essence of the thing. As Bowker and Star (1999) remind us, "People often cannot see what they take for granted until they encounter someone who does not take it for granted" (p. 291). Without being able to find nonlearning spaces, we fall into the default state of positing that all states are learning states. Research on tacit knowledge and implicit learning, that is, learning that is so well known to us that we are often unaware of it as it happens (e.g., Csikszentmihalyi's 1990 "flow" state), has important implications for nonlearning spaces.

Research on sensory and perceptual processes also plays an important role in our primary learning processes, for it is at this physiological level that we first begin to collect data from our surrounding environment (Libet 2004). Just as our data-collection capabilities are defined by our biological design, so too is our ability to learn (Gazzaniga 2008). Indeed, as Evans (2004) reports, our estimates of the amount of time that has passed are influenced directly by the complexity of the tasks we are undertaking at the time: therefore, "the experience of duration constitutes a physiological response to both self and situation, which is, in principle, independent of any objective temporal attributes of a particular event or situation" (p. 21). Moreover, it may be that sensory-perceptual experience orders our experience of time prior to cognitive processes. Sensory-perceptual experience is first represented as a combination of the time it takes for perceptual moments to be captured by the cortex, for the neurons to fire and distribute information, and the short-term memory to register the end of one event and the beginning of another. Sensory-perceptual experience at the level of our most basic physiological operations, thus, marks the smallest grain-size of "time" that we are able to process (Evans 2004, pp. 24–25).

So the past, at the level of automaticity in our decision-making processes, plays a central role in our emotional and cognitive interpretation and evaluation of external environmental cues. Bargh and Chartrand (1999), moreover, describe how this feature of our sensory-perceptual apparatus does not diminish us as learning beings: "the evaluations we've made in the past are now made for us and predispose us to behave in consistent ways; the goals we have pursued in the past now become active and guide our behavior in pursuit of the goal in relevant situations; and our perceptions of the emotional and behavioral reactions of others makes [sic] us tend to respond in the same way, establishing bonds of rapport and liking in a natural and effortless way. Thus 'the automaticity of being' is far from the negative and maladaptive caricature drawn by humanistically oriented writers . . . ; rather, these processes are in our service and best interests—and in an intimate, knowing way at that" (p. 476).

Of course, understanding the details of our perceptual and information processing, though illuminating as an element of the instruction and learning complex, is outside the scope of this book. Still, conceptualizing ourselves as biological beings rather than as purely cognitive beings does have implications when we consider our learning processes and environments. If, for example, our experience of the perceptual moment *now* has an outer limit of two to three seconds (between perceptual attention shifts), then time cannot be viewed as an objective reality but, instead, must be interpreted as a function of our subjective (i.e., constructed) physiological organization of temporal events. To stress the potential distinctiveness of our biological structure, Evans (2004) notes that, although human vision is trichromatic (i.e., employs three dimensions via three color channels and three types of photoreceptors), some animals such as rabbits are dichromats (employing two dimensions) and some are tetrachromats such as pigeons (employing four dimensions) (pp. 42–43). Our perception of color "reality," then, can be viewed as one of a range of biological potentials, where viability rather than optimal development is the evolutionary norm. The "technology" of our biological structure, therefore, mediates our understanding of both time and space, just as aural processes influence how much information we can communicate by speech and olfactory processes influence our memory structures.

Accounting for sensory-perceptual processes as part of a continuum from environmental cues to individual cognitive processing to actions within the task environment is not merely an academic exercise, but will ultimately allow me to elaborate on a sociocognitive perspective toward instruction and learning with technology. A sociocognitive perspective sidesteps traditional dichotomies between cognitive and social theories of learning by factoring sensory-perceptual processes into the equation. Accounting for learners as biological and cognitive entities, moreover, expands the sociocultural perspective articulated by Sutherland, Robertson, and John (2004) that "the mental functioning of an individual has its origins in social life" (p. 410). That is, information-processing theories of cognition have been accused of ignoring processes that occur outside "the mind," but my contention is that this may be a difference in metaphorical interpretation. For cognitivists, a definition of "the mind" as symbol processor does not deny the instrumental nature of sensory-perceptual information (traditionally privileged by behaviorists) or one's environment (privileged by social constructivists). However, cognitivists would certainly distinguish between individual processes and problem-solving environments rather than, as Bredo (1994) suggests, viewing "mind [as] an aspect of person-environment interaction itself" (p. 24). Although Bredo (1994) is correct in asserting that "Knowledge is thus (in a situated interpretation) inseparable from the occasions and activities of which it is the product" (p. 29), it would be an error to argue that knowledge therefore cannot be generalized across occasions and activities.

If nonlearning spaces exist at all, they are most likely consigned to rare human moments, moments where time and narratives of past, present, and future are temporarily frozen or sidestepped. Indeed, it is likely that nonlearning spaces are contingent upon our sensory-perceptual attention processes. In part, it is difficult to conceptualize the nature of such nonlearning moments because, as Henning (2004) asserts, it is difficult to imagine spaces where "Formal and abstract learning is not privileged in any way and is not viewed as inherently better than or higher than any other type of learning" (p. 144). Even this sentence suggests that beyond formal learning, there is only informal learning and, beyond that, well, we can proceed only to be or to act. But it is similarly difficult to imagine either of those states without learning being involved. As Readings (1997) states, "Change comes neither from within nor from without, but from the difficult space, neither inside nor outside, where one is" (p. 29).

Figure 2.4 is a reinterpretation of Seels et al.'s (2004) and Rice, Huston, and Wright's (1982) model of developmental changes, interests, and attention regarding television, organized around Evans's (2004) discussion of the perceptual nature of "real" time

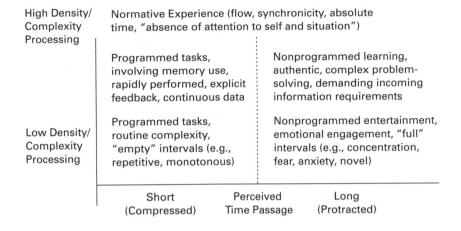

High Density/
Complexity
Processing

Normative Experience (flow, synchronicity, absolute
time, "absence of attention to self and situation")

Programmed tasks, involving memory use, rapidly performed, explicit feedback, continuous data	Nonprogrammed learning, authentic, complex problem-solving, demanding incoming information requirements

Low Density/
Complexity
Processing

Programmed tasks, routine complexity, "empty" intervals (e.g., repetitive, monotonous)	Nonprogrammed entertainment, emotional engagement, "full" intervals (e.g., concentration, fear, anxiety, novel)

Short (Compressed)	Perceived Time Passage	Long (Protracted)

Task Perceived as:

Familiar......................... Moderately novel .... Novel
Simple.................... Of intermediate complexity .... Complex
Wholistic .... Integratable .... Incongruous
Redundant .... Somewhat regular..................... Inconsistent
Repetitive .... Partially ordered..................... Unpredictable
Expected.......................... Recognizable........................ Surprising

Figure 2.4
Processing density and perceived time passage (adapted from Evans 2004, pp. 17–21; Seels et al. 2004, p. 265).

and learner processing/task complexity. The graphic is instructive in that it highlights how our biological mechanisms transform our experience of time (and space). Thus, when we consider the design and experience of artificial learning environments, it is not surprising to note that their most profound influence on our experience, too, will be in how they influence our basic perceptions of space and time. In short, time is technologically mediated and socially constructed as much as it is sensory-perceptual and cognitive.

The X-axis moves from low-density to high-density requirements in terms of human information processing; so, for example, a low-density task might be driving on a well-known route to a routine location, and a high-density task might be operating a complex air-traffic control console. The Y-axis ranges from short (compressed) perceptual time passage through long (protracted) time passage. Expressions that capture compressed time passage include "Time rushed/flew/raced by," and expressions that capture prolonged time passage include "Time dragged on/passed at a snail's pace/ stood still." Notably, our memories of past events tend exhibit time compression (Evans 2004, p. 129).

When time passes quickly while we are watching an entertaining movie, it is not because we are experiencing a demanding information-processing situation but because our emotional engagement is high. Thus it is erroneous to conclude that an engaged learner is necessarily learning a great deal. Inversely, when time moves slowly while we are calculating our monthly budget, it is not necessarily because budget activities are easy to perform (since they involve calculation, memory use, are often done quickly, require error checking), but, rather, because the task is well known but the processing requirements are high. As well, the subjective well-being of the learner-viewer is certain to interact with perceptions of the task at hand; that is, if the learner feels invigorated versus tired, comfortable versus anxious, enthusiastic versus bored, and so on (Daniels 2000), this will have an affect on his or her perception of the task. Issues of entertainment, information, instruction, and engagement and their interaction with space and time, as esoteric as they may at first appear, turn out to play a critical role in how we understand and conceptualize technology-rich learning environments.

2.3 Higher Learning

Given the individual potentials and contextual constraints for learning found in our work and leisure worlds, we need to deal with the following essential question: if we agree, as Gee (2000) argues, that tasks and activities drive community practice, that process demands and functions override traditional structures (i.e., departments, borders, boundaries), that generalization is preferable to specialization, and that knowledge (and, indeed, cognition) is distributed rather than individual (pp. 518–519), how do instructors educate these so-called knowledge workers of the future?

The question of educating "workers" presumes that it is our responsibility to prepare learners for a work life (which may or may not include preparing them for a personal one). Some educators are uncomfortable with this position, arguing instead that our responsibility is only to cultivate fine young men and women (i.e., citizens) for the "public good" in a democratic society. Higher education, they maintain, is not in the business of preparing employees–workers–human capital for successful corporate lives "determined by values of the marketplace" (Duderstadt 1999/2000, p. 40). Stromquist (2007) suggests a less flattering economic reality: "As attention is paid to practical problem-solving rather than to knowledge and reflection that are not produced for sale, it may be asserted that research focusing on knowledge for truth and critique has been significantly curtailed. Within universities, the determination of crucial knowledge is becoming less predicated on autonomous and internal definitions of what is important and relevant, and more on external definitions of what will sell" (p. 7).

Although this debate is an important one and, too often, one that is passed over for more pragmatic (i.e., productive) issues of research, funding, program development, student enrollment goals, and placement statistics, it represents a moot position if we accept that higher educational institutions are, foremost, institutions and, as such, are firmly placed in the American market-driven techno-workplace-preparation system. Undergraduate degrees granted in the years 1970 and 2000, thus, dropped in more esoteric majors such as English from 64,342 to 51,419 and education from 176,307 to 105,566, whereas, in application-oriented majors such as business, degrees granted more than doubled from 114,729 to 265,746 and increased an exponential 20 times in computer science, from 2,388 to 41,954 (Miller 2005, p. 94, reporting U. S. Department of Education, National Center for Education Statistics, http://nces .ed.gov/). Indeed, our *relevance* to the real market-driven world is a reputation that we work hard to protect and promote. Our educational idealism thus uncomfortably rubs up against our attention to *U.S. News*, *Money Magazine*, *Forbes*, and *Newsweek* rankings of educational institutions.

It may be a dodge to hold the position that the purpose of higher education is educating future generations of environmentally responsible, civically connected, rhetorically sensitive individuals who believe in personal and cultural development as well as the organizational conduct and success of the institutions that they do labor for, but for the time being that is the position that I will attempt to maintain. Yet it is also quite reasonable to stop occasionally and ask ourselves, as do Fischer, Greenbaum, and Nake (2000), "Do people learn because they want to increase their 'market value,' or do they learn because they care for a sustainable communal life and for their personal development?" (p. 512). Have we, as Needleman (2003) argues, "placed the satisfaction of desire above the cultivation of being?" (p. 6). Most likely it is reductivist to assume, as many educators believe, that where political, civil, and individual freedom is concerned the status of the consumer-learner is equal to the status of the citizen-learner (cf. Mattelart 2000, p. 105).

So I work for an institution in the business of educating and instructing learners on content areas that I have spent a considerable amount of time studying, learning, contributing to, and applying. My institution has a great many goals that I may or may not share, and I contribute to and participate in the activities that I am trained for or interested in, most notably activities related to classroom- and technology-based instructional settings. With Levine (1997), I suspect that

many faculty . . . probably do not worry enough about the difference between what they do professionally and what they get paid for, how much they get paid for it, what decisions their institutions make and how they make them. For many who read the world's politics in complex and theoretical ways, the sorts of grubby, chancy, particularist, opportunistic activities of administrative offices get translated too quickly into systemic analyses that make ideology too important and too pervasive for what is actually going on—which are usually . . . desperate, unsystematic efforts to keep the operation going, the faculty paid, the public undisturbed, the money coming in, and the intellectual activities of the university proceeding excellently. (p. 36)

Therefore, while it is important for me to periodically consider how institutional, economic, and social forces enhance and constrain my ability to inquire and instruct in these settings, the research indicates that—with or without me—a great many transformational changes are afoot.[2]

When Kerr (2002) points out that "Now it is the turn of higher education to go the way of agriculture, industry, transportation, and military endeavors—and those all went a long way" (p. 16), he is speaking of the digitization of traditional organizations and processes. Rex Davenport, the editor of *T+D*, views the Congress requirement in the early 1990s for learning institutions to provide 50 percent of their courses via distance education to qualify for federal student assistance as "for the traditional brick and mortar institutions, . . . a shot across the bow. Get relevant and get aggressive. Understand the disconnect between your institution and the educational needs of all parts of society—especially the workplace" (Davenport 2006, p. 8). Indeed, higher education has been shifting its conventional instruction to distributed instruction most intensely during the last decade.

Colleges and universities are aggressively moving courses and even entire certificate and degree programs onto the Web. During the 1997 academic year, for example, the National Center for Educational Statistics estimated that one-third of the universities in the United States offered distance education courses online (Lewis et al. 1999). Tabs (2003) found that, only three years later, these numbers had increased significantly: "During the 12-month 2000–2001 academic year, 56 percent (2,320) of all 2-year and 4-year Title IV-eligible, degree-granting institutions offered distance education courses for any level or audience (ie., courses designed for all types of students, including elementary and secondary, college, adult education, continuing and professional education, etc.)" (p. iii), with approximately 90 percent of public two-year and four-year institutions offering online courses. Collis (2002) reports "62 percent of the thirty-six hundred accredited institutions of higher education offered distance learning courses in 2000" (p. 181). Actual percentages and exact definitions of what constitutes an online course or defines the parameters of an institution of higher learning differ, but one theme pervades the research literature: More and more courses are moving online.

Part of the exploration of alternative conceptions of conventional classroom-based instruction is a response to a new generation of learners who were born into the World Wide Web. Burkhardt et al. (2003) report that in 2002, 65 percent of American children between 2 and 17 use the Internet, with children between 13 and 17 watching television less (3.1 hours) than they do using digital media (3.5 hours) (p. 6). Compare these 7 hours of media use to the 2 hours spent by elementary students on reading, language arts, and mathematics estimated by Goodman (1990, p. 31), and one can anticipate a learning population that differs from any other in educational history. According to Madden (2003), 47 million Internet users had done research for school or training online in March 2000; and, by September 2002, that number had grown

34 percent to 63 million users. DeBell and Chapman (2006) report, "About 91 percent (53 million persons) of children age 3 and over and in nursery school through grade 12 use computers" (p. iii). Allen and Seaman (2008) note that "Online enrollments have continued to grow at rates far in excess of the total higher education student population, with the most recent data demonstrating no signs of slowing" and more than "3.9 million students . . . taking at least one online course during the fall 2007 term" (p. 1). Given that approximately 21 million teenagers between the ages of 12 and 17 report using the Internet and 78 percent of that population primarily at school (16 million), online instruction and learning in higher education promise to be with us for some time to come (Hitlin and Rainie 2005, p. 1). These learners, according to De Alva (1999/2000) and Biggs (2003), have numerous expectations in terms of higher educational institutions:

1. These students want to complete their education while working full-time.
2. They want a curriculum and faculty that are relevant to the workplace (vocationally oriented).
3. They want a time-efficient education.
4. They want their education to be cost-effective (and costs have increased).
5. They expect a high level of customer service (and class sizes are growing).
6. They want convenience (Biggs 2003, p. 2; De Alva 1999/2000, pp. 55–56).

Notably, the learners-as-consumers model of educational interaction is a problematic one because (a) if universities are able to maintain their altruistic goal of serving the public good, learners may not be satisfied with the workplace preparation offered by some institutions; (b) although customers of financial institutions *expect* high returns on their investments in limited amounts of time, the *business* of financial institutions does not allow this promise to be made; so too are learners subject to the complexities of resources that are brought together to provide them with rigorous and useful courses and programs; (c) universities serve many constituents, not simply learners, and are therefore going to be continually faced with decisions that require trade-offs between satisfying one customer base versus another; and (d) convenience, which presumes agreement and a "good fit" and frictionless progress, is not the responsibility of higher learning institutions (i.e., many more applicants would like to attend Yale or MIT than are admitted, which is, again, similar to the situation with financial institutions).

Naidu (2003) lists seven additional factors, beyond learner responsiveness, that have also come together to increase WBI use and deployment in higher education:

1. The increasing accessibility and decreasing cost of information and communications technologies.
2. The capacity of information and communications technology to support and enrich conventional educational practices through resource-based learning and synchronous and asynchronous communication.

3. The need for flexible access to learning opportunities from distributed venues such as the home, workplace, and the community learning center, as well as the conventional educational institution.

4. The demand from isolated and independent learners for more equitable access to educational opportunities and services.

5. The belief among many educational institutions that the application of information and communications technology will enable them to increase their share in an increasingly competitive educational market.

6. The need, among educational institutions, to be seen to be "keeping up with the times" in order to attract the attention of parents, students, and donors.

7. The belief and the expectation that e-learning will reduce costs and increase productivity and institutional efficiency (pp. 251–352).

This latter argument, that the cost of instruction will decrease, is the most common promise in the higher education literatures, second only to the argument that instructional technologies allow unprecedented access to higher education. As Pascarella and Terenzini (1998) assert, "new teaching and learning technologies have made possible the 'anywhere, anytime' delivery of instruction and student learning. . . . Many believe that these technologies not only provide wider access to higher education but that they will also increase instructional effectiveness (through their greater flexibility to accommodate varying learning styles) and instructional productivity (through reduced costs and increased numbers of learners served)" (p. 160). Selber (2004b), though, notes that arguments regarding access for the disenfranchised are as erroneous as arguments related to productivity improvement: "This myth, which is particularly appealing in a time of shrinking fiscal resources, inspires distance education initiatives that increase enrollments and workloads but not faculty positions, intranets and e-mail exchanges that unrealistically inflate communication expectations. . . . But there is very little evidence right now to suggest that computers actually reduce instructional costs in any significant manner, or that they enhance the research and teaching productivity of faculty members" (p. 5; cf. Bryant, Kahle, and Schafer 2005).

Although Graham (2004) mistakenly describes the challenge for e-learning to be replicating conventional education, he presents a realistic overview of the costs of fundamental technological change in higher education settings, arguing that, given the uncertainty involved in any large-scale technological effort, "The calculation of benefits has to be made time and again for specific proposals and particular systems" (p. 311).

Saba (2003) echoes Graham's (2004) cautiousness, asserting that the following variables contribute to the increasing complexity of distance education in this country:

• global, social, and economic developments;
• industrial and postindustrial organizational structures;

• media attributes involved in the production and presentation of instructional materials;
• learner traits of various kinds and their interaction with media attributes;
• myriad factors related to teaching and tutoring as well as the formation of learning communities;
• individual differences in perception, information processing, cognition, motor behavior, and affective states; and
• an increasing variety of attributes in emerging digital media, such as virtual reality-based tele-immersion and tele-presence (pp. 7–8).

Saba's (2003) "variables" can be distilled roughly as social and organizational factors, media-technology developments, instructional elements, and learner issues, all coming together to provide fertile ground for arguments in favor of educational access or market opportunity.

In this respect, Lanham's (2002) summary of the basic assumptions driving our "brick-and-mortar" universities stands in sharp contrast to the educational landscape described by Graham (2004) and Saba (2003). Informed by the alternative structures organizing emerging virtual universities, Lanham's (2002, pp. 160–176) list of ten assumptions that organize most campuses stands in stark contrast to the demands being placed on contemporary educational institutions during this and the coming decades:

• *Assumption 1*—The ideal education is face-to-face, one-on-one education.
• *Assumption 2*—Higher education, in its ideal form, proceeds in a setting sequestered in both time and space.
• *Assumption 3*—The education that every university offers should be generated in-house by a resident faculty employed full-time for this purpose.
• *Assumption 4*—The ideal pattern of employment for a university faculty is one that combines a maximum of narrowness and inflexibility in job description with a maximum of job security: the tenure system.
• *Assumption 5*—The purpose of the university administration is to protect the faculty from the outside world.
• *Assumption 6*—University faculties are animated by a purity of motive different from, and superior to, the world of ordinary human work.
• *Assumption 7*—Universities are unique institutions. As such, they cannot be meaningfully compared to any others.
• *Assumption 8*—Inefficiency is something to be proud of.
• *Assumption 9*—The new electronic field of expression does not change what we are doing but only how we are doing it.
• *Assumption 10*—The university lives in the same kind of economy it has always lived in.

These intersecting issues not only capture the breadth of research literatures related to distance education but also cross individual, group, organizational, and national boundaries, producing a broadly defined area for investigation that centers on instruction and learning with technology. If even two or three of Lanham's (2002) assumptions are realized during the next several years, academic "business" as we currently understand it will experience elemental shifts that ripple through preparation, career development and advancement expectations, unit and institutional goals, and visions for what it means to prepare a new generation of learners (Levin, Ben-Jacob, and Ben-Jacob 2000). It is not surprising, then, that Austin (2003) describes future academic work as a career path that will have to meet fiscal challenges with increased investments in information society and new technologies, strategic support of an increasingly diverse student population, and the transformation from traditional "brick universities" to "click universities" (p. 121).

However, it should be noted that Austin's (2003) article in *Review of Higher Education* is one of the only articles published in that journal since 2002 that includes a discussion of the role of technology in institutions of higher learning, a somewhat alarming discipline-specific detail considering the dramatic changes facing higher education as a result of globalization, increased demands for alternative forms of education, and technology. Table 2.2 summarizes Hanna's (2003) description of this dramatic shift from a collegial to managerial to entrepreneurial orientation (or from traditional to extended traditional to for-profit adult-centered; cf. Hanna 1998). These developments parallel changes in the nonacademic workplace (Asaolu 2006).

Table 2.2

The changing cultures of higher education (adapted from Hanna 2003, p. 76)

	Collegial	Managerial	Entrepreneurial
Orientation to Change	Conservers	Pragmatists	Originators
Leadership	Stewardship	Preservation	Visionary
Values	Faculty program	Administrative efficiency	Client-oriented
Decision Making	Restricted, shared internal	Vertical, top-down	Horizontal, shared with stakeholders
Support Structures	Program-driven	Rule-focused	Learner-focused
Key Messages	Quality	Efficiency	Market-driven
Communication Strategies	Internal	Vertical, formal	External/internal, horizontal, informal
Systems and Resources	Duplicated according to need	Stable, efficient, and preorganized	Evolving "as needed"
Key Messages	Stick together	Don't rock the boat	Seize the day

But higher education is unprepared for the challenges that moving information and education online invite. Not only have educational researchers struggled in the academy for status and centrality against the forces of disciplinarily located educational efforts, but academic disciplinary structures are designed to solve particularized problems that do not tend to anticipate coresponsible ownership of the very constructs that emerging technologies tend to challenge: collaboration, information, learning, communication, methodology, and instruction (cf. Younglove-Webb et al. 1999).

Such fundamental changes require, according to Scenters-Zapico and Cos (2003), a radically comprehensive approach to problems and processes: "the new millennium's rhetoricians will be required to produce their own interactive multimedia presentations, with the triumphs going to rhetoricians skilled in many disciplines' knowledge and talents. As Athenians had to possess what we might today call 'multidisciplinary knowledge and skill' in order to survive and thrive in a demanding democracy, so students today must possess the multidisciplinary knowledge and technological skills to succeed in a multimedia age" (p. 64). Indeed, Scenters-Zapico and Cos (2003) conclude that multimedia technologies "atomize" disciplinary divisions by adding a sixth canon, interactivity, to the five rhetorical (i.e., multidisciplinary) canons of invention, arrangement, style, memory, and delivery (p. 65). It is therefore not surprising that innovative curricular developments in the humanities are centering themselves on digital media (Miller, Carter, and Gallagher 2003) and that engineering programs are grounding themselves in communication, social, ethical, and environmental studies (Vaezi-Nejad and Olabiran 2005).

Felder (2006) echoes the call for dramatic curricular revision to meet the demands of a new engineering economy. Graduates who "will continue to find jobs in the new economy" will need to be

• creative researchers, developers, and entrepreneurs who can help their companies stay ahead of the technology development curve;
• designers capable of creating products that are attractive as well as functional;
• holistic, multidisciplinary thinkers who can recognize complex patterns and opportunities in the global economy and formulate strategies to capitalize on them;
• people with strong interpersonal skills that equip them to establish and maintain good relationships with current and potential customers and commercial partners;
• people with language skills and cultural awareness needed to build bridges between companies and workers in developing nations (where many manufacturing facilities will continue to be located); and
• self-directed learners, who can continue to acquire the new knowledge and skills they need to stay abreast of rapidly changing technological and economic conditions (p. 96).

Globalization, multidisciplinarity, cultural awareness: essential words for a new era. As Salomon (1993) stresses, "In a rapidly changing world, one of the most crucial outcomes one expects of education is students' ability to handle *new* situations and meet *new* intellectual challenges" (p. 128). And there can be no doubt that fundamental assumptions about the world we live in are being radically realigned as we write (Newman 2008).

Unfortunately, in this regard our academic disciplinary structures confound as much as they comfort us in our attempts to understand instruction and learning with technology. Some of this problem has developed as a result of our uneasy relationship with historical developments in distance education, instructional technology, and networked education, which unfortunately has tended to emphasize technologies for delivery rather than transformation (Rickman et al. 2003; Shearer 2003). One would hypothesize that the opposite might be the case, given that distance education in the United States has a well-established history of over one hundred years dating back to primary paper and postal delivery systems (Pittman 2003; Wallace 2003); but, as Lyotard (1979, 1984) points out, "It is reasonable to suppose that the proliferation of information-processing machines is having, and will continue to have, as much of an effect on the circulation of learning as did advancements in human circulation (transportation systems) and later, in the circulation of sounds and visual images (the media)" (p. 4).

Distance education programs in this country date back to 1892, when Penn State and the University of Chicago developed the first correspondence programs (Pittman 2003; Wang and Gearhart 2006). Bastiaens and Martens (2000) also note the existence in Germany of correspondence courses on stenography as early as 1840. So the advent of the World Wide Web did not create the opportunity for distance education but, rather, vitalized conversations about the role of distance education, independent study, and adult learning in traditional academic institutions (Rogers 2000).

2.3.1   A Brief History of Technologies for Instruction and Learning

Peters (2003) divides the history of distance education into three distinct stages, beginning with print, incorporating alternative media such as radio and television, and, ultimately, combining interlinked media via multimedia technologies. James and Gardner (1995) describe four generations of distance education:

Generation One encompasses basic correspondence study including not only print materials, but also other mailable materials, including audio- and videocassettes. Audio and video teleconferencing are included in the *second generation*, whereas *Generation Three* relates primarily to computer technology capabilities. *Generation Four* includes some technological techniques that are not yet commonly used and more sophisticated options for the future (such as virtual reality or video desktop). (p. 23)

Related to these information design developments, Wisher and Curnow (2003) describe four more recent stages of video-based media use for instruction:

Video-based instruction has progressed from *the audiovisual stage* (1940s and 1950s) to *the educational media stage* (1960s and 1970s) to *the instructional technology stage* (1980s to mid-1990s) to what might be called *the Internet stage* (circa 1994). The antiquated terminology of the audiovisual heydays—fluorescent chalk, lantern slides, anamphoric lenses, lenticual screens, pantographs, and telemation devices—has been replaced by a new nomenclature: instant messaging, bandwidth, browsers, video streaming, and graphical user interfaces to name a few. Undoubtedly, the future will offer new video avenues for the learner. Virtual reality . . . , the handheld, wireless Web . . . , and spatially immersive visual displays that project stereo images on three walls and the floor are examples of the changing medium of instructional video. (p. 238)

Notably, radio, television, and perhaps the Internet have similar "histories" of hyperpromise and underestimation with regard to education, although the Internet's penetration in the United States dwarfs that of radio and television—three years for the Internet, fifteen for television, and thirty for radio (Asaolu 2006, p. 338). It is also worth noting that radio did not "rent out airtime" until between 1922 (bought from Great Britain's British Marconi in 1919 by an American consortium that included AT&T, Westinghouse, and General Electric, and incorporated as RCA); that the first educational television program in 1959, Sunrise Semester, which broadcast an instructor speaking before a lecture-style class as its format, ultimately became the semi-government-sponsored Public Broadcasting Service (PBS); and, in the late 1980s, that PBS faced serious educational budgeting problems and was forced to resort to providing educational content and single programs rather than developing its own content fully (Freed 1999; Mattelart 2000). Still, distance educational offerings via cable television have continued to find loyal audiences in urban locations since the 1950s (Wang and Gearhart 2006). For this reason, Tomlinson-Keasey (2002) stresses interaction over the particular medium involved, and she distinguishes television from the Internet specifically: "The ways in which students interact with the professor, other students, and the course content remain an important wild card in online courses and technologically mediated programs. Television was supposed to bring universal, high-level expertise into American classrooms, but the predicted benefits were never realized, at least in part because students' interactions with the medium were passive and teachers' engagement with the material during and following telecasts was awkward and cumbersome" (pp. 150–151).

As with radio and television, WBI is both *means* of education and a *mode* of education. On the one hand, WBI applications can be explored and employed that allow a range of educational objectives; on the other hand, WBI applications embed a host of cognitive and social understandings about the nature of human activities that they have been designed to support. Thus, a discussion list presumes that chronology and subject labeling are critical for understanding the content of and rationale for the human-to-human dialogue. Learning Management Systems (LMSs) that separate users into builders, designers, teachers, and students instigate a particular view of the subsequent learning space, one that reinforces the view that instructors do not design information but, rather, provide it, and that those who develop learning environments cannot simultaneously play the role of students who are evaluated by teachers. Learner control, in this educational space, most surely does not include being able to develop "rooms" that the teacher is not allowed to enter.

At the most abstract level, the contemporary debate between advocates of alternative educational approaches and sponsors of conventional, face-to-face instruction can be viewed as nothing less significant than struggle between time and space. As Cantelon (1995) states:

> The so-called traditional university also provides . . . examples of the tension between time and space. Historically, the university consisted of a space-time equilibrium based on an agricultural society. The green campus quadrangle, with or without walls, enclosed a particular space set aside for the purposes of what was called higher learning. Still, in the minds of many, a university is primarily a physical location. Most think of college in physical or spatial terms: a plot of land on which sits a library, a chapel, and an Old Main. Indeed, for most of the twentieth century, higher education has been afflicted with what has been called an edifice complex, investing a very large percentage of its available funds in buildings and their maintenance. (pp. 8–9)

This "edifice complex," too, plays out in historical discussions of distance education, except that technology becomes the new architecture (i.e., the delivery truck) and instruction and learning the foundation. Or perhaps instruction and learning become the architecture and technology the foundation (i.e., platform). Orel (1995), too, describes the "symbolics of power" represented by centralized technologies, writing that hospitals have been resistant to the simplification or distribution of hospital equipment to maintain the users' awareness that the medical community, and not its customers, are at the controls (pp. 88–89). Winner (1995), as well, highlights the *political artifacts* that make up our experience, that is, artifacts that "strongly condition that shared experience of power, authority, order, and freedom in modern society" (p. 147). In both these institutional settings, then, instruction, learning, and technology are problematically separated into wisdom (*sophos*), skill (*techne*), and thing (*pragmata*), ignoring the obvious and exciting interaction between the constructs. After all, *techne* is simultaneously a craft *and* an art, a practice and a way of knowing (Verbeek 2005). Give users the ability to learn outside the walls of the institution and users begin to question their relationship with the institution.

In an attempt to resist describing contemporary distance education efforts in purely technical terms, Dabbagh and Bannan-Ritland (2005) and Kearsley (2000) outline general themes that distinguish traditional learning environments from Web-based ones (see table 2.3).

Table 2.3
Traditional versus Web-based learning environments (adapted from Dabbagh and Bannan-Ritland 2005, p. 4; Kearsley 2000, pp. 4–10*)

Traditional Learning Environment	Web-Based Learning Environment
Bounded	Unbounded
Real time	Time shifts: asynchronous communications and accelerated cycles
Instructor-controlled	Decentralized control (student centered)
Individual learning*	Collaboration and community*
Linear	Hypermedia: multidimensional space, linked navigation, multimedia (multisensory)
Juried, edited sources	Dynamic, real-time information (exploration)
Stable information sources	
Structured problem-solutions*	Authenticity*
Familiar technology	Continuously evolving technology

Setting aside for a moment the potentially amplified dichotomy between traditional and technology-based learning environments presented in table 2.3, it is most useful to review Asaolu's (2006) comparison of contemporary technology developments (table 2.1) and Hanna's (2003) changing cultures of higher education (table 2.2), to begin to understand the organizational, social, and cultural forces that are interacting with our rapidly developing technological capabilities.

2.3.2 Thorny Problems

The optimism of some researchers about the sweeping reforms to higher education that will come as a result of information technologies are, one must admit, somewhat infectious. Indeed, it requires a delicate touch to be the one to counter each of Kearsley's (2000) themes with a counter theme—for example, where there is connectivity there must be solitude and reflection, where there is unboundedness comes a desire for parameters, development of shared knowledge requires individual understanding, and so on.

And such a delicate position is made all the more difficult to maintain given explosive changes being reported in the world of work around us. As Engeström (2000) writes:

The valid message and challenge is that the economic, technological, political, and cultural conditions of work are being radically transformed. This transformation includes widening gaps between the rich and the poor, both globally and within nation states. The transformation also includes radical qualitative changes in the structure and contents of work, a major facet of which is increasing horizontal movement across organizational, occupational and cultural boundaries and the emergence of what I've called "knotworking." If education is to remain relevant, educators need to study carefully these changes and build on their internal contradictions and emergent learning processes from below, rather than continue preaching the right answers from above. (pp. 533–534)

Dede (2002), similarly, argues that "the fundamental barriers to employing . . . technologies effectively for learning are not technical or economic, but psychological, organizational, political, and cultural" (p. 25). Duderstadt, Wulf, and Zemsky (2005) note, "the benefits of IT [information technology] investments will require the co-evolution of technology, human behavior, and organizations" (p. 38). Certainly, the debate over the viability of online instruction versus the potential threat that such instruction poses to more traditional forms of instruction and the controversy over resource allocation that favors the development of online education versus classroom-based instruction are part of this larger organizational and political landscape, leading Duffy and Kirkley (2004a) to assert that

contrasting perspectives characterize the polarized discussions that have arisen around distance education. On the one hand, it is viewed as the new revolution in education, extending the reach of education to those who cannot come to campus, making education more affordable, providing new models for lifelong learning (e.g., through communities of practice), and reforming teaching practices through the emphasis on student discussion and activity, and the elimination of the lecture as central teaching activity. On the other hand, distance education is seen as lowering the quality of instruction, a moneymaking rather than educational enterprise, an environment where cheating cannot be controlled, and an environment that threatens the teaching role both through the lack of any physical constraints on class size and potentially leading to the disaggregation of the roles of faculty. (p. 4)

If one views technical-mediation as transformational, it is also necessary to view online instruction and learning historically and holistically. First, when Bates and Poole (2003) compare instructional settings as they existed in the 1300s to distributed instructional situations currently being offered jointly by the University of British Columbia and Tecnológico de Monterrey in Mexico, readers are forced to acknowledge that most higher educational settings resemble more the lecture situations of the 1300s. Similar to technology, educational innovations are an admixture of extraordinary promise and incremental advances. To Bates and Poole (2003), the only way to clearly imagine traditional (face-to-face) instruction is to return to scenarios that existed prior to the invention of the Gutenberg press, even though many contemporary rules, behaviors, and designs for instructional settings are borrowed from these ancient settings. Second, rather than parsing instructional approaches into rigid categories such as "traditional" versus "online" (using only digital applications to display and distribute class materials and to facilitate class discussions) versus "blended," which, according to researchers, represents a hybrid of the two models (Collis and

Moonen 2001; Rovai and Jordan 2004), a comprehensive notion of instruction and learning can only evolve if one views these approaches as part of a greater continuum (Wallace and Weiner 1998). Thus, when Allen and Seaman (2008) attempt to define the approaches according to how much of a percentage of the course content is delivered online, the distinctions between the three categories become arbitrary and impossible to maintain. According to the authors, when more than 80 percent of one's instruction is delivered online, a course is defined as online; courses with 30 to 79 percent online are defined as blended or hybrid; courses with 1 to 29 percent online are defined as Web facilitated; and courses with 0 percent online are defined as traditional (p. 4). But how does one determine content percentages, what it means to be online, and whether instructional processes ought to be factored into the calculation?

Whatever the case, the greatest challenge facing both instructors and learners is the completely online course, whether augmented by audiovideo conferencing or text-based in nature. The challenges of working in an online-only instructional environment have been well documented in the research, including isolation effects (Burgess 2003), instructional pacing challenges (Gay and Hembrooke 2004), attrition issues (Neuhauser 2002), and learner motivation problems (Wang and Gearhart 2006), to name a few. And face-to-face instruction has well-documented shortcomings as well, including encouraging one-way transmission of content (Fetherston 2001), problematic instructor–learner contact ratios (Phillips 2005), and a shortage of effective methods of evaluation (beyond student feedback and nonrandomized peer review processes).

The difficulty with the identification of blended instruction as a *third* alternative approach to instruction is that, as long as I have been a practicing instructor (since the early 1980s), I have always employed blended instruction in my courses—that is, if augmenting one's instructor-learner face-to-face interaction with e-mail communication constitutes digital augmentation. As a researcher interested in online information design and evaluation, the real challenge was in adapting to an educational system that required teaching three courses per semester when, during graduate school, I had been trained and encultured primarily as a researcher. Applying my research training to *the problem of instruction*, in turn, heightened my uneasiness by revealing a host of educational journals across disciplines and drawing on dissimilar literatures and traditions. Over time I learned, as Petraglia (2003) summarizes, that

For most of the West's history, education proceeded without anything really like learning theory to guide choices. Vague ideals such as *phronesis* and "liberal education" characterized the teleology of education for well over 2000 years. Education was rooted largely in social values, conventions, and precedent rather than in any theories of human cognition and of the kinds of learning contexts that might best accommodate learning. (pp. 165–166)

In addition to internal institutional constraints on education, instructors of this generation are also institutional by-products of what Kerr (2002) calls "Shock Wave

II." Shock Wave II, in American institutions of higher learning, is a combination of external forces that are having a profound influence on what we do. According to Kerr (2002), dynamics that dominate our definition of higher learning include emerging electronic technologies, the DNA revolution, expanding demographic realities, increased competition for public sector resources, competition for students from the for-profit sector, increased assessment efforts aimed at improving primary and secondary education, the impact of a globalized economy, and controversies over appropriate models for the (post)modern university (pp. 2–4). So too are we beginning to strain at growing demands for education from emerging populations such as midcareer advancement audiences and senior citizens interested in lifelong learning opportunities (p. 7).

2.3.3 Nonsignificant Spaces

Rather than evoking the host of issues that we anticipate will result from a digitized academic landscape, two questions almost always arise when one turns to the topic of online education. First, which is *better*, traditional instruction or online courses? And, second, following naturally from the first, will online education lead to the destruction of "brick-and-mortar" educational institutions? Unfortunately, the dichotomy between face-to-face instruction and online instruction reduces much of what is interesting about the transition and interaction between traditional forms of instruction and emerging ones.

The research on distance education, correspondence courses, and extension teaching is about seventy-five years old and almost always supports the widely cited "no significant difference" phenomenon (Russell 1999). No other study related to distance education has received the attention of Russell's (1999) oft-cited summary of "no significant difference" findings contained in publications documenting the use of technology in instructional contexts. As Russell (1999) states explicitly, in the foreword of the book, "The good news is that these no significant difference studies provide substantial evidence that technology does not denigrate instruction" (p. xiii). This position toward technology is powerful rhetorically in that it allows Russell (1999) to argue simultaneously *for* and *against* technology integration in education: the claim that "This [no significant difference] fact opens doors to employing technologies to increase efficiencies, circumvent obstacles, bridge distances, and the like" can thus be followed immediately with the claim that no significant difference "also allows us to employ cheaper and simpler technologies with assurance that outcomes will be comparable with the more sophisticated and expensive ones as well as conventional teaching/learning methods" (p. xiii).

Thus Russell (1999) concludes, "The fact is that the findings of comparative studies are absolutely conclusive; one can bank on them. No matter how it is produced, how it is delivered, whether or not it is interactive, low tech or high tech, students learn equally well with each technology and learn as well as their on-campus, face-to-face counterparts even though students would rather be on campus with the instructor if that were a real choice" (p. xviii). Significantly, Meyer (2002) writes that, of the 355 media comparison studies published between 1928 and 1998 (Russell 1999), the review focused on performance measures (usually determined by grades or test scores) and student satisfaction. Only 40 out of the 355 studies (approximately 9 percent) included computer-based instruction (Meyer 2002, p. 14). Bernard et al. (2004b), in addition to pointing out that the rigor, quality, and sample sizes of the studies compared differ, notes that "an accepted null hypothesis does not deny the possibility that unsampled differences exist in the population; it means only that they do not exist in the sample being studied" (p. 383). Similarly, Arbaugh and Hiltz (2005), in their review of the shortcomings of existing research on asynchronous learning networks (ALN), argue that in addition to measuring traditional learning outcomes such as grades (on examinations or in the course) and perceived learning/satisfaction (via surveys), researchers should consider measuring collaborative examinations, projects and portfolios, and participation (that is, the number, frequency, and length of comments).

So hundreds, perhaps thousands of comparative studies of classroom teaching versus alternative media for delivering educational content—whether via cassette, videotape, television, or over the Internet—have reported that distance education courses are no less effective than traditional, face-to-face courses offered at most educational institutions. Rice, Hiltz, and Spencer (2005) thus assert "One rather broad conclusion of these kinds of studies is that there probably is no necessary (at least not simple or linear) causal relationship between the use of any particular new medium and success in teaching or learning" (p. 230). Lockee, Burton, and Cross (1999) point out, however, that comparison studies provide distance education advocates with the data to support "the [formidable] front-end investments needed in course development, delivery infrastructures, teaching technologies, and support staff" (p. 35). Technology advocates add that emerging technologies are capable of providing as much interaction between instructors and their students as instructors can manage (Mesher 1999). Bates and Poole (2003) conclude bluntly: "Asking whether online learning or any other technology is more or less effective than face-to-face teaching is not helpful. We know the answer: all other things being equal (which they never are) there is no statistically significant difference" (p. 72).

Indeed, technology advocates make broader claims than that, although reviewing their claims about what WBI *does* versus what it *promises* to do is an important exercise. Promises that WBI holds for instructors and learners, we are informed, include the following:

• "With current WBT development tools, there is almost no limit to the level of interactivity that can be included" (Barron 1998, p. 259).

• "It is relatively easy to incorporate (and encourage) communication between the instructor and the students" (Barron 1998, p. 364).

• "[Blended learning initiatives] increase sales per employee; improve sales productivity; improve employee job satisfaction" (Bersin 2004, p. 24).

• "It was estimated that the cost of taking a 40–60 hour IT course in person would be $2000, as compared to only $500 if taken online" (Capper 2001, p. 243).

• "the virtual delivery of education found in technology-mediated distance education . . . frees the teacher and learner from the constraints of time and place" (Carchidi 2002, p. 3).

• "The absence of temporal and spatial constraints means greater flexibility for teachers and students" (Curran 2001, p. 118).

• "Ease of access to a fast and relatively low-cost means of communication allows students to contact their tutors easily (and often) and—in principle, at least—receive an early response" (Curran 2001, p. 118).

• "E-learning solutions facilitate the delivery of the right information and skills to the right people at the right time" (Downey et al. 2005, p. 48).

• "The flexibility of e-learning systems allows individuals to be trained at a variety of locations, and often at their own convenience and pace, therefore avoiding the time and expenses associated with traditional training methods" (Downey et al. 2005, p. 48).

• "Increased participation, responding to larger class sizes, higher student-to-staff ratios, overcrowded classrooms, reduced interaction, and cramped physical class spaces" (McCormack and Jones 1998, p. 18).

• "Increased communication, . . . [as] it is commonly reported that people talk more electronically (via e-mail or a chat program) than they do in a face-to-face situation" (McCormack and Jones 1998, p. 21).

• WBI is "accessible to learners at a time, place, and pace that is convenient to them" (Naidu 2003, p. 353).

• "The ability to increase activity and interactivity with the help of adaptive learning programs" (O. Peters 2003, p. 98).

Critics of distance education, however, interpret "no significant difference" to mean that because there is no evidence that alternative-format courses do anything to enhance, improve, or enrich students' learning experiences, performance, or subjective satisfaction, administrators ought to invest their energy in trying to reduce class sizes and on improving instructor salaries and existing teaching facilities (Noble 1998; Oppenheimer 1997). To this end, Noam (1995) stresses that technology cannot facilitate effective teaching and learning, but that the cornerstones of good teaching must always involve "mentoring, internalization, identification, role modeling, guidance, socialization, interaction and group activity" (p. 249).

But "good teaching" is an elusive goal no matter what media we employ. Meyer (2002), in addressing the issue of quality in online learning, summarizes the critical issue: "Because we have not achieved a definitive answer on quality for more traditional classroom situations, perhaps it is unwise to expect such clarity for online learning" (p. v; cf. Bransford et al. 2004). Naidu (2003) notes that "In the midst of all this interest in and proliferation of e-learning, there is a great deal of variability in the quality of e-learning and teaching"; but adds, "However, this shouldn't be any surprise as there are just as many instances of poor and reckless face-to-face teaching as there are instances of excellence in that regard as well" (p. 354). Felder (2006) argues that "Nowhere in most engineering curricula do we provide a systematic training in the abilities that most graduates will need to get jobs—the skills to think innovatively and holistically and entrepreneurially, design for aesthetics as well as function, communicate persuasively, bridge cultural gaps, and periodically re-engineer themselves to adjust to changing market conditions" (p. 96). Koschmann et al. (1996) and Spiro et al. (1992) note that conventional, face-to-face instructional approaches often produce individuals who

• fail to develop valid, robust knowledge bases;
• have difficulty reasoning with and applying knowledge;
• are unable to reflect on their performance and continue the process of learning;
• oversimplify in their understanding of new concepts;
• compound earlier oversimplifications with larger networks of consequential misconception;
• work well with some forms of information but not with others (for example, visual versus textual versus auditory media); and
• are often rewarded for limited-duration learning that is tested in context and immediately (Spiro et al. 1992, p. 62).

These individuals hold reductive worldviews that, according to Spiro, Collins, and Ramchandran (2007), are "made up of events and phenomena that are orderly, predictable, decomposable into additive elements, non-contingent, and well structured" (p. 19); and unfortunately, these individuals tend to view "learning as best accomplished by approaches that lead to representations that are simple and highly general (capturing a topic with a single schema, prototype example, set of general principles and definitions, etc.), compartmentalized or 'chapterized'" (p. 20). These are the same learners that Sawyer (2006) describes as tending to treat new knowledge as unrelated to prior knowledge, to viewing course materials as discrete facts and procedures, to memorizing rather than understanding materials, and to managing new knowledge poorly without understanding how to reflect on its purpose or their personal strategies for learning (p. 4).

In addition to holding distance education to a standard that may not exist in conventional instructional settings, a clearly defined distinction between online and conventional instruction is difficult to maintain; and defining what it means to be *better* is an issue as well. For this reason, Saba (2000) asserts that traditional empirical comparative studies can benefit significantly from data derived from emerging methodologies such as discourse analysis, open-ended interviewing, and so on. Other researchers, for example Hiltz and Goldman (2005), simply acknowledge that both traditional and online instruction

have strengths and weaknesses. The relative effectiveness of an ALN is contingent not only on access to the necessary hardware and software facilities, but also on the teacher conducting the course in a manner that fits the characteristics of the medium, the nature of the course materials, and the characteristics of the students; also, on students being motivated and able to participate actively and regularly. It is the instructor who must take the primary responsibility for building a sense of connectedness and community in an online course. (p. 11)

Hiltz and Goldman (2005), in emphasizing effective instruction and its relationship with media choice in learning situations, represent a growing number of researchers who view the instructional challenge as a complex one made up of far more than the applications that we use. Gunawardena and McIsaac (2004), for example, describe the inevitable rethinking of comparative research, "from early media comparison studies that yielded 'no significant differences' which were clearly conducted to justify distance education as a worthwhile endeavor, to research that is focusing on critical pedagogical, design, and sociocultural context issues based on theoretical constructs in the field and related fields such as communication" (p. 387).

Despite the need for more sophisticated research on instruction, Meyer (2002) laments that "it continues to be true that the majority of articles published on distance education, Web-based education, and quality continue to be position papers, personal experiences, and advice to others contemplating a Web-based course" (p. 17). Clearly a thorough investigation of the research on distance education is called for, but the investigation would benefit from an approach that is not oriented around comparative media controls and grade outcomes. Certainly the research supports the simple notion that media types and learning should not be viewed as a one-way interaction: instructional situations are more complex than that.

So one major "lesson" of Russell's (1999) "no significant difference" report, bluntly put, is that technology does not inherently solve pedagogical problems. Indeed, technology can cause pedagogical problems or invent new ones—but technology does not necessarily have to cause problems. Technology is never transparent to the problems that we aim to solve using it. The reservations that some instructors express about the inability of emerging technologies to solve age-old teaching problems are frequently appropriate and should not be ignored. At the very least, technology always adds another layer (or various interdependent layers) to the initial problem at hand. Dynamic, interactive software may initially heighten user motivation to learn or increase anxiety over user abilities to learn; but, over time, solid principles of effective pedagogy almost always prove more successful than novelty and alternative media alone. So technology is never something that one adds to the instructional design process after establishing goals and strategies for achieving them. Technology interacts with, heightens, and complicates pedagogical aspirations. As Wisher and Curnow (2003) observe, "The underlying theme of the findings are [sic] really quite simple: If the classroom environment is replicated, the learning outcomes are replicated, ie., the 'no significant difference' phenomenon" (p. 328).

Finally, the "no significant difference" report comes dangerously close to presenting itself as an argument from ignorance or *argumentum ad ignorantiam*: proposition A is not known to be true, therefore A is false. Because the empirical evidence does not "prove" that technology improves learning, we erroneously hold that technology does not improve learning. As Walton (1999) asserts, "The argument from ignorance, analyzed this way as a dialectical fallacy, could be described as an exaggerated statement of the results of a discussion. It is the tactic of implying that the discussion has already successfully reached the closing stage, whereas in reality, it should be seen as still being in the argumentation stage" (p. 375).

The sophistication of this type of argument cannot be underestimated, even if its use is unintentional, because it shifts the task of establishing the most effective way to teach in the classroom to advocates of technology rather than defenders of conventional classroom-based teaching. Walton (1999), in his examination of fallacious uses of *argumentum ad ignorantiam*, thus concludes:

Fallacious arguments from ignorance are often connected with, first, a reversal of burden of proof, and second, a difficulty in fulfilling that burden, once it has been reversed, especially in cases where genuine evidence is difficult to find. In such cases, a failure to find evidence that might help to defend one against the charge may result in the charges going ahead purely on a basis of innuendo. Instead of fitting into the larger body of evidence to play its correct role in shifting a balance of consideration by presumption, the *argumentum ad ignorantiam*, in such a case, has an impact far out of proportion to its real weight, and functions as a basis for leading to a conclusion solely on the basis of slander and innuendo. (pp. 375–376)

Naming whether our intellectual context demands an argument and supporting evidence *for* technology use in instruction or evidence *against* technology use in instruction can teach us a great deal about both our position and our audience's position, beliefs, and attitudes about technology. Ultimately, of course, there are no easy answers, and proof is only available in particularized educational contexts. It is difficult to establish whether my daughter's "after school" immersion in multiplayer environments supplements or detracts from her *formal* educational endeavors, but it is also clear that the majority of her middle-school friends are spending time in these spaces with her. Extracting technology use from her learning is as problematic as ascribing importance to either school-based learning or workplace learning without acknowledging the powerful social and cultural forces influencing both (Tuomi-Gröhn and Engeström 2003a).

Several complex developments have been explored in this chapter. First, emerging technologies are rapidly conflating the learning worlds (work, leisure, and educational) that envelop and engage us. Second, models of productivity and efficiency drive many of our discussions about the influence of technology on instruction and learning. Third, comparative media studies have tended to dominate the research, and, as a result, few researchers have begun to map the emerging and multidisciplinary literatures related to instruction and learning with technology.

If we assume that the learning worlds we once inhabited were easily separable and maintained distinct problems, activities, communication rules and roles, environments and artifacts, and that this is no longer true, how might we begin to strategically map the research relevant to instruction and learning with technology? What are the theoretical implications of moving beyond our preoccupation with productivity and efficiency, and what assumptions might guide subsequent investigations?

Because technology, instruction, and learning are moving targets, and indeed, because learners are adapting rapidly to the pervasiveness of technologies in their everyday lives, reviewing the numerous research literatures that touch on issues important to these learning worlds is imperative. In addition to journals devoted to distance education and e-learning, a host of disciplinary interests come into play when we consider instruction and learning with technology, including, for example, educational, instructional, and communication technology; the teaching and learning sciences; communication and information design; human–computer interaction and ergonomics; training; adult education; and workplace studies. It quickly becomes apparent that the question is "What research field (i.e., theory, method, practice, and conceptual foundation) is *not* being profoundly altered by technology and our contemporary computing landscape?"

3 Research Conversations

In this chapter, I review and examine the prodigious efforts of researchers interested in instruction and learning with technology in general and distance education specifically. I present 300 peer-reviewed research journals related to instruction and learning with technology and organize them broadly according to traditional disciplinary boundaries, with the goal of positioning us for interdisciplinary conversations about the complex relationship between instruction, learning, and technology.

. . . there is a new profession of trail blazers, those who find delight establishing useful trails through the enormous mass of common record.
—Vannevar Bush (1945, p. 108)

When Cato grumbled that Isocrates's students wasted their whole lives on education and would have to use their knowledge to plead before Minos in the underworld, he presaged the plight of all those long-distance runners probing the complexity of human affairs.
—Merrill D. Whitburn (2000, p. 237)

3.1 Conversations and Commonplace Assumptions

Kenneth Burke (1941) has eloquently applied the metaphor of a "parlor" to describe the human condition. We enter the parlor at birth, arriving late, and find others already engaged in a host of conversations about every topic conceivable. We do not understand the full meaning of any of the conversations because we have no knowledge of the starting points, goals, or of previous references and exigencies guiding the existing topics. Ultimately, though, we listen in and figure out the conversations, assumptions, commonplaces, and conventions, and we become comfortable with and are able to contribute to the conversation. Upon our death, we depart the parlor: "the hour grows late, you must depart. And you do depart, with the discussion still vigorously in progress" (p. 111). And so the conversation in the parlor continues and advances ad infinitum.

But where do we identify the research conversation regarding distance education specifically, and instruction and learning with technology in general? In attempting to respond to this epistemologically daunting question, it is first necessary to address the question: *why* must we identify the research conversation regarding distance education? Elucidating the host of scholarly conversations about distance education requires an examination of five assumptions so common in the literature as to have become veritable topoi for researchers interested in contributing to the field. Yet, as with all topoi, the commonplace assumptions require identification and elaboration; and these elaborations in turn act to inform a principled structuring of potential research conversations regarding distance education.

As such, this chapter has not been designed to serve as a typical review of the literature for several reasons. First, such reviews exist for researchers interested in instruction and learning with technology (e.g., Allen et al. 2002; Bernard et al. 2004a,b; Larreamendy-Joerns and Leinhardt 2006; Sitzmann et al. 2005). Second, several educational researchers such as Boote and Beile (2005) have accurately captured the difficulty of constructing traditional literature reviews in education, which arises because educational researchers frequently cannot assume they are "communicating with a well-defined audience about commonly accepted problems . . . where disciplinary research . . . is based on a canon of shared knowledge" (p. 3). Topoi often serve unarticulated canonical roles; thus, this chapter is more accurately represented as an argument for multidisciplinarity that puts forward five position statements drawn from research *about the research* on instruction and learning with technology collected across disciplines.

3.1.1   Assumption 1: Distance Education in Higher Education Is Growing

Indeed, more and more courses and entire degree programs are being offered online (Allen and Seaman 2008; Mehlenbacher et al. 2000; Meyer 2002; Tabs 2003), and, therefore, the reasoning follows that distance education is an important object of study. In their landmark (2000) report, the Web-Based Education Commission urged the administration and 107th Congress to make distance education a centerpiece of national education policy: "The Internet is perhaps the most transformative technology in history, reshaping business, media, entertainment, and society in astonishing ways. . . . But for all its power, it is just now being tapped to transform education" (p. 1). Only three years before, Benyon, Stone, and Woodroffe (1997) revealed a more cautious perspective, noting that "Although even we see great potential in the technology [of the Web], we feel that we need better tools and a better understanding of the pedagogic impact which Web-based courseware will have" (p. 216). In this respect, practitioners, instructors, and policymakers could certainly benefit from the systematic study of distance education.

One could argue, however, that before distance education receives increased research attention, it would be reassuring to capture how traditional instruction has benefited from similar research attention. Although some researchers have suggested that systematic studies of instructional activities in face-to-face classrooms are rare (Bernhardt, Wojahn, and Edwards 1990; Chenowth et al. 1999; Duffy and Kirkley 2004a), others argue that extensive teaching and learning research exists (cf. Bransford et al. 2000) but that it appears to have had little influence on the way face-to-face instruction is commonly conducted (Sutherland et al. 2004). That is, practice in the classroom has remained stable for over a century, despite Koschmann et al.'s (1996) criticism that face-to-face instructional approaches often produce individuals who fail to develop rich knowledge bases, have difficulty reasoning with and applying knowledge, oversimplify new conceptual understandings, and compound those oversimplifications with larger misconceptions. As Fetherston (2001) points out, the "transmissive" approach or what Schank and Menachem (1991) refer to as the "sponge method" still dominates higher education classrooms; and the transmissive approach errs in assuming that learner exposure to content equals learning:

Commonly, most internal courses at universities involve a lecture and tutorial format in which content is delivered in lectures and discussed at tutorials. The unspoken assumption behind this approach is that delivery of the content results in learning of the material. This transmissive approach assumes a strong link between the means of education, the lecture and the tutorial, and the ends, the learning. Most of the time, lecturers who have delivered the material assume that students have learned. This traditional approach is reliant on inputs, and the key input is exposure to content for a specified time.

For external students, materials delivered by the Web offer access to easily updated textual materials, some limited interactivity and access to audio and video that can be streamed in real time. This makes it technically possible for them to watch a lecture in real time without attending the university. But viewed in terms of pedagogy, this use of the Web for this purpose is a transmissive (and delivery) mode of learning. Indeed, the Web has been likened to nothing more than a 24 hour-a-day glorified whiteboard. . . . While for some external students this transmissive approach can be attractive because of its instrumental nature, from a pedagogical view it does not necessarily result in the best learning. (pp. 27–28)

Duffy and Kirkley (2004b) have also noted that the transmissional model of instruction, where instructors present information and learners, in turn, assimilate it, "is reflected in the widespread notion that 'moving a course to the Web' is a matter of designing the content for the Web. In many of these cases, there is not even a mention of the learners and what they will do" (p. 108). This perspective is extended even more problematically into arguments that technology in and of itself cannot improve instruction (Clark 1983, 1994; Hestenes, Wells, and Swackhamer 1992). Instructional success with technology, then, requires that technology use be based on sound instructional design principles (Katz and Rezaei 1999). Advocates of more traditional (i.e., nontechnological) approaches to instruction find this argument appealing for several reasons:

1. it preserves the privileged position of content providers and instructors by stressing that *their* expertise—not technology—is driving the instructional process;
2. it minimizes the dramatic influence of the artifacts that we use to accomplish actions and emphasizes the actions themselves (as though actions can exist apart from the technologies that enable and constrain them); and
3. it places technological integration (which involves considerable uncertainty) *after* instructors and instructional content.

As Froke (1995) summarizes, "Classroom instruction was placed on a pedestal from which it has not been displaced as the only instructional system in which the encounters of teacher with student and student with student could satisfy the pedagogy of all time. An intervening technology among teachers and students was only a last resort" (p. 62).

At best, computer display of traditional subject matters enhances the novelty of the experience for certain audiences and sometimes their recall of the materials (Webster and Ho 1997). But Duffy and Kirkley (2004b) warn against privileging the role of instructional *content* in the overall learning process. Resources for learning, they argue, are but one part of everyday instructional situations: "Knowledge is not contained in those resources, but rather the knowledge is in the goal-oriented use of those resources in a specific context and for a specific purpose. What is learned is a function of the learner's goals and is impacted by the constraints and affordances of the particular situation" (p. 109).

Finally, highlighting the increase in online instruction in higher education draws our attention away from other less obvious assumptions about online instruction, for example, that it is *inevitable* or *necessary*. These assumptions are deeply grounded in the same premises that support and promulgate the myth of technological progress. And although it is probably true that technology will always be with us, it is not necessarily true that technology will always improve human civilization. We can learn a great deal from the technologies that we design and build, but it is dangerous to assume that technologies will *teach* us. Technology advocates will argue most persuasively that technologies enhance human performance; but histories of technology suggest that technologies often transform us, and occasionally to our detriment.

Ravenscroft (2001), in this respect, takes pains to repeat that "electronic learning" began in the 1950s, and to stress that

We should be mindful of this and initiatives since then when we consider the current feverish interest and activity in exploiting maturing Internet technologies. . . . Are these initiatives properly exploiting the highly interactive, communicative and participative possibilities provided by contemporary technologies? Or are we simply replicating or augmenting "conventional" approaches to teaching and learning, locally or at a distance, in ways that downplay the opportunity to re-evaluate "what it actually takes to learn" and thus ignoring ways of developing more innovative and improved pedagogical practices. (p. 133)

So although it is certainly a reality that distance education is here to stay (Meyer 2002; Web-Based Education Committee 2000), calling for disciplinary status and respect in response to practitioner need is unlikely to produce a sustained, broadly conceived research base. More likely, distance education research will find an audience with other researchers interested in instruction and learning with technology if it is thought provoking, well designed, results in rigorous analyses and compelling conclusions, influences the design of practical artifacts, or is potentially useful either to practitioners or to researchers attempting to solve instructional problems in their own disciplines.

Revised Assumption 1: The intersection of technology, cognition, instruction, and learning is an essential object of inquiry for all education providers. Accelerated technological developments cross traditional disciplinary borders and demand that research be drawn from multiple disciplinary perspectives.

3.1.2 Assumption 2: Distance Education Is More Effective/Equal to Traditional Education

Diaz (2000) has noted that "A large portion of distance education research has been devoted to comparative studies of distance and traditional methods of education" and warns that "This type of question is premised on the implicit yet rarely mentioned assumption that 'traditional' education is the ideal mode of educational delivery and thus can serve as the 'gold standard' against which all other forms of 'alternative' education should be measured." Indeed, Bernard et al. (2004a), in their analysis of the methodological shortcomings of distance education versus "traditional classroom instruction" research, observe, "it was the limited descriptions of the classroom condition that [we] found most wanting" (p. 186). It seems premature to frame distance education around comparative studies, especially when in controlling for media and contextual differences we defeat the purpose of the comparisons from the outset (Brown and Wack 1999; Sener 2005).

Further, Phipps and Merisotis (1999) challenge the quality of the comparative research, concluding that "there is a relative paucity of true, original research dedicated to explaining or predicting phenomena related to distance learning" (p. 2) and that "the overall quality of the original research is questionable" (p. 3). Dillon and Gabbard (1998), in their review of the research on hypermedia versus pencil-and-paper learning outcomes, are highly critical of the research: "Taking the literature as a whole, it is disappointing to report that statistical analyses and research methods are frequently flawed. . . . Failure to control important variables for comparative purposes, lack of adequate pretesting of learners, use of multiple *t* tests for post hoc data, and even the tendency to claim support for hypotheses when the data fail to show statistically significant results all suggest that the basis for drawing conclusions from this literature is far from sturdy" (p. 345).

Sitzmann et al. (2005) in their meta-analysis of Web-based training versus classroom-based instruction, similarly note, "One limitation of meta-analysis is that highly rigorous and less rigorous research designs are included in the same analysis" (p. 199). Add to this criticism the challenge of identifying just what the parameters of the object of inquiry are in cases where conventional and online instruction are compared, and one has to acknowledge the highly interpretive stance required to conduct meta-analyses. For this reason, Meyer (2002) summarizes much current thinking about Russell's (1999) "no significant difference" findings as follows:

The perception is that most studies done on distance education or the use of technology are poorly designed and prone to incomplete analyses. That certainly is true of the simple comparison study, where student outcomes (such as course grades) for an online course are compared with a traditional course. It is the source of the "no significant differences" phenomenon, where possible intervening forces are ignored and the researcher and instructor are the same person, further muddying the results. (pp. iv–v)

Rather than focusing on developing tightly controlled studies, distance education researchers can benefit from strengthening their understanding of the interaction between how people learn (cf. Bransford et al. 2000) and the research on how best to design online instruction (Clark and Mayer 2003). Tallent-Runnels et al. (2006), as well, note, "While recent research literature defines online delivery systems, few studies actually focus on instruction and learning online" (p. 117). Thus, as recently as 2000, the American Federation of Teachers, as part of its guidelines for broad principles in distance education (http://www.aft.org/about/resolutions/2000/distanceed .htm), has argued that "Research on the effectiveness of distance education for particular subjects and different students should be accelerated."

Revised Assumption 2: The "no significant difference" phenomenon captures learner outcomes in terms of objective tests and instructor grades but needs to incorporate other significant factors in the learning process, for example, how learner backgrounds and knowledge influence learning processes and outcomes, how technologies enhance and impede learner tasks and activities, the instructional influence of technology on social dynamics, and the nature of the learning spaces that we inhabit and the artifacts that we create.

3.1.3 Assumption 3: Distance Education Is a Means of Education
This assumption removes the comparative impulse by negating the influence of distance education (equated with technology) altogether. Distance education, in this

scenario, is simply a means of educating and, thus, serves as a platform for instruction and learning. This assumption finds support in Clark's (1983) assertion that technologies are "mere vehicles that deliver instruction but do not influence student achievement any more than the truck that delivers our groceries causes changes in our nutrition" (p. 445). Fetherston (2001) separates technologies from instruction when he concludes, "Be it calculator, TV, cassette recorder, videodisc, or computer, its use needs to be tempered with reference to sound pedagogical principles" (p. 34). Nichols (2003), as well, echoes this position: "The choice of e-learning tools should reflect rather than determine the pedagogy of a course; *how* technology is used is more important than *which* technology is used" (p. 3). Indeed, Polin (2004) observes that "software tools are themselves neutral devices, and they derive their power from the cultural surround in which they are used" (p. 46). This perspective is particularly problematic, dichotomizing technology and technological context. Verbeek (2005) summarizes it succinctly:

Technology itself follows no particular direction, neither toward a completion nor toward destruction. Only human beings can give it direction; it is in itself neutral, and it requires guidance. It is in no position to give itself ends and is only the mean for realizing ends provided by human beings. Technology now appears as a task or challenge for human beings, calling for them to ask to which ends they want to apply it, and which not. (p. 39)

It follows that, if successful instruction and learning are produced with or without technological delivery, the study of instruction and learning should therefore be our first priority. Of course it might be argued that, just as the grocery truck does not cause changes in our nutrition, so too it is problematic to assume that we will always use groceries in ways that guarantee nutritional change. Transmissional delivery or the "shaping" of instruction, with or without technological mediation, might or might not result in learning.

Emphasizing the role of instruction and learning at the conceptual expense of technological issues is, ironically, a by-product of Russell's (1999) "no significant difference" report. That is, Russell's (1999) historical review of media comparison studies requires, as its main operating premise, agreement that *two separate constructs* or educational forms can be identified when we describe distance versus traditional instruction. Rather than beginning with the first natural question that arises whenever one examines a new thing, that is, what is the old thing and how does the it differ from or contain the same attributes as the new, the operating assumption becomes that there is a difference (or that there is no difference) and that this difference warrants attention before proceeding with a full discussion of the emergent state of things. In this view, distance education is a form that is *not* traditional instruction; moreover, the focus of the discussion is on the form of instruction rather than on the function in terms of our educational processes or instructional goals. Separating form from function is, of course, a classic fallacy in document design (Schriver 1997), interface design (Shneiderman 1987), and computer-based text studies (Unsworth 1997). As Gunawardena and McIsaac (2004) point out,

Technological advances have already begun to blur the distinction between traditional and distance education settings. Time and place qualifiers are no longer unique. The need to test assumptions and hypotheses about how and under what conditions individuals learn best, leads to research questions about learning, teaching, course design and the role of technology in the educational process. (p. 363)

Moreover, the role of technology in the educational process cannot be emphasized strongly enough. Russell's (1999) argument, that "The good news is that these no significant difference studies provide substantial evidence that technology does not denigrate instruction," reinforces the tool metaphor for technology rather than framing technology as transformative. Other researchers contribute to this misconception by adding that, since technology cannot improve instruction, it is critical that researchers focus primarily on instructional design and instruction rather than on technological issues (Clark 1983, 1994; Hestenes, Wells, and Swackhamer 1992; Katz and Rezaei 1999).

Of course, separating technology from instruction is impossible. As Selber (2004b) notes, "It is often claimed that computers have produced an enormous number of positive changes in higher education, changes that have vastly improved the social as well as instructional landscape that students and teachers inhabit. The trouble with such an unqualified claim is that it grants a level of autonomy to technology that simply does not exist" (p. 233). Technologies that reallocate classrooms across time and space necessitate a rearticulation of what we value as natural about our centralized, "traditional" classrooms. As Lanham (2002) correctly asserts, "The digital medium is not a neutral conduit any more than print was. . . . The rhetoric of digital expression is already in use across academic life, at least in embryo, and its implications are clear enough and profound" (pp. 175–176).

The question of *quality* also raises the issue of instructional efficiency and assessment, although too often higher-quality instruction translates to learners participating more, feeling satisfied with, or achieving more (i.e., getting a higher course grade) rather than on less tangible educational variables including instructors learning more, the ability to present content that has not been previously available or possible (e.g., abstract mathematical reasoning), or other variables that are not measurable using traditional instruments such as multiple-choice and short-answer tests (cf. Neuhauser 2002). Again, it is erroneous to assume that sound instructional design principles can exist apart from the context, content, instructor influence, class personality, or dimensions and disciplinary focus of the instructional space (Grabinger 2004). Technology is not something to be added on afterward, self-contained or at best containing instructional approaches; instead, it interacts with instructional approaches intensely. Indeed, some technology-instructional mixes produce unanticipated surprises or outcomes that could not have been discovered before attempting to integrate technology into the instructional situation in the first place (or the reverse, as with the practices of gaming, wikis, and iPods created for noninstructional purposes being incorporated into instructional environments).

Feenberg (1999) makes a more direct assertion, writing, "To reduce technology to a mere causal function is to miss the results of a generation of social science research" (p. 169). Technology, he argues, is as fundamental to human civilization as money and power—where the point of money is utility, of power, effectiveness, and of technology, productivity. Ultimately, he states, "Those in charge of technological choices (who are not necessarily technicians) interpose devices between the members of the community, unburdening them at both the communicative and the physical levels" (p. 169).

Thus, perspectives on the role of technology in education can be placed on a continuum from negative (Dumont 1996; Fabos and Young 1999; Noble 1998; Oppenheimer 1997) to neutral (Clark 1983, 1994; Russell 1999) to positive (Dibiase 2000; Kozma 1991; Singh, O'Donoghue, and Worton 2005), where positive arguments are made every time researchers publish descriptive case studies that suggest that pedagogy dominates technology in technology-based instructional settings or that negate or minimize design, practice, and evaluation challenges that occurred in context (cf. Mehlenbacher 1997).

Revised Assumption 3: Technological mediation of instruction is inevitable, whether we are describing traditional lecture-style presentations or virtual reality simulations. At both ends of the technology-instruction continuum, how the act of learning is transformed and how we assess whether learning has occurred are the essential issues.

3.1.4 Assumption 4: Distance Education Is a Discipline

If distance education practice is pervasive, augments traditional conceptions of education (rather than necessarily improving or detracting from them), and involves emerging technological methods of instructional mediation, surely distance education deserves the status of a discipline. A discipline can be defined as a branch or department of knowledge (either a science or an art) aimed at practice or exercise rather than at developing abstract theory traditionally associated with a doctrine. Garrison (2000) explicitly links the development of a discipline with knowledge- and theory-making:

Theory is a coherent and systematic ordering of ideas, concepts, and models with the purpose of constructing meaning to explain, interpret and shape practice. Theory can provide a perspective that reduces complexity while suggesting generalizability. The organized body of knowledge we call theory is an abstract and parsimonious constellation of articulated constructs for the express purpose of understanding and guiding practice. (p. 3)

Institutions of higher education, at the faculty level, contain two foundational units: organizational and conceptual. Organizational units, that is, colleges and departments, are the recipients of hiring resources, funding, instructional demands, and institutional support (Slaughter and Rhoades 2004). Conceptual units, best represented by programs, often frame the organizational unit's growth extrainstitutionally in addition to defining disciplinary developments within the organizational units. These units have sometimes compatible and occasionally competing goals, expectations, and demands. For example, Pfeffer (1993), in his review of paradigm development in the academy, that is, the degree of consensus within fields over theory and methodology, found that outcomes of development influenced resource allocations, funding, productivity, job satisfaction, turnover, salary, and tenurability (p. 602). Frost et al. (2004), thus, describe the numerous challenges inherent in any academic attempt to form interdisciplinary initiatives in the face of traditional departmental and disciplinary structures and constraints; and Jones (2005) is pessimistic about university-based and necessarily interdisciplinary efforts to find funding support for Internet studies (p. 236).

Abbott (2002), noting that the number of academic disciplines in the United States has remained incredibly stable during the twentieth century, concludes, "The American system of disciplines thus seems uniquely powerful. Because of their extraordinary ability to organize in one single structure research fields, individual careers, faculty hiring, and undergraduate education, disciplinary departments are the essential and irreplaceable building blocks of American universities" (p. 210). In addition to acting as scaffolding for the primary academic organizational unit, the department, disciplines also support intellectual and academic identity formation:

Disciplines legitimate our necessarily partial knowledge. They define what it is permissible not to know and thereby limit the body of books one must have read. They provide a specific tradition and lineage. They provide common sets of research practices that unify groups with diverse substantive interests. Often, these various limits and canons are quite arbitrary. What matters is not the particular canonical writer or method but rather the legitimation of knowing only the one or the other. (Abbott 2002, p. 210)

Petraglia (2003) is refreshingly direct about the power of disciplinary thinking in the academy:

To indulge in some purposely masculinist metaphor, disciplinarity is, at root, about virility, about demonstrating that one has the intellectual balls/bullocks/*cojones* to cut it in the sphere of academic endeavor. Furthermore, this is not a quiet demonstration; disciplines must often publicly wave their gonads at the rest of the academy and go *mano a mano* with administrators, departmental and college-level curriculum committees, and other disciplines with which there is a dispute over turf.

Thus the need to be accorded disciplinary status is not a nicety but a necessity in the modern academy; it is accompanied by perceptions of methodological rigor and theoretical integrity, and it is ultimately rewarded with material resources, tenure lines, and publishing opportunities. The reasons for this center on the regulating and commoditizing nature of disciplines and the global expansion of a knowledge economy that, far from stumbling, seems to be more ideologically unchallenged than ever before. We have yet to find any real "cure" for disciplinarity's obvious shortcomings. Though we may rail against the arbitrariness and restrictiveness of disciplinarity, we continue to play by its rules, for they are, both figuratively and literally, the rules of the academy. (p. 155)

We play by the rules of disciplinary status for good reason, given their inseparability from modern conceptions of theory building. As Collins (2002) explains:

What the creation of disciplines did was to give specific groups of scholars the power to recruit their own members according to their own criteria; thus the founding period of disciplines is also the founding period of systematic theories. Theories, or our conceptions of distinctive methods and ways of framing subject matters, are what give disciplines the rationale to reserve a set of salaried positions for persons who operate in a particular network of discourse. Disciplinary theories and methodologies operate as frameworks for credentialing colleagues and students. Theories are the cultural expression of scholars' guilds. (p. 33)

Thus, identifying a *discipline* of distance education is terribly difficult or, worse, a doomed exercise in principle. Kanuka and Conrad (2003), for example, describe distance education as part of the growing collection of "e-terms" that include distance learning, distributed learning, computer-based learning, Web-based learning, virtual classrooms, digital collaboration, hybrid learning, mixed mode delivery, and blended learning, and assume that the "basic tenets of learning" will be altered by their development (cf. Shale 2003). Kanuka and Conrad (2003) argue for the continued and consistent use of the term "distance education" to describe "a pedagogical phenomenon that is independent of the communication medium" and that finds its historical roots in teaching and learning via correspondence courses. The authors warn that "As educators, we must resist the seduction of catchy labels and the temptation to mark our intellectual territory by layering new jargon over the old. We must name the enterprise in ways that meaningfully, clearly, and responsibly reflect the function of each particular teaching and learning process and are thereby acceptable to both the academic community and those participants whose engagement in distance education reflects its state of growth and innovation" (p. 392). Jones (2004) unapologetically accepts the usefulness of the term "e-learning," noting that "'e-learning' is one of many terms currently used to describe the use of information technology to support teaching and learning. Rather than argue about the ambiguities and differences among the various terms, this paper will use 'e-learning'" (p. 54). After a review of the various definitions given to e-learning, though, Servage (2005) bluntly concludes that "'E-learning' is a confused and confusing field, fragmented into multiple disciplines and emphases" (p. 306).

Distinguishing between instruction and learning with technology and distance education, therefore, can be accomplished by drawing on Gunawardena and McIsaac's (2004) definition of distance education as "issues related to learning and pedagogy in technology mediated learning environments" (p. 364), where broader technology issues can be stated to include learning and pedagogy set in environments that allow nontechnologically mediated interaction (e.g., the face-to-face classroom).

Finally, although distance education has developed out of the practice of instruction, this does not undermine its potential as a discipline, for, as Petraglia (2003) points out, a discipline can be viewed both from a research and an instructional perspective:

Disciplinary frameworks are comprised of shared jargon, commonplaces, methods of inquiry, topics deemed worthy of investigation by those who claim to operate within the discipline, etc. But this collection of parts fails to capture the whole of the concept. A discipline (from the Latin *disciplina*) originally denoted not only a process of discovering and arranging knowledge, but the practice of reproducing that knowledge-making process in others. And so a more complete etymology of "discipline" would tie the word to both Greek and Latin conceptions of knowledge generation *and* to pedagogy. (p. 152)

Indeed, Garrison (2000) has described distance education as "a field of practice," and concludes, "Theory in distance education must evolve to reflect current and emerging practices of designing and delivering education at a distance" (pp. 13–14). But grounding distance education in practice is likely to contribute to its being subsumed organizationally and conceptually under preexisting departments and programs. This would locate it as a subdiscipline, field, specialty, or applied endeavor. Notably, however, activities as instrumental to our everyday lives as designing interactive systems have similarly been observed to cut across innumerable fields involving people (sociology, psychology, ergonomics, cultural studies, anthropology), technologies (electronic and software engineering, multimedia studies, systems design, computer programming, communications materials), activities and contexts (business, organizational psychology, knowledge management, information science), and design (human–computer interaction, architecture, information design, engineering design, graphic design) (Benyon, Turner, and Turner 2005, p. 22).

Revised Assumption 4: Identifying and harnessing opportunities for publication in both theoretical research journals and practitioner venues, establishing a strong research funding base, and leveraging existing relationships with information technology units across campus to enhance departmental and college structures closer to home will serve to strengthen the programmatic status of distance education.

3.1.5   Assumption 5: Distance Education Research Will Improve Practice

Assumption 5 is problematic in two ways. First, it presumes that distance education research is of consistently high quality in its execution. In his description of what constitutes "research worth publishing," Moore (2004) stresses effective data-collection and methodological rigor only after establishing careful attention to prior research and persuasive presentation of existing versus new knowledge (cf. Lockee, Moore, and Burton 2001):

> The main reasons for [article] non-acceptance . . . is that people gather data that answers a question that is *not grounded* in previous research and/or is so specific to a particular program that it is of little value beyond that program, which together contribute to a disconnection between the empirical part of the research and the theoretical. A good article includes not only good data, gathered by a technically sound method and well analyzed, but a rationale for the research that explains in a persuasive way why, in terms of knowledge as reported in the literature, there is meaning and significance in that data. In other words, to be publishable, the question about which you have gathered data has to be grounded in a good review of previous research and then have conclusions that show how it fills a hole in that previous state of knowledge. (Moore 2004, p. 127)

In addition, as Lawless and Brown (2003) point out, "the complexity and novelty of instruction via the Web has many researchers attempting a variety of procedures to figure out what needs to be studied and how these factors can best be observed and measured. As the knowledge of Web-based instruction advances, we will need to continue to explore new approaches to research and alter our understanding of instructional processes and learning outcomes" (p. 229). Emerging research sites and characteristics demand flexible and creative research approaches.

Second, the assumption takes as a given that research feeds into practice in a unidirectional manner. Instead, theory should always be informed by practice, and practice without theory, however rudimentary, is impossible. Indeed, replicability and "certainty" are only possible in laboratory settings (if at all); most human activities are instead a perplexing balance of competing interests, values, desires, trade-offs, and acts of supreme satisficing (Bazerman 1988; Cooper and Bowers 1995; Latour 1988; Latour and Woolgar 1979; Nelkin 1978). Learning, technological development, design, and theory testing are therefore the most ill structured of ill-structured problems, and they require an "experiential semantics"—to use Rheinfrank, Hartman, and Wasserman's (1992) expression—a language that emphasizes their qualities as objects, their meanings as objects in the world, and our experiences with them. Assuming a one-way transmission from theory to practice, or from practice to theory as some researchers have advocated (Koumi 2005), is naive. Schön (1983) blames our preference for theory over practice, or "technical rationality," for our lack of interest in how humans perform tasks, noting that "the concept of 'application' leads to a view of professional knowledge as a hierarchy in which 'general principles' occupy the highest level and 'concrete problem solving' the lowest" (p. 24).

Thus, Miller (1994a) observes that "the greater the respect we have for the making of knowledge than for the making of tools and techniques," the more "widespread [our] tendency to consider technology as just 'applied science,' the direct use of the universalized knowledge created by science to solve specific practical problems" (p. 92). It is this general assumption that leads Garrison (2000) and others (e.g., McIsaac and Blocher 1998) to relegate practice to something that occurs after theory or something that is informed by theory. As Garrison (2000) states, "The challenge is to provide theory that will explain and anticipate distance education practices for a broad range of emerging educational purposes and experiences," even while admitting in the same paragraph that "Conceptual confusion is created with the advent of new terminology (virtual, open, distributed and distance education), new technologies, new program demands, new audiences, and new commercially competitive providers" (p. 1).

Carmean and Haefner (2002), in their discussion of "deeper learning principles" (that learning is social, active, contextual, engaging, and student owned), stress the importance of designing learning environments around these goals. Although we can be certain that the technological settings that are built to exhibit or that augment these principles will influence learning outcomes, how much or how little is a research question that requires continual elaboration. Indeed, one might argue that the pervasiveness of technology will not only influence instruction and learning but also increasingly influence the fundamental nature of data collection and analysis via model exploration and simulation applications, data modeling, and advanced visualization instruments (Bruce and Levin 1997; Voithofer 2005).

Finally, Nichols (2003) describes the relationship between theory and practice as a reciprocal one, where "Theory provides a yard stick for evaluating practice, though it may be adjusted by findings from practice that show the theory to be inadequate" (p. 2). Constructing and arguing about the design of systems (theoretical ones and computational ones) can serve as the unifying activity of both researchers and practitioners (Fischer 2000; Mehlenbacher et al. 2005). Ravenscroft (2001) unifies theory and practice by advocating that educational technologists adopt "design as theory" and view "learning theory, technology and context in the design of educational interactions, in ways that treat designs, like theories, as something that are developed, validated, evaluated and refined rather than 'delivered.' These models are also prescriptive, so we can generate predications about the impact on learner knowledge and behavior, whilst still evaluating their effectiveness and identifying unanticipated uses and advantages, rather than just 'trying them out and seeing what happens'" (p. 150).

Revised Assumption 5: Beyond detailed and rigorous collection of data and thoughtful presentation of research results and implications, research gains its status in the context of use, whether by other rigorous researchers or by reflective practitioners. Balancing the goal of generating abstract principles for instruction and attending to those principles in context of use is critical to the development of a "science" of instruction and learning with technology.

3.2 Returning to the Parlor with Designs on the Conversation

Dillon (1994), describing the complexity involved in attempting to classify any information into types, has noted that "Classification of concepts, objects or events is the hallmark of developed knowledge or scientific practice and to a very real extent, typologies can be seen as a measure of agreement (and by extension, progress) in a discipline" (p. 72). Gunawardena and McIsaac (2004), too, stress that "Theories are necessary because they help us to understand, communicate and predict the nature of a discipline or a field of practice, its purpose, goals, and methods" (p. 359).

So how do we characterize that conversation now, once we have unpacked the complex of assumptions that influence our exchanges? Orrill, Hannafin, and Glazer (2004) describe the state of the conversation bluntly: "Literally thousands of studies related to computers and learning have been published during the past three decades. The problem has been one of making sense of the enormous, and growing, body of available research" (p. 335). Moreover, Berge and Mrozowski (2001) in their review of almost 900 research articles in distance education during the 1990s found that almost 75 percent of the research involved descriptive studies. Lee, Driscoll, and Nelson (2004) in their review of research from 1997 to 2002 found that approximately 30 percent of the articles involved case studies. And Roblyer and Knezek (2003) in their analysis of articles published in the 1999–2003 issues of the *Journal of Research on Technology in Education* found that 87 percent of the articles focused on "evaluations or descriptions of programs, implementation methods, or usage characteristics" (p. 69). So, too, Nichols (2003) laments that

the vast bulk of literature in eLearning is practice-based and is typically presented in a descriptive format. The majority of conference presentations consist of a "here's what we did and here's the evaluation" format which do little for transferability to other institutions or even other courses. In addition, the body of literature appears fragmented and there are few common terms used consistently. It is unlikely that eLearning practice will continue to evolve unless the theoretical underpinnings of eLearning are explored and debated, providing a wider platform and a common philosophy for eLearning development. (p. 8)

The literature on e-learning (i.e., distance education), and the research related to instruction and learning with technology in general, is indeed a vast bulk. Álvarez and Kilbourn (2002), in their creative review of literatures related to information society studies, argue that such efforts "should be viewed as an educational problem, one that has implications for how we construct curriculum and for how we teach about the

Information Society, particularly in the field of educational technology." The concern is that, for researchers motivated to engage in the conversation associated with instruction and learning with technology, it is critical that we be able to articulate the parameters of those literatures, to identify critical issues for further research, and to establish future directions for research energy and development.

Bull et al. (2005) explicate the issue directly:

Lack of consensus on research questions and methodologies. For the first twenty years, educational technology research focused on the question: "Is a technology-based method better than a non-technology-based one?" Eventually, this strategy was deemed ill-conceived and unproductive. Yet no more useful paradigm has emerged to take its place. Future research must focus on yet-to-be-articulated research questions. (pp. 218–219)

Wallace (2003) warns that "many of the articles that have appeared in recent years about online learning are anecdotal or promotional" (p. 244), as are the "rash of how-to books, describing techniques for developing and teaching online courses . . . found in bookstores" (p. 243). Mortimore (2000) stresses that researchers "demand evidence, rather than anecdote, for answers" (p. 22). Gunawarden and McIsaac (2004) concur, urging that researchers "Avoid microanalyses" and "descriptive studies" and "Identify and develop appropriate conceptual frameworks from related disciplines such as cognitive psychology, social learning theory, critical theory, communication theory and social science theories" (p. 389). In reading broadly from literatures related to instruction and learning with technology, distance education researchers can begin developing a database of issues underemphasized in any single discipline. For example, in their review of research on computer-mediated communication (CMC), Romiszowski and Mason (2004) outline the similarities and differences between oral or textual discourse forms and active versus passive participation in group development—uncommon in the distance education research—while also stressing synchronous and asynchronous communication and interactivity—familiar and important subjects in the distance education research.

Empirical research approaches to educational research are generally privileged here, not to ignore the politics of positivism but because the empirical genre traditionally provides persuasive grounding for arguments (cf. Fahnestock 2005) and demands careful and rigorous attention to the identification, definition, and explication of its objects of inquiry.[1] It is not enough to write that a particular instructional approach led to more effective instruction without thoughtfully defining the instructional approach in question or one's interpretation of "more effective." Ross and Morrison (2004), however, articulate the common challenge that researchers face in attempting to apply their findings to real-world problems:

Given their long tradition and prevalence in educational research, experiments are sometimes criticized as being overemphasized and conflicting with the improvement of instruction. However, experiments are not intrinsically problematic as a research approach but have sometimes been used in very strict, formal ways that have blinded educational researchers from looking past results to gain understanding about learning processes. To increase their utility to the field, experiments should be used in conjunction with other research approaches and with nontraditional, supplementary ways of collecting and analyzing results. (p. 1041)

Thus, numerous researchers have explored alternative methodological approaches modeled on design rather than notions borrowed from decontextualized science (Buchanan 1992, 1995, 2001; Manzini 1995; Simon 1969, 1981), such as cognitive design (Quinn and Wild 1998), design research (Barab and Squire 2004; Collins 1996; Collins, Joseph, and Bielaczye 2004), practice-based research (Levy 2003), design experiments (Brown 1992), sociocultural instructional design (Grabinger 2004), and learner-centered design (Norman and Spohrer 1996; Quintana et al. 2006). Design is by nature multidisciplinary and invites an inevitable tension between general advice and specific design problems: design is at its core both *constructive* and *argumentative*. Design is a *constructive* task in as much as it ultimately demands synthesis in an act of producing a technology; design is *argumentative* in that research designers must be able to justify design decisions, to assess critically the trade-offs in alternative designs, and, in general, to discuss design problems with others or persuade them to adopt particular solutions.

Buchanan (1992) stresses the importance of this perspective toward design, writing "The power of design as deliberation and argument lies in overcoming the limitations of mere verbal or symbolic argument—the separation of words and things, or theory and practice that remains a source of disruption and confusion in contemporary culture. Argument in design thinking moves toward the concrete interplay and interconnection of signs, things, actions, and thoughts" (p. 20). Hannafin and Kim (2003), as well, call for integrated approaches to educational design that explicitly connect theory to practice:

The primacy of each discipline seemingly obviates the need to account for the Web's affordances in a principled way; a myriad of tacit problems emerge related to design and use, not the research questions themselves. Since discipline-specific frameworks are inherently insulated, it has proven difficult to aggregate findings across fields and define questions and associated methods that are truly unique to individual disciplines. The questions are often unique to a discipline, but design and use of the Web are not. When it comes to Web design, our disciplines have far more linking than separating them; we have yet to leverage that shared interest. Web-based teaching and learning researchers need common design principles across disciplines that can be elaborated and refined within disciplines. (p. 350)

Being able to identify with a degree of confidence what conversations one is responsible for as one goes about framing research problems and questions, outlining appropriate methodologies for addressing those problems, and contributing new knowledge to the area in question (while carefully acknowledging the limitations of one's methodological stance) are inherent to any research endeavor that hopes to be replicated either through further investigations or through citations and collaborative problem solving.

And therein lies the uncomfortable dilemma. The greatest reason to devote one's energy to doing research related to distance education and to instruction and learning with technology is that an exponentially growing number of journals both focus on and publish materials related to the subject. Because of this, it is difficult—even among leaders in the "discipline"—to reach consensus on just what are the major journals in the "field." Inversely, the greatest reason to avoid doing research related to distance education is precisely because it is so difficult to identify clear parameters for the field and its research, and this leads to some of the greatest arguments against even considering distance education as *being* a field.

And for good reason, since a field grounded in any and all disciplines, particularly without clear objects of study motivating its research questions, is rhetorically problematic (Cooper and Bowers 1995; Latour 1988). Related to this, the history of robust theoretical developments in distance education reveals ample situations where theorists have drawn on the literature and methods of particular disciplines (for example, communication theory, cognitive psychology, or information and instructional design) and rigorously applied those approaches to the distance education area. Of course, it might be argued that the history of social science research is filled with examples where the origin of many a new, substantive area (for example, the philosophy of science, the rhetoric of science and technology, or the sociology of religion, to name some of dozens) is derived from more established disciplinary foci.

3.3   Future Conversations and Peer-Reviewed Research

The citation that headlined this chapter, from Whitburn's (2000) *Rhetorical Scope and Performance*, highlights the paradox of establishing one's scope or focus carefully versus limiting one's investigation to the purely pragmatic. In terms of distance education and instruction and learning with technology, pragmatic research often focuses primarily on what is instructionally or institutionally unique to a particular situation, efforts that stress the "feel good" dimensions of instruction and learning with technology, or issues that apply directly to decision or policymaking in particular contexts. In Cato's view, the purpose of a lifelong education might well be to find arguments for defending a lifelong education "before Minos in the underworld"; and Whitburn (2000) uses this perspective to anticipate the challenge presented by the contemporary desire to find high-speed solutions even while we simultaneously understand that complex solutions require significant study and time-consuming reflection.

Whitburn (2000) charges that problem solvers who highlight the importance of time-efficient and practical solutions may in fact "themselves be guilty of impracticality if they think that problems can be approached in bits and pieces that are tailor-made to human capabilities. Specialization is an anthropocentric lie that humans have been using for 24 centuries to delude themselves" (p. 238). The problem of identifying the scope of the research literatures related to distance education and instruction and learning with technology may well result in a similar realization—that the related literatures, fields, subfields, and specializations all require our acknowledgment and consideration.

Along with a detailed understanding of the numerous journals related to distance learning and e-learning, we may also want to become familiar with the myriad of journals devoted to educational, instructional, and communication technology, and to the emerging journals related to the teaching and learning sciences. Assuming the dramatic influence of multimedia elements on designs for instruction and learning, we will certainly draw on research on communication and information design. Anticipating the transformational interaction between technologies, tasks, and humans, we will need to be familiar with the research on human–computer interaction and ergonomics. Indeed, understanding that the landscape and demographics of audience for distance education go beyond higher education settings, we will want to be familiar with the literatures related to training, adult education, and the workplace. And, finally, we will hope to keep abreast of research developments related to distance education that are located in the humanities and social sciences, as well as in the science, technology, engineering, and mathematics disciplines.

So where does all this bring us? Full circle, with more venues for publication than we can ever hope to know well and an uncomfortable sense that something is missing every time we do a literature review on a research question that falls under the general area of instruction and learning with technology. In reading widely about instruction and learning with technology, we perhaps fall victim to our academic training, of pursuing what Cubitt (1998) describes as one of the "rituals of entry," and therefore are "condemned to pursue the object-world down endless shelves of signification in pursuit of the impossible object of desire, total knowledge, total control" (p. 11). This is not necessarily a novel situation. Writing of the historical "impact of the brute abundance of books," Hobart and Schiffman (1998) observe "printing gave individuals access to a previously unimaginable number of books, overloading them with diverse and contradictory information" (p. 89). Thankfully, partaking in the scholarly conversations on distance education and instruction and learning with technology gives us far more room for errors of omission than the metaphor of browsing a library, even though part of the ritual of entry is to learn over time that "complete coverage" of any subject matter is impossible.

Still, in an attempt to reveal a traditional desire for well-defined parameters and models of research on the subject, we can begin to outline eight broad clusters of research and to group English-language journals that address subjects that fall under those clusters. Following Bain et al. (1998), one begins by reviewing an enormous number of peer-reviewed articles from any discipline that publishes research on instruction and learning with technology. The first phase of the analysis involves the classification of peer-reviewed journals into particular research clusters based on "global impressions formed through the constant comparative method" (Bain et al. 1998, p. 167). Detailed notes are taken as part of this informal, iterative process.

Journal names were collected with the assistance of half a dozen published researchers who focused on instruction, learning, and technology studies; colleagues were continuously asked to review the working list of journals and provide input into their applicability or importance; and graduate students reviewed journal and article contents under particular clusters and compared them to journal and article contents under other clusters. Journals with less than one article per year on instruction, learning, and technology were eliminated. Still, because many of the journals listed here contain specific articles that arguably refuse to respect parameters, the eight research clusters related to instruction and learning with technology are but one possible way of organizing the research literatures. Elaborating on distinct differences and similarities between the research clusters and the conceptual field established by the journals contained within them will be an important next phase in the ongoing analysis.

Finally, because the landscape described by table 3.1 is an accelerated, evolving one, we can continue to challenge our most motivated and creative graduate students to find another method of organizing the research that reduces the cognitive dissonance we experience while participating in the conversation.

Although non-peer-reviewed journals and magazines (e.g., *Campus Technology*, *Contemporary Education*, *Education Week*, *Sloan-C View*) have been omitted to keep the list in the hundreds, research published in these forums is often of great value and occasionally points to trends that the peer-reviewed journals are slower to identify. To illustrate the thorniness inherent in any attempt to characterize multidisciplinary research according to only peer-reviewed journals and the higher-level goal of organizing those journals into meaningful research clusters, it is useful to look closely at one journal that falls under only one of the research clusters. The *Journal of the Learning Sciences* (JLS), under the research cluster entitled "Teaching and Learning Sciences," provides a "multidisciplinary forum for exploration of issues in learning and education and for fostering strategies of teaching to allow the impact of cognitive sciences on education practice." The journal incorporates research from psychology, psychiatry, education, and anthropology, and its abbreviated description is that it is a "forum for the presentation of research on training and learning."

Kolodner (1991), in the opening editorial of the first issue of JLS, describes how articles will "discuss learning in real-world situations; propose teaching strategies or educational environments based on what we know about learning; report on the

Table 3.1

Research clusters and 300 associated peer-reviewed journals related to instruction and learning with technology

Research Clusters	Peer-Reviewed Journals	
Distance Education and E-learning (29)	*American Journal of Distance Education**	*International Review of Research in Open and Distance Learning*
	Asian Journal of Distance Education	*Internet and Higher Education*
	Distance Education	*Journal of Asynchronous Learning Networks*
	E-Learning	*Journal of Distance Education*
	E-Learning and Education	*Journal of Educators Online*
	European Journal of Open, Distance, and E-Learning	*Journal of e-Learning and Knowledge Society*
	Indian Journal of Open Learning	*Journal of Interactive Learning Research*
	Innovate: Journal of Online Education	*Journal of Online Learning and Teaching*
	Interactive Learning Environments	*Online Journal of Distance Learning Administration*
	International Journal of Distance Education Technologies	*Open Learning: The Journal of Open and Distance Learning*
	International Journal of Learning Technology	*Quarterly Review of Distance Education*
	International Journal of Instructional Technology and Distance Learning	*Texas Journal of Distance Learning*
	International Journal of Web-based Learning and Teaching Technologies	*Turkish Online Journal of Distance Education*
	International Journal on E-Learning	*USDLA Journal*
	International Journal of Interactive Technology and Smart Education	
Educational, Instructional, and Communication Technology (45)	*AACE Journal*	*Interactive Multimedia Electronic Journal of Computer-Enhanced Learning*
	Australasian Journal of Educational Technology	*International Journal of Educational Technology*
	Association for Learning Technology Journal	*International Journal of Education and Development Using ICT*
	Behavior and Information Technology	*International Journal of Instructional Media*

Table 3.1
(continued)

Research Clusters	Peer-Reviewed Journals	
	British Journal of Educational Technology	*Journal of Computing in Higher Education*
	Canadian Journal of Learning and Technology	*Journal of Computing in Teacher Education*
	Computers and Education	*Journal of Educational Computing Research*
	Computers in Human Behavior	*Journal of Educational Multimedia and Hypermedia*
	Contemporary Issues in Technology and Teacher Education[a]	*Journal of Educational Technology and Society*
	Cyberpsychology and Behavior	*Journal of Information Technology Education*
	*Education and Information Technologies***	*Journal of Instruction Delivery Systems*
	Educational Media International	*Journal of Interactive Instruction Development*
	Educational Technology	*Journal of Interactive Media in Education*
	Educational Technology Research & Development	*Journal of Research on Technology in Education*
	Education Technology Review	*Journal of Technology and Teacher Education*
	Educational Technology and Society	*Journal of Technology Education*
	Educause Quarterly	*Journal of Technology, Learning, and Assessment*
	E-Journal of Instructional Science and Technology	*Learning and Leading with Technology*
	Electronic Journal for the Integration of Technology in Education	*Learning, Media, and Technology*
	First Monday	*Media, Culture, and Society*
	Interactive Educational Multimedia	*Techné: Research in Philosophy and Technology*
		Technology and Culture
		Technology, Pedagogy and Education
		The Information Society

Table 3.1
(continued)

Research Clusters	Peer-Reviewed Journals	
Teaching and Learning Sciences (42)	*American Educational Research Journal*	*European Journal of Education*
	Applied Cognitive Psychology	*Instructional Science*
	Assessment in Education: Principles, Policy, and Practice	*Innovations in Education and Teaching International*
	British Educational Research Journal	*International Education Journal*
	British Journal of Educational Psychology	*International Journal of Educational Research*
	Cambridge Journal of Education	*Journal of Applied Psychology*
	Canadian Journal of Experimental Psychology	*Journal of Educational Psychology*
	Cognition and Instruction	*Journal of Experimental Education*
	Cognitive Science	*Journal of Experimental Psychology: Learning, Memory, and Cognition*
	Cognitive Psychology	*Journal of Instructional Psychology*
	College Teaching	*Journal of the Learning Sciences**
	Contemporary Educational Psychology	*Learning and Instruction*
	Current Directions in Psychological Science	*Learning Environments Research*
	Current Issues in Education	*New Directions for Teaching and Learning*
	Educational Psychologist	*PsychNology Journal*
	Educational Psychology in Practice	*Psychological Science*
	Educational Psychology Review	*Review of Educational Research*
	Educational Research and Evaluation	*Studies in Learning, Evaluation, Innovation, and Development*
	Educational Researcher	*Technology, Instruction, Cognition, and Learning*
	Educational Studies	*Theory into Practice*
	Electronic Journal of Research in Educational Psychology	*Australian Educational Researcher*

Table 3.1
(continued)

Research Clusters	Peer-Reviewed Journals	
Communication and Information Design (36)	*Argumentation*	*Journal of Digital Information*
	Assessing Writing	*Journal of Library Services for Distance Education*
	Business Communication Quarterly	*Journal of Technical Writing and Communication*
	Canadian Journal of Communication	*Journal of the American Society of Information Science*
	College Composition and Communication	*Journal of the American Society of Information Science and Technology*
	College English	*Journal of Visual Literacy*
	Computers and Composition	*Kairos: A Journal for Teachers of Writing in Webbed Environments*
	Document Design	*Language, Learning, and Technology*
	Human Communication Research	*Management Communication Quarterly*
	IEEE Transactions on Professional Communication	*Quarterly Journal of Speech*
	Information Design Journal	*Rhetoric Society Quarterly*
	Information Research	*Technical Communication*
	Journal of Academic Librarianship	*Technical Communication Quarterly*
	Journal of Advanced Composition	*Technology in Society*
	Journal of Business Communication	*TEXT Technology*
	Journal of Business and Technical Communication	*Visual Communication*
	Journal of Communication	*Written Communication**
	Journal of Computer-Mediated Communication	
	Journal of Design Communication	
Human–Computer Interaction and Ergonomics (13)[b]	*ACM Transactions on Computer–Human Interaction*	*Interacting with Computers: The Interdisciplinary Journal of Human–Computer Interaction**
	ACM Transactions on Information Systems	*International Journal of Human–Computer Interaction*
	Applied Ergonomics	*International Journal of Human–Computer Studies*

Table 3.1

(continued)

Research Clusters	Peer-Reviewed Journals	
	Ergonomics	*Journal of Usability Studies*
	Ergonomics in Design	*Personal and Ubiquitous Computing*
	Human Factors	*Theoretical Issues in Ergonomics Science*
	Human–Computer Interaction	
Training, Adult Education, and the Workplace (59)[c]	*Academy of Management Journal*	*Journal of Behavioral Decision Making*
	Academy of Management Learning and Education	*Journal of Business and Psychology*
	Academy of Management Review	*Journal of Career Assessment*
	Administrative Science Quarterly	*Journal of Education and Work*
	Adult Education Quarterly*	*Journal of Education for Business*
	Adult Learning	*Journal of Employment Counseling*
	Advances in Developing Human Resources	*Journal of Experiential Education*
	California Management Review	*Journal of European Industrial Training*
	Cognition, Technology and Work	*Journal of Management Development*
	Computer Supported Cooperative Work	*Journal of Managerial Psychology*
	Convergence: The International Journal of Research into New Media Technologies	*Journal of Occupational and Organizational Psychology*
	Educational Gerontology	*Journal of Organizational Behavior*
	Education and Training[d]	*Journal of Organizational Behavior Management*
	European Journal of Work and Organizational Psychology	*Journal of Organizational Change Management*
	Gender, Work, and Organization	*Journal of Vocational Behavior*
	Human Performance	*Journal of Workplace Learning*
	Human Resource Development International	*Knowledge Management Research and Practice*
	Human Resource Development Quarterly	*Management Learning*
	Human Resource Development Review	*MIS Quarterly*

Table 3.1

(continued)

Research Clusters	Peer-Reviewed Journals	
	Human Resource Management	*New Directions for Adult and Continuing Education*
	Human Resource Management Review	*Organization*
	Human Systems Management	*Organizational Behavior and Human Decision Processes*
	International Journal of Human Resource Management	*Organizational Dynamics*
	International Journal of Lifelong Education	*Organization Science*
	International Journal of Productivity and Performance Management	*PAACE Journal of Lifelong Learning*
	International Journal of Training and Development	*Peabody Journal of Education*
	International Review of Industrial and Organizational Psychology	*Performance Improvement Quarterly*
		SAM Advanced Management Journal
		Studies in Continuing Education
		Studies in the Education of Adults
		The Learning Organization
		Work and Occupations
Education in the Humanities and Social Sciences (55)	*American Journal of Education*	*Journal of Education for Business*
	Annual Review of Psychology	*Journal of Environmental Education*
	Anthropology and Education Quarterly	*Journal of Experimental Psychology: Applied*
	Assessment and Evaluation in Higher Education	*Journal of Experimental Psychology: Human Perception and Performance*
	Assessment Update	*Journal of Experimental Social Psychology*
	Basic and Applied Social Psychology	*Journal of Further and Higher Education*
	Change	*Journal of General Psychology*
	College Quarterly	*Journal of Higher Education*
	Communication Education	*Journal of Higher Education Policy and Management*

Table 3.1
(continued)

Research Clusters	Peer-Reviewed Journals	
	Communication Quarterly	Journal of Management Education
	Decision Support Systems	Journal of Management Information Systems
	Electronic Network Applications and Policy	Journal of Nursing Education
	Equity and Excellence in Education	Journal of Nutrition Education and Behavior
	Higher Education Quarterly	Journal of Statistics Education
	Higher Education Research and Development	Journal of University Teaching and Learning Practice
	Information and Management	Language Teaching Research
	Innovative Higher Education	Linguistics and Education
	International Journal of Inclusive Education	Oxford Review of Education
	International Journal of Teaching and Learning in Higher Education	Quarterly Journal of Experimental Psychology
	International Journal of Testing	Research in Higher Education
	Issues in Accounting Education	Review of Higher Education*
	Journal of Agricultural Education	Roeper Review
	Journal of Allied Health	Social Science Computer Review
	Journal of Applied Business Research	Sociology of Education
	Journal of College Science Teaching	Studies in Higher Education
	Journal of Criminal Justice Education	Teachers College Record
	Journal of Dental Education	Teaching in Higher Education
		Teaching of Psychology
Education in Science, Technology, Engineering, and Mathematics (21)	American Biology Teacher	International Journal of Mathematical Education in Science and Technology
	Bioscience Education E-Journal	International Journal of Science Education
	BMC Medical Education	Issues in Science and Technology
	Computer Science Education	Journal of College Science Teaching
	Educational Studies in Mathematics	Journal of Computers in Mathematics and Science Teaching

Table 3.1

(continued)

Research Clusters	Peer-Reviewed Journals	
	European Journal of Engineering Education	*Journal of Computing Sciences in Colleges*
	IEEE Transactions on Education	*Journal of Natural Resources and Life Sciences Education**
	International Journal of Computers in Mathematical Learning	*Journal of Science Education and Technology*
	International Journal of Electrical Engineering Education	*Medical Education*
	International Journal of Engineering Education	*Medical Teacher*
		Technology Teacher

*See tables A through H in the appendix for a detailed analysis of journals followed by an asterisk (*). Articles published during the last five or more years of each journal are identified and informally classified according to the five dimensions of everyday instructional situations, described in chapter 6. Currently one journal from each research cluster (e.g., *Distance Education and E-learning, Education, Instruction, and Communication Technology,* and so on) is summarized: the journals include the *American Journal of Distance Education, Education and Information Technologies, Journal of the Learning Sciences, Written Communication, Interacting with Computers, Adult Education Quarterly, Review of Higher Education,* and the *Journal of Natural Resources and Life Sciences Education.* Although an exhaustive review of the contents of each journal presented here is not feasible, this type of long-term project would provide an invaluable resource for researchers and students studying instruction and learning with technology.

[a]Only teacher-education journals related specifically to technology are included, because the majority of teacher-education journals (e.g., *Asia-Pacific Journal of Teacher Education, European Journal of Teacher Education, Journal of Teacher Education, Teachers and Teaching: Theory and Practice,* and *Teaching and Teacher Education*) emphasize K–12 settings, which are outside the scope of this book (e.g., the *Journal of Computers in Mathematics and Science Teaching*). Journals related to counseling that could be placed under Training, Adult Education, and the Workplace or Education in the Humanities and Social Sciences (e.g., *Counseling and Human Development, Journal of Humanistic Counseling, Education and Development,* and *Journal of Counseling and Development*) are not included for the same reason.

[b]The emphasis on practice in human–computer interaction and ergonomics is evidenced by the number of excellent (peer-reviewed) magazines not included in this list of journals, including, for example, *ACM SIGCHI Bulletin* (1982–2000), *Communications of the ACM* (1958–present), *eLearn* (2001–present), *Interactions* (1994–present), and *Ubiquity* (2000–present). The Association for Computing Machinery (ACM) Digital Library (http://portal.acm.org/dl.cfm) separates publications under journals, magazines, transactions, proceedings, and newsletters, even though peer-reviewed research articles can be found in each of these venues. Similar to journals on distance

Table 3.1

(continued)

education, ACM journal and magazine publications have seen significant growth since 1990, from 1 journal in 1954, to 3 in 1974, to 16 in 1994, to 38 in 2006 (Boisvert 2006).

[c]After receiving feedback from numerous researchers who align themselves with training, adult education, and studies emphasizing workplace settings, and collecting their lists of recommended journals related to these areas, I reviewed each journal's contents for the last five or more years. Some of the journals, highly recommended by these researchers, contained very few articles related to instruction and learning with technology, including, for example, the *Academy of Management Review*, *Employee Assistance Quarterly*, *Journal of Economic and Social Measurement*, *Personnel Psychology*, and the *Journal of Workplace Behavioral Health*.

[d]Interestingly—beyond the trade magazines *Industrial and Commercial Training*, *T+D*, and *Training*—the only peer-reviewed journals devoted to training in the workplace that actually use the word "training" in their titles are *Education and Training*, the *International Journal of Training and Development*, and the *Journal of European Industrial Training*. The academic discomfort with issues in training (viewed as vocational and industrial) versus education (conceptualized as progressive and democratizing) can currently be seen in the tension between traditional adult and higher education programs and human resource development programs housed in U.S. universities. The dichotomy is a historical one and rests on the erroneous assumption that training focuses only on skills and education focuses only on conceptual knowledge, as though information types can be decontextualized and labeled for consumption outside of learner contexts, instructional needs and goals, and tasks being performed. The dichotomy is also ironic given recent calls for improved workplace preparation in higher educational settings (Felder 2006).

application of these teaching strategies and environments; address related issues; report on experimental work; be theoretical; report on methodologies; be about learning per se; and cover knowledge representation issues, reasoning issues, and social issues that impact learning or are affected by learning" (p. 3). Although all the articles published in JLS address issues related to instruction and learning, articles that relate to technology or that focus on the learning behaviors of adult learners (loosely defined as university-level or beyond) versus K–12 students are highlighted. See table C in the appendix for an analysis of JLS issues from 1999 to 2007.

Broadening our investigation of the scholarly conversations that are germane to the study of instruction and learning with technology, we are able to articulate the tentative beginnings of a tabular map of our multidisciplinary object(s) of inquiry. This tabular map is only possible if we adjust our view of distance education and instruction and learning with technology from a research interest in the service of other, better-established disciplinary histories. Indeed, one might argue that instruction and learning with technology is at the heart of any disciplinary effort.

To accomplish this effort, we have to acknowledge that the study of technology, cognition, instruction, and learning is multidisciplinary and complex, and that how we assess whether learning has occurred—beyond end-of-course outcomes—is the essential challenge. Our multidisciplinary research interest demands multidisciplinary principles for practice and the development of strong theoretical and pragmatic collaborations. And in organizing the vast research literatures related to instruction and learning with technology around eight broad research clusters, we can begin to build a common reference "library" for designing a science of instruction and learning with technology.

Mining the research literatures from numerous disciplines produces a surprising by-product: the realization that various conversations about the nature and composition of instruction and learning with technology are playing out just out of earshot of one another. Transplanting discussions taking place outside their mainstream disciplines, researchers have been developing research-based theories of instruction and learning for well over thirty years, and few researchers have made the effort to compare and contrast these theories. We lack both a shared understanding of our primary objects of inquiry—that is, learning, technology, and instruction—and a language for comparing and contrasting visual representations of theoretical arguments. In the next chapter, after attempting to define our core objects of inquiry, I set about reviewing numerous theories of instruction and learning presented in peer-reviewed journals across disciplines in the form of visual arguments.

4   Models of Instruction and Learning with Technology

Following operational definitions of learning, technology, and instruction, I provide in this chapter an overview and analysis of a dozen models of instruction and learning with technology derived from the peer-reviewed research. Although some distance education researchers claim that there is a paucity of theory on instruction and learning with technology, a multidisciplinary perspective toward research related to the area reveals the opposite.

Researchers and theorists of learning are extremely weak when it comes to pointing out what needs to be learned.
—Yrjo Engeström (2000, p. 527)

The best material model for a cat is another, or preferably the same cat.
—Arturo Rosenblueth and Norbert Wiener (1945, p. 320)

How do researchers and practitioners interested in instruction and learning with technology proceed given the explosion in relevant peer-reviewed journal articles? More importantly, how do we construct operational models of instructional situations that can serve to guide our investigations of the influence of emerging technologies on the teaching and learning process?

Part of the problem created by exponentially growing research literatures related to instruction and learning with technology is the result of our pragmatic desire to define our research gaps and contributions modestly. Contrary to recommending that educational researchers live expedient publishing lives, Murphy and Woods (1996) anticipate a future where "knowledge researchers diligently trac[e] the sources of their ideas and vigorously outlin[e] how their particular study adds to the current body of knowledge research. The more the recorded histories and chartings of a territory such as knowledge are examined, the more likely future explorers are to recognize landmarks that have guided those before them and avoid pitfalls that have waylaid others" (p. 144). This optimism is difficult to maintain given increasing pressures on junior and senior researchers to live productive publishing lives (i.e., to generate higher numbers of articles, books, conference papers) versus prodigious publishing lives (i.e., to engage in limited but intense research efforts that produce a limited number of publications requiring years of research, collaboration, and writing to produce) (cf. MLA 2007).

Carr-Chellman (2006), in her study of 17 educational technology faculty who received tenure between 1999 and 2004, found that they published an average of 15 articles each for a total of 252 separate articles distributed across 120 distinct journals (p. 9). Hickson, Bodon, and Turner (2004), in their study of research productivity in communication, found that the number of articles required to establish researchers in "the top 100 most prolific researchers" grew from 15 to 23 articles between 1990 and 2001. This is a significant increase over little more than a decade and confirms the hypothesis that, at least in fields such as communication, the publication of a greater number of articles is a trend. In terms of the natural sciences, Bruss, Albers, and McNamera's (2004) analysis of 127 textual excerpts from the *Philosophical Transactions of the Royal Society of London* between 1800 and 1997 reveals that word concreteness and imagability (i.e., ease of visualizing), acquisition speed, cohesiveness, and positive connectives have all decreased over time, suggesting that articles have increased in complexity as well as number over the last one hundred years. This increase in quantity and complexity comes at a price, least of which, as Bowker and Star (1999) point out, is the disappearance of everyday categories that maintain the infrastructure of our lives:

In the past 100 years, people in all lines of work have jointly constructed an incredible, interlocking set of categories, standards, and means for interoperating infrastructural technologies. We hardly know what we have built. No one is in control of infrastructure; no one has the power centrally to change it. To the extent that we live in, on, and around this new infrastructure, it helps form the shape of our moral, scientific, and aesthetic choices. Infrastructure is now the great inner space. (p. 319)

Educational journals with a technology focus have seen dramatic growth as well. Research journals related to distance education and e-learning have enjoyed unprecedented development over the last two decades, from 4 peer-reviewed journals prior to 1992, to 10 by 1998, to 29 by 2005. The number of journals related to educational, instructional, and communication technology, too, have increased exponentially. Five journals devoted to the area existed before 1985 (*Computers and Education*, the *International Journal of Instructional Media*, the *Journal of Research on Technology in Education* [originally named the *Journal of Research on Computing in Education*], *Learning and Leading with Technology*, and *Media, Culture, and Society*), 16 existed by 1995, and, between 1996 and the present, those 16 grew to 45 peer-reviewed journals (see table 3.1 for a listing of the journals under these broadly-conceived research categories).

Indeed, Morello (1995), writing of "innovation for innovation's sake" in the design world, could be describing the rapid development and distribution of academic research articles related to instruction and learning with technology:

The result is the modest specific average quality of any item. . . . This "inflation of simultaneous proposals" can certainly be considered as a beneficial peculiarity of the market philosophy, but it is also a malefic peculiarity of the overdominant importance of a badly organized distribution system. (pp. 161–162)

Perhaps the (academic) business of knowledge making, regulation, and distribution ought not be described using consumer-market terminology, although academic research articles can certainly productively be viewed as products or processes with multiple purposes (intended and not), audiences (researchers, practitioners, students), shareholders (publishers, administrators, media representatives), and venues (conferences, proposals, academic–industry collaborations). And one natural by-product of this expanding market is bound inevitably to be more systematic means of synthesizing and "managing" the flow of information. Thus, Morello's (1995) recommendation for theorists (in this case, academic researchers) is to instruct

1. society itself, of the principles of a useful, clear, and severe judgment about products and related matters, starting in the primary schools (a sort of civil service);
2. enterprises, designers, and marketers, of the nature, quality, and quantity of their responsibilities and the ground of their collaboration; and
3. themselves, of the importance and the impact of intellectual integrity and probity (p. 75).

An additional part of the atomization of academic disciplines and publishing problem results from the nonstable nature of technology development itself. Pascarella and Terenzini (1998) have identified the uneasy relationship between fast-moving objects of study and the methodologies that we use to understand them:

Methodological challenges arise from the sheer number and diversity of information technology–based instructional approaches. The number of such instructional media is further complicated by the fact that multiple forms are often used in the same course. The possible combinations and permutations are staggering. Add to this picture the fact that the technologies themselves are changing as current ones are enhanced or become obsolete and new ones, unthought of three years (or months) ago, emerge. The range and volatility of instructional information technologies not only present serious research design problems, they may also produce a fragmentation that will put knowledge development itself at risk of bogging down in a flood of studies based on single course, single learning settings (let alone single institutions) which have few characteristics in common whether in their independent or dependent variables. (pp. 161–162)

Orel (1995) summarizes that "we realize more and more that the *means* (the technology) and the *result* (the expected normality) are not two different entities. The power to own the means also has an effect on the expected result" (p. 81). Bowker and Star (1999) state more bluntly, "we have—along with many researchers in the field of social informatics—demonstrated empirically that invisible organizational structures influence the design and use of systems: the question is not whether or not this occurs but rather how to recognize, learn from, and plan for the ineluctable presence of such features in working infrastructures" (p. 323). Academic researchers with institutional libraries that provide them with access to thousands of databases containing peer-reviewed journals and associated research articles related to instruction and learning with technology are bound to have a decided advantage over practitioners working in isolation on similar and complex problems. Indeed, as practitioners gain access to the resources available to them via the Internet and self-regulating blog and wiki communities, mainstream media, research, and academic sources will certainly be faced with growing challenges to their traditional authoritarian status, including interface and access issues, rapid change and heightened learning curves, information overload, and the "technostress" that accompanies these developments (Johnson and Magusin 2005; Wilder and Ferris 2006).

Therefore, it becomes increasingly important, given the ill-structuredness of the research on instruction and learning with technology, that researchers strive for what Bazerman (1988) calls "rhetorical self-consciousness" when we are interpreting, contributing, critiquing, amending, and elaborating on existing research. Bazerman (1988, pp. 323–329) suggests that researchers and research consumer-users can begin to achieve rhetorical self-consciousness by applying the following heuristics:

1. consider your fundamental assumptions, goals, and projects;
2. consider the structure of the literature, the structure of the community, and your place in both;
3. consider your immediate rhetorical situation and rhetorical task;
4. consider your investigative and symbolic tools;
5. consider the processes of knowledge production; and
6. accept the dialectics of emergent knowledge.

Bazerman's (1988) call to researchers parallels Selber's (2004b) recommendation that "rhetorically literate" learners be versed in persuasion (interpreting and applying both implicit and explicit arguments), deliberation (acknowledging that ill-defined problems demand thoughtful representation and time), reflection (demanding both articulation and critical assessment), and social action (defining all technical action as social action) (p. 147).

In this rhetorical-educational spirit, I have reviewed some of the more formidable assumptions driving our interpretations of the revolution in instruction and learning with technology, in addition to introducing some of the learning worlds that are driving us to examine online instruction and learning inside and outside of the academy, across disciplines, and in various instructional contexts. An overview of the literatures related to instruction and learning with technology provides us with an overwhelming number of established and developing conversations that we should be reviewing as we identify and contribute to the larger questions driving our parallel investigations.

At the heart of the matter are sets of fundamental questions that are almost too embarrassing to admit. For example, what do we mean when we talk about *learning*? What do we know about effective *instruction*? What is it that we are referring to when we speak of *technology*? As we begin to answer these (surprisingly) complex questions, we in turn produce a host of related questions that require considerable research: How do prior knowledge and learner background influence learning? What do we mean when we promise that tailoring instruction to particular learner types *improves* learning? Are some technologies superior to others for some instructional approaches? Beyond textual instruction, how to we design amalgamates of media types such as audio, video, graphic, and animated elements that support learning?

This chapter provides some preliminary definitions of learning, technology, and instruction, as well as reviewing several models of instruction and learning with technology that have been constructed by researchers during the last thirty years.

4.1 On Learning

Learning has been systematically studied by cognitive psychologists for several decades (Anderson 1995; Bransford et al. 2000; Clark 2005; Mayer 2001; Perkins 1993; Simon 1979). A cognitive information-processing model of learning involves the following critical information–human interactions:

• *Information and comprehension* (attention, selection, working memory, cognitive workload)
• *Representation and integration with existing and available knowledge* structures (encoding, strategies for potential storage in long-term memory, information mapping, schemas, and interaction with external resources)
• *Retrieval and development of new connections* between the new information and the existing state of understanding (reviewing, associative reasoning, mental models, conceptual organization, and interaction with external resources)
• *Construction and elaboration toward a richer understanding* of the subject matter, leading to expert understanding and/or behaviors (practice, reorganization of material for problem setting, plan and goal development, propagation, and situational exigencies).[1]

Hede and Hede (2002), addressing learning that involves simultaneous interaction with multimodal media elements, stress learner attention as critical to the learning process. Learners' problem-solving approaches, combined with motivation, cognitive engagement, intelligence, and reflection, influence how learners attend to and control visual input (textual, graphical, video, and animated) and auditory input (narration, instructions, cues, and music). Learner attention and time spent on the learning task are fundamental to the learning process. As the amount of input increases, learners must compensate by increasing the amount of cognitive information processing (i.e., working memory) applied to the learning situation (see figure 4.1).

The initial goal, then, is to find ways to facilitate multilevel learning, that is, learning that involves a combination of factual and conceptual knowledge, the ability to apply that knowledge, and feedback on learner progress. Connecting this goal to understandable learning tasks and activities, designing learning environments that encourage discussion and on-task behaviors, and, in doing so, drawing on technologies and artifacts that support these efforts follows naturally from the initial goal. As the number of tasks, the need for navigation, and the types of interactivity unrelated to the primary learning objectives and goals increase, the amount of on-task learning necessarily decreases. Ultimately, shifting learning to doing, learners are able to focus less on strategies for searching and more on identifying information patterns, production detection and automatic action, and the nuances of their context: these abilities distinguish the experienced from the inexperienced (Bransford et al. 2000).

Carmean and Haefner's (2002) "deeper learning principles" provide an instructional turn to Hede and Hede's (2002) model of multilevel learning. Deeper learning and the instructional principles that support it, Carmean and Haefner (2002) argue, are *social*, *active*, *contextual*, *engaging*, and *student owned*. Learning is social when it involves apprenticeship, cooperation, prompt rich feedback, and contact time between learners and learners and between instructors and learners (Chickering and Ehrmann 1998). Active and engaging learning incorporates situated, real-world problems and is designed around practice and reinforcement (Brown 1992; Marchese 1998, 2002). Contextualized learning, similarly, reinforces prior knowledge, applies to learners, requires considerable knowledge construction, and is concrete rather than abstract (Merrill 2002). Finally, Carmean and Haefner (2002) note that learner- or student-owned learning demands that learners creatively organize new knowledge, take control of their planning and learning tasks, and are allowed time for synthesis and reflection (see also Bransford et al. 2000).

Other concepts integral to an information-processing model of learning include the limited capacity assumption (Chandler and Sweller 1991), dual coding or channeling (Mayer 2005), cognitive workload (Mayer and Moreno 2003; Sweller 2005), mental representation and modeling (Johnson-Laird 1983), and cognitive flexibility (Spiro et al. 1992), and these processes all focus on the learner's ability to manage incoming information in real time. Clark and Mayer (2003) provide an excellent summary of how these cognitive principles can inform instruction.

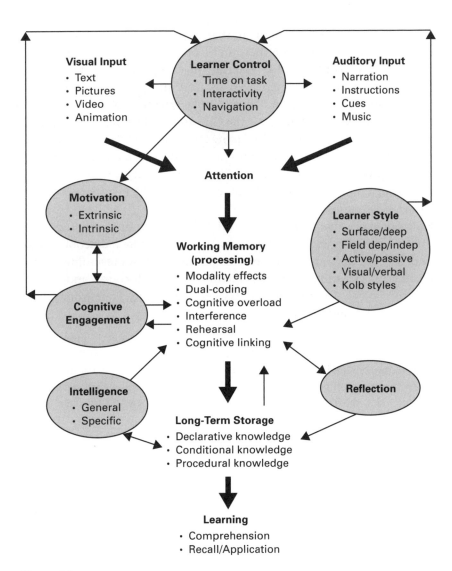

Figure 4.1
Integrated model of multimedia effects on learning (adapted from Hede and Hede 2002).

Berninger and Richards (2002) remind us that a learner's "functional systems involve many different components that have to be orchestrated and thus the complexity of the learning process" (p. 317). Even at the comprehension stage of the learning process, humans are actively engaged in acquiring incoming information (auditory, haptic, visual, or textual) and in selecting, interpreting, and sorting in microseconds the resulting information for possible storage in long-term memory. Dietz (2005) describes human activities as involving individual abilities (e.g., selecting, interpreting), coordination activities (communicating with others), and production activities (acting with others), and this simple division of learning foci enables us to begin conceptualizing a more integrated picture of learning that incorporates cognitive and social views of learning.

Engeström (2000) agrees that a broader definition of learning incorporating social dynamics, situated cognition, and human activity theory is required, describing individual models of learning as promulgating an "enlightenment view of learning." What is missing in such views of learning is an emphasis on dialectics, discourse, and instructor-learner transformation. An enlightenment view of learning, Engeström (2000) argues, maintains problematically that

Learning is a fairly simple matter of acquiring, accepting, and putting together deeper, more valid facts about the world. Of course, this tacitly presupposes that there are teachers around who already know the facts and the needed course of development. Inner contradictions, self-movement, and agency from below are all but excluded. It is a paternalistic conception of learning that assumes a fixed, Olympian point of view high above, where truth is plain to see. (p. 530)

The picture of learning that Engeström (2000) is taking issue with here is a natural outcome of the transmissional model of instruction, a model that represents learning as an entity or object rather than as an event or process. Engeström's (2000) description of learning naturally accounts for instructional activities, learner motivation and engagement, social interaction, and complex learning environments. Likewise, existing views of learning informed by deterministic notions of technology present information as stand-alone and modular rather than as a developed and developing part of the learning process. Attending to the interaction between learning and technology thus enriches our understanding of our basic learning processes. As Krendl and Warren (2004) note, "The focus on individuals' attitudes toward, and perceptions of, various media has begun to introduce a multidimensional understanding of learning in relation to media experiences. Multiple factors influence the learning process—mode of delivery, content, context of reception, as well as individual characteristics such as perceived self-efficacy and cognitive abilities" (p. 69).

Unfortunately, many discussions of learning emphasize the polar ends of the landscape between purely cognitive and social, the one position stressing information-processing models, and the other, constructivist ones. Indeed, one cannot talk about or read research on learning that does not draw contrasts between cognitive or information-processing views of learning and social or constructivist ones. The historical tension between cognitive and social perspectives on learning have never been greater than during the last several decades. Cognitivists argue that social constructivists have tended to oversituate learning and, in doing so, have become advocates of theories of learning that are nonpragmatic and difficult to evaluate. Social constructivists maintain that knowledge cannot be removed or decontextualized from application or context and that cognitivists are behaviorists who liken cognition to limited computer-processing models.

Certainly cognitivists owe a great deal to historical behaviorist traditions (see, e.g., Anderson 1995; Anderson et al. 2004). And certainly behaviorism serves as the great and convenient straw man of the modern psychological tradition, to hear social constructivists frame historical developments in the field. But the relationship between these research traditions is not that straightforward, and these exaggerations further heighten the tensions between the two groups.

Thus cognitivists have accused social constructivists of wresting knowledge away from the individual learner entirely, leaving them with only specific learning circumstances and nongeneralizable contexts for learning. Barab and Plucker (2002), indeed, have squarely set cognitivism under "traditional" learning theories and maintain that "Educators . . . have fallen victim to a circular logic: Traditional, entity-based theories, placed knowledge in the head of the learner, which led to the creation of educational systems that focused on transmitting content into individual minds" (p. 165). Lave (1996), too, asserts that "Common theories of learning begin and end with individuals (though these days they often nod at 'the social' or 'the environment' in between)" (p. 149). Contrary to this assertion, however, Simon (1969, 1981) does more than nod to context when he writes, "The proper study of mankind has been said to be man. But I have argued that man—at least the intellective component of man—may be relatively simple, [but] that most of the complexity of his behavior may be drawn from man's environment" (p. 159).

Most behaviorists and cognitivists would generally agree that effective learning occurs when the instructional content, medium, setting, and desired learning outcome are similar in composition. Additionally, similar to behaviorists, cognitivists continue to stress the importance of thoughtful sequencing of conceptual and procedural content in well-designed steps (Burton, Moore, and Magliaro 2004, p. 13). Social theorists, influenced by Vygotsky (1978), stress that all learning involves a complex interaction between individuals, artifacts, and societal elements in a purposeful and communal process. Notably, a Vygotskian perspective (1978) also values the relationship between novices and experts, a research focus shared by many cognitivists (Chi, Feltovich, and Glaser 1981; Simon 1979).

Both perspectives on learning, as well, share the belief that the transmission of knowledge is a two-way process and that instructors need to acknowledge and respond to the constructed nature of all learning. As Benbunan-Fich, Hiltz, and Harasim (2005) remind us, "knowledge has to be discovered, constructed, practiced, and validated by each learner" (p. 21); and, in order to accomplish this, each learner must interact with a community of learners, in effect, to test through trial and error various developing versions of the "knowledge within the head of the learner." Importantly, Benbunan-Fich et al. (2005) stress that constructivist theories of learning should not be confused with the "Pedagogical methods [that use] this approach, including collaborative learning, creat[ing] learning situations that enable learners to engage in active exploration and/or social collaboration, such as laboratories, field studies, simulations, and case studies with group discussion" (p. 21). These instructional activities emphasize having learners actively *do* something as part of their learning experience; and, although research supports the benefit of learning-by-doing (Bransford et al. 2000), the *doing* and the knowledge to be acquired must be closely aligned.

In addition, cognitivists and social constructivists are sometimes misrepresented as focusing only on individual learning versus environmental, social, or group learning. Instead, as Anderson et al. (2000) stress, "The cognitive approach should not be read as denying the value of learning in group activity, and the situative approach should not be read as denying the value of learning by individuals working by themselves. The difference between the perspectives involves different ways of focusing on learning activity, but both perspectives provide accounts of learning that can occur in groups and in solitary activity" (p. 11).

In reviewing the research and practical influence of emerging technologies on instruction and learning, whether framed cognitively or situationally, it is often useful to focus first on how individuals learn and then to broaden one's object of inquiry to include artifacts, other learners, and other environmental or contextual variables (Winn 2003). To this end, Newell and Simon (1972) admit taking a pragmatic approach to the development of information-processing theory:

It is difficult to test theories of dynamic, history-dependent systems. The saturation with content—with diverse meaningful symbolic structures—only makes matters worse. There is not even a well-behaved Euclidean space of numerical measurements in which to plot and compare human behavior with theory. Thus, this book makes very little use of the standard statistical apparatus. (p. 13)

Contrary to the criticisms of cognitive perspectives toward psychology, Newell and Simon's (1972) description of the interplay between general models of cognition and context anticipates recent developments in the field. As Winn (2004) summarizes:

There is evidence that cognitive activity is not separate from the context in which it occurs. . . . Thinking, learning, and acting are embedded in an environment to which we are tightly and dynamically coupled and which has a profound influence on what we think and do. What is more, evidence from the study of how we use language . . . and our bodies . . . suggests that cognitive activity extends beyond our brains to the rest of our bodies, not just to the environment. (p. 80)

Evans (2004) echoes this position as well, stating "The world we perceive to be out there is as much a product of cognition in a human body as it is the result of an external reality. . . . Hence, our world-view as human beings is exactly that, a view from one possible ecologically viable perspective among many possible perspectives" (p. 8). Davies (1995) agrees, as least where our perception of time is concerned, noting that "We must face up to the fact that, at least in the case of humans, the subject experiencing subjective time is not a perfect, structureless observer, but a complex, multilayered, multifaceted psyche. Different levels of our consciousness may experience time in quite different ways" (p. 266). Vosniadou (1996) also argues for this perspective in a much less speculative manner, recommending that "What is needed is to change our conception of the mind from that of a symbol manipulating machine to that of a developing, biological system that functions and evolves within a complex physical, social, and cultural environment" (p. 2). Vosniadou's (1996) conclusion rests, interestingly, on the initial success of cognitive science research where, she writes, "the turn to instructional interventions and experiments as a means of doing basic science happened precisely *because the epistemology of cognitive psychology could not provide an adequate learning theory to explain the results that it had itself produced*" (pp. 100–101).

Anderson et al. (2000), situating studies of cognition and learning in formal educational settings, take a much more collaborative position:

The cognitive and situative perspectives also provide valuable complementary analyses of school learning. For example, in mathematics education the cognitive perspective provides important analyses of information structures in conceptual understanding and procedures that are needed for students to succeed in the tasks emphasized in most mathematics curricula. . . . The situative perspective provides important analyses that emphasize students' participation in socially organized activities of learning, including patterns of classroom discourse and the opportunities to learn how to participate in the learning practices that their classrooms support. . . . A more complete cognitive theory will include more specific explanations of differences between learning environments, considered as effects of different contexts, and a more complete situative theory will include more specific explanations of individual students' proficiencies and understandings, considered as their participation in interactions with each other and with material and socially constructed conceptual systems. (p. 12)

It can be argued, then, that demanding adherence to either a cognitive or a social perspective toward instruction and learning with technology is unnecessary and counterproductive. These perspectives might, instead, emphasize a particular dimension of a larger sociohistorical or even anthropological methodological stance toward the study of human psychology in general (Cole and Engeström 1993). With this

Table 4.1
Alternative views of the same learning activities or processes

Approach	Emphasis	Specific Methods
Biophysical	Physical, motor, neurological	Electronencephalography (EEG), ERPs, fMRI, MEG, NIRS, PET, TCDS
Behavioral	Behavior, perception, tasks	Direct observation, trial and error, punishment-reward, time-stamping
Cognitive	Mind as container (attention, retrieval, mental models, cognitive overload)	Talk-aloud protocols, computer modeling, quantitative experimental designs
Organizational	Tasks in context	Activity theory, genre analysis, case study approach, social network analysis
Social	Human interaction, groupwork	Situativity theory, discourse analysis, critical realism, political theory
Cultural	Community, social conventions	Anthropological approaches to situativity and community formation, structural and poststructural analysis, phenomenology
Historical	History, events, chronology	Economical, sociological, narrative, critical theory

orientation, we would be able to draw on various quantitative and qualitative traditions, constructing alternative conceptions of the learning process depending on our methodological viewpoint (see table 4.1).

Beginning one's investigation with a sociocognitive orientation provides opportunities for framing instructional situations as both profoundly personal and individual and intensely sociocultural in nature. Barab and Plucker (2002) find that the literatures on legitimate peripheral participation, distributed cognition, activity theory, and situated cognition offer promising developments in this direction, writing, "talent [knowledgeable skillfulness] is not in the head or in the environment, but in the variables of the 'flow itself'" (p. 178). Hutchins (1995) as well concludes that "most learning in . . . setting happens in the doing, the changes to internal media that permit them to be coordinated with external media happen in the same process that bring the media into coordination with one another" (pp. 373–374). This perspective certainly finds support in recent research on mindful learning, which, according to Langer (2000), stresses perspective rather than the assimilation of context-free facts: "When we ignore perspective, we tend to confuse the stability of our mind-sets with the stability of the underlying phenomenon: All the while things are changing and at any one moment they are different from different perspectives, yet we hold them still in our minds as if they were constant" (p. 221).

4.2 On Technology

In addition to defining what we mean by learning, it is especially useful here to define as explicitly as possible what we mean by technology, because interpretations of what is and what is not technology are often limited to artifacts alone. That is, most attempts to define technology tend to do so without reference to technology users' prior knowledge, expectations, contexts for use, and user perceptions of newness, complexity, and dangerousness. The problem with defining technology out of the context of its use and, therefore, as directionless, is that we are then reduced to definitions that almost always invite exceptions to the rule we have just established: technology either includes everything from simple instructional instruments or devices or focuses on complex digital applications or systems, it either consists of limited or multiple parts, it either acts alone or requires other technologies to function, it either demands secondary training or is intuitively usable, or it works without secondary power sources or with them (i.e., electricity). Transparent technologies, the pencils of our time, thus become *tools* because we can only view the relationship between their function and their users as a one-way interaction. *We* use pencils; pencils do not use us.

This perspective toward technology, in turn, invites an atheoretical position toward technology. As Verbeek (2005) asserts, "Things belong to the realm of praxis and must be approached pragmatically" (p. 78). He offers instead a view of technology as relationally dependent on nature and context:

Things, in short, disclose a world. When somebody uses a tool or piece of equipment, a referential structure comes about in which the object produced, the material out of which it is made, the future user, and the environment in which it has a place are related to each other. But that this is so, according to Heidegger, generally appears only when a handy or ready-to-hand tool or piece of equipment breaks down. When this happens, the tool suddenly demands attention for itself. The reliable dealings we are used to having with the tool are ruptured, and instead of withdrawing from our attention the tool suddenly forces itself upon us. Someone sits at a word processor focused on the text at hand and all of a sudden the computer freezes. The trustworthy world that developed around the computer—the open books, the keyboard, the screen, the cup of coffee; in short, the entire mutually referring network . . . is abruptly destroyed. . . . Its transparency is transformed into opacity. The computer no longer can be conveniently utilized in the practice of writing, but abruptly demands interaction with itself. The relation with the world around the computer that took place "through" it is disturbed. Only when it starts up again and everything works without a hitch is the world that was destroyed again restored. (pp. 79–80)

A view of technology as transformative undermines the myth of technical transparency. Whenever human beings interact with technology, learning is inevitably a part of the process; and, unfortunately, humans rather than machines are frequently held responsible for breakdowns. Thus Butler (1996), tracing the history of usability engineering studies during World War II, states without irony that at that time "equipment complexity began to exceed the human limits of safe operation" (p. 61), a character-ization that stresses human error rather than excessive complexity as the origin of the usability problem. In terms of computer applications, then, an interface is perceived, interpreted, understood, and used depending on the knowledge that users bring to the situation and the tasks that they are attempting to accomplish. And, as Shneider-man (1987) reminds us, we then require both factual and conceptual knowledge about the *computing domain* (the particular application and its functionality), the *task domain* (experience, complexity, frequency of exposure), and the mapping of the tasks to the application at hand. As well, it is rare for a given user to exhibit expertise in task behaviors alone, given that using the Web, for example, demands a host of activities, including reading to do (to perform a task), reading to learn (to learn about some-thing), reading to assess (to figure out a document's contents or usefulness), reading to learn to do (to acquire knowledge for completing tasks later), reading for pleasure with our information goals in check, and so on (Redish 1988, 1993).

The more complex a tool gets or the more historically contextualized, the more likely we are to describe that tool as an instrument, device, application, technology, or system (from least to most complex). Asaolu (2006) summarizes three levels of technology in terms of their historical development: *before 3200 BC* (low-level technol-ogy), *3500 BC to date* (intermediate-level technology), and *1950 AD to date* (high-level technology). Low-level technologies include primitive tools and machines; are natural, adapted, or manufactured; and include such artifacts as spears, hammers, levers, and wheels. Intermediate-level technologies are manufactured for generalized use and employ natural forces such as wind, water, and combustion. High-level technologies are standardized and automated (Fordist) and can serve the mind (via information and communication) as much as the body (ICT) (Asaolu 2006, p. 336).

One can quickly surmise that, were we to push harder on the distinctions between low-, intermediate-, and high-level technologies, distinctions between Asaolu's (2006) stages of technological development would become difficult to maintain. Indeed, the levels of technology represent three calendar times that are far from equal in duration. That is, *1950 AD to date* is an inordinately brief technological flash in time compared to the two prior chronological snapshots. Yet the *1950 AD to date* level also contains the rapid development of computer technologies from mechanical and hardwired devices (of the 1950s) to bulky machines with primitive input–output mechanisms such as punch cards (of the 1960s), to dumb terminals and command-line interfaces (of the 1970s), to first-generation graphical interfaces (of the 1980s), to browser-based comput-ing (of the 1990s), to three-dimensional, social, and simulated environments of today.

Orel (1995) captures the product–user relation of these three levels of technology with the descriptions *closed-objects and users* (i.e., humans using fixed technologies as directed), *open-objects and utilizators* (i.e., humans interacting with building-block technologies allowing multiple possibilities), and *self-technologies and experimenters* (i.e., humans directing distributed technologies for their own purposes) (pp. 87–88).

As our technologies become more complex, so do our interactions, intentions, and expectations for them.

Comparing the technological setting of a traditional classroom to a smart classroom highlights the increased demands that surround and pervade the subject matter being discussed (similar subjective workload demands have been observed when comparing paper to Web-based instructional materials; cf. Emerson and MacKay 2006). One primary difference between a traditional classroom and a smart classroom is the training, skills, and expectations that we bring to the setting. To be prepared to use a traditional classroom, instructors need to supply their own books, reading materials, and lecture notes or lesson plans. In some cases, they may provide their own writing implements (e.g., chalk or erasable markers).

In contrast, a smart classroom requires significantly more knowledge on the part of instructors. The University Computing and Communications Services support group at California State University, Sacramento (CSUS), recommends that instructors preparing for network access in their smart classrooms consider the following additional requirements:

To gain access to the CSUS campus network in a Smart Classroom, you will need to have a 10baseT Network Interface Card that is compatible with your computer (we suggest 3Com and Intel cards). The network card must be recognized by your operating system: Windows 95, 98, ME, 2000, NT, and XP or Mac OS 8, 9, and X. If required, we suggest you have a professional install the network card. Additionally, you will need to have Category 5 network cable. (http://webapps2.csus.edu/smartclassrooms/smart-classrooms-faq.aspx)

Instructors on the CSUS campus, therefore, are likely to require additional support even before entering a smart classroom and, even when prepared, are likely to spend more time interacting with the classroom "aids" than they would in a traditional, well-known instructional space. The instructional "payoffs" can be numerous of course, including instructional relevancy, novelty, multiple display opportunities, data analysis and manipulation possibilities, ready-made instructional materials for reuse, and so on. But claims that building "smartness" into instructional settings improves instructional effectiveness at less "cost" (the least of which being the new demands placed on the instructors who use them) are highly exaggerated.

To connect Asaolu's (2006) overview of historical developments in technology with our present instructional circumstances is a difficult task, partly because we are often faced with the immediacy and demands of current technologies and partly because historical accounts of the relationship between technology and instruction are often postnarratives that omit the challenges, misdirections, and failures associated with technological creation and adoption. Still, it is worthwhile to at least briefly place current technologies into historical context if only to encourage a perspective that invites us to consider the range of loosely defined "technological" artifacts that have influenced our instructional contexts (see table 4.2).

Table 4.2
Historical perspectives on technology related to instruction and learning

Technology	Familiar–Unfamiliar	Simple–Complex	Stand-alone–Support required	History
Books	familiar	simple	stand-alone	Around 1450, Gutenberg press, first English print shop, 1458; 1500s, books of instruction or "hornbooks" consisting of text and illustrations (after Ramus's educational reform movement)
Chalk	familiar	simple	stand-alone	Antiquity, for writing on "a small flat rectangular piece of stone found at Thera" in 15th century BC (Olson 1974, p. 1); colored fluids for "ink" date back to Egypt and China, 2000 BC
Pencil, markers	familiar	simple	stand-alone	Graphite, 1564; patented, 1795, most common instructional artifact in the historical and contemporary classroom
Chalkboard, blackboard, whiteboard, smartboard	familiar	simple to complex	stand-alone	1800s, initially "lapchalks," railroad travel allows distribution of wall-sized versions in 1840s (Great Exposition of London held in 1851); 1960s, replaced by steel boards with porcelain enamel; 1990s allergy fears popularize whiteboards
Slide projector, LCD projector and screen (slides)	familiar but technical	simple to complex (to repair)	stand-alone to support required	1676, Magic Lantern (or Sturm Lantern) is invented; "Hyalotypes" become common around 1875; 2004, LCD projectors are replacing carousel-based projectors; leads ultimately to integration of artificial projection with real-time viewing and interaction

Table 4.2
(continued)

Technology	Familiar–Unfamiliar	Simple–Complex	Stand-alone–Support required	History
Telephone, cellular phone	familiar but technical	simple to complex (to repair)	stand-alone to support required	1870; patented, 1876; by 1877, first regular telephone line completed; by 1880, almost 50,000 telephone lines exist in the U.S. and, by 1900, 10 percent of households had phones; first touch-tone produced in 1941, eight years before publication of Shannon's (1949) *A Mathematical Theory of Communication* (Urbana: Univ. of Illinois Press); phone used to augment correspondence education; cellular phones expand data delivery considerably but it takes 37 years, until 1977, for commercial availability in America
Photographs, film	familiar to use, technical to produce	complex to use and repair	training and support required	1877, famous stop-action galloping horse pictures; 1888 development of single-lens camera used to make first moving picture sequences; 1891, Edison invents Kinetoscope, patented in 1993 (first "parlor" in New York City in 1894); 13 *Soldiers of the Cross* films, Australia, 1901; Warner Bros. studio purchases Vitaphone sound system in 1926; 1927's first "talkie," *The Jazz Singer*; 1922's first color film, *The Toll of the Sea*, used Technicolor with subtractive two-color process throughout; projection issues result in limited educational use
Sound systems	familiar but technical	simple to complex (to repair)	stand-alone to support required	1898 patent for telegraphone; Alexander Graham Bell's 1857 ear phonautograph (used the inner ear from a human cadaver and represents a macabre page in the history of biomechanical inventions); introduction of sound-on-film educational companies in late 1920s

Table 4.2
(continued)

Technology	Familiar–Unfamiliar	Simple–Complex	Stand-alone–Support required	History
Radio	familiar but technical	simple to complex (to repair)	stand-alone to support required	1907 patent for wireless telephony; formation of British Marconi; U.S. incorporation in 1922, moving from music and local programming to drama and news by 1940 with Edward R. Murrow's "Radio News" (central medium in 1930s); by 1950, 94 percent of American households own radio sets
Television	familiar to use, technical to produce	simple to complex (to repair)	stand-alone to support required	1902, use of visual sequences for instruction; 1904, patent for color television system; BBC is started in 1936; by 1949, 10 million monochrome TVs have been sold; popular in distance education from late 1970s until early 1990s
Wireless remote controls, microphone, mouse	familiar	complex to use and repair	stand-alone to support required	1950, Zenith "Lazy Bones"; "Flash-matic" invented by Adler in 1955; "clickers" in large-class formats are becoming popular
Networked micro, home, personal computer (PC)	often complex to use, technical to troubleshoot	complex to use and repair	training to support required	First Electronic Numerical Integrator and Computer (ENIAC) completed in 1945; second Electronic Discrete Variable Computer (EDVAC) completed in 1952; from mainframe (1960s) to mini (late 1970s) to micro (early 1980s); early use in education includes Plato; currently multimodal (two-way audiovideo, asynchronous and synchronous Web-based)[a]

Table 4.2
(continued)

Technology	Familiar–Unfamiliar	Simple–Complex	Stand-alone–Support required	History
VCR/DVD player (videotapes and DVDs)	familiar but technical	simple to complex (to repair)	stand-alone to support required	1972, first VCR for home use; 1977, first VHS VCR; 1999, first HD-compatible VCR; rapidity of developments has shifted to replayable cable television market that is displacing VCR centrality in the home
Internet, World Wide Web	familiar to use, increasingly familiar to produce	simple to complex (to program)	stand-alone to support required	1969, first computer message sent from UCLA to Stanford and, same year, the Advanced Projects Research Agency Network (ARPANET) formed; 1973, DARPA initiates the Internetting project: TCP/IP Protocol Suite developed; 1986, NSF begins development of NSFNET (major communication backbone); Berners-Lee develops World Wide Web (WWW) in 1991; by 1996, around 45 million people use the Internet and, by 2004, between 600 and 800 million users worldwide; Federal Networking Council (FNC) defines word "Internet" in 1995
Document reader/camera	familiar but technical	simple to complex (to repair)	stand-alone to support required	Mid-1990s priced alone with video conferencing systems around $50,000 but, today, priced at around $10,000; allows spontaneous interaction between instructors and any materials that fit on the flat screen projection unit
Mobile devices (laptops, PDAs, phones)	familiar to use	simple to complex (to design)	stand-alone to support required	First portable computer produced in 1981 (Osborne 1); in 2005, 21 percent of all computers sold in U.S. are portable; propelled by broadband ubiquity and cellular messaging, online social networking explodes in early 2000s from its humble beginning in the form of Friendster in 1997.[b]

Table 4.2
(continued)

[a] Networked personal computers at once demand a table of their own that describes the use of databases, multi-user domains, hypertext and multimedia systems, Web-based first- and second-generation applications, laptop and mobile computing uses, and virtual world environments. This table is designed to describe broader technological developments related to educational settings and, so, only touches on some of these virtual technologies briefly.

[b] Because this table serves as a synopsis of the histories of various technologies, only a small number of interesting details are provided, along with a brief timeline of the pace of adoption in the United States. Where possible, references for "invention" dates are supported by articles or books and, in some cases, the inventors.about.com Web site provides secondary support (http://inventors.about.com/od/astartinventions/a/FamousInvention.htm). Other invaluable resources include the following: on the printing press, see Hobart and Schiffman (1998), Olson (1974); on books, see Madej (2003); on pencils, see Petroski (1989); on chalk and the chalkboard, see Barclay's (February 2001) "The Chalkboard" (Reed Magazine, http://web.reed.edu/reed_magazine/Feb2001/features/Chalkboard/chalkboard_index .html), the University of Oxford Museum of the History of Science's (2005) poignant *Bye-bye blackboard . . . From Einstein and Others* (http://www.mhs.ox.ac.uk/blackboard/), and Roy (1993); on radio and television history, Casson's (1910, 1999) *The History of the Telephone* (University of Virginia Library Electronic Text Center, http://etext.lib.virginia.edu/etcbin/toccer-new2?id=CasTele.sgm&images=images/modeng&data=/texts/english/modeng/parsed&tag=public&part=all); on cellular technology, see Bellis's *Selling the Cell Phone, Part 1: History of Cellular Phones* (http://inventors.about.com/library/weekly/aa070899.htm); on interesting film history details, see Dirks's (1996, 2006) *Timeline of Influential Milestones and Important Turning Points in Film History, Pre-1900s: Film History by Decade* (http://www.filmsite.org/filmh.html); on video used specifically for instruction and training purposes, see Wisher and Curnow (2003); on the slide projector, see Bellis's *Magic Lantern—Slide Projector* (http://inventors.about.com/od/mstartinventions/a/magic_lantern.htm); on document cameras and alternative video-display technologies, see Time, Inc.'s (2003) "Smart Conference Rooms" (http://www.timeinc.net/fortune/services/sections/fortune/tech/2003_07smart.html); for an entertaining history of VCRs, see Hain and Browne's (1994, 2005) *Total Rewind: The Virtual Museum of Vintage VCRs* (http://www.totalrewind.org/); for a well-designed overview the history of computing, see PBS's (1996) *Triumph of the Nerds: The Rise of Accidental Empires in Silicon Valley* (http://www.pbs.org/nerds/), and, for an excellent summary of information technologies and accessibility, see Vanderheiden and Zimmermann (2002); for thorough histories of the Internet, see Banks (2008), the Internet Society history resources (http://www.isoc.org/internet/history/), and Elon University/Pew Internet Project's *Imagining the Internet: A History and Forecast* (http://www.elon.edu/predictions/); for data on mobile device use, see Ladner (2008); for research on social networking, see Boyd and Ellison (2007), Greenhow (2008), Mehlenbacher (2008), and National School Boards Association (2007).

Table 4.2 consists of five columns. The first column, arranged roughly in chronological order, lists technological developments that have either had significant influence on instructional processes or that have been thought to have potential for instruction use. Experimental technologies have been left out of the table deliberately, saving those discussions for our review of learning environments and artifacts later in the book. Notably, except for the radical exceptions of the personal computer, Internet, Web, and contemporary mobile devices, most of the technologies described in table 4.2 are designed to generate, display, distribute, and view instructional content or to facilitate communication at a range of proximities. Prior to the advent of the computer, technologies that encouraged modes of communication that allowed many-to-many interactions were limited; our instructional and historical habit of one-to-many communication has resulted in a host of technologies that allow only one-to-many communication, or perhaps one-to-many technologies have limited our notions of instruction to that instructional approach.

Column 2 of table 4.2 describes technology in terms of familiarity versus unfamiliarity, where familiarity refers to the technology's "taken-for-grantedness" or "naturalization" as an object in our world (Bowker and Star 1999). In the context of use, most of the technologies described, prior to the computer, tended to be familiar. The *Oxford English Dictionary*, interestingly, defines "familiar" as something that pertains to one's household or family, to people and their relations, and to physical proximity. Thus technologies that feel nonpersonal, distant, and disconnected from our social selves and lives are frequently thought of as alienating, technical, and abstract.

Column 3 describes technologies on a continuum from simple to complex and allows us to see how context influences our perceptions of the utility and friendliness of technologies around us. Complex, as a noun, verb, and adjective, is generally not a desirable state or process. That is, in repair situations, even the most familiar and intimate technologies (e.g., the family alarm clock) become foreign to us, complex and intimidating.

Column 4 describes technology as ranging in "learnability" from stand-alone use to training and support required. Many contemporary technologies, in part because of our lack of familiarity with them, require some form of training and initial support to encourage adoption. Historical technologies, as well, can require a considerable learning curve if used in advanced ways (e.g., I once sat in a one-day workshop with a handful of Ph.D.s learning how to use a multifeatured telephone system).

Column 5, the most detailed column, provides a telegraphic overview of the history of the technology being described. As has been suggested, these sorts of summaries tend to reproduce "facts" that adhere to chronological and superficial understandings of the complex histories of the technologies in question. They also, however, can give us a quick picture of the interconnections between technological developments and the satisfying illusion that "the next great technological advance" is part of an inevitable, natural, and predictable flow of human conceptions. Chronological perspectives toward technology also provide some insights into the nuanced relationship between invention, implementation, and adoption that all new technologies encompass.

In reviewing technologies that have infiltrated formal learning environments, then, it is critical to emphasize their sociocultural underpinnings. Even technologies that are traditionally assumed to be transparent—pencils, typewriters, algebra, writing—are inexorably embedded in our cultural upbringing, enculturation, and educational systems. Each technology has a specialized production history, particular ergonomic, distribution, and storage features, developing display and presentation aspects, and a task vocabulary that develops out of long-term use and acceptance. Isolating an individual artifact and labeling it instructional, therefore, requires a historical understanding of the artifact and its relationship with learning activities. Technologies are cultural by-products and, as Hatch and Gardner (1993) remind us, "Cultural forces influence the kinds of skills people can exhibit, the way those skills are developed, and the purposes to which they are directed" (p. 167).

Thus, a technology as rudimentary as the graphing calculator, for example, has been shown to fundamentally alter traditional mathematics instruction in terms of

• what mathematics learners are able to do (strengthening the interaction between algebraic and graphical representations of functions);
• how learners are able to learn mathematics (allowing easy axis adjustment and "zooming");
• the speed with which graphical representations can be generated, encouraging some instructors to design more complex ("real-world") problems for learners;
• how confident learners feel about mathematics problem solving;
• the way instructors structure class time, allowing much more small-group laboratory work and less lecturing;
• the manner in which learners approach problems, increasing the amount of learner-to-learner collaboration and data sharing; and
• the amount of instruction and time required to make sure that learners don't simply use the graphing calculators without understanding the underlying mathematical concepts (Wilson and Krapfl 1994).[2]

In addition to dramatically influencing learning activities and tasks, graphing calculators as technology also inform the subject matter and instructional activities required of instructors.

4.3 On Instruction

Instruction in higher education is often relegated to hallway conversations and the scholarship of teaching and learning workshops hosted by faculty centers for teaching and learning, rather than assigned as an area that is critical to the university mission of knowledge making and inquiry. But research on instruction, similar to research on technology, is simultaneously pervasive and dispersed across disciplines. It may be that, as one of Feenberg's (1999) paradigm mediums, instruction operates tacitly in everything researchers do, or that the well-worn theory–practice dichotomy in the academy sets instruction firmly in the domain of practice, where few aim to stray. Certainly, the perception, held by the general public as well, is that university faculty who receive teaching awards and who are not well known for their research might as well begin seeking alternative employment immediately.

As well, instruction is generally viewed inappropriately as the mere presentation of known facts, knowledge, and the true state of the world. Säljö (2003) attributes this misconception to erroneous understandings of both instruction and learning:

Our collective assumptions of what learning is all about are still heavily coloured by the traditional metaphors of the exercise of mental facilities and the shaping of physical action as the prototypes of learning: to learn is to copy until perfection is reached. The corresponding metaphor of teaching is one of instruction functioning as a conduit in which information and knowledge, packaged in an easily digestible format, are poured into the minds of pupils. In both these metaphors, learning is essentially a passive and reproductive process; what people learn is a limited set of skills that can be defined as such and that should transfer to new situations. (pp. 319–320)

Petraglia (1998) suggests that this view is supported by the tacit assumptions we bring to most instructional situations: "the very idea of education presumes that students are developing, rather than merely exhibiting, already existing knowledge and skills and that the classroom is structured hierarchically with the teacher as the central authority who must be empowered to legitimize and regulate student learning" (p. 161). His recommendation, instead, is that we negotiate postmodernist denials of objective reality on the one side and the privileging of the knowledge constructed by learners over instructional authority on the other side, by

adjusting our pedagogical stance to one that persuades learners rather than informs them—in other words, taking the rhetorical turn. . . . Chief among [the challenges posed by that] is that of overcoming our ingrained beliefs about persuasion and education on the one hand, and an uncritical embrace of antifoundationalism on the other. Constructivism without a dialogic and argumentative dimension either sets up a false and unnecessary antagonistic dichotomy pitting the educator against the learner—a dichotomy that has at stake the question of whose real world is to be acknowledged—or else it prompts a kind of "anything goes" response that serves no one's interests, least of all the students'. Instead, an argumentative framework acknowledges that teachers and educational institutions have objectives, but learners have real worlds that may be an obstacle in achieving them. (p. 163)

Or it may be that, as anyone who has ever served as an instructor can attest, Bruner's (1966) statement that "Perhaps the greatest problem one has in an experiment of this sort [teaching] is to keep out of the way" (p. 70). This sentiment finds ready support in numerous well-worn quotations regarding the centrality of the learner to all instructional experiences, including Albert Einstein's "It is a miracle that curiosity survives formal education," Beatrix Potter's "Thank goodness I was never sent to school; it would have rubbed off some of the originality," and George Bernard Shaw's "A fool's brain digests philosophy into folly, science into superstition, and art into pedantry. Hence University education."

This desire to keep instructors out of the way of a learner's personal learning process, however, does not mean that we should leave instruction entirely to the learner, as research on discovery learning and free exploration confirm. De Jong and van Joolingen (1998) warn that instructional support is critical to the success of exploratory learning efforts, including providing learners with support in generating hypotheses, designing experiments, making predictions, and regulating their learning processes. It also does not mean that we should leave instruction to our technologies, as appealing as some writers make that sound: Ravetz (1996), for example, notes, "My own private fantasy is that much of standard teaching even at the University level could be left to the machines, and students could then explore the human side of it all—history, literature, philosophy, whatever—either with multimedia equipment or even with a teacher" (p. 54).[3]

Both of these representations of learning emphasize learners who, we presume, are able, motivated, and strategic enough to shape their own learning objectives and methods for assessing whether or not they have learned what they hoped to learn. But learners are only one part of what it takes to create successful instructional situations: we also require meaningful learning tasks and activities, productive and structured social dynamics, well-conceived instructional activities, and learning environments that foster mutual support and creative trial and error. In short, we must balance what we know about how learners think, believe, and act with what we know about how to design effective instruction.

Instruction, at the most basic level, involves the communication of declarative knowledge (facts, guidelines, knowing what), conceptual knowledge (concepts, principles, knowing why and when), and procedural knowledge (tasks, actions, knowing how) between an instructor or instructional "text" (where contemporary texts can include video, audio, simulation, or multimedia objects) and a learner. How much or little conceptual versus procedural instruction one communicates, moreover, has been shown to reduce error rates among learners asked to complete high- or low-level tasks following instruction, with conceptual instruction best suited to high-level tasks and procedural instruction well suited to both high- and low-level tasks (Lin and Salvendy 1999). Online instruction involves an interdependent relationship between these levels of knowledge in both the instructional content (domain knowledge) *and* the instructional environment (operating knowledge).

Unfortunately, the difficulty that researchers have defining *instruction* probably leads to difficulties we encounter when trying to define *Web-based* instruction. WBI, as it is often defined, tends to stress either the technological context within which instruction and learning occurs or the learning itself, which may explain why definitions of WBI are often conflicting or confusing. Again, instruction as an object prefaced by the adjective "Web-based" suggests that other instantiations of instruction are equally possible, such as face-to-face or traditional instruction. To speak of laboratory-based or field-based or inquiry-based instruction would seem awkward, because laboratories and fields and inquiry-guided situations as actions highlight learning and learning processes. To describe them as instruction rather than as instructional activities or, better, as types of learning, would seem problematic. Being relegated to adjectives, technology-mediated instruction thus subordinates technology to content and, further, reinforces our view of instruction as being stand-alone content that is delivered rather than centered around action.

Synonyms for WBI also include e-learning, online teaching and learning, distance education, distance learning, Web-based training, computer-assisted learning, computer-assisted learning, flexible learning, and technology-rich instruction. Botkin and Kaipa (2004) observe that, although academics tend to prefer *distance education* to business's *e-learning*, both use *Web-based learning* (p. 410). These etymological debates are to be taken seriously given that it is difficult for any field of research to develop cohesive programs without being able to find agreement on the terminology that defines its object or objects of study. For this reason, interpreting the Web in WBI as referring to the global network of multimedia information that is readily accessible for communication broadens the grain-size of our analysis and encourages strengthened dialogue with researchers interested in instruction and learning with technology in general.

Instruction, broadly defined, accounts for instruction with vocational, hands-on, and performance-related training goals in mind, versus "education," which is broader in its definition. Dabbagh and Bannan-Ritland (2005) view distance learning, online learning, and WBI as concentric circles with WBI in the center: distance learning includes "Pedagogical models or constructs, distributed learning, open or flexible learning, knowledge-building communities"; online learning includes "learning technologies and delivery models, virtual classrooms, knowledge networks, asynchronous learning networks, WBI"; and WBI includes instruction "Supported through the use of Web-based authoring tools and course management systems" (p. 22). Relan and Gillani (1997), similarly, conceive of WBI as a space for "the application of a repertoire

of cognitively oriented instructional strategies implemented within a constructivist
. . . and collaborative learning environment, utilizing the attributes and resources of
the World Wide Web" (p. 43). Notably, both definitions highlight the learning context
(i.e., one that is Web-based) surrounding instruction. Researchers use the phrases Web-
based learning (WBL), Web-based instruction (WBI), and Web-based education (WBE)
interchangeably (e.g., McCormack and Jones 1998; MacDonald et al. 2002).

"Web-based education" brings in a host of issues and interactions not addressed
here directly, including admissions processes, program development and institutional
support structures, mentoring and advising, attrition issues, cost and institutional
scalability, and placement and workforce preparation considerations. As well, education can occur without instructor support or specific instructional goals framing the
learning event (e.g., we can learn during a PBS special or a family dinner, although
instruction was not likely the motivating goal of either event). Interestingly, education
can be viewed on the one hand to encompass instruction and can include policy and
administrative issues; and, on the other hand, education can be described as limiting
in its emphasis on instruction in formal versus informal contexts. WBI is preferable
to the industry's favorite term, "Web-based training" (WBT), because training does
not necessarily require declarative or conceptual knowledge exchange; and it is preferable to the term "e-learning," because electronic learning can include VCRs, television,
audiotape recorders, and so on. Finally, instruction can be both a noun, or "direction,"
and an action (as in "to practice teaching"), whereas instruction also allows for settings
outside traditional K–12 structures.

Ultimately, the involuted interactions between how we instruct, what we want
learners to know (cognitive), how they solve problems (attitudinal and affective), the
tasks we want them to accomplish (behavioral), and the technologies that mediate
these processes (symbolic) demand careful consideration. Once we begin to acknowledge this complexity, we are then able to develop conceptual pictures of the relationships between particular instructional approaches, learning contexts, and technological
settings. One potentially useful way to view the relationship between learning, technology, and instruction is as a process from cognitive demands, through technology-
based problem solving, to technology use. Table 4.3 offers one such representation,
explicitly connecting learning and complex problem solving with the integration of
ICT use and activities.

Table 4.3, despite its inelegance, is a labor-intensive synthesis that draws on theory
from information technology, educational assessment, and cognitive science research.
Quellmalz and Kozma's (2003) explication of the relationship between learning,
problem solving, and ICT serves as a base that integrates Anderson and Krathwohl's
(2001) extension of Bloom's (1976) taxonomy for learning, Simon's (1979) learning
terminologies, and Slack et al.'s (2003) structural levels of learning. Slack et al. (2003)
were influenced significantly by Biggs and Collis's (1982) qualitative method for

Table 4.3

ICT assessment framework (adapted from Quellmalz and Kozma 2003, p. 395; augmented with Anderson and Krathwohl 2001; Simon 1979; Slack et al. 2003, p. 309)

Cognitive Demands	ICT Knowledge and Skill for Solving Complex Problems	Strategies for Technology Use
Declarative knowledge/ prestructural/ comprehension	• Identify/list required domain information • Identify features and functions of technology tools	• Identify media types • Specify basic operating characteristics
Unistructural factual knowledge	• Recognize, describe, express • Identify uses of tools	• Identify features • Identify functions • For each tool group and specific tool, identify appropriate uses
Procedural knowledge/ integration with existing structures	• Perform steps • Operate tools • Reproduce, instruct, design	• Follow directions • Use algorithms • Produce components and complete operations
Schematic and strategic knowledge	• Plan strategies and procedures	• Analyze problems • Identify needed and given information and pose questions • Specify design for data/ information collection • Specify analysis plans • Choose appropriate tools • Specify product form and content
Multistructural	• Access and organize information and data • Represent and transform information and data	• Specify search purpose/topic • Navigate directories • Generate Web searches • Search multiple representational formats • Generate representations from data or phenomena • Transform data from one form to another
Develop new connections/relational/ conceptual	• Analyze and interpret information and data • Abstract, model, critique	• Take and record measurements • Identify information/data • Apply quantitative and qualitative procedures • Understand and compare data and information • Infer trends/patterns • Produce solutions/findings • Use modeling and visualization tools to investigate, compare, test

Table 4.3

(continued)

Cognitive Demands	ICT Knowledge and Skill for Solving Complex Problems	Strategies for Technology Use
Extended abstract/ develop toward a richer understanding	• Critically evaluate	• Evaluate relevance, credibility of information, data, representations • Evaluate quality of plan, conduct, analysis, argument, conclusions
	• Communicate ideas, findings, arguments • Reflect, elaborate, tutor, reframe	• Express questions, ideas clearly and appropriately • Present ideas, findings in alternative formats appropriate for audience • Present supported argument/ findings
	• Design product	• Compose product to fit constraints, appropriate for audience, purpose
	• Collaborate to solve complex problems and manage information	• Plan project work and roles • Contribute relevant information • Fulfill task assignment • Incorporate and integrate others' information and views

assessing learner outcomes, entitled the "Structure of the Observed Learning Outcomes" (SOLO) taxonomy (which, unfortunately, given the usefulness of the long-term research, is memorable more as a name than as acronym that details numerous potential learning outcomes).

The next section—in an effort to explicitly bring learning, instruction, and technology under a single perspective—reviews several of a growing number of models of instruction and learning with technology. The goal of this review is twofold: (1) to show the range of interpretations of various researchers interested in the area; and (2) to develop a framework for everyday instructional situations that accounts for existing research and that, ideally, simplifies the terminology that we use to describe these constantly evolving objects of study.

4.4 Sociocognitive Models of Formal Instructional Situations

The models of instruction and learning outlined in this section are excerpted from the original author-researchers' published articles. In addition to the traditional and strategic overview of existing literature that plays a role in most articles and chapters summarizing perspectives toward instruction and learning with technology, collecting graphical representations of theories provides considerable opportunity to compare and contrast the terminologies and principles organizing different researchers' methods for describing teaching and learning. Clearly, these graphic models are meant to persuade readers to adopt or cite a particular perspective toward a particular research theory. As with the empirical discourse that frames these diagrams of models in development, all the visuals displayed in a given research article are designed with a particular audience, purpose, and rhetorical situation in mind. Diagrams, in combination with textual explanations, often facilitate the understanding of complex hierarchical and sequential relationships, in addition to being more memorable than textual or auditory descriptions (Guri-Rozenblit 1988). Indeed, Hill (2004) has pointed out that because visual representations are interpreted as being more vivid, viewers tend to respond to them more emotionally, and "persuasive elements that instantiate strong emotions in the audience tend to have an extraordinary amount of persuasive power" (pp. 35–36).

To be sure, visual representations of the models of instruction and learning with technology developed by researchers are arguments in support of particular worldviews. Despite this, however, the potential vagueness, simplification, ambiguousness, amplification, or lack of explicit textual propositions has been documented in the research (Rosner 2001). Visual designs have a well-documented history of creation, consumption, convention development, and adaptation (Kostelnick 2004; Tufte 1983, 1990). Similar to Hill (2004), Blair (2004) argues that visual representations are particularly effective as arguments because of their "evocative power" and, more importantly, because they present sometimes complex arguments in believable snapshots that presume familiarity with the underlying argument and that, therefore, instantiate agreement without encouraging dialectical consideration. Hampton (1990), as well, reminds us that we must "realize that rhetoric is functioning in a state of information overload and that the critic must know what information is being eliminated as well as what information is being given" (p. 355).

Thus Lynch (1991) describes the importance of interpreting conceptual illustrations in the context of scientific processes and discourse:

Diagrams are not isolated representations. . . . An appreciation of the picture's conceptual and documentary functions can be gained only when one places it within a cross-referential network. This network includes various other textual features—captions, headings, narratives, and other tables, graphs, photographs and pictures—as well as the practices within which these textual features have a role. (p. 209)

Taylor and Blum (1991) stress that in diagrams "space and time remain virtually unrepresented" (p. 284) with time momentarily frozen and space captured by the two-dimensional frame of the page. Their conclusion is one that audiences for visual diagrams of instruction and learning with technology need to consider carefully: "that 'reality' does not dictate any unique representation" (p. 291) and, therefore, that arguments embodied in diagrams represent a subtle interaction between texts and visuals in the construction of theory.

Kress and van Leeuwen (1996) view visuals as communication representations that have been historically subordinated, interpreted primarily as expressive—produced for "pleasure, entertainment and immediacy of apprehension" (p. 30)—rather than as articulated "rational and social meanings" that can be analyzed (p. 20). But even a quick glance at the models of instruction and learning with technology outlined in this section invites preliminary analysis, especially given the range of representations, geometrical organizations, and emphases presented by the different models' originators.

Graphical representations of instruction and learning with technology come in various forms, as tables, grids, process diagrams, ecological representations, flowcharts, input–output processes, concentric circles, Venn diagrams, and triangles. Anderson (2004), for example, places learners and instructors (from top to bottom) in the center of his model of online learning. Learners and instructors are brought together by a knowledge–content interface (center), and interact within a community of inquiry via structured learning resources (from left to right). The model also accounts for the continuum from instructor-guided, collaborative learning through independent learner study and factors into its design community-based versus individually driven organizations. Thus, Anderson (2004) notes that, although "community binds learners in time, forcing regular sessions or at least group-paced learning" (see collaborative learning and community of inquiry interactions on the left side), less structured and more scalable online learning environments can be achieved by encouraging independent study and interaction between learners and course content (see independent study and structured learning resources on the right side). At the center of the instructional situation is the "knowledge–content interface," which can be interpreted either as the instructional space that learners and instructors share or as the complex interaction between content and learning itself (see figure 4.2).

Interestingly, Anderson (2004) connects the tools that learners use explicitly to the types of learning tasks and activities they engage in, which most likely exaggerates the influence of particular applications on the range of actions they afford and the transformative and social uses of technologies. Finally, Anderson (2004) includes instructor collaboration as part of his model, in contrast with many models of instruction and learning with technology. It is probably fair to assume that instructors, especially when using alternative methods for instruction, are prone to engaging in more discourse with their colleagues, administrators, and technical specialists than are instructors working in conventional teaching contexts.

Astleitner and Steinberg (2005), in their meta-analysis of gender effects on Web-based learning, present an integrated model of Web-based learning that distinguishes

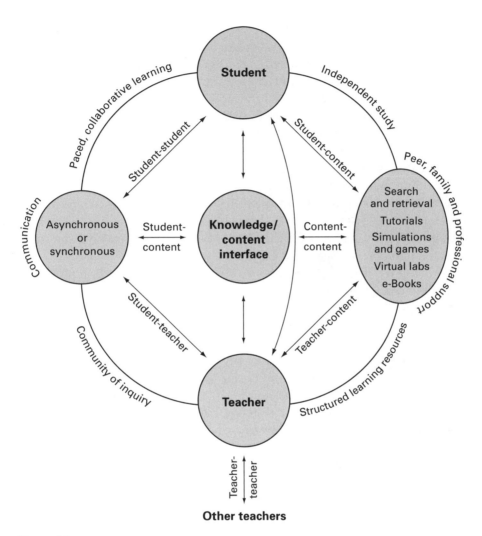

Figure 4.2
Model of online learning showing types of interaction (adapted from Anderson 2004, p. 49).

human from course and technology characteristics and that stresses learning outcomes related to learner interest, knowledge, and satisfaction: "Individual learners, groups of learners, instructors, instructional systems, and learning materials realize—based on human characteristics, technology, and course attributes—instructional events which support learning" (p. 51). Balanced across the top, from left to right, are human characteristics (which can include both instructors and learners), technologies for learning, and the context for the instructional situation. Interactions can occur between learners, groups, instructors, systems, and materials, and instructional events are equated with support that is provided for learning. Between these actors and actions and instructional outcomes (e.g., interest, knowledge, satisfaction) reside motivational, cognitive, and emotional processes. The model is top-down and balanced, privileging human actors, technologies, and contexts for learning. Although outcomes are built into the instructional situation, the model allows for both transmissional and transformational interpretations (see figure 4.3).

One of the earliest studies of computer-facilitated learning (CFL) environments in higher education was produced by Bain et al. (1998). In contrast to a top-down process model from input to outcomes, Bain et al.'s (1998) characterization of CFL environments is therefore largely descriptive in nature (see table 4.4).

Bain et al.'s (1998) study involved 36 projects funded between 1993 and 1996 by the Committee for the Advancement of University Teaching in Australia, and included learning environments from the sciences, medicine, and humanities that employed technology "to enhance teaching and learning" (p. 167). What distinguished Bain et al.'s (1998) work from many other researchers was their interest, not in how computer-facilitated learning environments *might* support instruction, but in how they currently did. The authors explain, "we are interested in how CFL is actually used because, from an educational perspective, that is what we need to know to understand its likely impact on student learning" (p. 165). Notably, the authors' categorization of computer-facilitated learning environments did not account for either learner backgrounds or prior knowledge or for learning outcomes specifically (p. 178). The grounded description, interpretation, and case studies presented by Bain et al. (1998) are necessarily exploratory and invite the use of a tabular format that is presented in both short and detailed form.

The online interaction learning model that Benbunan-Fich, Hiltz, and Harasim (2005) propose includes four "inputs" (the technology-media mix, the individual student, the instructor, and the group and organizational setting) and five "outputs" (access, faculty satisfaction, student learning, student satisfaction, and cost-effectiveness) separated by "learning processes," which include the "amount and type of interaction/activity, individual vs. collaborative learning, and perceived media sufficiency (richness, social presence/community)" (pp. 23–24). Their representation of inputs forms an approximate symmetry and balance, suggesting that the attention

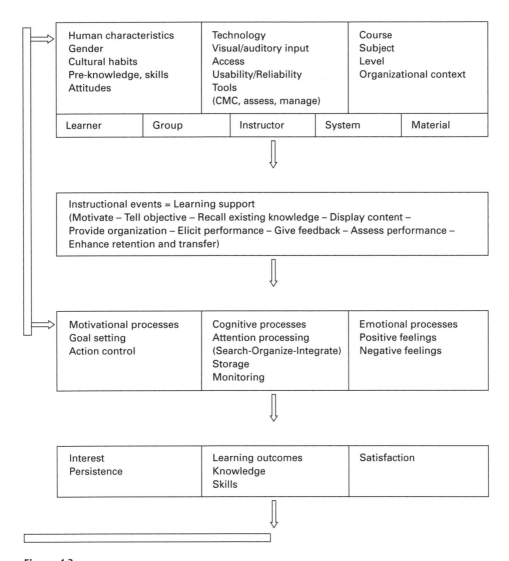

Figure 4.3
An integrated model of Web-based learning (adapted from Astleitner and Steinberg 2005, p. 50).

Table 4.4

Qualitative dimensions of computer-facilitated learning (from Bain et al. 1998, pp. 172–173)

Dimension	Details
Learning framework	*Facilitated* Learning opportunities encourage active exploration of the subject/ content matter and challenge students to build their own knowledge representations. *Guided* Learning opportunities encourage students to explore the subject/ content matter, but the process is actively guided through feedback, model answers, or good practice exemplars. *Structured* The learning opportunities provided are highly structured. Information is provided and students are given set tasks to perform using the given information.
Origin of knowledge	*Student/collaboration* Knowledge results from the reasoned interpretation of information. Different but equally valid interpretations of the same information are possible. *Academic/discipline* Knowledge is drawn form a well-defined discipline base with a received interpretation.
Learning directions	*Student-managed* Students given the freedom or opportunity to explore their own lines of reasoning or questioning within the knowledge domain. *Teacher-managed* Teacher controls the flow of information, questioning and directing within the program. Students free to review aspects of choice but the paths are laid down by the teacher.
Knowledge focus	*Conceptual/procedural reasoning* Development of higher-order thinking, reasoning, and metacognitive skills used in conjunction with discipline concepts, principles, and procedures. *Conceptual/procedural knowledge* Disciplinary content, concepts, and principles and the associated procedural skills are developed. *Case-based reasoning* Professional reasoning or decision-making skills in the application of knowledge to case-based problems are developed.

Table 4.4
(continued)

Dimension	Details
Learning process	*Knowledge construction/challenge* Students challenged to consider information presented from different perspectives or reconsider their own understandings so as to construct new interpretations. *Knowledge elaboration/challenge* Students provided with learning opportunities that extend and/or challenge existing conceptual understanding or interpretive skills, allowing them to explore consequences of their interpretations. *Knowledge synthesis/elaboration* Students required to synthesize knowledge from various sources often to solve case-based problems. Through this process, their conceptual understanding may be elaborated. *Knowledge elaboration* Students invited to explore nuances of concepts, find new examples, and extend their existing understanding of the concepts. *Knowledge emulation* Ideas/concepts connected and understandings developed in line with the received wisdom of the discipline. The aim is for students to be able to emulate expert understanding and thinking. *Knowledge assimilation* Factual knowledge presented in a fairly fragmented way with little structuring, elaboration, or transformation required of the students who, instead, are to assimilate the knowledge.

given to each dimension is similar. By outlining the dimensions of the particular course in question, the authors suggest that disciplinary and institutional factors influence instructional situations as much as technologies, instructors, and learners. Reading from top-left to bottom-right suggests that technology variables are privileged over student characteristics. Input–output models for learning, notably, are highly transmissional in nature. Benbunan-Fich et al. (2005) summarize the inputs that inform instructional situations in general and WBI specifically as shown in figure 4.4.

In contrast to Anderson (2004), Biggs, Kember, and Leung (2001) have developed a general model of learning—the presage-process-product (3P) model—that is *explicitly* process-oriented and that views "student factors, teaching context, on-task approaches to learning, and the learning outcomes" as a "dynamic system" (see figure 4.5).

Biggs et al.'s (2001) model, as a flowchart form similar to the models of Anderson (2004) and Astleitner and Steinberg (2005), reinforces hierarchies and depicts, as Kress and van Leeuwen (1996) state, "the world in terms of an actively pursued process with a clear beginning and an end (or 'input' and 'output,' 'source' and 'destination,' 'raw materials' and 'finished product')" (p. 85). In all such cases, one of the difficulties with applying a process–product orientation to instruction and learning is that it is difficult

Technology	Course
• Mode (media mix) • Time dispersion • Geographical dispersion • Software functionality • Reliability • Media bandwidth	• Course type • Class size • Type of subject • Institutional context
Instructor Characteristics	**Student Characteristics**
• Skills • Effort • Pedagogical model	• Motivation • Ability (GPA) • Skills/knowledge • Attributes (e.g., age, sex) • Learning styles

Figure 4.4
Inputs informing instruction and learning (adapted from Benbunan-Fich, Hiltz, and Harasim 2005, p. 24).

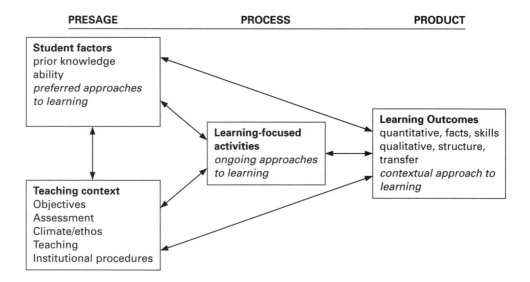

Figure 4.5
The presage-process-product (3P) model of teaching and learning (adapted from Biggs, Kember, and Leung 2001, p. 136).

to know where process ends and product begins. More importantly, many of the products that we hope will reveal that the process of learning has occurred often give us only glimpses of the applicability and long-term influence of our instruction on learners. Activity theory has shown us that, along with the various instruments and artifacts that make up typical instructional events, understanding what we do as instructors, how we communicate with learners, and what they in turn must do in order to exhibit that learning has occurred are varied and context dependent.

Bransford et al. (2004) revive Jenkins's (1978) model of instruction, a model that notably has no explicit instructor category (although the category of teaching and learning activities emphasizes instruction). Interestingly, though, the model reinforces "overarching categories" (i.e., content, activities, tasks, and learners) and "subordinates" (i.e., modality of content, formal instruction, transfer, knowledge), and these structures are presented hierarchically in the form of a pyramid (Kress and van Leeuwen 1996, pp. 81–84).

The appeal of Jenkins's (1978) model is its explicit identification of criterial tasks as an important feature of instruction and learning (see figure 4.6). Criterial tasks highlight recognition, recall, and transfer of learner characteristics, instructional activities, and content features, revealing the importance of prior knowledge to all learning events. Content is at the top and center of the tetrahedral configuration, activities move from left into tasks on the right, and all these elements come together at the bottom with the learner. Although the model is not transmissional in its organization, Bransford et al. (2004) do build successful transfer of new learning into the instructional situation.

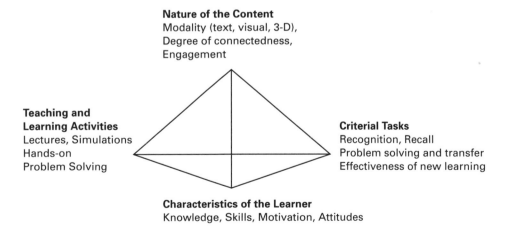

Figure 4.6
Jenkins's (1978) tetrahedral model (adapted by Bransford et al. 2004, p. 212).

Bryant, Kahle, and Schafer (2005), in a summary of the distance education research geared at accounting academicians, present a model of distance education that emphasizes the role of an instructor, a learner, a mode of communication, and an educational organization. Interestingly, the Bryant et al. (2005) model overlaps in notable ways with the models of Anderson (2004) and Biggs et al. (2001), highlighting instructor–student interactions mediated by technology (see figure 4.7).

Planning and support figure prominently in the Bryant et al. (2005) model, being the only activity that is represented in two nodes. As a flowchart form, their model is no less complex than Anderson's (2004) model; but the use of rectangles rather than circles suggests a more formal relationship between the actors, activities, institutions, artifacts, and outcomes portrayed.

Dabbagh (2005) and Dabbagh and Bannan-Ritland (2005) present one of the most thoroughly researched, theory-based design frameworks for e-learning, in the symbolic form of a triangle with circles moving from instructional strategies to learning technologies to pedagogical models and back to instructional strategies again. They thus highlight "the interaction between pedagogical models, instructional strategies, and learning technologies to facilitate meaningful learning and knowledge building" (Dabbagh 2005, p. 26) and reinforce the assumption that well-developed models of learners ought to inform instruction, which ought to inform technology choice and implementation. Interestingly, Dabbagh (2005) does not have instructional strategies being informed by particular learning technologies; this oversight suggests that her model is an ideal one, where designed technologies always support instructional tasks, activities, and strategies rather than enforcing or detracting from particular instructor–learner interactions (see figure 4.8).

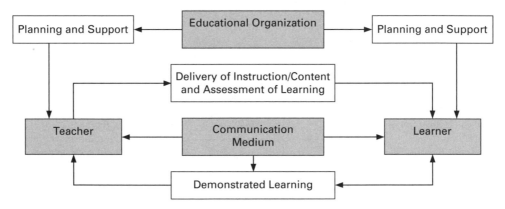

Figure 4.7
Model of distance education (adapted from Bryant, Kahle, and Schafer 2005).

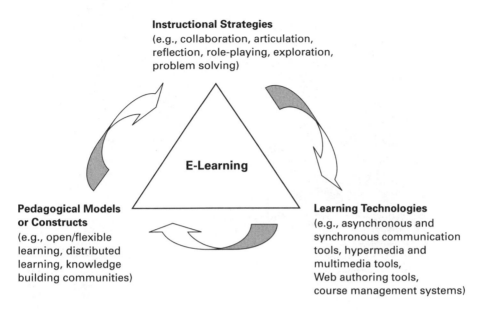

Instructional Strategies
(e.g., collaboration, articulation,
reflection, role-playing, exploration,
problem solving)

E-Learning

**Pedagogical Models
or Constructs**
(e.g., open/flexible
learning, distributed
learning, knowledge
building communities)

Learning Technologies
(e.g., asynchronous and
synchronous communication
tools, hypermedia and
multimedia tools,
Web authoring tools,
course management systems)

Figure 4.8
A theory-based design framework for e-learning (adapted from Dabbagh 2005).

As Dabbagh (2005) summarizes it: "These three components form an interactive relationship in which pedagogical models or constructs grounded in the situated cognition view inform the design of E-Learning by leading to the specification of instructional and learning strategies that are subsequently enabled or enacted through the use of learning technologies" (p. 32). Finally, Dabbagh (2005) views her contribution as having theory-into-practice utility: "Educators and instructional designers can think of this model as a theory-based or grounded design framework that guides the design of E-Learning" (p. 32).

So diagrammatic representations of models for instruction and learning with technology can be either representations of an ideal or desired (future) state or representations of a generalized (present) reality. In the case of Dabbagh (2005), influencing the future design of e-learning environments is the goal; and, therefore, it is not surprising that instructional strategies are shown influencing technological decisions that may be desirable but, in most educational institutions and corporate training environments, are also highly unusual.

Garrison, Anderson, and Archer (2000), interestingly, remove technology as a variable in their model, stressing instead the sociocognitive relationship between higher-education teachers and students as mediated by discourse, content, and instructional setting. In the form of a Venn diagram, Garrison et al. (2000) thus emphasize the

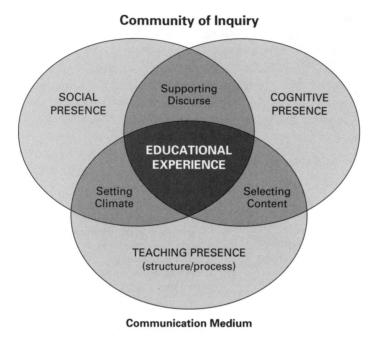

Figure 4.9
Elements of an educational experience (adapted from Garrison, Anderson, and Archer 2000).

interdependent relationship between individual learning, social dynamics, instructional activities, and communication medium (see figure 4.9).

In their learning model developed while building a program in management education and training for the advanced technology sector, MacDonald and colleagues (MacDonald et al. 2002; MacDonald and Gabriel 1998; MacDonald et al. 2001; MacDonald and Thompson 2005) drew on research from distance education and adult learning and consulted with industry experts to produce the "demand-driven learning model" (DDLM) for Web-based learning. After Bransford et al.'s (2004) use of Jenkins's (1978) model of instruction and Dabbagh's (2005) framework for e-learning, MacDonald et al. (2001) present their DDLM hierarchically in the form of a triangle, only, in their model, learning outcomes occupy the privileged position at the peak of the triangle. According to MacDonald et al. (2001), DDLM proposes "a high-quality standard of 'superior structure,' grounded in consumer (learner) demands and recognizes the needs of instructors and designers" (p. 19). An anticipated result of this "consumer" orientation and its stress on quality is that program outcomes and evaluation are highlighted (see figure 4.10).

Richards (2006) describes his model of online learning situations as follows: "An integrated notion of ICT-supported learning environments is presaged by an initial

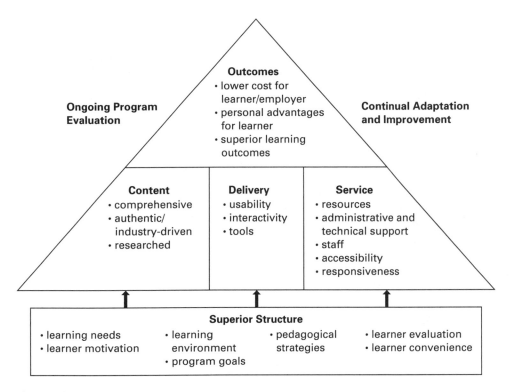

Figure 4.10
Demand-driven learning model (adapted from MacDonald and Gabriel 1998; MacDonald et al. 2001, 2002; MacDonald and Thompson 2005).

recognition that both *pedagogical* and *technological* perspectives involve three convergent principles of design and development: the organization of *information*, the facility for *communication* and some convergent mode of 'user interaction'" (p. 244). In Richards's (2006) view, discussions about the details of synchronous versus asynchronous communication tools reveal a narrow perspective toward technological use in educational contexts. Instead, he advocates a tightly coupled relationship be maintained between the design of instruction and our goals and support for instructor-to-learner, learner-to-learner, and learner-to-computer interaction (see figure 4.11).

Richards (2006) does not explicitly elaborate on the spatial and temporal details of instructional situations and, instead, places interaction design at the center of instructional "Commun(ity)ication," pedagogical orientation, subject matter, means of communication, open versus closed technical settings, and informational artifacts (which could include hardcopy resources). In the same (2006) article, Richards elaborates on the framework by emphasizing the importance of instructional goals for both

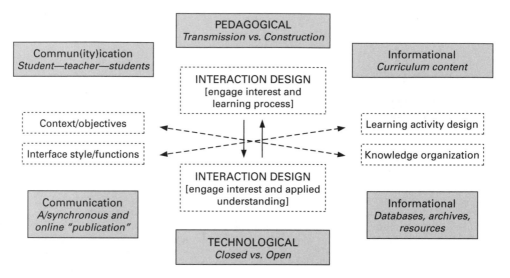

Figure 4.11

Pedagogical process, technological infrastructure, and convergent interactivity (adapted from Richards 2006, p. 245).

performance and knowledge making, interactions between one's learning community and learning environment, and between content and process through activity-reflection or doing-thinking cycles (p. 252). The model that he presents, therefore, highlights the interdependent relationship between interaction design and instructional design.

In contrast to the communication triangle evoked by Dabbagh's (2005) visual model of e-learning and Richards's (2006) boxed process model, Shea, Pickett, and Pelz's (2003) model of online learning environments is represented as a series of circles in the form of a Venn diagram. As such, their model presents a rich representation of the dynamics involved in any instructional situation and is particularly notable for its attempt to integrate the work of other theorists. One unfortunate by-product of model development in the research related to instruction and learning with technology is that many efforts appear to develop out of context of other similar efforts. Drawing on Bransford et al.'s (2000) emphasis on the importance of creating learner-, knowledge-, and assessment-centered learning environments, on Chickering and Gamson's (1987) widely cited seven principles of effective undergraduate instruction, on Anderson et al.'s (2001) conceptual framework for teacher presence, and on Garrison, Anderson, and Archer's (2000) emphasis on creating successful communities of inquiry in higher education, Shea, Pickett, and Pelz (2003) present a multilayered picture of online learning environments.

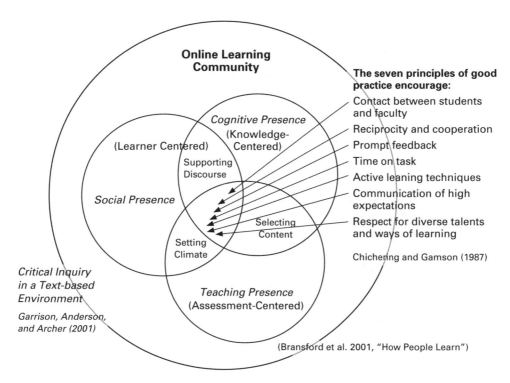

Figure 4.12

A conceptual framework for high-quality, higher education, online learning environments (adapted from Shea, Pickett, and Pelz 2003).

Shea et al.'s (2003) conceptual framework presents itself as a series of concentric circles, where the broadest instructional goal is the creation of online learning communities and the "procedures" for facilitating this process are Chickering and Gamson's (1987) principles for effective instruction (see figure 4.12).

As primary shapes, circles contrast with triangles and rectangles as organisms and ecologies contrast with technologies and systems (cf. Kress and van Leeuwen 1996). Hierarchies are impossible to identify explicitly (beyond the numerical seven principles listed on the upper-right-hand corner of the visual), and—since the top-left area is left to white space—identifying the most important information in the visual is difficult.

The conceptual breakdowns of the variables outlined by Benbunan-Fich et al. (2005), Astleitner and Steinberg (2005), and Bransford et al. (2004) are certainly defined in less detail by other researchers, and it is worth reiterating that the research developing conceptual models of instruction is broadly distributed and rarely acknowledges similar models being developed across disciplinary or field boundaries. Thus,

Siedlaczek (2004), reporting on her M.Ed. thesis study of five community college instructors' perceptions of the differences between face-to-face and online instruction, develops a graphical representation quite similar to existing models, although the link to these other research efforts is difficult to identify relying on traditional citation tracking.

Figure 4.13 highlights how technology, administrative, learner, instructor, and community issues interact in online instructional environments.

Similar to Anderson (2004), Siedlaczek (2004) interprets online environments as a series of symmetrical circles joined by unidirectional and multidirectional lines. Technology and administrative issues feed into the dynamics of teaching in an online environment and do not receive feedback and information from it. This is somewhat problematic unless institutional computing and administrative decisions are made completely apart from instructional goals and planning; and, with increased multidisciplinary instructional assessment, this disconnect is less common. Similar to Bryant et al. (2005), Siedlaczek's (2004) incorporation of unidirectional arrows requires elaboration. For example, are we to assume that the learners somehow interact with online environments, but that those environments do not interact back? Moreover, given Siedlaczek's (2004) ambitious attempt to capture the social and cultural elements of institutions that factor into instruction and learning with technology, it is surprising that no mention is made of financial constraints or costs associated with these instructional initiatives, perhaps because costs would cut across and through most of the clusters represented in figure 4.13.

Learners and instructors, again, factor significantly into the instructional situation. Learner attributes include learning styles, role, and characteristics and skills, and instructor issues include teaching style, strategies, role, course design, motivation, and characteristics and skills. For Siedlaczek (2004), then, teaching in an online environment represents a culmination of the particular factors brought into the environment, highlighting instructional space as a separate construct. At the bottom of her model diagram is the learner–instructor relationship and learning communities, a presumed outcome of technology, administrative, instructor, and learning dynamics. Learning communities and instructional relationships are influenced by learners, instructors, and the online environment, but are only secondarily related to technology and institutional policies and procedures. Finally, the lines from learners and instructors to instructional relationships are partial ones, suggesting that relationships and learning communities are not an assumed by-product of learner–instructor interactions.

Each of the sociocognitive models of formal instructional situations reviewed here emphasizes and deemphasizes particular dimensions of our object of inquiry. Because instruction, learning, and technology are interdependent, we begin to see how it becomes necessary to conceptualize them as ecological dimensions rather than as categories or parts given their amorphous subject matters, external and internal forms,

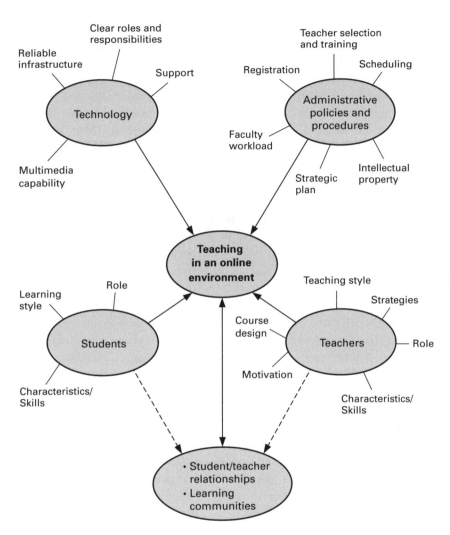

Figure 4.13
Factors affecting teaching in an online environment (adapted from Siedlaczek 2004).

and contexts. Keeping in mind that graphical representations of the state of anything are arguments for a particular way of looking at the thing, table 4.5 summarizes the models of instruction and learning with technology reviewed here (Anderson 2004; Astleimer and Steinberg 2005; Bain et al. 1998; Benbunan-Fich, Hiltz, and Harasim 2005; Biggs, Kember, and Leung 2001; Bransford et al. 2004; Bryant, Kahle, and Schafer 2005; Dabbagh 2005; Garrison, Anderson, and Archer 2000; MacDonald and Gabriel 1998; MacDonald et al. 2001, 2002; MacDonald and Thompson 2005; Richards 2006; Shea, Pickett, and Pelz 2003; Siedlaczek 2004). Where possible, dimensions have been collapsed when the details describing a particular dimension overlapped considerably.

Reviewing numerous models of instruction and learning with technology drawn from various disciplines highlights the need for a common language for describing face-to-face instructional situations through to virtual learning environments (and all realizable and potential instructional situations in between). The models of teaching and learning reviewed here tend to emphasize (1) learners, (2) instructors, (3) instructional strategies, (4) content, (5) group interaction, (6) learning outcomes, and (7) institutional context. The framework for everyday instructional situations developed in chapter 6 will emphasize some of these dimensions (learners and group dynamics), deemphasize others ("outcomes" and institutional contexts), and argue for the importance of still others (learner tasks and activities and learning environments and artifacts).

Clearly, our object of study cannot be reduced to obvious, measurable, input–output processes; nor can it be carved cleanly into process–product scenarios. Instruction and learning with technology is as complex an object of study as the gestures, words, images, and media that embody our everyday lives as biological learning beings.

Indeed, our attempt to define learning has revealed numerous competing viewpoints, emphases, and research-based disputes. For our purposes, we have defined learning multidimensionally as a sensory-perceptual, cognitive, affective, and social activity that involves comprehension, integration with existing knowledge, development of new connections, and elaboration toward a richer understanding. Instruction, or the communication of declarative, conceptual, or procedural knowledge, is mediated by technology that is understood through its historical context (from familiar, simple, and stand-alone to unfamiliar, complex, and scaffolded). Finally, the review of numerous visual representations of models of instruction and learning with technology that have been generated by researchers across disciplines, and their subsequent analysis, has revealed elements of these models that are surprisingly similar.

We have established that our learning worlds are collapsing in on each other, that the literatures related to instruction and learning with technology are as generalized as they are specific, and that models that can inform a global view of instruction and learning with technology are being developed across fields with few attempts to

Table 4.5
Learning dimensions from reviewed models of instruction and learning with technology

Dimension	Details	Source
Student characteristics; learner factors	• Knowledge, skills, motivation, attitudes • Gender, cultural habits, preknowledge, skills, attitudes, motivational processes, goal setting, action control, cognitive processes, storage, monitoring, emotional processes, positive feelings, negative feelings, interest, persistence, learning outcomes, knowledge, skills, satisfaction • Motivation, ability (GPA), skills/knowledge, attributes (e.g., age, sex), learning styles • Prior knowledge, ability, preferred approaches to learning • Learner, planning, instruction, communication medium, demonstrated learning • Learning style, role, characteristics/skills	• Anderson (2004) • Astleitner and Steinberg (2005) • Benbunan-Fich et al. (2005) • Biggs et al. (2001) • Bransford et al. (2004) • Bryant et al. (2005) • Siedlaczek (2004)
Instructor; teacher characteristics	• Teaching style, strategies, role, characteristics/skills, motivation, course design • Gender, cultural habits, preknowledge, skills, attitudes, motivational processes, goal setting, action control, cognitive processes, storage, monitoring, emotional processes, positive feelings, negative feelings, interest, persistence, learning outcomes, knowledge, skills, satisfaction, teacher-teacher • Teacher, planning, delivery of instruction/content • Skills, effort, pedagogical model	• Anderson (2004) • Astleitner and Steinberg (2005) • Benbunan-Fich et al. (2005) • Bryant et al. (2005) • Siedlaczek (2004)
Learning framework or direction; instructional events or strategies; teaching and learning activities	• Paced, collaborative learning; independent study; peer, family, and professional support; structured learning resources; community of inquiry; communication • Facilitated, guided, structured, student/collaboration, academic/discipline • Learning-focused activities, ongoing approaches to learning • Lectures, simulations, hands-on problem solving • Collaboration, articulation, reflection, role-playing, exploration, problem solving • Transmission versus construction	• Anderson (2004) • Bain et al. (1998) • Biggs et al. (2001) • Bransford et al. (2004) • Dabbagh (2005) • Richards (2006)

Table 4.5
(continued)

Dimension	Details	Source
Knowledge focus; material; nature of content; technology; system; learning technologies	• Asynchronous or synchronous, knowledge/content interface, search and retrieval, tutorials, simulations and games, virtual labs, e-books • Reliable infrastructure, clear roles and responsibilities, support, multimedia capacity • Student/collaboration, academic/discipline, conceptual/procedural reasoning, conceptual/procedural knowledge, case-based reasoning • Modality (textual, visual, 3-D), degree of connectedness, engagement • Technology, visual/auditory input, access, usability/reliability, tools (CMC, assess, manage), course, subject, level, organizational context, mode (media mix), time dispersion, geographical dispersion, software functionality, reliability, media bandwidth • Asynchronous and synchronous communication tools, hypermedia and multimedia tools, course management systems • Curriculum content, communication (a/synchronous), and online 'publication'), technological (closed vs. open), informational (databases, archives, resources), interaction design • Content (comprehensive, authentic/industry-driven, researched), and delivery (usability, interactivity, tools)	• Anderson (2004) • Astleitner and Steinberg (2005) • Bain et al. (1998) • Benbunan-Fich et al. (2005) • Bransford et al. (2004) • Dabbagh (2005) • MacDonald et al. (2005) • Richards (2006) • Siedlaczek (2004)
Group characteristics; interaction	• Student–student, student–content, content–content, teacher–content, student–teacher, student–content • Gender, cultural habits, preknowledge, skills, attitudes, motivational processes, goal setting, action control, cognitive processes, storage, monitoring, emotional processes, positive feelings, negative feelings, interest, persistence, learning outcomes, knowledge, skills, satisfaction • Social presence, supporting discourse, cognitive presence, selecting content, teaching presence (structure/process), setting climate • Commun(ity)ication (student–teacher–students) • Social presence, supporting discourse, cognitive presence, selecting content, teaching presence (structure/process), setting climate, critical inquiry, seven principles of good instruction • Student–teacher relationships, learning communities	• Anderson (2004) • Astleitner and Steinberg (2005) • Garrison et al. (2000) • Richards (2006) • Shea et al. (2003) • Siedlaczek (2004)

Table 4.5
(continued)

Dimension	Details	Source
Learning process; criterial tasks; outcomes	• Motivate, tell objective, recall existing knowledge, display content, provide organization, elicit performance, give feedback, assess performance, enhance retention and transfer • Knowledge construction/challenge, knowledge elaboration/challenge/knowledge synthesis/elaboration, knowledge elaboration, knowledge emulation, knowledge assimilation • Quantitative, facts, skills, qualitative, structure, transfer, contextual approach to learning • Recognition, recall, problem solving and transfer, effectiveness of new learning • Lower cost for learner/employer, personal advantages for learner, superior learning outcomes	• Astleitner and Steinberg (2005) • Bain et al. (1998) • Biggs et al. (2001) • Bransford et al. (2004) • MacDonald et al. (2005)
Context; course; administrative policies and procedures	• Course type, class size, type of subject, institutional context • Objectives, assessment, climate/ethos, teaching, institutional procedures • Educational organization and support • Resources, administrative and technical support, staff, accessibility, responsiveness • Registration, teacher selection and training, scheduling, intellectual property, strategic plan, faculty workload	• Benbunan-Fich et al. (2005) • Biggs et al. (2001) • Bryant et al. (2005) • MacDonald et al. (2005) • Siedlaczek (2004)

identify, let alone synthesize, these conversations. The critical and persuasive role of visual representations of models has also been introduced. Now we turn to two dichotomies, between science and nonscience and between theory and practice, that undermine the development of a third, multidisciplinarity perspective that is gaining momentum in various research literatures. Taking a rhetorical design perspective, complemented by contemporary research in human–computer interaction and design studies, allows us to move beyond what appear to be irreconcilable states of disagreement or incompatibility between theorists and practitioners.

5   Designs for Learning

Given the exponential rate of publishing on instruction and learning with technology, traditional dichotomies between science and nonscience and between theory and practice become difficult to maintain. Understanding the relationship between these endeavors is critical if we hope to develop theories we can apply and to understand how our applications embody working theory. A third, integrative rhetorical design perspective is proposed.

All men and women require a liberal art of design to live well in the complexity of the framework based in signs, things, actions, and thoughts.
—Richard Buchanan (1992, p. 14)

Engineering, like poetry, is an attempt to approach perfection. And engineers, like poets, are seldom completely satisfied with their creations.
—Henry Petroski (1982, p. 83)

As we have seen, claims that a dearth of theoretical models for instruction and learning with technology exist may have been overexaggerated. The previous chapter contained only a few of the models that researchers have described in various journals published across several disciplines. Here it is worth elaborating on a central lesson that came out of the review of the literatures related to instruction and learning with technology in higher educational settings. Numerous content experts from many academic disciplines appear to view instruction, learning, and technology as reasonable areas for intellectual investigation and publishing within their own disciplines, resulting in a distribution of research related to these subjects that makes it exceedingly difficult to "consider the structure of the literature, the structure of the community, and our place in both," to restate one of Bazerman's (1988) ideals for rhetorically sensitive researchers. Ironically, education, literacy, and technology—three of the five paradigm mediums that serve as the fundamental topoi of human civilization (Feenberg 1999)—are acceptable subjects for research no matter what one's disciplinary training. And, doubly ironic, no matter what one's disciplinary training—unless that discipline is engaged in the theoretical study of education, literacy, and technology—these objects of inquiry tend to be interpreted as part of the practical arts. Reduced to skill (*techne*) and thing (*pragmata*), they then become something that learners are expected to acquire incidentally, over time and through practice, outside the disciplinary subject matter being studied. Since the business of any academic discipline is to produce and disseminate knowledge related to that discipline, however, and since instruction has been historically (and uncomfortably) linked to the mission of disciplinary knowledge production, (distance) education operates ipso facto as a subset of any disciplinary research interest.

The relationship between knowledge production and instruction, it has been noted, is an uneasy one, and research on distributed instruction already maintains a precarious status in various disciplines, similar to technology education and to rhetoric and writing instruction. Hence, numerous textbooks on research methods devoted to particular disciplines often add the obligatory "format the document" section (assuming software application and document design knowledge), "write up the report" (assuming composing and disciplinary knowledge), or "present the data" (assuming visual communication knowledge). These disciplinary afterthoughts overlook the transformative role of language use, argument, and consensus building in all disciplinary knowledge making. Centralized writing instruction, as well, has found it difficult to influence the practices of writing-in-the-disciplines because instructors trained in those disciplines believe that their discourse problems are unique to their subject matter and methods and are therefore nongeneralizable (despite considerable research suggesting the contrary, e.g., Bazerman and Paradis 1991; Faigley and Hansen 1985; Gilbert and Mulkay 1984; Myers 1990; Prelli 1989; Rymer 1988). Conversely, instructors motivated to cover as much of their *own* subject matter content as possible in a semester-long course have tended not to view writing as integral to their instructional goals and curricular efforts.

Buchanan (2001) observes that "design, like rhetoric, was practiced as a craft and profession before it became a subject of theoretical speculation" (p. 188), and the same can be argued for theoretical speculation on the subjects of instruction, writing, learning, and technology. Technology-specific instruction, for example, tends to occur on the margins of academic instruction, and is often assumed without preparation, training, or time devoted to the subject in most academic courses. Similarly, technology-focused courses in curricula devoted to reading and writing instruction suffer the same minimized status. This has resulted in, at best, an evolutionary approach to integrating theory on instruction, writing, learning, and technology into the courses offered in various disciplines or, at worst, a haphazard development that enjoys infrequent faculty attention, revealed in statements such as "our new group of students are dreadful writers" or "even our graduate students mistake using Google for doing library research."

In addition to being invisible and practical arts owned by all disciplines, instruction, writing, learning, and technology simultaneously demand consideration as part of the study of *any* subject matter. Thus, the tension between those advocating the creation of a stand-alone discipline for instruction and learning with technology and those motivated to see these subject matters integrated across the curriculum is, in large part, a methodological one. Two of the most enduring academic dichotomies—between science and nonscience and between theory and practice—unnecessarily fracture the perspective required to address the complex relationships between instruction, learning, and technology, given that these objects of inquiry demand an approach that integrates *techne*, *pragmata*, and knowledge or *sophos*.

5.1   Science and Nonscience

Discussions about one's "worldview"—or less dramatically, methodological perspective—often describe either the difference between scientists and nonscientists (e.g., technicians, artists, the general public) or between scientists who practice quantitative methods and those who practice qualitative ones. Thus, Gieryn's (1983) overview of the historical differences between scientists and mechanicians (i.e., inventors and engineers) provides an excellent starting point for ways that we can view *design* as the integration of theory (or argumentation) and practice (or construction). According to Gieryn (1983), scientists can be distinguished from mechanicians in the following ways:

1. Scientific inquiry is the fount of knowledge on which the technological progress of inventors and engineers depends.
2. Scientists acquire knowledge through systematic *experimentation* with nature; because mechanicians and engineers rely on mere observation, trial and error, and common sense, they cannot explain their practical successes or failures.
3. Science is theoretical. Mechanicians are not scientists because they do not go beyond observed facts to discover the *causal principles* that govern underlying *unseen processes*.
4. Scientists seek *discovery of facts* as ends in themselves; mechanicians seek inventions to further personal profit.
5. Science need not justify its work by pointing to its technological applications, for science has nobler uses as a means of intellectual discipline and the epitome of human culture (pp. 786–787).

These propositions, of course, are false. This is somewhat surprising given the perception, promulgated by the mainstream media and accepted without much resistance by the general public, that *pure* science exists and that its methods inform our practice and policy in a unilateral way (Solomon 2001). The relationship between nature (objective reality) and technological representations of nature (imitation), however, has become increasingly blurred, and as a result the contrast between experimentation (highlighting control) and observation (highlighting viewer–object inseparability) has decreased (Kari and Rozenberg 2008). An educational example is that we no longer have to *attend* real-time lectures held on our campuses but, sometimes, can view them via Web-streaming configurations broadcast to our laptops. Although in these cases we can announce that we have watched a lecture, we cannot claim to have attended it, and deciphering the exact difference between the one and the other is similar to establishing how viewing the ocean floor with the assistance of a long-range sensor influences, alters, represents, and rearranges our perceptions and descriptions of the actual ocean floor.

Jablokow (2005) describes a scientific universe that differs significantly from Gieryn's (1983) twenty-five-year-old system when he writes, "There are new expectations for today's scientists, and they are staggering: more solutions, to more complex and difficult problems, delivered at increasing speeds (with shorter and shorter timelines), and subject to increasing demands for higher accuracy with a decreasing tolerance for failure" (p. 533). Similarly, Powell and Owen-Smith (2002) unpack the historical conception of researcher, stating: "The traditional view of the university researcher as a dedicated and disinterested, though passionate, searcher for truth is being replaced in the life sciences by a new model of the scientist-entrepreneur who balances university responsibilities and corporate activities in the development of new compounds and devices designed to improve human health and generate revenues for the investigator, the university, and investors" (p. 108).

So too, recently, has the science of learning been increasingly held accountable in terms of how much or little it can help us improve instruction and education. As Czubaroff (1997) reminds us, "The empiricist-instrumental-pragmatic concept of knowledge needs to be complemented with a social vision of knowledge—a vision rooted in the traditions of praxis, practical reason, and ancient civic wisdom" (p. 69). And so must our pragmatic views of the relationship between instruction, learning, and technology be challenged by dynamic social interpretations that place knowledge making in context. This challenge does not require that educational researchers embrace postmodern or relativist approaches or discard empirical facts altogether. As Weiss (2000) has argued in his review of the influence of postmodern theory on organizational science, "a typical problem with relativist approaches" is that "While their original appeal is based on an interesting criticism of mainstream work, their advocates tend not to be interested in actually carrying out the work necessary to provide the evidence that would build support for their view" (p. 729). Weiss (2000) concludes assertively, "In the absence of such research evidence, [postmodernists] are left merely to repeat their critique; they run out of things to do or say and eventually seek yet newer alternative positions from which to criticize the rest of us" (p. 729). A more moderate position is held by King and Frost (2002), who maintain, "The pitfall is not in the belief that new knowledge can be applied productively; that belief has been amply justified. Rather, it is in the confidence that knowledge per se can readily transcend the inherently ambiguous nature of things as we find them in the world" (p. 21).

If we accept that theory and practice are inextricably bound as activities and that achieving persuasive generalizability depends on one's audience and purpose, it becomes clear that the historical fissure between science and nonscience has been maintained by dated conceptions of scientist (or designer) as lone producer, communicating outcomes *after* the action has taken place, and accepting feedback for incorporation into the *next* published or manufactured artifact.

Bereiter (1994) offers a most useful perspective toward *science as progressive discourse* that describes scientific activities as profoundly community-driven (cf. Pfeffer 1993). A view of science as progressive discourse stresses the importance of four kinds of commitment: of *mutual understanding, empirical testability, expansion,* and *openness.* All these commitments require "some sacrifice of immediate self-interest" to the argument being forwarded, as well as a commitment to:

1. Work toward common understanding satisfactory to all. . . . It is to be distinguished from a willingness to compromise, which presumes that opposing sides will not alter their beliefs but that each side will yield just enough to achieve a practical resolution of conflicts.
2. Frame questions and propositions in ways that allow evidence to be brought to bear on them. What counts as evidence may itself be disputed; the commitment is to seek out things that opposing sides will accept as evidence and to frame the discourse in ways that build on such evidence.
3. Expand the body of collectively valid propositions. . . . A commitment to expand (in number, scope, or connectedness) . . . the body of the collectively valid implies a willingness to maximize the basis from which new conclusions may be drawn, thus increasing the possibilities of an advance in understanding over the understandings originally brought into the discourse.
4. Allow any belief to be subjected to criticism if it will advance the discourse. . . . This challenge is not done willy-nilly, however, but is conducted in the course of trying to resolve some impasse or to achieve some higher goal. (Bereiter 1994, p. 7)

Rather than focusing on how our sensory experiences account for in-the-world realities (given the increasing number of simulated realities that currently make up our worlds), we might argue that Bereiter's (1994) "empirical testability commitment" instead emphasizes learning through experimentation, introspection, and collaboration. This position, moreover, allows us to explore alternative data collection and analysis approaches. Van der Aalsvoort and Harinck (2000) provide a concise historical overview of the strengths and weaknesses of alternative methods for studying social interaction. Their summary includes empirical methods, ethnomethodological approaches, linguistic methods, and multimethod pluralism. This latter "approach," also referred to as the "paradigm of choices" (p. 8), finds its origins in the 1970s when researchers grew tired of defending the parameters of their particular research programs and began focusing on understanding the phenomenon at hand. Some educational researchers, as well, have called for a reevaluation of dichotomous views toward quantitative and qualitative methods for assessing teaching and learning (cf. Murphy and Woods 1996). Gunzenhauser and Gerstl-Pepin (2006) describe our current environment as "a postparadigmatic context in which epistemologies, theoretical perspectives, and methodologies are open for interrogation" (p. 342).

The development of our postparadigmatic context can also probably be tied to Gleick's (1999) observations on our Western hunger for acceleration and alternatives and to the development of a host of technologies that facilitate data collection and analysis available to the typical research team. Whatever the methodological research choice, van der Aalsvoort and Harinck (2000) conclude by recommending that researchers study prolonged and persistent engagement, highlight their particular research context, collect data from multiple sources and informants, represent numerous participants for study, and carefully consider issues of generalizability and sampling (pp. 18–19). These recommendations ought to resonate with researchers from any research tradition; and, indeed, as Harpine (2004) suggests, "Syllogism, deductive logic, inductive logic, the argument from authority, empirical observation, and hypothesis testing are widespread in diverse human societies" (p. 355), so these research methods are not necessarily even owned solely by Western scientists and empirical researchers.

Of course, achieving efficient versus fully satisfying solutions necessitates expediency in our community decision-making processes, and so Bereiter (1994) adds that the commitments to science as progressive discourse do not hold for all forms of discourse. One exception is legislative discourse which, he notes, is different because

> Governments have to act, and this often means that legislators cannot talk on until they reach an understanding satisfactory to all. They have to resort to compromise or majority rule. . . . In science, however, the discourse process itself is always open to question, and methodological disputes are common. (p. 7)

Bereiter's (1994) observations provide a middle ground for the increased interest in alternative data-collection methods in the sciences of instruction and learning with technology, in addition to supporting an approach to instructional situations driven by pragmatism and pluralism versus a neo-positivist philosophy of science. Both Bereiter's (1994) emphasis on science-as-discourse and Buchanan's (1992, 1995, 2001) conception of design as an exploration of "concrete integrations of knowledge that will combine theory with practice for new productive purposes" aim to generate a "new liberal arts of technological culture" (Buchanan 1992, p. 6). Both draw on a unifying rhetorical tradition that addresses theory and practice. In addition, both authors highlight the benefits of developing a research agenda that balances theory and artifact development, evaluation, and the generation of useful heuristics for both researchers and practitioners.

Bereiter (1994) and Buchanan (1992, 1995, 2001) differ on several critical points, however. First, Bereiter (1994) suggests that, just because scientific discourse sounds at times as though it maintains a faith in the existence of objective reality, this does not mean that scientists are naive enough to hold this worldview: scientific discourse is organized around consensus, agreement, methodological replicability, and disclosure to minimize individual self-interest in the name of the enterprise (cf. Gilbert and Mulkay 1984 for insights into the self-depreciatory realism of many practicing scientists engaged in the "search for truth"). Second, Buchanan (1992) directly distinguishes between neo-positivists (i.e., empiricists) and design practitioners, although his stance is weakened when he notes that "The test [of a design], of course, is whether experiments in innovation yield productive results, judged by individuals and by society as a whole," naming this as "the measure of objectivity in contemporary design thinking" (p. 11), a position that itself has a neo-positivist ring to it. Bereiter (1994) states that the goal of scientific discourse is progression rather than positive or quantifiable contributions to society as a whole. These differences emphasize the tension between traditional perspectives of scientific inquiry as value based versus value ridden and bring issues of the relationship between theory building and practice to the foreground.

5.1.1 Theory and Practice

While writing this book, I submitted a conference proposal outlining the four or five theories related to instruction and learning with technology that were beginning to inform an initial framework for instructional situations. Although the proposal was accepted, one of the reviewers wrote:

This paper seems like a good fit for this [group] but it is not really a research paper. Instead the author(s) is attempting to develop a conceptual model for designing and evaluating WBI. I assume that eventually this framework can be turned into some kind of tool that could be used to analyze WBI, but at this point this just seems to be foundational, review of the literature kind of work. Since this is a research conference, I think this framework is a bit premature and has not been tested/validated in any way, so is not yet ready for primetime.

The reviewer is correct that the work described in the proposal was preliminary, was not a "research paper," and did not describe an empirical study that involved random assignment of participants and a control group or validation of an instrument, although it is fair to assume that not everyone would interpret a research conference as a conference devoted to quantitative and qualitative empirical research papers. Research, instead, involves the application of convincing methods for the systematic study of objects that are carefully defined and elaborated upon. Quantitative or qualitative studies are aimed at contributing to the development of theories of and practices in instruction and learning with technology. In addition, we have seen that contributing empirical studies to a fast-growing, diverse, and disciplinarily isolated research literature on instruction and learning with technology will ultimately result in a more comprehensive understanding of our subject matter.

Morris's (1967) first hypothesis of model creation serves as a useful defense for the presentation of a framework for everyday instructional situations prior to validation or operationalization: "The process of model development may be usefully viewed as a process of *enrichment* or *elaboration*. One begins with very simple models, quite distinct from reality, and attempts to move in evolutionary fashion toward more elaborate models which more nearly reflect the complexity of the actual . . . situation" (p. B-709). Morris (1967) is particularly candid in stating, "Starting simply gets things moving and thus tends to relieve some of the tension. It does, however, require a certain amount of poise or 'guts' to back off from a complicated problem and begin with a simple conceptual structure" (p. B-709). In this respect, one could argue that a broadly conceived review of the numerous literatures that should (or could) be relevant to the general topic of instruction and learning with technology would seem a worthwhile first step in the process of approaching the problem.

Defining "foundational, review of the literature kind of work" as premature, then, reveals an important tendency among social scientists studying the topic of instruction and learning with technology, for several additional reasons. First, it is quite possible to gain validation for an instrument that measures uninteresting or irrelevant phenomena. Second, although identifying a research gap to frame an empirical study without a rich understanding of a discipline or field's structure is quite possible (and perhaps common), this practice presents severe problems for researchers over time as they work to incorporate particular empirical findings into larger frameworks for understanding the object(s) of study. Such is certainly the case with the abundant research on media comparison and learning styles, where hundreds and perhaps thousands of studies have confused rather than clarified the primary issues at stake. Thus, a carefully controlled empirical study that compares one type of bulletin board application to another—a research contribution that will likely find publication—does not necessarily contribute to our understanding of how to use a bulletin board for instruction. As Lewis, Perry, and Murata (2006) elaborate, "the very qualities that suit an [educational] innovation to controlled trial may handicap it at the later stage of dissemination," such as "external specification that limits local sense of ownership; simplification that enables easy transport and wide usability but compromises quality; creation of a compromise 'Swiss Army Knife' version that contains features for many sites but is not well adapted to any one; and emphasis on fidelity to the original design that stifles continuing improvement" (p. 8).

Theory and practice are as inevitable as trial and error, involving sometimes tightly and sometimes loosely coupled feedback from actions to ideas and back again. Unfortunately, in our race for easy solutions or satisfactory compromise, we are often guilty of relying on simple prescriptions, anecdotal experience, and personal guidelines or principles to inform our actions (hence my ongoing discomfort with any "workshop" that promises to help me design, teach, learn, speak, write, or live more effectively, with greater ease, and especially *in less time*). With complex tasks, efficiency is often counterproductive if the ultimate goal is effectiveness. Bluedorn (2002), as well, observes that since our individual goal is to prolong gratification, minimizing the amount of time we devote to pleasurable tasks such as reading is (ironically) counterproductive (p. 105). In other instances, building elaborate understandings of simple relationships between things is critical. Or, put bluntly, we are wise not to hurriedly cross the street without first developing an elemental theory of how traffic direction works.

A more dramatic example of the position that theory needs practice for grounding (and even the word "grounding" betrays our tendency to view practice as *below* theory) can be found in Johnson-Laird's (1983) argument that "theory should be describable in the form of an *effective procedure*" (p. 6). Card, Moran, and Newell (1983) distinguish between theory-based and empirically derived applied sciences, noting that developing common frameworks allows researchers to both anticipate and describe phenomena meaningfully. Schön (1983, 1987), although not as computational in his review of the relationship between theory and practice, laments the privileged position that theory generally holds over practice, as *high* theory is set as the aspiration and in-the-trenches application as the necessary outcome.

Both theory and practice involve, in addition to problem solving, problem *setting*. Schön (1983) defines problem setting as "a process in which interactively, we *name* the things to which we will attend and *frame* the context in which we will attend to them" (p. 40). Importantly, the more contingent our situation, the more difficult the act of identifying the appropriate problem; as Schön (1983) asserts, "when the ends are confused and conflicting, there is as yet no 'problem' to solve" (p. 41). But this is also the quintessential reflective moment where it is paramount that we commit ourselves to, as Dewey (1991) notes, "Active, persistent, and careful consideration of any belief or supposed form of knowledge in the light of grounds that support it and the further conclusions to which it tends" (p. 6). Importantly, this elaborate cognitive process requires effort, and Dewey (1991) emphasizes that, prior to sincere inquiry, learners must experience "a state of perplexity, hesitation, doubt" (p. 9) that results in sincere curiosity. It is in this uneasy moment that potential problem solvers are able to generate *problems* that require solutions.

Orrill, et al. (2004) present a framework for interpreting the research on learning and instruction with technologies distinguishing between "foundation" research (psychology, engineering, computer science, information management), "application" research (instructional design, educational technology), and "theory-building" research (the learning sciences). Foundational research, according to Orrill, Hannafin, and Glazer (2004), emphasizes "developing fundamental knowledge about technology and its use that is necessary before an innovation or instructional approach can be considered for use in educational settings, while concurrently defining underlying principles and processes for use-inspired research" (p. 336). Application research, in contrast, stresses the "application of principles in the real world" and not the creation of theories or principles designed to influence the real world (p. 340). Finally, theory-building research merges foundation and application research, iterating between theory and design, and employing a range of research methodologies suited to particular contexts for use (p. 345).

With the exception of the problematic dichotomy between foundation and application research, Orrill et al.'s (2004) elaboration of theory-building research is appealing, particularly in terms of its focus on designers as audience. Hill et al. (2004), similarly, direct research toward practice explicitly, suggesting that researchers need to explore best practices in research, expand best practices directly into use, examine both formal and informal learning environments, and elaborate on the role of intentional and incidental learning in both face-to-face and online learning situations (p. 453). Reigeluth (1999), as well, recommends an instructional-design theory that is "*design-oriented* (focusing on means to attain given goals for learning or development), rather than description oriented (focusing on the results of given events)" and that "identifies *methods* of instruction (ways to support and facilitate learning) and the *situations* in which those methods should and should not be used" (p. 6).

Research and practice are often characterized as unrelated enterprises; but the distinction is, at some levels, an arbitrary one, given emerging qualitative approaches to data collection, the emphasis that many funding organizations place on the generation of applicable research by "scientist-entrepreneurs," and the misconception that practice is not exactly what researchers do when they are engaged in academic research: after all, conceiving, organizing, planning, implementing, and managing research *is* a practice. Equipment, instrument validation, technological enhancements, visual models of scientific theories, and peer-reviewed research articles are the socially constructed artifacts (i.e., products) of the practice of research. Indeed, academic researchers can even find research artifacts devoted to the study of knowledge making and research activities themselves in journals such as *Knowledge in Society*, *Research in Higher Education*, and *Theory into Practice*.

But the theories that we are striving to build in the face of exponential technological developments are only one end of the continuum: new technologies are the other. We develop a theory of online discussion in a text-based environment, and our theory is informed by inevitable comparisons between the social and gestural communication cues that inform face-to-face and not online interaction. Technologies appear that allow us to interact in real time via audiovideo conferencing, and our theory requires modification, perhaps as significant as drawing on an entirely untapped research literature, for example, video- or film-production theories and processes. Most engaging conversations about research with colleagues from other disciplines, thus, tend to be guided by attempts to explicitly define the specifics of one's terms and to make connections via questions such as "Is that similar to such-and-such a technology?" or "How are you defining x?" (where x is the construct being examined, built, or tested). Similar process descriptions for scientist-theoreticians and nonscientist-practitioners are required—processes that invite interactions that are exploratory, iterative, experimental, generative, and creative. Such processes can productively be developed within the framework of a rhetorical design perspective.

Speaking directly to the development of a "theory of instruction," Bruner (1966) summarizes both the *prescriptive* and the *normative* nature of theories. To Bruner (1966), theories outline "rules concerning the most effective way of achieving knowledge or skill" and provide "a yardstick for criticizing or evaluating any particular way of teaching or learning"; simultaneously, theory "sets up criteria and states the conditions for meeting them" and the "criteria must have a high degree of generality" (p. 40). This perspective informs his four major elements of any theory of instruction:

1. Specify the experiences which most effectively implant in the individual a predisposition toward learning—learning in general or a particular type of learning.
2. Specify the ways in which a body of knowledge should be structured so that it can be most readily grasped by the learner. . . . (the merit of a structure depends upon its power for *simplifying information*, for *generalizing new propositions*, and for *increasing the manipulability of a body of knowledge*).
3. Specify the most effective sequences in which to present the materials to be learned (*that is, tasks*) [parentheses mine].
4. Specify the nature and pacing of rewards and punishments in the process of learning and teaching. . . . The timing of the shift from extrinsic to intrinsic and from immediate to deferred reward is poorly understood and obviously important. (pp. 40–42)

Bruner (1966) then elaborates on the learner's setting for instruction, describing it as a mix of predispositions (i.e., affordances), the structure and form of knowledge, sequence and its uses, and the form and pacing of reinforcement (pp. 42–51). The setting for instructors involves activating problem solving, managing structure and sequence, and administering reinforcement and feedback (pp. 57–70). The setting for learners, therefore, is highly complex and involves an intense interaction with the instructor and the subject matter and an interplay between learning tasks and instructional approaches. Bruner's (1966) theory of instruction, then, marries general science with particular practice, and highlights the considerable challenge that educational researchers face in identifying, understanding, and acting on larger educational processes.

5.2 Rhetorical Design

Design is what academic researchers do when they construct knowledge and contribute new studies and publications for dissemination via peer-reviewed academic research journals (Rowland 2004). Design is what practitioners do when they conceive and craft technical solutions for instructional situations using a combination of general (i.e., theoretical) knowledge and situational (i.e., practical) knowledge. Design is what instructors and instructional designers do when they explore and manipulate the capabilities of enterprise-level LMS applications and synthesize research and textbook materials for use in instructional situations. Indeed, design is what we expect successful learners to do when we attempt to teach them to interpret, select, analyze, present, and creatively apply new knowledge to their prior understandings and to novel problem situations (Fischer 2006).

Design is always constrained by our conceptions of audience, purpose, and situation (or exigency) and design solutions always represent themselves as trade-offs rather than as correct or incorrect answers. A rhetorical design perspective also attempts to honor both an empirical dimension (toward building *generalizable* theories of behavior) and an artistic dimension (toward building *particularized* knowledge that can be applied successfully to problems in various domains). Some researchers, however, hold that scientific and design approaches to problem solving are incompatible with one another. In his critique of purely scientific approaches to problem solving, Buchanan (1995) advocates the development of design theories that account for both the prescriptive and the normative dimension of complex problem solving. The essential tension for Buchanan (1995) is between neo-positivist knowledge building and design knowledge making:

Design is partly rational and cognitive, and partly irrational, emotive, intuitive, and noncognitive. It is rational to the extent that there is conscious understanding of the laws of nature; it is irrational to the extent that the sciences have not yet succeeded in revealing the laws of complex phenomena. Indeed, there is reason to believe that design will always retain an irrational or intuitive component, because there are properties of materials and forms that possess aesthetic and spiritual appeal for which no scientific explanation seems possible. (p. 50)

Invention is central to technical, scientific, communication, and instructional design. Miller (1979) suggests that our inability to approach problems creatively (i.e., to invent) and the tendency, instead, to focus on issues of form and style, set the historical division between science and rhetoric in motion:

The collapse of invention as a rhetorical canon is complementary to the rise of empirical science. If the subject matter of science (bits of reality, inartistic proofs) exists independently, the scientist's duty is but to observe clearly and transmit faithfully. The whole idea of invention is heresy to positivist science—science does not invent, it discovers. Form and style become techniques for increasingly accurate transmission of logical processes or of sensory observations; consequently, we teach recipes for the description of mechanism, the description of process, classification, the interpretation of data. (p. 614)

The actual practice of design, however, demands that we determine the best possible solution under the current circumstances, and, more often than not, theoretical prescriptions have a difficult time meeting this demand. As Pea (1993) reminds us, "one central aspect of work in design is that it is very commonly posed, or at least thought about, in terms of *trade-offs*. A designed thing is, of course, but one choice among many possibilities that were considered, and even more possibilities that were never considered" (p. 73). Design, therefore, is "wicked," messy, and inexact. Schön (1987) characterizes the mess that we must confront as follows:

Designers put things together and bring new things into being, dealing in the process with many variables and constraints, some initially known and some discovered through designing. . . . Designers juggle variables, reconcile conflicting values, and maneuver around constraints—a process in which, although some design products may be superior to others, there are no unique right answers. (p. 42)

5.2.1 Wicked Twenty-First-Century Knowledge Work

Outcomes without correct answers are, in a word, "wicked"—and wicked objects can be lawless, formidable, unpleasant, wonderful, potentially harmful, and occasionally playful. These contradictory characterizations sound as though they conflict with descriptions of contemporary knowledge work, but the term "wicked" actually captures the contingent, borderless problem spaces that most distributed learners inhabit. Kukla et al. (1992) define wicked problems as having the following attributes:

1. *There is no definitive formulation of the problem.* Because these systems are large and constantly changing, the person solving the problem does not have all the information needed to understand the problem fully.
2. *There is no "stopping rule" to tell when the problem is solved.* The problem solver can never conclusively answer the question "Have I done enough?"
3. *There is no immediate nor ultimate test of whether the system design is successful.* The system design process has unbounded consequences, and there is no way to conduct comparative analysis.
4. *There is no single, identifiable "cause" of a problem.* The problem may be a symptom of other problems, and the solution will change depending on how the problem is formulated. (Kukla et al. 1992, p. 43)

Buchanan (1992) traces the origins of the term "wicked problems" to early 1960s formulations of Horst Rittel (summarized in Rittel 1972). Churchman (1967), similarly, defined wicked problems as "that class of social system problems which are ill-formulated, where the information is confusing, where there are many clients and decision makers with conflicting values, and where the ramifications in the whole system are thoroughly confusing. The adjective 'wicked' is supposed to describe the mischievous and even evil quality of these problems, where proposed 'solutions' often turn out to be worse than the symptoms," (p. B-141). Buchanan (1992) notes that Karl Popper (1972) first used the term "wicked" to characterize complex problems, whereas Churchman (1967) was intentionally emphasizing the moral dimensions of design and planning. For Buchanan (1992), *indeterminacy* is the key attribute of wicked problems, and, therefore, wicked problems are nonprogrammable and must be interpreted rhetorically (p. 16).

Wicked problems also hold a certain amount of immediacy; for this reason, it is all the more important to stop occasionally and review research on instruction and learning with technology to help us understand what is working and what is not in the virtual learning spaces currently being developed. Verbeek (2005) captures this balancing act between action and reflection as follows:

The facts that technological artifacts can be conceived as constructions, always exist in a context, and are interpreted by human beings in terms of their specific frameworks of reference do not erase that fact that systematic reflection can be undertaken of the role that these contextual and interpreted constructions play concretely in the experience and behavior of human beings. That "the things themselves" are accessible only in mediated ways does not interfere with our ability to say something about the roles that they play, thanks to their mediated identities, in their environment. (p. 113)

A rhetorical design perspective, therefore, does not exclude the application of empirical methods to the problems at hand but rather views the data collected within those frameworks in the context of theory and practice, that is, of understanding *and* making. As Heidegger (1968) eloquently points out, "thinking itself is man's simplest, and for that reason hardest, handiwork, if it would be accomplished at its proper time" (p. 16). Such a perspective, as well, allows us to balance the interests of instructors and learners by acknowledging the constructive nature of the technologies that we use to mediate and evaluate their mutual efforts and outcomes. Edelson (2002) posits that, although empirical and design research employ different forms of support, their arguments are aimed at accomplishing the same ends:

Traditional empirical methods gain their strength from statistical sampling. . . . The strength of theories developed through design research comes from their explanatory power and their grounding in specific experiences. . . . A design research theory is compelling to the extent that it is internally consistent and that it accounts for the issues raised during the design and evaluation process.

    Finally, . . . design research is not, in fact, incompatible with traditional outcome-based evaluations. If the nature of any theory is such that a minimum level of certainty is required before it should be applied, then the theory should be evaluated empirically before it is applied, whether the theory was developed through design research or otherwise. (p. 118)

Design and empirical research, therefore, need not be treated as though they are mutually exclusive enterprises if we adopt a rhetorical design perspective toward inquiry and knowledge making that emphasizes the construction of good reasons or arguments for specific decision-making situations. So, although Edelson (2002) is correct in asserting that designers can benefit from employing empirical methods in their design processes, Buchanan (1995) and especially Cross (1995) are also right to hold that the indeterminacy of all design situations distinguishes design from empirical research: "design problems . . . are not the sort of problems or puzzles that provide all the necessary and sufficient information for their solution. Some of the relevant information can be found only by generating and testing solutions; some information, or 'missing ingredient,' has to be provided by the designer" (Cross 1995, p. 108). Complex research problems, in general, require continuous testing and revision, and a rhetorical design perspective therefore is particularly useful for its emphasis on trail and error between individuals and their environment as part of the inquiry process.

So, when we consider the challenge of "preparing workers with skills for the twenty-first century," we are actually addressing aspects of the design process that are too often already established for traditional learners, namely, problem finding, problem setting, and communicating the results. Perkins (1993) notes that, unfortunately,

Conventional education does virtually all problem selecting for students, deciding which problems are worth doing and, often, in what order. Then the assignments stop. And we are puzzled when students do not see opportunities in everyday life to apply what they have learned. Such a mishap is commonly called "lack of transfer." But this is something of a mis-diagnosis, because it fails to recognize that the students have never had a chance to learn the process we are hoping they will transfer—problem selection. The surprising thing is not that learners commonly miss "real-life" applications, but that from time to time students find some. (p. 113)

Problem setting requires a sophisticated understanding of the audience or audiences experiencing the problem and conceptualizing its solution, the frequency and severity of challenges presented by the problem, the demands posed and the complexity involved in solving it, and the characteristics of the environment and artifacts that make up the setting of the problem space. In all such situations, problem recognition must be followed at the most general level by the creative identification of potential courses of action and approaches for evaluating the success of those alternatives. Designers employ numerous strategies for generating alternative interpretations, including selection, comparison, explanation, organization, annotation, representation, elaboration, and categorization. And, finally, communicating one's results—or constructing one's argument(s)—is far more complex than traditional grammatical, formatting, and tool-centered treatments (e.g., the proverbial equivalent of "write up the report") would suggest. Argumentation involves not only elements of production such as choosing, evaluating, and creating, but also social exigency such as commitment, composition, coordination, and expression. Research that further elaborates on these twenty-first-century skills will inevitably arise when we carefully examine the tasks and activities that we set for contemporary learners.

5.3   Usable Instruction

A usability perspective toward instruction and learning with technology would surely emphasize how technology supports or impedes learner tasks (i.e., interaction) with instructional materials and artifacts, whereas a rhetorical perspective would maintain that the relationship between a rhetor and audience (i.e., the instructor and the learner) ought to be the foundation on which all other instructional issues rest. Instruction and learning with technology requires both orientations.

Indeed, contemporary problem settings demand both perspectives. Jost (2003) argues dramatically that "any intelligent use of rhetoric to define a problem . . . means *re*thinking for our own times the commonplaces that past thinkers invented and made use of: imagination and reason, fact and value, means and ends, particular and general laws, universal truths and contingent probabilities, arts and sciences, theory and practice, and more. This rethinking comes back in spades if we redefine education (or business) itself 'as' a habit of rhetorical rethinking, that is *as* training in *practical* arts of inquiry, argument, interpretation, and judgement in concrete but historically indeterminate subject matters" (p. 16). And, as Hauser (2004) reminds us, "Rhetoric is a practical discipline; it has a strong tradition that merges theory and *praxis* in the concrete conditions of performance, especially as these are realized in democratic societies" (p. 42).

Everyday technologies imbue instructional situations, demanding the rights and privileges of sophisticated rhetors. In this respect, if we hold that any technology is *theory in practice* (or artifact as theory; cf. Carroll and Kellogg 1989), we might begin to view technologies as exhibiting particular characteristics and therefore as rhetorical in their own right. Maintaining this rhetorical perspective, easy descriptions of instructor-as-input, learner-as-input, technology-as-input, and learning-as-output become difficult to maintain. If our learning environments and artifacts require us to *re*think their particular and general laws of behavior, our interactions with space become highly contingent and personal. Instructional artifact becomes instructional argument, and artifacts only serve to support or impede the rigor, multidimensionality, and richness of the ensuing dialectic.

Usability research and evaluation locates its beginnings in early research on human-information processing theory (Newell and Simon 1972; Simon 1969, 1981; 1979) and human–computer interaction (Card, Moran, and Newell 1983; John 2005). Understanding humans as technology users necessitates an understanding of humans as audience, where audience is understood in the postmodern sense as actively engaged information producers and consumers, or "pro-sumers" and "co-producers" (Lyotard 1979, 1984; Mattelart 2000; Ryan 1994). In the early 1990s, issues of usability were brought to the forefront by advances in human–computer interaction, including direct-manipulation interfaces and affordable home computing that finally highlighted application-based rather than operating system–driven computing. Almost overnight, a conceptual explosion in studies that emphasized usability testing and evaluation appeared on the research landscape (e.g., Adler and Winograd 1992; Bias and Mayhew 1994; Dillon 1994; Duffy, Palmer, and Mehlenbacher 1993; Duin 1993; Dumas and Redish 1993; Hackos and Redish 1998; Lee 1999; Lindgaard 1994; Mayhew 1999; Mehlenbacher 1993; Nielsen 1994, 1997, 1999; Nielsen and Mack 1994; Rubin 1994; Schell 1986; Skelton 1992; Trenner and Bawa 1998).

At the most general level, usability involves the application of social science research and theories of computer and information technology to the challenge of designing artifacts that are useful to and usable by humans. With the goal of improving the design of artifacts, researchers and practitioners collect data via interviews (Brenner, Brown, and Canter 1985; Brown and Canter 1985; Dumas 2001a), surveys (Babbie 1973, 1975), talk-aloud protocols (Bainbridge 1999; Cooper and Holzman 1983; Ericsson and Simon 1984), videotape analysis (Ball and Smith 1992; Kendon 1990), and so on.[1]

Assuming that technology plays a critical role in all our interactions, that is, taking a view of technology as mirror rather than as tool, it becomes apparent that new approaches to research and practice on instruction and learning with technology are required. Contemporary rhetorical theory and design studies offer one way of framing our emerging instructional situations. A rhetorical design perspective allows us to view educational reforms related to instruction and learning with technology as construction and argumentation. Making instructional arguments, by its very nature, requires taking a position of humility rather than inhabiting the traditional stance of facilitator (i.e., guiding others toward the truth) or, worse, of lecturer (i.e., transmitting or translating the truth).

Buchanan (1992), in his "Wicked problems in design thinking," advocates just such a comprehensive "study of the traditional arts and sciences toward a new engagement with the problems of everyday experience, evident in the development of diverse new products which incorporate knowledge from many fields of specialized [design] inquiry." He outlines "four broad areas in which design is explored," and these areas, interestingly, can all be applied to the design of everyday instructional situations:

1. the design of *symbolic and visual communications* (e.g., graphic design, book production, scientific visualization, communication of information, ideas, and arguments through photography, film, television, and computers);

2. the design of *material objects* (e.g., the form and appearance of everyday products and the relationship of those products and human beings);

3. The design of *activities and organized services* (e.g., how physical resources, instruments, and humans interact in strategic and meaningful ways); and

4. The design of *complex systems or environments for living, working, playing, and learning* (e.g., traditionally, systems engineering, architecture, and urban planning and, more recently, how humans interact with their environments in balanced and functional ways) (pp. 9–10).

These four broad areas center around the audience, user, reader, learner, or—to employ a frequently used twenty-first-century label—the information "consumer." Thus, Bransford et al. (2004), influenced by Wiggins and McTighe (1997), recommend that instructors focus on their ideals in terms of learner understanding (i.e., background and knowledge) and, therefore, consider "the idea of 'working backwards' by beginning with a clear articulation of goals for student learning and then deciding how various teaching strategies might help us achieve these goals" (Bransford et al. 2004, p. 231). But Carroll (1990) complicates this recommendation by reminding us of the inherent and strained relationship between the instruction that we design and what adults actually *do* (i.e., their tasks and activities) when they learn to use computers:

It is surprising how poorly the elegant scheme of systems-style instructional design actually works. . . . Everything is laid out for the learner. All that needs to be done is to follow the steps, one, two, three. But, as it turns out, this is both too much and too little to ask of people. The problem is not that people cannot follow simple steps; it is that they do not. People are thrown into action; they can only understand through the effectiveness of their actions in the world. People are situated in a world more real to them than a series of steps, a world that provides rich context and convention for everything they do. People are always already trying things out, thinking things through, trying to relate what they already know to what is going on, recovering from errors. In a word, *they are already too busy learning to make much use of the instruction.* (p. 74; emphasis mine)

As our ability to design rich and complex learning environments grows, the challenge of capturing learner attention in strategic ways and of generating instructional materials and artifacts (i.e., communications, objects, and activities) increases as well. Instruction and learning with technology, then, are as much artistry as they are engineering. And this creative balance makes it difficult to work backward toward the learner, since such an approach presumes a determinate end point to begin from. Rhetorical perspectives on design and sociocultural perspectives on instructional design call into question our certainty about learners, their learning needs, and their contexts (Grabinger 2004). Human problem solvers, instead, interact intensely with the feedback(s) that they get from their environment, testing and revising on the fly,

adapting their plans according to the opportunities and constraints of the ill-structured problems they are trying to solve, and setting iterative goals for themselves along
the way (Suchman 1987).

Instructional "design," then, is the act of combining the elements of content and
display to effectively present instructional content in a way that promotes learning
through organized instructional resources and user interfaces that are not confusing,
dissatisfying, or cognitively taxing. Indeed, the benefit of taking a rhetorical design
perspective toward instruction and learning with technology is that it can help us
achieve three goals: understanding theory and practice regarding instruction and
learning with technology, building usable learning environments that facilitate the
various dimensions of everyday instructional situations, and encouraging an interdisciplinary, multimethodological approach to studying, designing, and evaluating
instructional situations and learning events. As Naidu (2003) writes, "A big advantage
of setting a design task as the basis for the study of the subject matter . . . is the variety
of cognitive tasks required to move from a conceptual idea to a product. These include
*information gathering, problem identification, constraint setting, idea generation, modeling
and prototyping,* and *evaluating*" (p. 360). Notably, these activities anticipate the very
abilities that we hope to inculcate in our learners; and so, naturally, deriving our
instructional tasks and activities from the research questions and problems that inspire
us has potential.

5.3.1 Triangulating Individuals, Activities, and Artifacts

The "interface" and the context for communication between the instructor and the
learner has always mediated the instructional message or dialectic exchange. Pure
Socratic models of instruction are an ideal, beginning with instructional interactions
mediated by orality, through visual and textual symbolic exchange (literacy), and
culminating in the technological facilitations of the last fifty years (Ong 1982). As has
been established, educational researchers often mistakenly interpret technology as an
additional element beyond the pristine instructor–learner transmissional relationship,
erroneously implying that technological mediation confounds human-to-human
interaction (Clark 1983) or that it merely represents "clever technical achievements"
(cf. Fetherston 2001). This argument results in an odd compulsion to decouple the
study of instruction and learning from the technical contexts in which it occurs or,
worse, to study instruction and learning in traditional contexts, without acknowledging that these contexts are as artificial as the human-made farms that Simon (1969,
1981) has described.

Inversely, educational researchers assume that instructor–learner–computer interaction is "better" because there are more ways for communication to occur (via sound,
graphics, animation, and so on), an odd spin on the erroneous empirical notion that

having more data improves our ability to understand our objects of inquiry. This argument has led researchers to treat instruction and learning with technology as though it is something entirely new and without precedent. Thus Serdiukov (2001) concludes that this three-way communication event is "more advantageous as it expands the opportunities for learning by allowing interaction between all three components of the model whether face-to-face or at a distance through the Internet: Student-Teacher, Student-Computer and Teacher-Computer" (p. 21). Importantly, as Hannafin and Kim (2003) warn, not only does this naive attitude about the importance of interface design in the learning process produce poor learning interfaces, but as well, "Ironically, researchers make similar basic design decisions—pacing, control, font, color—but we often fail to recognize their influence on our research findings" (pp. 349–350).

Any interface between instructor-as-rhetor and learner-as-audience will invite breakdowns that Winograd and Flores (1986) define as "situation[s] of non-obviousness, in which the recognition that something is missing leads to unconcealing (generating through our declarations) some aspect of the network of tools that we are engaged in using" (p. 165). Transparency is undermined the moment a breakdown occurs, and, the less familiar instructors and learners are with the interface(s) used to mediate their instructional experience and the audiences for whom the instruction is designed, the more likely it is that breakdowns will occur, given the wickedness of design activities in general.

Few usability researchers, however, have paid tribute to the rhetorically grounded, audience-oriented perspective that they embrace. This is particularly unfortunate given the powerful insights that can be gained by explicitly connecting designer-user with task, artifact, and context. Audience as construct has received considerable theoretical treatment from classical and contemporary rhetoricians (Aristotle 1926; Bitzer 1968; Cicero 1949, 1970; Miller 1985; Toulmin 1958). Here, of course, we not defining rhetoric as the study of mere style, eloquence, or "languaging" as one colleague pejoratively summarized it. This perspective is a by-product of the marginal position that rhetoric holds in the contemporary arts and sciences, which Petraglia (2003) argues began with "Peter Ramus [circa 1543] whom we discredit with shaving off and giving to other disciplines all the really interesting bits of rhetoric and leaving the reduced study with the crumbs of eloquence" (p. 157). Given the popular conception of rhetoric as "the crumbs of eloquence," and more often as crumbs that cannot be trusted to reflect the true nature of the original dish, it is not surprising that Simons (1989) has lamented, "When 'rhetoric' is used in reference to scientists, textbook writers, reporters, and the like, it is frequently a term of derision, a way of suggesting that they have violated the principles held high in their professions" (p. 3). Petraglia (2003) notes, to counterbalance this popular misconception of rhetoric, that "Throughout most of the Western experience, it was commonly assumed that early training in rhetoric laid

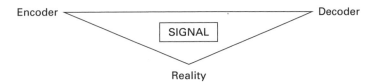

Figure 5.1
Kinneavy's (1971, p. 61) communication triangle.

the necessary groundwork for further disciplinary education and imbued knowledge with a sense of occasion and appropriateness" (p. 157).

It is from this groundwork, though, that we can begin to elaborate on the major dimensions of a rhetorical design perspective for everyday instructional situations. Thus, for effective communication to occur, the speaker or author must adopt the presentation and treatment of the message to those who will hear or read it. Not surprisingly, the principle of audience orientation and the goal of applying it to concrete information design situations is a complex proposition. We begin with Kinneavy (1971), who represents all communication events as a triangle (see figure 5.1).

Kinneavy's (1971) communication triangle is notably grounded in transmissional terminology (of encoders and decoders) and is instructional in that it highlights the relationship between individuals and context and between messages and community. The Encoder, or orator, framed by reality or a context for communicating, generates a message that, in turn, is understood and interpreted by a Decoder, or audience, in context. Bahri and Petraglia (2003) explicitly connect cognitive science with rhetorical theory, defining "rhetorical intelligence" as "the cognitive abilities required for inquiry, and interpretation with a view to pursuing argument and change" (p. 4). Booth's (2003) definition of rhetoric extends this perspective toward rhetoric to emphasize community: "Rhetoric is the art of discovering warrantable beliefs and improving on those beliefs in shared discourse—the art of appraising and pursuing *reasons* for changing beliefs and practices" (p. vii). Ultimately, this preliminary transmissional triangle enjoys considerable elaboration in recent research on activity-centered design (Engeström 1999; Gay and Hembrooke 2004), work-centered design (Ehn 1988; Hart-Davidson, Spinuzzi, and Zachry 2006; Moran, Cozzi, and Farrell 2005; Suchman 1983), and ecologically centered design (Barab and Roth 2006; Kaptelinin, Nardi, and Macaulay 1999; Nardi and O'Day 1999; Spinuzzi 2002), where an activity consists of motivation driving the activity, goals for completion, actions, intentional goals, and routine actions. Thus, work, applications, and artifacts are evaluated by how they support a range of human activities (Bødker 1991).

These lines of thinking have influenced the development of what Cole and Engeström (1993) call their "basic mediational triangle." Their triangle places medium

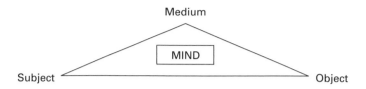

Figure 5.2
Cole and Engeström's (1993, p. 5) mediational triangle.

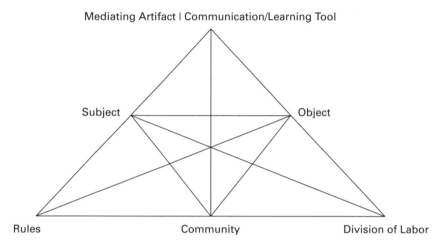

Figure 5.3
Application of Engeström's (1999) activity analysis and Cole and Engeström's (1993, p. 8) mediational triangle extended to communication and learning (adapted from Gay and Hembrooke 2004, p. 5).

or artifact at the top and subject (rhetor-designer), object (audience-user) at the bottom, and "mind" in the center (see figure 5.2).

Gay and Hembrooke (2004) elaborate on Cole and Engeström's (1993) basic mediational triangle, producing a configuration that highlights the role of factors beyond a rhetor and an audience. Activity theory, here, is connected to human–computer interaction to represent "dynamic change, tool mediation, and social construction of meaning" in action (see figure 5.3).

In Gay and Hembrooke's (2004) triangle, we can see the advantages of viewing design situations as comprising designers, users (i.e., communities), tasks and activities, and artifacts and environments. The dimensions that make up this approach, in turn, have implications for our general efforts to develop workable frameworks for everyday instructional situations. As well as being reminiscent of Kinneavy's (1971) theory of communication, Gay and Hembrooke's (2004) addition of a third-tier set of influences that are focused primarily on the social dynamics of a given community process elevates design beyond the individual level (cf. Preece 2001). That is, one vivid advantage of viewing human design processes at the activity level is that one's perspective must shift from individuals and trial and error at the single-task level and expand to emphasize inherently social issues such as conflicts, disagreements, "interactions, ambiguities, and complexities" (Gay and Hembrooke 2004, p. 16) among individuals and activities. This reorientation, in turn, allows for a view of design that includes construction, argumentation, and ongoing evaluation:

A period of search and questioning begins as new models and metaphors are considered and new solutions and designs are developed. After the initial series of trials and testing of designs in actual settings, new priorities and approaches emerge, followed by periods of reconceptualization, revision, and redesign. Ultimately, the entire cycle is repeated until some resolution, new stability, or closure is achieved. (Gay and Hembrooke 2004, p. 11)

Thus, designers build interfaces (complex, multilayered networks of signals) within given contexts of use that are understood and interacted with by user communities. Importantly, the interfaces are no longer constrained by platform, space, or time, often inhabiting the "anywhere and anytime" global communication construct reserved for everything "24/7." The design of instruction, thus, is distributed geographically and temporally and becomes a placeless act of rearticulation, imitation, remediation, and pseudo-replication. In the case of instruction and learning with technology, instructors design instructional lessons that are (presumably) understood and responded to by learners in given instructional contexts. Rhetorically sensitive instructional designers, in Fleming's (2003) view, would require an understanding of five interrelated issues:

1. *Circumstantial knowledge*: . . . an understanding of the people, places, events and history of the situation;
2. *Verbal formulae*: recurring linguistic patterns that make up the discursive repertoire of a particular community and particular discursive situations;
3. *Common sense*: that collection of truths, presumptions, values, and preferences that is operative in a community;
4. *Models of textual development*: conceptual patterns and structures that organize everyday argumentative thinking in a community; and
5. *Logical norms*: deep-seated logical knowledge, general warrants, rules of inference, and other "universal" principles that authorize arguments. (Fleming 2003, pp. 105–106; cf. Bazerman 1988)

This perspective is echoed by Spinuzzi (2006) when he highlights rhetoric as central to the effective preparation of future knowledge workers:

Knowledge workers need to become strong rhetors. Rhetoric, which is too often glossed as "lying," is the study of argumentation and persuasion . . .—and net workers sorely need to understand how to make arguments, how to persuade, how to build trust and stable alliances, how to negotiate and bargain across boundaries. Rhetoric was deployed in modular work, but in more limited ways due to the silos and compartmentalization that characterized that form of work organization. . . . In knowledge work, which is intricately and unpredictably connected, with everyone on the border, workers need to find themselves doing this rhetorical work with nearly everyone.

Central to the *business* of formal instruction is a rhetorical design perspective where learners come to understand ways of knowing (inquiring, analyzing, interpreting, synthesizing, etc.) and articulating through shared discourse sophisticated arguments within particularized disciplines of knowledge. Such a perspective toward instruction is no less fundamental than arguments in favor of design over empirical approaches, invention over discovery, or sociocultural over behavioral emphases.

Analogous conversations have played out in various disciplines—for example, in linguistics, where the debate has been over syntactic versus semantic interpretations of language (Evans 2004; Tomasello 1995), in computer science, where the debate has been over information-processing versus language-action and semiotic perspectives (Vera and Simon 1993; Winograd and Flores 1986), in graphic design, where the debate has been over grammatical versus rhetorical analyses of images and words (Buchanan 1992; Buchanan and Margolin 1995), and in psychology and cognitive science, where the debate has been over cognitive versus social models of learning (Anderson et al. 2000; Fahnestock 2005). In all of these debates, it is reductivist to conclude that semantic, language-rich, social models have won out; but it is realistic to say that models that account for the historically competing interests between particularization and generalization, arts and sciences, and current-traditional and rhetorical perspectives seem a desirable multidisciplinary theoretical goal.

Berlin's (1987) description of the evolution of twentieth-century approaches to rhetoric (from objective to subjective to transactional) anticipates the roots of some of the educational misconceptions about the relationship between instruction, learning, and technology. An objective position toward instructional technology would hold that technology (or language, for that matter) operates as a "sign system, a simple transcribing device for recording" observable realities in the world (p. 7). Subjective positions toward instructional technology ground "truth either within the individual or within a realm that is accessible only through the individual's internal apprehension" (p. 11); hence the popularity of "learner-centered" and constructivist articulations of the missions of online instruction. And, finally, a "transactional rhetoric" of instructional technology, in Berlin's (1987) framework, "is based on an epistemology that sees truth as arising out of the interaction of the elements of the rhetorical situation: an interaction of . . . subject, object, audience, and language" (p. 15). Instructors, instructional content, interaction and communication, learners, and technologies thus intermingle to *produce* learning situations—learning situations cannot be situated on top of technologies any more than knowledge making can be separated from language use (Brown 2002a). Kinneavy's (1971) characterization of communication is thus problematic given its easy separation of rhetor from audience from situational reality, as though any of these situational elements ever operates without shaping the others.

So, the roles that technologies play in terms of instruction and learning and human behavior and action, in general, ought to be topics of considerable interest to researchers in usability and human–computer interaction. A contemporary extension of the rhetorical design perspective with an emphasis on interfaces between humans and technologies, usability research attempts to balance both theory and practice, is grounded by the mantra that effective communication/design requires having a sophisticated understanding of one's user (i.e., audience), and appreciates both the cognitive and social dimensions of human action, community, and learning.

The audience-oriented (interface/instructional) designer's essential tension is between studying general design guidelines or knowledge of specifics (e.g., Inaba, Parsons, and Smillie 2004) and principles or knowledge of universals derived from the research (Marshall, Nelson, and Gardiner 1987; Smith and Mosier 1984) and in applying them to real design problems. The source of the tension between "general advice" (facts) and "specific design problems" (values) lies with the design process itself: design is at its core both *constructive* and *argumentative*. Design is a *constructive* task in as much as it ultimately demands synthesis in an act of producing a technology; design is *argumentative* in that the designer must be able to justify design decisions, assess critically the trade-offs in alternative designs, and, in general, discuss design problems with others or persuade them to adopt particular solutions. As well, design is learning in that it almost always involves negotiation with impasses, errors, and imperfection (Petroski 1982, 2003). As Winograd (2006) summarizes:

On the one hand, the designer works with available materials . . . to create artifacts with desired behavior and appropriate use of resources. On the other hand, the designer takes the perspective of the people who live with and alongside the system, with primary concern for their action and experience. This balancing act is vital to all kinds of design, from architecture and urban design to the design of consumer devices. (p. 71)

In this respect, designers differ markedly from traditional research academicians, in purpose and in epistemological orientation. Czubaroff (1997) summarizes the academician's dilemma when she writes:

Few academicians today are willing to dispense with the distinction between "facts," conceived as empirically and intersubjectively verifiable statements about "what is," and "values," conceived as end states, principles, qualities, or items of experience which are regarded as desirable or undesirable by human beings. Nonetheless, the recognition that statements of fact may be intersubjectively verified as empirically true or false only within specific conceptual frameworks which themselves cannot be verified as true or false, and the recognition that these conceptual frameworks are themselves theoretical constructs created and motivated by human purposes and values, have [led] numbers of scholars to conclude that the fact–value distinction is not a strict dichotomy and that the idea of truth is not strictly commensurate with the idea of factuality. (p. 70)

A rhetorical design perspective allows researchers to connect our goals of better understanding instruction in context, to elaborate on learning in both formal and informal settings, and to describe face-to-face and artificial learning environments that interact with instructors and learners to produce interesting instructional outcomes. Moreover, a rhetorical design perspective encourages a multimethodological perspective, organized as we are around the goal of designing learning environments that are highly engaging and that elevate instructor-learner knowledge making and application. This, in turn, makes it particularly important that we draw on research that has as one of its central objects of inquiry the technologies that mediate our interactions with other learners.

Thus we turn our focus to the usability of designs and to human–computer interaction, which—surprisingly—are relatively new developments, at least in the computer science research literature. Adler and Winograd (1992) aptly label the challenge of understanding humans, learning, and the technologies that we create as "the Usability Challenge," arguing that we need to commit ourselves to "a foundational shift in our thinking and practice." This foundational shift places

a premium on designing for learning—learning at three levels. First we need to design equipment that supports the kind of learning in which users come to understand how and why the system works as it does. Second, the equipment needs to be designed to support the kind of learning in which users discover how to adapt and extend the technology to satisfy the demands and contingencies of their work better. And finally, we need to create a design process that allows us to learn how better to tackle these daunting usability challenges. (p. 13)

Despite this challenge to designers and researchers, a 1996 Association for Computing Machinery 50th Anniversary Symposium summarizing perspectives in computer science contained eight articles devoted to human–computer interaction out of a total of sixty-eight across ten general research areas, including for example, architecture, operating systems and networks, and programming languages (Tucker and Wegner 1996). Usability and human–computer interaction research are still very much novel areas for inquiry in the computer science world; depending on whom you ask and what source you consult, both have histories of almost three decades (using Card, Moran, and Newell 1983, as a seminal starting-point). Ergonomics or the study of industrial products and processes, proper, finds its beginnings following World War II. Early academic studies of the subject published in journals such as *Applied Ergonomics* (1969–present) and *Ergonomics* (1957–present) and proceedings papers published in the Human Factors and Ergonomics Society conferences (1972–present) emphasized topics such as economic production cycles; nuclear power plant and aircraft cockpit design and testing; panel layouts and automation processes; workspace design; human posture, stress, and limitations; the aeronautics space industry; and so on.

As well, the limited historical attention to usability issues can be tied to the dominance of waterfall methods that pervade the computer science, programming, and design communities (Royce 1970). This method privileges pseudo-scientific approaches to design that are linear and highlight planning, development, and implementation at the expense of "evaluation," which always falls at the end of the development cycle. Hackbarth (1997) thus describes the design process as a series of steps, with designers "diagnosing" the users in terms of what they need to know and assessing what they already know, through design, procurement, production, and refinement, or summative evaluation and revision. Hackbarth (1997) also admits that his characterization of the process of creating WBI "has a linear structure, later steps surely inform earlier ones" and that "at any point we may have to 'take a few steps back' to revise our assessments, tests, procedures, materials, and yes, even our objectives" (p. 194).

Kalous (2005), in a recent review of a variation of rapid prototyping or extreme programming, describes REDD (Rapid E-Learning Development and Deployment) as a method that is designed to streamline the development of online learning environments. The method, an abbreviated version of the dominant instructional design approach, ADDIE (Analysis, Design, Development, Implementation, and Evaluation), involves selecting a team, managing outside relations (approvals and deadlines, communication processes), gathering and approving content, and the predictable final action of evaluation. To this end, evaluation is described by Kalous (2005) almost as an afterthought: "Now that the project is completed, it's ready to be tested. The ideal pilot group is a mixture of intended participants and SMEs (for quality assurance purposes)" (p. 28). Indeed, Wiens and Gunter (1998) describe the three stages of WBI as design, development, and delivery (pp. 95–96), leaving evaluation out of the process altogether.

Such atheoretical conceptions of design have led some critics, such as as Laurillard (2002), to call for the realignment of research and teaching and for teaching methods that support students in the generic skills of scholarship, not mere acquisition of knowledge" (p. 22). Laurillard (2002) believes that this realignment can be augmented by technology with the development of "a collective R&D program that builds design tools, or Generic Learning Activity Models (GLAMs), for supporting students in learning the skills of scholarship" (p. 25). Similarly, Achtenhagen (2003) describes an approach to knowledge acquisition that stresses action, introducing the concepts of *Lernhandeln* (roughly, "learn-acting" in German) and *Handlungsorientierung* ("action orientation"). A focus on *Lernhandeln* and *Handlungsorientierung* emphasizes the following:

• Action orientation includes acting and thinking.

• It does not mean unreflected assimilation to use specified tasks in school or at the workplace; critical thinking is basic.

• The individual shall be able to generate adequate actions in carrying out specified tasks. This includes an internal modeling of situations and the given system and the ability to change a situation step by step; the ability to master routine tasks, but also new tasks, by developing mental representations of modes of problem solving.

• Action orientation should improve the quality of learn-acting by providing content-related but also social-communicative experience and experiences with one's own behavior, including meta-cognitive activities. (Achtenhagen 2003, p. 141)

Although Weber (2003) criticizes the "materialist" underpinnings of the *Lernhandeln* approach (*Handlungsorientierung* actually derives from *ökonomische Handlungskompetenz* or "occupational competencies"), she also stresses some of the additional strengths of the *Lernhandeln* orientation, including its focus on complex issues and problems, on relevancy, and on the interaction between situated learning and the generation of "codified knowledge, theories and heuristics, algorithms and techniques" (pp. 161–162).

It is clear that the wicked problems that this generation of learners-designers face demand innovative strategies for approaching them. Importantly, these designs for learning merge theory and practice and focus on data generalization and model building versus data use and system refinement. Sensitive to Spinuzzi's (2003) distinction between method and methodology, our problem solvers understand that "A *method* is a way of investigating phenomena," whereas "a *methodology* is the theory, philosophy, heuristics, aims, and values that underlie, motivate, and guide the method" (p. 7). Strategies for approaching problems effectively require that we understand the subtle assumptions that influence and constrain our investigations. Kincheloe and Tobin (2006) summarize it simply:

In this complex context we understand that even when we use diverse methods to produce multiple perspectives on the world, different observers will produce different interpretations of what they perceive. Given different values, different ideologies, and different positions in the web of reality, different individuals will interpret what is happening differently. We never stand alone in the world, especially when we produce knowledge. We are connected and constantly affected by such connections in every step of the research act. Understanding these aspects of the connections between the knower and the known modifies the very way we approach knowledge, research design, research method, and interpretation. (p. 7)

These strategies can also inform, as Nerur and Balijepally (2007) propose, part of a new way of thinking about design that is open ended, exploratory, and constructive. Nerur and Balijepally (2007) distinguish between traditional views of design and what they call an "emergent metaphor of design," noting that these orientations differ in process, goals, problem-solving strategies, learning approaches, and theoretical or philosophical roots. Traditional views of design tend to be formal and procedural, and tend to distinguish formulation from actual design processes and aim at optimization rather than artifacts that are adaptive, responsive, and flexible. Moreover, traditional views of design are organized around means–ends analyses of design problems, thus requiring a fixed view of the environment in question and assuming control and predictability. The philosophical roots of traditional design views tend to be based on the scientific method and are therefore somewhat positivist, in contrast to emergent metaphors of design which are influenced by pragmatism, action learning theory, and phenomenology. Emergent metaphors of design, thus, are generative, exploratory, interactive, collaborative, opportunistic, and dialectic in nature (p. 82).

During the last two decades, usability researchers and practitioners have applied their methods not only to hardware but also to productivity software, direct-manipulation interfaces, secondary support systems, documentation, and most recently to online learning environments. This extension of objects of inquiry in usability research is congruent with Dumas's (2003) argument that usability testing can be performed at various stages of almost any designed product—with all software, hardware, audience types, for cooperative use, in various stages of design, and for all secondary support materials delivered with the primary product (p. 1099). Although Rappin et al. (1997) have observed that "The requirements of interfaces designed to support learning are different than for interfaces designed to support performance" (p. 485), it is unclear how and in what ways what we know about usable interfaces does not apply generally to performance applications as well as learning environments.

The most natural and least troubling extension of usability evaluation to instruction and learning with technology is to design and test online learning environments for how closely they follow Rubin's (1994) process for conducting usability testing (e.g., Veldof 2003) or for how successfully or poorly they address Nielsen's (1994) heuristics for usable design (e.g., Downey et al. 2005). After all, at the most basic level, learners working in an artificial learning environment can be described as users who have a set of tasks (i.e., what did you *do* . . .?) that they want to accomplish within the environment (or class) using a given set of applications (via an interface). Arguments over whether the online learning environment is stand-alone, tutorial-based, secondary support, or Web-based do not negate the general issues being addressed. As Smith, Newman, and Parks (1997) remind us, "It is obviously possible to assert that the Web is so different from anything that has ever gone before that all previous usability research is irrelevant. However, on the face of it, the Web can be regarded as predominantly hypertext, and, over the last decade, much effort has been expended on hypertext usability research" (p. 68).

It is in this spirit that detachment from the particularized features of online learning environments seems prudent. Focusing instead on the characteristics-in-use of online learning environments and interfaces reveals that researchers have begun to develop a series of interrelated principles for design that we can put into practice. The most frequently cited list of interface attributes is Nielsen's (1994) ten heuristics for usable design, which he generalized from usability evaluations of eleven applications and approximately 250 usability problems. Numerous researchers have discussed in detail the various parameters that need to come together to produce what we experience as a usable, well-designed interface (see table 5.1).

But educational researchers have only begun to explore the usefulness of usability in general (Flowers 2005) and in the design and evaluation of educational technology (Buzhardt and Heitzman-Powell 2005). While some researchers have applied these heuristics directly to the testing of educational technology in general (Lee 1999) and online learning environments specifically (Benson et al. 2002; Koohang and Weiss 2003; Wang and Yang 2005), others have argued for more synergistic collaborations between usability and online learning researchers (Squires and Preece 1999; Zaharias 2004a,b).

After all, the human–computer interaction foundations of usability research began with a focus on studies of learning, specifically on novice–expert studies of humans playing chess and solving complex mathematics and physics problems (Chi, Feltovich, and Glaser 1981; Simon, 1979). This shared interest in human tasks and on developing sophisticated methods for describing them (Jonassen, Hannum, and Tessmer 1989) promises to contribute to the development of theories of e-learning usability. A usable (artificial) learning environment, therefore, would be useful (it does what we want it to do), effective (it allows us to perform our tasks quickly and proficiently), learnable (it enables us to learn how to do our tasks), flexible (it has system integrity and tolerates our errors), and satisfying (it encourages us to continue using the interface).

Notably, Collins and Berge (1995) and Relan and Gillani (1997) do not highlight the technical artifacts that make up these online environments any more than we would expect social historians studying classroom instruction to focus on the furniture that makes up the typical instructional setting. It is important while considering the complex of interactions and developing affordances that comprise a typical online instructional environment, however, to note that a typical elementary school classroom is brimming with technologies and instruments, although the technologies are so familiar that we often fail to acknowledge their existence. A thing's affordance, according to Pea (1993), "refers to the perceived and actual properties of [the] thing, primarily those functional properties that determine just how the thing could possibly be used" (p. 51), and "the psychology of everyday things" (to use Norman's 1990 initial phrase) influences our interaction with all artifacts. Pea (1993) even goes so far as to argue that things "literally carry intelligence *in* them, in that they represent some individual's or some community's decision that the means thus offered should be reified, made stable, as a quasi-permanent form, for use by others" (p. 53). More accurately, things might be said to carry information in them—in the original sense of

Table 5.1

Comparison of research-based features of online learning environments and interfaces (adapted from Lee 1999; Mehlenbacher et al. 2005; Nielsen 1994; Quesenbery 2003; Tilson et al. 1998)

Research-Based Features of Online Learning Environments and Interfaces

Lee's (1999) multimedia	Mehlenbacher et al.'s (2005) WBI	Nielsen's (1994) software applications	Quesenbery's (2003) computer systems	Tilson et al.'s (1998) e-commerce
Learnability	Educational (in facilitating and promoting learning)	Match between system and real world Recognition rather than recall Help and documentation	Easy to learn (how well the product supports both initial orientation and deepening understanding of its capabilities)	Simplicity (do not compromise usability for function) Support (make assistance proactive) Obviousness (make objects and their controls intuitive)
Performance effectiveness	Economical (in terms of time and resources for learners, instructors, and tertiary users)	Visibility of system status User control and freedom Consistency and standards	Effective (completeness and accuracy with which users achieve their goals)	Encouragement (make actions predictable and reversible)
Flexibility	Efficient (in terms of resources, task support, and time)	Flexibility and efficiency of use	Efficient (speed and accuracy with which users can complete their goals)	Versatility/flexibility (support alternative interaction techniques)
Error tolerance and system integrity	Ergonomically effective (capacity for producing desired results)	Error prevention Help users recognize, diagnose, and recover from errors	Error tolerant (how well the design prevents errors, or helps with recovery from those that do occur)	Accessibility (make all objects accessible at all times)
User satisfaction	Equitable (equally usable by all learners)	User control and freedom Aesthetic and minimalist design	Engaging (degree to which the tone and style of the interface makes the product pleasant or satisfying to use)	Satisfaction/feedback (create feeling of progress and achievement) Personalization (allow users to customize)

"being informed"—and our intentions and interactions with them produce particular outcomes.

The expression "Technology is the stuff that doesn't work" is helpful in understanding the relationship between the artifacts that inhabit our world and our interactions with them, whether a familiar, comfortable, positive one or a strange, tense, or negative one. Intention and affect are what humans bring to the artifacts; and, although artifacts do not literally *not work*, it is true sometimes that we do not work well *with* them. Indeed, our strained relationship with technology is exemplified by the staggering $121 million in revenue that "For Dummies" books published by IDE generated in 2000 alone (Kreitzberg and Shneiderman 2001).

When our relationship with a technology becomes familiar, in the positive sense, we often focus our attention on other, less fluid relationships. To remember that an erasable marker is a technology, we need to remember the first time we worked with one, made complex by our familiarity with historical technologies such as chalk—we adjusted our writing manner, the weight we applied to our writing hand, how much we were able to brush against new writing with our hand before smudging or erasing prior notes, our writing pace, our expectations about the readability of text, and so on. Familiar technologies feel like utilities, similar to electricity. Few of us need to know much about the workings of electricity in order to benefit from it. However, the ever-present reality for designers is that, as Winograd and Flores (1986) remind us, "In creating new artifacts, equipment, buildings, and organizational structures, . . . breakdowns will show up in our everyday practices and in the tools we use" (p. 163).

So even the act of naming the technologies in a contemporary classroom can be a difficult one. My daughter, closing her eyes and remembering her classroom, lists the following items: "A projector, trash can, papers, pencils, student cubbies, gradebook, curriculum book, lesson plans, bookshelves, books, transparencies, chairs, a chalkboard, notebooks, computers, post-its, protractors, tables, toys, puzzles, posters, plants, art supplies, chalk, charts, art, room dividers, flipcharts, candy (for rewards), circle areas drawn on the floor, project areas, and lots of other stuff." Even without her teacher and the other students in the room, this is an environment rich with devices, teeming with educational and noneducational artifacts.

Moll, Tapia, and Whitmore (1993) describe such a list of artifacts as "culturally mediated systems of . . . living knowledge" (p. 159) that are deeply rooted in the history and sociocultural setting of classroom-based education. As Schank (2005) observes, "The equivalent of a fully equipped kitchen is sometimes very expensive to recreate" (p. 153). So too with technical representations of well-known classroom artifacts, except that these familiar artifacts allow us to internalize their operational characteristics and to focus almost entirely on the actions that they allow us to accomplish. Bonk and Dennen (2003) note, "Most e-learning tools available . . . provide templates and guidelines for warehousing students and providing static course material. However, assistance in developing rich situations for collaborative knowledge construction, information seeking and sharing, reflection, debate, and problem-based learning is generally overlooked in the design of standard courseware tools" (p. 332).

Although this chapter concludes with a state of design practice that is less than satisfactory, reviewing the enduring dichotomy between what is defined as science and what is defined as nonscience has revealed how this dichotomy has served as a powerful backdrop for current divisions between theory and practice. These divisions, in turn, have resulted in a situation that has made it difficult for members of two discourse communities to benefit fully from important work being carried out in each community. By highlighting similarities between the activities of theoreticians and practitioners, I have outlined a useful alternative that is responsive to wicked contemporary problems, a rhetorical design perspective that allows us to benefit from the considerable research on usability, human–computer interaction, and design studies.

In the next chapter, I examine the formal instructional situations that unfold every day in higher educational settings. The context for learning is pragmatically centered on the learning environment within which instructors and learners interact and perform the majority of their instructional activities, tasks, and learning. Drawing on the models discussed in the previous chapter, I further elaborate on a framework for everyday instructional situations that embraces instruction and learning events involving various degrees of technology involvement.

6 A Framework for Everyday Instructional Situations

Instruction and learning with technology can be characterized and contextualized by describing *all* learning or *everyday* instructional situations. Everyday instructional situations consist of five interdependent dimensions: learner background and knowledge, learner tasks and activities, social dynamics, instructor activities, and learning environment and artifacts.

In the last three or four years, I've moved from focusing on becoming a better learner to spending more time learning how to unlearn.
—John Seely Brown (2002b, p. 69)

What can we know? That is, what can we be sure we know, or sure that we know we knew it, if indeed it is at all knowable. Or have we simply forgotten it and are too embarrassed to say anything? . . . By "knowable," incidentally, I do not mean that which can be known by perception of the senses, or that which can be grasped by the mind, but more that which can be said to be Known to possess a Knownness or Knowability, or at least something you can mention to a friend.
—Woody Allen (1989, pp. 28–29)

Given the increased demands for strategic and flexible learning across the learning worlds that define us, and the necessary foregrounding of instruction and learning with technology in our everyday lives, we have outlined a rhetorical design perspective toward theory and application that embraces uncertainty, negotiation, construction, and argumentation. Theories, artifacts, and activities, from this perspective, *always* have a purpose and an audience and are therefore both expressive and pragmatic.

Within this context, we can forward a framework for everyday instructional situations, choosing the term "framework" deliberately, as preferable to both "model" and "theory." Although skepticism over the ambitiousness of the expression "everyday instructional situations" is perfectly reasonable, it too is an expression selected carefully from a range of possibilities. Finally, since in all matters of naming and categorization we inevitably address the nuances of terminological choice, it is useful also to introduce an additional expression, "terministic screens," into the discussion.

Burke (1966) defines terministic screens as "filters" that allow observers *different* views of the *same* objects. Burke (1966) uses examples of photographs of the same things using different color filters and descriptions of dreams when interpreted by a Freudian, Jungian, Adlerian, or practitioner of some other school (pp. 45–46), and states that "*many of the 'observations' are but implications of the particular terminology in terms of which the observations are made.* In brief, much that we take as observations about 'reality' may be but the spinning out of possibilities implicit in our particular choice of terms" (p. 46; emphasis his). Although Burke (1966) is quick to point out that his definition of terministic screens does not necessarily address the truth or falsity of what we report, he does note that particular terministic screens not only help us to select and sort reality according to the language we use but also force us "to track down the kinds of observation implicit in the terminology [we] have chosen, whether [our] choice of terms was deliberate or spontaneous" (p. 46). As Winograd (2006) confesses, "however valuable a theoretical perspective may be, it is never the whole story. A theory is by its nature a partial account of reality—a set of blinders through which some aspects of the world are highlighted and others become invisible" (p. 72).

When we elect to describe a framework for everyday instructional situations, then, we acknowledge, as Burke (1966) does, that "We *must* use terministic screens, since we can't say anything without the use of terms; whatever terms we use, they necessarily constitute a corresponding kind of screen; and any such screen necessarily directs the attention to one field rather than another. Within that field there can be different screens, each with its ways of directing attention and shaping the range of observations implicit in the given terminology" (p. 50). But we can also hold to his goal of avoiding "mere relativism" by assuming that any terminology used to describe reality has as its primary goal that "all members of our species conceive of reality somewhat roundabout, through various *media* of symbolism" (p. 52). The moral, then, is that we need to use our terms very carefully and to insist that others employ the same care, reflection, and precision in the choice of their descriptions of the objects of inquiry that they describe (cf. Bowker and Star 1999; Fenwick 2006).

The term "framework" is therefore preferable to "theory," since effective theories often incorporate procedural or predictive qualities, and it is premature to make such claims. A theory of everyday instructional situations would require a detailed description of how instructional situations are created, how they are interpreted by individuals, and how they are articulated between individuals. A framework, in the most literal sense, aims to describe the fundamental structure underlying a concept, technology, or system, and the system that is being described here is derived from an extensive review of the literatures informing instruction and learning with technology (see table

3.1). Second, similar to Dillon's (1994) distinction between a framework and a model, we can view a framework as consisting of the generic dimensions of the phenomenon and a model as being more specific and connected to particular instances. The structure that describes everyday instructional situations, however, can change in terms of the emphasis and importance placed on particular dimensions in different instructional situations. In self-directed, informal learning situations, for example, learners will rely less on direct instructional intervention and feedback, relying most likely on computer-based interactions or instructional materials designed for general audiences rather than specific ones; social dynamics will play a reduced role in self-directed interaction, and learner–content interaction will best characterize the situation.

In this respect, a useful goal is to outline at the roughest possible level the basic dimensions of instruction and learning with technologies. Dillon (1994) argues that any proposed framework must be accurate, relatively noncomplex, suitably generic, and modifiable in the light of feedback (p. 123). These are lofty objectives, and one of the reasons for carefully reviewing the various literatures related to instruction and learning with technology is to begin to categorize the numerous ways that researchers characterize the dynamics involved in general and technology-rich instructional situations. This effort, in turn, can enrich our developing framework as it applies to alternative theoretical and practical contexts. As Bonk and Dennen (2003) promise, "Frameworks . . . lead to more focused research agendas, enhanced tool and courseware designs, prominent course and program comparison benchmarks, well-planned instructor training programs, accessible pedagogical materials and reports, and better overall online teaching and learning environments. As courses and programs for online learning mount, there will be additional (and perhaps better) frameworks, perspectives, and models that can assist in improving Web-based teaching and learning" (p. 346).

The word "everyday" accounts for both formal and informal instructional situations. In contrast to Kalantzis and Cope (2004), who setup a dichotomy between everyday and educational learning, the goal here is to describe instructional situations as being both amorphous and deliberate, unorganized and efficient, and endogenous and exophoric (p. 39). "Everyday" reminds us that learning is commonplace (i.e., pervasive), that it has emotional, sensory-perceptual, cognitive, and social dimensions, that it has a repetitive quality, and that it is common or ordinary in the sense that every day requires or demands learning of us.[1] Importantly, all instructional situations require the existence of instruction, either provided directly by a human or from instructional materials such as text, graphics, examples, overheard discussions, demonstrations, feedback systems, multimedia, and so on. The benefit of human-to-human instruction is that learners are able to ask questions, seek elaborations, and tailor the instruction to fit their needs; the benefit of human-to-instructional materials is that learners are able to use the materials whenever they want, to read and review them as many times as necessary for understanding, and to return any time for reminders or to access additional instructional materials. Conceptual information is often best suited to human-to-human instructional situations (where informational give and take encourages elaboration and explanation), whereas procedural information is best suited to human-to-material instruction (where just-in-time access to particular types of information is able to occur close to the job at hand). It is also apparent that what is at one moment defined as informal learning at another can be enthusiastically appropriated for use in formal instructional situations as with the contemporary integration of gaming into formal instructional contexts (Dickey 2005; Squire 2006; Venkatesh and Speier 2000). For this reason, Solomon, Boud, and Rooney (2006) warn that "It seems that by naming everyday learning as informal learning, this kind of learning can only be understood in relation to what it is not, that is formal learning" (p. 12).

The term "instruction" is preferable to "teaching" because it reduces our tendency to presume the immediate involvement of a human instructor in situations where learning can or does occur. Learners use instructional materials, whereas it is more common to think of teaching materials as having instructors as their audience. As well, "instruction" does not evoke the infantilizing connotation of the word "teaching," both in the way instructors are characterized and in terms of the anticipated K–12 audiences that they frequently address. K–12 instruction and learning—and the numerous associated discussions, debates, policies, think-tank spokesgroups, national, regional, and local associations and advocates—at times appears to be an instructional "black box"; for this reason, our focus is limited to educational contexts involving "adults" that characterize most institutions of higher learning.

Gunawarden and McIsaac (2004) have stressed that researchers need to "Move beyond media comparison studies and reconceptualize media and instructional design variables in the distance learning environment" (p. 389). Researchers, they argue, should consider methodological approaches that both "Generate a substantive research base by longitudinal and collaborative studies" and "Identify and develop appropriate conceptual frameworks from related disciplines such as cognitive psychology, social learning theory, critical theory, communication theory and social science theories" (p. 389). Saba (2003) has noted as well that "If distance education theory is to be paradigmatic, it has to explain education when instructor and learner are under the same roof as well as when they are not" (p. 10).

In our summary of models of formal instructional situations, we saw that several features or dimensions of instructional situations received substantial, repeated consideration. Elsewhere I have argued that it is useful to generalize to all (or everyday) instructional situations before immediately turning to online learning environments (Mehlenbacher 2002). The models reviewed emphasized learners, instructors, instructional strategies, content, group interaction, learning outcomes, and institutional context. The model presented here collapses instructors with instructional strategies, views content as being shared by learners, instructors, and social dynamics, and sets learning outcomes and institutional contexts outside our focus of attention. See table 6.1 for an elaboration of the five dimensions—or "important parameters for defining various educational ecosystems" (Bransford et al. 2004)—of everyday instructional situations.

The five dimensions are informed by the research from the eight research clusters (table 3.1) and the summarized models of instruction and learning with technology (table 4.5) outlined earlier, as well as drawing heavily on cognitive science and information-processing perspectives toward learning on the one hand and rhetorical and design theory applied to technology on the other. A sweeping generalization might hold that the research related to distance learning and e-learning and to educational, instructional, and communication technology features numerous articles that focus on learner background and knowledge and learning environment and artifacts, that journals related to the teaching and learning sciences have tended to foreground learners and social dynamics, and that journals related to communication and information design emphasize instructor and learner tasks and activities. Articles related to instruction and learning with technology that emphasize each of the five dimensions of instructional situations, of course, can be found across clusters (see appendixes A–H).

Balancing the descriptions of Krendl and Warren's (2004) "merging" literatures and Álvarez and Kilbourn's (2002) "fragmented" ones, we can argue that the literatures relevant to learning and instruction with technology exhibit the equivalent of a high-speed ripple effect, partly due to the proliferation, reliance on, and ill-defined nature of online research journals and digital libraries (Ekman 2000; Friedlander 2002), and partly due to the complex of issues related to the inter- and extradisciplinary research area of instruction and learning with technology. Unfortunately, rather than being able to wait for the tides to recede in order to identify patterns, we find ourselves, midripple, attempting to understand and predict the patterns that result from the network of subparallel ridges and furrows produced by the effect. Table 6.1 should therefore be interpreted as an introduction to the five dimensions of everyday instructional situations in addition to relevant activities or attributes connected with those dimensions in the research literature.

Notably, these dimensions are broad in nature and are not intended to capture the subtle complexity of the relationships between dimensions. For example, the relationship between learner activities and social dynamics in most instructional settings is going to be heightened by the number and intensity of collaborative projects introduced by the instructor, the richness of the instructions and tasks assigned, and how well or poorly the learner groups are conceptualized, prepared for collaboration, and managed. Instructor activities and learner tasks can overlap in terms of the applications used (e.g., posting to a class discussion list) but not in terms of the rhetorical and

Table 6.1

Five dimensions of everyday instructional situations[a]

Dimensions of Instructional Situations	Relevant Activities or Attributes
Learner Background and Knowledge	• highlighting role of learner characteristics and prior knowledge • applying skills and abilities, learning and technology experiences, standardized test taking, and general educational success to various learning contexts • comprising of the biological attributes (age, gender, race/ethnicity), abilities (cognitive, physical), personal identity (learning style, attitude, motivation, self-monitoring), literacies (computer, domain, textual, visual), and sociocultural context (family, economic, geographic, organizational) of learners in formal and informal instructional situations
Learner Tasks and Activities	• focusing on the nature of tasks (e.g., requirements, procedures, importance, frequency, time, complexity), user behaviors and expectations, and human problem-solving activities • involving actions with learning materials, exercises, goals, processes (e.g., reading to learn, reading to learn to do, reading to analyze, reading to compare, confirm, correct) • emphasizing individual or distributed learner activities related to discovering, sampling, comparing, referring, organizing, illustrating, and generalizing
Social Dynamics	• drawing on computer-mediated communication, collaboration and groupwork, social cognition, and communities of interest • comprising of socioemotional-affective-cognitive interactions between learners and instructors, learners and learners, learners and content, learners and interfaces, instructors and content, instructors and interfaces, instructors and other instructors, content and content, and institutional support structures • requiring responsiveness, social relationships and abilities, personal styles, strategies for scheduling, group management, immediacy, and self-assessment
Instructor Activities	• stressing authentic problem-based goals for instruction in projects and learning activities • adapting to audience, communication of content, objectives, prior knowledge, information exchange, topic elaboration, topic pacing and flow, sequencing, methods of evaluation, and immediacy of feedback • understanding of subject matter, theories of knowledge, pedagogy, and reflective abstraction

Table 6.1
(continued)

Dimensions of Instructional Situations	Relevant Activities or Attributes
Learning Environment and Artifacts	• moving from drill-and-practice to computer-assisted learning to Web-based artifacts that facilitate learners, their tasks, and the purpose and goals of the instruction • selecting instructional artifacts (e.g., reading and writing applications that support viewing, managing, and disseminating individual and shared documents), promoting mentoring and open exchange of ideas, discussion, pacing and flow, meaningful sequencing, methods of evaluation, and immediacy of feedback • optimizing ergonomic design for usability, comfortable, functional, and aesthetic, promoting discussion face-to-face, virtually, and design for two and three worlds, supporting one-to-one, one-to-many, and many-to-many communication and exchange

[a]Earlier versions of this table appear in Mehlenbacher (1998) and Mehlenbacher et al. (2000, p. 179) as the five dimensions of an instructional situation characterizing Web-based and conventional classes. Versions also appear in Mehlenbacher (2002, 2007b), and in Mehlenbacher et al. (2005).

instructional purpose (e.g., for the instructor it may be to summarize the contributions; for the learners it may be to argue in favor of one approach versus another).

Because our goal is to capture the fundamental dimensions of everyday instructional situations initially, it is not necessary to explicitly define where one dimension ends and where another begins, nor is it necessary to capture the rich interplay between dimensions. In the manner of an Escher print, figure 6.1 represents the five dimensions of everyday instructional situations graphically, suggesting how one or more dimensions, when grounding another, serve to figure the dimension under investigation. Thus an instructor interested in engaging learners in higher-level research activities might construct a simulated publishing environment that emphasizes collaborative peer review and conceptualize issues related to learner background and knowledge, tasks and activities, social dynamics, and environment and artifacts under instructor activities. Still, to one degree or another, all five dimensions are required to produce an everyday instructional situation.

Figure 6.1 appears to be a tessellation; tessellations, however, involve repeated use of a single shape to cover a plane surface, without gaps or overlapping between the shapes, like the tiles of a washroom floor. Tessellations cannot have any gaps and cannot overlap one another, as does this particular noncircular Venn diagram. Hexagons, squares, and triangles can tessellate; octagons and pentagons cannot. And

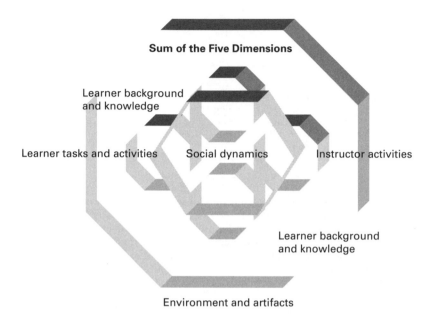

Figure 6.1
Figuring and grounding the five dimensions of everyday instructional situations.

instruction and learning with technology can be improved in certain situations and not in others, lacking as tessellations do mathematical precision and replicability.

All instructional situations can therefore be described as involving learners (with particular biological, cognitive, affective, socioeconomic attributes), tasks (read this poem, solve this mathematical problem, measure this flame), social dynamics (one-way explanation, discussion, groupwork), instructional activities (expectations, methods, objectives), environments (seminar rooms, classrooms), and artifacts (whiteboards, chairs, pencils) for learning.

Distinguishing between the five dimensions is simplified by presenting exaggerated instances of problematic versus ideal realizations. Thus, one can imagine the following instructional possibilities:

Problematic versus Ideal Learner Attributes: Situations where learners are disengaged, unprepared, not present, unwilling to change their beliefs or attitudes, versus situations where learners are highly motivated, on-task, competent, engaged, driven by high intrinsic needs for content, exchange, and mastery.

Problematic versus Ideal Task Design: Situations where tasks are poorly constructed, that is, poorly articulated, arbitrary or unrelated to the course content, inauthentic, require more time than is available, or demand skills the learners have not acquired, versus situations where tasks are authentic, engaging, well defined instructionally but complex and tightly coupled with the instructional goals, content, and opportunities for future application.

Problematic versus Ideal Social Dynamics: Situations where instructors provide one-way transmission of instructional content without considering or even imagining prior learner knowledge and without encouraging or permitting learner questions, feedback, or elaboration, where instructional materials are limited and poorly designed or constructed, and where learners engage in limited interaction with the instructor and with other learners, versus situations where instructor-to-learner, learner-to-learner, learner-to-task, learner-to-content, and learner-to-personal-learning interests and goals are engaging and thoughtfully conceptualized, designed, and implemented.

Problematic versus Ideal Instructional Activities: Situations where the primary interaction is between learners and the course textbook and reading materials, where lessons are organized around lectures in which instructors present information one-to-many and discourage questions from learners, versus situations where instructors are knowledgeable and learners are studious and reflective about materials that present multiple views of the content, where activities are anchored, instructional goals are carefully articulated, and real-world trial and error is encouraged.

Problematic versus Ideal Environment and Artifacts: Situations where the learning environment and artifacts are limited to auditory presentation of course content and inflexible learner positioning (e.g., in rows of chairs) allows little or no room for individual or group work, where note-taking and questions are discouraged, where learner competition is high and homogeneous classroom behavior is the norm, where lighting is poor, air quality stale, and the aesthetic experience unpleasant, versus situations where dialogue is encouraged and facilitated by the surroundings, where both individual and group work are supported, and where a combination of media allow spontaneous generation of higher-level thinking, exchange, analysis, synthesis, modification, review, and application.

Education, therefore, can be viewed as a continuum of transactional "offerings" where the specifics of media and mediation are less important than their variety and quality. Derived from Moore's (1992) emphasis on the interaction between learners and instructors and between learners, instructors, and the overall instructional design of a course (i.e., social dynamics and instructional activities), "transactional distance" can be either large (i.e., involving high structure and low dialogue) or small (i.e., encouraging low structure and high dialogue). In this light, it seems more appropriate to frame different educational approaches in terms of whether they are same-time same-place instruction, same-time different-place instruction, or flexible-access instruction. Ultimately, it may be that the development of descriptive terminologies characterizing mediated instructional events requires a historical turn rather than a futuristic orientation (cf. Berlin 1987). Online instruction, strictly speaking, subverts or forces us to reorganize space and time, especially if our instructional bias has been toward privileging the instructional organization of space and time that applies to conventional classrooms.

Thus, finding a general language for describing everyday instructional situations is the only way we can begin to organize our research, practice, and ideals for supporting effective learning experiences. A third method of organizing the five learning dimensions of everyday instructional situations, then, might elaborate on ideal learning experiences in either face-to-face or online settings (see table 6.2).

In the remaining sections, an elaboration of the five dimensions of everyday instructional situations is given. Importantly, these are tentative overviews of each dimension, only touching on the vast literatures represented by the eight research clusters described earlier. The research reported, therefore, should be read directly where possible given the goal of touching on the widest possible range of studies related to each particular dimension. Summarizing numerous studies, after all, limits any researcher's ability to describe carefully the particular details of a given study, its context, and the control structures driving the research. The literature review organizing our description of each dimension is meant to serve as catalyst for researchers interested in the scholarship characterizing that particular dimension (in lieu of the book-length consideration each dimension rightly deserves).

6.1 Learner Background and Knowledge

Users, learners, and audiences in general are changing, growing, and collapsing in ways that are difficult to anticipate (Hill and Mehlenbacher 1998; Oblinger and Oblinger 2005). Moreover, as Weinberger (2007) observes, users are also "finding one another in the digital world and forming real social groups, not because they share essential demographic traits but because they're talking to one another" (p. 118). Yet we also understand that the background and knowledge that learners bring to any learning situation can greatly determine what they learn, how much they learn and, ultimately, how long and in what ways they are able to apply that learning. As Hannafin and Land (1997) encapsulate, "Knowledge must be assimilated; perceptions of value, meaning, and importance must be tentatively derived; existing knowledge must be evaluated concurrently with new knowledge; and understandings must be reconstructed accordingly" (p. 170). Most instructors can recount numerous experiences with students who came to them with little or no experience in the instructors' particular subject matter and who, by semester's end, turned out to be proverbial geniuses with the material. Conversely, instructors can describe students who seemed, either deliberately or out of some cruel cosmic set of limitations, to be unable to grasp even the most basic tenets of their subject matter.

Of course, both of these examples where learners appear to defy our initial instructional estimation of their capabilities can also be explained by the critical role of

Table 6.2

Five dimensions and ideal experiences for learners in face-to-face and online environments[a]

Dimensions of Instructional Situations	Ideal Experiences for Learners	
	Face-to-Face Environment	Online Environment
Learner Background and Knowledge	Facilitates individual reflection and group activities, extrinsically motivating, active, verbal, involving various media types serving individual learner preferences and cognitive styles	Highly goals directed, carefully monitored, self directing, encourages intrinsic motivation and a positive attitude toward working alone, presents materials in various modalities
Learner Tasks and Activities	Focused on whiteboard content, encouraging note-taking and active reading, balancing media elements and working with artifacts that have real-world applications	Focused on content and schedule, balances visual and textual information, facilitates cognitive and metacognitive strategies for future learning
Social Dynamics	Socially comfortable and inclusive, supportive, encouraging mutually-defined goals, task-oriented, open and scaffolded interchange	Provides real-time, interruptible, bi- or multi-dimensional, social situations, balances affective and task-oriented goals strategically
Instructor Activities	Discussion-oriented, mixture of activities, highlights practice and application of theory, involves learners in objective setting and evaluation processes	Goal-/criterion-directed, controlled sequencing, availability of inquiry options, responses evaluated quickly, exploratory, visual
Learning Environment and Artifacts	Small, comfortable, free of distractions, designed for discussion, groupwork, with ample table space and artifacts that support or extend learner opportunities for scaffolded exploration, manipulation, analysis, and creation	Focused visually, instructional goals and accompanying materials separated from navigation, encouraging multiple paths of discovery via questions and answers, stressing interpersonal as well as task-oriented communication and resource sharing

[a]Influenced by Gilbert and Moore (1998), Hannafin and Land (1997), Kirkley, Savery, and Grabner-Hagen (1998), Mesher (1999), Najjar (1998), and Savery (1998).

context in the learning process; and, so, any emphasis on learner background and knowledge should be approached with caution. The context within which learners are asked to display prior knowledge and understanding profoundly influences their success or failure: thus it is not surprising that successful auto mechanics can fail to be able to identify engine difficulties without access to the actual engines themselves (rather than illustrations of those engines).

At the most general level, learning audiences can be defined as impatient, task-oriented, unforgiving, and disdainful of anything they perceive to be condescending, jargon-ridden, or overly technical in nature (Mehlenbacher 2003). As well, and most importantly, learners are not motivated to stop what they are doing to learn. As Pasmore (1994) observes:

There's an old joke about the fellow who returns his chain saw because it doesn't work well. When the clerk starts the saw to check it out, the fellow asks, "What's that noise?" Although it sounds like this fellow is really dumb, I feel the same way each time I learn to do something with one keystroke on my computer that used to take four or five. I have a sort of inner calculus that tells me when my frustration has built up to a point that it's time to read my manual. If I'm in the middle of something important, I'll wait a bit longer; if I have free time, I may look at the manual just out of curiosity. I'm sure that my learning would be faster if I took a concentrated course, many of which are available at the university for a nominal fee. But that much concentrated time is hard for me to find. So I waste time by seconds and minutes instead, which I'll bet in the span of a year add up to a lot more than the time I would spend in the course. (p. 77)

Between instructional activities, tasks designed to facilitate learning and group interaction, and the development of learning environments and artifacts that are conducive to learner development, fall learners and the backgrounds and knowledge they bring to everyday instructional situations. Importantly, the dynamics between these instructional dimensions can be well conceived and engaging and, still, individuals immersed in some contexts may fail to learn. But if learners are invested in and committed to learning in a given context and are unable to learn, a careful review of the instructional activities, artifacts, and situation will most certainly reveal shortcomings in the some part of the design of the learning situation surrounding the learner.

It is not enough, however, to assume that understanding our learners will improve our ability to instruct them. Schwartz, Martin, and Nasir (2005) note that "Despite the contention that a better understanding of the mechanisms of thought should lead to better models of instruction, the usefulness of cognitive psychology for the development of productive teaching practices is uncertain," and they posit that "A critical challenge . . . is to develop methods and measures that yield prescriptions, not just descriptions, of learning" (p. 21). Still, Kirkley and Duffy (2000) state, "One of the looming challenges educators face today is understanding how student diversity and uniqueness impacts the complex process of learning. Affective and cognitive factors are increasingly examined as we seek to understand how to teach and support the *whole learner*" (p. 21). For this reason, Gibson (2003) laments that only 20 percent of the articles published in the *American Journal of Distance Education*, Australia's *Distance Education*, and Canada's *Journal of Distance Education* from the late 1980s to the mid-1990s focus on learners and learning (p. 147). The relationship between understanding our learners, their prior knowledge, readiness for learning, self-regulatory skills, and future ability to creatively apply new understandings is intimately connected to our notions of effective instruction.

Indeed, it is almost a truism and has been widely supported by the research that the more thoroughly we understand the prior experiences, knowledge, problem solving skills, attitudes, and expectations of learners, the more likely it is that we will be able to meet them where they are with new information and understandings (Anderson 1995; Bransford et al. 2000; Hiltz and Shea 2005; Jenkins 1978; Simon 1979). For this reason, Bransford et al. (2004) define "learner centered" instruction as the act of "connecting to the strengths, interests, and preconceptions of learners and helping them learn about themselves as learners" (p. 215). The notion that learners are *not* "empty vessels" waiting to be filled with new content is integral to understanding how learning occurs and how instruction should be organized and presented. Importantly, however, we are never able to fully "analyze" our "target group of learners" and "ensure that the instruction is appropriate and relevant" (Fowler 2003, p. 37). Audience definition is cocreated by instructors and learners, and direct interactions between audience attributes, instructional organization and presentation, and learning outcomes are difficult to establish with confidence.

As well, although *expertise* is often held to be something that is exhibited by the instructor, increasingly it is held to be a quality that is less easily defined and perhaps only contingent and domain specific in nature. As we have moved increasingly from conventional face-to-face to online environments, our definition of learning audience has also broadened. Online, the primary audience for instruction is still *learners*; but, increasingly, the secondary audience is *instructors*. In these new environments, instructors are subject to a host of new learning curves and uncertainties that many of them have not had to deal with in traditional instructional spaces (Minielli and Ferris 2005). In addition, various new learners come together in WBI environments. Tertiary audiences involved and contributing to sophisticated online courses include, for example, instructional designers, technical specialists, administrators, program coordinators, librarians, support staff, and research and teaching assistants. Highlighting the multiple audiences that can be involved in the WBI planning, design, implementation, delivery, and evaluation process is a critical first step in beginning to understand the complexity of the move from conventional to online learning environments.

We have learned from more than twenty years of cognitive science research that both experienced and inexperienced learners develop rich mental models of learning tasks and concepts, sometimes used synonymously with prototypes and schemata, that guide them as they apply knowledge to a given situation and acquire new knowledge for use in new situations (Johnson-Laird 1983). Winn (2004) distinguishes between mental models and schemata, suggesting that the former "is broader in conception than a schema because it specifies causal actions among objects that take place within it" (p. 90). Critical to the formation and development of mental models is the process of selective perception, wherein learners actively emphasize or deemphasize information depending on prior knowledge and information familiarity. As well, given the integral role of selection in the problem-formation process, some researchers argue that it is critical to creativity and innovation in learning (Csikszentmihalyi 1996; Reid and Petocz 2004).

Selective perception is also a process that minimizes cognitive workload (which is always hopelessly limited), particularly as tasks grow in complexity (i.e., are longer in duration, require higher accuracy, and demand more working memory) and as learners develop their expertise in a given domain (through prior experience and similar interpretive outcomes). Feinberg, Murphy, and Duda (2003) further elaborate on the importance of cognitive load learning theory, which involves sensory memory, working memory, and long-term memory, distinguishing between *intrinsic* cognitive load (instructional content) and *extrinsic* cognitive load ("any cognitive activity engaged in because of the way the task is organized or presented, not because it is essential to attaining relevant goals," p. 107). Quellmalz and Kozma (2003) describe intrinsic cognitive load as being optimized by working *with* technology and extrinsic cognitive load as being an effect *of* technology:

What complicates how we measure cognitive load is the various different causes that contribute to its level, some of them supportive of learning and some detrimental. If our attention is split between two different information types or if modality types demand either auditory or visual processing, cognitive load is increased. And both of these demand types are intensely connected to the nature of the instructional content, how much or little redundancy is represented in the information, and on other design features of the instruction.

Effects *of* technology are those residual changes in students' cognitive capacity that result from the use of technology to learn. Effects *with* technology are those performances that students display while equipped with a cognitive tool, such as a visualiser, analysis package, or a model builder. From the latter perspective, some cognition is performed by the person and some by the technology that they use. (p. 291)

The prior knowledge or mental models that learners bring to any information, therefore, can be vital to providing them with strategies and heuristics for managing the processing event. Johnson-Laird (1983) views mental models as integral to human meaning-making, writing:

mental models play a central and unifying role in representing objects, states of affairs, sequences of events, the way the world is, and the social and psychological actions of daily life. They enable individuals to make inferences and predictions, to understand phenomena, to decide what action to take and to control its execution, and above all to experience events by proxy; they allow language to be used to create representations comparable to those deriving from direct acquaintance with the world; and they relate words to the world by way of conception and perception. (p. 397)

The importance of developing working user models cannot be overemphasized, especially as we move instructional situations online. Although the usefulness of user models to the designers of instructional materials has been questioned, user modeling has operated as a foundational strategy for human–computer interaction and usability researchers for several decades (cf. Card, Moran, and Newell 1983). Still, Allen (1996) has warned that believing that our representations of the mental models of users will predict user expectations and behaviors is naive:

User models can predict users' preferences in a general way; but . . . they can break down when they are employed at too specific a level. This result is a salutary reminder that models are just that: simplified versions of a complex reality. Forcing users to fit stereotypes is a recipe for information-retrieval disasters. (pp. 42–43)

On the opposite end of the continuum, defining the knowledge that makes up part of a learner's mental model at too general a level of specificity is equally problematic. Brewer (1987) distinguishes between "global" and "instantiated" schemas, where the former are general and abstract and the latter are more detailed to eliminate nonproductive generalizability. A more dogmatic way of interpreting this principle is Williams's (2004) assertion that "Knowledge is meaningful and relevant only to the extent it supports a skill(s) required to accomplish the work activity" (p. 115). Winograd and Flores (1986) put it more simply: "In driving a nail with a hammer (as opposed to thinking about a hammer), I need not make use of my explicit representation of the hammer. My ability to act comes from my familiarity with *hammering*, not my knowledge of *a hammer*" (p. 33). This is a very process-oriented and pragmatic way to describe the relationship between knowledge and activity, and it is appealing for those very reasons. Discussions about the formation, composition, and utility of "knowledge" in educational research too often become so abstract that it is difficult to identify the requisite skills, learning activities to be taken, instructional objectives required to meet learner needs, and anticipated outcomes (a term used by assessment specialists much more comfortably than educational researchers) for learning events. Perkins's (2008) distinction between possessive, performative, and proactive knowledge is helpful, here, because proactive knowledge allows us to describe learner abilities, dispositions, and strategies for deploying knowledge successfully in different contexts.

What we do agree on, however, is that all learners fit somewhere along the continuum from novice to expert or from inexperienced to experienced. The labels of these continua are not synonymous and frequently depend on whether a researcher's orientation is cognitive, developmental, or sociocultural. Cognitivists have tended to prefer the novice–expert continuum, although they have been criticized for drawing too strong a distinction between the two states of expertise. The novice–expert label is also somewhat problematic given that some researchers (e.g., Duffy, Palmer, and Mehlenbacher 1993) have elaborated on the impossibility of true expertise in complex, ill-defined problem domains such as computing and technology contexts. The problem with the inexperience-to-experience continuum is that these terms conflate abilities (i.e., cognitive and physical) with personal attributes or dispositions such as attitude, motivation, self-monitoring strategies, and "life" experience.

So the background and knowledge that learners bring to any learning situation can significantly influence what they learn, how much and for how long they learn, and their ability to apply that learning. In this respect, the benefit of identifying a rich repository of learner attributes and capabilities is, we assume, that knowledge of our audiences for communicating improves our ability to design and evaluate our instruction. Thus, learners engaged in everyday instructional situations will bring the following general attributes to the event (see table 6.3).

Table 6.3 organizes learners, generally, from individual physical and cognitive to social and communal attributes, although factors that comprise each learner attribute (e.g., abilities as cognitive and physical) are sorted alphabetically to avoid privileging particular factors. Thus, although geographical factors may be a more powerful indicator of learner behavior than family issues, "family" precedes "geographic."

Hiltz and Shea (2005), summarizing the research on learner profiles and online learning, state that we know the following about successful students:

On the individual level, students who are motivated, self-directed, and confident about having the computer skills necessary to use the technology are those who are most likely to thrive in the ALN [asynchronous learning networks] environment. Often, these are students who are older than traditional on-campus undergraduates. Females seem on the average to be somewhat more comfortable in ALN courses than are males, perhaps because of their generally higher verbal skills and their greater tendency to enjoy collaborative learning styles. (p. 163)

This perspective highlights much of what is difficult about the task of identifying the factors that contribute to an individual's ability to learn, especially in technology-mediated environments. Here we have a host of variables, none of them explicitly elaborated upon, that all apparently contribute to a learner's ability to do well in an ALN environment (in itself, a construct that requires explicit definition for comparison's sake): Personal attributes influence learning (e.g., motivation, self-direction, confidence, and learning style), as do biological ones (e.g., age, gender), as do literacies (e.g., verbal ability). The particular context of the studies that informed the assumptions about learner attributes influencing success online are not described, and, ultimately, one might argue that the attributes could just as easily describe successful learners in *any* context.

Table 6.3
Characterizing learners, their background and knowledge

Learner Attributes	Factors for Each Learner Attribute
Biological Attributes	Age: children, adults, seniors Gender: male, female, masculine, feminine Race/ethnicity: Caucasian, African-American, Asian, etc.
Abilities	Cognitive: learning capacity, intelligence scores, prior knowledge, testing ability, educational level Physical: ambulatory, haptic, visual, auditory
Personal Identity	Attitude/motivation: orientation toward task, engagement, affective expectations, intention (Davies 2006), self definition, esteem levels, self-sufficiency (Meyer 2002) Learning style: reflective, sequential, deductive, inductive, flexibility (James and Gardner 1995) Self-monitoring: strategies for assessing own learning progress, metacognitive abilities, internal sphere of control (Hiltz and Shea 2005)
Literacies	Computer: training or education with technology, platform- and application-specific familiarity, adaptability, problem solving, task experience, novice or expert, prior online experience Domain: knowledge of application area, education, testing capability, time management skills, academic accreditation, general knowledge of scientific, economic, multicultural, and global principles governing expertise (Burkhardt et al. 2003) Textual: reading level, verbal ability, ESL/International, basic numeracy Visual: experience with scientific and data visualization, various media information types, spatial systems, simulation, virtual reality environments
Sociocultural Context	Family: parents' education, expectations, primary language, educational involvement Economic: high, low income, support and living expenses Geographic: rural, urban, low or concentrated populations, developed, developing countries Organizational: large or small, private, public, educational or production

In the sections that follow, the five general learner variables—related to biological attributes, abilities, personal identity, literacies, and sociocultural context—are elaborated upon with the goal of developing a working definition of what we mean by learner background and knowledge. Since the research on learner knowledge and attributes is disparate and considerable, this is not meant to be a comprehensive review. Rather, empirical and theoretical research on the subject is briefly touched upon and useful references for further and detailed investigation are provided. Some issues or controversies related to learner variables are also raised for consideration.

6.1.1 Biological Attributes

Biological attributes are those human characteristics that are most routinely used to categorize empirical participants, including *age*, *gender*, and *race*. Although one can categorize a given sample using refined biological attributes, it is always useful to keep traditional categorizations in mind. Thus, for example, although gender is generally either male or female (notably, in that order), some researchers choose to divide their sample group into biological male, biological female, masculine, feminine, and so on.

A review of biological attributes and their relationship to learning processes invites book-length treatment in and of itself, so this discussion is necessarily cursory and aimed more at highlighting general demographic trends than at elucidating the subject matter thoroughly. A radical perspective on the role of biological attributes and learning might be that, depending on the influence of sociocultural variables on one's behavior, biological factors should not play a critical role in all but bio- and sensory-physical processes rather than cognitive ones. Still, given the predominance of these attributes as variables in the instruction and learning with technology literatures, it would be irresponsible to ignore them. Indeed, our increasingly technologized society and the global trends toward accessible education for all have heightened the importance of these variables for some researchers.

According to the U.S. Department of Commerce (2001) census figures, 26 percent of the U.S. population is under 18 and 12 percent is over 65 years of age, a combined total of almost 40 percent. Our preoccupation with the remaining 62 percent of the population, aged 18 to 65, is rooted in our focus on what constitutes the labor-capable percentage of the population; but, as Fischer (2000) reminds us, information overload is a lifelong condition. Indeed, MacPherson (2006) cites one child development expert's concern that children are exhibiting early characteristics of "problem-solving deficit disorder" as a result of increased time with technology and decreased time engaged in simple play activities. This should not come as a total surprise given that, as DeBell and Chapman (2006) point out, "About two-thirds of children in nursery school and 80 percent of kindergarteners use computers," and "about 23 percent of children in nursery school use the Internet" (p. iv).

On the other end of the continuum, with a median per capita income that is 67 percent higher than the general population (Keller 2001), the elderly are also electing to exercise their educational options in increasingly creative and technical ways. Because it has been observed that older adults (mean = 72 years) perform less effectively than younger adults (mean = 21 years) in terms of free memory recall and rehearsal strategies (Ward and Maylor 2005), human–computer interaction researchers have begun to devote serious attention to the needs of "senior" users related to computing technologies (Rau and Hsu 2005). Indeed, this interest in senior users is sure to increase as dramatically as the growth in our older population—from a global population of less than 17 million people over 65 years old in 1900 to as many as 2.5 billion by 2050 (Bogin 2001, p. 263). Hawthorn (2000) notes that older users will tend to have more difficulties with vision, hearing, response time, long-term attention (at least in terms of fatigue), and short-term memory abilities. Ziefle and Bay (2005) found that older adults (mean = 55.5 years) solved fewer tasks, spent more time on tasks, made more detour steps, and had more difficulty understanding the features of cell phones than younger adults (mean = 23.1 years). Given the specialized needs of older users, Hawthorn (2000) argues that interface designers have a professional obligation to aim for "intergenerational fairness" in their designs. Plaisant et al. (2006) agree, citing research that suggests that, although no less receptive to new technology than younger users, older users continue to experience accessibility and usability challenges.

In university settings, gender demographics have seen significant changes during the last forty years as well. The majority of learners enrolled as undergraduates in U.S. higher education institutions are women, and the majority of learners taking classes online are also women (Kramarae 2003). Astin (1998) notes that, between 1966 and 1996, the number of women aspiring to pursue graduate degrees in all disciplines at American universities increased from 40.3 percent to 67.7 percent, and increases in doctoral and advanced professional degrees grew 411 percent (p. 116). Whereas in 1967, 66.5 percent of male and 44.5 percent of female college students believed that "activities of married women are best confined to the home and family," in 1996, 30.8 percent of male and 30.8 percent of female college agreed with this position (p. 119).

These changes have been less dramatic in activities related directly to technology use, perhaps because this generation of 18- to 24-year-olds has been using the Internet since elementary school (Salaway and Katz 2006). Dholakia (2006), citing a recent PEW Internet report, notes that although the gap between male and female use of the Internet in the United States is dropping, males still traditionally use the Internet more than females, while women use the Internet more than men in the home (55.1 percent versus 44.9 percent) and more men than women access the Internet from both the home and work (61.4 percent versus 38 percent). Indeed, DeBell and Chapman (2006) report that "In contrast to the 1990s, when boys were more likely than girls to use computers and the Internet, overall computer and Internet use rates for boys and girls are now about the same" (p. v). Dholakia (2006) does suggest, however, that the gendered-male orientation of contemporary technology has still resulted in tendencies to stereotype females, promote aggressive gaming formats, promulgate male-dominated discussion groups, and support increases in Internet pornography (p. 237). These social and cultural factors might explain why, according to Knezek and Christensen (2002), research shows no differences in attitudes toward computers in first grade but, by the seventh grade, research suggests that boys enjoy computers more than girls. These patterns are further complicated by information technology preferences related to academic major (Salaway and Katz 2006), such as in the decline of women receiving computer science undergraduate degrees from 37 percent in 1985 to 22 percent in 2005 (National Science Foundation 2007).

Eldred and Hawisher (1995) have described in some detail the potentially equalizing nature of computer-mediated communication environments, although Selfe and Meyers's (1991) study of gender communication suggests that the equalization phenomenon may not be as empowering for females as earlier researchers had hypothesized. Thus, Cooper and Weaver (2003) not only report higher levels of anxiety among females of all ages when interacting with computers, but they also note that social context further challenges female comfort with computing:

Our search of the literature finds very few differences in males' and females' competence with the computer, when they are using information technology by themselves. As soon as computing becomes public, however, the arrangement of the social context can make an enormous difference in the way people feel and think. Computer anxiety becomes exacerbated in public. Girls and boys become more motivated to conform to their social stereotypes, to the detriment of the girls' performance on the computer. (p. 65)

This is not to suggest, however, that gender does not influence online behavior and interaction in notable ways. Still, recent research suggests that sociocultural developments, for example, the distributed involvement of males and females and users of various age groups in the use of online learning materials, may be streamlining the responses of these populations. Neuhauser (2002) has noted that age, gender, and Internet experience do not yield significantly different perceptions of WBI activities, although Koohang and Durante (2003) report significantly more positive perceptions of WBI corresponded to years experience with the Internet. Fahy (2002), for example, examined 356 student postings (i.e., 2,558 sentences and 44,599 words) from a fifteen-week graduate course in distance education, and found that male students used almost 50 percent more intensifiers (e.g., very, only, every, never, always) than females, and the intensifier "very" twice as often as females; the results for qualifiers (e.g., but, if, may/might, I think, often, probably, though) were less obvious, with females using them 57 percent more than males, and the qualifier "I think" more than 68 percent of the time (p. 12). Interestingly, males used over 13 percent fewer words in their postings (p. 16). Fahy (2002) concludes, "The influence of these communicative forms may be subtle, but findings such as these suggest they are real and that they may constitute an important, if yet poorly understood, part of the gestalt of online distance learning" (p. 19).

While Fahy (2002) admits that distinctive patterns of linguistic usage among males and females is difficult to capture, Bussey and Bandura (1999) argue that gender is exceedingly difficult to fix as either a strictly biological construct or as a socially constructed one. They maintain that, rather than being "a unitary monolith," traditional notions of gender tend to ignore "the vast differences among women and the similarly vast differences among men depending on their socioeconomic class, education, ethnicity, and occupation. The practice of lumping all men and women into dichotomous gender categories, with men preordained for agentic functions and women for expressive and communion functions similarly comes in for heavy criticism" (p. 683). Numerous individual gender characteristics, thus, are influenced by parental, peer, media, educational, occupational, and broader sociocultural factors. Acknowledging that challenges experimental control and invites the application of innovative data-collection approaches. Still, notably, Wizemann and Pardue (2001) and the Committee on Understanding the Biology of Sex and Gender Differences, Board of Health Sciences Policy, conclude that "Being male or female is an important fundamental variable that should be considered when designing and analyzing basic and clinical research" (p. 173).

Keller (2001) has argued that demographic issues influencing higher education ought to be the first strategic priority of administrators for the next several decades. Among the more notable changes taking place in the demographics of higher education are racial configurations, according to Keller (2001). Of the almost 500,000 foreign students who enroll in U.S. universities, analysts anticipate an increase in students from Muslim and African countries, of the three-quarter of a million legal immigrants admitted to the United States each year, approximately 200,000 enter on student, work, or tourist visas and do not return to their countries of origin; and, finally, mixed marriage and cohabitation practices have created a new international reality that educators have only begun to acknowledge.

For this reason, researchers have begun to examine the interaction between racial variables and technological ones in terms of technologically rich teaching and learning practices. Clearly, patterns of use are worth documenting. According to the Bureau of Labor Statistics (2005), Asians use computers and the Internet at work more than Caucasian users, in addition to blacks and African Americans, Latinos, and Hispanics. Not surprisingly, the higher one's education, the more likely one is to use the Internet at work; and, again not surprisingly, the "most commonly reported task" reported by the 77 million computer users at work is using e-mail.

Remarkably, though, discussions about computer-mediated communication have emphasized, when they have focused on demographic features influencing user behavior at all, variables such as gender, while frequently deemphasizing other factors, such as race and age. Racial and power dynamics in educational and noneducational settings, whether online or off, are an area of research that is growing, and the majority of studies report that populations such as Native and Latin Americans gain much needed access to education via distributed learning systems (Stewart 2004). Part of the reason for this omission is that the computer-mediated communication (CMC) literature, in general, has tended to assume that CMC has an equalizing effect on traditional power dynamics. Thus, Carabajal, LaPointe, and Gunawardena (2003) summarize the benefits of CMC as follows: "Status development and differentiation is likely based upon influential messages rather than hierarchical status based on physical and social cues such as gender, race, socioeconomic status, and physical features. . . . The simultaneous submission of messages to all members of the group facilitates the free exchange of ideas, the sharing of multiple perspectives, and the creation of an interpersonal distance resulting in an equalizing effect on participation" (p. 222).

Although it is probably safe to assume that a confluence of demographic variables such as gender, race, socioeconomic status, and education, in addition most importantly to writing ability, influence participation and the quality of interactions online, it is more likely that the these variables play a crucial role in social dynamics online. Wolfe (2000), for example, observed segments of four undergraduate English classes, two computer-mediated and two face-to-face, and found that white males participated more in face-to-face classes, followed by Hispanic women, Hispanic men, and finally by white women. Interestingly, white female participation increased by more than 50 percent when the conversation took place online, a pattern of behavior not shared with the Hispanic women, who dropped 11 percent and who preferred the computer-mediated less than the face-to-face environment. White women preferred the online environment most, and, notably, white males preferred it least.

The combined development of diversity and access initiatives in usability, design, and computer research, combined with the widespread popular appeal for audiences both surprisingly young and increasingly aged, demands that practitioners and researchers interested in further supporting existing educational audiences and engaging emerging ones begin to pay careful attention to the biological attributes of their learners and how these attributes influence their learning processes in face-to-face and online instructional situations.

6.1.2 Abilities

Learner abilities are largely biological and can be broadly categorized as *cognitive* or *physical*, where cognitive abilities have been described using various typographies (e.g., learning capacity, intelligence scores, prior knowledge, testing ability, educational level) and physical abilities tend to focus on numerous sensory-motor capabilities (ambulatory, haptic, visual, auditory). Dillon and Gabbard (1998) stress that "meta-analyses of individual differences studies indicate that general ability is the single best predictor of performance on most tasks, and such findings have relevance to all forms of human–computer interaction as well" (p. 339). Certainly, the general cognitive abilities of learners can be viewed as a central aspect of higher-level task processing, comprehension, and learning outcomes, especially as learners move from well-learned instructional settings (face-to-face) into less familiar ones (online). Physical abilities, too, play an essential role in learning ability especially in regards to technology access and usability, and thus to instruction and learning with technology in general.

Clark and Feldon (2005), though, remind us that general ability does not equal intelligence (what they call "fluid reasoning ability"): "Indeed, studies of experts in a variety of fields have found no correlation between fluid ability and performance" (p. 105). Because practice and a wide range of other historical and contextual issues factor into successful performance and expertise in any domain-specific activity, it turns out to be impossible to distinguish expert behavior and performance from cognitive ability without factoring in time and exposure to particular problem sets into the equation. For this reason, novices tend to struggle more with unstructured instructional materials than experts, although lack of structuring at some level impedes any individual's ability to learn.

Still, Kolatch (2000) suggests that it is critical for designers to understand the cognitive abilities of their user-learners if designers aim to anticipate the information needs that those users bring to interactions with instructional materials. Sutcliffe et al. (2003), thus, explicitly connect cognitive variables (e.g., limited attention span or impaired formation of long-term memory) to dialogue and display issues (e.g., limit distractions, reminders) and to repair and training recommendations (e.g., keep explanations short). To this end, researchers have created brain–body interfaces that account for various cognitive abilities, including users who have suffered brain injuries (Cole and Dehdashti 1990; Doherty et al. 2002); and centers such as the Trace Research and Development Center at the University of Wisconsin–Madison (http://trace.wisc.edu/) have amassed hardcopy and online resources for designers interested in various audience types.

It is also useful to distinguish, as Hannafin et al. (2003) do, between *cognitive* and *learning* factors: cognitive factors are the processes involved in learner interpretation, comprehension, and understanding (gathering abilities), whereas learning factors are the processes or strategies that learners apply to the activity of learning new facts, procedures, or concepts (organizing abilities). Cognitive factors include prior knowledge, metacognition, system knowledge, self-efficacy, cognitive and learning styles and preferences, and motivation (pp. 246–249); learning factors involve learning context, opportunities for active learning, resources, applications, and scaffolding (pp. 250–253).

Anticipating the physical abilities of different learners is, in some ways, much more complex because it involves user abilities that include ambulatory, haptic, visual, and auditory considerations. Certainly, as instruction moves online, issues of access for diverse audiences is becoming more and more important (Shneiderman 2001). Luczak, Roetting, and Oehme (2003) remind us that our heightened expectations in terms of computational output devices are a relatively recent development. The first generation of computers used printers, lamps, and teletypes to provide user information; then, in the 1970s, displays that used monochrome cathode ray tubes (CRTs) provided us with elemental, alphanumerical characters. Only in the mid-1980s were full-screen CRTs with direct-manipulation interfaces, color, and graphics made the mainstay of our computing interactions. Over this brief period of time, alternative output devices (i.e., auditory, haptic, and ambulatory, in order of emphasis) have been slow to emerge, and only during the last several decades have we seen developments in this area that warrant educational attention (Ware 1997).

Haptic interfaces, according to Iwata (2003), are "feedback devices that generate sensation to the skin and muscles, including a sense of touch, weight, and rigidity" (p. 206). Haptic devices have been designed to apply force (either through partial- or full-body equipment), to simulate larger spaces (treadmills, sliding, or pedaling devices), or to heighten human-to-virtual object interaction (finger or foot pads). Moyle and Cockburn (2005) outline the twenty-year history of mouse-based gesture systems and the decade-long development of Web browser–based gesture systems, arguing that considerable research still needs to be done on interactions as elemental as mouse and pen click-and-drag interfaces. Loomis and Lederman (1986) have explored notions of tactual perception, and Mynatt (1997) has described systems that support blind users; and, recently, some experimental applications have used sound to denote visual patterns for blind users (Adams-Spink 2005). Stone (2001) divides haptic issues into developments in *teleoperation* (human extension of manipulation and sensing) and *telepresence* (natural interaction, sometimes via exoskeleton structures, in simulated environments).

Iwata (2003) notes that, whereas the design of visual displays has benefited from a century of activity, haptic interface design is still in its infancy. Minogue and Jones (2006) note as well that haptic research has generally been ignored by educational technologists, who have focused instead on auditory and visual modalities and interfaces; but they add that recent research on virtual learning environments (e.g., O'Hagan, Zelinsky, and Rougeaux 2002) offers to broaden our interest in kinesthetic, embodied, and tactile learning processes. Brewster (2003), reviewing research on perception, notes that whereas our visual abilities are limited (we see the world through a view of 80 degrees laterally and 60 degrees vertically), our auditory experiences allow data to be collected from all around us, although at a much lower resolution (p. 222).

As well, although we are frequently overloaded with visual information, auditory input is often underutilized by our environment and artifacts. Finally, Kaye (2004) outlines a detailed program for olfactory research, noting that humans have approximately 1,000 olfactory receptors for assessing smells in the world. For these and other reasons, future technological applications that facilitate nonvisual modalities are most certain to receive additional interest and development.

6.1.3 Personal Identity

Personal identity is an invented construct meant to capture those individual and preferential aspects of human behavior that are exceedingly difficult to isolate empirically, including *attitude/motivation*, *learning style*, and *self-monitoring* capabilities. It is ironic that the psychological literature often refers to the personal identities of human beings as "individual differences" (Jonassen and Grabowski 1993), and that, at least in methodological terms, these differences are frequently framed as confounding what we know about general human behavior. Of course, methodologically there are many benefits to building the generalizations that we make about human behavior based on a subject pool of more than one individual and his or her behavior; but it is sometimes easy to forget that the observed behavior of one individual is often where our idea for experimentally testing an hypothesis about human behavior *begins*.

Learner attitudes and motivation toward learning comprise several observable features, including their general orientation toward the task at hand, their level of engagement in the activity, their affective expectations regarding the learning event, and whether or not they intend to learn from the situation. While reading a PDF version of an article related to this manuscript, for example, I am actively engaged in learning new material and attempting to interpret it in light of what I know, am hopeful that the article will contribute to my writing efforts in general, and am interested enough to suspend all other activities until I have finished reading the article (or writing into this text using the article).

Conversely, a learner who is not engaged in a learning activity will tend to allow distractions to enter the processing event, will be difficult to engage, and is unlikely to be able to see or imagine any benefits being derived from learning the new materials. So relegating learner attitude to a *noncognitive* category is clearly reductivist. As Evans (2004) asserts, "emotions are related to specific neurological mechanisms and processes, they constitute real experiences, we perceive these experiences and are 'aware' of these experiences via consciousness" (p. 31). Messick (1996) argues for a more integrative perspective, writing, "Speaking of borders between personality and intelligence, one view is that intellect includes procedural skills, declarative knowledge, metacognitive processes, and volition while personality encompasses emotion, temperament, character, and motivation" (p. 358).

Davies (2006) distinguishes between motivation to learn and intention to learn in terms of processing order. Motivational factors influence learner choices about learning and intention, as a "volitional state is post-decisional" (p. 9). Intention, then, involves both action and effort, whereas motivation can involve both although it need not. Davies (2006) concludes that specific features that undermine learner intention include designing tests that do not require study or effort, setting deadlines that are disconnected from instructional content, designing materials at an inappropriate level of difficulty, using assessment instruments that do not measure the instructional learning objectives, and applying ineffective pedagogical strategies given the particular learning situation (p. 22).

Montgomery, Sharafi, and Hedman (2004), focusing on learner engagement related to working with information technology, define the three features of "engagement mode" and relate each feature to Csikszentmihalyi's (1990) notion of flow, which emphasizes a balance between learner ability and task complexity (cf. Chen 2007). According to Montgomery et al. (2004), learners who are enjoying an activity (evaluation), or how much they can control the activity (locus of control), or a goal related to the performance of the activity (focus of motivation) tend to have more positive learning experiences (p. 335). Of course, one's level of engagement in a learning activity is likely to influence the amount of time one devotes to that activity, and some authors advocate that spending more time doing anything that is important to us is the key to achieving joie de vivre in general. As Andrews (2006) summarizes, "At the core of joie de vivre are enthusiasm, exuberance, excitement, energy, and spontaneity" (p. 96), and idealized visions of engaged learners certainly exhibit these characteristics. Perhaps engagement's centrality to our learning selves is why Borgmann (1995) defines it as "the symmetry that links humanity and reality," noting that "Human beings have certain capacities that prefigure the things of the world; and conversely what is out there in the world has called forth human sense and sensibility. . . . Engagement is to designate the profound realization of the humanity-reality commensuration" (p. 15).

Crick, Broadfoot, and Claxton (2004), in their efforts to develop an effective lifelong learning instrument, describe an individual's "learning identity" as "the beliefs, values and attitudes about learning, self and knowledge held by the learner" (p. 249). Personal identity and learning ability are inextricably bound together; but researchers are unclear on the exact attributes of identity that lead to what Crick et al. (2004) call one's lifelong "learning energy" or what Bussey and Bandura (1999) describe as "self-efficacy." As Bussey and Bandura (1999) have observed:

people are self-organizing, proactive, self-reflective, and self-regulating, and not just reactive organisms shaped and shepherded by external events. The capacity to exercise control over one's thought processes, motivation, affect, and action operates through mechanisms of personal agency. Among the mechanisms of agency, none is more central or pervasive than people's beliefs in their capacities to produce given levels of attainments. Unless people believe they can produce desired effects by their actions, they have little incentive to act or to persevere in the face of difficulties. Perceived efficacy is, therefore, the foundation of human agency. (p. 691)

Motivation is one of the most commonly cited attributes of successful learners, both online and off-line. Learner motivation can be connected to self-defining characteristics such as self-esteem and self-sufficiency, and these attributes can accentuate personality dimensions that can contribute to motivated behaviors, such as openness to new learning experiences, optimism, and extraversion. Heinström (2003) has explicitly connected attributes such as neuroticism, extraversion, openness to experience, agreeableness, and conscientiousness to the information-seeking behaviors of learners. Kemp (2002) describes learner resilience and persistence attributes that contribute to success in undergraduate studies as "the ability to make things better, persistence at working through difficulties, and the confidence to make the most of bad situations" (p. 74). Kemp's (2002) notion of persistence complements traditional cognitive definitions of motivation by inviting a notion of motivation that is strongly tied to the existence of positive or negative environmental factors that may support or impede learner progress. Garrison's (2003) definition of motivation folds both internal and external attributes into the definition of motivation:

Without some sense of control, it is very difficult for students to assume responsibility for their learning and to achieve deep and meaningful outcomes. Motivation in the form of commitment to a learning goal and the tendency to persist is most essential for self-directed learning. Control and choice strengthen motivation, which in turn builds a sense of responsibility. However, as necessary as a sense of control is, without appropriate support and guidance learners may not persist or achieve the desired educational outcomes. (p. 165)

Colquitt, LePine, and Noe (2000), summarizing numerous studies of learning motivation in training situations, note that learners tend to be more motivated if they have high achievement motivation, limited anxiety, a high internal locus of control, are conscientious, and report a competitive orientation. Importantly, though, the authors note that situational variables such as a poor work climate and limited peer and management support can undermine even highly motivated learners.

Another way of framing motivation is to reduce it to a trial-and-error process where goals and intentions are formulated and tested according to the features and designs of situated tasks in a given learning environment. In this respect, then, learner motivation can be both individually defined and enhanced or constrained by the learner's situation. Learner motivation, then, has a temporal dimension that is organized around the initial intentions of the learner and the affordances presented by the learning situation or context. Pea (1993) provides a memorable description of the creative ways that learner motivation or desire and the opportunities and constraints presented in a particular context interact, noting:

With a *task* desire, one has a clear goal and intention, and the need is to specify an action with a particular means. If I am freezing in a cabin, my task desire for warmth may make the affordance of a chair for burning much more salient than its affordance for sitting. If my task desire were different, different properties of the chair would matter. (p. 55)

Further elaborating on learner *desire* or personal investment, Maehr and Meyer (1997), in their excellent review of the research related to motivation, divide issues of motivation into direction (where energies are invested), intensity (number of activities attempted or finished), persistence (number of activities attempted or time spent), quality (levels of engagement), and outcomes (observable performance). These motivational foci, in turn, can have individual, situational, or interactive emphases.

Tomlinson-Keasey (2002) constructs an image of online learners that assumes increased motivation, writing, "In the new course configurations, students assume increased responsibility, no longer waiting passively for the instructor to entertain, to indicate what is on the exam, or to interpret the readings. The professor will provide the structure for the course and design the materials, but students must negotiate their own way through the lessons" (p. 148). This image does not, however, find much empirical support, and, indeed, the resistance of learners to the work necessarily involved in learning is more likely the norm rather than the exception.

Bures, Abrami, and Amundsen (2000), in their study of 79 students drawn from five courses using the same online conferencing software, found that learners who did not expect their online contribution level to influence their course performance (i.e., their grade) contributed less than those who were motivated to contribute to improve performance. Moreover, data suggest that motivated learners characterize their online conferencing as being more satisfying if they believe it contributes to their learning outcomes.

Hiltz and Shea (2005), drawing on a sample of approximately 40,000 students who were part of the SUNY Learning Network from 2000 to 2002, found that the most frequent reason for choosing online courses "related to schedule conflicts stemming from academic, work, family, and other commitments" (p. 147). Hiltz and Shea (2005) conclude that students who match four or more of the following characteristics are likely to perform poorly in online courses:

• Does the student have an external locus of control?
• Does the student have low self-efficacy regarding [his or her] computer skills?
• Does the student have low self-efficacy regarding the course content?
• Does the student lack previous experience with online courses?
• Did the student enroll solely because of course availability?
• Does the student have a low [log-in] rate for the course home page?
• Is the student reading and writing few messages on the class forum?
• Is the student quiet or non-responsive in the online chat room? (Hiltz and Shea 2005, p. 152)

Learning styles has been the focus of more research than perhaps any other aspect of personal identity (James and Gardner 1995; Neuhauser 2002). Although learning styles have been shown by some researchers to influence the way learners access information (Kolb 1984; Sadler-Smith and Riding 1999; Schmeck 1988), researchers in general disagree over what exactly learning styles *are*. James and Gardner (1995) note that "No universally accepted terminology exists to describe learning style and its various components; however, how people react to their learning environment is a core concept. Although the terms *learning style* and *cognitive style* are sometimes used interchangeably, the term *learning style* appears more regularly in print; it also appears to be the broader term" (pp. 19–20). Liu and Ginther (1999) view "learning style" and "cognitive style" to be synonymous, stating that "Generally, cognitive styles are more related to theoretical or academic research, while learning styles are more related to practical applications" and that "Cognitive/learning styles measures conventionally lie somewhere between aptitude and personality measures." It might be argued, in addition, that cognitive styles reflect human attributes or processes that tend to be fixed over time, whereas learning styles are easier to alter over time with instruction, motivation, trial and error, and experience.

One strong proponent of learning styles and their influence on both learning and the design of instruction is Felder (1993), who suggests that learners can be characterized broadly according to five learning style questions:

• What type of information does the learner preferentially perceive: sensory—sights, sounds, physical sensations, or intuitive—memories, ideas, insights?
• Through which modality is sensory information most effectively perceived: visual—pictures, diagrams, graphs, demonstrations, or verbal—sounds, written and spoken words, and formulas?
• With which organization of information is the learner most comfortable: inductive—facts and observations are given, underlying principles are inferred, or deductive—principles are given, consequences and applications are deduced?
• How does the learner prefer to process information: actively—through engagement in physical activity or discussion, or reflectively—through introspection?
• How does the learner progress toward understanding: sequentially—in a logical progression of small, incremental steps, or globally—in large jumps, holistically?

In dramatic contrast to this position, Dillon (1994), who has reviewed the research on cognitive styles, finds that much of it is lacking in either construct validity or predictive value:

Cognitive style can loosely be defined as the manner in which people process and respond to information and rests on an assumption that individuals can be distinguished in terms of characteristic processing and response. . . . Few of these putative styles have been shown to predict design performance reliably (or much else for that matter) but the idea of cognitive style remains seductive and has given birth to the notion that designers might manifest distinctive styles of reasoning that could be identified and used to aid design education and to develop computer-aided design (CAD) tools. (p. 24)

So, although the research literature has tended to focus on learning styles as they relate to online instruction, and although the construct is both appealing and important to instructional designers, it is still a controversial issue that more often than not produces no significant differences for researchers in both online and face-to-face environments (Neuhauser 2002). Indeed, learning style measures have continued to show no significance in terms of behavior and performance within evolving virtual reality learning environments (Chen, Toh, and Ismail 2005).

The first problem is with the expression itself: learning styles. What the surveys designed to elicit student learning styles are actually informing us about are learner *preferences for media and information presentation* as they relate to their learning strategies, not actual learning styles in any concrete sense of the term. Learners may have preferences for how their information is designed and delivered, and these preferences may determine how easy or difficult it is for them to integrate new information into their existing knowledge; but this does not mean literally that learners are applying styles to their use of those materials that differ significantly (in the empirical sense) from each other. Learners, rather, have generalizable methods for processing information and for understanding the interaction between form and content (perceptually, cognitively, and affectively).

Thus, James and Gardner's (1995) argument that "using technology alone without considering individual differences articulated by learning styles is futile" (p. 27) is problematic in that it assumes a natural relationship between technology-based instruction and learning styles that is just as relevant to traditional instructional settings and because learners who "suffer" through conventional lectures are still quite able to learn if properly prepared, motivated, and cognitively engaged (Schwartz and Bransford 1998). Audience-oriented information presentation may make learning less difficult, but it is not required for learning to occur, with or without technology. Or, as Dillon and Greene (2003) argue, "the most important goal of all education, including distance education, is to help learners learn how to learn. Even if the concept of learner styles were a valid construct, our ultimate goal should be to help learners learn in a variety of situations and under a variety of conditions, because that is the nature of the learning society in which we live" (p. 238).

Messick (1996) sees the problem of *match* as critical to the cognitive style challenge. Reviewing three possible pedagogical approaches—directing instruction to learner styles, exposing learners to both preferred and weaker stylistic preferences, and interacting between instructional approaches and an understanding of learner preferences for instruction. The problem, Messick (1996) concludes, "is not just that the problem of match is technically intricate, but that it is profoundly value laden. The question of *what* should be matched is the problem of prescription; the question of *how* to match is a problem of educational technology; the questions of *purpose* and *locus of choice* are problems of social values and ethics" (p. 369). And the ultimate paradox is that learners' choices in instruction are inevitably informed and constrained by their cognitive styles, creating a deterministic feedback loop between instructional design and audience preference.

"Self-monitoring," "metacognitive monitoring," and "self-regulated learning" are often used interchangeably to describe learners' higher-level conception of themselves as learners, the progress they are making toward achieving their learning goals, and the trial-and-error planning they bring to novel learning situations. Antonietti, Ignazi, and Perego (2000) explicitly connect metacognition to learner tasks and activities, as consisting of "beliefs and knowledge about the strategies which can be used to carry out a task—when a strategy may be useful, what skills the strategy requires, how much time must be spent in applying the strategy, what obstacles may be encountered, what benefits may be derived and so on—and self-evaluation about one's aptitude, promptness and habits to adopt such strategies" (p. 3).

Zimmerman (2002) notes that self-regulated learning involves "(a) setting specific proximal *goals* for oneself, (b) adopting powerful *strategies* for attaining the goals, (c) *monitoring* one's performance selectively for signs of progress, (d) *restructuring* one's physical and social context to make it compatible with one's goals, (e) managing one's *time use* efficiently, (f) *self-evaluating* one's methods, (g) *attributing* causation to results, and (h) *adapting* future methods" (p. 66). Although Ruban and McCoach (2005) stress the importance of overall ability (as defined by high school and admission tests) on the grades that learners receive in higher educational settings, they conclude that "it is possible that beyond a certain level or cut-off score, the relationship between ability and later achievement may be less strong or absent altogether, because other variables such as motivation, self-regulation, and environmental influences come into play and exert greater influence" (p. 496). Research on the characteristics and performance of self-regulating learners has supported this hypothesis (Montalvo and Torres 2004). Finally, Smith, Murphy, and Mahoney (2003) validated a learner questionnaire using 107 undergraduate university students and found that self-direction or self-management of learning was a strong indicator of learner success in "resource-based learning delivery that is online" (p. 63), but Arbaugh (2004) notes that self-management of learning is an ability that may require more than a single-course online experience to develop fully.

It is clear, then, that issues related to learning styles, attitudes about learning and learning ability, self-motivation and personal drive, and the ability to monitor one's learning strengths and weaknesses all factor significantly into every learner's processes for engaging in instructional situations. Researchers therefore have increasingly sought to integrate affect into their initially cognitively constrained notions of learner knowledge and behaviors.

6.1.4 Literacies

Counter to the popular definition of literacy as reading and writing, literacy is actually a plural object form. Learners bring various literacies to every instructional situation, literacies that are both individual and social in origin and, therefore, difficult to explicate definitively. A cultural-historical approach grounded in the theory of distributed cognition highlights, for example, the complex temporal interaction between individual, community, environment, and artifacts simply for learning to read (only a small part of what it means to be literate). As Cole and Engeström (1993) summarize, "the cognitive processing involved in learning to read is not an individual matter," but rather is distributed among instructors, learners, other learners, and the artifacts and environments that shape them. Reading, then, according to Cole and Engeström (1993), represents a movement from the constraining "expected future state, mature reading" through to "the development of the to-be-acquired new system of mediation, mature reading" (p. 23).

Literacy, then, is distributed. For the purposes of elaboration, literacies can be divided roughly into four interdependent areas: *computer*, *domain*, *textual*, and *visual* literacy. Six general conclusions about literacy, after Warschauer (2002), apply to all four of the literacy areas:

1. There is not just one, but many types of literacy;
2. The meaning and value of literacy varies in particular social contexts;
3. Literacy capabilities exist in gradations, rather than in a bipolar opposition of literate versus illiterate;
4. Literacy alone brings no automatic benefit outside of its particular functions;
5. Literacy is a social practice, involving access to physical artifacts, content, skills, and social support; and
6. Acquisition of literacy is a matter not only of education, but also of power.

Importantly, defining multiple literacy types suggests that learners can develop abilities, skills, and knowledge of particular, specialized fields that have identifiable rules for signification, interpretation, production, and evaluation. Literacies are *learned*. Thus, the distinction between one type of literacy and another is difficult to maintain unless one elevates the analysis above to, for example, textual and print letters or words and visual images and graphic designs. After all, at the most abstract level, textual and visual literacy can both be interpreted as symbolic communication systems with a host of cognitive and social rules for use and interpretation, as can computer, digital, media, and information literacy. The pivotal step in one's interpretation of literacy, for this reason, is simply that there are multiple types and that they all involve comprehension, interpretation, evaluation, communication, and production competencies. As Olson (2005) concludes, literacy always involves metarepresentation, that is, "learning to think not only about the world but learning to think about one's representations of the world" (p. 61).

"Computer literacy"—often used interchangeably with "Internet," "digital," and "media literacy"—refers to the ability, training, and general education that learners have with technology, their ability to work with various technological artifacts and in numerous environments flexibly and creatively, and the length and intensity of their exposure to computers in general. Conversancy with computers is almost a requirement to function in contemporary learning environments; as Freese, Rivas, and Hargittai (2006) state, "the Internet is becoming increasingly *proto-normative* in that more and more services are being moved online with the expectation that individuals (or surrogates) are informed Internet users" (p. 237). Indeed, Ba, Tally, and Tsikalas (2002) found that—of the nine low- and ten middle-income families they studied— most of the children spent between two and three hours per day using computers for social and leisure activities, and that computer use interacted with computer and Internet access, parental attitudes toward computing, the children's peer groups, and how much their schools emphasized computing. Computer literacy is most frequently defined as the ability of learners to work with particular operating and programming environments, applications, and software configurations, although Ba et al. (2002) argue that troubleshooting abilities, alternative purposes, communication and Web literacy inform a broader view of what it means to be digitally literate.

Unfortunately, a common tools approach has tended to dominate educational definitions of computer literacy. Bartholomew (2004), for example, describes a statewide effort to define computer literacy that resulted in learners being expected to show proficiency through hands-on production tests in six areas: operating system and general computer information, word processing, spreadsheets, database, presentations, and Internet and e-mail (p. 325). Taking an application-based view of computer literacy is most likely as limiting as taking a grammatical view of textual literacy and further research is needed to address this developing competency issue. Certainly most educators agree, too often tacitly, that learners are unlikely to succeed in higher education without basic computing capabilities, but how much capability and of what nature are questions open to debate. Shneiderman's (1987) distinction between user knowledge at the syntactic level (i.e., rule-based behavior with and knowledge of computer applications) versus the semantic level (i.e., understanding of computational environments and general operating structures) seems germane to this discussion and allows us to consider levels of computer literacy that go beyond applications and particular tasks.

Either way, whether or not learners entering higher education settings are "computer literate" is a topic of some debate. According to Rickman and Grudzinski (2000), more than one-quarter (n = 1,682) of the student population at one northwestern state university want information technology used during approximately 40 percent of their class time, but not more than 50 percent of the time. Wang and Artero (2005) surveyed 657 students at a public university to establish basic Internet literacy skills as well as to report their behavior patterns using the Web. The authors end up focusing their discussion on the students' information literacy skills, noting that the students required development in these skills, and defining information literacy as "identifying the information needed to address a given problem or issue, finding the needed information, evaluating the information, citing the information and using the information responsibly" (p. 80).

Murray and McPherson (2006) reviewed the online reading strategies of non–English speaking learners and recommend that "explicit instruction in the vocabulary, elements and structure of Web pages" (p. 153) reduces learner disorientation, a finding similar to general studies of user interactions with online texts (Selber, Johnson-Eilola, and Mehlenbacher 1997). More studies of the online reading patterns of non–English speaking learners are certainly required given the increasingly international audiences for online instructional materials, and the conflation of textual, digital, visual, and information literacies should not be viewed as a solution to the problems learners experience with online materials.

Human–computer interaction and usability researchers have spent a considerable amount of energy elaborating on user types, backgrounds, and behaviors. One aspect of this research that is particularly relevant to discussions about literacy is user "experience" (Chi, Feltovich, and Glaser 1981; Chi, Glaser, and Rees 1982). Kearsley (1988), for example, describes three dimensions of user experience: expertise with the computer, with particular application software, and with particular task domains. Certainly as we continue to move instruction and learning activities online, our need to define computational knowledge and skills as a *basic* requirement of learners increases. As well, for this reason, domain literacy (e.g., scientific knowledge, academic discourse, hands-on collaboration and communication, and so on) requires specific attention.

Domain literacy, which is not necessarily directly correlated with cognitive capacity, refers to the competency or expertise that learners develop with particular subject matters, areas, or contents. Unfortunately, domain expertise in higher educational settings is often established through standardized and subject-matter testing and the distribution of grades, rather than through theoretical and applied mastery of subject matters *in context of use*. Burkhardt et al. (2003) argue that general knowledge of scientific, economic, multicultural, and global principles governing learner expertise is increasingly important for "digital-age literacy" (p. 15).

Textual literacy is most frequently associated with reading traditional print materials, but also includes writing, speaking, listening, and fundamental numerical abilities such as arithmetic and elementary mathematical reasoning. The problem with assuming that literacy involves *only* textual literacy is that contemporary information-managing learners are increasingly and routinely confronted with nontextual symbols that demand understanding, interpreting, categorizing, and evaluating. It is thus not surprising to find authors such as Thirunarayanan (2006) concluding erroneously that "Such limited and primarily alphabet-based definitions of literacy may have been appropriate, and perhaps even sufficient, until the emergence of sophisticated tools of information and communications technologies. . . . These new and versatile technologies will slowly but surely initially diminish and then eventually altogether do away with peoples' reliance on soon to be obsolete skills such as reading and writing." Thirunarayanan (2006) proposes that, eventually, a "Personal Thoughteracy Assistant" (PTA) will be created that contains "a combination of audio, video and text" and that allows users to transcend the limited alphabetic literacy that we currently celebrate. In his example of the PTA in use, however, it worth noting that thoughteracy will be achieved first through the visual interpretation of images, through the ability to navigate to additional, related information, through reading and interpreting a graphical timeline, by understanding a brief narrative history of the subject in question, and, finally, by reviewing several articles published in peer-reviewed journals. The PTA, Thirunarayanan (2006) adds, "can provide many views of the content such as a 'historical view,' 'context view,' 'story view,' 'relevance view,' and 'applications view.'"

Several aspects of Thirunarayanan's (2006) characterization of thoughteracy are problematic, the least of which is the integral role that traditional *reading* (whether from images, textual narratives, interfaces, or audiovisual contents) plays in this new and improved age of ICT. Of course, Thirunarayanan's (2006) elevated thoughteracy has already been elaborated in contemporary critical views of literacy that frame literacies as both textual and nontextual, functional and critical, social and political, and that allow us to analyze, discover, manipulate, and critique structures around us (Gee 1990; Selber 2004a). We now acknowledge, as Cubitt (1998) writes, that "If language and gesture are technologies, then surely technologies must also be understood as languages and gestures" (p. 124). Johnson and Magusin (2005) thus define information literacy very broadly to include "visual literacy, digital literacy, media literacy, network literacy, computer literacy, and basic literacy" (p. 51). A rhetorical design perspective, as well, reinforces this view toward multiple literacies. After the arguments of McLuhan (1964), we are increasingly challenged to understand both the influence of media themselves *and* of the content they disseminate as worthy of careful study.

Visual literacy, which increasingly demands scientific and data visualization capabilities, involves the ability to understand various media information types and environments including conceptual, descriptive, and symbolic modalities. "Visual literacy" is sometimes used interchangeably with "media literacy" and "information literacy" (and we have already seen "information literacy" used interchangeably with "computer literacy" and "Internet literacy"). According to Chauvin (2003), "visual literacy" is the term used most frequently by researchers with art, design, psychology, and production experience, whereas media literacy specialists are often most interested in *mass* media (Lunenfeld 1999), information literacy experts in library and information science (Allen 1996), and writing theorists in multimodal uses of the word (Hull and Nelson 2005).

Jones-Kavalier and Flannigan (2006) note that distinctions between digital and visual literacy are becoming difficult to maintain as technologies for generating nontextual representations proliferate. The definition of visual literacy that they forward, therefore, assumes the visual manipulability that we have come to assume via computation:

Visual literacy . . . emerges from seeing and integrating sensory experiences. Focused on sorting and interpreting—sometimes simultaneously—visible actions and symbols, a visually literate person can communicate information in a variety of forms and appreciate the masterworks of visual communication. . . . Visually literate individuals have a sense of design—the imaginative ability to create, amend, and reproduce images, digital or not, in a mutable way. Their imaginations seek to reshape the world in which we live, at times creating new realities. (p. 9)

Numerous other researchers with different disciplinary backgrounds share this argument for a perspective that embraces both textual and visual literacy (e.g., Bernhardt 1993; Hodes 1998; Tufte 1983, 1990). Indeed, Kress and van Leeuwen (1996) take the argument for a unified vision of textual and visual literacy to a more emphatic level, asserting that "the opposition to the emergence of a new visual literacy is not based on an opposition to the visual media as such, but on an opposition to the visual media in situations where they form an alternative to writing and can therefore be seen as a potential threat to the present dominance of verbal literacy among elite groups" (p. 16). Similar challenges to the primacy of textual literacy can be found in recent characterizations of a new generation of visual learners (Weeks 2007).

The conflation or confusion over how many different types of literacies there are and the nature of the knowledge required for them, has led some researchers to articulate multiple literacy approaches. Selber (2004b), for example, outlines what he describes as a computer multiliteracies program that consists of three categories: *functional*, *critical*, and *rhetorical*. The distinctions between these perspectives are fundamental, with a functional orientation stressing computers as tools, learners as users, and outcomes as employment; a critical orientation viewing computers as cultural artifacts, learners as interrogators, and outcomes as informed critique; and a rhetorical literacy defining computers as hypertextual media, learners as producers, and outcomes as reflective praxis (p. 25). Interestingly, Selber's (2004b) notion of rhetorical literacy embraces all four of the literacy types (computer, domain, textual, and visual), and connects explicitly with the rhetorical design perspective outlined in the previous chapter.

Finally, Lea (2004) elaborates further on how our growing knowledge of learner literacies can be explicitly applied to course design, suggesting that instructors take care to account for both learners' current and prior literacy practices, acknowledge the epistemological importance of both written and multimodel texts, adopt a global view of all the texts used in given instructional contexts, eliminate dichotomous stances toward academic and nonacademic literacies, factor in the role of power in all literacy use, practice literacy use as evidence of learner engagement versus acculturation, and carefully articulate the integral relationship between literacies and technologies (p. 744).

6.1.5 Sociocultural Context

Bonk and Cummings (1998) have suggested that "Learning is most effective when differences in learners' linguistic, cultural, and social backgrounds are taken into account" (p. 84), but just how instructors go about accomplishing this goal is an area that requires considerable focused research. These issues are sure to increase in importance as international educational initiatives gain momentum. Several factors that have been connected to learner motivation and achievement include *family* influences, *economic* factors, *geographic* dynamics, and *organizational* variables.

Baker, Scher, and Mackler (1997) have summarized the research on how family and home influences significantly improve children's motivations to read, and, since older children with positive attitudes toward reading have been shown to have higher reading achievement scores, one might conclude that parents who engage in shared storybook reading and who encourage leisure reading can influence their children's future learning behaviors. As well, Metcalf (2003), in her UK study of the role of part-time work, family, and income demographics and their influence on higher education enrollments, found that higher education participation was significantly tied to parental education, which, in turn, was tied to class and income factors.

Defining learners or audiences in terms of their demographic characteristics—for example, their level of education, geographical location, or by economic standing—is not new and finds its roots in the North American Industry Classification System (see http://www.ntis.gov/products/naics.aspx), a system that influences most contemporary marketing analyses of audiences and their tastes and preferences. Economic standing has been shown repeatedly to influence Internet and computer usage (U.S. Department of Commerce 2004; Shneiderman 2001); and one would anticipate that this, in turn, should influence the systems accessed.

Downey et al. (2005), in their study of the relationship between culturally diverse participants' ratings of the usability of a WBI application, found that participants with high collectivism scores on a cultural survey instrument ranked system satisfaction higher than those with high individualism scores (p. 58). Thus, according to the authors, participants from countries where a higher acceptance of uneven power distribution and collectivism versus individualism prevail (e.g., China, India, Indonesia, Malaysia, and Singapore) tend to show higher system satisfaction. Although the study involved a small number of participants (30) being trained at an international workshop, the findings certainly point to the inevitable relationship between technology acceptance and cultural expectations. Smith et al. (2004) have outlined a preliminary metalevel taxonomy of "cultural attractors" that Web site designers should consider carefully, including color use, use of culturally specific symbols, culturally specific iconography, branding and signification, and linguistic cues (p. 72).

Distance education researchers have only begun to explore the wider institutional and organizational factors that influence learner success or failure. Shaffer (2005) outlines a preliminary model of socioeconomic variables surrounding DE programs and, although his model is complex and compelling, he also admits that it is untested at this point. Larger issues of geography, marketing, employment rates, societal and institutional recognition, and funding availability influence program variables such as application rate and acceptance, financial aid, faculty satisfaction and quality, and graduate rates and placement. Most certainly these macro-level, sociocultural issues influencing learner success educationally require additional research. Indeed, identifying sociocultural similarities and differences of importance to instruction and learning with technology represents a considerable challenge. Levine and Norenzayan (1999), for example, found that the "pace of life" (defined by average downtown walking speed, postal service exchange times, and the accuracy of public clocks) was significantly faster in economically productive countries with colder climates and individualistic cultures. Such findings certainly suggest that cognitive models of learners can benefit from developing cultural analyses.

For the most part, the present analysis thus far has focused on instructors, learners, tasks, social dynamics, and formal and informal learning environments at the expense of organizational, extrainstitutional, national, and international factors that come together to shape everyday instructional situations. As the tide of globalization that in part is prompting distributed education continues to advance, research investigating the troubling interaction between developing countries and impoverished technological landscapes will grow in importance. Selfe and Hawisher (2006) remind us that "The dynamics of the relationship among technology, literacy, poverty, and human development remain difficult to identify and are overdetermined. Indeed, the nations that might benefit the most from technological innovation are in the worst position to exploit it" (p. 254). Research that brings these factors to the surface and elaborates on different contexts for learning and instruction with technology promises to contribute to this discussion.

6.2   Learner Tasks and Activities

Tasks unite learner behaviors, facilitate social dynamics, inform instructional activities, and are framed by learning environments and artifacts. Mapping the relationship between learners and their goals, activities, and the tasks that make up those activities is at the heart of any attempt to understand either traditional face-to-face instruction or online instruction. As Tomlinson-Keasey (2002) reminds us, "Technologically mediated instruction requires the involvement of the student and flounders when students are passive" (p. 150). But more than that, the self-management of study and reflection related to the subject matter, comprehensive approaches to the instructional materials at hand, and the number of hours per week spent on-task have been shown to distinguish high-achieving learners from low ones (Smith and Smith 2006). Not surprisingly, learners who spend more time on-task tend to learn more (Bransford et al. 2000), and learners who spend more time using computers tend to be more comfortable with computers (Litchfield, Oakland, and Anderson 2002). In short, complex learning tasks and subject matters demand learner energy, motivation, attention, reflection, feedback, and trial and error.

Thus, Kozma (1991) states that any media used for learning will succeed or fail based on attributes of the tasks and the characteristics of the learners involved:

Whether or not a medium's capabilities make a difference in learning depends on how they correspond to the particular learning situation—the tasks and learners involved—and the way the medium's capabilities are used by the instructional design. Tasks vary in their situational characteristics and in the demands they place on the learner to create mental representations of certain information and to operate on that information in certain ways. Learners vary in their processing capabilities, the information and procedures that they have stored in long-term memory, their motivations and purposes for learning, and their metacognitive knowledge of when and how to use these procedures and information. (p. 182)

This is largely because tasks that are well known in conventional, face-to-face instructional settings are sometimes subtly and sometimes radically altered in online learning spaces. Thus, the activities involved in attending an online class are sharply reduced, while simultaneously the tasks involved in submitting assignments is made more complex; online, the task of improvisationally arranging a meeting "after class" with a colearner to go over class notes is fragmented across time (is class held synchronously?), space (are you ever really *with* a colearner?), technology (does the online environment support individual information exchange or do colearners tend to converse *outside* the WBI space?), and learning artifacts (what are the roles of studying and note-taking online?). As Hannafin et al. (2003) argue, "Many performance-oriented tasks, traditionally mentored or demonstrated in live situations, are difficult to convey effectively in virtual environments. Methods and techniques associated with complex performance via WBLEs [Web-based Learning Environments] need to be identified and validated across domains and tasks" (p. 254).

Researchers interested in the differences and similarities between educational technologies and conventional, hardcopy learning materials have long been interested in how different media influence learner behaviors, comprehension, motivation, and engagement. Dillon and Gabbard (1998), in their review of quantitative research on hypermedia's influence on learning, note that the tasks that learners attempt to perform—such as reading-to-learn versus reading-to-do—affect the success of their user experience with hypermedia versus paper-and-pencil instructional materials: "while it seems that paper offers significant advantages over hypermedia in some comprehension tasks, those tasks (or subtasks) that involve substantial amounts of large document manipulation, searching through large texts for specific details, and comparison of visual details among objects are potentially better supported by hypermedia" (p. 331). Dillon and Greene (2003), in their review of the relationship between learner attributes and distance education, recommend that "we should turn our focus from learner traits to learner approaches and develop instruments that we can use to help us learn more about the relationship between approaches to study and performance" (p. 242). Their recommendation is that, by altering instructional approaches online, we can begin to understand how learners succeed rather than merely describing traits that learners bring to learning situations beforehand.

6.2.1 Defining Tasks

Before we can understand how to design and evaluate instructional approaches, we need to understand instructor and learner activities, and these activities can be defined even more explicitly at the level of single tasks. At its most general level, a task refers to any portion of work to be accomplished, work that usually involves labor or difficulty. That is, we generally do not refer to activities that are pleasurable as *tasks* but, rather, as something we do. And yet at the cognitive level, playing chess is clearly a complex task that has served as a powerful metaphor for other "real-world" tasks (cf. Simon 1969, 1981; 1979).

In cognitive science, a task is any human activity that is made up of a series of subtasks, some that are conscious (for example, crossing the street) and some that are unconscious (for example, looking to the right or to the left prior to or while crossing the street). Williams (2004) emphasizes the discrete nature of tasks, their relationship to interaction (with applications, one's environment, or other humans), and the importance of being able to identify task beginnings and endings (p. 80). Dillon (1994) notes that tasks might further be elaborated upon by focusing on cognitive, perceptual, and physical elements, where physical elements dominate face-to-face versus online interactions. And Norman (1993) compares experiential cognition to reflective cognition, blurring the distinction between what we traditionally define as subconscious and conscious task processing. Experiential cognition is automatic and well learned, and, Norman (1993) emphasizes, "the appropriate responses [are] generated without apparent effort or delay" (p. 22). In contrast, reflective cognition involves choice and decision making: "Reflective thought requires the ability to store temporary results, to make inferences from stored knowledge, and to follow chains of reasoning backward and forward, sometimes back-tracking when a promising line of thought proves to be unfruitful. This process takes time" (p. 23).

Over time, our definition of task has generally grown more realistic, meaning we have generally acknowledged that tasks cannot be easily algorithmitized or parameterized. Thus, a relatively simple task involving basic, familiar concepts and procedures such as ordering lunch in a restaurant can be subjected to a fine-grained task analysis that involves a host of potential choices, situational determinants, and numerous embedded decision points. Most tasks, therefore, involve certain processes, often require the use of applications that invite their own host of tasks, and end in an awkward merging of the two separate knowledge domains. The challenges inherent to algorithmitizing definitions of task contrast sharply with our tendency to describe tasks in terms that suggest that tasks are entities that we can calculate, rate, or estimate.

Tasks can be categorized according to various parameters: in terms of frequency, time spent performing the task, the difficulty involved in recognizing that the task requires performing, the delay between acknowledgment and actual performance, the difficulty involved in learning and in performing the task, the challenge of recognizing when the task has been finished, the likelihood and consequences of inadequate performance, and the criticality of the task performance in relation to the person engaged in the task, the community that person belongs to, and the overall activity involved. As well, tasks can be better understood by collecting information about the individual and environmental variables that surround them, that is, the entry-level skills and knowledge, attitudes, biases, and needs of user-learners and the physical and organizational compositions of their environment. Williams (2004) advocates collecting data via market surveys, observation, interviews, questionnaires, checklists, attitude scales, critical incident descriptions, task analysis, task design, deficiency analysis, and user and/or subject-matter ratings for user, task, and environmental characteristics (p. 79).

Because the focus here is on tasks in the broader context of both designing and offering instruction, Williams's (2004) elaboration on the terms *importance*, *frequency*, *time*, *complexity*, and *difficulty* is particularly noteworthy:

- *Importance*: How important the task is to the overall responsibility.
- *Frequency*: How often the task is (or is expected to be) performed.

• *Time*: The typical time the task takes (or is expected to take) to perform.
• *Complexity*: Rating on the relative complexity of the task.
• *Difficulty*: Rating on the difficulty of the task (it may be appropriate to specify both physical and mental difficulty in some cases). (Williams 2004, p. 101)

Indeed, Miller, Lehman, and Koedinger (1999) stress that "careful selection and analysis of the tasks that frame microworld use is essential if such environments are to lead to the learning outcomes imagined for them" (p. 305). Because designing the instructional materials housed in an online environment (or the general environment, for that matter) is an ambitious undertaking, it is often necessary to begin with tasks that are performed frequently rather than tasks that the instructor believes are important. Although one might imagine that these considerations would highlight the same tasks, considerable experience with the usability testing of WBI materials suggests the direct opposite. Thus, where instructors tend to spend a great deal of time working out the nuances of important conceptual definitions and methods for applying them in context, most learners focus much more time and attention on the class schedule, due dates, and assignment explanations. In fact, instructors rarely have students ask to elaborate in detail on sentence-level descriptions of their class notes online, but they do have a great many students inquire after the particular meaning of this or that sentence in their assignments section, even after they have revised those assignment instructions many times for many different classes of learners.

6.2.2 Illusive Authenticity and the Design of Tasks

Figuring out mismatches between instructor conceptions of the task and learner representations of the task is probably one of the greatest challenges instructors face. Of course, task descriptions and attributes can thwart easy explication, in addition to learner expectations and backgrounds and the particular social dynamics of the learning situation. Many of these compelling instructional issues have been brought to the foreground by researchers interested in authenticity in education.

Indeed, few expressions find as much use or as much enthusiasm in educational circles as the term "authentic." Herrington, Oliver, and Reeves (2003) limit their focus on authentic activities to formal learning environments, noting that researchers such as Petraglia (1998) have argued persuasively that authenticity is a largely constructed educational concept and that true authenticity depends on a complex interrelationship between learners, situations, and tasks. For this reason, I routinely ask myself, when engaged in personal learning *moments* (e.g., reading an article or book that helps me to understand an issue more fully or conceptualize a complex matter more strategically), what it is about the moment that could be emulated in formal instructional settings and what aspects of the moment are highly personal, individually motivated, and of uncertain immediate use (if I am even able to articulate usefulness in a particular moment). Thus, we should always remember that tasks have both an objective dimension and a subjective one, where the latter represents the learner's perceived experience of the task, whether as simple, dull, complex, or highly engaging (Campbell 1988). While tasks or activities can be interpreted as having particular features or characteristics, these features are always interacting with learner backgrounds and knowledge.

Ten principal characteristics of authentic activities, according to Herrington, Oliver, and Reeves (2003), include the following:

• *Authentic activities have real-world relevance*: Activities match as nearly as possible the real-world tasks of professionals in practice rather than decontextualized or classroom-based activities.

• *Authentic activities are ill defined, requiring students to define the tasks and subtasks needed to complete the activity*: Problems inherent in the activities are ill defined and open to multiple interpretations rather than easily solved by the application of existing algorithms. Learners must identify their own unique tasks and subtasks in order to complete the major task.

• *Authentic activities comprise complex tasks to be investigated by students over a sustained period of time*: Activities are completed in days, weeks, or months rather than minutes or hours. They require significant investment of time and intellectual resources.

• *Authentic activities provide the opportunity for students to examine the task from different perspectives, using a variety of resources*: The task affords learners the opportunity to examine the problem from a variety of theoretical and practical perspectives, rather than allowing a single perspective that learners must imitate to be successful. The use of a variety of resources rather than a limited number of preselected references requires students to distinguish relevant from irrelevant information.

• *Authentic activities provide the opportunity to collaborate*: Collaboration is integral to the task, both within the course and the real world, rather than achievable by an individual learner.

• *Authentic activities provide the opportunity to reflect*: Activities need to enable learners to make choices and reflect on their learning both individually and socially.

• *Authentic activities can be integrated and applied across different subject areas and lead beyond domain-specific outcomes*: Activities encourage interdisciplinary perspectives and enable students to play diverse roles, thus building robust expertise rather than knowledge limited to a single well-defined field or domain.

• *Authentic activities are seamlessly integrated with assessment*: Assessment of activities is seamlessly integrated with the major task in a manner that reflects real-world assessment, rather than separate artificial assessment removed from the nature of the task.

• *Authentic activities create polished products valuable in their own right rather than as preparation for something else*: Activities culminate in the creation of a whole product rather than an exercise or substep in preparation for something else.

• *Authentic activities allow competing solutions and diversity of outcome*: Activities allow a range and diversity of outcomes open to multiple solutions of an original nature, rather than a single correct response obtained by the application of rules and procedures.

A critical attribute of authentic tasks is their tendency to contain many subtasks, some well defined and some ill defined in nature. Thankfully, Hilton (2003) found that learners who approve of the use of challenging scenarios in instruction also accept that they are difficult or very difficult to do. Truly authentic tasks frequently demand— as an initial step in approaching them—the need to actually discover, decide, and prioritize the subtasks required to attain a satisfactory outcome. Indeed, establishing just what one views as a satisfactory outcome may be the true first task. Godshalk, Harvey, and Moller (2004) note that, when designing specific procedures for authentic tasks, instructors need to attend to "the design of learner tasks such that learners faced with ill-structured domains are asked to examine these domains through tasks that require them to disown their beliefs (even temporarily), process information adaptively, and assemble it into flexible knowledge structures" (p. 525). These tasks anticipate learner abilities that Engeström (2000) has observed in the workplace and refers to as "knotworking," which requires "interdependency between multiple producers" in addition to "Rapid negotiation and improvisation with constantly changing configurations of partners" (p. 533). In this respect, authentic learning tasks belong to Weinberger's (2007) "miscellaneous order," where "the only distinction between metadata and data is that metadata is what you already know and data is what you're trying to find out" (p. 104). Certainly, the attributes of authentic problems, then, have a great many things in common with the dimensions of wicked problems outlined earlier.

Problem-based learning (PBL) is one of the better-documented approaches for foregrounding authenticity in learning and is grounded in constructivist learning theory. Constructivist theorists tend to elaborate more fully on the social dimensions of teaching and learning, although this does not mean that they view cognitive theories of learning as incompatible with their own. PBL was first implemented in 1968 as part of the M.D. program at McMaster University in Hamilton, Ontario, Canada, and Smith et al. (2005) have argued that—coupled with cooperative groupwork—PBL can "advance academic success, quality of relationships, psychological adjustment, and attitudes toward the college experience" (p. 10). Savery and Duffy (1995) summarize the four principles of PBL as follows:

• Understanding is based on experiences with content, context, the learner's goals, and so on, and these factors are inextricably woven together. Thus, understanding is a construction that is unique to the individual.

• Meaning is not transmitted, although it may be tested for compatibility with the meanings of others. From another perspective, cognition may be regarded as being distributed rather than individually localized.

• Puzzlement is the factor that motivates learning (thus, puzzlement works as a stimulus for learning and, in turn, influences the organizational content learned).

• Social negotiation and the ongoing testing of the viability of existing concepts in the face of personal experience are the principal forces involved in the evolution of knowledge.

Constructivist theorists advocate a radical change in the way instructors approach their learners, subject matters, and methods of presentation. Given the ill-structured nature of many learning situations facing learners, constructivists aggressively challenge the instructional role of authority figure, master teacher, or sage, advocating instead a vision of instructor as coach, guide, mentor, or facilitator.

Kozma et al. (2000), following this reasoning, frame their principles for instruction in studies of scientists' actual professional activities, arguing that "Given the practices of scientists and the needs of students, we have derived some specifications for the design of representational environments to support the investigations of these knowledge-building communities" (p. 138). As science education researchers, Kozma et al. (2000) agree with numerous other cognitive science and human–computer interaction researchers that in classroom or virtual environments, learners need to be able to:

• *Generate representations* that express their understanding of underlying entities and processes (Representing). A term from cognitive psychology, this stage involves learners attempting to understand their situation or problem as they work through it. How learners characterize their problem is critical to developing a representation of their state and the possible solutions that are available given the constraints of the situation. The prior experience of learners and their ability to apply that experience to interpret their particular situation greatly influences the form of their representation.

• *Access information* related to the problem (Discovering). With detection or representation of the impasse accomplished, learners must access information that will help them solve the problem. This can be a significant challenge for learners and involves working with their notions and names for the information and the terminology of the resources they are working with (Furnas et al. 1987; Gomez, Lochbaum, and Landauer 1990; Landauer et al. 1993).

• *Navigate information* related to the problem (Selecting). In selecting or defining a topic, learners begin navigating the document or online information space. Many of the methods for navigating online are different from navigating hardcopy texts (despite the emulation of familiar touchstones such as tables of contents and indexes).

Issues of navigation are frequently cited as the major difference between hardcopy and online text use and grow in importance as more and more online spaces aim to support social navigation effectively (Buscher and Hughes 2003). Keyes, Sykes, and Lewis (1989) recommend that designers chunk information, provide queues about hierarchy, filter out irrelevant material, mix modes to appeal to various audience types, and abstract or simplify complex concepts.

• Use these representations to *identify, explain, and analyze phenomena* at the observable and metaphorical level in terms of subject matter under general and particular consideration (Sampling, Annotating, and Illustrating). To accomplish this, learners must be able to comprehend text and graphics, and text and graphics must therefore be designed effectively (Barker 1998; Schriver 1997).

• *Take an epistemological position* that representations correspond to but are distinct from the phenomena they observe and their understanding of it (Comparing).

• Use language in social context to *communicate* or *transfer* understanding and make explicit connections across representations that convey relationships between different representations and between symbolic expressions and the phenomena they represent that are appropriate for different purposes (Kozma et al. 2000, p. 136) (Illustrating and Representing).

Another way to highlight the nuanced structure of tasks is to take them out of their natural context (face-to-face instructional situations) and to conceptualize them as designed for alternative or emerging contexts. Because online "microworlds" are represented by and as computer interfaces, it becomes important to understand the user tasks and activities that characterize human–computer interaction, general problem-solving activities, and information literacy demands (see table 6.4).

Developments in humanities computing have also led researchers to formulate summaries of primary activities related to research in the humanities. Unsworth (2000) describes these activities as "scholarly primitives," where primitives are "some basic functions common to scholarly activity across disciplines, over time, and independent of theoretical orientation" (p. 1); and Jessop (2005) has explored how these primitives might be applied not only to research but to teaching and learning in the humanities. Unsworth's (2000, p. 1) "self-understood" functions of high-level research include the following activities:

• Discovering
• Annotating
• Comparing
• Referring
• Sampling
• Illustrating
• Representing

Table 6.4
General problem-solving tasks for the twenty-first century[a]

General problem-solving tasks for the twenty-first century

	Allen's (1996) task behaviors	Association of College and Research Libraries' (2000) information literacy abilities	Mehlenbacher's (1992) online tasks	Norman's (1990) human activities
Define information goal (e.g., Where do I begin? What is expected of me?)	Recognition of the problem	Determine the extent of information needed	Set an information goal to represent task (combine prior knowledge and information goals)	Form a goal
Navigate and select information (e.g., Where am I in this process? When am I finished?)	Identification of alternative courses of action	Access the needed information effectively and efficiently	Navigate to new or related topics and choose relevant topics	Form an intent Specify actions Do actions
Scan for relevancy and focus (e.g., What do I do now? What do I do next?)		Evaluate information and its sources critically	Scan the information	See what happens
Understand and interpret information (e.g., How do I interact with the materials? How do I get more/less information?)		Incorporate selected information into one's knowledge base	Attempt to understand the information (read the online text and graphics)	Interpret it
Evaluate information goal and success of inquiry (e.g., How am I doing? Did I achieve my goal?)	Evaluation of the alternatives in order to select a course of action	Evaluate information and its use	Revise information goal based on feedback	Evaluate outcome
Apply information to various contexts (e.g., Does the given solution apply to this particular case? What changes or modifications are required to apply what I have learned?)		Use information effectively to accomplish a specific purpose Understand the economic, legal, and social issues surrounding the use of information, and access and use information ethically and legally		Evaluate outcome

[a]Adapted from Allen (1996, p. 13); Association of College and Research Libraries (2000); Mehlenbacher (1992, p. 37); Norman (1990, p. 48).

The reason for drawing on Unsworth's (2000) discussion of "scholarly primitives" is that, rather than stressing which comes first—learning or technology, instructor training or learner reform—in fact, a thoughtful and thorough understanding of *tasks* ought to drive instruction and learning with technology. That is, these primitive academic tasks among faculty-instructors ought to be shared by student-learners, as authentic faculty research activities too ought to be shared with students. After all, "discovering" in the rhetorical tradition is often replaced by inventing, since discovering emphasizes *uncovering* or *exposing to view* something previously hidden, unclear, or undisclosed, and that perspective toward problem definition suggests that a set objective solution or truth is out there waiting to be unmasked. As we have seen, in a world defined by wicked problems, no such guarantees can be assumed; contemporary learners are frequently inventing or, rather, *creating*, *imagining*, or *producing* by mental activity or collaboration.

Unsworth (2000) does not provide extensive definitions of the tasks or activities that make up each of his scholarly primitives; but, in some ways, their definitions are so clear that we frequently deemphasize their instrumentality in most instructional situations and problem-solving endeavors. In brief, learners are annotating whenever they create notes or elaborate on any subject matter; comparing whenever they identify the differences and similarities of one object or concept with another; referring whenever they attribute something to a person, place, or thing as the ultimate source or cause; sampling whenever they attempt to explain, model, or identify parallels to a given case; illustrating whenever they describe by example or analogy to elucidate or explain a subject further; and representing whenever they specify the character or quality of something (either positively or negatively) through artificial resemblance. Notably, instructional situations often call for these actions on the part of learners without ever really identifying, describing, or developing their capacities to perform them.

Mayer (2001), in his overview of major ways that knowledge can be structured and the processes involved in active learning (cf. Feinberg, Murphy, and Duda 2003), provides a compelling cognitive contrast to Unsworth's (2000) scholarly primitives. Given our focus on tasks and activities, I have taken liberties with Mayer's (2001) separation between knowledge structures and learning processes by translating them into action verbs followed by Mayer's (2001) descriptions and examples (see table 6.5).

Another way of framing Unsworth's (2000) scholarly primitives and Mayer's (2001) active learning processes in instructional situations is to quickly review their similarity with other conceptions of human problem-solving behaviors and tasks (cf. tables 4.3 and 6.4). Advocating a design-oriented approach to problem solving, Buchanan (1995) creatively extends what he describes as Simon's (1969, 1981) "thought processes of creating, judging, deciding, and choosing as the real subjects of the new intellectual

Table 6.5
Knowledge structures and active learning processes[a]

Name	Description	Example
Selecting	Learner pays attention to relevant words and pictures in a multimedia message to create a word base and an image base	In viewing a narrated animation on lightning formation, learner pays attention to words and pictures describing each of the main steps
Organizing	Learner builds internal connections among selected words to create an coherent verbal and pictorial model	Learner organizes the steps into a cause-and-effect chain for the words and for the pictures
Integrating	Learner builds external connections between the verbal and pictorial models and with prior knowledge	Learner makes connections between corresponding steps in the verbal chain and in the pictorial chain and justifies the steps on the basis of knowledge of electricity
Comparing	Learner compares and contrasts two or more elements along several dimensions	Comparison of two theories of learning with respect to nature of the learner, teacher, and instructional methods
Generalizing	Learner describes main idea and supporting details	Presentation of thesis for the major causes of the American Civil War along with evidence
Classifying	Learner analyzes a domain into sets and subsets	Description of a biological classification system for sea animals

[a]Adapted from Mayer (2001, pp. 52–53).

trade among cultures and disciplines" to produce a matrix outlining the "pattern of rhetoric in twentieth-century design" (Buchanan 1995, p. 45). Buchanan's (1995) pattern divides design into conceptual verbs and objects or subject matters, that is, into inventing and communicating signs and images (messages), judging and constructing physical objects (products), deciding and planning actions and services (processes), and, finally, evaluating and integrating ideas and systems (environments) (p. 45).

Buchanan's (1995) description of what problem solvers do when designing can be compared to Bruce and Levin's (1997) four-part division of the activities that we engage in when using educational technologies: inquiry, communication, construction, and expression (influenced by Dewey 1943). The appeal of this orientation is its focus on its use of instructional approaches to organize technological activities (see table 6.6):

In a review of National Science Foundation Applications of Advanced Technologies funded in 1996, Bruce and Levin (1997) found that 70 out of 73 of the projects focused on technologies that facilitate inquiry and communication, that three of the projects

Table 6.6
Media use and the learning tasks and activities associated with them[a]

Media Use	Learning Tasks and Activities
Inquiry	• Theory building—technology as media for thinking: Model exploration and simulation tools, visualization software, virtual reality environments, data modeling (defining categories, relations, representations), procedural and mathematical models, knowledge representation (semantic network, outline tools), knowledge integration • Data access—connecting to the world of texts, video, data: Hypertext and hypermedia environments, library access and ordering, digital libraries, databases, music, voice, graphics, video, data tables, graphs, text • Data collection—using technology to extend the senses: Remote scientific instruments accessible via networks, microcomputer-based laboratories (with sensors for temperature, motion, heart rate), survey makers for student-run surveys and interviews, video and sound recording • Data analysis: Exploratory data analysis, statistical analysis, environments for inquiry, image processing, spreadsheets, programs to make tables and graphs, problem-solving programs
Communication	• Document preparation: Word processing, outlining, graphics, spelling, grammar, usage, and style aides, symbolic expressions, desktop publishing, presentation graphics • Communication—with other students, teachers, experts in various fields, and people around the world: Electronic mail, asynchronous computer conferencing, synchronous computer conferencing (text, audio, video), distributed information servers, student-created hypertext environments • Collaborative media: Collaborative data environments, group decision support systems, shared document preparation, social spreadsheets • Teaching media: Tutoring systems, instructional simulations, drill and practice systems, telementoring
Construction	• Control systems—using technology to affect the physical world, robotics, control of equipment, computer-aided design, construction of graphs and charts
Expression	• Drawing and painting programs, music making and accompaniment, music composing and editing, interactive video and hypermedia, animation software, multimedia composition

[a]Adapted from Bruce and Levin (1997).

involved technologies for construction, and that none of the projects involved media for expression.[2] This finding is supported by Roberts's (2003) study of teaching faculty at a Scottish university whose major use of the Internet was, first, "to update their own knowledge of subject information for teaching," and, second, "to direct students to relevant Websites for subject resources" (p. 145). Other potentials for Internet use in teaching, including supporting independent, self-paced learning and managing distributed groupwork and discourse, remained largely unexplored, encouraging Roberts (2003) to conclude, "teachers' conceptions need to develop from instructivist, information transmission mode to constructivist, learning facilitation mode" (p. 127).

More recently, Raubenheimer et al. (2007) observed a purposeful sample of twenty faculty at North Carolina State University with experience teaching in technology-rich classrooms across disciplines, class sizes, and subject matters. Faculty were interviewed and observed, student work was gathered, and each of four research observers wrote a case record and performed cross-case analysis. Observations were based on an observation instrument (with an inter-rater reliability of 89 percent among the observers) that addressed, among other things, technology use by the instructors and instructor behavior and lesson implementation. In addition to noting that faculty instruction was essentially teacher centered, Raubenheimer et al. (2007) found that instructor use of technology in the classroom was primarily to communicate information, a conclusion in keeping with the common faculty perception that the purpose of teaching was "for students to learn the content and/or structure of the discipline."

Similar to the tasks and activities identified by Bruce and Levin (1997) are the North Carolina State University LITRE (Learning in a Technology-Rich Environment) Committee's four general activities related to student learning, knowing, and doing (Margolis 2004). Comprised of faculty from numerous disciplines, distance education and information technology specialists, and administrators across colleges, the LITRE Committee has worked for several years to amass research and best practices related to student engagement with instruction and technology. To that end, their inquiry-based instructional approach grounds the majority of their technology discussions (see table 6.7).

Developing effective instruction on problem solving, empirical inquiry, research from sources, and performance activities—always firmly rooted in the disciplinary structures that represent them—represents a truly wicked twenty-first-century challenge for instructors (cf. Fleming 2003). But they can also serve to orchestrate meaningful comparison and contrast across disciplines and to help researchers interested in instruction and learning with technology to articulate higher-level educational goals for learners unfamiliar with the discourse of their fields. As well, a focus on tasks that support these processes—that is, of finding the problem, representing it, planning a problem solution, executing the plan, checking the solution, and reflecting to consolidate learning (Pea 1993, p. 66)—quickly highlights the need for a view of tasks

Table 6.7

Student learning: Four ways of knowing and doing[a]

Activity	Explication
1. Problem solving	
Definition	A way of knowing and doing that involves an initial state and an end state and some difficulty in moving from the initial state to the end state and consists of overcoming and attaining the end state
Common ways of knowing and doing	(1) Finding or being given a problem; (2) defining the problem; (3) determining various possible solutions, ways of attaining end state; (4) evaluating the solution; (5) applying the optimal solution to the problem
Variations	(1) designing a product; (2) applying specialized knowledge; (3) finding sources that provide pertinent information
Question for technology education	What kinds of technology and technology education do we provide students to best enable them to solve problems in ways appropriate to their fields of study?
2. Empirical inquiry	
Definition	A way of knowing and doing that consists of answering questions by drawing conclusions from systematic inquiry based on empirical data
Common ways of knowing and doing	(1) Asking or being given a research question; (2) designing or being given a research method for answering the question; (3) applying deliberate and thorough observational skills; (4) organizing, summarizing, and presenting data; (5) coming to conclusions based on the data
Variations	(1) hypothetical empirical inquiry; (2) descriptive empirical inquiry; (3) prospective empirical inquiry
Question for technology education	What kinds of technology and technology education do we provide to students to best enable them to engage in empirical inquiry appropriate to their fields of study?
3. Research from sources	
Definition	A way of knowing and doing that involves academic investigation using primarily library and Internet resources, the "research paper"
Common ways of knowing and doing	(1) Asking or being given a research question; (2) locating relevant primary and secondary sources to answer the question; (3) critically evaluating the sources; (4) marshalling the evidence to answer the research question
Variations	Varies according to discipline. Doing the research is not an end in itself, rather a means of learning about and entering into the conversation of the discipline
Question for technology education	What kinds of technology and technology education do we provide to students to best enable them to engage in academic research appropriate to their disciplines?

Table 6.7
(continued)

Activity	Explication
4. Performance	
Definition	A way of knowing and doing that results in an artifact which has value in and of itself but, more importantly in terms of learning, as direct evidence of the performance, a student's ability to successfully apply art and technique
Common ways of knowing and doing	Depends on the discipline
Variations	Depends on the discipline
Question for technology education	What kinds of technology and technology education do we provide to students to best enable them to engage in the modes of performance appropriate to their disciplines?

[a]Adapted from Margolis (2004, p. 53).

that moves toward complex individual and social activities and the artifacts and environments that support or undermine them.

6.2.3 Moving from Tasks to Activities, Artifacts, and Environments

The tasks that we construct for learners—similar to the attributes and abilities of learners themselves—are not generated in a vacuum. Tasks interact with each other, with learners and other learners, with instructional goals, activities, and learning outcomes, and with the artifacts and environments that comprise everyday instructional situations. For this reason, it is prudent to divide tasks into individual and social activities to account for the complex of factors that come together to support or impede learner engagement, production, task-completion, and coordination.

Dietz (2005), applying Winograd and Flores's (1986) conversation-as-action model of human–computer interaction, separates human abilities into *forma* (form), *informa* (content), and *performa* (engagement) abilities and describes how we apply these abilities to either coordinating or producing in given sociotechnical contexts.

Performa abilities, according to Dietz (2005), are related primarily to personal identity factors, and learner motivation and metacognitive awareness play a significant role in the amount of engagement learners bring to a given task or set of tasks. Informa abilities are connected to cognitive and problem-solving abilities, and forma abilities connect performa and informa activities to social dynamics and learner literacies, wherein learners are expected to take their problem-solving abilities and to create or produce artifacts that are persuasive, informative, and useful. Tasks, then, combine individual abilities with coordinating discourse and actions with production processes.

The importance of Winograd and Flores's (1986) influence on contemporary perspectives toward computing use cannot be underestimated for, as Winograd (2006) reminds us:

In imposing a language-action framework on information technology, we emphasize the action dimension over the more traditional dimension of information content. As an orienting theory, this perspective reveals the underlying structure that drives and gives meaning to the activities of people using an information system. It offers the possibility of making that structure visible to the participants in a way that enables them to act more effectively when effective coordination is a necessity and cannot be taken for granted. (p. 72)

Developments in technology and computing, then, need to be grounded in human action and activities to become meaningful. But technology and computing, in turn, alter our perceptions of what skills, knowledge, and attitudes are necessary for defining what it means to act meaningfully. Thus, with the widespread use of powerful mechanisms for exploring digital library repositories, Thelwall (2004) stresses that "search skills in education [are] widely recognized, becoming a part of information literacy and triggering the publication of entire books devoted to various forms of online searching." Moreover, contemporary reviews of the literature—grounded as they are in heightened online archiving and search capabilities—can be expected to draw on multidisciplinary resources much more routinely, and this "increased serendipity," to use Thelwall's (2004) expression, will require researchers who both have interdisciplinary skills in evaluating out-of-field research and are comfortable with collaborative models of researching and writing.

The emerging roles of researchers interested in instruction and learning with technology, of instructors aiming to create technology-mediated educational experiences, of learners intent on harnessing alternative methods to generate worthwhile outcomes, and of administrators motivated to support institutional climates that facilitate the creative use of technologies in education are all design-oriented. Brown (2000) interprets the increased need for these skills on the contemporary erosion of trust and recommends "triangulation," that is, "taking bearings not on the information alone but also on its context" (p. 1). Cross (1995) summarizes design studies to produce four core features of design ability that capture many of the tasks and activities outlined by Dietz (2005), Mayer (2001), and Unsworth (2000). Design involves the resolution of ill-defined problems, the adoption of strategies for producing solutions, the application of multiple perspectives, and the use of "nonverbal, graphic/spatial modelling media" (Cross 1995, p. 111).

Importantly, these activities are usually prompted by cognitive dissonance and the general learner orientation, "How do I . . . ?," with the answer being provided in the context of learning to do. The challenge is to build online instructional environments that promote primary learning and task accomplishment and, therefore, reduce secondary distractions due to ill-conceived user interactions. As Squires (1999) has asked, how can usability goals "be contextualized in terms of the complex tasks involved in learning" (p. 465)? And this, of course, is a question that can be applied as much to face-to-face instruction as it has been to online instruction. In Margolin's (1995) words, "Most products support traditional patterns of activity rather than create new ones" (p. 136); this assertion is particularly true of technology use for instruction and learning.

One way of moving our attention away from content delivery and in the direction of task orientation is to conceptualize designs for learning based on learner questions. Mehlenbacher and colleagues (Mehlenbacher 2003; Selber, Johnson-Eilola, and Mehlenbacher 1997; Tomasi and Mehlenbacher 1999), focusing on online documentation design, propose that these learning questions can be organized around six information types and questions applied to instructional content and interfaces (table 6.8).

Another way of explicitly connecting learning tasks to the design of artificial instructional environments is to begin with what we know about human cognition and learning processes. Van Merriënboer and Kester (2005) provide a most useful summary of cognitive principles that inform the design of tasks, support, procedures, and practice, and that can, in turn, assist the designers of learning environments and artifacts to build systems that support effective learner actions and activities (see table 6.9).

Table 6.8
Six information types and questions applied to instructional content and interfaces[a]

Information type	Questions for instructional content	Questions for instructional environment
Goal exploration	What am I trying to accomplish in this program, course, lesson, module?	What can I accomplish in this environment?
Definitional and descriptive	What is this particular content? How am I expected to use or apply it?	What is this particular feature? What is it used for?
Procedural and immediate	How does this work? What parts work to create whole understanding?	How do I do this? What steps does this require?
Diagnostic and state explication	What did that mean? How is this related to prior information? Where am I in the material?	What just happened? Huh? Where am I?
Example-based and medium term	How is this content useful? Is it the same as previous content? How do elaborations fit into the bigger picture?	How does this example work? How do I copy it step-by-step? What are the various parts?
Conceptual and long term	How does this course material fit with previous courses? Why is this lesson included in the course materials? How do these examples solidify my overall understanding of the materials?	How do all these application features work together? What would I like to learn how to do in this environment if I only had the time?

[a]Adapted from Mehlenbacher (2003, p. 533).

Table 6.9
Prominent multimedia principles[a]

Principle	Example
Learning tasks and learning in simulated task environments	
Sequencing principle	Learners start with only a few elements and continue with models with increasingly more elements
Fidelity principle	Learners begin with textual examples, move to video representations, to simulations, and end with real-world examples
Variability principle	Learners prepare examples for different contexts of use, audiences, and systems
Individualization principle	Learners are assessed and examples that have them work with their difficulties or misconceptions are presented
Training-wheels principle	Learners have numerous tasks and options blocked until they perform specific tasks and then options are added as they become necessary for learner progress in working with more complex tasks
Completion-strategy principle	Learners evaluate existing examples and then redesign the examples and, finally, design their own examples
Supportive information and learning from hypermedia	
Redundancy principle	Learners first produce a limited descriptive example and then develop a complex example with working parts and structuring
Self-explanation principle	Learners articulate their understanding of an example and describe it and how it works
Self-pacing principle	Learners are able to view examples and control how they are presented and the support information that is provided with them
Procedural information and electronic performance support systems	
Temporal split-attention principle	Learners building an example are given just-in-time instruction on how to perform the task while they are doing it
Spatial split-attention principle	Learners work on an example and present a separate analysis of the example while they work with it
Signaling principle	Learners analyze an example and produce an example of someone working on the example in a step-by-step fashion
Modality principle	Learners work with simulated example and explain the example textually or orally
Part-task practice and drill and practice	
Component-fluency principle	Learners work with example and repeat tasks using the same or different examples until they are fluid with the class of example in general

[a]Adapted from van Merriënboer and Kester (2005).

Designing learner tasks and activities so that cognitive and learning processes, information goals, and group dynamics are supported by the instructional environment thus becomes a central goal when conceptualizing everyday instructional situations.

6.3 Social Dynamics

Interaction, of course, is as essential to a meaningful life as it is to successful instructional situations. Indeed, Csikszentmihalyi and Rochberg-Halton (1981) view our involvement in social interactions as an essential means for evaluating our "personhood":

Moving from a personal to a social perspective does not change the nature of the criterion. The same considerations that define a positive state of the individual apply to the social system, except that we move from the level of personal consciousness to that of community. The relevant consideration shifts from order and disorder within persons to order and disorder between persons. Entropy in a social system exists when the intentions of people conflict with one another; when the same information is interpreted as positive feedback by some and as negative by others; and when the psychic energy investment of some people makes it more difficult for others to attain an ordered state. When a group is in an entropic state the intentions of its members cancel out each other instead of contributing toward each person's goals. (pp. 10–11)

Very few topics receive as much attention as social dynamics and the role of interaction, collaboration, and community in the instruction and learning with technology research literature (Jonassen et al. 2005). Gunawardena and McIsaac (2004), listing current trends in distance education, outline the following critical issues for researchers interested in instruction and learning with technology:

• *The distance learner*: Topics such as race, gender, learner independence (availability of options), academic self-concept, competence (ability, skill, motivation), support (human and artifacts), critical thinking, group dynamics abilities, self-efficacy, learning strategies, and learner readiness (pp. 380–381).
• *Interaction and learning*: Topics such as synchronous versus asynchronous communication, processes and types of learning, exchange patterns and knowledge making, cognitive presence, international variations (pp. 381–382).
• *Social dynamics*: Topics such as socioemotional-affective interaction (encouraging, task orientation, supporting), role of moderation and facilitation, information exchange, and methodological issues (pp. 382–383).
• *Social presence*: Connected to social dynamics, as well as group cohesion, motivation, social equality, social richness, instructor immediacy, learner satisfaction (pp. 383–384).

• *Cultural context*:   Topics such as nonnative student participation, globalization, multicultural course design, issues of language, gender, conflict management styles, and varying technical capabilities (pp. 384–385).

• *Distance education as a complex system*:   Topics such as learner support, design, teaching, communication, and especially transaction, housed under a systems theory approach (p. 386).

• *Rethinking comparative studies*:   Problems such as research design issues, lack of usefulness, and confounded results due to media issues or control group challenges, framed within discussions of the utility of emerging research methods such as ethnography (p. 386).

Although these research areas are listed as nonparallel issues, it is possible to interpret them in a more chronological fashion. Initial studies comparing online with face-to-face instruction, having been revised to emphasize the creative application of emerging methods for studying online instruction, could potentially help us view distance education as a complex system made up of interacting learning dimensions. Foundational studies of the attributes of distance learners can be augmented by analyses of social presence, dynamics, and online interaction. And, finally, understanding the relationship between learners, their tasks, and the social interactions that they engage in to accomplish their tasks can, in turn, help us to better understand the social and cultural contexts that characterize learning situations (cf. Clark and Mayer 2003; Medsker and Holdsworth 2001).

Social dynamics in instructional situations, at the most fundamental level, include communication, interaction, dialogue, or discussion between an instructor and a learner (with eight variations). Whether facilitated by oral, visual, or written communication or technology-mediated interaction, social dynamics provide the glue that holds an instructional situation together. Saba (2003) stresses the centrality of communication to instruction when he notes that "separation can be bridged by communication technology, a fact demonstrated by teachers and students everywhere. But if students and teachers are separated by the total absence of dialog, as occurs in many classrooms across the country and around the world, bringing them together until they stand nose to nose will not offer a solution" (p. 17). Wagner (2006) argues that interaction is essential to effective instruction, noting that learners interact for a myriad of worthwhile outcomes including participation, communication, feedback, elaboration, motivation, negotiation, discovery, and exploration (pp. 47–48).

Given the acknowledged importance of social dynamics to effective instruction, it is not surprising that Chickering and Gamson's (1987) seven principles for how to teach effectively at the undergraduate level, as well as their application to online environments (Chickering and Ehrmann 1998), have been so widely cited (cf. Shea, Pickett, and Pelz 2003). Mehlenbacher et al. (2000) provide a summary of Chickering et al.'s results applied specifically to online writing instruction (see table 6.10).

Table 6.10

Chickering and Gamson's (1987) seven principles of "Good Practice in Undergraduate Education" compared with writing instruction and online instruction[a]

Good Practice in Education	Good Practice in Writing Instruction	How Online Instruction Could Facilitate Good Practice
Encourages contact between students and faculty	Small class sizes (national standards recommend less than 20) and emphasis on the complete writing process	Ease of student access to faculty through e-mail and electronic conferencing
Encourages cooperation among students	Collaborative peer review, group exercises, and collaborative writing	Ease of collaboration and perceived sense of online "community"
Encourages active learning	Constant student application of precepts and guidelines	Students more willing to challenge authority and to take less conventional communication roles
Gives prompt feedback to students	Frequent feedback on drafts and revisions from both teachers and other students	Use of help desks, hotlines, and other course management and user assistance resources
Emphasizes time on-task	Courses designed around writing tasks, emphasis on process from drafting through revision	Network tracking systems can monitor student use of particular materials and provide students with the opportunity to read and review materials as often as they require
Communicates high expectations	Emphasis on practice and on revision and peer review for continued improvement	Models of excellence available online, Web dissemination of student work emphasizes importance of quality, call for continued involvement in online class "experiments"
Respects diverse talents and ways of learning	Emphasis on meeting the needs of different audiences, use of diverse strategies	Provides different paths to objectives and alternative representations of instructional materials, self-paced, flexible access

[a]Adapted from Mehlenbacher et al. (2000).

Part of the appeal of Chickering and Gamson's (1987) and Chickering and Ehrmann's (1998) summary of effective instruction is its emphasis on the numerous forms of interaction required in any instructional situation. Social interaction, broadly defined, can take eight forms (Anderson 2003b):

1. learners interacting with instructors, or visa versa;
2. learners interacting with other learners;
3. learners interacting with content;
4. learners interacting with interfaces;
5. instructors interacting with content (form and function);
6. instructors interacting with interfaces;
7. instructors interacting with other instructors; and
8. content interacting with content (Anderson 2003b).

Because content always has an author or authors, issues of learner interaction with content can fall under instructor activities as well as social dynamics, given the postmodern perspective that—once a text has been articulated—readers actively engage in constructing both a detailed picture of the author/instructor and of the information in context. Social dynamics in a face-to-face instructional situation, though, would tend to involve humans engaged in real-time oral exchanges and discussions centered on the instructional content at hand. Secondarily, instructor feedback on learner contributions in the form of text also constitutes social dynamic action. And finally, instructional content generated by the instructor (text, audio or visual elements, and constructed simulations, etc.) can also be represented as social in nature, although exchanges between learners and multimedia elements, that is, the interface features of multiple modalities, are not experienced as personal or real-time exchanges (Tu and Corry 2003).

These eight forms of interaction, however, should not be viewed as distinct or isolated, and we should also not privilege any particular interaction (e.g., the instructor interacting with content or with learners or a group of learners). Hatch and Gardner (1993) stress the distributed nature of all such instructional interactions, writing, "Intelligence is enmeshed in all of a person's activities, past and present, and embedded in the local settings and cultures in which those activities are carried out. . . . The individual's intelligences, interests, and concerns are formed in interactions with peers, family members, and teachers, constrained by available materials, and influenced by cultural values and expectations" (p. 171). Steinkuehler (2006), as well, views online learning communities—even when formed around multiuser video games—as a rich embodiment of human action and discourse: "One of our challenges in the analysis of human activity (and therefore, situated cognition, in all its messiness) is to ground our interpretations not only in the microdetails of what people do *and* say, but also, and just as critically, in broader claims about the 'forms of life' that render those activities meaningful (e.g., the values, identities, worldviews, and philosophies that function in ways that enable us to recognize when one is being a particular sort of someone, doing a particular sort of something, and not something or someone else)" (pp. 49–50).

Importantly, then, although instructors can be successful in facilitating learner discussion and interaction, this does not mean that group interaction will always be positive or enjoyable for the individuals involved. As Jackson (1998) observes in terms of argumentation theory, "The unrestricted openness of public discussion on the Web presents a challenge . . . to find a balance between a commitment to 'first-order conditions' for critical discussion such as the unrestricted right to raise questions and make claims, and a basic practical recognition that the exercise of this right by very many people produces discourse that is essentially unexamined and unproductive. Letting everyone 'have their say' means accepting and archiving false assertions, irrelevant objections, repetitions, blatant abuses such as argument ad hominem, and other argumentative missteps" (p. 190).

Instructors who provide well-designed anchors that promote online classroom discussions are likely to enjoy greater student participation (Guzdial and Turns 2000), but still the depth and intensity of the discussion depends on learner involvement and engagement. Lipponen (2000) observes that three distinct modes of discourse dominate online discussions: social-oriented, fact-oriented, and explanation-oriented interactions. Finding creative instructional methods that encourage learner-generated explanations then becomes a worthwhile goal. But the influence of others on our performance is not always that straightforward. Kiesler and Cummings (2002), for example, note that research on distributed work suggests that, when working on well-defined tasks around others, our efficiency and motivation increases; it follows that, when working on ill-defined tasks, we experience increased stress and are more easily distracted. In work situations that demand multitasking, individuals outside groups often attend to the most immediate tasks versus the highest-priority tasks. When task and outcomes are distributed, individuals can exert greater focus without having to attend to the needs of others. Thus, in cases where learners require autonomy and reduced interruptions, virtual communication is ideal. If, however, instructors hope to heighten informal communication, learner efficiency and motivation, or voluntary learner involvement, working online poses very real challenges.

Kiesler and Cummings (2002), therefore, hypothesize that even with technological means to communicate at their disposal, humans are less likely to work efficiently and to collaborate voluntarily on projects without daily physical contact and frequent informal communication. Indeed, the authors report that beyond thirty meters physical distance, people are significantly less likely to create strong social ties, a finding that is supported by Kraut et al. (2002), who observe that "researchers with the most similar interests were more than four times as likely to publish together if their offices were on the same corridor as they were if their offices were on different floors of the same building, and researchers whose offices were in different buildings almost never collaborated regardless of their research interests" (p. 138). Proximity encourages more frequent informal communication, as well as accidental or coincidental encounters.

Interaction, whether face-to-face or online, does not create effective instruction. Interactions can be effective or ineffective in either context. Wang and Gearhart (2006) argue that the quality of online interaction is determined by a host of contextual variables, including "(a) beliefs and perceptions, (b) teacher direction, (c) learner motivation, (d) learning styles, (e) nature of the task, (f) media, (g) technical support, and (h) immediacy of feedback" (p. 65); and only two of these variables distinguish online from face-to-face contexts. So, for example, learner motivation can be very high but, when confounded by limited instructor input, ill-defined learning tasks, or a communication interface that is unwieldy and difficult to use, social dynamics can be ineffective or unsatisfying; inversely, a motivated instructor with well-defined learning tasks and an elegant interface cannot overcome the resistance of unmotivated learners.

Brown and Renshaw (2000), organizing collaborative classroom activities around collective argumentation, write that instructors should focus on the following primary tasks:

• Allocating management of the problem-solving process to the group;
• Facilitating cooperation between students by reminding them of the norms of participation;
• Participating in the development of conjectures and refutations;
• Modeling particular ways of constructing arguments;
• Facilitating class participation in the discussion of the strengths and weaknesses of a group's coconstructed argument;
• Introducing and modeling appropriate language for different curriculum areas; and
• Providing strategies for dealing with the interpersonal issues that arise when working with others. (Brown and Renshaw 2000, p. 53)

Because social dynamics are so foundational to all instructional situations, it is not surprising that they intersect frequently with learner background and knowledge (experiences and understanding), learning tasks and activities (actions and discourse), instructional activities (mutual understandings and trust), and the primary learning environment and artifacts on hand (rules and procedures and established processes). Wang and Gearhart (2006), as well, stress the centrality of social dynamics, linking them to learner motivation (i.e., "content relevance, learner confidence, task challenge, learner curiosity, learner control, and learner satisfaction," p. 66) in addition to demographic characteristics such as professional background, age, and gender. Moreover, social dynamics online and off are so central to contemporary learning and problem solving that research on the subject can be located across disciplines and subdisciplines.

From the distance education research, Carabajal, LaPointe, and Gunawardena (2003) rely on a transmissional model to describe group development online. Although social dynamics are not likely to be captured by a process algorithm, their perspective provides a clear means for researchers to describe their particular emphases. Researchers, they argue, tend to focus on member characteristics, attitudes, and skills, groups, tasks, settings, and learning cultures (i.e., entry elements); on roles, participation, communication patterns, and group histories (i.e., process elements); or on decision quality, production processes, or learner satisfaction (i.e., outcomes) (pp. 225–229).

Tu and Corry (2003) further elaborate on the process elements that organize asynchronous learning discussions, highlighting the importance of discussion duration (two-week long being preferable to one-week long), class size (small groups being preferable to large), depth of threads (shallow being preferable to deep discussion levels), frequency of discussion/postings (established being preferable to open ended), moderation requirements (structured being preferable to unstructured), instruction for discussions (articulated being preferable to assumed), and quality and evaluation criteria (responses that integrate multiple views and that suggest reflection being preferable to single entry postings). Drawing on Collison et al.'s (2000) argument that rubrics for evaluating online discourse are critical, Tu and Corry (2003) stress that the "Rules of Netoric" need to be explicitly spelled out for learners (cf. Anderson et al. 2001).

In instructional situations, social dynamics are in principle designed to reiterate, reinforce, and generate shared knowledge. Gunawardena and McIsaac (2004) summarize, "The process by which the contributions are fitted together is interaction, broadly understood, and the pattern that emerges at the end, when the entire gestalt of accumulated interaction is viewed, is the newly-created knowledge or meaning" (p. 382). This perspective toward interaction, in turn, leads to a four-part approach to data collection and analysis, where online interactions can be reviewed for the

1. Type of cognitive activity performed by participants (questioning, clarifying, negotiating, synthesizing, etc.);
2. Types of arguments advanced throughout the debate;
3. Resources brought in by participants for use in exploring their differences and negotiating new meanings; and
4. Evidence of changes in understanding or the creation of new personal constructions of knowledge as a result of interactions within the group (p. 382).

Ellis et al. (2005), from the personnel psychology literature, found that teams that received as little as 2.5 hours of training (on teamwork, declarative and procedural information related to a given project, and for practice) performed more effectively across several measures. The authors trained 124 introductory management students (of a total of 260), organized into 65 four-person teams, and the teams that received training demonstrated significantly greater proficiency in task coordination, planning, and group problem solving.

Walther and Bunz (2005), two computer-mediated communication researchers, studied 44 students, enrolled in senior undergraduate classes at two major research universities, as they worked together to produce six review papers using synchronous discussion lists and chatrooms. After finishing each paper, participants were asked to fill out a Likert-scale assessment of how well or poorly their group adhered to the following rules of effective communication as defined by a social information-processing theory of communication: starting promptly, communicating often, acknowledging group members' messages, explicating expectations and progress, organizing and multitasking content, and honoring deadlines. Interestingly, everything but organizing content correlated with the instructors' evaluation of the group's finished papers, and the authors speculate that having set rules of interaction to follow strengthened the group members' rankings of trust in their group members and processes as well.

From the teacher preparation area, Larson (2000) found that the six high school instructors that he studied viewed discussion as serving several purposes: "as recitation, a teacher-directed conversation, an open-ended conversation, a series of responses to challenging questions, a guided transfer of knowledge to the world outside the classroom, and as practice with verbal interaction skills" (p. 666). And just as the learning environment is grounded in instructional goals and rules for instructor–learner interaction, so too does technologically mediated communication demand the establishment of protocols for exchange and meaning making, perhaps more so as visual and gestural information are often severely limited. In this respect, classrooms can be viewed as rich rhetorical sites for study, with tightly constrained rules for the use of time and space, if one adopts Darwin's (2003) definition of rhetorical theory as the study and practice of human exchange, "an art of working with (and sometimes against) one's relationships with others in order to address contingent situations" (p. 25).

Research on virtual teamwork therefore highlights the importance of tasks, information exchange, trust, and especially time on group processes and products. Alexander (2002), in his study involving 1,600 information systems freshmen, gave learners the choice of working face to face or online in groups of four to six members. Interestingly, only 96 students elected to work in face-to-face groups; Alexander (2002) noted that these groups benefited from increased social interaction as part of the experience. The virtual teams worked significantly more on their own, produced permanent records that they used as part of their e-mail exchanges, and encountered the usual problems in e-mail communication (nonclarity, misinterpretation, etc.). Most importantly, the virtual teams frequently had little time to build trust between their members. Thus, team members who did not become immediately involved quickly fell out of the groups, and immediacy of responses was critical to ongoing team member identification.

Ergonomics researchers Klein and Miller (1999) return specifically to the problem-solving research to generate their framework for distributed planning processes. All team planning, they argue, involves

- detecting the problem
- gathering information
- representing the problem
- formulating a course of action
- detailing a course of action
- evaluating the plan
- managing the planning process
- managing the resources available to the planners
- managing information routing strategies (p. 212).

Klein and Miller (1999) explicate how planning processes depend considerably on resource and environmental variables. Thus, planning is more difficult under time pressure, when resources are scarce, when integrated rather than modular, when developed in complex or unpredictable problem-solving environments, and when high precision is required or low feedback is offered (pp. 217–218). Moreover, DeSanctis and Monge (1999) suggest that collaborative tasks aimed at resolving conflict and building consensus tend to be easier to accomplish face to face than online (p. 697), so a motivated group of learners with ample resources can still encounter significant challenges if their individual perspectives on the task at hand are divergent rather than convergent. Murphy (2003), for this reason, stresses traditional team-building processes such as relying on agendas, encouraging open exchange, establishing strategies for disagreement, and clearly assigning tasks and activities, especially in virtual groupwork (p. 26). Tolmie and Boyle (2000), in their review of factors that contribute to success in higher educational learning environments, list the following influences:

- size of group (less than six per team in large classes)
- knowledge of other participants (familiarity and face-to-face interaction improves virtual teamwork)
- student experience (better experienced communicators function more effectively)
- clarity about task (shared understanding of the task optimizes problem solving)
- ownership of task (shared negotiation over selected task heightens group interaction)
- need for system (required virtual interaction improves group purposefulness)
- type of system and prior experience of CMC (training and usability heighten group progress) (pp. 122–123).

Maznevski and Chudoba (2000) add that "the higher the task's required level of interdependence, the more communication incidents will be initiated" (p. 485). So although convergence may be desirable, tightly coupled task work tends to require a higher frequency of interaction in order to succeed.

For an understanding of how social dynamics outside traditional instructional settings function in the everyday lives of learners, it is also productive to review some of the research on professional and contextual work activities and practices. Gay and Hembrooke (2004), for example, gave 45 undergraduate students in a communications class wireless laptop computers in exchange for tracking all their Web browsing and communication activities for an entire semester. It was recommended that students use the computers to complete their course assignments, including lectures, group discussions, collaborative groupwork, and final projects. Interestingly, although students reported feeling free from space and time and at ease in being able to interact with friends and classmates, they also admitted that wireless computing encouraged distractedness and addictive usage patterns. In addition, as "temporal and spatial boundaries blurred, so did the social roles, communal expectations, norms, behaviors, and types of interactions that were associated with those spaces" (p. 55) (whether those spaces were labeled home, work, recreational, study, etc.). As one student reported in his or her journal at the conclusion of the experiment:

These tools [the laptops and wireless access] have offered me increased freedom over the course of the semester. The freedom is not the equivalent of increased free time, but rather the freedom is the increased opportunity to make choices as to how I choose to participate in class, complete assignments, and conduct my usual computer-related activities. (p. 56)

Incredibly, students spent an average of three to seven hours a day on the Internet, with the majority of their activities involving e-mailing or instant messaging. One student reported that, prior to wireless access, she had accessed her e-mail approximately three times a day; after being connected, she found herself checking e-mail as many as twenty-five times a day. She closes her journal entry admitting, "Still, I could not erase my access to the Internet or increase my will power. I found myself purposefully leaving this tool at home when going to study" (p. 58). Yet, despite this admission, students, according to Gay and Hembrooke (2004), continued to report that "They felt that they had better concentration when they were doing more than one thing" (p. 62). This may explain why, as Caruso and Kvavik (2005) report in their study of more than 17,000 American undergraduates, more than 90 percent own cell phones, 66.6 percent own personal computers, 55.6 percent own laptops (p. 3), 99.7 percent use e-mail, 98.9 percent create documents related to schoolwork, and 98.4 percent rely on the Internet for university assignments (p. 5).

Gay and Hembrooke (2004) stress, however, that students who attended lectures with laptops performed lower on recall and recognition tests than students who attended lectures without. So, although wireless laptop computing clearly helps students to collaborate on and build networks around the instructional materials and deadlines, it is also clear, as Gay and Hembrooke (2004) conclude, that "Students and faculty have limited visions of how systems should be integrated into learning environments" (p. 71). In particular, the authors stress the importance of nontechnical factors in the technology-learning mix, such as social protocols and norm setting, project management strategies, task-oriented guidance, and group roles and participation expectations (cf. Bugeja 2007).

6.3.1 Mortar Communication and Networked Interactions

Cazden's (1988) study of face-to-face classroom discourse should be required reading for anyone interested in building, designing, managing, or evaluating online interactions in instructional spaces. Cazden (1988) argues that the three fundamental features of classroom discourse are the language of control, of curriculum, and of personal identity, which play out in the articulation of propositional (or referential, cognitive, or ideational) information, the establishment and care of social relationships, and the communication of speaker identity and attitudes (p. 3).

But Cazden (1988) is also interested in capturing the numerous ways that classroom discourse differs from everyday discourse. Notably, others have extended and refined Cazden's (1988) early work, and thus Brown et al.'s (1993) research provides compelling comparative data. They found that classroom goals could be distinguished according to individual and communal responsibility, mutual respect, an orientation around discourse, and rituals and agreed-upon rules of participation.

Similar to Brown et al. (1993), Cazden (1988) notes that "one objective of education in many classrooms . . . [is] to inculcate in learners at the beginning of their school career some new criteria for appropriate ways of talking in school, and even appropriate topics for that talk as well" (p. 16). This inculcation plays out in several variations on the same instructor–learner interaction rules. Instructors Initiate an exchange, learners Respond, and instructors Evaluate (IRE) (p. 29); or, in more extended exchanges, a "Topically Related Set (TRS)" contains several initiate–respond–evaluate sequences depending on how deeply the topic is covered, with "The basic and conditional sequences . . . ordered within each set, and evaluations . . . at the end of set, but not necessarily after each student response within them" (p. 36). It should be noted that, within these rules of classroom discourse, Cazden (1988) is careful to build "improvisation" or "the competence to adapt tacitly known schemata to inevitable moment-to-moment variations in a complex environment" (p. 45). Indeed, in online instructional settings, Cazden (1988) suggests that not only is temporality disrupted but also the instructor control over single sequences is undermined by the development of "multiple threads" (p. 67).

But social dynamics online, in addition to displacing face-to-face patterns of interaction, are central to the online experience. Indeed, more than two decades ago, Williams (1981) wrote, "a technology is always, in a full sense, social" (p. 227). And Gilbert and Moore (1998) add to this perspective that "social interaction can directly foster instructional interaction" (p. 31), although researchers are careful to remind us that online interaction can never "duplicate face-to-face classroom instruction" (Cook 1995, p. 39). Roblyer and Wiencke (2003), therefore, distinguish instructional from social interaction between instructors and learners, understanding of course that all "interaction is achieved through a complex interplay of social, instructional, and technological variables" (p. 85). Their model of interaction in online instructional environments involves students exchanging social and instructional messages with each other and an instructor communicating instructional content and activities with the support of distance technology (p. 82).

Roblyer and Wiencke (2003) are no doubt aware that they have created a closed circle to characterize both the formal learning situation and their learners' experiences in it (ignoring for a moment their use of a masculine symbol for the instructor and images of learners that are primarily female). An increasingly important aspect of any characterization of contemporary learners, however, requires the acknowledgment that our formal instructional settings are in a constant battle with outside, informal learning opportunities and computer-based life distractions. Sutherland et al. (2004), observing the range of out-of-school multimedia projects that students routinely engage in, report, "Results of the teacher questionnaire administered to all teachers in the project schools and interviews with partner teachers indicate that the majority of teachers are not aware of the nature and extent of students' expertise that relates to their out-of-school uses of ICT" (p. 418).

Contributing to our understanding of classroom discourse as moving beyond classroom walls (actual or virtual), technologies continue to alter well-established patterns of interaction. Lévy (2001), in his description of the different types of interactivity, shows how technologies can facilitate interactions that are unidirectional, reorganizational, or involving, depending on the medium (see table 6.11).

Bonk and Dennen (2003) adapt Cummings, Bonk, and Jacobs's (2002) matrix for describing the flow of communication between instructors and learners, instructors and instructors, instructors and practitioner-experts, and learners and instructors. Table 6.12 summarizes the dynamic.

Bonk and Dennen (2003) argue that the interaction matrix "widens one's views on the range of online participants, the forms of online instruction, the degree and type of interactions online, and the online environments that may soon be common" (p. 336). The inclusion of practitioner-experts, moreover, allows for a variety of potential interactions, for example, with technical and instructional support experts, administrators and assessment specialists, and representatives from outside institutions.

Table 6.11

The different types of interactivity[a]

Communication system	Linear message, not modified in real time	Interruption and reorientation of the information stream in real time	Involvement of the participant in the message
One-way distribution	• press • radio • television • cinema	• multimodal database • static hyperdocuments • simulation without immersion or the ability to modify the model	• single-participant video games • simulation with immersion (flight simulators) but without possible modification of the model
Dialogue, reciprocity	• mail • correspondence between two people	• telephone • videophone	• dialogs that take place through virtual worlds, cybersex
Multilogue	• correspondence networks • publication systems in a research community • e-mail • electronic conferences	• multiparticipant teleconference or video conference • open hyperdocuments accessible online, written and read by a community • simulation (with the ability to act on the model) as a medium for community debate	• multiuser role playing in cyberspace • multiparticipant video games in "virtual reality" • communication through virtual worlds, continuous negotiation of participants with their image and the image of their shared situation

[a]Adapted from Lévy (2001, p. 65).

6.3.2 Virtual Barriers to Community Formation

Dieberger (2003) has argued that "Although many people may access an information system at the same time, most systems maintain the illusion of a dedicated resource and the only indication of a large number of users simultaneously accessing a system might be an unusually slow response time. Humans are social animals, but our social skills are mostly unused in today's information systems" (p. 293). Not only do technologies tend to support collaboration poorly, but humans have also only recently begun to acknowledge that contemporary, complex problems *demand* teamwork and collaboration in order to solve them. Technologies are not simply social, then, but need increasingly to be designed and used for social purposes. As Jablokow (2005) asserts:

We must collaborate, bringing together the combined expertise and experience of several (or even many) individuals in order to solve the problem at hand. But in order to collaborate effectively, we will need to know more—and about different things. Collaboration is not

Table 6.12

E-Learning communication flow among instructors, learners, and practitioners-experts[a]

	To Learners	To Instructors	To Practitioners-Experts
From Instructors	• Syllabus, schedule, profiles, tasks and tests, lecture notes and slides, feedback and e-mail, resources, course changes	• Course resources, syllabi, lecture notes and activities, electronic forums, teaching stories and ideas, commentary	• Tutorials, online articles, listservs, electronic conferences, learning communities, news from discipline/ field, products to apply in field
From Learners	• Models or samples of prior work, course discussions and virtual debate information, introductions and profiles, link sharing, personal portfolios, peer commenting or evaluation	• Class voting and polling, completed online quizzes and tests, minute papers, course evaluations and session feedback, reflection logs, sample student work	• Resumes and professional links, Web page links, field reflections and commentary
From Practitioners-Experts	• Web teleapprenticeships, online commentary and feedback, e-fieldtrips, internship and job announcements	• Survey opinion information, course feedback, online mentoring, listservs	• Discussion forums, listservs, virtual professional development, team explorations and communities

[a]Adapted from Bonk and Dennen (2003, p. 336); Cummings et al. (2002, p. 5).

instinctive in humans, and so as a start, we must learn how to collaborate, so that our very efforts at collaboration do not pose a greater problem than any one we have originally come together to solve. (p. 533)

Preece (2001) has done considerable research on the relationship between online communities and usability and notes that sociologists have been struggling to find fixed definitions of community for well over fifty years, frequently electing to focus on the physical characteristics of community such as boundaries, location, and size. Preece (2001) defines online community as "any virtual social space where people come together to get and give information or support, to learn or to find company" (p. 348). Preece (2001) suggests that three elements influence the sociability of an online community: purpose (i.e., interest, reasons for belonging), people (i.e., individual, social, and organizational needs met and roles), and policies (i.e., protocols and policies for normative behavior) (p. 349).

Koch (2003) similarly defines communities as groups of people who not only share perceived commonalities, but also share the following attributes: a boundary (common interest, idea, context); sense of membership; ongoing interaction; and collaborative, mutual support (p. 447). Gay and Hembrooke (2004) provide an interesting contrast to Preece (2001) and Koch's (2003) characterization of online community formation, stressing the challenges of maintaining effective interaction online:

• CMC may disrupt the natural flow of conversation and lead to misinterpretation by removing discourse from its context;
• Participants are sometimes overwhelmed by technology, task, and communication issues;
• Different modes of interaction afford different experiences within the information space;
• Artifacts and objects play an instrumental role in mediating group activities;
• New social protocols need to be established for people to work effectively in CMC environments;
• CMC masks social cues and cultural differences;
• CMC does not guarantee increased participation and interaction among colleagues;
• Lack of social cues in CMC enables some people to become antagonistic toward others compared to copresent communication;
• Some people need more structure and guidance than others;
• Differences in participation rates are due to personal choice, time constraints, inadequate access, and fear of being judged;
• CMC can accommodate flexible communication patterns (p. 51).

Online, people are initially brought together as a result of their shared interest in a course, instructional approach, program of study, or subject matter. Incidental issues influencing membership in an instructional community can include factors as secondary as instructor reputation, timeliness of the course offering, or work-family scheduling constraints. Because many learners join instructional communities with initially low-level understandings of the purpose and usefulness of the involvement, the usability of the online environment is particularly important, including how the environment supports dialogue and social interaction, information design, navigation, and general access (Preece 2001, pp. 349–350).

Créplet, Dupouët, and Vaast (2003) describe a case study of a French biology laboratory and find it advantageous to distinguish between epistemic communities and communities of practice. Epistemic communities, they maintain, involve "a group of agents sharing a common goal of knowledge creation and a common framework allowing the shared understanding of this trend" (p. 45). Influenced by Lave and Wenger (1991), the authors describe communities of practice as consisting of "groups of persons engaged in the same practice, communicating regularly with one another about their activities. Members of a community of practice essentially seek to develop their competencies in the practice considered" (Créplet, Dupouët, and Vaast 2003,

p. 47). Communities of practice, then, according to the authors, highlight "the achieve-ment of an activity," and "knowledge creation is an unintended spill-over" (p. 45). Instructors interested in the relationship between community formation, mainte-nance, and learner development will find a fruitful metaphor in Créplet, Dupouët, and Vaast's (2003) detailed description of the roles of scientists and technicians in the laboratory group. Critical to the success of this particular laboratory community were what the authors called "interface persons," individuals "who belong to two social worlds simultaneously and make them communicated through their unique double memberships. Moreover, they lie at the periphery of these two social worlds in order to be acquainted at a minimum to the two cultures" (p. 60).

Interface persons in many instructional situations end up being the high-performing learners who understand, communicate (i.e., translate), and negotiate instructor expectations, guidelines, and principles of effective practice (provided in the form of "boundary objects" such as instructional materials or instructor–learner discourse), while at the same time interacting with and engaging in learner-to-learner knowledge-formation activities. This "boundary-spanning" role offers tangible and intangible rewards to interface persons and simultaneously produces tensions at the edges of both communities. And, finally, it should be noted that instructors cannot, in principle, create communities of practice in their classrooms online or off—com-munities of practice are necessarily voluntary and self-managed and, therefore, resist instructional formalization.

Indeed, numerous researchers (Brown 2000a; Chickering and Ehrmann 1998; Squires and Preece 1999) explicate social learning in formal instructional situations as including cognitive apprentice structures; rich, timely feedback; high learner–instruc-tor interaction; and cooperation and a sense of safety among learners. This latter goal, for a positive and kind learning environment, is not always the way discourse spaces organize themselves on the everyday Web. As Waldstein (2005) notes in his study of one active political newsgroup, discursive strategies that include resistance, domina-tion, exclusion, and control are certainly found in even the most liberal online discus-sions. Taboada (2004) summarizes bulletin board message structures as involving argumentation, personal attacks on other posters, discussions of the strengths and weaknesses of a given position or product, or requests for advice. Finally, Wang and Gearhart (2006) view online interaction as a complex dynamic that involves group composition, learning tasks, learner engagement, external resources, instructor's role, quality feedback, formative assessment, time flexibility, and time management vari-ables (p. 80).

More recently, researchers have begun to elaborate on the relationship between successful problem solving in groupwork and other compelling variables, including age, gender, ability, and friendship (versus acquaintance). Kutnick and Kington (2005), for example, found that paired girls who were friends performed highest on science reasoning tasks and paired boys who were friends performed lowest. These findings were consistent across grade levels (one, three, and five) and across teacher-assessed ability levels (low, medium, and high).

Stelzer and Vogelzangs (1995) stress that the number-one challenge facing the designers of WBI environments is how to generate a high level of instructor–learner interaction, given that the greatest difficulty experienced by online students is feeling isolated and keeping their motivation high. For this reason, Lynch (1998) emphasizes the importance of planning, early in the development process, for the integrated use of communication applications as part of the instructional goals of an online course. Carefully anticipating how Web pages, discussion lists, chat environments, whiteboards, commenting and annotation software, and e-mail or listservs will work *together* can allow e-learning designers to anticipate some of the general problems online learners and instructors are likely to encounter. If effectively managed, online interaction has been shown to positively influence learner interest, participation, perceived satisfaction, and concentration levels (Casarotti et al. 2002, pp. 36–37).

The relationship between learner engagement online and learner participation and interaction with others is a significant one. Deka and McMurry (2006), for example, found that although instructor-initiated interaction with learners did not influence success (in terms of final grades), learner-initiated interaction with instructors did. Thus learners—in particular, ones with strong reading comprehension abilities and confidence in their learning processes—who actively sought out instructor feedback, input, and guidance tended to perform better than learners who did not.

Van Eijl, Pilot, and de Voogd (2005), describing a blended undergraduate English literature class, allowed 61 students to choose either team-based or individual study. Teams could be self-selected by the students and were composed of four or fewer students. Thirty-four students elected to work collaboratively (56 percent) and 27 students (44 percent) chose to work individually. Interestingly, higher-performing students chose to work collaboratively rather than alone (a significant difference); indeed—and this may have been a result of this preference for collaboration among strong students—the collaborations resulted in higher grades than the individual work. Finally, collaboration in the course did not result in differences between the groups in terms of time spent on the course, perceived difficulty of the quizzes, coherence in course work, and evaluation of the course. In terms of instructor time committed to either collaboration or individual student work, a trade-off was noted; while group projects result in fewer products to evaluate, group projects also require additional feedback and instructor management.

Hiltz and Goldman (2005), summarizing interviews with 20 faculty about how their shift from traditional teaching and learning had changed after moving online, provide three excerpts that stress time and thoughtfulness:

I do think that in terms of [comparisons with] face-to-face, it's a better learning experience. They have time to think about the materials, digest it and internalize it.

With ALN, with text, you have a lot more time to think about what they are really asking.

What was interesting is the comments you get—in many ways they are more thoughtful. They [learners] have more time to reflect. (p. 6)

Because the online instructional space requires largely textual communication between instructors and learners, learners too have new challenges to address, for example, how to manage the instructional discussions, the online instructional materials, and the nuances of the particular instructional environment. In this respect, the instructor's expectations about discourse, timeliness, the openness of the instructional tasks, and the expectations of other learners all interact with the learning environment's features, design, and support materials. As Buscher and Hughes (2003) remind us, face-to-face interactions are made up of a complex of informational cues: "Through our position in relation to others, our posture, movements, the direction, intensity and duration of our gaze, and other finely tuned embodied actions, we occupy a place in the encounter, where we make available to others what actions they can reasonably expect us to take" (p. 98). It is this high-speed and "flexible display" of social cues and informational heuristics that are almost always lacking in current online environments. Shea, Pickett, and Li (2005), in their study of 913 higher education faculty and their concerns about online teaching, observe that "Perhaps the most frequently cited variable in discussions of quality in online learning is interaction"; but they also note that interaction can be framed as an argument for adoption for instructors who want to provide access to more learners or as an argument against adoption for instructors who feel overwhelmed by the challenge of managing heightened interactions.

Kennedy and Duffy (2004), in addition to highlighting the importance of interactions between instructors and learners and between learners and other learners (cf. Moore and Kearsley 1996), also elaborate on the critical role that administrators and "key players in the providing institution" play in orienting learners to the online environment, including the importance of user's guides and introductory tutorial materials that frame the learning experience for learners. As well as noting the importance of administrative, instructional, and technical support specialists, Kennedy and Duffy (2004) stress the importance of online instructors collaborating with other instructors either formally (through training and program coordination activities) or informally (through shared materials, online classroom "war stories," and mentoring relationships) (p. 207). Kirkwood and Price (2006) concur, writing that "Course development and presentation is rarely confined to an individual or small group of staff and decision-making can be complex and have unexpected repercussions" (p. 10).

Beyond instructor-learner interaction, Anderson (2003a) has elaborated on the importance of learner interaction with content and instructor interaction with content. Researchers have also begun to parameterize the nature of interaction, listing the attributes of any interaction as including the direction of the initiation (Song 2003), immediacy (Woods and Baker 2004), presence, frequency, duration, depth, task relatedness, and learning satisfaction (Hackman and Walker 1990).

In conclusion, Dieberger (2003) predicts that future learning environments will ultimately anticipate the critical nature of social dynamics in the process of instructing and learning:

Future information systems will be populated information spaces. Users of these systems will be aware of the activities of others, and what information they find useful or not. They will be able to point out and share information easily and even guide each other. These systems therefore will be social spaces. (p. 293)

And our virtual social spaces, similar to our colocational social spaces, will encourage collective behaviors and issues of communication, exchange, privacy, ownership, and group and conflict management. These latter issues, as much as the challenges inherent in our design of such systems, pose the most significant problems for institutions and individuals working in learning environments of the future.

Østerlund and Carlile (2003), in reviewing relational knowing and practice theory, note that researchers tend to privilege either the individual or the social:

This split has [led] to two theoretical constituencies that rarely account for each other. . . . Those who focus on the individual, his or her knowledge actions, intentions, or goals leave the nature of the "world" or environment relatively unexplored. Others emphasize the world and its structures, while individuals and social structures are assumed to exist as uniform entities. (p. 3)

Theories of situated cognition and practice attempt to undermine this dichotomy, allowing for individual differences and the cognitive reformulation of social and organizational processes, expectations, and norms (Nova 2005).

Van den Hooff et al. (2003), in their survey of a community of professionals gathered for information exchange and a community of professionals in the health care sector, found that "knowledge sharing is directly influenced by identification, trust, communality and connectivity, and not mediated by ability and willingness to share" (p. 135). Identification with one's community involves feelings of belonging, solidarity, and bonding. Trust is established when one feels that members of the community will help when problems occur and are dependable, reliable, and supportive. Communality is achieved when one works well with one's community, actively contributing to and helping members of the community, with the members of the community in turn providing a shared information base and sharing relevant information that supports work. Finally, according to van den Hooff et al. (2003), a connected community communicates efficiently both internally and externally, overcoming common barriers to time and distance (pp. 128–129).

It should also be noted that research on argumentation in general (Hample 2000) suggests that individuals making arguments or requests edit their positions both in consideration of harm to others and for relationship maintenance reasons, as well as for internal effectiveness and notions of truth and relevance. Thus, facilitating the creation of classroom community is a double-edged sword, where arguments and debate may be increased if social relationships are not strong or edited if social relationships are intense. Instructors might encourage open and organic information sharing among their learners, but how their learners' behaviors are influenced by the encouragement is difficult to gauge.

Gunawardena, Lowe, and Anderson (1997) provide a five-phase model of online interaction that is particularly rich and useful (see table 6.13). In the same article, Gunawardena et al. summarize findings related to their model that came out of reviewing the transcripts collected over a three-week asynchronous forum for 25 professional trainers on the implications of teaching and learning technologies for workplace training. The data, if one's goal is to attain the knowledge construction phase of interaction, were not encouraging:

Phase I   Sharing/comparing information, 191 postings
Phase II   Discovering dissonance, 5 postings
Phase III Negotiating meaning/coconstruction of knowledge, 4 postings
Phase IV   Testing/modifying proposed synthesis, 2 postings
Phase V   Stating/applying newly constructed meaning, 4 postings (p. 427).

Gunawardena, Lowe, and Anderson (1997) conclude: "The transcript analysis model showed us, however, that professional discourse, though often valuable, is not congruent with the active construction of knowledge" (p. 427). Accalogoun, Sunal, and Nichols (2006) applied Gunawardena et al.'s (1997) interaction analysis model to transcripts collected from 28 elementary teachers enrolled in a four-week summer graduate methods course and observed similar results: there was no interaction for knowledge construction, and interactions of all phases decreased each subsequent week (Accalogoun, Sunal, and Nichols 2006, p. 138).

Finally, taking a very instructor-centered position on online interaction, Schwier and Balbar (2002) note that there are no easy guidelines for managing communication in online instruction. Instructors, though, will benefit from careful planning, from flexible facilitation, from attending to learner-to-learner interactions, and from being open to ongoing discourse experimentation.

This characterization of the often nuanced and sometimes labile nature of interaction in everyday instructional situations seems limiting. Certainly it fails to capture the intense importance of community engagement in our everyday lives. Community,

Table 6.13

Interaction analysis model for examining social construction of knowledge in computer conferencing[a]

Phase I: Sharing/Comparing Information

• A statement of observation or opinion
• Statement of agreement from one or more other participants
• Corroborating examples provided by one or more participants
• Asking and answering questions to clarify details of statements
• Definition, description, or identification of a problem

Phase II: Discovering/Exploring dissonance or inconsistency among ideas, concepts, or statements

---

• Identifying and stating areas of disagreement
• Asking and answering questions to clarify the source and extent of disagreement
• Restating that participant's position, and possibly advancing arguments or considerations in its support by references to the participant's experience, literature, formal data collected, or proposal of relevant metaphor or analogy to illustrate point of view

---

Phase III: Negotiating/Co-constructing meaning or knowledge

• Negotiation or clarification of the meaning of terms
• Negotiation of the relative weight to be assigned to types of argument
• Identification of areas of agreement or overlap among conflicting concepts
• Proposal and negotiation of new statement embodying compromise, co-construction
• Proposal of integrating or accommodating metaphors or analogies

---

Phase IV: Testing/Modifying proposed synthesis or co-construction

---

• Testing the proposed synthesis against "received fact" as shared by the participants and/or their culture
• Testing against existing cognitive schema
• Testing against personal experiences
• Testing against formal data collected
• Testing against contradictory testimony in the literature

Phase V: Stating/Applying newly-constructed meaning

• Summary of agreement(s)
• Applications of new knowledge
• Metacognitive statements by the participants illustrating their understanding that their knowledge or ways of thinking (cognitive schema) have changed as a result of the conference interaction

---

[a]Adapted from Gunawardena et al. (1997, p. 414).

after all, helps us define ourselves and our relation to the world. As Cubitt (1998) asserts, "Identity, gender, nation, are abstractions we have woven out of the endless flickering of community, derivations from the void which we drape, fold and knit about ourselves to keep us warm, and to stop our selves from leaking out" (p. 20). Schwier and Balbar's (2002) reminders, and Leinhardt and Steele's (2005) conclusion that "Dialogue-based instruction is difficult" (p. 157), in this light, are remarkably understated. Even as one places social dynamics at the center of the five dimensions of everyday instructional situations, it becomes increasingly difficult to keep its boundaries from spilling over into individual learning, activities, instruction, and the learning spaces designed to contain them all. It is also clear, as Spinuzzi (2003) asserts, that online community processes rarely achieve what face-to-face processes are able to achieve:

Compare the relatively impoverished set of online communication mechanisms typically used in software development . . . and online university courses . . . with the wide range of civic mechanisms (including genres) that geophysical communities use to carry out their forensic, epideictic, and deliberative activities: voting, award ceremonies, legislation, juries, and hundreds of others. Without such civic mechanisms and a rich ecology of genres to support them (from ballots to legal briefs to award speeches), workers can swap solutions, but those solutions will tend to be reactionary rather than proactive and forward looking. (pp. 217–218)

Redirecting our instructional focus from transmissional perspectives toward technology-mediated communication to relational and activity-based models of interaction provides fresh insights into the role of social dynamics in everyday instructional situations. After Nardi (2005), we can then begin to explore how media function to support or constrain our affinity with other learners (through informal communication, eating and drinking, shared experiences in common spaces, and touching), our commitment to them (through continuous communication in activities of shared interest), and our attention to them (through negotiated availability and eye, voice, visual, or textual contact). Technologies that influence community interaction are central, therefore, to understanding learners, communicating and designing shared instructional activities, and to developing "safe" learning environments that foster security, task-oriented engagement, risk taking, honesty, and the open exploration of values, beliefs, and ideas (cf. Holley and Steiner 2005; Strange and Banning 2001).

6.4 Instructor Activities

Assuming motivated, prepared, and capable learners, authentic and engaging learning tasks and activities, a well-developed sense of shared purpose and community, and an environment that facilitates exploration, trial and error, scaffolding, and mutual respect, we can now attempt to characterize instructional activities and—possibly but not necessarily—knowledgeable, well-trained, pedagogically astute instructors. It is very important that we emphasize the various dimensions brought together in any given everyday instructional situation to remind ourselves that (a) effective instruction does not guarantee that learning will occur, (b) transformational learning experiences are inordinately rare and wonderful occasions, and (c) a "passion for one's subject matter" is certainly laudable but will falter hopelessly in the face of apathy, rote memorization, isolated learners, and a stuffy lecture hall with poor acoustics.

In our framework for everyday instructional situations, instructors are purposefully placed under the general heading of "instructional activities" to acknowledge the increasingly decentered role that they are being encouraged to take. The appeal of constructivist approaches to learning—extended somewhat unnaturally to an "approach" to instruction, what Bereiter (2002) refers to as a "degraded form of constructivism common to education, where it means roughly 'hands-on' learning and the avoidance of direct instruction" (p. 466)—has placed the manner in which instructors construct knowledge on the same level as the way that learners construct knowledge. This position of instructional uncertainty has been further exacerbated by a postmodern concept of the university where knowledge itself has been relegated to argument and belief systems. In addition, instructors in our framework for everyday instruction fall as much under learners, with their various backgrounds, knowledge, and concerns, as do students and instructional designers expected to support faculty content development (Petherbridge and Mehlenbacher 2007). Thus, one worthwhile goal of researchers interested in instructor attributes is to begin organizing what we learn about instructors in terms of their biological attributes (age, gender, race/ethnicity), their abilities (cognitive and physical), their personal identity (attitude/motivation, teaching style, and self-monitoring or reflective practice), their literacies (computer, domain, textual, and visual), and the sociocultural context and preparation that brought them to teaching (family, economic, geographic, and organizational). Viewing instructors as learners, moreover, encourages researchers to acknowledge the importance of learners, learning tasks and activities, social dynamics, and learning environments and artifacts to the overall production of effective learning situations.

At the risk of falling into well-worn prescriptions for instructional behavior that are difficult to decipher—even for instructors motivated to do so—it is useful to first summarize some of the considerable research that has been carried out on how people learn. Indeed, over the last twenty years, in addition to learning a great deal about how people learn (Bransford et al. 2000), we have also learned a great deal about how to design effective instruction. Although instructor beliefs, personal style, and knowledge clearly set the tone for effective instruction, they are not the sum of what is required to encourage and facilitate successful learning. Learners require authentic learning activities, multiple views of the subject matter, strategic and supportive scaffolding of important concepts, procedures, and skills, and a safe environment that allows engaged trail and error. Table 6.14 operates as a "cheat sheet" for any instructor's office door, reminding us of certain incontestable instructional ideals.

As table 6.14 suggests, research on learning and on learners offers instructors and instructional designers a rich source of information for exploring, designing, and assessing alternative strategies and approaches to instruction. This section is not meant to provide researchers and practitioners with a comprehensive picture of the instructional activities that inform everyday instructional situations; indeed, a great many excellent peer-reviewed journals currently exist that focus significantly on the design and evaluation of instruction (e.g., *Cognition and Instruction*; *Instructional Science*; *Learning and Instruction*; *Technology, Pedagogy, and Education*; and *Technology, Instruction, Cognition, and Learning*). This section will also not dwell on the research-based benefits of supporting collaborative learning (e.g., cooperative, virtual, distributed, team-based, group-focused) activities in the classroom, as those issues have been covered as part of the social dynamics dimension.

Instead, we briefly focus here on (1) issues related to instructor background, training and preparation, style, presence, immediacy, motivation, and time on-task (encouraging constructivist, learner-centered approaches), (2) new realities being generated by technology-mediated instruction and learning (e.g., understanding online information, user-learner interactions with online texts, information genres), and (3) recent research on the roles of narrative and argumentation organized around shared models and worked examples.

6.4.1 Successful Instructors

Successful instructors operate as consultants, guiding and bringing expertise to situations where the knowledge or processes for deriving solutions are contingent or unknown, and this orientation, for many, requires a significant reorientation. Successful instructors cannot act merely as content experts for others, explaining or showing something, whether facts, skills, principles, or general subject matter. Content experts do not necessarily have expertise in presentation, pedagogy, organization, and technology, and instruction is not merely function to pedagogical, andragogical, or technological form. Indeed, the title, "content expert," does not accurately describe what a successful faculty-teacher represents, as a rich definition of expertise would involve not only domain- and task-specific knowledge but also context-specific flexibility: an "expert," then, would be able to redefine and redesign his or her subject matter for multiple audiences. Reviewing the role of faculty in the development of the virtual postsecondary educational organization, Carchidi (2002) asks, "How will content providers play a role in shaping the organizational system beyond that of merely being viewed as an input to the system or a nominal check on quality?" (p. 221). Borgmann (2000), turning the question to learners, adds, "What the student needs are higher

Table 6.14

Sample of high-level principles for effective instruction[a]

Learner-Based Instruction (Bonk and Dennen 2003)	Seven Principles (Chickering and Gamson 1997)	Learning Activities (Dabbagh and Bannan-Ritland 2005)	Learning to Teach (Ramsden 2003)	Postmodern Education for Generation NeXT (Taylor 2006)
Facilitates, does not dictate Varies forms of mentoring and apprenticeship	Encourages **contact** between students and faculty	Promotes authentic learning activities Promotes articulation	Engages learners at their level of understanding Explains materials plainly Learns from learners about teaching and teaching improvement	Uses active and creative methods to facilitate significant learning experiences
Establishes a safe environment and a sense of community	Encourages **cooperation** among students	Promotes collaboration and social negotiation Promotes role-playing activities	Uses teaching methods and academic tasks that require thoughtful and cooperative learning	Helps students develop meaning through real life application
Exploits potential of the medium for deeper student engagement Explores recursive assignments that build from personal knowledge	Encourages **active** learning	Promotes problem solving Promotes hypothesis generation Promotes self-directed learning	Encourages learner independence	Ends the teaching pedagogy Moves to learning-centered academic paradigm Obligates students to bring information
Uses public and private forms of feedback Embeds thinking skills and portfolio assessment into assignments	Gives prompt **feedback** to students	Promotes coaching Promotes scaffolding	Improvises and adapts to new demands Gives high-quality feedback on learner work	Provides meaningful assessments

Table 6.14
(continued)

Learner-Based Instruction (Bonk and Dennen 2003)	Seven Principles (Chickering and Gamson 1997)	Learning Activities (Dabbagh and Bannan-Ritland 2005)	Learning to Teach (Ramsden 2003)	Postmodern Education for Generation NeXT (Taylor 2006)
Varies forms of writing, reflection, and other activities Uses explorations to enhance content	Emphasizes **time** on-task	Promotes reflection	Shares love of subject Makes material stimulating and interesting	Focuses on student engagement
Provides clear expectations and prompts task structuring	Communicates high **expectations**	Promotes modeling and explaining	Makes clear what has to be understood, at what level, and why Uses valid assessment methods	Teaches "up" educational taxonomies
Allows choice Looks for ways to enhance the learning experience	Respects **diverse** talents and ways of learning	Promotes multiple perspectives	Shows concern and respect for learners Focuses on key concepts and misunderstandings, rather than on covering ground	Offers multiple learning options

[a]Adapted from Bonk and Dennen (2003, p. 335); Chickering and Gamson (1997); Dabbagh and Bannan-Ritland (2005, p. 206); Ramsden (2003, pp. 86–87); Taylor (2006, pp. 52–53).

order skills, learning how to learn, finding whatever information is needed, and solving problems generally. . . . The goal, then, of education in cyberspace is to produce the learner, the person who has learned how to learn but otherwise knows nothing" (p. 206).

A rich definition of teachers, that is, instructors with depth, is that they operate in indeterminate situations to produce artifacts that are both functional (i.e., are economically and ecologically responsible, useful, usable, and learnable) and aesthetically satisfying (i.e., meet the emotional, historical, physical, and personal needs of user-learners). Indeed, Borgmann (1995) defines designers in a way that is strikingly similar to some definitions of educators in general: "Designers are professionals in that they have been entrusted by society with a valued good and are hence accountable not only to the immediate desires of society but also for the well-being of the good that is in their care" (p. 18). Wang and Gearhart (2006) thus conclude, "Ideally, course designer and course instructor should be the same person" (p. 18).

Rather than focusing on the one-way communication of course content, instructors need to communicate instructional objects through discussion, elaboration, confirmation, sharing, questioning, introducing and pacing, and adapting. Moreover, at this particular stage of technological development designed to support instruction, instructors must creatively move across learning environment features by using structured discussion lists, e-mail, phone- and text-based cellular technologies, chatrooms, text- and visual-based synchronous environments, and instructional artifacts such as documents, process descriptions, specifications, and group and classroom coordination tools designed to support the management of instruction. As Kintsch (1990) recommends, instructors also "need clearer definitions of the goals of instruction in terms of how a particular content is to be used" (p. 185), or learners need to be informed that their *use* of a particular instructional process or product is part of their problem situation. As much as possible, online learners need to be able to take an active role in the learning process, not only for motivational reasons but also for practical ones: instructors cannot possibly hope to keep up with the incoming requests for their "direction" if learners default to them as the single authority for the class content.

Instructor activities drive most formal educational experiences and are organized around the presentation and pedagogical style of instructors and the flexibility of their subject matter and media choices. Backer and Saltmarch (2000) remind us that higher education instructors have been slow to move online, noting that "There is a small (but growing) cohort of early adopters of technology in universities but the majority of professors are either non-users or just beginning to explore multimedia and the World Wide Web in the classrooms" (pp. 1–2). For this reason, O. Peters (2003) admits his misgivings about the movement of instruction onto the Web in a series of questions:

Will many teachers be tempted to use these expensive and extraordinarily versatile technological tools in a one-dimensional manner, to imitate and perpetuate and aggravate traditional teaching and learning down to the very last detail? Will many restrict themselves to recording their lectures on video, transferring them to a CD-ROM, and then feeding them into the virtual university? Will others simply have their teaching texts digitized and placed on the Internet, wrongly viewing the Internet as mainly an instrument for distribution? Will universities use the new media just to extend conventional instruction to remote groups through satellite and video conferencing? (p. 98)

One way of avoiding Peter's (2003) prognostication is to imagine reviewing "instructors" as "designers" (cf. Borgmann 1995). After all, the primary distinction between teachers, instructors, or faculty and instructional designers is assumed to be that the former are content (i.e., function) experts and the latter have expertise in presentation, pedagogy, organization, and technology (i.e., form). Once again, it is highly problematic to set up unnatural dichotomies between context and content, medium and message, or form and function if we aim to fully conceptualize the communication of information or instructional materials. Alternative labels to designers, such as, for example, media specialists or technology-support specialists are equally problematic, since these conceptions also remove subject matter from technological, instrumental, and instructional design and, as such, reduce design to the "coverboard of lacks or inadequacies of production" (Morello 1995, p. 72) or to mere "surface aesthetics" (Borgmann 1995, p. 17).

Notably, a face-to-face instructor who simply lectures to his students, taking the occasional question along the way, can still be a forceful educational motivator; otherwise, lectures would not play such an interstitial role in the everyday life of university campuses. Movshovitz-Hadar and Hazzan (2004), for example, in an analysis of the lecture plan and performance of an award-winning mathematics lecturer, derived six principles for effective instruction that can just as surely be applied to online instructional materials and situations. Effective lecturers provide top-down descriptions of main ideas, provide examples to illuminate definitional terminology, present in self-contained modules, stop occasionally to provide the big picture of where a unit belongs in the overall instructional plan, create a relaxed atmosphere, and help listeners distinguish between important and less important ideas being presented (p. 814).

These lecture-based strategies for effective lecturing, interestingly, are quite compatible with Schnotz's (2005) summary of empirical evidence related to instruction using text and visuals, stressing the importance of coherence and contiguity (i.e., words and pictures are preferable to words alone), modality (i.e., pictures and spoken text are preferable to written text), sequencing (i.e., pictures before text explanations are preferable to pictures after text explanations), and reading ability and prior knowledge (i.e., pictures benefit poor readers more than good readers) (pp. 60–63).

It may be that, just as the current generation of instructors find their most comfortable stance as lecturers, the next generation of instructors will emulate more facilitative, multimodal stances influenced by digital interaction and dialogue. Whatever the case, we can expect, as Johnston (1996) observes, that "There is overwhelming evidence that one of the most influential factors in determining how teachers teach is their own experience as students," and that "For university teachers who have been exposed to little other than very traditional lectures, it is difficult for them to think about their own teaching in any other way." This instructor-as-apprentice model, indeed, has a well-established history that began with the early use of another powerful technological invention: the text. As Borgmann (2000) notes,

In antiquity and the Middle Ages, when texts were rare and precious, the sharing of texts through reading them aloud, the *lectio* in Latin, became central. As medieval instruction developed, lectors (readers) became instructors too. They would not only recite but also comment, explain, and illuminate the text. In time, such reading and instruction came to be known as *lectura*, whence our word "lecture." Thus lecturers became the warrantors and anchors of a text. Through their person they would bring the meaning of a text alive in reality, that is, at a particular time and place. Lecturing, along with the institution it developed in, the university, has passed into contemporary higher education. (p. 204)

Two variables that make this historical educational situation work are instructor presence and immediacy, and these two variables play central roles in the success of online instruction as well. Bess (1998) elaborates on the differences between face-to-face lecturing and discussion, comparing lecturers to theater "performers on stage" and discussion faculty to "group psychologists." Lecturers must be, according to Bess (1998), "skilled in presentation—at sensing audience cues, at visual and auditory dynamics, at story telling, at mystery mood creation, at unraveling conundrums, and at dénouement," and discussion leaders must exhibit "Skills of developing formal and informal leadership, group culture, group norms, and effective communication" (p. 6). Technologies designed for online communication, however, resist clean distinctions between performer and facilitator roles. Murphy and Ciszewska-Carr (2006), for example, note that synchronous and asynchronous interactions between instructors and learners are both similar to and different from face-to-face settings:

Compared to the asynchronous, the synchronous environment affords voice. Compared to teleconferencing, it's more convenient and supports easier interactivity. Compared to the face-to-face classroom, it's constrained by spontaneity and intimacy. The instructors can't orient themselves as if they were in a face-to-face classroom because individuals in these environments share the same time and space. However, in a Web-based synchronous environment, they share time but not space. They can't orient themselves as if they were in an asynchronous environment. There, neither time nor space is shared.

Instructor immediacy thus plays a critical role in interactions that occur "at a distance," a notion that is either ironic or paradoxical or both. Immediacy is a term that has temporal, relational, and, importantly, genre dimensions. Instructors generate messages and share them with audiences, and audiences, in turn, form expectations and understandings of the messages based on their relationship to the instructor and understanding of the mode of communication mediating the messages. Importantly, each of the elements in this communication event is fluid rather than static; therefore the influence of instructors, the readiness of students for learning, and the conduciveness of the environment to engaging discourse and learning can differ from context to context. As Hara and Kling (2001) highlight, online "Students reported confusion, anxiety, and frustration due to the perceived lack of prompt or clear feedback from the instructor, and from ambiguous instructions on the course Web site and in e-mail messages from the instructor" (p. 68).

Instructor time plays a crucial role in the construction of instructor immediacy, as well. Keeton (2004) conducted in-depth, open-ended interviews with eight faculty and found that, not only did they assume having between 7 and 48 hours (mean = 24 hours) to respond to learner questions (p. 80), they also reported "that teaching well online is more time-consuming than teaching F2F [face to face]" (p. 77). In addition to estimations that it takes twice or three times as much time and effort to plan and prepare for online courses, higher education faculty also face a growing number of competing challenges for their attention, including increased class sizes, teaching loads, and accelerated publishing and funding competition. Kramarae (2003) adds that "The difficulty of dealing with too much e-mail was a recurring theme in the interviews with many university professors" (p. 264). Without questioning the expectations of learners, Wang and Gearhart (2006) describe the problem of instructor immediacy as follows:

In Web-based instruction, learners generally expect the instructor to respond to their messages as soon as possible, even in asynchronous communication such as e-mail and discussion board. When feedback is delayed or withheld, learners often send e-mails to the instructor to check if the instructor has received their messages or not. If the instructor does not respond to learners' follow-up messages, learner expectation can easily turn into frustration, and motivation for further learning can be seriously affected. (p. 68)

Importantly, Tomlinson-Keasey (2002) warns against reductivist interpretations of the shifting role of faculty as instructors, noting, "The changing role of the professor in a wide range of technologically mediated courses has been reduced to aphorisms such as 'the sage on the stage becomes the guide on the side.' While this notion conveys some of the obvious differences between traditional and online settings, it does not capture the range of changes that take place" (p. 146). Holmberg (2003) frames new demands on instructors in terms of learner empathy and belonging: "Such feelings are fostered by lucid, problem-oriented, conversation-like presentations of learning matter expounding and supplementing the course literature; by friendly mediated interaction between students, tutors, counselors, and other staff in the supporting organization; and by liberal organizational-administrative structures and processes. Factors that advance the learning process include short turnaround times for assignments and other communications between students and the supporting organization, suitable frequency of assignment submissions, and the constant availability of tutors and advisors" (p. 82). Sutherland et al. (2004), as well, warn that many informal learning situations will be difficult to transfer into formal learning situations given the complexity of the materials and the importance of structured instruction that anchors complex content.

Dziuban, Shea, and Arbaugh (2005) do not assume that online instructors will adapt "guide on the side" personas seamlessly, but they do highlight the multiple roles facing instructors as they move online. They state, "As instructors make the transition to the online environment, their roles change quickly and dramatically. The new demands can conflict with the customary demands typically encountered in face-to-face teaching, specifically in course organization and presentation, interaction with students, student assessment, maintaining office hours, and organizing course materials" (p. 170). And Rodriquez and Nash (2004) further highlight the new demands facing instructors, writing, "It cannot be assumed that faculty members are automatically effective online instructors just because they have published in prestigious journals and are respected in their fields or because of their success in a face-to-face classroom setting" (p. 75).

Thus, while Ruhleder (2004) notes that some instructor activities online remain similar to face-to-face interactions (e.g., providing new information, encouraging peer response to questions, and facilitating learners helping to clarify questions for other learners), other practices are altered in important ways. These practices include, for example, setting the tone and pace of the discussion, controlling learner interaction by moving on or changing topics, and discouraging learner interruptions to the information dissemination. The "flow" of the online "lecture" is disrupted, to paraphrase Ruhleder (2005, p. 86).

With instructional constructs as fundamental as flow being challenged by the distributed classroom, clarifying exactly how instructors *learn* how to effectively facilitate face-to-face or online classes increases in importance. Glyn (2004), drawing on facilitator education and development, suggests that instructors can prepare for new approaches to teaching through (1) skill-based, guideline-driven facilitation, (2) theory-based facilitation based on observed practice, (3) facilitation that highlights the presence and attributes of the instructor, and (4) facilitation that emphasizes the political dynamics of facilitation (p. 125). An extensive literature on instructor training and preparation exists, and this research area is, not surprisingly, increasingly important to higher education institutions motivated to improve instruction in general (Austin 2003; Crawford 2003; Petherbridge and Mehlenbacher 2007).

6.4.2 Instructor Knowledge and Activities for Instruction

But our instructor is also operating in a domain that, less than twenty years ago, did not exist except in the imaginations of hypertext visionaries (Shneiderman 1987). This new landscape demands a host of high-level skills, knowledge, and roles. Yang and Cornelious (2005) note that numerous factors influence the perception on the part of faculty that teaching online is not only very different from teaching in face-to-face settings but is also more difficult: online instructors need to be aware that their fundamental roles and responsibilities change, that interpersonal interaction and social dynamics are altered, that alternative technical and instructional support structures are needed, and that new learner expectations about instructor accessibility, responsiveness, and flexibility force a reevaluation of standard practices that occur around traditional instruction. Bransford et al. (2000, p. 242) argue that, to effectively integrate technology into teaching, instructors need to

- develop expertise in subject content and teaching,
- develop understanding of theories of knowledge,
- develop understanding of pedagogy as a discipline,
- understand principles of learning and apply to them as learners,
- have opportunities to learn from recent research and cognitive discoveries, and
- develop models for lifelong learning that guide their own career planning and teaching.

Anderson et al. (2001) provide what they call "macro-level comments about course process and content" and describe how instructors need to manage instructional processes and discourse while also providing instructional content (see table 6.15).

Kreber and Cranton (2000) divide the knowledge that instructors need to exhibit into three categories: *instructional knowledge* gained through content reflection, *pedagogical knowledge* gained through process reflection, and *curricular knowledge* gained through premise reflection. Instructional knowledge involves knowing how to develop and organize teaching materials and to prepare lessons that adhere to learning objectives and effective evaluation measures. Pedagogical knowledge involves understanding how to motivate different learners, to employ various instructional methods strategically, to facilitate learner-to-learner interaction, and to help learners overcome difficulties through specific techniques for learning, meaningful feedback, and self-assessment. Finally, curricular knowledge involves maintaining the big picture of a course, being able to redirect instruction as necessary, and being able to articulate the benefits learners may experience as a result of a course (pp. 479–481).

Notably, Kreber and Cranton (2000) do not include information literacy or technology in the repertoire of knowledge that instructors need to acquire as part of their professional identity. This is not entirely surprising since we are only just beginning to understand some of the enduring effects of even "primitive" information technolo-

Table 6.15

Parameters of teaching presence[a]

Indicators	Examples
Instructional design and organization	
Setting curriculum	"This week we will be discussing...."
Designing methods	"I am going to divide you into groups, and you will debate...."
Establishing time parameters	"Please post a message by Friday...."
Utilizing medium effectively	"Try to address issues that others have raised when you post."
Establishing netiquette	"Keep your messages short."
Facilitating discourse	
Managing agreement/disagreement	"Compelling counterexample. Care to respond?"
Reaching consensus/understanding	"Joe and Mary are saying essentially the same thing."
Encouraging contributions	"Thanks for thoughtful response."
Setting climate for learning	"Feel free to contribute your feelings on the subject."
Prompting discussion	"Any additional thoughts on the issue?"
Assessing efficacy	"I think we're a little off track here."
Directing instruction	
Presenting content/questions	"The text reports.... What do you think?"
Focusing discussion	"Perhaps we've covered that topic."
Summarizing discussion	"Initially, Mary argued ... but we still haven't addressed the following."
Assessing and feedback	"Good point but we also need to consider...."
Diagnosing misconceptions	"Try using the ruler feature in MS Word."

[a]Adapted from Anderson et al. (2001, p. 6).

gies such as e-mail on instructor and learner relationships and roles. Duran, Kelly, and Keaten (2005) in their survey of 124 faculty from a private university and 135 faculty from a public university ($n = 259$), found that instructors perceive the major motivation for learners' e-mailing them is to make "excuses" for late work or absences, to ask about a course, or to express concern over grades (p. 167). Other notable themes included the instructors' perception that e-mail is not face-to-face communication ("Nothing beats face-to-face communication, then phone conversations, e-mail is *way* back as a distant third . . . it is convenient"), that e-mail is time-consuming ("making the faculty member be available 24/7 and therefore you're never far from work"), that e-mail makes in-depth dialogue difficult ("It is an acceptable way to communicate 'nuts and bolts' information but not nuanced material"), and that e-mail encourages

unacceptable informality (p. '170). Ultimately, Duran et al. (2005) report that "faculty
. . . feel that their relationships with students have not improved as a result of e-mail
and that a majority of their e-mails come from a few students" (p. 172).

Dabbagh and Bannan-Ritland (2005), in contrast to Kreber and Cranton (2000), do
include knowledge of technology or "comprehension of new learning technologies"
in their overview of the competencies required of online instructors, in addition to
stressing the importance of team building and management skills, an emerging instructional goal that receives limited attention even though many instructors now routinely form learner teams as part of their instructional activities. Additional broad
competencies include effective interpersonal communication and feedback, administrative and support service skills, knowledge of how to conduct needs assessments,
and development of a systems perspective of thinking (p. 49). The importance of
having a systems perspective, for Dabbagh and Bannan-Ritland (2005), is that it allows
instructors to assess their face-to-face versus online teaching experiences, to review
research related to instruction and learning with technology, and to follow institutional policies related to distance education and online learning that provide the
context for their instruction.

Viewing instructional situations, whether experienced online or off, as consisting
of the same five dimensions allows us to select from a range of instructional strategies.
The important question, then, is not which strategy is more or less effective, but which
strategy is more or less effective given one's audience, learning tasks, instructional
goals, and learning context. It might be argued that effective online instruction
requires a particularly structured approach to task conceptualization and elaboration.
Anecdotally, one of the benefits of teaching online is that it encourages instructors to
design their traditional face-to-face materials so that task instructions are understandable, comprehensive, and concise. In this respect, Williams's (2004) overview of
instructional "techniques" is most useful, especially when combined with Bonk and
Dennen's (2003) instructional emphasis on learner communication, shared text creation, and community-building activities (see table 6.16).

Other pedagogical activities that Bonk and Dennen (2003) recommend include
scavenger hunts, voting and polling, interactive peer and guest commenting, peer
feedback roles, gallery tours and the publishing of learner work, symposia, and guest
experts (p. 343).

6.4.3   Pacing, Time On-Task, and Learning without Instructors

Particular instructional activities do not produce learning. Instruction can be thoughtfully designed, conceptualized, and delivered and still learning does not necessarily
have to occur; inversely, dialogue, materials, or sensory modes (i.e., aural, visual,
tactile, taste, and olfactory information) never intended to *instruct* can provide rich
learning experiences for learners implicitly and explicitly. This instructional position

Table 6.16
Conventional and online instructional activities

Instructional Activity	Description and Variations
Lecture^	Presents instructional content to learner. In the strictest case, learners are not able to actively respond during presentation
Tutorial^	Consists of presentation of instructional content, query for assessment of learning, and re-presentation or remediation, when learner has not met criteria
Drill and Practice^	Involves repeated presentation of instructional material, followed by testing of acquisition, until the responses meet criteria
Inquiry or Generative^	Involves presentation of data, information, etc., in response to learner's inquiries. In some cases, the form and order of presentation is adaptive based on previous responses by the learner
Demonstration^	Learner is shown how something operates, is performed, etc., by being taken through the appropriate steps, actions, and/or decisions required
Role Playing or Structured Controversy^*	Primarily interactive, with participants assuming or being assigned specific roles in the interaction. Typically attempts to simulate real world and includes debate and compromise
Games^	Can be paper-and-pencil exercises or computerized. Usually closely approximates the real world in that data used by the learner are the same, but normally operates in a compressed time frame
Topical/Article Discussion^*	Can be structured (guided) or unstructured. Questions, prepared in advance, directed to learners to guide discussion along preconceived path. Restricted within predetermined boundaries to ensure group stays on track. In unstructured discussion, learning experience controlled by participants who also provide subject matter expertise. Participants also provide direction and effort toward reaching desired goal
Simulation^	Involves representation of real-world environment (data conditions, etc.) in simulated manner. Not real-time (actually occurring in a system at that current time). Participants, individually or as teams, represent users or decision makers and perform same kinds of operations and make same types of decisions they might make in a real-life situation
Explorations or cases^*	Learners either evaluate existing articles or generate reading packets related to specific topics. Can involve real-time generation of data or models and reflection on connection to subject matter at hand. Cases can involve testing, collaborative work, or problem-solution responses
Evaluation^	Discrete or combined analysis of responses or readings for purpose of deciding next portion of instruction to provide
Hands-on Practice^	Makes use of actual system equipment, or simulated versions, to provide authentic experience to learner

Table 6.16
(continued)

Instructional Activity	Description and Variations
Supervised Practice^	Practice done under direct supervision of instructor, supervisor, etc.
On-the-job Practice^	Practice performed in job environment with actual system, equipment, and supporting materials (e.g., job aids)
On-the-job Performance^	Actually performing certain activities on the job, instead of in instructional environment, as a means of learning them

*Adapted from Bonk and Dennen (2003, pp. 341–342).
^Adapted from Williams (2004, pp. 123–124).

supports both a traditionalist stance—that instructors have something to teach learners or that certain concepts are difficult to learn without the support of instructors—and a constructivist one—that learners bring their own prior knowledge and worldviews to instructional situations. And this argumentative stance, as Petraglia (1993) asserts, "acknowledges that teachers and educational institutions have objectives, but learners have real worlds that may be an obstacle to them" (p. 163).

But the *real* worlds that learners bring to contemporary instructional situations are as artificial as they are tactile, and even "tactile" as a descriptor fails to acknowledge the considerable grounds being made in haptic human–machine interactions (Iwata 2003). My daughter, who had used the words "C'puter" and "e-mail" by the time she turned two, now routinely mixes natural with synthetic terminology to describe the world that she inhabits: sunrises appear "pixelized" and oceans are interactive, computer dialogue boxes are named "Okay screams" and "The Internet always knows where your house is." Mass media video permeates our understandings, and our understandings have increased from less than 10 frames per second (fps) in the early 1980s to as many as 100 fps in experimental gaming environments.

Noting the changes over time in audience expectations of pacing and sequencing in film-editing techniques, Gleick (1999) observes, "We no longer need to see the man getting out of the car, and closing the car door, and walking up the steps, and knocking, and entering. The camera can jump from car to living room without leaving us behind" (p. 197). So too with modern media for communication: our learners' expectations are that information will be transmitted quickly, minimalistically, and with limited attention to affective and relational information elements. Our technological realities are, some researchers note, making it increasingly difficult to capture rules or "netiquettes" for behavior and conduct in human-computer-augmented communication (Gay and Hembrooke 2004).

It is also difficult to establish which came first: humans attending to screen-based information minimalistically or screen-based information speeding past humans too quickly to facilitate understanding or allow reflection. Online instruction and, as provocative as multimedia and the Web appear, much of the information that we skim, scan, and read online is still primarily textual. As single instructors translate their once-hardcopy stand-alone computer "lecture notes" into online instructional content, or as groups of instructional designers and content experts work together to produce online materials meant to exist beyond the instructional "life-cycle" of any single instructor, so too will the line between *human* and *textual* instructors become blurred. And as we enter into the domain of learning from online texts, a new complex of issues will arise as some traditional issues recede (e.g., poor oral presentation skills, badly organized notes, or lack of instructor presence or engagement). Cubitt (1998) reinforces how reading online information is subtly familiar to and differs from reading hardcopy texts:

It is tempting to see in Internet communications an entirely new mode of reading, one which eliminates the specificities of place and time, the vertigo of distance, to produce an ecstasy of pure interface between text and reader. But netsurfing still respects the older distributions of reading, though modified and accelerated: the histories of interactive marginalia, of dedicated spaces and times for reading, specifically the textual negation of place in a really engrossing read and the universalisation of space in the library. But the net also derives its metaphors of surfing and browsing from a nomadic reading, neither negating place nor universalising it, but wandering, and taking the hereness and nowness of place with it as unstill reference point. (p. 6)

Quality time on-task and learner engagement, clearly, are instructional goals that are difficult to argue with. Goodman (1990) provides a research-based summary of strategies for increasing learner time on-task, such as instructing more and testing less, encouraging total learner participation, maintaining enthusiasm, correcting learner errors quickly, rewarding learner engagement, and emphasizing momentum and group interaction (p. 86). Hannafin et al. (2003) write, "To-be-learned knowledge and skills can be organized and sequenced to optimize efficiency, but this may well come at the expense of deeper, more reflective learning; reflection can be increased as well, but typically with less *efficiency*" (p. 255; emphasis added). Similarly, Clark and Linn (2003) recommend that more time be spent on fewer topics to facilitate deeper knowledge integration of complex science topics. If we presume that much human learning involves trial and error, but that errors reduce efficiency, it might be argued that learning is, at its core, inefficient.

Moreover, research on the differences in terms of effort and time for instructors teaching online versus face to face points to another layer of complexity in terms of the efficiency versus effectiveness issue. According to Hislop and Ellis (2004), although their seven online instructors spent only slightly more time working with students than their face-to-face colleagues, the 24/7 nature of online instruction and the larger amount of energy required over limited durations at certain points in the semester are most certainly what have led faculty to report that teaching online requires significantly more time (cf. McKenzie et al. 2000).

To this admixture of complexities, we invite the motivated and enthusiastic instructor, aiming to engage students in addition to actually teaching them something. Plowman (2005) provides a memorable overview of how our enthusiastic instructor might describe effective teaching:

Teachers prompt a sense of coherence and understanding in learners by moving between adapting, sequencing, tailoring, and reviewing materials and eliciting, supplementing, and monitoring learners' responses. Teachers use these professional skills to sustain learning discourses and to ensure that classroom activities and processes rarely seem fragmented, although they are manifold and diverse. Ultimately, teachers want to feel assured that learners are getting the story straight. (p. 55)

But identifying whether learners are "getting the story straight" is not that straightforward. To begin with, learners have a creative way of producing their own social learning networks in the form of friendships, collaborations, study groups, and so on. In addition, a major part of the learning that takes place in contemporary educational institutions occurs after hours and outside established learning spaces.

Between the unanticipated social consequences of technological learning processes and the tentative instructional frameworks for managing these processes falls a rapidly changing instructional content and presentation. Plowman (2005) stresses the increasing complexity that exists when technology interacts with instruction, pointing out that as instructors learn to develop instructional materials beyond texts and two-dimensional graphics, the responses of learners to alternative media become less predictable:

Interactive media superficially appear to combine media with which people are already familiar, such as film, television, and books, but we cannot directly transfer what we have learned about making meaning from such texts. The structure of interactive media differs from that of traditional media because it switches mode between video, text, animation, graphics, sound, and silence; there are combinations of different media on the screen at the same time; users can control pace, sequence, and activity, and there is no fixed running time. These attributes are potentially beneficial, but they are also responsible for the multiplicity of pathways and disruption of the flow of the user's experience, especially as it is sometimes difficult to predict the required user input or system response at the foci of interactivity. The narrative is easily suspended and altered, and this can thwart or confuse the learner's expectation so although concepts of sequence, connection, causality, and linearity are implicit in definitions of narrative, they are not directly applicable to interactive media. (p. 61)

And it is the moments *between* the multimedia objects that offer the greatest possibility for user misinterpretation and error. The learner can navigate away from the instructional sequence or replay an animation element because it is aesthetically interesting rather than substantially helpful in terms of the instructional objectives at hand, or the learner can pause long enough to allow distractions unintended or unwanted by the designer of the interactive environment. Plowman (2005) refers to these moments between elements as "lacunae or gaps in the text where interactivity is evoked" (p. 61) and stresses that these gaps are the places that most learners make choices, and not all of the choices can be easily anticipated. Users proceed through iterations of trial and error. Plowman's (2005) study, unfortunately, confirms this: "learners lacked overall strategies for dealing with a task because they preferred to try out different possibilities fairly arbitrarily at the computer. The lure of interactivity meant that they seemed reluctant to reflect on the task with which they were engaged" (p. 72).

But engaging learners in reflection of the subject matter at hand is a fundamental goal. Indeed, learners who understand the subject matter will be able to answer Schank's (2005) essential questions for establishing if material being taught is teachable in the first place: what are the skills that comprise this subject, can I name them, can I practice them, and am I able to tell if someone is doing them correctly (pp. 76–77)?

As we have seen in terms of the one-way transmissional television medium (see figure 2.3) and perceived passage of time related to learner processing and task complexity (see figure 2.4), technology-mediated interactions that increase psychocognitive interaction and learner engagement are goals that designers aim to facilitate. Biggs (1999) summarizes these interactions in his research on learner study habits (see figure 6.2).

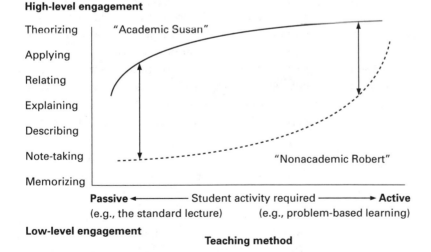

Figure 6.2
Student orientation, teaching method, and level of engagement (adapted from Biggs 1999, p. 59).

Biggs (1999) outlines how learning activities interact with particular teaching approaches in addition to "the academic orientation" of learners to produce learner engagement. As well, the interactions we have described between learner background and knowledge, learning tasks and activities, and instructor activities, here, are organized around the notion of engagement, where engagement is assumed involve high levels of learner processing and task complexity.[3]

Of course, for instructors to begin fully engaging their learners, high-level reflection on their own particular teaching style, instructional content, and the media they intend to employ becomes necessary (Reeves and Reeves 1997; Vosniadou et al. 1996). Table 6.17 summarizes two methods of orienting one's instructional style.

As with all general principles for practice, continua of instructional orientations are useful when viewed as heuristics for thinking about one's instruction, but they ultimately resist easy application over time or in context. It is one thing to know, for example, that differences exist between step-by-step, procedural instruction and scaffolded, facilitative instruction; it is quite another matter to identify when and under what circumstances one applies the former versus the latter approach, or a combination of the two. Tutorial-style technical instruction, thus, often demands a highly flexible approach that integrates both instructional styles, between specifying specific interface keystrokes or interactions and articulating higher-level writing and design goals.

6.4.4 Understanding Online Learning

If instructors, content, instructional activities, and learner engagement all invite their own treatises, it is not surprising that the dramatic movement of instruction online both challenges and vitalizes what we understand about the business of instruction. Acknowledging that the primary difference between traditional and online instruction is that the instructional setting consists of online products and processes might at first seem a minor point of difference, but the acknowledgment quickly returns us to the most essential of questions: (1) What do we know about instruction in general, and (2) What about the online setting adds to, takes away from, or alters our definition of instruction?

Notably, although the instructional potential of the Web has been described, Thomson, Greer, and Cooke (2001) are generally negative about how much of this potential has been realized:

The potential of the Web as a resource for instructional use is tremendous. Unfortunately, the poor design of most of the Web renders it practically useless in any real pedagogical setting; especially where a learner is seeking structured instruction. Poorly designed instructional hypermedia applications often fail to provide any real instruction to the intended learners. Instead learners become frustrated and confused by the choices presented and often fail to form a

Table 6.17
Two instructional approaches offering a range of orientations[a]

Instructional Approaches: Continua of Orientations

From Reeves and Reeves (1997)	From Vosniadou et al. (1996)
Pedagogical philosophy, from instructivist to constructivist	Interactive versus passive learning
Learning theory, from behavioral to cognitive	Fun versus serious learning
Goal orientation, from sharply focused to general	Natural versus efficient learning
Task orientation, from academic to authentic	Learner control versus chalkboard control
Source of motivation, from extrinsic to intrinsic	Grounded versus abstract learning
Teacher role, from didactic to facilitative	Scaffolding versus step-by-step learning
Metacognitive support, from unsupported to integrated	Modeling versus telling, and
Collaborative learning strategies, from unsupported to integral	Reflective versus reactive learning
Cultural sensitivity, from insensitive to respectful	
Structural flexibility, from fixed to open	

[a]Adapted from Reeves and Reeves (1997, pp. 60–63); Vosniadou et al. (1996).

solid understanding of the concepts the instructional site is attempting to communicate. (p. 633)

Looking at what research tells us about the design of paper materials and online documents created to support and instruct readers is one place to begin examining the instrumental role that texts play in learning and teaching humans how to accomplish their learning goals. It is important to note, however, as Schriver (1997) has pointed out, that although "Documents play a role in almost everyone's daily activities . . . surprisingly, knowledge about creating documents for audiences is not yet well developed" (p. 3). Understanding how people process documents does not necessarily teach us how to design them, although at the very least one can assume that a richer understanding of audience always contributes to the communication and design process.

A commonly held misperception about documentation and the development of new technological interfaces is that, eventually, interfaces will be so well designed that designers will be able to eliminate the need for supplementary texts, documentation, online support, and training. Surprisingly, this widespread myth finds support among human–computer interaction and usability researchers who, one might maintain, ought to know better. The popular joke that results is, if the system is poorly designed, documentation will fix it; if the documentation is poorly designed, training will fix it; if the training is poorly designed, the help desk will fix it; and so on.

This myth finds its support in the myth of transparency described earlier, in addition to the problematic belief that providing text that elaborates on the features of the task or the interface is all that is required, whether that information is well or poorly designed. As Borgmann (2000) eloquently elaborates, "Transparency . . . is anything but transparent and casts its own shadows of enigma and confusion" (p. 175). Simply providing text or moving text online does not necessarily guarantee that the needs of user-learners will be served. Poor hardcopy materials are going to produce poor online materials; and, interestingly, well-designed hardcopy materials will not necessarily produce usable online materials (Selber, Johnson-Eilola, and Mehlenbacher 1997; Tomasi and Mehlenbacher 1999).

Audience understanding turns out to be as critical to design success as media constraints and opportunities. To this end, designers of instructional texts continue to rely on basic rhetorical principles first outlined by Aristotle (1926) from classical antiquity. Indeed, the five-step documentation design process has been elaborated in detail by contemporary rhetorical theorists (Bazerman 1988; Bitzer 1968; Burke 1969; Kinneavy 1971; Miller 1985) and information designers alike (Draper 1998; Fawcett, Ferdinand, and Rockley 1993; Hayes 1989; Schriver 1997). Document design involves determining the purpose of the information (i.e., what is being written about, for whom, and the objectives of the information), selecting the communication medium, organizing the information using appropriate organizational patterns, and formalizing and evaluating the organization (Fawcett, Ferdinand, and Rockley 1993, pp. 44–45).

Although human–computer interaction researchers draw on theories of language (e.g., by drawing syntactic versus semantic levels of user comprehension) to understand how humans *communicate* with computer interfaces, they tend to describe interfaces in design terms rather than writing ones. Still, the relationship between writing, design, and reading cannot be underestimated. In a thought-provoking and extensive series of studies, Landauer et al. (1993), Furnas et al. (1987), and Gomez, Lochbaum, and Landauer (1990) explicate the challenge that learners can be expected to have with any interface design:

Any two people [are] unlikely to agree on the "best" term, so the common expedient of a one word command, file name, or table label will usually fail to put a user in touch with [the desired] data. . . . Moreover, while, on average, each person can think of four or five different terms that might suit an "information object," the total number of terms so offered by, say 100 people is in the order of 30. The chance that four or five terms offered by one person will match any one of the four or five offered by another is no greater than 50%. (Landauer et al. 1993, p. 76)

In terms of readers, contrary to generalizations often made about the superiority of hardcopy to online information, Dillon (1994) finds the results on reading speed, accuracy, fatigue, comprehension, and preference generally unconvincing:

• *Speed*: "the evidence surrounding the argument for a speed deficit in reading from VDUs [video display units] is less than conclusive. A number of intervening variables, such as the size, type and quality of the VDU may have contaminated the results and complicate their interpretation" (Dillon 1994, pp. 31–32).

• *Accuracy*: "investigations of reading accuracy from VDU and paper take a variety of measures as indications of performance. Therefore two studies, both purporting to investigate reading accuracy may not necessarily measure the same events. The issue of accuracy is further complicated by the presence or absence of certain enabling features (e.g., search routines) and the potential to alter information structures with hypertext applications" (p. 34).

• *Fatigue*: "It would seem safe to conclude that users do not find reading from VDUs intrinsically fatiguing but that performance levels may be more difficult to sustain over time when reading from average quality screens. As screen standards increase over time this problem should be minimized" (p. 35).

• *Comprehension*: "it would seem as if reading from VDUs does not negatively affect comprehension rates though it may affect the speed with which readers can attain a given level of comprehension" (p. 37).

• *Preference*: "preferences are shifting as screen technology improves or as readers become more familiar with technology" (p. 37).

Dillon (1994) does conclude, however, that two difficulties are experienced more by the users of online information than hardcopy documents: "The major differences appear to occur in manipulation which seems more awkward with electronic texts and navigation which seems to be more difficult with electronic and particularly hypertexts" (p. 42). Wang and Gearhart (2006), though, emphasize that the nature of the instructional content influences learner interaction with online texts, noting that interactivity will be decreased by content modality options, illegibility, readability, relevance, task challenge, programmed feedback, and learner opportunities for input and control (p. 98).

Because the audiences for hardcopy and online texts are potentially exponential, research on human–computer interaction and text usability has tended to focus on categorizing and understanding the tasks and activities that users are likely to engage in while using interfaces. Prior to task-oriented models for documentation (Barker 1998; Coe 1996; Duffy, Palmer, and Mehlenbacher 1993), manuals and online systems were frequently organized around system features and topics rather than human needs and goals (Goodall 1991). Notably, instructional information can still facilitate human text-processing abilities when designers establish a hierarchy of topics, chunk information into meaningful units, and maintain a consistency of topics so that readers can establish thematic continuity (Kintsch and Vipond 1979; Kintsch 1986). However, designing instruction around the tasks that learners bring to the information elevates the text from being readable to being usable. When users encounter an impasse in their performance, they redefine their tasks or subgoals in order to resolve their impasse with the primary system. An impasse—similar to Winograd and Flores's (1986) workplace *breakdown*—represents a mismatch between information and use.

Working in concert with the general tasks that users perform using computer interfaces are the information goals that they bring to their specific tasks. Ummelen (1997) distinguishes between information types, arguing that users either want procedural information ("how to do it," instructions, syntactical elaboration) or declarative information ("how it works," explanatory, conceptual elaboration). Carroll and colleagues (Carroll et al. 1987; Carroll 1990; van der Meij and Carroll 1995) assert that adult learners are only interested in procedural, task-supporting information; however, other researchers (Charney, Reder, and Kusbit 1991; Mirel 1999) extend minimalism to account for learning situations that involve complex technologies and information types.

Although empirical research does not reveal differences in reading speed, accuracy, fatigue, comprehension, and preference between hardcopy and online information, differences do exist. As we have discussed, rather than merely "displaying" information online, we are indeed altering our relationship with information in subtle yet profound ways. Despite this, online information is still frequently seen as a simple extension of printed materials (Brockmann 1990); and researchers continue to be compelled to compare and contrast paper versus online documentation to justify the rapid contemporary movement online (Barnett 1998), a tendency that unfortunately has been replicated again and again by educational technologists motivated to justify their explorations into online instruction and learning.

Minimalist design, which has had a dramatic influence on research related to online information, has had much less influence on research and practice in communication, information, and educational technology. In brief, minimalists maintain that designing systems that improve the user's ability to quickly accomplish tasks is a critical goal for online documentation designers (Carroll 1990), yet this focus may limit designers to providing skills-based training rather than imagining ways of supporting long-term user performances. For this reason, Gery (1991) asserts that many online documentation systems have "done little more than speed information searches" (p. 23). Not only do users continue to have problems with their application programs, but they also encounter problems with the accompanying online help (Duffy, Palmer, and Mehlenbacher 1993; Pratt 1998). Van Dam (1987) warns, therefore, "Don't copy old bad habits; think about new organizations, new ways of doing things, and take advantage of this medium" (p. 3).

Many hypertext efforts have largely ignored this call to action and simply *automate* the printed documentation of a system or application by moving paper-based manuals online. In doing so, they do not address the need to integrate information with task performance (Norman 1993) but, instead, simply transfer inefficiencies inherent to paper information online. But establishing what it means to take full advantage of hypermedia is complicated by its historical interaction with print-based development methods. Research on media differences reveals a complex relationship between humans, the tasks they are attempting to accomplish, and the documents they are using to support those task activities.

As Redish (1988) observes, hardcopy books use conventions that are more familiar to users and that rarely require "system" knowledge or the special skills with navigation routinely required of online documents. Yet whereas information within individual print manuals is often (although not always) located more quickly than in online manuals, online libraries of documents allow users to locate the appropriate online book more quickly (Barnett 1998; Landauer 1997). The research conflicts on exactly which medium is preferable for which user situation (Barnett 1998; Grice 1989). Thus, measuring user performance and analyzing results from usability testing may not be easily comparable (Grice and Ridgway 1993; Mehlenbacher 1993).

So, although designers converting print-based to online information may be tempted to place versions of their hardcopy documents online without significantly rethinking core design issues, such time-saving strategies are bound to create problems. Because of the interplay between user, task, primary workspace, and secondary materials, differences between print and online materials can play a critical role in user success. Selber, Johnson-Eilola, and Mehlenbacher (1997) outline the physical differences between hardcopy pages and computer displays in terms of four parameters:

• *Resolution*: Computer screens are much harder to read because their resolution is lower and physical displays reduced.

• *Display area*: Computer screens rarely allow readers to view more than one page at a time and limit readers' abilities to mark their position in the document via marginal notes, dog-tagging, and so on.

• *Aspect ratio*: The horizontal–vertical ratio of most computer screens (4 × 3) realigns traditional designer and reader expectations in terms of white space, and so, unfortunately, most computer screens invite reduced white space and therefore a reduction in overall scanability and readability.

• *Presence*: The static nature of hardcopy documents invites readers to assume that it is less likely to disappear or to change from one user situation to another; ironically, the dynamic, interactive nature of online documents provides critical opportunities for user customization or information tailoring.

Rhetorical differences between print and online information are more difficult to establish, in part because research conflicts on the strengths and weaknesses of the alternative media. Selber, Johnson-Eilola, and Mehlenbacher (1997) summarize three

major differences between print and online information as organizational, navigational, and contextual:

• *Organizational*: Users read print and online documents in both linear and nonlinear
ways, although online information frequently uses dynamic and associative structures
that invite users to organize and reorganize information in various ways.
• *Navigational*: The spatial comfort that holding a printed book can provide is often
lost to users, and they find themselves having trouble getting a sense of text that
includes an accurate, global understanding of the online information they are accessing (Haas 1989).
• *Contextual*: User interactions rely heavily on contingent, situated, recursive actions
rather than on contextual plans (Beabes and Flanders 1995; Boy 1992; Suchman 1987;
Winograd and Flores 1986), and, therefore, documents must begin with a focus on
the contexts and purposes of use rather than on the formal characteristics of different
document types (see table 6.18).

As well, we have long known that users tend to avoid reading computer documentation whether online or off (Mehlenbacher, Wogalter, and Laughery 2002; Rettig
1991), but reading for complete comprehension online is even rarer than reading a
user manual (Duffy, Palmer, and Mehlenbacher 1993). The argument that no one reads
online information is an oversimplification. Rather, no one reads online information
unless they think they have to or need to and, when they do read online information,
they satisfice, skip, scan, and skim. As Redish (1993) reminds us, "You can't assume
that, just because you wrote a document, people will read it" (p. 15). Moreover, when
people do read instructional documents, they still tend to fail to accomplish their
tasks.

Allen (1996), describing the relationship between theories of bounded rationality
and online design, posits the following general principle:

People can, and frequently do, engage in information avoidance. They interact with their environment by limiting their intake of information, ignoring information if it is associated with
negative outcomes, and taking information shortcuts. Organizations are frequently equally irrational in their collection, processing, and use of information. (p. 119)

Although avoidance may not be the most accurate word to describe what human
beings do when they interact with information systems, it does capture what *appears*
to describe user behaviors with instructional and informational materials, help systems,
and user documentation (Mehlenbacher 2003).

Thus, the most commonly cited shortcoming of documentation is that it is too
complex or that it focuses too much on the features of the primary technologies that
it is created to support (Sullivan and Flower 1986). Baecker et al. (2000) summarize
the problem directly: "Documentation typically consists of lengthy prose interspersed
with screen snapshots, but users don't read manuals and typically find online help

Table 6.18
Physical and rhetorical differences between print and online information[a]

Physical Differences	Pages	Screens
Resolution	70–1200 dots/inch	50–100 dots/inch
Display Area	Generally larger	Generally smaller
Aspect Ratio	Generally taller than wide	Generally wider than tall
Presence	Physical	Virtual
	Static	Dynamic
	2-D interactive	3-D interactive
	Immutable	Mutable

Rhetorical Differences	Pages	Screens
Organizational	Linear	Linear and nonlinear
	Familiar	Familiar and unfamiliar
	Hierarchical	Hierarchical and nonhierarchical
	Logical/deductive	Logical/deductive
	Fixed	Associative and dynamic
Navigational	Familiar	Familiar and unfamiliar
	Limited	Robust
	Static	Static and dynamic
Contextual	Generally rich	Generally poor

[a]Adapted from Selber et al. (1997, p. 1621).

unhelpful" (p. 20). As Carroll and his colleagues (Carroll et al. 1987; Carroll 1990; van der Meij and Carroll 1995) have asserted since the 1980s, most instructional manuals would benefit dramatically from a considerable reduction in size. The same is probably true of online instructional materials.

Documents designed for learning adults should highlight procedural, task-supporting information. Brockmann (1990) stresses that task-oriented documents appeal to adults who, most of us agree

• are impatient learners and want to get started quickly on something productive;
• skip around in manuals and online documents and rarely read them fully;
• make mistakes but learn most often from correcting such mistakes;
• are best motivated by self-initiated exploration; and
• are discouraged, not empowered, by large manuals that decompose each task into its subtask minutiae (p. 113).

For this reason, Davis (2003) recommends that instructional designers motivated to facilitate text-based learning should include explicit text structures, well-defined learning objectives, question-and-answer formats, pretesting structures, reading instructions, metacognitive prompts, numerous well-constructed graphics, posttesting environments, and feedback cycles (p. 292).

The expressions, "Users are idiots" and "Students can't be taught unless they want to learn" find their roots in the perception of human beings that the troubles they experience interacting with the world are *their* responsibility. But designers of information can learn a great deal about their designs from the difficulties that users and learners experience trying to work with them. Poor design helps people work poorly with documents. Thus, it is not surprising that, even as far back as twenty years ago, Odescalchi (1986) found that users of a software-oriented manual expressed higher dissatisfaction, committed more errors, and were less productive than when using task-oriented materials. Importantly, the human characteristics described here do not translate into "online information users are idiots"; rather, they teach us a great deal about the widespread and inappropriate design of information itself.

Putting all of the responsibility for user-learner problems with instruction on the designers of instructional materials, however, is also an exaggeration. Human beings are creative problem-solving entities and, as such, can be particularly creative about making errors. Schriver (1997) notes that almost 94 percent of the users she observed blamed themselves for the problems they encountered while using software applications. User-learners, for example, frequently hold mistaken models of the problems they are working with and misapply these errors to emerging problems (Kay and Thomas 1995). Moreover, initial misconceptions can produce "problem tangles" that lead to increasingly confusing mismatches between instruction and user-learner representations of the original problem (Mack and Nielsen 1994; Mirel 1998).

Unfortunately, most designers of online instruction presume that, beyond the immediate instructional materials they are producing, few other information types need to be provided for users. Nothing could be further from the truth. Primary products are surrounded by numerous support materials, and all these materials present similar challenges in terms of design and evaluation. Barker (1998) provides a table of "Sample Titles for Software Manuals and Help Systems" (p. 158) that provides an excellent starting point for listing some of the support materials that can augment primary online instructional materials (see table 6.19).

Brockmann's (1998) analysis of technical communication as narrative or genre has implications for instruction in both online and face-to-face contexts. Genres consist of the following established features:

• *Tone*: For example, the instruction manual genre usually employs the "you-attitude" tone in which audiences are directly addressed in second-person pronouns.
• *Length*: For example, the instruction manual genre tends to be a text under 100 pages rather than 21 volumes.
• *Weave of text and graphics*: For example, the patent genre includes illustrations, and their words refer to them frequently (p. 118).

Table 6.19
Information titles/genres and a brief description of typical contents[a]

Information Titles/Genres	Description of Contents
Product packaging and labeling*	Product highlights, marketing reviews, screenshots, and sometimes brief installation instructions (often managed by information technology support specialists)
Read-me file*	Last-minute bug fixes, feature updates, and information about errors in documentation (often a negative introduction, unfortunately, to the system)
Maps^	Representation that provides a "big picture" of the system, showing the relationship between features and tasks (also referred to as "sitemaps")
Demos^	Series of hands-on introductions of task as users watch and occasionally interact with system (often part of product announcements or integrated into tutorials)
Getting started guide*	Brief overview of system and introductory features and a walkthrough of some basic system features
Error messages*	Feedback that indicates a user or system error has occurred (frequently poorly written or unhelpful)
More info^	Option that is sometimes provided as part of dialog boxes describing error messages and that provides diagnostic feedback or additional information to help users understand the error state that they are in and how to overcome it
Online guide, coach, or wizard*	Embedded user assistance aimed at taking users step-by-step through tasks (sometimes called "intelligent" help)
Context-sensitive help messages*	Rollover, mouseover, or bubble information that supplements icons or system features
Help or online help system†	Help on using help, table of contents, alphabetic index, search engine, and procedural information
User's guide	Procedures for most system functions
Reference manual or reference guide	Reference or support-level information designed primarily for experienced users
Quick reference card or pocket reference	Brief overview of commands, menus, icons, and essential system information
Manual	Parts of traditional user's guide, installation information, and reference section (all-inclusive title)
Tutorial	Series of lessons that introduce basic (and sometimes advanced) features of the system
Online documentation*	Parts of traditional user's guide, installation information, and reference section (all-inclusive title)
Communication center^	Resource that provides an area for two or more users to work and talk together synchronously or asynchronously to solve problems

Table 6.19

(continued)

Information Titles/Genres	Description of Contents
Third-party information†^	Additional access to information and support produced by third-party companies or communities (method of strengthening user self-sufficiency while simultaneously off-loading responsibility for system shortcomings or limitations)
WBI*	Combination of many of these titles/genres, some produced by the enterprise-level LMS providers, some by intra- and extra-institutional information technology support specialists, and some produced by experienced (model) instructors and application specialists

^a^Extension of Barker (1998, p. 158).

*Adapted from Mehlenbacher (2003, p. 535).

†Adapted from Novick and Ward (2006, p. 18).

^Adapted from Smart (2003, p. 220).

6.4.5 Online Instruction as Narrative and Argumentation

Finding creative and powerful ways to instruct and to design instruction, then, is an act of telling and narrative construction. As with misconceptions about rhetoric, many view storytelling as the opposite of truth telling, even though telling of any kind involves identifying, selecting, and organizing events in the most meaningful arrangement for understandability and memorability. Telling is, as Fisher (1984, 1987) argues, less about fabrication than it is about finding good reasons, part of a narrative paradigm for human behavior. As Fisher (1984) summarizes:

The presuppositions that structure the narrative paradigm are: (1) Humans are essentially story-tellers; (2) the paradigmatic mode of human decision-making and communication is "good reasons" which vary in form among communication situations, genres, and media; (3) the production and practice of good reasons is ruled by matters of history, biography, culture, and character along with the kinds of forces identified in the . . . language action paradigm; (4) rationality is determined by the nature of persons as narrative beings—their inherent awareness of *narrative probability*, what constitutes a coherent story, and their constant habit of testing *narrative fidelity*, whether the stories they experience ring true with the stories they know to be true in their lives . . . ; and (5) the world is a set of stories which must be chosen among to live the good life in a process of continual recreation. (pp. 7–8)

Journet (1990), describing the relationship between science and narrative storytelling, emphasizes the integral role of narrative in any act of knowledge construction:

In the act of constructing narrative, a writer imposes temporal and sequential order on a mass of data by selecting and arranging "significant" events. The writer's decisions about how significant events relate to one another are the product of a particular theoretical orientation or conceptual framework. Narrative is thus a way of constructing knowledge that is important to any discipline that depends on historical explanation. (p. 164)

Although their results were tentative, Bearman, Cesnik, and Liddell (2001) compared learner performance using two virtual patient tutorials, one designed to emphasize narrative and the other problem solving. Their results suggest that "There is some evidence to support the value of a narrative design for virtual patients which are to be used to teach communication skills" and, interestingly, that narrative design influences learners' use of open-ended questions and language that is more appropriate to the patient situation (p. 830). The authors hypothesize that the narrative design encouraged a stronger rapport with the patient, which, in turn, resulted in learner communication behaviors appropriate to the situation at hand. Whether or not these situational skills would transfer to more general patient-learner communication abilities is an issue that the researchers did not investigate.

Strongly connected to the role that narrative reasoning plays in instruction, the practice of organizing materials around exemplary models or examples has also received attention in the research. Of course, teaching by example is not a new phenomenon. Indeed, Isocrates, in *Against the Sophists*, argues that the instructor "must in himself set such an example of oratory that the students who have taken form under his instruction and are able to pattern after him will, from the outset, show in their speaking a degree of grace and charm which is not found in others" (Norlin 1928, 1954, p. 18). But whether narrative frameworks are the optimal method of passing on instructional experience from one instructor to another is still under debate.

More recently, Atkinson et al. (2000) review the considerable research on worked examples and recommend that well-designed examples in instruction exhibit both interexample and intraexample features. Interexample features include the existence of multiple examples and forms per problem, surface features that encourage deep structure comprehension, and examples that are close to the problem assigned; intraexample features include the integration of example parts, the use of multiple modalities (e.g., aural, visual), subgoal structures that are clear and understandable, and issues of completeness in terms of the example provided (p. 203). Subjects where worked examples have been shown to improve learner performance over direct instruction include physics (Ward and Sweller 1990), mathematics (Zhu and Simon 1987), and programming (Tomasi and Mehlenbacher 1999).

Reed and Saavedra (1986) and Renkl (2005) as well have argued strongly for the importance of concrete examples in problem-solving instruction and design. It is critical that instructors and designers distinguish carefully between a knowledge of specifics (i.e., guidelines) and a knowledge of universals (i.e., principles). Both concepts appear to share similar goals for providing learners with methods of conduct, application, or operation, and both specifics and universals define the delicate balance between conceptualizing and doing. Examples (i.e., models) represent the complex instantiation of guidelines; that is, good examples always precede good guidelines for writing, designing, or behaving. Examples embrace guidelines, and guidelines presented in the context of real-world examples often reflect differing levels of complexity, generalizability, and usefulness. Where guidelines problematically deemphasize the influence of context, examples are defined by it.

Renkl (2005) recommends that the following instructional activities related to "worked-out examples" facilitate deeper understanding for learners:

• The *self-explanation elicitation guideline*. Learners perform better by explaining to themselves how examples work.
• The *help guideline*. Learners often require additional information, after prompting for self-explanation, to develop content knowledge.
• The *easy-mapping guideline*. Learners benefit from well-integrated procedures, text, and pictures.
• The *structure-emphasizing guideline*. Learners benefit from structural rather than surface descriptions of the example.
• The *meaningful-building block guideline*. Learners working on subproblems are more likely to succeed with the complete problems (pp. 232–238).

The practices of combining narrative fidelity, rich examples and models, and thoughtful principles for organization are developing instructional strategies that require additional research. But initial investigations in instructional design and in math, science, and technology education are encouraging.

In instructional design, Grabinger's (2004) comprehensive "sociocultural" perspective toward the design, development, and evaluation of research about instruction and learning with technology is particularly intriguing. Grabinger (2004, pp. 51–53) distinguishes sociocultural from traditional instructional design across four dimensions—how instructional designers view learning, the roles of learners and teachers, instruction and the environment, and the use of tools. Whereas traditional instructional design treats learning as a performance error, as the sharing of modular knowledge elements, and as controllable "through the precise arrangement of information, practice, and testing," sociocultural instructional design views learning as collaborative and generative, involving enculturation into a community of learners driven by authentic problems, and as continual, mediated, and constructed.

In contrast to traditional instructional design, where instructors organize the information to be learned, treat learners as being similar to one another, and focus on the clarity of the delivered content, sociocultural instruction stresses instructor–learner collaboration, allows for individual learner differences, and privileges the role of learners in the learning process. In sociocultural instruction and environments, learning is evolving and participatory, interactive and ongoing. Learning is not decontextualized, assigned, or based on assessment strategies such as end-of-course tests as with traditional instructional design. Finally, with sociocultural instructional design, tools are not viewed as delivery mechanisms or as devices to be learned apart from the course content but, rather, as technologies for augmenting the learning process and community development. Although Grabinger's (2004) dichotomy between traditional and sociocultural instruction design is, perhaps, too cleanly drawn, the important argument being put forward here is that design needs to be viewed as a complex interplay between conception, inception, and reception, all deeply connected to the educational context within which design and evaluation serve to balance one another.

Grabinger's (2004) analysis of the differences between traditional and sociocultural instructional design resists being dichotomously reductivist. Indeed, he admits that "the design distinctions . . . are fuzzy and often interact and blend together in creating the most efficient and effective learning environments" (Grabinger, Aplin, and Ponnappa-Brenner 2007). Importantly, we find here another characterization of instruction and learning with technology that emphasizes learners and the learning process, teachers, and the environment and tools dimensions. Sociocultural instructional design moves our focus away from behavioral understandings of individual designers and learners toward a view of instructors and learners deeply engaged in real-world environments with authentic communities of practice. As such, Grabinger (2004) and Grabinger et al. (2007) provide us with a perspective that accounts for both emerging models of higher educational instruction and studies of workplace learning. Although technology, demoted to "tool use," suffers the usual instrumental characterization (not deserving of instructional attention "as a means to an end") and instructors are still held as having considerable influence over the success of instructional situations, a sociocultural instructional design perspective provides us with a useful language for connecting theory with practice in design.

In science education, Linn (2000) and colleagues (see a special 2000 issue of the *International Journal of Science Education*, *22*, 8, on their Knowledge Integration Environment or KIE system and process) echo Bonk et al.'s (Bonk and Cummings 1998; Bonk and Dennen 2003) learner-centered principles in the form of four overriding science education goals. Their learner-centered principles in science education are organized around four instructional goals: making science accessible, making thinking visible, helping students learn from each other, and promoting lifelong science learning. In order to make science more accessible, instructors encourage learners to build more and more powerful scientific principles over time and to investigate personally relevant problems, and provide scaffolded activities that encourage inquiry. Accessibility is heightened by visibility, so scientific processes are modeled, explanation is encouraged, and data are represented from various perspectives. Learners share their understandings and are shown how to engage in supported and respectful interactions. As a lifelong learning process, science education allows diverse information sources, facilitates reflection and personal data collection, and involves long-term science project experiences (Linn 2000, p. 782).

Linn (2006) elaborates on this framework in terms of general design thinking, describing research that supports the following activities or patterns: orient, diagnose, and guide; predict; observe; explain; illustrate ideas; experiment; explore a simulation; create an artifact; construct an argument; critique; collaborate; and reflect (pp. 251–252). Moreover, the framework promotes a lifelong view of instruction and learning that encourages visualization, learner collaboration, and authentic problem solving in context.

Conversely, Bell (2000) found that learners with more dynamic process-oriented views of science produce more complex arguments (as determined by the number of warrants and evidence provided). Rittle-Johnson and Koedinger (2005) describe how scaffolding can facilitate process orientation, and write that "(a) story contexts may be useful scaffolding for introducing new tasks or problem types, (b) visual representations may facilitate problem solving, and (c) scaffolding intermediate procedural steps and then fading the scaffolding may support learning and problem solving" (p. 342).

Although research has recently emphasized learner attributes and prior knowledge and how to facilitate social dynamics both face to face and online, instructional activities can be broadened to encompass these dimensions. Effective instructors are masters at anticipating their learners' needs, understandings, confusions, and questions. Instructors also increasingly recognize that team-based problem-solving activity drives most disciplinary knowledge-making efforts and corporate organizational trends, so learner-to-learner interactions that are satisfying and that produce creative solutions are desirable. Somewhat absent from these discussions of instruction and learning, however, are the places and spaces that we inhabit and that inhabit our learning moments. When we frame instruction as a "classroom management" challenge (whether the classroom walls are real or digital, or a combination of the two), we open ourselves up to the future of instruction, of spaces and artifacts designed to enhance or augment instruction and learning. It is in the cocreation of these spaces that instructors, designers, and learners are beginning to see how learning, too, resides, takes up, is situated in, and occupies environments as much as we do.

6.5 Learning Environment and Artifacts

The development of instructional environments and artifacts that facilitate interaction, learning, problem solving, discovery, and analysis is in its embryonic stages. Currently, enterprise-level Learning Management Systems (LMSs) and the potentials of open source educational environments comprise our worldview for the most part (Berggren et al. 2005; von Hippel and von Krogh 2003). As well, in educational and ICT circles, conversations among the "geek chic" have turned to the implications of serious games (de Freitas 2006; Dickey 2005; Foreman et al. 2004; Mann 1996; Squire 2006) and social networking spaces for education (Boyd and Ellison 2007; Greenhow 2008; Mehlenbacher 2008; National School Boards Association 2007).

However, it is useful to begin the conversation at the nonvirtual beginning, where humans interface with the "natural" (i.e., not human-made) world, to remind ourselves that a great many root developments remain as yet unexplored. Evans (2004) provides an enthralling description of the relationship between human beings and the natural world in which we live, revealing our cognitive, emotional, and physiological interdependence on environment:

The wake–sleep cycle in humans is regulated by the detection of light, and controlled by the suprachiasmatic nucliei, located above the crossing of the optic nerve in the mid-brain. Clearly, a wake–sleep cycle, which closely parallels the Earth's own day–night rhythm, and moreover, which has a physiological mechanism for ensuring the internal cycle remains entrained with the geo-physical cycle, allows a diurnal organism to sleep when there is no light and function when there is. The point is that the nature of the environment which an organism inhabits necessitates responses from the organism in order to function more effectively (and hence ensure survival). These behavioural responses . . . can lead to physiological responses (i.e., evolutionary change which enhance biological morphology). (p. 42)

Given the interdependent relationship between physiological human functionality and behavioral, cognitive, emotional, social, and cultural organization and sense making, it requires no elaborate stretch of the imagination to understand how the technical experiments with simulated realities of the last several decades have profound implications for the design of everyday learning. As Zimbardo and Boyd (2008) remind us—with a human processing speed of approximately four hertz compared to more than three gigahertz for contemporary personal computers—"We are hertz machines in a megahertz world" (p. 30).

So, when we move into the realm of the artificial, we are enthralled by the opportunity to reinvision environments to our particular specifications and likings, while, simultaneously, common sense forces us to acknowledge that at some levels we may be getting in over our proverbial heads. As Weinberger (2007) offers apothegmatically, "Information is easy. Space, time, and atoms are hard" (p. 5). Our early forays into virtual spaces were elemental and hopeful "Pong" simulations consisting of straight lines that moved horizontally and vertically to return a square ball from one side of a dividing center line to another, the ping of contextual detail removed entirely from the game space. As memory, display, peripheral, and computing power have grown, exponentially over the last few short decades, our virtual spaces and the artifacts they embody have grown in complexity as well—what could initially be described as Crayola representations of hastily rendered storyboards have developed into full-bodied, three-dimensional, multicolor imitations of reality. Artificial learning environments should not be viewed as a *genre* of instruction but, rather, as an artform that allows instructors to create *any* genre of instruction using them.

The technology of virtual or simulated spaces, here, is taken at its broadest level to include human-made artifacts, defined after Cole and Derry (2005) as dualistic in nature:

By virtue of the changes wrought in the processes of their creation and use, artifacts are *simultaneously ideal (conceptual) and material*. They are material in that they have been created by modifying physical material in the process of goal-directed human actions. They are ideal in that their material form has been shaped to fulfil the human intentions underpinning those earlier goals; these modified material forms exist in the present precisely because they successfully aided those human intentional goal-directed actions in the past, which is why they continue to be present for incorporation into human action. (pp. 211–212)

Emerging learning environments have been variously described as artificial learning environments, ICT-supported and computer-facilitated learning environments, microworlds, dynamic simulated situations, and multiuser participatory domains, where only some human problem-solving processes are controlled by the learner-user and some are controlled by the environment, situation, or context of use established by the learning space. Within such spaces, learner attention, selection, and manipulation of relevant data are carried out in concert with the system's temporal and spatial release and display of information and events (Hoc 2005).

Könings, Brand-Gruwel, and van Merriënboer (2005) prefer the term "Powerful Learning Environments" (or PLEs) and recommend that such environments need to support four high-level stages of the learning process:

First, prior knowledge and experiences of the student must be activated, in order to build new knowledge on pre-existing knowledge. Second, new skills or knowledge must be demonstrated to the student through modelling. Third, the student should have the opportunity to apply their new knowledge and skills. Fourth, the newly acquired skills and knowledge must be integrated into real-world activities of the student. (p. 647)

Advocating that PLEs be designed to serve the aims of modern education, Könings et al. (2005) stress the importance of self-regulated learning in all instructional situations. PLEs designed to support Könings et al.'s (2005) and Merrill's (2002) stages of learning are organized around authentic tasks and activities that engage learners in individual and collaborative problem solving, articulation, and reflection. The combined perspectives of instructors, educational designers, and learners interact with the environment, and the environment, ideally, adapts itself to the motivations and capabilities of learners as they acquire knowledge and apply it to new contexts.

PLEs should be flexible and open to revision, for recent research on situated cognition, context, and sociocultural perspectives toward learning invites a blurring of just where individual cognition ends and social-environmental knowledge-making (i.e., "the wild") begins (Hutchins 1995). Though we may still maintain that individual cognition is central to the enterprise of learning, this cognition is framed by the activities (defining a problem, reviewing known solutions, becoming familiar with the constraints of the problem situation, and so on) and the sociocultural environments (practices, culture, conventions, standards) of everyday learning situations. The learning situation is formal insofar as it is designed by *instructors* (or with instructors present) or informal insofar as it is self-defined, motivated, and aimed at outcomes tied more to personal learning goals than to institutional ones.

Researchers interested in evaluating training (Mahapatra and Lai 2005) and traditional instruction (Hoey, Pettitt, and Brawner 1997), influenced by Moore (1992) and the pervasiveness of information technology in general, suggest that as more instructors move their classrooms online, an additional uncharted type of interaction will become increasingly important: learner–environment interaction (see Khan 1997 and Moore and Kearsley 1996 for numerous chapters that focus specifically on this dimension). The environment in general refers to the physical or distributed site for learning, which may include specific online applications that learners interact with such as e-mail and listserv programs, MOOs (multi-user domains, object-oriented), chatrooms, network file exchange platforms, discussion lists, and computer-conferencing software (Eldred and Hawisher 1995). Environments may be well designed and easy to navigate, convenient, reliable, accurate, and comprehensive, or they may be the opposite. But regardless of whether environments are well or poorly designed or historically significant, they do inform our definition of self and of tasks.

The type of information, artifacts, elements, and events contained within these environments has powerful consequences for the way we constrain and extend prior understandings. Thus, books, articles, reference materials, and notes serve to facilitate self-guided study, whereas exercises, practice labs, and experiments invite coaching; demonstrations privilege content and encourage instructor control, whereas peer discussions and projects distribute learning across instructional participants (cf. Wenger and Ferguson 2006).

Designers of virtual instructional environments, however, have only begun to make use of what we already know about learning in everyday contexts. In this regard, Perkins (1993) views as woefully inadequate the instructional uses of knowledge that we have gained from watching problem solvers in context:

First, in rich contexts of inquiry and indeed in most everyday activities we find immense physical support systems for cognition; these support systems speak to all four facets of the access framework, providing (1) needed knowledge, (2) accessible representations, (3) efficient retrieval paths, and (4) constructive arenas (scratch pads, work benches, etc.) that support the making of things and the structuring of ideas. Second, the best use of these physical support systems is an art. It is not so commonly found. And conventional instruction does little to acquaint students with this art. (p. 96)

The question is, can art be engineered? Certainly Petroski (1982) believes so, with an important qualification: "Engineering, like poetry, is an attempt to approach

perfection. And engineers, like poets, are seldom completely satisfied with their creations" (p. 83). Lunenfeld (1999) has also acknowledged the gulf between idealized
and actual designs, warning that "Too many contemporary observers churn out theories that offer fantasies of fully accessible, fully immersive virtual realities where gender
and identity are untethered from the body; that literalize the metaphor of cyborg life;
that obsess on the ever-titillating concept of teledildonics. The trend is to discuss the
implications of technologies (especially where something could go) rather than to
analyze the technologies themselves (where they are)" (p. xix).

Where we are technologically is a long way past the glowing green typefaces and
Pong interfaces of the 1970s. Notably, however, we are also some distance from fully
immersive virtual realities and cyborg interactions. Thus the look and feel of e-mail
applications have evolved quickly by some measures, from their initial laboratory-
based conception in the 1960s, to their pervasive use by over 70 million users on a
daily basis in 2004, up 37 percent from 2000 (Rainie and Horrigan 2005). But those
of us who were introduced to e-mail applications prior to 1980 have not witnessed
the revolutionary applications that figure in popular films such as *The Minority Report*.
"You've got mail" is an old joke at this point but is still an element of millions of
e-mail users' interactions with their computers today. Figure 6.3 provides snapshots
of four generations of e-mail interfaces, revealing the incremental technological
advances that user-learners have adapted to habitually.

E-mail is not simply another version of memo-based communication, nor has
it completely changed communication as we understand it. As Ducheneaut and
Watts (2005) remind us, "E-mail is an evolving sociotechnical phenomenon" (p. 12).
We find ourselves once again caught between marketed promise and sociocultural
compromise.

At this particular point in time, most online learning environments take the form
of enterprise-level (i.e., complex) Learning Management Systems (LMSs). LMSs include
various applications for facilitating discussions, content import and export functions,
assessment tools, document sharing, calendaring and course management, and for
tracking learner progress in online courses (Petherbridge and Mehlenbacher 2007). A
typical LMS presents learners with multiple levels of interaction including the browser
interface, the LMS features, the online course structure and organization, and the
instructional materials that make up each instructional module. Not only are learners
challenged by multiple levels of interaction, but instructors are also subject to significant learning curves as they respond to the unpleasant effects of creeping featurism
and deceptive intuitiveness. Norman (1990) coined the term "creeping featurism," and
Schriver (1997) ultimately defined it as "manufacturers' seeming obsession with adding
newfangled features to their products" (p. 227). The desire to provide as many functions and features as possible in each new release of a product was very popular
in the 1980s but, with luck, is losing some momentum these days as user-friendly

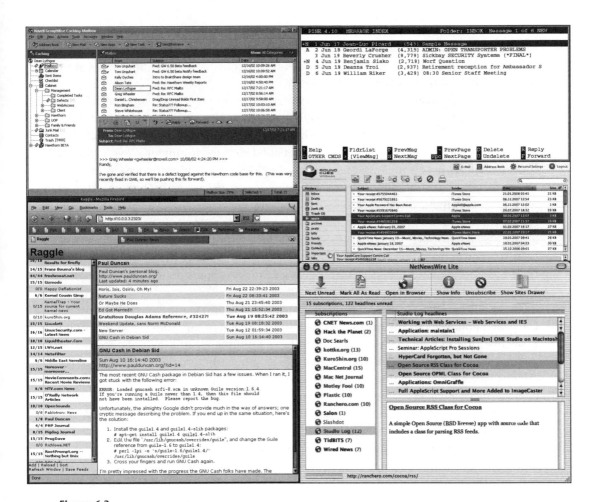

Figure 6.3
Four generations of e-mail interfaces.

products become more important to consumers (Benjamin 2007; Zeven 2006). Creeping featurism, in part, helps explain why Microsoft Word 4.01 required less than 1 MG, whereas, depending on how many add-ons users choose, MS Office 2007 now requires more than 1500 times that memory.

The learning environment and artifacts that surround everyday instructional situations are as varied as the learners, activities, social dynamics, and instructional opportunities that inhabit them, but design, architecture, interface, communication, and educational researchers have long understood that environment plays a pivotal role in any learning event. Strange and Banning (2001) summarize the idea as follows: "it appears that environments exert their influence on behavior through an array of natural and synthetic physical features, through the collective characteristics of inhabitants, the manner in which they are organized, and as mediated through their collective social constructions" (p. 200). Similarly, Mountford (2001) notes, "Spaces have heuristic power over their inhabitants and spectators by forcing them to change both their behavior (walls cause us to turn right or left; skyscrapers draw the eye up) and, sometimes, their view of themselves" (p. 50).

In describing a learning environment, therefore, it is pragmatic to establish specifically the parameters of the learning situation we are describing. Soloway et al. (1996) explicitly ground their description of learning environments and their application to instructor pedagogy, in their case software designed to support the learner desire for growth, diversity, and motivation. Importantly Soloway et al. (1996) do not interpret context in its broadest sense, and a discussion of the full sociocultural context for contemporary online education in higher educational settings falls outside the scope of this book as well.[4] Even at the institutional level, instructional issues quickly become educational, administrative, and societal issues. Grossen's (2000) definition of an institution, here, has implications for any discussion of the interaction between cognitive and social dimensions of learning: "The notion of 'institution' (which, by the way, is rarely explicitly defined) has two inter-related meanings: according to the first, institutions are social organisations gathering a group of people whose aim is to achieve predetermined goals (for example teaching or healing) and to produce material or symbolic goods; according to the second, institutions are sets of laws, rules, norms, values, reciprocal expectations, tacit assumptions, common representations, routines, which are constituents of social organisations" (p. 22).

For the purposes of our examination, then, we limit definitions of learning environment to the immediate instructor–learner context, whether a classroom, software environment, museum, or coffeeshop. Here, Burns and Hajdukiewicz's (2004) distinction between one's general environment and one's "work environment" is useful:

The work domain describes *why* and *where* work needs to be done, the components and resources available for fulfilling the domain purposes, the functions of these resources, and the principles, relationships, and constraints that govern domain behavior. Activities include the tasks and procedures that need to be performed to achieve particular goals, the strategies for performing these tasks, troubleshooting, decision-making, and coordination. Activities can be considered as the *what*, *when*, and *how* associated with action in the work environment. People and technology define the capabilities, competencies, organization, role allocation, responsibilities, communication, and culture in the work environment. These characteristics can define the *who* when considering the work environment. (p. 250)

Work environments for learning, increasingly, occur inside and outside of formal educational institutions, and considerable research emphasizes not only workplace (corporate, manufacturing, and service) and educational (higher education, high school, middle school, and elementary) settings, but also, more recently, leisure (home, community center, athletic, and religious) settings (Fraser 1998). All these settings share fundamental attributes such as location, equipment and artifacts, instructional structures, relationships with time, space, grouping, separation, and rules for discourse use.

At the most basic level, the traditional school classroom, elementary through graduate school, has remained an eerily stable architectural reality for many decades. At any of these educational levels, researchers have noted that settings can be organized in either closed or open designs. Interestingly, even open environments contain rules for and assumptions about how the humans interacting with them will behave, interact, and communicate. Closed environments are often more explicit about the rules for instructor–learner conduct than "open" ones. For example, Ivinson (2000), in her analysis of the dynamics and setting that characterize primary school classrooms, outlines a continuum from restricted but visible through open but less visible (see table 6.20).

Ivinson (2000) interprets the local setting of the classroom as an intensely relational one and stresses that "Different forms of relationship have different consequences for learning" (p. 91). As well, we can identify in Ivinson's (2000) description of the environment for elementary instruction variables that interact with and inform the learning dimensions of everyday instructional situations. Within one's environment, place, equipment, and wall displays form the setting for learner and instructor activities and tasks and help define the kinds of discourse that are encouraged and discouraged. Social dynamics, instructional activities, and learner engagement with instructional materials, in turn, are informed by whether instructional spaces are open or closed, complex or simple, time consuming or temporally constrained.

Higher educational settings exhibit similar reconfigurations as well, in terms of both brick-and-mortar and simulated architectures, with experience from simulated environments informing developments in traditional domains. Dordai and Rizzo (2006), thus, note that the "echo-boom generation" (learners born between 1980 and 1995) expect to be able to define their own versus university spaces (*my* space versus *our* space). Moreover, they are a generation that assumes 24/7 campuses that allow

Table 6.20
Classroom contexts: Distinct domains and associated classroom activities[a]

Domain	Closure/restricted, visible pedagogy	Openness/less restricted, invisible or less visible pedagogy
Place	• specialist space (e.g., art room, hall) • furniture positioned in lines, rectangles • rectangular and square tables • tables face teacher's table or board • children have their own place • storage room at individual places	… in the classroom … in groups … round tables … tables face each other … places are communal … individual drawers in communal trolley
Equipment	• children own personal everyday equipment (e.g., pencil, pen) • children keep subject specific items (e.g., exercise books, text books) • children can access specialist equipment (e.g., apparatus, paint brush)	… everyday equipment is communal … kept in communal places … teacher controls specialist equipment
Curriculum structuration	• activity has an identifiable beginning • activity has a set procedure • activity has an identifiable end	… arises in an ad hoc way … the procedure is novel … the end is contingent
Time intervals	• regular and often (predictable) (e.g., happens each day or week) • short time cycle (e.g., a few minutes)	… irregular and infrequent … long time cycle (e.g., across a term)
Setting and grouping	• ability groups • assigned to groups for activities • equipment for specific (activity) groups • seated in specific groups • groups have a different teacher	… no ability groups … work individually … all use same equipment … individual places … same teacher
Space and movement	• restricted (e.g., children sit in a fixed place) • homogeneous (e.g., the same place for each activity) • teacher strongly controls movement	… less restricted (children occupy a variety of seats) … diverse (e.g., different places for different activities) … children have autonomy
Wall displays	• curriculum subject oriented (e.g., gives information, functional) • child's name appears • label indicates subject • teacher's individual style • hierarchical (e.g., sample of the "best work")	… child-centered (e.g., illustrates "creativity") … no names used … label indicates topic … school aesthetic code … equal (e.g., every child is represented)
Teacher's classroom discourse	• subject focused (e.g., instructional) • subject criteria made explicit • sameness emphasized	… child focused (e.g., regulative, moral) … individuality emphasized … difference encouraged

[a]Adapted from Ivinson (2000, pp. 73–74).

them to tailor-design their educations, educations as sustainable and revisable as their campus grounds.

Notably, however, many of the challenges faced by the designers of simulated learning environments are challenges faced by the designers of real-world architectural campuses. Strange and Banning (2001) define all human environments as a combination of the following components:

- physical condition, design, and layout (viewed as a continuum from deterministic to possibilistic with probabilistic in between);
- characteristics of the people who inhabit them (producing congruence or incongruence with differentiation and consistency determining how a fit is achieved);
- organizational structures related to their purposes and goals (degree of complexity, centralization, formalization, stratification, production, efficiency, and morale); and
- inhabitants' collective perceptions or constructions of the context and culture of the setting (p. 5).

In contrast to real-world architectural learning environments, simulated spaces are designed to support a new form of person–environment interaction where general environments are able to adapt locally to the motivations, needs, desires, and abilities of learners. It is no longer science fiction to interact with simulated environments where half the objects—for instance, tables and chairs—are generated by an augmented reality system while the other half exist in real space (Knight 2005a). In addition to offering new opportunities for engaging learners and heightening presence, the instructional implications are literally just around the artificial corner. Importantly, the goal is not to build complex learning environments but, rather, to design developmental environments. Table 6.21 summarizes Strange and Banning's (2001) characterization of the differences between complex and developmental environments.

An example of a developmental environment in progress is Ziv, Ben-David, and Ziv's (2005) simulation-based medical education (SBME) environment. The environment allows learners to experience the complex problem solving that is required to "manage" medical mistakes (e.g., mistaken patient identities, adverse drug reactions, incorrect diagnoses) via simulation. SBMEs allow learners to experience life-threatening situations, exploring, interpreting, and learning from decisions that might otherwise result in dire outcomes. Such learning opportunities, of course, cannot be arranged using actual medical contexts, particularly in problem situations that required immediate determination of patient problems and corrections to the current course of action. SBMEs thus allow learners the luxury of participating in, reflecting on, and sharing with other learners their reactions to intense learning situations without exposing the learners or others to physical harm. SBMEs find their design metaphors, features, and affordances in approximations of real-world activities within which professionals practice and learn.

Table 6.21
Complex organizations versus developmental environments[a]

Complex Organizations	Developmental Environments
• Uniformity, simplification, and routinization of procedures	• Appreciation for the unique and creative
• Minimize conflict and variance	• Encourage complexity, diversity, and controversy
• Centralize substantive decisions	• Maximize responsibility of participants in making decisions (role-taking)
• Clear stratification of authority and responsibility	• Encourage personalism and community by minimizing status and power
• Formalize and specify regulations for accurate accountability	• Minimize formality to create levels of ambiguity and flexibility in response to individual need
• Maximize achievement per unit of time and resource	• Maximize time and resource per unit of achievement
• Interactions based on functional responsibilities	• Interactions based on personal modeling and mentoring
• Minimize risk taking to maximize efficient use of resources	• Encourage opportunities for risk taking to maximize educational effectiveness

[a]Adapted from Strange and Banning (2001, p. 74).

6.5.1 Conventional Learning Spaces

Designing online environments that facilitate interactivity, authentic engagement, learner motivation, and that enhance opportunities for scaffolding and exploratory learning is a wicked problem because it is contingent on human-to-human communication (and miscommunication), including temporal, technical, organizational, social, and, increasingly, geographical constraints. Pea (1993) is correct in asserting, "On close inspection, the environments in which humans live are thick with invented artifacts that are in constant use for structuring activity; for saving mental work, or for avoiding error, and they are adapted creatively almost without notice. These ubiquitous mediating structures that both organize and constrain activity include not only designed objects such as tools, control instruments, and symbolic representations like graphs, diagrams, text, plans, and pictures, but people in social relations, as well as features and landmarks in the physical environment" (p. 48). Moreover, by nature, all artifacts resist seamless interaction with humans, their activities, habits, particularities, affective motivations, and long-term goals (or all humans resist seamless interaction with artifacts). As Barab, Evans, and Baek (2004) note:

Throughout history, humans have constructed . . . tools that influence their transformation and likewise tools embedded in social interactions have triggered human development. In essence, humans and their environment mutually transform each other in a dialectical relationship.

Culturally, these tools and the knowledge pertinent to their continued use are passed from generation to generation. (p. 201)

Since our rhetorical design perspective frames design, technology, and learning as interactive, iterative processes of discovery and trial and error, the research on human–computer interaction, design, and usability is an important resource for approaching the design of learning environments. Unfortunately, however, most usability research has tended to focus on usability testing and evaluation rather than on usability issues in general and on usability issues applied in the beginning and throughout the design process (Allen 1996). At the same time, the development of alternative forms of technology-mediated instruction is clearly connected to the explosion in research on instruction and learning. Methods for evaluating their influence on learning become increasingly important as instructional situations become easier to imagine and design. Lunenfeld (1999) thus stresses a proactive rather than reactive vision for the design of simulated learning environments: "Rather than thinking of the digital media and environments . . . as though they possessed the stability of painting or architecture, better to embrace their mercurial qualities and conceptualize them as being somehow evanescent, like theatrical performances or dance recitals" (p. xx). Allen, Otto, and Hoffman (2004), too, suggest that transmissional metaphors of media deemphasize the enveloping nature of contemporary media. For this reason, they recommend defining medium in environmental terms:

Applying this metaphor to human affairs seems particularly relevant in an era when electronic information pervades virtually every aspect of everyday life. Our perceptions of the planet earth are influenced by world-wide "supermedia" events . . . even as we are surrounded by "info-cocoons" patched together from components such as facsimile machines, computers, copiers, cellular phones, radios, TVs, and video games.

. . . the notion of media as channels for transmitting information is limited because it tends to ignore many of the modalities of perception and action that people use when interacting with contemporary computer-based media. (p. 221)

So instruction occurring in conventional spaces is evolving to match developments in nonconventional ones. Although the context of the face-to-face classroom is well known and has a documented historical and social evolution (Tyack 1974), many of these studies minimize the role of emerging technologies in the learning spaces. Online, instructors, learners, tasks (i.e., instructional tasks that interact with interface feature tasks), and social dynamics all play out in ways that are both familiar and unfamiliar to us. Thus, many of our basic assumptions about and strategies for approaching these learning dimensions require modification simply because of evolving changes in our learning environments.

One way that face-to-face educational environments are fundamentally different from online ones is noted by Cazden (1988) early in her analysis of traditional classroom discourse:

Classrooms are among the most crowded human environments. Few adults spend as many hours per day in such crowded conditions. Classrooms are similar in this respect to restaurants and buses or subways. But in such places simultaneous autonomous conversations are normal, whereas in classrooms one person, the teacher, is responsible for controlling all the talk that occurs while class is officially in session—controlling not just negatively, as in a traffic policeman does to avoid collisions, but also positively, to enhance the purposes of education. (pp. 2–3)

So "improvements" brought about by simulated learning environments, unfortunately, do not need to be as radical as we might hope for decision makers to consider investing in technology. As Anson (1999) notes, "At many institutions, administrators are realizing that creating a state-of-the-art multimedia course out of, for example, 'Introduction to Psychology,' which may enroll up to five hundred students, represents a major improvement. The quality of faculty lectures is uneven; they come at a high cost; and they are often delivered in settings not conducive to learning—hot, stuffy lecture halls with poor sound systems and ailing TV monitors hung every few rows" (p. 271).

Much of our disappointment with current online learning environments, therefore, is less a feature of media themselves and more a function of the current state of the virtual learning environments themselves. As Allen, Otto, and Hoffman (2004) suggest:

The ergonomic utility of many media environments is based on metaphors and mechanics that invite users to participate in worlds populated by semiautonomous objects and agents—ranging from buttons and windows to sprites and computer personas. Attempts to model user engagement with these worlds as the processing of symbols, messages, and discourse are limited because the channel-communications metaphor fails to specify many of the modalities by which humans interact with situations. These modalities include locating, tracking, identifying, grasping, moving, and modifying objects. There is a profound, but not always obvious, difference between receiving communication and acquiring information through these interactive modalities. (p. 215)

Rather than framing the discussion in terms of successful or unsuccessful implementations of instruction or learning (even the word "implementations," as we have pointed out, suggests that face-to-face instruction and learning should be viewed as *different* from online learning and instruction), it is more productive to look carefully at the interaction between instructional and learning settings and the related acts of instruction and learning that play out in the different domains (cf. Winn 2003). One quickly realizes that the "no significant difference" debate has been stripped of its most interesting meanings, if by "difference" one only means difference according to end-of-semester test scores or course grades.

"Difference," according to the (online) *Oxford English Dictionary* (OED), refers to "The condition, quality, or fact of being different, or not the same in quality or in essence; dissimilarity, distinction, diversity; the relation of non-agreement or non-identity *between* two or more things, disagreement." Rather than emphasizing the mathematical etymology of "difference," which stresses difference in terms of "The quantity by which one quantity differs from another" or "the remainder left after subtracting one quantity from another," we need instead to take a descriptive rather than causal approach to instruction and learning. Online instruction and learning, then, would be elevated from its common status—as an "electronic platform" as one colleague misguidedly put it, or as a "treatment to be applied" as another remarked—to an alternative space. To draw on recent research discussions related to architectural and online social navigation (Höök, Benyon, and Munro 2003), online instruction and learning would inhabit alternative "'places' where social interactions are encouraged and which are visible through the configuration of the space and how people conceive of the various interactions in it" (p. 9).

Viewing Internet-based information as a platform for content is even more reductive than viewing it as a method of disseminating information. At least with the latter, one is acknowledging that Internet-based information is both a process and a product. More importantly, rather than sitting underneath the critical layer of content, the Internet transforms the content into something somewhat similar to and yet quite different from its traditional hardcopy instantiation. "Instantition," here, is selected deliberately to highlight the possibility that moving hardcopy information online may or may not improve one's interaction with the resultant content. Cubitt (1998) captures this tension when he describes the human colonization of cyberspace:

> This visualization of cyberspace as a new terrain expresses itself in metaphors that move between building a new world and revealing it, staking claims to a preexisting turf and laying the ground for its existence. The amazing commonality of the net is so easy to love. But the visual metaphors of net and matrix predate that passion, writing the map grid over the unformed universe inside the network of computers. I do not mean, here at least, that cyberspace, or even dataspace, is merely a reflection or a reproduction of existing social relations. Rather, it is a project of and a projection from those conditions. (pp. 83–84)

So, in the case of the online OED, it would be a profound misrepresentation to suggest that using the online instantiation of the dictionary is either better or worse than using the hardcopy book(s). The hardcopy mini-version of the OED (two volumes) requires a magnifying glass to read its entries and demands a considerable amount of bookshelf space. The hardcopy OED, moreover, is difficult open and flatten for optimal reading. The online OED provides a powerful search mechanism that offers readers options for pronunciation, spellings, etymology, quotations, and a date chart; allows readers to cut-and-paste entries directly into their word processing documents; enables them to select the author of a given quotation for additional citation information; and even provides them with learning resources if they are interested in using the dictionary for instructional purposes. Other features allow them to join the OED

Online listserv and to view new words or receive quarterly updates or a "word of the day" e-mail message. The hardcopy OED has sentimental value as a graduation gift and is difficult to move.

We do know from interacting with software via traditional e-mail, instant messaging, or discussion forums that computer-mediated communication is made necessarily more complex by the additional workload required to learn and manipulate the interface *and* to engage in the act of communicating. Plowman (2005), moreover, stresses that in any instructional situation, our computational interactions further complicate our instructional goals and our desire to facilitate effective group dynamics in general:

These [computational] procedures and operations are not a feature of interaction with teachers or traditional linear media, but they can get in the way of understanding and achieving learning goals when activity is computer based. Procedural and operational talk is more seamless in classrooms where teachers are available to direct activities. Although teachers may request everybody to stop what they are doing and listen, accomplished teachers are able to integrate the new instructions or move in a new direction without disrupting the flow of teaching and learning. Such scenarios are based on energetic, reflective, and resourceful teachers; it is acknowledged that some classroom activity falls short of this ideal, and teacher talk is often monologic or variations on a pattern of initiation/response/evaluation. (p. 56)

It remains to be seen whether the expression "get in the way of understanding" needs to be applied to the role of technology in human communication acts, given that so much of what we currently define as communication has become difficult to distinguish from technologically mediated communication. I have communicated with four people today but none of these communications has been face-to-face; and, even in a real-time work environment, much of the day's communication will still involve technology (e.g., telephone, slide-projector augmented communication, and e-mail). So, not surprisingly, agreement about what exactly constitutes an "online" environment is not easy to reach.

A cursory review of several researchers' descriptions of online learning environments, for example, reveals that "online" can be understood in terms of its features or materials or its functions and services. Table 6.22 summarizes the major attributes of online learning environments.

If we cannot agree on the terminology used to describe online learning environments, we can at least establish the language we will use to approach the design and evaluation of such systems.

6.5.2 Interactive Learningscapes

De Souza (2005) elaborates on how online environments might more effectively support learner-user activities that are less reparative than epistemic, writing that they would encourage problem approximation, formulation, knowledge reorganization,

Table 6.22
Attributes of online learning environments[a]

Features (Chapman 2005)	Materials (Collins and Berge 1995)	Functions (Ingraham et al. 2002)	Services (Peters 2003)
Ability to coordinate course registration, scheduling, learning programs	Web-based course administration (e.g., syllabi, course readings, registration, attendance, participation records)	Links to student records and other MIS systems Provides student tracking and assessment tools	Electronic administration of distance students' files
Resource management, content integration, repositories	Reference textbooks (e.g., hyperlinked and/or multimedia "deep archival reference" books or bibliographic databases)	Be or support database-driven active pages	
Material distribution, reporting	Lectures (e.g., guest lecturing or lecture notes or slides integrated with graphics and video/audio clips)	Easy to use staff and student user interface Easy access on and off campus Allows student note-taking, search, printing Secure environment	Teaching in continuing education Online seminars, drill, practical training, tutorials
	Laboratory simulation and experimentation (e.g., animations, case studies, interactive media)	Supports full range of multimedia file formats	
Online conferencing, collaborative tools	Collaborative learning (e.g., brainstorming, networking, project-based collaboration, mentoring in real-time)	Provides feedback Supports student collaboration, discussion groups	Electronic advisory service for potential students
Tracking student accomplishments, learning assessment, learner testing, profiling, assessment	Recitation, assignments, grading (e.g., online quizzes, tests, drills, automated feedback)	Flags new changes made since student last visited	Electronic drill exercises, correction of written assignments Evaluation of course development
	Virtual educational institutions (e.g., nonprofit course delivery servers like Virtual Online Universities)		Access to university library

Table 6.22

(continued)

Features (Chapman 2005)	Materials (Collins and Berge 1995)	Functions (Ingraham et al. 2002)	Services (Peters 2003)
Online help features		Provides effective online help for instructors and students	

[a]Adapted from Chapman (2005, pp. 1151–1152); Collins and Berge (1995, pp. 238–240); Ingraham et al. (2002, p. 39); Peters (2003, pp. 92–95).

solution evaluation, and the generation of multiple solution types (p. 105). Such systems would formalize our arguments about the transformative nature of human–artifact interactions, producing analyses and understandings that could not be reached without the benefit of the artifact in question.

Finding ourselves able to design environments and artifacts that supplement or replace these types of instructor–learner interactions, the important question becomes "How do we now conceptualize 'interactivity' and 'activity'?" As Rose (1999) asserts, "if the words 'interactive' and 'interactivity' proliferate in texts on educational computing, it is despite their apparent lack of denotative value" (p. 43). Two of the common meanings that Rose (1999) cites are a high degree of learner control and an information-rich environment. Another recent discussion defines interactivity very differently, deriving its definition from conversation analysis: the extent to which messages in a sequence are related to each other, as shown by a high level of agreement, use of first-person pronouns, and other features (Rafaeli and Sudweeks 1997). Instructional and multimedia designers often describe the use of video/audio clips, simulations, forms to fill out, and collaborative learning technologies as interactive. Yet emerging technologies and user trends continue to redefine interactivity not only in terms of the duration of time and interaction between media output but in terms of how learners are allowed to manipulate and manage media objects. How, for example, does the interactivity of Web-based video programming (cf. Hansell 2005) where users are able to view, sort, and augment their original view with secondary subject matter compare to the conversational give-and-take of a chat environment? At the very least, researchers need to think more carefully about online interactivity and why we value it.

In our desire to promote active learning, we may be guilty of promoting more interactive learning environments, environments that give immediate responses to learners but that do not necessarily facilitate reflection or a careful examination of all the materials and tasks. Thus Najjar's (1998) assertion that "an interactive user interface appears to have a significant positive effect on learning" is tempered by his acknowledgment that multimedia features can distract rather than focus, that low-aptitude learners appear to benefit more from multimedia than high-aptitude learners, and that interactivity influences users in different ways depending on their motivational level, age, and the methods used to test them on their learning (pp. 314–315). Rose (1999) identifies the quintessential tension between learner reflexivity and the interactive experience when she notes that, although researchers "valorize learner control, non-linearity, and flexibility as interactivity's defining characteristics," skeptics of the power of interactivity might also imagine "the shadowy figure of the disavowed other lurking behind these wide-eyed adventurers: the shadow of a child sitting mesmerized and immobile before the computer, only her index finger on the mouse moving occasionally as a stream of images passes in a more or less predetermined sequence before her glazed eyes" (p. 45). An "interactive" learning environment does not necessarily invite learner activity and engagement.

Of course, as Internet speed and development suites become less of an issue, online educational environments are certain to become even more interactive, but the price may be that more reflective learners fare poorly for the design "upgrade" and considerable multiple literacies involved in learning to work successfully in emergent environments. One way of conceptualizing developments in online environments over that last thirty years is summarized in table 6.23.

Table 6.23

Online design as linguistic, extralinguistic, metaphorical, space-time dynamics

Linguistic	Extralinguistic	Metaphoric	Space-time
Textual	Static, list-making, linear	Accounting, descriptive categorization	Independent
Hypertextual	Limited graphics, text-based, nodes, links	Encyclopaedic, footnotes, layered content	Primary and Secondary Textuality
Oral/Pictorial	Iconic/2D graphics	Narrative, landscape, event-based	Independent and Dependent
Multimedia	Iconic, graphics, multimodal	Interactive television, action and objects, scripts	Programmed Entertainment
Simulation	Actions, objects, scripts, 3D graphics and animation	Buildings/ transportation systems, puzzle-like	Refined, manipulated, rule-based
Two worlds	Actions, scripts, 3D graphics and animation	Symbiotic, sensophysical and environmental feedback looping	Organic, centered on individual perceptions and priorities
Three worlds	Conceptual artifacts, intelligent environments, open-ended spaces	Symbolic, sensophysical and artifact-rich environments and interactions	Conceptual, centered on individual manipulation and multiple viewpoints

To begin imagining how learners will become increasingly conversant with increasingly complex simulated environments, we need only think about our relationship with textual reading. As Ryan (1994) reminds us, reading is *already* a highly interactive event—we have just internalized the mechanisms that define that interactivity:

> Increasing the reader's participation in the creative process, and thereby questioning such distinctions as author/reader, actor/spectator, producer/consumer, has been a major concern of postmodern art. This does not mean that without these efforts reading would be a purely passive experience: theorists . . . have convincingly demonstrated that a world cannot emerge from a text without an active process of construction, a process through which the reader provides as much material as she derives from the text. But the inherently interactive nature of the reading experience has been obscured by the reader's proficiency in performing the necessary world-building operations. (pp. 16–17)

As online educational environments provide more opportunities to input information, to receive immediate feedback, and to "build worlds," the interaction between learners and the features of their learning environment may change, and instructors need to be aware of such shifts in audience orientation and environmental usability. With hardcopy texts, such issues do not exist beyond the parameters of page turning, searching, and the accessing of special sections (e.g., answers, examples, review, exercises). Similarly, in face-to-face classrooms, attending to details of the classroom setting or environment often reduces the amount of attention that students are able to place on the instructional content (except in cases where instructors invite students to attend actively to each other, a shared text, or supplementary overhead materials). It seems critical, then, to avoid collapsing interactive learning with active learning behaviors.

Collins (1996) further distinguishes between *interactive*, *active*, and *passive* learning, noting that

> The costs and benefits of active learning vs. passive learning are probably well known, but the costs and benefits of interactive learning vs. active learning are less well known. The costs of high interactivity are a lack of thoughtfulness by the student because things move fast, and a lack of problem finding and construction by students because everything they do is responsive to some situation. The benefits of high interactivity are that students receive immediate feedback on the success of their actions, they find such environments extremely motivating, and they are very active trying out different skills and strategies. (p. 352)

Although we all agree that, in conventional classrooms, active learning has many advantages over passive learning, it may be that moving online encourages what Dumont (1996) describes as "the paradox of the active user," a user who is highly motivated to accomplish goals quickly but whose "skills tend to converge at relative mediocrity" (p. 195). Thus, active users can be particularly good at moving quickly though a series of low-level tasks to reach a well-defined goal, but they may not fully understand the underlying complexity of the environment they are using. Active users, for example, may know how to search the Internet for specific information in order to complete a research assignment, but they may not reflect on the instructor's goals to have students learn how to efficiently and effectively sift through online information as a way to strengthen information gathering and to promote advanced learning opportunities. Reflective learners, on the other hand, may understand the importance of learning how to use the software and also of understanding the overall instructional goals and content of the online course. They may develop a richer picture of the learning environment as a space where interface design and functionality can sometimes overshadow or even compete with the Web site's educational merit and instructional purpose.

6.5.3 Designing for Two Worlds

The most powerful metaphor for online learning environments is currently an architectural one, although cultural critics, educational technologists, and library scientists have also characterized online spaces as vast spatiotextual repositories or as ecological spaces (Allen, Otto, and Hoffman 2004; Barab and Roth 2006). Mitchell (1999) argues that successful online spaces support accessibility (by providing "Digital Downtowns and Cyber Siberias"), visibility (by including attractive "Logical Landmarks"), and loyalty (by encouraging communities that "Stay Around") (pp. 123–127).

Buscher and Hughes (2003) describe accessibility as "sociability" (the attraction of people by other people) and visibility as "reciprocity of perspective" (mutually shared views of the same space), and point to the need for system intersubjectivity ("spatial grammars" that build on "commonsense knowledge") (p. 102). Although the inspiration for structures that draw on commonsense knowledge (e.g., urban landscapes) without compromising integrity have yet to be developed, the authors suggest that designers explore the continuum between static online spaces populated with recognizable structures and dynamic spaces where users build their own microworlds. Erickson and Kellogg (2003), in addition to visibility, list awareness (of others) and accountability (related to social beliefs, customs, and norms) as being critical to the success of "socially translucent systems," that is, systems where it is "easier for users to carry on coherent discussions; to observe and imitate others' actions; to engage in peer pressure; to create, notice and conform to social conventions" (p. 19). Koch (2003) equates the awareness and sociability of a system's features as contributing to its "matchmaking" abilities by relationship discovery and cooperative partnering. And finally, Konstan and Riedl (2003) and Svensson and Höök (2003) both recommend that some form of filtering be available so that users are able to deemphasize irrelevant information and focus on information germane to their particular problem-solving context.

The flexibility of online social spaces, therefore, is in its infancy. Arnold and Smith (2003) remind us that "computer-mediated communication and communities that rely heavily on these new media are confronted with significant limitations: lacking social cues, making do with gaps or lags in feedback, and dealing with 'noise,' for example. Communication becomes relatively 'thin,' reducing the context that communication partners effortlessly share in face-to-face situations" (p. 466). McGrath and Munro (2003) capture the informal nature of many learning encounters in their description of typical work environments:

Chance meetings, recruited conversations, seeing what people are doing or reading, seeing when people are available, unplanned, unforced, social interaction, the ability to ignore people politely when passing them in the corridor—our work-lives are made up of these things. We might view these things as "by-products" of co-location. They are often difficult to support, or even absent in systems given to flexible workers. (p. 176)

The authors posit that systems need to anticipate these types of "casual navigation" by providing users with opportunities to colocate virtually, exchanging both formal and informal messages and collecting and sorting information for problem solving and future use.

And because human–environmental interaction also depends on the visuospatial capabilities of learners, Allen, Otto, and Hoffman (2004) posit that—as human interaction with particular online environments increases—the ideal is for such interactions to become *routine*. Thus, the authors maintain:

In everyday activity, the *routinization* of such effectivity-affordance pathways renders them "transparent" to the individual's conscious awareness.

Factors that influence the transparency and learnability of these pathways include:

(a) Availability of opportunities that users will perceive as relevant to his or her needs, wants, or interests;
(b) Tightness of coupling in real time ("feedback")—basically the immediacy and resolution with which users can perceive the results of his or her own actions;
(c) Invariants or regularities in the relationship between the users' actions and perceptions; and
(d) Opportunities for sustained and repeated engagement. (Allen, Otto, and Hoffman 2004, p. 228)

Routinization and well-conceived designs that *afford* effective, creative, and satisfying interactions are therefore central to the instructional challenge at hand. An affordance, initially defined by Gibson (1966), cannot easily be altered by human needs and, according to Pierskalla and Lee (1998), is "something invariant, objective, real, physical, and psychical. Affordances are offered, provided, or furnished by the environment and made available to the perceiver (either for good or ill)" (p. 71). Barab and Roth (2006) extend Gibson's (1966) notion of perceptual affordances in their elaboration of affordance networks, which "are extended in both time and space and can include sets of perceptual and cognitive affordances that collectively come to form the network for particular goals sets. Affordance networks are not entirely delimited by their material, social, or cultural structure, although one may have elements of all these; instead, they are functionally bound in terms of the facts, concepts, tools, methods, practices, commitments, and even people that can be enlisted toward the satisfaction of a particular goal" (Barab and Roth 2006, p. 4). Tuomi-Gröhn and Engeström (2003b) add that interactions with affordances should be viewed as both cognitive and social:

The affordances that enable our activities are properties of artifacts that have been designed so that those activities can be supported. The functions of these properties as affordances are shaped by social practices. People learn these practices, including the utilities of affordances, mainly by participating in them along with other people. The range of situations that provide affordances for an activity constitutes an important aspect of the socially constructed meanings of the properties of those situations. (p. 25)

As we reviewed at some length in "Designs for Learning," taking a rhetorical design perspective toward the design and evaluation of learning environments has considerable potential. Moreover, these learning environments need not be either natural or simulated, but can represent combinations of the two. As Buchanan (2001) notes:

In approaching design from a rhetorical perspective, our hypothesis should be that all products—digital and analog, tangible and intangible—are vivid arguments about how we should lead our lives. The arguments provide alternatives for the short-term tasks and activities of everyday living, but they also have long-term implications that are subtler and less easily understood. Products embody cultural values and knowledge drawn from many fields of learning, and products express values and knowledge in a complex debate conducted not in words but in nonverbal language. Of course, we are referring to the classic products of design, found in graphic communication and industrial objects. But the hypothesis also applies to the newer, more complex products of the digital medium. The new digital or electronic medium, whose rhetorical forms are now under creation in the leading design schools and in industry, represents a blending of modes of communication, a synthesis of images, words, artifacts, and a blending of actions, environments, and systems of use that are both physical and cultural. (p. 194)

Redfern and Naughton (2002) outline six research directions for collaborative virtual environments (CVEs) that elucidate the challenges facing the designers of immersive environments. CVEs need to be designed to better support work–artifact collaboration, What You See Is What I See (WYSIWIS), chance meetings, peripheral awareness, nonverbal communication, and design for two worlds (pp. 205–206). The majority of the six research areas address ways that CVEs might ideally imitate colocational collaboration. Colleagues working closely together, after all, are able to provide each other with both explicit and nonintrusive feedback in terms of individual

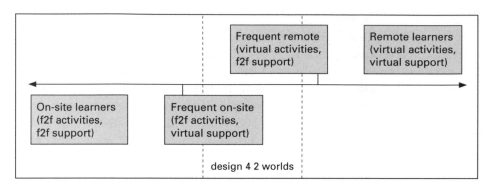

Figure 6.4
Continuum from face-to-face through virtual learning environments (with design for two worlds in center).

and group activities, focuses of attention, task progress, and other peripheral but useful coordination.

Redfern and Naughton's (2002) list is, in some ways, not entirely surprising in its reliance on traditional face-to-face interaction as a source of issues not yet satisfactorily addressed by simulated environments. But the notion of *design for two worlds* is a particularly important design aim. Certainly, prior to simulated reality, experiencing two worlds happened when readers-users worked with hardcopy manuals while committing actions in real time, "toggling" between textual information and physical tasks in real time. Broadening this task from working in a conventional instructional space to inhabiting virtual environments helps us anticipate the opportunities and challenges facing future instructional designers (see figure 6.4).

Increasingly, sophisticated learning environments will demand two-world designs that are flexible, supportive, and aesthetically engaging. Both mobile, distributed artifacts (e.g., laptops, cell phones, intelligent input–output devices, and audio-video recording and production handhelds) and wireless, connected artifacts (e.g., networks, USB devices, Internet-enabled interaction systems) will be required. Some of these technologies will control individual-to-group information dissemination (e.g., interactive whiteboards), and some will encourage self-directed learning (e.g., wizards, intelligent tutoring systems). Moreover, these environments will acknowledge that learning involves many activities and that innovative spaces need to achieve both openness and sectional interaction. Thus, some spaces will need to support presentational activities and others to facilitate social, informal, and collaborative work (Joint Information Systems Committee 2006).

Orel (1995), in his review of vital self-technologies, such as home-based diagnostic instruments, well-being or relaxation devices, and hygiene products, observes that—

just as traditionally hospital-based medical technologies are increasingly being recon-
ceptualized for home and personal use—so too is it inevitable that "self-education" or
"cognitive self-technologies" represent "the future of the knowledge sector" (p. 82).
Educational technologies then will represent a continuum from centralized institutional IT services through distributed computing access through home-based interaction with other home-based learners through mobile and wearable learning technologies.
"Do-it-yourself" will become an instructional goal of progressive educational technology specialists (consider, e.g., the recent popularity of iPods and iPhones for educational module delivery), where "do" will involve Unsworth's (2000) scholarly primitives
and "it" will involve whatever we mean by learning. Assessment of educational progress, however, will likely remain centralized and monolithic, similar to the medical
community's maintenance of health-care accreditation and licensing processes.

The point here is that "toggling" may not accurately capture how technologies spill
over from public spaces to private ones, and the implications for "real-world campuses" is therefore difficult to anticipate. Orel (1995) argues that understanding the
opportunities and constraints of different "localities of use" will become a driving
challenge for designers but, from an instructional perspective, more likely understanding our goals in terms of the *materials* with which learners will work and the *manner*
in which this work is accomplished will provide the ultimate challenge (p. 83). Nardi
and colleagues (Nardi and O'Day 1999; Nardi and Whittaker 2002) thus stress, "A key
question for the design of a media ecology for distributed work is, How much face-
to-face communication is needed?" (Nardi and Whittaker 2002, p. 102). Framing the
problem around the tasks and activities that we hope to accomplish, the range of distances available to us, the amount of time available, and other aspects of our learning
context allows us to transcend our perspective single-machine model of technology
use in instructional settings.

Stevens (2000), in his comparison of a professional architecture company and a
middle school classroom, laments that "the multiple technologies in use in the classroom have highlighted the unique affordances of paper for the collaboration of
student designers and contrasted these to the relative inadequacies of the computer
tools" (p. 395). Olson et al. (2002), as well, in their observations of the behaviors of
six teams in "radically collocated work," note that members were able to move quickly
between tasks and subtasks, to share informal solutions and on-the-job training sessions, and benefited significantly from shared artifacts that were constantly visible,
changeable, tactile, comprehensive, and highly spatial. Resisting the conclusion that
paper is *preferable* to technology in some situations, however, Stevens (2000) instead
describes instruction designed for two worlds:

Another implication of this study is that the issue should not be conceived of in "either–or"
terms (i.e., either computers or traditional learning technologies). As research in computer-
supported cooperative work has shown so vividly over the last decade . . . , settings are nearly

always inhabited by a combination of old and new, digital and analog, standardized and ad hoc. From these combinations, hybrid practices emerge . . . , in which movement across the digital-and-paper divide become fluid and functional. For educational settings, the implied principle therefore is the maintenance of media diversity. (p. 395)

Interestingly, Smith (2001), in a study that compared three treatment groups ("pilots" interacting to solve problems, "consultants" watching and talking with pilots, and "copilots" alternating between pilot and consultant every 40 seconds), found that pilots and copilots performed better on the online posttest than the consultants, indicating that *any* interaction (beyond observation and talk) is superior to no interaction at all. Smith (2001) concludes that interaction in a "game-like" environment enhances learner performance because "The additional sense information, the integrated visual, tactile, propioceptive and motor processes associated with the hand–eye coordination of interactively solving spatial problems, provides a scaffolding for learning mental image-based transformations, such as mental rotation, particular to that *spatial domain* (system of shapes). . . . Hands-on/interactive situations provide additional advantages such as involvement, greater attention and motivation." Although cognitive load theorists might hypothesize that learning and doing could compete with one another, in this case—given that learning and doing are aligned conceptually—learner workload is not adversely affected.

Colella (2000), too, argues, "Much of our imagination about how computers can be used to enable new kinds of learning in the sciences is constrained by the box and the monitor motif of the computer" (p. 472). Acknowledging that "there are human ties to interactions in real space that are lost in cyberlearning" (p. 475), Colella (2000) elaborates on an emerging trend in educational computing called "participatory simulations," where the technological "localities of use" involve groups of learners in real-time role-playing via mobile computing devices. In addition to embedding learners in an engaging simulation that would be difficult to emulate without technological augmentation, Colella (2000) outlines the following design principles for constructing simulations for two worlds:

• *Keep the technology unobtrusive*: This encourages imaginative engagement that enhances belief in the game's major metaphor (pp. 491–492).

• *Add coherent, consistent rules to the experiential world*: This allows learners to manipulate structures and features of the microworld without necessarily detracting from their personal involvement (pp. 492–493).

• *Recreate scientific phenomena in interpersonal space*: This connects learner investment to physical experience by having learners *act* in participation with the simulation (pp. 493–494).

• *Facilitate similar but nonidentical experiences*: This requires that individual learners act in groups to explore and understand the simulation (pp. 494–495).

• *Enable students to devise their own solutions*: This highlights learner representations rather than "correct" solutions, although this feature requires thoughtful facilitation (pp. 495–497).

The same guidelines can be applied to the use of contemporary mobile technologies such as smart cell phones, wearable devices, tablet computers, and PDAs. Gayeski (2007) notes that, in the United States, PDAs and computer laptops currently outnumber traditional desktop computers and that approximately 80 percent of the nine million handheld computers are synchronized with computers located in the workplace (p. 148). These devices place simulations into the palms of our hands and allow us to interact in real time with the environments that surround us. Moreover, these devices distribute our tasks and activities across time and space.

Finally, Brown (2002b), drawing on Brown and Duguid's (2000) social theory of information, describes the need for instructional designs that capitalize on social, informational, and physical spaces:

What makes a great simulation is not the absolute fidelity of the simulation, but how it encourages dialogue, how it leads students to play with it collaboratively, and how it functions as a boundary object for constructing their own understandings of it. Knowledge is information that has been internalized and integrated into our frameworks. To facilitate student learning we need to design spaces that encourage and scaffold conversations that do that. This means considering not only the social and informational spaces, but also the physical space and how all three of these spaces combine to promote the kinds of conversations we are talking about. (p. 54)

6.5.4 Conceptual Artifacts

Bereiter's (2002) provocative book, *Education and Mind in the Knowledge Age*, points us to a third developmental space that has received little attention as a result of our preoccupation with the dichotomy between the internal workings of individuals and the external constructions of the outside world. Bereiter (2002) elaborates extensively on Popper's (1972) definition of *three worlds*—the physical, the mental, and the idea world—arguing that to properly develop theories of instruction and learning suited to the knowledge age we need to acknowledge the growing importance of issues related to the world of ideas (see Popper 1992 for an elaboration of *world 3*). This world, according to Bereiter (2002), consists of "conceptual artifacts" that have their own particular histories, can be described, compared, evaluated, applied in different ways, and that differ according to how much learners understand and use them (p. 65).

Conceptual artifacts have similarities to Miller's (1994b) description of genres in that they have both structural and pragmatic dimensions: "in their *structural* dimension, [they] are conventionalized and highly intricate ways of marshalling rhetorical resources such as narration and figuration. . . . In their *pragmatic* dimension, genres not only help real people in spatiotemporal communities do their work and carry out their purposes; they also help virtual communities, the relationships we carry around in our heads, to reproduce and reconstruct themselves, to continue their stories" (p. 75). Bereiter's (2002) conceptual artifacts and Miller's (1994b) genres are referred to as "focal artifacts" by Roth et al. (1999). Focal artifacts "provide anchors or bridges across varying discourse communities and across different physical, geographical, and social organizations of participants (although the artifacts may have different meanings to the different parties involved)" (Roth et al. 1999, p. 298). They accomplish this by structuring the "interactional physical space" and the "temporal evolution of the activities" (p. 316). For Roth et al. (1999), then, learning can be found "in relationships between people, artifacts, social configurations, and physical arrangements" (p. 337).

Focal or conceptual artifacts, therefore, can be characterized as objects constructed of discourse that not only exhibit unintentional affordances but also that are designed with intentions to do certain things and affective responses to having things done to them. Similarly, for Bereiter (2002), conceptual artifacts "are human constructions like other artifacts, except they are immaterial and, instead of serving purposes such as cutting, lifting, and inscribing, they serve purposes such as explaining and predicting" (p. 58). He defines conceptual as "discussible ideas, ranging from theories, designs, and plans down to concepts, like unemployment and gravity" (p. 64). Artifacts he defines as "human creations" that "are created to some purpose" (pp. 64–65).

The instructional opportunities presented by the ideas-as-artifacts argument is elucidated eloquently by Bereiter (2002) when he describes what it means to understand another person (pp. 102–103) and "Newton's theory" (pp. 109–110). In brief, Bereiter (2002) identifies eleven elements of understanding that we can enumerate here by describing another complex idea, what it means to understand technology:

1. Understanding technology "depends on your relationship to it" (p. 109). Understanding differs depending on whether you are a programmer, a teacher, a document designer, an administrator, an author of how-to technology books, a parent, an instructional designer, an academic researcher studying technology, or a politician.
2. Understanding is critical to acting intelligently in relation to technology. What it means to understand technology depends on who you are and how intelligently you are able to act in relation to technology, managing technical specialists, deciphering research on technology, guiding learners as they become familiar with specific types of technology, or supporting technical activities.
3. Understanding interacts with interest. That is, it is difficult to imagine someone who has no interest in technology being able to claim an understanding of it.

4. Understanding technology requires some understanding of systems theory and logic, the social and cultural forces that shaped and are shaped by technology, and so on.

5. Understanding technology does not mean that one can explain it. Explanation, however, could play an important part in developing and extending its understanding.

6. Just as "no single correct, complete, or ideal understanding" (p. 110) of technology can exist, there can be identifiably incorrect understandings.

7. Conversations about technology generally emphasize the construct or artifact itself, its importance, foundations, strengths and limitations, and so on.

8. Understanding is often conveyed through narratives containing key ideas such as progress, innovation, adoption, social and cultural influences, and so on. Incomplete or incoherent narratives reveal problems with understanding.

9. A *deep* understanding of technology requires knowledge of deeper things related to it such as state-of-the-art developments and historical developments of fundamental machinery and systems.

10. Insightful problem solving is possible with deep understanding.

11. Deep involvement with technology, for various audiences, situations, and contexts, is required for deep understanding.

Bereiter (2002) concludes emphatically that "We should treat the understanding of conceptual artifacts in the same commonsense way we treat understanding of material objects—as inhering in the relationship between the person and the object rather than as a characteristic of a different kind of object located in the person's mind" (p. 111). He does not, however, argue that conceptual artifacts are easily distinguished from some complex material artifacts (such as the design of an automobile from the automobile itself), and adds that establishing exactly what constitutes a conceptual artifact (e.g., Newton's theory) and what does not (e.g., a song) is a formidable intellectual challenge.

As well as representing an intellectual challenge, the practical challenge of designing conceptual artifacts is as significant as the challenge facing the developers of instructional objects. As Fletcher, Tobias, and Wisher (2007) point out, "We do not yet have an adequate number of working examples of instructional objects or instances of their use to enable researchers to weigh outcomes and benefits, identify best practices, and establish workable definitions" (p. 100). However, just as there are numerous theoretical benefits of viewing technology as more than a tool and instruction as more than a treatment, Bereiter (2002) notes that "a broadened conception of tools is useful for thinking about human intelligence" (p. 477). How to approach the best design for the three worlds (i.e., intellectual processes in the mind, external objects in the world, and human-made artifacts connecting the two) thus represents an intriguing area for further exploration.

This line of inquiry encourages us to approach emerging technologies critically, at once appreciating how they allow us to communicate and interact in new ways, while at the same time pushing for artifacts that invite novel educational application. For example, virtual reality environments are useful for allowing real-time collaboration between participants located at great distances, but how can they be used to support learner investigations of alternative spaces, histories, narratives, and graphical realities? Beyond imitating a chalkboard, what do smartboards allow creative instructors to accomplish?

In addition to arguing for a three-world epistemology and conceptual artifacts, this chapter has outlined the potential benefits of viewing everyday instructional situations as comprising five interrelated learning dimensions: learner background and knowledge, learner tasks and activities, social dynamics, instructor activities, and learning environment and artifacts.

The dimensions, exacted from our research on the eight research clusters related to instruction and learning with technology broadly defined, are very much a work in progress. Although we have only begun to elaborate on the composition of each of the dimensions, we have made a useful start. We have established that learner background and knowledge comprise biological attributes, abilities, personal identity, literacies, and sociocultural variables. Learners begin from their various backgrounds to approach learner tasks, activities, and social dynamics that involve processes such as problem representation, information access and evaluation, integration, modification, and extension, and application for different purposes, audiences, and situations (either within learners or between them). Instructor activities and learning environments and artifacts interact to produce, support, and facilitate human understanding, learning, and knowledge making.

In the next chapter, we touch briefly on the implications of the present framework for everyday instructional situations. Most importantly, the framework is helpful for pointing the way to potentially useful methods of evaluating everyday instructional situations. As well, the framework encourages theoreticians to consider multidisciplinary and integrative approaches to instruction and learning with technology. Two particularly interesting avenues for consideration include studies of space and time in our mediated age.

7 Futures for Instruction and Learning with Technology

These diverse literatures we have been discussing—of distance education; computers and the humanities; educational, communication, instructional, and information technologies; the learning sciences; psychology; computer science; design; human–computer interaction; and rhetorical theory—position researchers interested in instruction and learning with technology to contribute in novel and, as yet, only tentatively explored ways. Theoretical and empirical investigations that explore the relationship between design and evaluation, space and time, and instruction and learning with technology are but a few possible areas for future research.

Understanding is to be judged according to its ability to produce further understanding.
—Carl Bereiter (2002, p. 444)

What the student, or at least the student who thinks, knows is that further study is required.
—Bill Readings (1997, p. 30)

It is tempting to conclude this book with a list of research-based instructional design principles. Even better, organizing those design principles around the five dimensions of everyday instructional situations that have been introduced would serve to exemplify one immediate application of a complex and frequently confusing research landscape on instruction and learning with technology. Table 7.1 is one example of how research-based recommendations for practice in online instruction might be generated from a review of a handful of research articles related to instruction and learning with technology.

So how do designers use this list of principles–guidelines in their efforts to design new artifacts? Again, research suggests that they in fact do not (Marshall, Nelson, and Gardiner 1987; Smith and Mosier 1984). Presenting a list of principles or guidelines for practice, however well articulated the design recommendations, has several well-documented shortcomings in terms of how well or poorly those guidelines are applied. First, research on the use of guidelines in the design of complex systems suggests that

Table 7.1

Recommendations for everyday instruction across five dimensions

Support Strategies	References
Learner Background and Knowledge	
• Allows novices to get familiar with complex notions without excessive cognitive load • Supports building of theories, beliefs, conceptual manipulation • Leads to deeper understanding (i.e., surpasses depth without support) • Empowers learners to extend thinking and process higher-order concepts • Supports learning of self-regulation and development of metaknowledge • Refines understanding through experience • Supports development of learner's "need to know more" information	Hannafin and Land (1997, pp. 182–184)
• Enables and encourages learners to explore different perspectives • Provides opportunities for reflection • Allows opportunities for articulation	Herrington, Oliver, and Herrington (2007, pp. 27–28)
• Integrates theoretical knowledge with participants' practical experience • Structures support and guidance for learning in all phases of learning process • Supports conscious reasoning and self-assessment, setting one's own (i. e., not set by the environment) learning goals (What do I know; What should I learn?)	Tynjälä and Häkkinen (2005, pp. 330–331)
Learner Tasks and Activities	
• Uses clear expectations and prompt task structuring • Embeds thinking skills and portfolio assessment as integral part of assignments • Explores recursive assignments that build from personal knowledge • Provides clear expectations and prompt task structuring • Varies forms of writing, reflection, and other pedagogical activities	Bonk and Dennen (2003, p. 335)
• Allows information retrieval from online archives and commercial databases • Supports individual and group presentations • Enables practice and experience using emerging technologies that may be intrinsically useful in today's society	Collins and Berge (1995, pp. 3–4)
• Provides ill-defined activities that have real-world relevance • Presents complex tasks to be completed over extended periods of time	Herrington et al. (2007, p. 27)
• Serves as resource for identification, evaluation, integration of various information • Acts as a medium of collaboration, exchange, and communication of ideas • Behaves as an international platform for expression and contribution of artistic/cognitive understandings and meanings • Works as a medium for participating in simulated experiences, apprenticeships, and cognitive partnerships	Relan and Gillani (1997, p. 43)

Table 7.1

(continued)

Support Strategies	References
Social Dynamics	
• Includes public conferencing, such as discussion lists using Listserv software • Allows interactive chat, used to brainstorm with teachers or peers and to maintain social relationships • Involves personal networking and professional growth and such activities as finding persons with similar interests on scholarly discussion lists • Supports peer review of writing, or projects involving peer learning, groups/peer tutorial sessions, and peer counseling	Collins and Berge (1995, pp. 3–4)
• Encourages collaboration and exchange between different groups of people (e.g., professional groups, people from different domains, experts and novices) • Facilitates real dialogue • Enables construction of new knowledge on the basis of others' contributions, sharing cognitive load • Externalizes group processes and increasing awareness of them • Involves tasks that force groups to collaborate and coordinate knowledge • Supports shared workspaces	Tynjälä and Häkkinen (2005, pp. 330–331)
Instructor Activities	
• Facilitates, does not dictate (i.e., allows choice) • Looks for ways to enhance the learning experience • Varies forms of mentoring and apprenticeship • Uses public and private forms of feedback • Uses student explorations to enhance course content	Bonk and Dennen (2003, p. 335)
• Mentors, advising and guiding students • Involves project-based instruction, either within the classroom or in projects involving community, national, or international problem-solving • Includes guest lecturing, promoting interaction between students and persons in larger community • Provides didactic teaching (i.e., supplying course content, posting assignments, or other information germane to course work) • Supports course management (e.g., advising, delivery of course content, evaluation, collecting and returning assignments) • Facilitates collaboration • Includes computer-based instruction, such as tutorials, simulations, and drills	Collins and Berge (1995, pp. 3–4)
• Engages learners in making sense out of what they know and in complex ideas • Supports metaknowledge about problem solving; addresses complex thinking versus rote memory and disassociation problem • Leads to deeper understandings and personal model building and refinement • Increases meaningful understandings and relationships with phenomena	Hannafin and Land (1997, p. 182)

Table 7.1

(continued)

Support Strategies	References
• Provides access to expert performances and models • Includes apprenticeship and scaffolding approaches to learning • Allows coaching of both instructor to learner and also learner-to-learner	Herrington et al. (2007, p. 27)

Learning Environment and Artifacts

• Diminishes oversimplification problem; supports flexible, decontextualized knowledge that can be applied outside of a particular context • Supports more complex and multifaceted understanding • Addresses complex learning goals issue • Deemphasizes misconceptions and passivity due to disassociated learning • Orients learners to interrelatedness of knowledge; learners use knowledge as tool • Presents abstract notions to be experienced, manipulated, scrutinized • Provides deeper understanding through getting to know phenomena; formulates and develops personal understanding and decisions	Hannafin and Land (1997, pp. 185–186)
• Includes computer mediation (for indexing, storing, searching, disseminating information) • Supports geographic independence ("learning is no longer restricted to the physical buildings of the learning institution, and consequently the problems of overcrowding start to disappear," p. 20) • Enables temporal independence (teachers and learners do not need to synchronize their meeting times and instructors have the ability to control their schedules; "Students no longer must compete with other students for the educator's limited time," p. 21) • Includes platform independence ("nature of the Web almost totally removes this problem" of relying on any particular hardware or software type, p. 21) • Provides a simple, familiar interface • Increases communication ("it is commonly reported that people will talk more electronically (via e-mail or a chat program) than they do in a face-to-face situation," p. 21) • Increases learner control	McCormack and Jones (1998, pp. 20–22)
• Hyperlinks textual material, incorporating pictures, graphics, and animation • Supports videotaped elaboration of subject matter, including interviews, and panel discussions • Hyperlinks multimedia elements such as simulations, graphics, and animations • Supports just-in-time access to range of electronic databases, search engines, and online libraries • Allows just-in-time access to coaching and assistance via telementors, e-communities, and peers	Naidu (2003, p. 353)

Table 7.1

(continued)

Support Strategies	References
• Integrates different forms of representation and different forms of learning activities (reading, writing, discussing, using metaphors, audio, visual, etc.) • Integrates e-learning with face-to-face learning situations whenever possible • Emphasizes links between authentic work activities, e-learning material, and virtual discussion	Tynjälä and Häkkinen (2005, pp. 330–331)

it is very difficult for designers to actually apply them (see, e.g., Chevalier and Ivory 2003; Mehlenbacher 1992; Schriver 1989a,b). Either the guidelines tend to be too general for a particular design situation or they tend to be too specific to apply to new design situations. As Henninger, Haynes, and Reith (1995) assert, guidelines "tend to be stated either at a high level of abstraction, making them vague and difficult to interpret in terms of a specific design context . . ., or at the level of interface widgets, making it difficult to design interaction strategies for different kinds of users" (p. 43). Design situations are, after all, inherently fast-paced, intuitive, and highly contingent upon evolving design constraints and opportunities. Sometimes guidelines are simply ideals that invite little disagreement except when the uncomfortable realities of resources and time are factored in—as with most "just-in-time" online support and assistance systems (Naidu 2003). Ultimately, relying on guidelines for instruction and learning with technology requires a leap of faith from describing what the research suggests that we have learned over the last thirty years to general principles for practice that are not necessarily supported by the context or experimental design specifics of the research or instructional situation.

Therefore, the application of general heuristics or open-ended questions that encourage certain design *perspectives* is more likely to encourage the flexible, creative, and particularized design and evaluation of online learning environments. Heuristics are not guidelines, and they are not principles; heuristics are general, context-sensitive issues that designers consider when making design decisions. Kirsh (2005) begins to get at the power of general perspectives toward the design of online learning environments when he argues that well-designed learning environments display "cognitive efficiency" (i.e., are "faster without more errors") and "cognitive effectiveness" (i.e., suggest "the idea of normal conditions") (pp. 162–163). And Baecker et al. (2000) challenge designers and evaluators to test their developing systems "in real use by real users in real work contexts over extended time frames" (p. 22).

Thus, as difficult as it is to resist Aristotle's argument that the objective of every "speech" is summary aimed at achieving happiness as a universal notion, researchers studying the complex interaction between instruction, learning, and technology must acknowledge that the future is a domain that is ultimately unknown. To conclude with table 7.1 would be to treat this book as a very long "speech," in effect to cut the conversation very short by providing a common ("applied") ending that satisfies most but that discontinues the many exciting conversations yet to be experienced.

But one of the major goals of this book has been, instead, to beckon researchers interested in instruction and learning with technology to begin considering the numerous and growing literatures that offer insights into our collective object of inquiry. Another aim has been to keep the speech from falling into inaccessible jargon or optimistic reductionism; and, where numerous digressions mark the presentation, the goal has been to simply enliven the discourse about instruction and learning with technology. Unfortunately, as Lewis, Amini, and Lannon (2000) correctly assert, "Subjectivity, by its nature, is nontransferable" (p. 41); so the most encouraging response this "speech" might achieve is to heighten or intensify our interest in the subject matter, in its multidisciplinary history, complicated present, and rapidly evolving futures.

With that aim in mind, we have covered an enormous amount of ground in this speech. We have outlined how contemporary connectivity has distributed traditional understandings of space and time and conflated the once separate domains of work, leisure, and learning. This discussion clarifies our growing sense that we are on an accelerated path toward technological solutions to the (technological) problems we ourselves have often created. Moreover, the hastened sensibility produced by artifacts and environments of our own making discourages us from stepping back and reflecting on our goals, plans, and progress using knowledge that we have already gained from our technological adventures of the not-too-distant past. But stepping back, assessing the numerous existing and potential research landscapes that can fruitfully contribute to our understanding, and reflecting carefully on our current and future goals for instruction and learning with technology is precisely what we need to do.

We have also highlighted the centrality of instruction and learning with technology to contemporary research production in the academy and, more importantly, have shown how perspectives drawn from numerous research literatures—with special emphasis on rhetorical theory and design studies—can be instrumental to the development of theory and practice on instruction and learning with technology. Teaching in higher education is a surprisingly undervalued art and craft but we need to hold, with Bahri and Petraglia (2003), that "Accepting a rhetorical pedigree requires that we not shy away from the importance of teaching and instead insist . . . that education merits our complete intellectual engagement" (p. 2). Moreover, we can now assume that understanding technology has become an irrefutable reality for contemporary educational researchers, and not a mere skill set for practitioners, gadgeteers, and technical specialists. Technological knowledge is integral to everyday life. As Verbeek (2005) concludes, "The design of technology thereby becomes no longer an internal technological affair, but appears to be a moral matter as well. Technologies are not merely functional objects that also have dimensions of style and meaning; they mediate the relations between human beings and the world, and thereby shape human experiences and existence" (pp. 235–236).

In an effort to (artificially) suspend the rapid acceleration of technological change encouraging a proliferation of academic journal publishing that promises to confuse as much as it helps, we have seen how characterizing the research literatures around eight broadly defined research clusters can help us purvey some order on an otherwise unruly range of journals and research emphases. This process is as exciting as it is destabilizing, given the inevitable datedness that becomes a routine feature of explicitly naming journals and related educational technologies. But this review is also instrumental in developing an appreciation of major challenges facing researchers interested in instruction and learning with technology. Indeed, a broadly conceived review of the research related to instruction and learning with technology supports the need for considerable additional analyses.

Part of our investigation has been to elaborate on a rhetorical design perspective that encourages a view of research, instruction, and learning as complex design activities. That elaboration, in turn, led to a summary of existing models of instruction and learning with technology that fed directly into the development of a conceptual framework for everyday instructional situations. The five dimensions of everyday instructional situations can serve as touchstones for researchers interested in a complex subject matter that spans numerous traditional and emerging disciplines. Moreover, it allows us to elevate the research conversation above well-traveled dialogues such as learning styles and student satisfaction, the benefits of interaction, media and "tool" introductions and instructions for use, distance education program popularity, enrollment and attrition details, and the question of which comes first, good teaching or expensive technology. For the record, those who support instruction in higher education rarely argue that purchasing more sophisticated technology will improve faculty teaching, although occasionally one hears promises that technology enhances student learning or supports "excellence" in teaching.

Another way to conceptualize the *problem* of instruction and learning with technology is to take a metalevel approach to the prolific generation of research on the subject. But in order to do this, productive researchers must step back from the landslide of nuanced studies they are adding to the pile and adopt the role of students new to the "discipline" of instruction and learning with technology. This requires time and reflection. As Sandoval and Millwood (2005) argue, referring to middle-school science students, "Engaging students in inquiry, even as it challenges their ideas about the nature of scientific phenomena, does not seem sufficient to challenge their ideas about the nature of inquiry itself. Doing that seems to depend on orchestrating and supporting a sustained epistemic discourse" (p. 52). This conclusion is at the crux of the challenge presented by any systematic attempt to evaluate or assess the methods that we use to produce the data that we analyze so that we might argue for or against certain positions. It may be that, rather than assuming that having our learners engage in the processes of data collection and analysis that represent our instructional perspective, our attention instead needs to be on the very processes of inquiry themselves. Such a perspective surely demands a multi- or interdisciplinary *distantia* (i.e., standing apart).

A recent long-term research program being carried out at Harvard University offers some hints at how we might begin conceiving of a wide-ranging research program on instruction and learning with technology. Within the broader framework of a three-year Harvard-based interdisciplinary study, Nikitina (2005) summarizes interviews with 30 faculty and 28 students involved in interdisciplinary programs at four U.S. universities. Their data suggest that three "cognitive moves" are frequently required whenever researchers and instructors engage in interdisciplinary work over time:

• overcoming monodisciplinarity (i.e., appreciation of alternative disciplinary views, identification of strengths and weaknesses in disciplinary perspectives, and acceptance or rejection of different disciplinary inputs),
• provisional integration (i.e., emergence of hybrid understanding and complex disciplinarity), and
• revising integration (i.e., questioning and critical probing of integration and rejection of the provisional integration as final and complete) (p. 413).

Understanding interdisciplinarity requires an understanding of what we mean by a discipline, which Nikitina (2005) suggests has three interrelated meanings: "(a) *discipline as culture*, referring to an academic or department affiliation or to a collaboration of people within the institutional structure; (b) *discipline as epistemology*, referring to the shared methodological tools and ways of knowing; and (c) *discipline as language*, referring to communication that uses a similar language or symbol system" (p. 393). Each meaning, in turn, draws on numerous sources of theory and terminology that guide subsequent thinking and work in each particular research and instructional context. And this investigation, in turn, brings us back to the multidisciplinary research conversations that we began mapping early in this project.

As such, integrative multidisciplinarity, or interdisciplinarity, holds promise for current and future researchers interested in instruction and learning with technology. Our framework for everyday instructional situations, consisting as it does of five dimensions of learning, can then be applied to our working understandings of the literatures on instruction and learning with technology. For instance, table 7.2 presents a matrix for organizing future research studies on the relationship between instruction, learning, and technology.

Table 7.2
Research initiatives organized around the five dimensions of everyday instructional situations

Research Matrix for the Five Dimensions of Everyday Instructional Situations

	Learner Background and Knowledge	Learner Tasks and Activities	Social Dynamics	Instructor Activities	Learning Environment and Artifacts
Learner Background and Knowledge		• Demographics and scholarly primitives • Learning styles and problem solving	• How different learners interact • Personality attributes and classroom conflict	• Perceptions of instructors • Understanding teaching styles	• Accessibility issues and usability • Designing for engagement
Learner Tasks and Activities	• Designing tasks for particular learners • Cognitive workload and authenticity		• Interfaces for collaborative work • Discourse moves in discussion lists	• Managing different tasks • Instructor comments and learner revision	• Tools for representing and analyzing texts • Applications for extending creativity
Social Dynamics	• Interaction between different learners • Linguistic variables and interaction	• Alternative group interaction and different task types • Cross cultural collaboration in class		• Instructor perceptions of asynchronous discussions • Interaction strategies and professional development	• Resources for augmenting learner collaboration • Peer review applications
Instructor Activities	• Diversity and inclusive instruction • Cognitive engagement online	• Simple versus complex problem use • Textual versus graphical lessons	• Group sizes and management • Managing group conflict		• Managing presence and authority • Building learning objects
Learning Environment and Artifacts	• Methods for audience analysis • Learner perceptions of multimedia lessons	• Applications for assignment submission and evaluation • Teaching critical thinking	• Software for measuring group productivity • Shared documents and group work	• Usable assignment structures • Program quality in WBI	

Reviewing the existing landscape for research on instruction and learning with technology, then, can be achieved in reverse. Research on how particular learner demographics such as age influence complex problem-solving activities in engineering would contribute to our understanding of how learner background and knowledge interact with learner tasks and activities. Tables A through H in the appendix show how we might begin to interpret emerging research at the level of individual peer-reviewed articles. Eight journals, one from each of the eight research clusters presented in table 3.1, have been informally tagged according to individual article emphases on one or more of the five learning dimensions presented in table 6.2.

Ultimately, researchers might construct interactive, visual artifacts that allow other research producers and consumers to access complex representations of the current "state" of research on instruction and learning with technology. Four possible "views" might include, from left to right, slide-rule views of research emphases across time, sizing views according to volume related to particular dimensions, connected document views that highlight relationships between topics, or content libraries with associated tags produced by different audiences for different purposes (see figure 7.1).

7.1 Design and Evaluation

Just as the relationship between research and practice in educational technology has been an uneasy one, so too has the historical relationship between educational technology and assessment or evaluation. As Marshall (1999) points out, "Our neglect of assessment may be due to the incremental and ad hoc way technology educators have approached curriculum building for technology and our unwillingness to address issues such as what learning theory tells us about ways technology is being used versus the way technology could be used" (p. 315). We conceptualize, build, and respond to our designs long before we are able to evaluate and refine them, at least when we apply traditional ISD (instructional systems design), Waterfall methods of engineering design, SCORM (sharable content object reference model), or ADDIE (analysis, design, development, implement, and evaluate) approaches to design (Shearer 2003). Thus, Curzon's (2003) description of the timeline for an effective instructional design project includes ten phases: project definition, research, requirements, setup, development and ongoing testing, final testing, production, publicity, review, and enhancement (pp. 15–19), where by "testing" he means debugging rather than evaluation.

In contrast, Bonk, Wisher, and Champagne (2007) list eight issues that evaluators of online courses need to consider when designing their evaluation: what measures will be collected in terms of learners; the instructor; the training required for the course; the tasks, activities, or pedagogical composition of the course; the technology tools employed; the course coherence and interactivity; the program, certificate, or

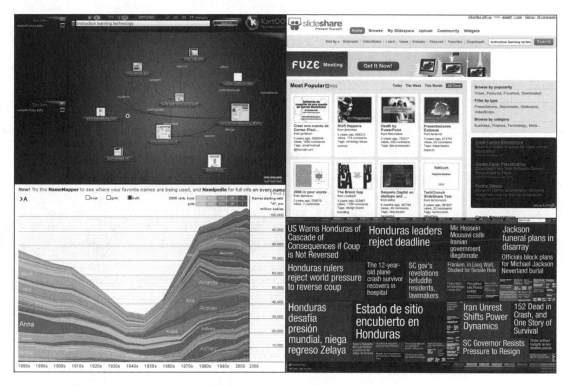

Figure 7.1
Potential visual representations of research clusters, journals and journal articles, and everyday instructional situations and learning dimensions. *Source*: From left to right, visual representations adapted from http://www.babynamewizard.com/voyager, http://marumushi.com/apps/newsmap/newsmap.cfm, http://www.kartoo.com/, and http://www.slideshare.net/.

degree objectives; and institutional or organizational factors (pp. 265–268). Each of these issues comes with a range of potential questions and approaches to data collection depending on the goals and the extensiveness of the evaluation effort.

Herron and Wright (2006) distinguish between assessment and evaluation, arguing that assessment focuses on student learning and evaluation focuses on programmatic issues. Assessment, then, measures learner readiness, formative progress, and summative learning outcomes. Broadfoot and Black (2004) view our contemporary emphasis on assessment and evaluation as part of the same orientation, describing how "the assessment revolution" permeates our institutions and policies:

We have become an "assessment society," as wedded to our belief in the power of numbers, grades, targets and league tables to deliver quality and accountability, equality and defensibility as we are to modernism itself. History will readily dub the 1990s . . .—as well as the early years of the new millennium—"the assessment era," when belief in the power of assessment to provide a rational, efficient and publicly acceptable mechanism of judgment and control reached its high point. It is probably no accident that this development came at a time when capitalism itself became transformed into a global system and the other trappings of globalization—instant international communication and the knowledge economy—also developed in previously almost unimaginable ways, a decade during which e-mail and the World Wide Web for example, have transformed all our lives. (p. 19)

Herron and Wright (2006) agree, noting that

At no other time in the history of higher education have there been so many inquiries into accountability for student learning, progress, and degree program viability. Funding for higher education has, in some states, been sharply reduced and any funding increase in the future may be linked to accountability. This climate of precise accountability for student learning creates severe constraints when a new learning format, such as online learning, is so rapidly growing in the number of students enrolled and the number of courses offered. (p. 47)

Again, we are wise to remind ourselves periodically that the history of technology is a history filled with both hyperpromise and underestimation. Even in the last three decades, technological developments have outstripped what we have learned about their influence on instruction and learning from the research (Roberts 2006), but the marketing promises that keep us close to the information technology trough are an economic force in and of themselves. Zane and Frazier (1992) contacted 15 educational software companies and found, uniformly, that "they did not perform any type of empirical evaluation of their software products as part of the development process" (p. 415). The authors conclude, "the warnings and suggestions made over the past decade [the 1980s] concerning the poor quality of educational software and the necessity for documenting learner improvement as a function of the software have to a large extent been ignored" (p. 415).

Notably, the framework proposed here for everyday instructional situations does not include an extensive discussion of the implications of summative evaluation or traditional assessment practices. Our focus has not been on traditional assessment practices that relate to instruction and learning with technology, for three reasons. First, the relationship between technology and learning (and human behavior in general) has tended to be reduced to pre- and posttests that ignore the interdependent relationship between human and technological spheres, and, therefore, studying controllable changes between learning *before* technology is introduced and learning *after* is problematic. Introducing technology into learning *changes* the context within which learning occurs; therefore, controlling for learning is effectively impossible. Second, traditional assessment efforts involve defining explicitly the objectives for instruction and whether or not those objectives were met, and this is an aspect of formal learning that tends to deemphasize the integral role that technology currently plays in the instruction and learning process. In terms of online instruction, Hannafin et al. (2003) thus argue that "Assessment practices have largely been mapped over from traditional teaching-learning approaches, but may not provide either suitable evidence of student learning or may simply emphasize those aspects of learning that are easy to assess" (p. 256). Third, although thoughtfully designed and implemented formative evaluations deserve center stage in the development of instruction and learning with technology, these are long-term and large-scale endeavors that need to involve information technology and distance education specialists, faculty and program administrators, planning and analysis experts, instructional designers, and educational researchers.

Collaborations have begun, however, with colleagues in the business of assessment, to develop extensions of the framework for everyday instructional situations that integrate assessment goals and methods into the study of instruction and learning with technology (Raubenheimer et al. 2007). Assessment efforts by other researchers that stress the interactions between instructors and learners in different disciplines and the learner's role in learning—elements of instructional situations that map closely onto the five dimensions of everyday instructional situations but notably exclude learning environments and artifacts—are also underway and show potential applicability to a wide range of educational contexts (Black and William 2006).

Currently, however, the learning that occurs around, outside, and without the direct approval of institutional instructors and outside the reach of "traditional teaching-learning approaches" seems most interesting. Numerous studies, for example, capture learner satisfaction without capturing explicit or, for that matter, implicit learning. As well, we have seen that an engaged viewer may not necessarily translate into a learning viewer. And finally, an emphasis on formative assessment runs the risk of interfering with what some consider the four most enthralling aspects of being an instructor: (1) attempting through trial and error to discover how much or little the prior knowledge and backgrounds of learners are interacting with the content being communicated, (2) creating learning experiences that are highly participatory, immersive, and that elicit moods that enhance learners' memories of the situation (cf. Branaghan 2001), (3) finding creative ways to integrate one's content with existing and emerging media, and (4) learning through trial and error what works and does not work for learners when they attempt to apply new information to complex problem situations.

In an attempt to offer at least the beginnings of a pragmatic program of research that is useful to designers interested in assessment and evaluation, table 7.3 draws on the considerable research devoted to the usability of performance systems and to WBI design (Bevan 1998; Mehlenbacher 2002, 2003; Nielsen 1994, 1997; Zaharias 2004a). From this considerable research base, we can begin to outline a set of heuristics for the designers and evaluators of online learning environments. The design heuristics

Table 7.3

Task-oriented usability heuristics for WBI design and evaluation[a]

Usability Heuristics for WBI Design and Evaluation	
Learner Background and Knowledge	
Accessibility[b]	Has the WBI been viewed on different platforms, browsers, at different connection speeds? Is the site ADA compliant (e.g., red and yellow colors are problematic for visually-challenged learners)? Have ISO-9000 standards been considered?
Customizability and maintainability	Does printing of the screen(s) require special configuration to optimize presentation and, if so, is this indicated on the site? Are individual preferences/sections clearly distinguishable from one another? Is manipulation of the presentation possible and easy to achieve?
Error support and feedback[c]	Is a design solution possible that prevents a problem from occurring in the first place? When learners select something is it differentiated from unselected items? Do menu instructions, prompts, and error messages appear in the same place on each screen? Is feedback of the appropriate type (textual, graphical, auditory) for the information being displayed? Do error messages plainly describe what action or assistance is available?
Navigability and user movement[d]	Does the site clearly separate navigation from content? How many levels down can learners traverse and, if more than three, is it clear that returning to their initial state is possible with a single selection? Can learners see where they are in the overall site structure at all times? Do the locations of navigational elements and general layout of text and graphics remain consistent? Is the need to scroll minimized across screens and frames within screens?
User control, error tolerance, and flexibility[e]	Are learners allowed to undo or redo previous actions? Can learners cancel an operation in progress without receiving an error message? Are multiple windows employed that can be manipulated easily? Do the instructional materials support the learner's workflow, allowing shortcuts if desired? Can learners annotate the instructional content themselves?

Table 7.3

(continued)

Usability Heuristics for WBI Design and Evaluation

Aesthetic appeal[f]	Is the screen design logical and minimalist (uncluttered, readable, memorable)?
	Are graphics or colors employed aesthetically and functionally, accompanied and identified in text, meaningfully labeled, and reducing unnecessary information where possible?
	Are distractions minimized (e.g., movement, blinking, animation, etc.)?
	Is the information design pleasant, engaging, attractive, fun, stimulating, or emotionally satisfying?
Consistency and layout[g]	Does every screen display begin with a title/subject heading that describes contents?
	Is there a consistent icon design and graphic display across screens?
	Do words and terms describe the same items throughout the site?
	Is layout, font choice, terminology use, color, and positioning of items the same throughout the site (<4 of any of these are usually recommended)?
Typographic cues and structuring[h]	Does text employ meaningful discourse cues, modularity, chunking?
	Is information structured by meaningful labeling, bulleted lists, or iconic markers?
	Are legible fonts and colors employed?
	Is the principle of left-to-right placement linked to most-important to least-important information?
Visibility of features and self-description	Are objects, actions, and options visible?
	Do learners have to remember information from one part of a dialogue to another?
	Are prompts, cues, and messages placed where learners will be looking on the screen?
	Do text areas have "breathing space" (i.e., white space) around them?
	Is white space used to create symmetry and to lead the eye in the appropriate direction?

Social Dynamics

Communication protocols	Are instructions provided for engaging with other learners online?
	Are instructions and resources related to collaboration, teamwork, and group processes provided?
	Have methods and guidelines for copyright, fair use, and the management of group rights been made available?
	Are documents, resources, and task instructions shared across learners?
Mutual goals and outcomes[i]	Are learners rewarded for communicating?
	Are communication applications provided that allow synchronous and asynchronous interaction?
	Do communication applications allow information revision, organization, and management?
	Are interactions organized around instructional objectives and task deliverables?

Table 7.3

(continued)

Usability Heuristics for WBI Design and Evaluation

Shared resources[j]	Does the environment support group presentation, analysis, problem solving, and artifact construction? Can learners control whether information and communication is private at the individual and group level? Are various media able to be exchanged with ease by learners? Can learners manipulate planning and scheduling resources individually and in groups?

Instructor Activities

Authority and authenticity[k]	Does the site establish a serious tone or presence? Is simple language used and jargon appropriate for the intended audience? Are learners reminded of the security and privacy of the site? Are humor or anthropomorphic expressions used minimally? Is direction given for further assistance if necessary?
Concurrency[l]	Are feedback and assessment made available for learner viewing? Are site features and materials germane, timely, and designed around learner needs and expectations? Is instructor-learner feedback thought provoking (e.g., encouraging elaboration, clarification, questioning)?
Intimacy and presence	Is an overall tone established that is present, active, timely, respectful, and engaging? Does the discourse model solidarity, acceptance, warmth, and trustworthiness? Does the site act as a learning environment for learners, not simply as a warehouse of unrelated links?

Environment and Artifacts

Completeness	Are levels clear and explicit about the "end" or parameters of the site (thus avoiding unnecessary learning)? Are there different "levels" of use and, if so, are they clearly distinguishable? Are the beginnings and endings of tasks easy to identify?
Examples and case studies	Are examples, demonstrations, or case studies of learner experiences available to facilitate learning? Are examples divided into meaningful sections (e.g., overview, demonstration, explanation, etc.)?
Help and support documentation[m]	Does the site support task-oriented help, tutorials, and reference materials? Is help easy to locate and access on the site? Is the help table of contents or menu organized functionally, according to learner tasks?

Table 7.3

(continued)

Usability Heuristics for WBI Design and Evaluation

Metaphors and maps[n]	Does the site use an easily recognizable metaphor that helps learners identify applications in relation to each other, their state in the system, and options available to them?
	Does the site provide a spatial layout and temporal organization that is meaningful for and among learners?
	Do graphics, videos, animations, and sounds contribute to the purpose and message of the site?
Organization and information relevance	Is a site map available?
	Is the overall organization of the site clear from the majority of screens?
	Are primary options emphasized in favor of secondary ones?
Readability and quality of writing	Is the text in active voice and concisely written (> 4 < 15 words/sentence)?
	Are terms consistently plural, verb+object or noun+verb, avoiding unnecessarily redundant words?
	Do field labels reside on the right of the fields they are closely related to?
	Does white space highlight a modular text design that separates information chunks from each other?
	Are bold and color texts used sparingly to identify important text (limiting use of all capitals and italics to improve readability)?
	Can learners easily understand the content of the information presented?
Relationship with real-world tasks	Is terminology and labeling meaningful, concrete, and familiar to the target audience?
	Do related and interdependent functions and materials appear on the same screen?
	Is sequencing used naturally when common events or narratives are expected?
	Does the site allow learners to easily complete their transactions or selections?
Reliability and functionality	Are all functions labeled clearly?
	Do all the menus, icons, links, and opening windows work predictably across platforms?
	Have important interactive features and multimedia elements been tested across platforms and browsers?

---

[a]Stewart, Hong, and Strudler (2004) have produced a useful instrument for evaluating the quality of online instruction based on learner assessments and that bears some similarity to the organization of table 7.3 (see pp. 146–150, or http://www.scsv.nevada.edu/~stewarti/mathweb/quest/intro.htm for an online version of the instrument). Basing their instrument on previous student evaluation research and the distance learning literature, Stewart et al. (2004) define quality in Web-based instruction across seven factors: (1) Instructor and peer interaction (questions 38–41, 44–51): Thoughtfulness of interactions, clarity, informality, encouragement, timeliness; (2) Technical issues (16a–d, 17a–d): speedy download and quality of graphics, audio, video;

Table 7.3

(continued)

(3) Appearance of Web pages (2–4, 7, 8): font versus content, overuse of bold, color, cluttering, animation, missing graphics/links; (4) Hyperlinks and navigation (9, 11, 13–15): information easy to find, meaningful hyperlinks, useful structure, layout; (5) Content delivery (30–32, 34–37): appropriate media use, examples, resources, assessment tools, instructional methods (e.g., case studies, discussions, etc.); (6) Online applications (20, 21a–c, 42): ease of use of audio, video, chatrooms, e-mail, simulations, and; (7) Class procedures and expectations (22, 23, 25–29): availability of help, introduction to technology, task-orientedness, clarity of grading, course expectations.

[b]Designers unfamiliar with the myriad of issues related to Web accessibility should begin by reviewing the W3C's (2006) Web accessibility guidelines, version two (http://www.w3.org/TR/WCAG20/). As well, the Trace Research and Development Center at the University of Wisconsin-Madison offers a warehouse of resources on accessibility and usability (http://trace.wisc.edu/).

[c]Stemler (1997) describes feedback in terms of the feedback that learners receive from instructors (e.g., "encouraging feedback") rather than as a feature of the interface (p. 343). Feedback where possible should be supported at the interface level so that instructors can focus on instructional activities, content, and social dynamics. Keeton's (2004) extension of Chickering and Gamson's (1987) instructional principles for online learning environments defines constructive instructional feedback as continuous, prompt, detailed, corrective, and learner-centered (p. 97). De Souza (2005) adds a type of interface "feedback" that will become increasingly important as instructors imagine courses that encourage design behaviors and outcomes of their learners, entitled "resignification," that is, interface feedback that encourages "a repurposing of the available signs" and the application of "many different things" when working in online environments (p. 112).

[d]Rouet and Potelle (2005) provide an excellent overview of principles for navigation in multimedia environments, for example, that explicit links are preferable to embedded ones, that shallow versus deep menu structures reduce user errors and search time, and that concept maps and other visual representations of the overall system augment user understanding.

[e]Burns and Hajdukiewicz (2004) offer an overlapping breakdown of criteria for usability that includes visual clarity, consistency, compatibility, informative feedback, explicitness, appropriate functionality, flexibility and control, error prevention and correction, user guidance and support, and system usability problems (pp. 208–286).

[f]Tractinsky, Katz, and Ikar (2000), in their study of Automatic Teller Machine (ATM) aesthetics and usability, note that "interface aesthetics has a major effect on a priori perceptions of ease of use, and perhaps more importantly on post facto evaluations of usability" (p. 140). For this reason the authors warn against "the unequivocal message expressed by the HCI literature" stating that function is more important than form. Agarwal and Venkatesh (2002) too stress the importance of evoking "emotional responses among users" and cite similar research on designing for "flow," "cognitive absorption," and "cognitive engagement" (p. 182). Of course the dichotomy between form and function is a problematic one in the first place, as stated elsewhere, and so aesthetic issues are included as a category for evaluating usability to emphasize the importance of aesthetics on perceptions of functionality and to see how much or little high aesthetic evaluations correlate with high perceptions of system usability. As Zaccai (1995) asserts, aesthetics "is totally

Table 7.3

(continued)

related to our ability to see a congruence among our intellectual expectations of an object's functional characteristics, our emotional need to feel that ethical and social values are met, and finally, our physical need for sensory stimulation" (p. 9). Indeed, along with an emerging focus on aesthetics, notions of pleasure, identity, comfort, stimulation, and "fun" have begun to find representation in the research literature (e.g., Blythe et al. 2003; Green and Jordan 2002; Schrepp, Held, and Laugwitz 2006). Importantly, animation can be highly functional: Betrancourt (2005) provides a thorough review of task-oriented animation use in instruction, although researchers still recommend minimizing the use of animated graphics (Ivory and Megraw 2005).

[g]George (2005), from talk-aloud protocols of nine users of a complex library Web site, found that top-to-bottom/left-to-right navigation strategies, color use, font size and labeling, information chunking, and global headings were all considered design priorities for the users (p. 178).

[h]Wang and Gearhart (2006) provide an excellent overview of text layout and legibility issues related to WBI specifically, noting that even text line length and line spacing contribute to the readability of online information (pp. 142–147); Schriver (1997) recommends that different font types, sizes, formats, and colors be used minimally and that sans serif is preferable to serif typefaces.

[i]Niesten and Sussex (2006) have described the role of lucidity and playfulness in Internet chat environments that has interesting potential for instructors interested in supporting productive online interactions and collaborative resource sharing. Extending traditional notions of learner assessment even further, Chickering and Mentkowski (2006) have described how building "valuing" into learner discourse can strengthen less tangible dimensions of interaction, that is, asking how one's values influence decision making, analyzing the role of groups, cultures, and societies in the value-generation process, and understanding how one's discipline stresses certain values and deemphasizes others (p. 227).

[j]Adler, Nash, and Noël (2006) summarize 12 issues for the designers of collaborative editing software that include time and space, awareness, communication, private and shared work spaces, intellectual property, simultaneity and locking, protection, workflow, security, file format, platform independence, and user benefit. Each of these issues needs to be addressed in the collaborative editing space that is part of the overall online learning environment.

[k]Not surprisingly, the general design of your course Web site can instill confidence in an audience's perception of your authority as an instructor. Hertzum et al. (2002) provide an interesting review of the literatures on authority, credibility, and trust issues related to online information. The Stanford Persuasive Technology Lab (2006) provides a useful list of Web site credibility guidelines with links to relevant and supporting research: http://credibility.stanford.edu/guidelines/. Finally, Witmer, Jerome, and Singer (2005) have constructed a questionnaire that assesses the "presence" established by simulated environments, hinting at the ultimate blurring of online instructors and virtual spaces.

[l]Roberts et al. (2005) have generated a 20-item survey instrument for evaluating university-wide distance education courses based on the Southern Association of Colleges and Schools Commission on Colleges' (2003) accrediting guidelines. Notably, instructor timeliness and other activities that encourage critical thinking factor largely in the instrument (pp. 61–62).

Table 7.3
(continued)

[m]Gräsel, Fischer, and Mandi (2000), in their empirical study of the influence of additional support influence on learner representations, found that "Additional information could only be used adequately by the students when it was presented in a contextualized manner *and* when students were supported by strategy instruction on how to use the information" (p. 302). Even when online learning environments provide useful instructional and reference materials, designers need to carefully consider providing secondary materials that support metacognitive activities among their learners.

[n]Shen, Woolley, and Prior (2006), describing a pilot project for a small group of Chinese users where they replaced the common "desktop" metaphor with a "garden" metaphor, show how culturally rooted metaphors have significant implications for international audiences (cf. Hsu 2006 for metaphor use related specifically to learning).

are organized according the five dimensions of everyday instructional situations, with learner tasks and activities incorporating interaction display issues.

These heuristics are only that: heuristics, created to generate intelligent questions and to encourage thoughtful discussion of the numerous dimensions involved in everyday instructional situations, online or off. When designers or evaluators of online instruction review these heuristics they are generally excited by their relationship with emerging research on instruction and learning with technology, their applicability to a range of technological environments and instructional materials, and their emphasis on learners and their tasks. But there are many other directions our extended consideration of instruction and learning with technology might just as fruitfully pursue.

As we have seen, developing a transformational perspective toward instruction and learning with technology necessarily complicates how we approach the subject, and this complication is a very good thing. Reductivist interpretations of the relationship between instruction, learning, and technology have enjoyed enough airtime. Many areas for future inquiry have only been tangentially explored, emphases as theoretically rich and compelling as the networked learning worlds that are rapidly being constructed around us. The question, then, becomes much more irresistible than how can we use technology to improve our teaching. Our complex object of inquiry, instruction and learning with technology, invites us to begin considering constructs as fundamental as *space* and *time* and to explore how they interact with the complex phenomena we are aiming to characterize and understand.

7.2 Space and Time

When advertisements on television claim that a new technology will "transport you to another dimension," they are not claiming that, while using their technology, we will be whisked away from our positions directly in front of the hardware that was designed to give us the simulated "real-world" experience. Neither were the technicians who designed the original flight simulators promising that actual flight would be achieved using their machines. But the promise of transportation from the here and now to wherever and whenever is neither novel nor entirely fanciful. As King and Frost (2002) suggest:

The ability to operate effectively across space, time, and divergent sociocultural contexts is one of the great triumphs of humans. This ability did not spring forth like Athena from the brow of Zeus, however. It was painstakingly created over centuries by the invention and deployment of technologies for selective disambiguation and ambiguation of critical issues, tasks, beliefs, values, and so on. (p. 20)

That our technologies reveal our priorities, visions, and ideals is also not astonishing. As we have seen, our relationship with technology is less a deployment than it is a feedback loop, where the technologies that we invent, in turn, invent us. Technologies created to support and augment instruction and learning, as well, reveal our assumptions about what constitutes effective instruction and optimal learning as much as they reveal our technological potentials. Thus, early technical efforts in distance education in Australia, according to Stacey (2005), developed out of pioneering sociocultural experiments with *invisible classes* and *external studies* programs (p. 254). As long as technological mediation is separated from our analyses of instruction and learning, we will continue to be susceptible to grim prognostications about higher education or idealistic prophesying about technologized workplaces, accelerated learning processes, and unfettered leisure spaces.

Our desire to control space interacts with our desire to manage time. Burgelman (2000) writes, "Apart from the search for means of survival like food and procreation, man has also been looking for ways to increase the speed of his actions by imitating what is happening elsewhere (conquering time) or by looking for what can be found over there (conquering space)." Viewed this way, travel by foot, vehicle, dialogue, print, telephone, telegraph, Internet, and so on are "nothing more than an application of the principles of mobility, interaction, and interactivity" (ibid.), decentering knowledge with communication as a cultural product.

One method of redefining mobility is by creating artificial spaces where the limits of our everyday movements and interactions can be ignored. For this reason, Needleman (2003) observes, "It is no exaggeration to say that the continuously accelerating influence of advanced technology is more and more rapidly changing nearly every pattern of human conduct in nearly every corner of the world: in family relations, in sexual morality, in the meaning and nature of work, in business, in religion, in the arts, in the nature of childhood and the instruments of education, in the meaning of love—the list is endless" (pp. 4–5). But, as Burgelman (2000) laments, our unquenching desire for simulated experiences produces an "ambiguity in our current experience of time and space, both seducing and revolting, [that] deserves our utmost attention."

Cooper (2006), reviewing the allure of biotechnical solutions to biological and social problems, thus warns that "In theory, we can keep solving these problems until we find ourselves in a world we cannot live in," reminding us that "Technology can liberate us at the same time as it undermines the conditions that might make such liberation meaningful" (p. 27). We produce technologized opportunities for distributed learning, approximate the costs and benefits, and our institutions incorporate these approaches into existing instructional formats without anticipating the radical and inevitable transformations that result. We are, to use Goodyear's (2006) term, the masters and victims of our race to achieve "time-space compression" (p. 89).

Murray (2006) takes a somewhat more radical, pro-cybernetic view of living and learning, positing that our interactions with the world, driven by circularity, feedback, and communications, are always acts of individualized construction: "We learn something new, and in the learning we change the phenomenon as we bring it into focus, provide it with attributes and communicate our observations to others, and we are changed by it, as it becomes part of our lives" (p. 217). In this respect, people do not extract information from their surrounding environment; rather, people and their environment are involved in a constant exchange of information, informing both the individual and the surrounding system—information and understanding are thus the "process of living *between* the observer and the system/environment" (p. 218). Murray's (2006) definition of teaching, then, is no less significant than the constant act of constructing environments.

Or, as Rowland (2004) has stated, "knowledge is messy, contextualized, seeks community, and travels on language" (p. 36). This perspective reminds us that, just as instruction cannot be removed from its situation of use, developing personal and group understanding and knowledge is an ill-structured and shared communication event. Our inability to easily delineate instruction, therefore, parallels our emerging lack of well-delineated territories where public and private spaces are clearly established and rules for engagement gain meaning from the walls that enclose us. As Kiesler and Cummings assert, "People use cues from their own and others' locations, such as functional activities associated with the location, artifacts, physical boundary cues, and physical distance signals, to establish territories" (Kiesler and Cummings 2002, p. 65), and these territories or "communication zones" in turn establish social bonds and frame "attentional contracts" (Nardi and Whittaker 2002, p. 85).

Distributed contact reallocates space and demands that we pay attention to time in new ways, on the one hand allowing us to interact anywhere, anytime, but, on the other, requiring that we negotiate time zones that were established prior to constraintless communication (Avital 2000). Proponents of traditional spaces, therefore, urge that virtual spaces overwrite the critical real-time dimensions of our everyday lives. Hallowell (1999) laments the loss of shared personal spaces, writing, "The human moment has two prerequisites: people's physical presence and their emotional and intellectual attention" (p. 59).

But we have established that it is counterproductive to detach human knowledge making, communication, artifacts, and learning from the contexts within which they are produced. Moreover, we have resisted drawing an easy dichotomy between individual cognition and environmental opportunities and constraints. Instead, we have incorporated into our view of instruction and learning with technology sensory-perceptual interaction and processing and a rich conception of communication, mediation, and artifact manipulation that draws on rhetorical theory, design studies, and usability research.

Instant and continuous connectivity perceived in near real time is a decade-old reality, as the intervals between naturally occurring and mediated events are separated by increasingly inconsequential intervals of time. Technologies are more capable of interacting with things at any time than the humans who work with them. As the culmination of capitalist mechanization, organizations can also produce, deliver, and serve at any time, unlike the individual human beings who make them up. Regularly scheduled human leisure is part of the clockwork, although organizations also provide technologies that promise to optimize "nonproductive" activities within these intervals, or to increase productivity during work time to allow for nonproductive benefits. In an etymological sleight of hand, interestingly, we can see mul-*time*-dia in our multimedia working, learning, and leisure spaces, where *mul-* invokes "to think about" and *-dia* is derived from the Greek for "through," separated by *time*.

Our perception can no longer be trusted to provide us with information that distinguishes the real from the artificial. Or, as Bush (1945) anticipated, we are awash in "conclusions which [we] cannot find time to grasp, much less remember" (p. 101). Communication and response interact instantaneously. No wonder Lakoff and Johnson (1980) note the dominance of monetary images in metaphors of time (p. 8). Indeed, time *is* money: it is exchanged, sold, hoarded, saved, spent. But we cannot exchange time for knowledge any more than we can instantaneously transmit information for understanding. Our experience of time and our experience of information are always situated and mediated.

Online instruction, the Internet, and our collapsing learning worlds have generated a fracture between our perceptual experience of time passage and normative time. Indeed, time is a social construct that we rarely *experience* without technological mediation; or, put another way, all our experiences are amalgams of self, mediator (whether biophysical, representational, schematic, or artifact-augmented), and environment (Arrow, Poole, Henry, and Moreland 2004). To speak of managing time, then, is highly problematic, and to hold that globalized information structures can bypass human community development and sustenance or minimize local and cultural difference and conflict is shortsighted.

Technology inserts itself between perceptions of time and notions of self. Writing of the initial navigational invention of the clock, Borgmann (2000) observes, "Here is an early example of information technology that yields information more instantaneously and easily while at the same time it disengages us from reality and diminishes our expertise, the latter being assumed by the machinery of the device" (p. 79). Technology does not understand time. But we have forgotten that, and thus, Bluedorn (2002) notes, "in many parts of our world, particularly the industrialized, bureaucratized world, temporal depths are much shallower than those in Augustine's time, the pace is faster, punctuality is a greater concern, life strategies are more monochronic, and time is believed to be not just more fungible, but absolutely fungible (even though that is not true)" (p. 245). Microsoft laments that people take an average of 11 minutes to find the information they are seeking on the Web and responds by developing more sophisticated search engines, deemphasizing the numerous human dimensions of any successful search, including problem setting, naming, knowledge of the search environment, specific finding activities, ability to assess results, coordination with others, time for reflection, and so on (Hoover 2007). Searching, in short, is not a technical problem. It is for this reason that Needleman (2003) concludes that "almost everything we call 'progress' is actually measured by the degree to which it enables us to conduct ourselves without the need to bring thought into conscious relationship with movement or feeling" (p. 140).

But a full exploration of how our relationship with space and time is being radically rewritten by technologies for instruction and learning is an additional book-length task. Now, though, we have run out of time. We have described how a transformational perspective toward technology-mediated instruction and learning highlights the theoretical, multidisciplinary, and significant nature of our object of inquiry. The technologies that we design for instruction and learning mirror what we value about effective teaching and ideal learning across disciplines. Just as technologies cannot be reduced to experimental treatments or heavy-handed media comparisons, so too must instruction and information be understood and designed with careful attention to audience, purpose, medium, and context.

Our overview of everyday learning has introduced us to converging learning worlds, and to numerous research conversations playing out across hundreds of research journals. Issues in instruction and learning with technology have a considerable history when we characterize them as communication and literacy events. A common theme of productivity, efficiency, and acceleration emerges from reviews of the role of technology in our learning lives. Ultimately, it will be useful to capture in more detail how emerging technologies are also rewiring our personal relationships, providing us with new opportunities for social and civic engagement, and producing novel spaces for self-expression and creative exchange. We have only begun to benefit from the instructional lessons that nonformal learning spaces can teach us.

Meta-analyses of the vast research literatures related to instruction and learning with technology have also helped us better articulate instruction, learning, and technology developments within and across disciplines. Reviewing visual representations of models of instruction and learning with technology from numerous researchers has allowed us to begin conceptualizing instruction and learning in general, historical, and detailed ways. This effort needs to be continued, to integrate emerging neurological research and sociocultural analyses into our existing cognitive and social discussions. Contemporary discussions about specific technologies need to be broadened to account for long-term historical patterns and developments as well as emerging spaces for instruction and learning.

Multidimensional viewpoints demand a reexamination of existing articulations of science and design and theory and practice. Dichotomies have been too sharply drawn between these worldviews, and that, in turn, has encouraged us to begin elaborating on a rhetorical design perspective toward instruction and learning with technology. With the wicked problem of how to characterize the research, design, practice, and evaluation of instruction and learning with technology before us, we have concluded by proposing a framework for everyday instructional situations. Our introduction to the five learning dimensions that form that framework is clearly only a beginning, but worth revision and extension. We have concluded by showing how the framework can be used to help us characterize our research, our implementations, and our mediated explorations of instruction and learning. Time permitting, reflections on the everyday nature of instruction, learning, and technology are only just beginning.

Appendix

Table A: *American Journal of Distance Education* **Analysis (2002–2007)**

American Journal of Distance Education Article Analysis (2002–2007) Year, Volume, Page Numbers, Authors, Title, Instructional Dimension			
2007, 21			
215–231	J. Hewitt, C. Brett, V. Peters	Scan rate: A new metric for the analysis of reading behaviors in asynchronous computer conferencing environments	SD EA
199–214	J. E. Hughes, S. McLeod, R. Brown, Y. Maeda, J. Choi	Academic achievement and perceptions of the learning environment in virtual and traditional secondary mathematics classrooms	LB EA
185–198	L. M. Shoaf	Perceived advantages and disadvantages of an online charter school	LB IA
145–164	B. H. Chaney, J. M. Eddy, S. M. Dorman, L. Glessner, B. L. Green, R. Lara-Alecio	Development of an instrument to assess student opinions of the quality of distance education courses	LB SD IA
133–143	P. F. O'Leary, T. J. Quinlan, Jr.	Learner-instructor telephone interaction: Effects on satisfaction and achievement of online students	TA IA
117–132	J. Gaytan, B. C. McEwen	Effective online instructional and assessment strategies	IA
93–104	J. Flowers, S. E. Cotton	Impacts of student categorization on their online discussion contributions	TA SD

American Journal of Distance Education Article Analysis (2002–2007)
Year, Volume, Page Numbers, Authors, Title, Instructional Dimension

77–91	T. M. Abdel-Salam, P. J. Kauffmann, G. R. Crossman	Are distance laboratories effective tools for technology education?	LB TA EA
61–75	C. G. Keeler, M. Horney	Online course designs: Are special needs being met?	LB IA EA
37–49	K. R. Barrett, B. L. Bower, N. C. Donovan	Teaching styles of community college instructors	TA EA
21–36	K. K. Seo	Utilizing peer moderating in online discussions: Addressing the controversy between teacher moderation and nonmoderation	SD TA
3–19	B. Offir, R. Bezalel, I. Barth	Introverts, extroverts, and achievement in a distance learning environment	LB EA

2006, 20

231–244	Hawkes, M.	Linguistic discourse variables as indicators of reflective online interaction	LB SD
211–229	Graddy, D. B.	Gender salience and the use of linguistic qualifiers and intensifiers in online course discussions	LB SD
191–193	Jeong, A.	Gender interaction patterns and gender participation in computer-supported collaborative argumentation	LB SD
163–179	Pomales-Garcia, C., Liu, Y.	Web-based distance learning technology: The impacts of Web module length and format	TA IA EA
143–161	Moisey, S. D., Ally, M., Spencer, B.	Factors affecting the development and use of learning objects	TA EA
93–107	Mabrito, M.	A study of synchronous versus asynchronous collaboration in an online business writing class	TA SD EA
65–77	Young, S.	Student views of effective online teaching in higher education	LB IA
39–50	Schumm, W. R., Webb, F. J., Turek, D. E., Jones, K. D., Ballard, G. E.	A comparison of methods for teaching critical thinking skills for U.S. army officers	TA EA
23–37	Richardson, J. C.	The role of students' cognitive engagement in online learning	LB IA
7–22	Harroff, P. A., Valentine, T.	Dimensions of program quality in Web-based adult education	IA EA

American Journal of Distance Education Article Analysis (2002–2007)
Year, Volume, Page Numbers, Authors, Title, Instructional Dimension

2005, 19

Pages	Authors	Title	Dimension
229–240	Popovich, C. J., Neel, R. E.	Characteristics of distance education programs in accredited business schools	EA
215–227	Hee, J. C., Johnson, S. D	The effect of context-based video instruction on learning and motivation in online classes	LB IA
197–214	Oriogun, P. K., Ravenscroft, A., Cook, J.	Validating an approach to examining cognitive engagement within online groups	LB SD
163–181	Yang, Y-T. C., Newby, T. J., Bill, R. L.	Using Socratic questioning to promote critical thinking skills through asynchronous discussion forums in distance learning environments	LB IA
149–162	Dongsong, Z.	Interactive multimedia-based e-learning: A study of effectiveness	LB EA
133–148	Garrison, D. R., Cleveland-Innes, M.	Facilitating cognitive presence in online learning: Interaction is not enough	LB IA
105–118	Stein, D. S., Wanstreet, C. E., Calvin, J., Overtoom, C., Wheaton, J. E.	Bridging the transactional distance gap in online learning environments	LB SD
87–103	Egan, T. M., Akdere, M.	Clarifying distance education roles and competencies: Exploring similarities and differences between professional and student-practitioner perspectives	LB TA
71–85	Adams, J., DeFleur, M. H.	The acceptability of a doctoral degree earned online as a credential for obtaining a faculty position	LB IA
51–64	Roberts, T. G., Irani, T. A., Telg, R. W., Lundy, L. K.	The development of an instrument to evaluate distance education courses using student attitudes	LB IA
37–50	Duphome, P. L., Gunawardena, C. N.	The effect of three computer conferencing designs on critical thinking skills of nursing students	LB TA
23–36	Morris, L. V., Wu, S-S., Finnegan, C. L.	Predicting retention in online general education courses	LB TA
5–22	Fahy, P. J., Ally, M.	Student learning style and asynchronous Computer-Mediated Conferencing (CMC) interaction	LB SD

American Journal of Distance Education Article Analysis (2002–2007)
Year, Volume, Page Numbers, Authors, Title, Instructional Dimension

2004, 18

225–241	Lee, Y., Driscoll, M. P., Nelson, D. W.	The past, present, and future of research in distance education: Results of a content analysis	EA
207–223	Giguere, P. J., Formica, S. W., Harding, W. M.	Large-scale interaction strategies for Web-based professional development	TA SD
199–206	Dupin-Bryant, P. A.	Pre-entry variables related to retention in online distance education	LB SD
169–185	Belanich, J., Wisher, R. A., Orvis, K. L.	A question-collaboration approach to Web-based learning	TA SD
151–167	Hanlon, L. L.	Accreditation of distance learning in the field of dentistry	LB EA
131–150	Stewart, I., Eunsook, H., Strudler, N.	Development and validation of an instrument for student evaluation of the quality of Web-based instruction	LB EA
103–114	Bender, D. M., Wood, B. J., Vredevoogd, J. D.	Teaching time: distance education versus classroom instruction	IA EA
89–101	Molinari, D. L.	The role of social comments in problem-solving groups in an online class	LB SD
73–88	Rose, M. A.	Comparing productive online dialog in two group styles: Cooperative and collaborative	LB SD
51–62	Edmonds, C. D.	Providing access to students with disabilities in online distance education: Legal and technical concerns for higher education	LB EA
39–50	Dupin-Bryant, P. A.	Teaching styles in interactive television instructors: A descriptive study	IA EA
21–38	DeTure, M.	Cognitive style and self-efficacy: Predicting student success in online distance education	LB EA
5–19	Kinash, S., Crichton, S. Kim-Rupnow, W. S.	Cognitive style and self-efficacy: Predicting student success in online distance education	LB EA

American Journal of Distance Education Article Analysis (2002–2007)
Year, Volume, Page Numbers, Authors, Title, Instructional Dimension

2003, 17

235–246	Murphy, E., Coffin, G.	Synchronous communication in a Web-based senior high school course: Maximizing affordances and minimizing constraints of the tool	SD EA
221–234	Oriogun, P. K., Cook, J.	Transcript reliability cleaning percentage: An alternative interrater reliability measure of message transcripts in online learning	SD EA
207–220	Levy, S., Beaulieu, R.	Online distance learning among the California community colleges: Looking at the planning and implementation	LB EA
173–187	Lee, J., Gibson, C. C.	Developing self-direction in an online course through computer-mediated interaction	LB SD
161–172	Winston, B. E., Fields, D. L.	Developing dissertation skills of doctoral students in an Internet-based distance education curriculum: A case study	TA EA
145–159	Benson, A. D.	Dimensions of quality in online degree programs	SD EA
119–128	LaPadula, M.	A comprehensive look at online student support services for distance learners	SD EA
99–118	Woods, R., Ebersole, S.	Using non-subject-matter-specific discussion boards to build connectedness in online learning	SD EA
77–98	Roblyer, M. D., Wiencke, W. R.	Design and use of a rubric to assess and encourage interactive qualities in distance courses	SD EA
45–57	Williams, P. E.	Roles and competencies for distance education programs in higher education institutions	EA
25–44	Jeong, A. C.	The sequential analysis of group interaction and critical thinking in online threaded discussion	LB SD
7–24	Stein, D., Glazer, H. R.	Mentoring the adult learner in academic midlife at a distance education university	LB IA

American Journal of Distance Education Article Analysis (2002–2007)
Year, Volume, Page Numbers, Authors, Title, Instructional Dimension

2002, 16

245–158	Cheurprakobkit, S., Hale, D. F., Olson, J. N.	Technicians' perceptions about Web-based courses: The University of Texas system experience	LB EA
227–244	Aragon, S. R., Johnson, S. D., Shaik, N.	The influence of learning style preferences on student success in online versus face-to-face environments	LB EA
205–226	Conrad, D. L.	Engagement, excitement, anxiety, and fear: Learners' experiences of starting an online course	LB EA
169–189	Thurmond, V. A., Wambach, K., Connors, H. R.	Evaluation of student satisfaction: Determining the impact of a Web-based environment by controlling for student characteristics	LB EA
151–168	Kanuka, H., Collett, D., Caswell, C.	University instructor perceptions of the use of asynchronous text-based discussion in distance courses	IA SD
131–150	Tu, C-H, McIsaac, M.	The relationship of social presence and interaction in online classes	IA SD
99–113	Neuhauser, C.	Learning style and effectiveness of online and face-to-face instruction	LB EA
83–97	Allen, M., Bourhis, J., Burrell, N., Mabry, E.	Comparing student satisfaction with distance education to traditional classrooms in higher education: A meta-analysis	LB EA
65–81	Kemp, W. C.	Persistence of adult learners in distance education	LB EA
37–52	Bisciglia, M. G., Monk-Turner, E.	Differences in attitudes between on-site and distance-site students in group teleconference class	LB EA
23–36	Litchfield, R. E., Oakland, M. J., Anderson, J. A.	Relationships between intern characteristics, computer attitudes, and use of online instruction in a dietetic training program	LB TA
5–22	Fahy, P. J.	Use of linguistic qualifiers and intensifiers in a computer conference	LB SD

Table B: *Education and Information Technologies* **Analysis (2001–2006)**

Education and Information Technologies Article Analysis (2002–2006) Year, Volume, Page Numbers, Authors, Title, Instructional Dimension			
2006, 11			
293–303	Fisher, T.	Educational transformation: is it, like "beauty," in the eye of the beholder, or will we know it when we see it?	IA EA
269–282	Carr, N., Chambers, D. P.	Cultural and organisational issues facing online learning communities of teachers	SD IA EA
217–237	van Weert, T. J.	Education of the twenty-first century: New professionalism in lifelong learning, knowledge development and knowledge sharing	TA IA EA
199–216	Watson, D.	Understanding the relationship between ICT and education means exploring innovation and change	IA EA
161–185	Kienle, A.	Integration of knowledge management and collaborative learning by technical supported communication processes	SD EA
121–135	Barak, M.	Instructional principles for fostering learning with ICT: Teachers' perspectives as learners and instructors	LB IA EA
33–69	Mishra, P., Yadav, A.	Using hypermedia for learning complex concepts in chemistry: A qualitative study on the relationship between prior knowledge, beliefs, and motivation	LB TA IA EA
7–20	Olofsson, A. D., Lindberg, J. O.	"Whatever happened to the social dimension?" Aspects of learning in a distance-based teacher training program	SD IA EA

Education and Information Technologies Article Analysis (2002–2006)
Year, Volume, Page Numbers, Authors, Title, Instructional Dimension

2005, 10

Pages	Authors	Title	Dimension
361–379	Goscinski, A., Campbell, M., Dew, R., Horan, P., Newlands, D., Rough, J., Silcock, J., Zhou, W.	An IT Bachelor degree using modern technologies to illustrate core concepts and principles and building generic skills	LB IA
341–360	Papastergiou, M.	Students' mental models of the Internet and their didactical exploitation in informatics education	LB EA
289–296	Kendall, M.	Lifelong learning really matters for elementary education in the 21st century	LB IA
277–287	Furr, P. F., Ragsdale, R., Horton, S. G.	Technology's non-neutrality: Past lessons can help guide today's classrooms	LB EA
157–163	Cannainn, S. O., Hughes, J.	Learning our way forward in eLearning: The story of *something fishy*	IA SD EA
147–156	Baron, G-L., Harrari, M.	ICT in French primary education, twenty years later: Infusion or transformation?	EA
111–123	Tattersall, C., Manderveld, J., van den Berg, B., René van Es, J.	Self organizing wayfinding support for lifelong learners	LB TA
83–110	Schewe, K-D., Thalheim, B., Binemann-Zdanowicz, A., Kaschek, R., Kuss, T., Tschiedel, B.	A conceptual view of Web-based e-learning systems	LB IA EA
67–82	Aiken, R. M., Bessagnet, M-N., Israel, J.	Interaction and collaboration using an intelligent collaborative learning environment	TA SD EA
51–65	Van Eijl, P. J., Pilot, A., de Voogd, P.	Effects of collaborative and individual learning in a blended learning environment	LB SD EA
33–49	Vandenberg, A.	Learning how to engage students online in hard times	IA EA
21–32	Nordkvelle, Y. T., Oldon, J.	Visions for ICT, ethics and the practice of teachers	TA IA EA
7–20	Law, N., Chow, A., Yuen, A. H. K.	Methodological approaches to comparing pedagogical innovations using technology	EA

Education and Information Technologies Article Analysis (2002–2006)
Year, Volume, Page Numbers, Authors, Title, Instructional Dimension

---

2004, 9

387–404	Drenoyianni, H.	Designing and implementing a project-based ICT course in a teacher education setting: Rewards and pitfalls	IA EA
377–386	Hawkey, K.	Assessing online discussions working 'along the grain' of current technology and educational culture	SD EA
355–375	Or-Bach, R., Van Joolingen, W. R.	Designing adaptive interventions for online collaborative modeling	SD EA
345–353	Kalogiannakis, M.	A virtual learning environment for the French physics teachers	IA EA
333–343	Pedersen, J.	Project work in the paperless school: A case study in a Swedish upper secondary class	SD EA
321–331	Klein, J.	The effectiveness of intuitive and computer-assistive educational decision making in simple and complex educational situations	TA IA EA
291–308	Nachmias, R., Mioduser, D., Cohen, A., Tubin, D., Forkosh-Baruch, A.	Factors involved in the implementation of pedagogical innovations using technology	IA EA
271–289	Wallace, M., Karpouzis, K., Stefanou, M., Maglogiannis, I., Kollias, S.	Electronic roads in historical documents: A student oriented approach	LB IA EA
255–270	Akbaba-Altun, S.	Information technology classrooms and elementary school principals' roles: Turkish experience	IA EA
239–253	Kordaki, M.	Challenging prospective computer engineers to design educational software by engaging them in a constructivist learning environment	SD EA
219–237	Milne, I., Rowe, G.	OGRE: Three-dimensional program visualization for novice programmers	IA EA
209–218	Hu, C.	Rethinking of teaching objects-first	IA EA
185–197	Wu, C-C., Lee, G. C., Lai, H-K.	Using concept maps to aid analysis of concept presentation in high school computer textbooks	IA EA
175–183	Hubwieser, P.	Functional modeling in secondary schools using spreadsheets	TA EA

Education and Information Technologies Article Analysis (2002–2006)
Year, Volume, Page Numbers, Authors, Title, Instructional Dimension

159–173	Dagdilelis, V., Satratzemi, M., Evangelidis, G.	Introducing secondary education students to algorithms and programming	TA IA
147–158	Petre, M., Price, B.	Using robotics to motivate 'back door' learning	TA IA
131–145	Haberman, B.	High-school student' attitudes regarding procedural abstraction	LB TA
117–130	Brinda, T.	Integration of new exercise classes into the informatics education in the field of object-oriented modeling	IA EA
109–116	McDougall, A., Boyle, M.	Student strategies for learning computer programming: Implications for pedagogy in informatics	LB TA
67–89	Markauskaitė, L.	Developing country-tailored policy for the provision of schools with educational software and content: The case of Lithuania	IA EA
47–66	Strickley, A.	Factors affecting the use of MIS as a tool for informing and evaluating teaching and learning in schools	IA EA
37–45	Jedeskog, G., Nissen, J.	ICT in the classroom: Is doing more important than knowing?	LB TA IA EA
21–35	Karagiorgi, Y., Charalambous, K.	Curricula considerations in ICT integration: Models and practices in Cyprus	IA EA
5–19	Farrell, G., Leung, Y. K.	Innovative online assessment using confidence measurement	IA EA
2003, 8			
369–379	Charistos, N. D., Teberekidis, V. I., Tsipis, C. A., Sigalas, M. P.	Design and development of a multimedia educational tool for interactive visualization and three-dimensional perception of vibrational spectra data of molecules	IA EA
345–368	Atif, Y., Benlamri, R., Berri, J.	Learning objects based framework for self-adaptive learning	TA IA
327–343	Fritze, Y., Nordkvelle, Y. T.	Comparing lectures: Effects of the technological context of the studio	IA EA
313–326	Loveless, A. M.	The interaction between primary teachers' perceptions of ICT and their pedagogy	IA EA

Education and Information Technologies Article Analysis (2002–2006)
Year, Volume, Page Numbers, Authors, Title, Instructional Dimension

Pages	Authors	Title	Dimension
267–285	Melle, A. V., Cimellaro, L., Shulha, L.	A dynamic framework to guide the implementation and evaluation of educational technologies	IA EA
245–266	Sheard, J., Ceddia, J., Hurst, J., Tuovinen, J.	Inferring student learning behavior from website interactions: A usage analysis	TA IA
229–244	Kolokotronis, D., Solomonidou, C.	A step-by-step design and development of an integrated educational software to deal with students' empirical ideas about mechanical interaction	LB TA EA
195–214	Van Weert, T. J., Pilot, A.	Task-based team learning with ICT, design and development of new learning	IA EA
179–193	Lazonder, A. W.	Principles for designing Web searching instruction	IA
165–177	Hawkey, K.	Social constructivism and asynchronous text-based discussion: A case study with trainee teachers	SD IA
147–164	Ki, W. W., Tse, S-K., Shum, M., Lam, H-C.	The introduction of a computerised network to support educational change in Hong Kong	IA EA
127–145	Tubin, D., Mioduser, D., Nachmias, R., Forkosh-Baruch, A.	Domains and levels of pedagogical innovation in schools using ICT: Ten innovative schools in Israel	IA EA
109–125	Breiter, A.	Public Internet usage points in schools for the local community—concept, implementation and evaluation of a project in Bremen, Germany	IA EA
83–95	Monk, M., Swain, J., Christ, M., Riddle, W.	Notes on classroom practice and the ownership and use of personal computers among Egyptian science and mathematics teachers	IA EA
67–81	Zahariadis, T., Voliotis, S.	New trends in distance learning utilizing next generation multimedia networks	IA EA
55–66	Ketamo, H., Multisilta, J.	Toward adaptive learning materials: Speed of interaction and relative number of mistakes as indicators of learning results	TA IA

Education and Information Technologies Article Analysis (2002–2006)
Year, Volume, Page Numbers, Authors, Title, Instructional Dimension

47–54	Moreira, D. A., Silva, E. Q.	A method to increase student interaction using student groups and peer review over the internet	SD EA
37–46	Kern, V. M., Saraiva, L. M., Pacheco, R. C. S.	Peer review in education: Promoting collaboration, written expression, critical thinking, and professional responsibility	TA SD
23–36	Mioduser, D., Nachmias, R., Tubin, D, Forkosh-Baruch, A.	Analysis schema for the study of domains and levels of pedagogical innovation in schools using ICT	TA IA EA
5–22	Pearson, M., Somekh, B.	Concept-mapping as a research tool: A study of primary children's representations of information and communication technologies (ICT)	LB IA

2002, 7

377–384	Lockhorst, D., Admiraal, W., Pilot, A., Veen, W.	Design elements for a CSCL environment in a teacher training program	TA SD EA
369–376	Knezek, G., Christensen, R.	Impact of new information technologies on teachers and students	LB EA
359–367	Cannings, T. R., Talley, S.	Multimedia and online video case studies for preservice teacher preparation	IA EA
351–357	White, B., Le Cornu, R.	E-mail reducing stress for student teachers	IA EA
343–349	Witfelt, C., Philipsen, P. E., Kaiser, B.	Chat as media in exams	TA SD
333–342	Drenoyianni, H., Selwood, I., Riding, R.	Searching using "Microsoft Encarta"	TA IA EA
323–332	Romeo, G., Walker, I.	Activity theory to investigate the implementation of ICTE	IA EA
313–312	Masters, J., Yelland, N.	Teacher scaffolding: An exploration of exemplary practice	IA
303–312	Yip, W.	Students' perceptions of the technological supports for problem-based learning	LB TA
295–302	Furr, P. F., Ragsdale, R. G.	Desktop video conferencing	SD

Education and Information Technologies Article Analysis (2002–2006)
Year, Volume, Page Numbers, Authors, Title, Instructional Dimension

287–294	Stacey, E.	Social presence online: Networking learners at a distance	SD EA
257–274	Khalid, H., Swift, H., Cullingford, C.	The new office technology and its effects on secretaries and managers	LB EA
237–255	Webb, M. E.	Pedagogical reasoning: Issues and solutions for the teaching and learning of ICT in secondary schools	IA EA
225–235	Panselina, M. E., Sigalas, M. P., Tzougraki, C.	Design and development of a bilingual multimedia educational tool for teaching chemistry concepts to deaf students in Greek sign language	LB TA EA
201–224	Montilva, J. A., Sandia, B., Barrios, J.	Developing instructional Web sites—A software engineering approach	IA EA
169–188	Komis, V., Avouris, N., Fidas, C.	Computer-supported collaborative concept mapping: Study of synchronous peer interaction	TA SD
137–154	Dougherty, J. P., Kock, N. F., Sandas, C., Aiken, R. M.	Teaching the use of complex IT in specific domains: Developing, assessing and refining a curriculum development framework	IA EA
127–135	MacKinnon, G. R., Vibert, C.	Judging the constructive impacts of communication technologies: A business education study	LB IA
93–109	Hartviksen, G., Akselsen, S., Eidsvik, A. K.	MICTS: Municipal ICT schools—A means for bridging the digital divide between rural and urban communities	LB SD
67–80	Gulz, A.	Spatially oriented and person oriented thinking—Implications for user interface design	LB IA EA
55–66	Milne, I., Rowe, G.	Difficulties in learning and teaching programming—Views of students and tutors	TA IA
41–53	Curran, K.	An online collaboration environment	EA
17–40	Tselios, N. K., Avouris, N. M., Kordaki, M.	Student task modeling in design and evaluation of open problem-solving environments	LB TA
5–16	Schrum, L., Hong, S.	From the field: Characteristics of successful tertiary online students and strategies of experienced online educators	LB IA

Table C: *Journal of the Learning Sciences* **Analysis (1999–2007)**

Journal of the Learning Sciences Article Analysis (1999–2007) Year, Volume, Page Numbers, Authors, Title, Instructional Dimension			
2007, 16			
523–563	Nathan, M. J., Eilam, B., Kim, S.	To disagree, we must also agree: How intersubjectivity structures and perpetuates discourse in a mathematics classroom	LB SD EA
485–521	van Amelsvoort, M., Andriessen, J., Kanselaar, G.	Representational tools in computer-supported collaborative argumentation-based learning: How dyads work with constructed and inspected argumentative diagrams	TA SD EA
415–450	Parnafes, O.	What does "fast" mean? Understanding the physical world through computational representations	LB TA IA EA
371–413	Squire, K., Klopfer, E.	Augmented reality simulations on handheld computers	LBIA EA
307–331	Hmelo-Silver, C. E., Marathe, S., Liu, L.	Fish swim, rocks sit, and lungs breathe: Expert-novice understanding of complex systems	LB IA EA
175–220	van Aalst, J., Chan, C. K. K.	Student-directed assessment of knowledge building using electronic portfolios	LB TA IA EA
81–130	Puntambekar, S., Stylianou, A., Goldstein, J.	Comparing classroom enactments of an inquiry curriculum: Lessons learned from two teachers	TA IA
5–35	Gottlieb, E.	Learning how to believe: Epistemic development in cultural context	
2006, 15			
549–582	Seymour, J. R., Lehrer, R.	Tracing the evolution of pedagogical content knowledge as the development of interanimated discourses	LB SD IA
537–547	Greeno, J. G.	Authoritative, accountable positioning and connected, general knowing: Progressive themes in understanding transfer	LB EA
499–535	Marton, F.	Sameness and difference in transfer	LB EA

Journal of the Learning Sciences Article Analysis (1999–2007)
Year, Volume, Page Numbers, Authors, Title, Instructional Dimension

Page Numbers	Authors	Title	Instructional Dimension
431–449	Lobato, J.	Alternative perspectives on the transfer of learning: History, issues, and challenges for future research	LB SD
379–428	Wells, G., Arauz, R. M.	Dialogue in the classroom	SD
331–377	Zohar, A.	The nature and development of teachers' metastrategic knowledge in the context of teaching higher order thinking	LB IA
301–329	Bielaczye, K.	Designing social infrastructure: Critical issues in creating learning environments with technology	EA
193–220	Marton, F., Ming, F. P.	On some necessary conditions of learning	LB IA
121–151	Dillenbourg, P., Traum, D.	Sharing solutions: Persistence and grounding in multimodal collaborative problem solving	TA EA
53–61	Hmelo-Silver, C. E., Azevedo, R.	Understanding complex systems: Some core challenges	LB EA
45–52	Lesh, R.	Modeling students modeling abilities: The teaching and learning of complex systems in education	LB TA
5–9	Sabelli, N. H.	Complexity, technology, science, and education	TA EA

2005, 14

Page Numbers	Authors	Title	Instructional Dimension
567–589	Hewitt, J.	Toward an understanding of how threads die in asynchronous computer conferences	TA SD EA
527–565	Muukkonen, H., Lakkala, M., Hakkarainen, K.	Technology-mediation and tutoring: How do they shape progressive inquiry discourse	TA SD EA
489–526	Lim, C. P., Barnes, S.	A collective case study of the use of ICT in economics courses: A sociocultural approach	TA EA
405–441	Fischer, F., Mandl, H.	Knowledge convergence in computer-supported collaborative learning: The role of external representation tools	SD EA
243–279	Dori, Y. J., Belcher, J.	How does technology-enabled active learning affect undergraduate students' understanding of electromagnetism concepts?	LB SD IA EA

Journal of the Learning Sciences Article Analysis (1999–2007)
Year, Volume, Page Numbers, Authors, Title, Instructional Dimension

201–241	Rummel, N., Spada, H.	Learning to collaborate: An instructional approach to promoting collaborative problem solving in computer-mediated settings	LB SD IA EA
161–199	Chi, M. T. H.	Commonsense conceptions of emergent processes: Why some misconceptions are robust	LB TA IA
69–110	Goldstone, R. L., Son, J. Y.	The transfer of scientific principles using concrete and idealized simulations	LB IA EA
5–34	Nasir, N. S.	Individual cognitive structuring and sociocultural context: Strategy shifts in the game of dominoes	LB TA

2004, 13

507–526	Godshalk, V. M., Harvey, D. M., Molter, L.	The role of learning tasks on attitude change using cognitive flexibility hypertext systems	LB TA
423–451	Pea, R. D.	The social and technological dimensions of scaffolding and related theoretical concepts for learning, education, and human activity	TA IA
387–421	Sherin, B., Reiser, B. J., Edelson, D.	Scaffolding analysis: Extending the scaffolding metaphor to learning artifacts	IA EA
337–386	Quintana, C., Reiser, B. J., Davis, E. A., Krajcik, J., Fretz, E., Duncan, R. G., Kyza, E., Edelson, D., Soloway, E.	A scaffolding design framework for software to support science inquiry	TA EA
305–335	Tabak, I.	Synergy: A complement to emerging patterns of distributed scaffolding	IA SD
273–304	Reiser, B. J.	Scaffolding complex learning: The mechanisms of structuring and problematizing student work	TA IA
265–272	Davis, E. A., Miyake, N.	Explorations of scaffolding in complex classroom systems	TA IA EA
165–195	Hudson, J. M., Bruckman, A. S.	The bystander effect: A lens for understanding patterns of participation	SD EA

Journal of the Learning Sciences Article Analysis (1999–2007)
Year, Volume, Page Numbers, Authors, Title, Instructional Dimension

2003, 12

183–218	Suthers, D. D., Hundhausen, C. D.	An experimental study of the effects of representational guidance on collaborative learning processes	TA SD IA
145–181	Zohar, A., Dori, Y. J.	Higher order thinking skills and low-achieving students: Are they mutually exclusive?	LB IA
53–90	Hammer, D., Elby, A.	Tapping epistemological resources for physics	LB IA

2002, 11

489–542	Barab, S. A., Barnett, M., Squire, K.	Developing an empirical account of a community of practice: Characterizing the essential tensions	TA SD IA
389–452	Clement, J. J., Steinberg, M. S.	Step-wise evolution of mental models of electric currents: A "learning-aloud" case study	LB TA IA
319–357	Sfard, A.	The interplay of intimations and implementations: Generating new discourse with new symbolic tools	TA SD EA
301–317	Schliemann, A. D.	Representational tools and mathematical understanding	TA SD EA
251–274	Forman, E. A., Ansell, E.	Orchestrating the multiple voices and inscriptions of a mathematics classroom	TA SD IA EA
217–249	McClain, K.	Teachers' and students' understanding: The role of tools and inscriptions in supporting effective communication	TA IA EA
105–121	Edelson, D. C.	Design research: What we learn when we engage in design	TA IA EA
63–103	de Vries, E., Lund, K., Baker, M.	Computer-mediated epistemic dialog: Explanation and argumentation as vehicles for understanding scientific notions	TA SD IA EA

2001, 10

417–446	Kurtz, K. J., Miao, C-H., Gentner, D.	Learning by analogical bootstrapping	LB TA SD
365–415	Umaschi Bers, M.	Identify construction environments: Developing personal and moral values through design of a virtual city	LB TA IA EA

Journal of the Learning Sciences Article Analysis (1999–2007)
Year, Volume, Page Numbers, Authors, Title, Instructional Dimension

281–322	Hay, K. E., Barab, S. A.	Constructivism in practice: A comparison and contrast of apprenticeship and constructionist learning environments	IA SD EA
265–279	Guzdial, M., Rick, J., Kehoe, C.	Beyond adoption to invention: Teacher-created collaboration activities in higher education	SD IA EA
223–264	O'Neill, D. K.	Knowing when you've brought them in: Scientific genre knowledge and communities of practice	TA SD IA EA
63–112	Barab, S. A., Hay, K. E., Yamagata-Lynch, L. C.	Constructing networks of action-relevant episodes: An in situ research methodology	TA SD IA EA
165–202	Kulikowich, J. M., Young, M. F.	Locating an ecological psychology methodology for situated action	IA EA

2000, 9

471–500	Colella, V.	Participatory simulations: Building collaborative understanding through immersive dynamic modeling	SD EA
437–469	Guzdail, M., Turns, J.	Effective discussion through a computer-mediated anchored forum	SD IA EA
373–401	Stevens, R. R.	Divisions of labor in school and in the workplace: Comparing computer and paper-supported activities across settings	SD EA
145–199	Jacobson, M. J., Archodidou, A.	The design of hypermedia tools for learning: Fostering conceptual change and transfer of complex scientific knowledge	LB EA
105–143	Kozma, R., Chin, E., Russell, J., Marx, N.	The roles of representations and tools in the chemistry laboratory and their implications for chemistry learning	LB EA
7–30	Resnick, M., Berg, R., Eisenberg, M.	Beyond black boxes: Bringing transparency and aesthetics back to scientific investigation	LB TA EA

Journal of the Learning Sciences Article Analysis (1999–2007)
Year, Volume, Page Numbers, Authors, Title, Instructional Dimension

1999, 8

391–450	Edelson, D. C., Gordin, D. N., Pea, R. D.	Addressing the challenges of inquiry-based learning through technology and curriculum design	TA IA EA
245–290	Lehrer, R., Lee, M., Jeong, A.	Reflective teaching of Logo	LB IA
215–244	Shapiro, A. M.	The relevance of hierarchies to learning biology from hypertext	LB IA
177–214	Ploetzner, R., Fehse, E., Kneser, C., Spada, H.	Learning to relate qualitative and quantitative problem representation in a model-based setting for collaborative problem solving	LB IA
71–126	Van Lehn, K.	Rule-learning events in the acquisition of a complex skill: An evaluation of Cascade	TA IA
41–70	Caplan, L. J., Schooler, C.	On the use of analogy in text-based memory and comprehension: The interaction between complexity of within-domain encoding and between-domain processing	LB IA
1–40	Chaney-Cullen, T., Duffy, T. M.	Strategic teaching framework: Multimedia to support teacher change	IA EA

Table D: *Written Communication* Analysis (1999–2007)

Written Communication Article Analysis (1999–2007)
Year, Volume, Page Numbers, Authors, Title, Instructional Dimension

2007, 24

223–249	Lee, C. K.-M.	Affordances and text-making practices in online instant messaging	SD EA

2006, 23

173–201	Swarts, J.	Coherent fragments: The problem of mobility and genred information	TA EA

Written Communication Article Analysis (1999–2007)
Year, Volume, Page Numbers, Authors, Title, Instructional Dimension

2005, 22			
224–261	Hull, G. A., Nelson, M. E.	Locating the semiotic power of multimodality	TA EA
166–197	Brandt, D.	Writing for a living: Literacy and the knowledge economy	TA EA

2004, 21			
236–241	Hayes, J. R.	Herbert A. Simon: 1916 to 2001	LB

2003, 20			
391–425	Faber, B.	Creating rhetorical stability in corporate university discourse: Discourse technologies and change	SD EA

2002, 19			
297–333	Wolfe, J.	Marginal pedagogy: How annotated texts affect a writing-from-sources task	TA IA

2001, 18			
26–60	Honeycutt, L.	Comparing e-mail and synchronous conferencing in online peer response	TA EA

2000, 17			
491–519	Wolfe, J.	Gender, ethnicity, and classroom discourse: Communication patterns of Hispanic and white students in networked classrooms	LB EA

1999, 16			
29–50	Chenoweth, N. A., Hayes, J. R., Littleton, E. B., Steinberg, E. R., Van Every, D. A.	Are our courses working? Measuring student learning	LB IA

Table E: *Interacting with Computers* Analysis (2001–2006)

Interacting with Computers Article Analysis (2001–2006)
Year, Volume, Page Numbers, Authors, Title, Instructional Dimension

---

2006, 18

1351–1370	Pandir, M., Knight, J.	Homepage aesthetics: The search for preference factors and the challenges of subjectivity	LB EA
1336–1350	Ben-Ari, M., Yeshno, T.	Conceptual models of software artifacts	LB TA EA
1310–1335	Kjeldskov, J., Stage, J.	Exploring 'canned communication' for coordinating mobile work activities	TA SD EA
1260–1277	Quayle, M., Durrheim, K.	When the chips are down: Social and technical aspects of computer failure and repair	TA SD EA
1215–1241	Fu, W-T., Bothell, D., Douglass, S., Haimson, C., Sohn, M-H., Anderson, J.	Toward a real-time model-based training system	LB TA EA
1186–1214	Scholtz, J., Morse, E., Steves, M. P.	Evaluation metrics and methodologies for user-centered evaluation of intelligent systems	TA EA
1170–1185	Eccles, D. W., Groth, P. T.	Agent coordination and communication in sociotechnological systems: Design and measurement issues	TA EA
1055–1069	Schrepp, M., Held, T., Laugwitz, B.	The influence of hedonic quality on the attractiveness of user interfaces of business management software	TA EA
956–976	Rodriguez, J., Diehl, J. C., Christiaans, H.	Gaining insight into unfamiliar contexts: A design toolbox as input for using role-play techniques	LB TA EA
891–909	Alty, J. L., Al-Sharrah, A., Beachham, N.	When humans form media and media form humans: An experimental examining the effects different digital media have on the learning outcomes of students who have different learning styles	LB TA EA
853–868	Garcia-Ruiz, M. A., Gutierrez-Pulido, J. R.	An overview of auditory display to assist comprehension of molecular information	LB EA
820–852	Shen, S-T., Woolley, M., Prior, S.	Toward a culture-centered design	LB EA

Interacting with Computers Article Analysis (2001–2006)
Year, Volume, Page Numbers, Authors, Title, Instructional Dimension

770–792	Hsu, Y-C.	The effects of metaphors on novice and expert learners' performance and mental-model development	LB EA
723–746	Kim, J., Kim, H., Park, K.	Toward optimal navigation through video content on interactive TV	TA IA EA
683–708	Ioannidou, I. A., Paraskevopoulos, S., Tzionas, P.	An interactive computer graphics interface for the introduction of fuzzy inference in environmental education	TA IA EA
665–682	Adler, A., Nash, J. C., Noël, S.	Evaluating and implementing a collaborative office document system	SD EA
556–567	Mills, S.	When humans need humans: The lack of use of computer-based ICT in distance pastoral care	IA EA
457–477	Kurniawan, S. H., King, A., Evans, D. G., Blenkhorn, P. L.	Personalising Web page presentation for older people	LB EA
432–456	van Setten, M., Veenstra, M., Nijholt, A., van Dijk, B.	Goal-based structuring in recommender systems	TA EA
410–431	Lekakos, G., Giaglis, G. M.	Improving the prediction accuracy of recommendation algorithms: Approaches anchored on human factors	LB EA
385–409	Kelly, D., Tangney, B.	Adapting to intelligence profile in an adaptive educational system	LB IA EA
356–384	Papanikolaou, K. A., Mabbott, A., Bull, S., Grigoriadou, M.	Designing learner-controlled educational interactions based on learning/cognitive style and learner behavior	LB TA IA EA
331–355	Wang, H-C., Li, T-Y., Chang, C-Y.	A Web-based tutoring system with styles-matching strategy for spatial geometric transformation	LB IA EA
265–282	Maes, A., van Geel, A., Cozljn, R.	Signposts on the digital highway: The effect of semantic and pragmatic hyperlink previews	TA IA EA
246–264	Norman, K. L., Panizzi, E.	Levels of automation and user participation in usability testing	TA EA
227–245	Hone, K.	Empathic agents to reduce user frustration: The effects of varying agent characteristics	LB IA EA

Interacting with Computers Article Analysis (2001–2006)
Year, Volume, Page Numbers, Authors, Title, Instructional Dimension

187–207	Lazar, J., Jones, A., Hackley, M., Shneiderman, B.	Severity and impact of computer user frustration: A comparison of student and workplace users	LB TA EA
47–70	Lindgaard, G., Dillon, R., Trbovich, P., White, R., Fernandes, G., Lundahl, S., Pinnamaneni, A.	User needs analysis and requirements engineering: Theory and practice	TA IA EA
21–46	Carroll, J. M., Rosson, M. B., Convertino, G., Ganoe, C. H.	Awareness and teamwork in computer-supported collaborations	SD IA EA
1–20	Détienne, F.	Collaborative design: Managing task interdependencies and multiple perspectives	SD IA EA

2005, 17

711–735	Bickmore, T. W., Caruso, L., Clough-Gorr, K., Heeren, T.	"It's just like you talk to a friend" relational agents for older adults	LB EA
660–671	Curzon, P., Wilson, J., Whitney, G.	Successful strategies of older people for finding information	LB TA EA
621–642	Dickinson, A., Newell, A. F., Smith, M. J., Hill, R. L.	Introducing the Internet to the over-60s: Developing an e-mail system for older novice computer users	LB EA
506–521	Markopoulos, P., IJsselsteijn, W., Huljnen, C., de Ruyter, B.	Sharing experiences through awareness systems in the home	SD EA
484–505	Abascal, J., Nicolle, C.	Moving toward inclusive design guidelines for socially and ethically aware HCI	LB EA
453–472	Evett, L., Brown, D.	Text formats and Web design for visually impaired and dyslexic readers—Clear text for all	LB EA
419–452	Sedig, K., Rowhani, S., Liang, H-N.	Designing interfaces that support formation of cognitive maps of transitional processes: An empirical study	TA IA EA
367–394	Hsu, Y-C.	The long-term effects of integral versus composite metaphors on experts' and novices' search behaviors	LB TA EA
317–341	de Souza, C. S.	Semiotic engineering: Bringing designers and users together at interaction time	LB TA EA
187–206	Käki, M., Aula, A.	Findex: Improving search result use through automatic filtering categories	TA EA

Interacting with Computers Article Analysis (2001–2006)
Year, Volume, Page Numbers, Authors, Title, Instructional Dimension

167–185	Faulkner, X., Culwin, F.	When fingers do the talking: A study of text messaging	TA EA
105–120	van der Velden, M.	Programming for cognitive justice: Toward and ethical framework for democratic code	LB EA
9–33	Kavanaugh, A., Carroll, J. M., Rosson, M. B., Reese, D. D., Zin, T. T.	Participating in civil society: The case of networked communities	LB SD EA

2004, 16

1133–1152	Rogers, Y., Lindley, S.	Collaborating around vertical and horizontal large interactive displays: Which way is best?	SDEA
1069–1094	Sanford, A., Anderson, A. H., Mullin, J.	Audio channel constraints in video-mediated communication	TA EA
989–1016	Zhou, Z., Cheok, A. D., Yang, X., Qui, Y.	An experimental study on the role of software synthesized 3D sound in augmented reality environments	LB TA EA
939–956	Sayers, H.	Desktop virtual environments: A study of navigation and age	LB TA EA
831–849	Sutcliff, A., Gault, B.	Heuristic evaluation of virtual reality applications	LB TA EA
799–829	Clemmensen, T.	Four approaches to user modeling—a qualitative research interview study of HCI professionals' practice	LB TA
769–797	Gwizdka, J., Chignell, M.	Individual differences and task-based user interface evaluation: A case study of pending tasks in e-mail	LB TA
657–681	Romero-Salcedo, M., Osuna-Gómez, C. A., Sheremetov, L., Villa, L., Morales, C., Rocha, L., Chi, M.	Study and analysis of workspace awareness in CDebate: A groupware application for collaborative debates	LB TA SD EA
635–656	de Souza, C. S., Nicolaci-da-Costa, A. M., da Silva, E. J., Prates, R. O.	Compulsory institutionalization: Investigating the paradox of computer-supported informal social processes	LB SD EA
615–633	Meira, L., Peres, F.	A dialog-based approach for evaluating educational software	TA EA
579–610	de Souza, C. S., Preece, J.	A framework for analyzing and understanding online communities	LB SD EA

Interacting with Computers Article Analysis (2001–2006)
Year, Volume, Page Numbers, Authors, Title, Instructional Dimension

557–578	Renshaw, J. A., Finlay, J. E., Tyfa, D., Ward, R. D.	Understanding visual influence in graph design through temporal and spatial eye movement characteristics	LB TA IA
507–521	Paddison, C., Englefield, P.	Applying heuristics to accessibility inspections	LB EA
411–430	Zajicek, M.	Successful and available: Interface design exemplars for older users	LB EA
403–410	Zajicek, M., Edwards, A.	Universal usability revisited	LB EA
377–401	Olsson, E.	What active users and designers contribute in the design process	LB TA
351–376	Park, S., Choi, D., Kim, J.	Critical factors for the aesthetic fidelity of Web pages: Empirical studies with professional Web designers and users	LB EA
295–309	Partala, T., Surakka, V.	The effects of affective interventions in human-computer interaction	LB EA
217–241	Oulasvirta, A.	Task demands and memory in Web interaction: A levels of processing approach	TA EA
183–215	Huart, J., Kolski, C., Sagar, M.	Evaluation of multimedia applications using inspection methods: The cognitive walkthrough case	TA EA
163–181	Rau, P-L. P., Chen, S-H., Chin, Y-T.	Developing Web annotation tools for learners and instructors	SD EA
115–132	Kabassi, K., Virvou, M.	Personalised adult e-training on computer use based on multiple attribute decision making	LB EA
93–113	Sillence, E., Baber, C.	Integrated digital communities: Combining Web-based interaction with text messaging to develop a system for encouraging group communication and competition	SD EA
63–91	Smith, A., Dunckley, L., French, T., Minocha, S., Chang, Y.	A process model for developing usable cross-cultural Websites	LB EA
45–62	Efendioglu, A. M., Yip, V. F.	Chinese culture and e-commerce: An exploratory study	LB EA
29–44	De Angeli, A., Athavankar, U., Joshi, A., Coventry, L., Johnson, G. I.	Introducing ATMs in India: A contextual inquiry	LB EA
7–27	Siala, H., O'Keefe, R. M., Hone, K. S.	The impact of religious affiliation on trust in the context of electronic commerce	LB EA

Interacting with Computers Article Analysis (2001–2006)
Year, Volume, Page Numbers, Authors, Title, Instructional Dimension

801–830	Decortis, F., Rizzo, A., Saudelli, B.	Mediating effects of active and distributed instruments on narrative activities	TA EA
783–800	Trouche, L.	From artifact to instrument: Mathematics teaching mediated by symbolic calculators	TA IA EA
759–781	Pargman, T. C., Waen, Y.	Appropriating the use of a Moo for collaborative learning	SD EA
737–757	Pargman, T. C.	Collaborating with writing tools: An instrumental perspective on the problem of computer-supported collaborative activities	SD EA
709–730	Béguin, P.	Design as a mutual learning process between users and designers	LB TA EA
693–707	Masino, G., Zamarian, M.	Information technology artifacts as structuring devices in organizations: Design, appropriation and use issues	SD EA
665–691	Rabardel, P., Bourmaud, G.	From computer to instrument system: A developmental perspective	TA EA
647–663	Folcher, V.	Appropriating artifacts as instruments: When design-for-use meets design-in-use	LB TA EA
577–602	Sutcliffe, A., Fickas, S., Sohlberg, M. M., Elhardt, L. A.	Investigating the usability of assistive user interfaces	LB TA EA
559–576	Lin, J., Laddaga, R., Naito, H.	Personal location agent for communicating entities (PLACE)	TA EA
479–495	Jones, M., Buchanan, G., Thimbleby, H.	Improving Web search on small screen devices	TA EA
429–452	Lindgaard, G., Dudek, C.	What is this evasive best we call user satisfaction?	LB TA EA
409–428	Rouet, J-F.	What was I looking for? The influence of task specificity and prior knowledge on students' search strategies in hypertext	LB TA
169–185	Price, S., Rogers, Y., Scaife, M., Stanton, D., Neale, H.	Using 'tangibles' to promote novel forms of playful learning	LB SD
109–119	Alm, I.	Designing interactive interfaces: Theoretical consideration of the complexity of standards and guidelines, and the difference between evolving and formalised systems	LB SD EA

Interacting with Computers Article Analysis (2001–2006)
Year, Volume, Page Numbers, Authors, Title, Instructional Dimension

91–107	Raybourn, E. M., Kings, N., Davies, J.	Adding cultural signposts in adaptive community-based virtual environments	LB SD EA
33–55	Lee, Y., Chong, Q.	Multi-agent systems support for community-based learning	LB SD EA

2002, 14–15

713–737	Sumi, Y., Mase, K.	Conference assistance system for supporting knowledge sharing in academic communities	TA SD EA
663–688	Stathis, K., de Bruijn, O., Macedo, S.	Living memory: Agent-based information management for connected local communities	TA SD EA
643–662	Beeson, I.	Exquisite variety: Computer as mirror to community	TA SD EA
601–618	Danielson, D. R.	Web navigation and the behavioral effects of constantly visible site maps	TA IA EA
575–599	Hertzum, M., Andersen, H. H. K., Andersen, V., Hansen, C. B.	Trust in information sources: Seeking information from people, documents, and virtual agents	LB IA EA
547–574	Elliott, G. J., Jones, E., Barker, P.	A grounded theory approach to modeling learnability of hypermedia authoring tools	LB IA EA
301–312	Burrell, J., Gay, G. K.	E-graffiti: Evaluating real-world use of a context-aware system	LB TA EA
271–299	Keates, S., Clarkson, P. J., Robinson, P.	Developing a practical inclusive interface design approach	LB EA
231–250	O'Hagan, R. G., Zelinsky, A., Rougeaux, S.	Visual gesture interfaces for virtual environments	TA EA
211–229	Thomas, B. H., Demczuk, V.	Which animation effects improve direct manipulation	LB TA EA
141–169	Picard, R. W., Klein, J.	Computers that recognize and respond to user emotion: Theoretical and practical implications	LB TA EA
119–140	Klein, J., Moon, Y., Picard, R. W.	This computer responds to user frustration: Theory, design, and results	LB TA EA

Interacting with Computers Article Analysis (2001–2006)
Year, Volume, Page Numbers, Authors, Title, Instructional Dimension

93–118	Scheirer, J., Fernandez, R., Klein, J., Picard, R. W.	Frustrating the user on purpose: A step toward building an affective computer	LB TA EA

2001, 13–14

15–29	Ahuja, J. S., Webster, J.	Perceived disorientation: An examination of a new measure to assess Web design effectiveness	LB TA EA
1–14	Turner, P., Turner, S.	A Web of contradictions	TA IA EA
695–716	Kohrs, A., Merialdo, B.	Creating user-adapted Websites by the use of collaborative filtering	LB EA
677–693	Ciancarini, P., Rossi, D., Vitali, F.	Designing a document-centric coordination application over the Internet	SD EA
655–676	Isenhour, P. L., Rosson, M. B., Carroll, J. M.	Supporting interactive collaboration on the Web with CORK	SD EA
631–654	Thomson, J. R., Greer, J., Cooke, J.	Automatic generation of instructional hypermedia with APHID	IA EA
549–580	Davis, S., Wiedenbeck, S.	The mediating effects of intrinsic motivation, ease of use and usefulness perceptions on performance in first-time and subsequent computer users	LB TA EA
527–548	Rodríguez, F. G., Silva, J. L. P., Rosano, F. L., Contreras, F. C., Vitela, A. I. M.	A student centered methodology for the development of a physics video based laboratory	TA IA EA
401–426	Phillips, P., Rodden, T.	Multi-authoring virtual worlds via the World Wide Web	EA
353–374	Pimentel, M. G. C., Ishiguro, Y., Kerimbaev, B., Abowd, G. D., Guzdial, M.	Supporting educational activities through dynamic Web interfaces	IA EA
325–351	Light, A., Wakeman, I.	Beyond the interface: Users' perceptions of interaction and audience on Websites	TA EA

Table F: *Adult Education Quarterly* Analysis (2002–2008)

Adult Education Quarterly Article Analysis (2002–2008) Year, Volume, Page Numbers, Authors, Title, Instructional Dimension			
2008, 58–59			
229–248	Eneau, J.	From autonomy to reciprocity, or visa versa? French personalism's contribution to a new perspective on self-directed learning	LB TA IA
61–82	Zembylas, M.	Engaging with issues of cultural diversity and discrimination through critical emotional reflexivity in online learning	LB IA EA
3–21	Chen, L-K., Kim, Y. S., Moon, P., Merriam, S. B.	A review and critique of the portrayal of older adult learners in adult education journals, 1980–2006	LB
2007, 57–58			
22–43	Kreber, C., Klampfleitner, M., McCune, V., Bayne, S., Knottenbelt, M.	What do you mean by "authentic"? A comparative review of the literature on conceptions of authenticity in teaching	TA IA
2006, 56–57			
26–45	Conceição, S. C. O.	Faculty lived experiences in the online environment	LB EA
308–322	Clark, M. A.	Adult education and disability studies, an interdisciplinary relationship: Research implications for adult education	LB IA
291–307	Taylor, E. W.	Making meaning of local nonformal education: Practitioner's perspective	IA
273–290	Dirkx, J. M.	Studying the complicated matter of what works: Evidence-based research and the problem of practice	IA
171–187	Nesbit, T.	What's the matter with social class?	LB IA
188–200	Harvey, B. J., Rothman, A. I., Frecker, R. C.	A confirmatory factor analysis of the ODDI Continuing Learning Inventory (OCLI)	LB SD

Adult Education Quarterly Article Analysis (2002–2008)
Year, Volume, Page Numbers, Authors, Title, Instructional Dimension

2005, 55–56

39–64	Ziegahn, L.	Critical reflection on cultural difference in the computer conference	SD EA
3–20	Kasworm, C.	Adult student identity in an intergenerational community college classroom	LB SD EA
269–287	Roberson Jr., D. N., Merriam, S. B.	The self-directed learning processes of older, rural adults	LB TA
200–219	Kotrlik, J. W., Redmann, D. H.	Extent of technology integration in instruction by adult basic education teachers	IA
182–199	Smith, R. O.	Working with difference in online collaborative groups	LB SD
116–128	Ponton, M. K., Derrick, M. G., Carr, P. B.	The relationship between resourcefulness and persistence in adult autonomous learning	LB TA

2004, 54–55

60–68	Merriam, S. B.	The role of cognitive development in Mezirow's transformational learning theory	LB TA
5–22	Cranton, P., Caruseta. E.	Perspectives on authenticity in teaching	LB IA
257–272	Birden, S.	Theorizing a coalition-engendered education: The case of the Boston women's health book collective's body education	SD IA
273–290	Suh Young Jang, Merriam, S.	Korean culture and the reentry motivations of university-graduate women	LB
174–192	Chang, W-W.	A cross-cultural case study of a multinational training program in the United States and Taiwan	LB IA
89–104	Sandlin, J. A.	"It's all up to you": How welfare-to-work educational programs construct workforce success	LB IA

2003, 53–54

277–293	Rager, K. B.	The self-directed learning of women with breast cancer	LB TA
81–98	Kasworm, C.	Adult meaning making in the undergraduate classroom	LB EA

Adult Education Quarterly Article Analysis (2002–2008)
Year, Volume, Page Numbers, Authors, Title, Instructional Dimension

2002, 52–53

27–43	Billett, S.	Toward a workplace pedagogy: Guidance, participation, and engagement	SD IA EA
281–298	Balatti, J., Falk, I.	Socioeconomic contributions of adult learning to community: A social capital perspective	LB SD EA
176–192	Yorks, L., Kasl, E.	Toward a theory and practice for whole-person learning: Reconceptualizing experience and the role of affect	LB SD
193–209	Drennon, C. E., Cervero, R. M.	The politics of facilitation in practitioner inquiry groups	SD IA
210–227	Rachal, J. R.	Andragogy's detectives: A critique of the present and a proposal for the future	LB IA
228–245	Brown, J. O.	Know thyself: The impact of portfolio development on adult learning	LB IA
140–154	Carney-Crompton, S., Tan, J.	Support systems, psychological functioning, and academic performance of nontraditional female students	LB SD EA

Table G: *Review of Higher Education* Analysis (1997–2008)

Review of Higher Education Article Analysis (1997–2008)
Year, Volume, Page Numbers, Authors, Title, Instructional Dimension

2008, 31–32

257–285	Locks, A. M., Hurtado, S., Bowman, N. A., Oseguera, L.	Extending notions of campus climate and diversity to students' transition to college	LB EA
185–207	Lindholm, J. A., Astin, H. S.	Spirituality and pedagogy: Faculty's spirituality and use of student-centered approaches to undergraduate teaching	LB IA

2007, 30–31

343–362	Cox, B. E., Orehovec, E.	Faculty–student interaction outside the classroom: A typology from a residential college	SD EA

Review of Higher Education Article Analysis (1997–2008)
Year, Volume, Page Numbers, Authors, Title, Instructional Dimension

2006, 29–30

| 425–450 | Pike, G. R., Kuh, G. D. | Relationships among structural diversity, informal peer interactions and perceptions of the campus environment | LB SD |

2005, 28–29

23–52	Perna, L. W.	The benefits of higher education: Sex, racial/ethnic, and socioeconomic group differences	LB
503–525	Zhao, C-M., Carini, R. M., Kuh, G. D.	Searching for the peach blossom Shangri-la: Student engagement of man and women SMET majors	LB
475–502	Ruban, L. M., McCoach, D. B.	Gender differences in explaining grades using structural equation modeling	LB
455–474	Hoffman, J. L., Lowitzki, K. E.	Predicting college success with high school grades and test scores: Limitations for minority students	LB
169–189	Olivas, M. A.	Higher education as "place": Location, race, and college attendance policies	LB EA

2004, 27–28

| 23–48 | Lattuca, L. R., Voigt, L. J., Fath, K. Q. | Does interdisciplinarity promote learning? Theoretical support and researchable questions | LB IA |
| 527–551 | Teranishi, R. T., Ceja, M., Antonio, A. L., Allen, W. R., McDonough, P. | The college-choice process for Asian pacific Americans: Ethnicity and socioeconomic class in context | LB |

2003, 26–27

| 119–144 | Austin, A. E. | Creating a bridge to the future: Preparing new faculty to face changing expectations in a shifting context | IA |

2002, 25–26

| 433–450 | Leppel | Similarities and differences in the college persistence of men and women | LB |

Review of Higher Education Article Analysis (1997–2008)
Year, Volume, Page Numbers, Authors, Title, Instructional Dimension

2001, 24–25

281–296	Fleming, J.	Who will succeed in college? When the SAT predicts black students' performance	LB TA
39–61	Toutkoushian, R. K., Smart, J. C.	Do institutional characteristics affect student gains from college?	LB
309–332	Kuh, G., D.; Hu, S.	The effects of student-faculty interaction in the 1990s	LB IA
219–235	Keller, G.	The new demographics of higher education	LB

2000, 23–24

469–490	Gates, G. S.	Teaching-related stress: The emotional management of faculty	IA
347–363	Cockrell, K. S., Caplow, J. A. H., Donaldson, J. F.	A context for learning: Collaborative groups in the problem-based learning environment	LB SD
299–318	Gatz, L. B., Hirt, J. B.	Academic and social integration in cyberspace: students and e-mail	LB SD
173–191	Colbeck, C. L., Cabrera, A. F., Terenzini, P. T.	Learning professional confidence: Linking teaching practices, students' self-perceptions, and gender	LB IA

1999, 22–23

367–390	Bella, M. L., Toutkoushian, R. K.	Faculty time allocations and research productivity: Gender, race and family effects	IA

1998, 21–22

151–165	Pascarella, E. T., Terenzini, P. T.	Studying college students in the 21st Century: Meeting new challenges	LB EA
115–135	Astin, A. W.	The changing American college student: Thirty-year trends, 1966–1996	LB EA
1–15	Bess, J. L.	Teaching well: Do you have to be schizophrenic?	IA

1997, 20–21

163–179	Kraemer, B. A.	The academic and social integrating of Hispanic students into college	LB SD

Table H: *Journal of Natural Resources and Life Sciences Education* **Analysis (1999–2008)**

Journal of Natural Resources and Life Sciences Education Article Analysis (1999–2008) Year, Volume, Page Numbers, Authors, Title, Instructional Dimension		
2008, 37		
63–68	Dai, J., Turgeon, A. J.	Loop-imbedded (non-linear) instruction modules: A novel delivery method for online learning	TA IA EA
8–13	Berzonsky, W. A., Richardson, K. D.	Referencing science: Teaching undergraduates to identify, validate, and utilize peer-reviewed online literature	LB TA IA
2007, 36		
139–146	Reuter, R.	Introductory soils online: An effective way to get online students in the field	IA EA
95–102	Motavalli, P. P., Patton, M. D., Miles, R. J.	Use of Web-based student extension publications to improve undergraduate student writing skills	TA IA
53–57	Helms, T. C., Doetkott, C.	An educational software for simulating the sample size of molecular marker experiments	TA EA
6–10	Helms, T. C., Doetkott, C.	Educational software for mapping quantitative trait loci (QTL)	TA EA
2006, 35		
174–182	Peterson, J., Launchbaugh, K., Pickering, M., Hollenhorst, S.	A comparison of computer-assisted instruction and field-based learning for youth rangeland education	LB TA IA
34–41	Speth, C. A., Lee, D. J., Hain, P. M.	Prioritizing improvements in Internet instruction based on learning styles and strategies	LB IA
2005, 34		
44–48	Mamo, M., Kettler, T., Husmann, D.	Learning style responses to online soil erosion lesson.	LB IA
13–16	McAndrews, G. M., Mullen, R. E., Chadwick, S. A.	Relationships among learning styles and motivation with computer-aided instruction in an agronomy course.	LB IA

Journal of Natural Resources and Life Sciences Education Article Analysis (1999–2008)
Year, Volume, Page Numbers, Authors, Title, Instructional Dimension

2004, 33			
106–110	Taraban, R. McKenney, C., Peffley, E., Applegarth, A.	Live specimens more effective than World Wide Web for learning plant material.	IA EA
102–105	Turgeon, A. J., Thompson, M. M.	Comparison of faculty workload in resident and distance environments: The case of a turfgrass management course.	IA EA
16–20	Riffell, S. K., Sibley, D. F.	Can hybrid course formats increase attendance in undergraduate environmental science courses.	LB EA
2003, 32			
52–56	Duke, J. M.	A Web-based interface for student peer review, problem-based learning, and peer pressure.	LB EA
2002, 31			
141–147	Gunn, R. L., Mohtar, R. H., Engel, B. A.	World Wide Web based soil and water quality modeling in undergraduate education.	IA EA
123–130	Sheppard, P. R.	Web-based tools for teaching dendrochronology.	EA
48–54	Popp, J. S., Annis, Jr., D. C., Keisling, T. C.	Using digital information technologies to provide Envirothon educational materials to contestants.	IA EA
16–19	Graves, A. R., Hess, T., Matthews, R. B., Stephens, W., Middleton, T.	Crop simulation models as tools in computer laboratory and classroom-based education.	EA
2001, 30			
97–103	Tan, S. C., Turgeon, A. J., Jonassen, D. H.	Develop critical thinking in group problem solving through computer-supported argumentation: A case study.	TA
9–13	Shoener, H. A., Turgeon, A. J.	Web-accessible learning resources: Learner-controlled versus instructor controlled.	LB IA

Journal of Natural Resources and Life Sciences Education Article Analysis (1999–2008)
Year, Volume, Page Numbers, Authors, Title, Instructional Dimension

2000, 29

149–154	Eick, M. J., Burgholzer, R. W.	Design and implementation of interactive online tutorials for introductory soil science courses.	IA
15–22	Jovanovic, N. Z., Annandale, J. G.	Soil water balance: A computer tool for teaching future irrigation managers.	EA
1–7	Wery, J., Lecoeur, J.	Learning crop physiology from the development of a crop simulation model.	LB EA

1999, 28

59–62	Hannaway, K. J., Hannaway, D. B., Shuler, P. E., Niess, M. L., Griffith, S., Fick, G. W., Allen, V. G.	World Wide Web curriculum design using national collaboration.	SD IA
53–56	Lippert, R. M., Plank, C. O.	Responses to first time use of Internet inservice training by agricultural extension agents.	IA EA

Notes

1 Everyday Learning

1. Beyond this list of Web 1.0 user experiences, we could also add Web 2.0 interactions with, for example, collaborative document, spreadsheet, database, and presentation applications such as Google Docs or Zoho or online social networking spaces such as Bebo, Delicious, Facebook, Flickr, LinkedIn, MySpace, Ning, Photobucket, Plaxo, Twitter, and YouTube (see Wikipedia's 2008 List of Social Networking Websites: http://en.wikipedia.org/wiki/List_of_social_networking _websites). Although some of these Web sites will no longer exist by the time this book goes to press, distributed communication environments and social operating systems are ineluctable technological realities. Global multimedia systems have become distributed interfaces and applications. For more specific information on key emerging technologies and trends, see EDUCAUSE Learning Initiative's (2008) *2008 Horizon Report* (Austin, TX: New Media Consortium, http://www .nmc.org/pdf/2008-Horizon-Report.pdf). Whenever possible, I will keep references to technology conceptual rather than specific to avoid dating the discussion and obscuring the larger issues of instruction and learning at hand.

2. On software built to predict future appearance based on current behaviors, see Knight's (2005b) "Mirror that reflects your future self" (NewScientist.com, February 2, available online: http://www.newscientist.com/article/mg18524856.200-mirror-that-reflects-your-future-self .html); and Lipson's (2007) "Hod Lipson Builds 'Self-Aware' Robots" (TED Talks, March, available online: http://www.ted.com/index.php/talks/hod_lipson_builds_self_aware_robots.html). On the design of emulative robots, see MIRROR, a three-year Information Society Technologies-funded project support by the Neuroinformatics for "living" artifacts Proactive Initiative, a project focused on building robots that "interpret actions performed by others" based on "a representation of the action during learning" and then imitates "complex behavior . . . based on this representation" (http://cordis.europa.eu/ictresults/index.cfm/section/news/tpl/article/ BrowsingType/Features/ID/73517; http://www.lira.dist.unige.it/projects/mirror/).

2 Learning Worlds

1. Tancer (2008), concluding that "we are what we click" (p. 203), shows how emerging analytics methods are being applied to how Internet users interact with approximately one million Web

sites across more than 150 industries, offering insights into complex user behaviors related to politics, pornography, pharmaceuticals, gambling, socializing, celebrities, market trends, individual phobias, and cultural fears, all search topics subject to their own particular seasonal fluctuations.

2. See Bousquet (2008) for a systematic and troubling account of how market-driven philosophies applied to higher educational institutions have resulted in the "casualization" and exploitation of a largely contingent instructional workforce (cf. Fish 2009).

3   Research Conversations

1. For an amusing insight into actual scientific practice and scientists' perspectives on the business of science, see Gilbert and Mulkay's (1984) *Opening Pandora's Box: A Sociological Analysis of Scientists' Discourse*. Gilbert and Mulkay (1984) capture the human side of a living "objectivist" in the following excerpt of an interview with a biochemist:

Everybody wants to put things in the third person. So they just say, "it was found that." If it's later shown that it was wrong, don't accept any responsibility. "It was found. I didn't say I believed it. It was found." So you sort of get away from yourself that way and make it sound like these things just fall down into your lab notebook and you report them like a historian. . . . Of course, everybody knows what's going on. You're saying, "I think." But when you go out on a limb, if you say "it was shown that" or "it was concluded" instead of "we conclude," it should be more objective. It sounds like you're taking yourself out of the decision and that you're trying to give a fair, objective view and that you are not getting personally involved. Personally, I'd like to see the first person come back. I slip into it once in a while. "We found." Even then I won't say "I." I'll say "we" even if it's a one-person paper. Can spread the blame if it's wrong [*laughs*]. (pp. 58–59)

4   Models of Instruction and Learning with Technology

1. Bereiter (2002) offers an insightful critique of strictly cognitive ("mind-as-container") or strictly social ("knowledge-outside-the-mind") perspectives toward learner "understanding," describing understanding as "the ghost in the taxonomy" (p. 94). The taxonomy Bereiter (2002) is referring to is Bloom's (1956) *Taxonomy of Educational Objectives* (produced by an American Educational Research Association-sponsored committee chaired by Bloom), but Bereiter could just as easily be criticizing any model of learning that moves learners through "levels" of understanding such as comprehension, application, analysis, synthesis, and evaluation (cf. Biggs's 1999 "identify, describe, analyze, theorize" hierarchy, p. 67). In these models, knowledge exists prior to the first level, comprehension, and all other levels represent alternative *uses* of that knowledge. To sidestep this critique, I have deliberately focused on information rather than knowledge. This allows us to include external resources as part of the repertoire of learners as well as take into account the situational exigencies that learners engage in while establishing how what they are learning will be applied.

2. Nickerson (2005) has documented the complex history of the slide rule, as well, both as an instrument that magnified human cognitive ability and as a technology influenced by conceptual, material, social, and economic historical developments. Wenzel's (1998–2009) "Museum of Pocket Calculating Devices" (http://www.calculators.de/) and Frolov's (1998–2009) Soviet Digital

Electronics Museum (http://rk86.com/frolov/calcolle.htm) provide thousands of historical images of calculators, reminding us that the range of interface possibilities for even technologies as rudimentary as calculators is potentially infinite. Finally, see Thimbleby's (2000) powerful critique of calculator design despite our well-structured understanding of arithmetic; and Trouche's (2003) exploration of the complex relationship between calculators, their use, and how learners understand in mathematics.

3. Bodemer et al. (2005) studied the interaction between technology and instruction by having 84 students in two groups work with static (hardcopy) and dynamic (computational) representations of a statistics problem. The static representations presented students with the problem prior to solution, after the solution, and in the process of being solved (active integration). Half the students then freely explored a data analysis application to work on the problem, and the other half were guided by structured hypothesis testing. Following student interaction with the representations, the authors tested the students for understanding in addition to collecting data on their interactions with the data analysis software while students talked aloud. Students provided with active integration performed significantly better on the post test with or without structured instruction during the use of the data analysis software. Structured instruction improved verbal understanding but not student retention. In a second experiment, the authors separated 48 students working on a mathematics problem into the two conditions and did not vary instructional support during the use of the data analysis application. In this case, textual and algebraic information were either presented with the representation or students were able to interactively integrate this additional information. Results suggested that having students interactively integrate addition instructional material enabled them to perform better on the post test. Clearly, instructional materials that support learner interaction with data are preferable to having students explore data unaided.

5 Designs for Learning

1. A separate book could be written on the data-collection approaches taken by usability researchers interested primarily in data for design's sake (cf. Genov 2005). Methods range from the strictly behavioral to highly social. Designers of instruction motivated to engage in learner-centered design efforts have a wide range of resources available to them. They can employ usability inspection methods, usability testing methods, or both. Common usability inspection methods include heuristic evaluations, guideline reviews and feature inspections, cognitive and pluralistic walk-throughs (Huart, Kolski, and Sagar 2004), consistency and standards inspections, formal usability inspections, and automated Web site evaluations. Information on how to generate a formal usability test report is summarized by Theofanos and Quesenbery (2005). Dumas and Redish (1993) and Rubin (1994) provide a pragmatic overview of usability testing in general. Usability testing of as few as five participants uncovers 80 percent of the severe usability problems (Dumas 2001c). Numerous researchers advocate the use of talk-aloud protocol data as a supplement to video data (cf. Card, Moran, and Newell 1983; Dumas 2001b; Mehlenbacher 1992; Newell and Simon 1972). Researchers have employed the method to construct models of writing (Hayes 1989; Hayes and Flower 1983; Swarts, Flower, and Hayes 1984), to study document creation (Odell, Goswami, and Herrington 1983), and to enhance the writing process (Hayes, Waterman, and

Robinson 1977). Other means of data collection include eye-tracking studies (Cooke 2005), tracking user-logs or analytics (Hahn 2003; Kantner 2001a,b; Sullivan and Lindgren 2006), surveying learners (Richardson 2004), focus groups (Kuhn 2000; Maughan 2003), remote usability testing (Perkins 2001), and participatory design (Spinuzzi 2005). The movement in learner-centered design and evaluation over the last decade (Quintana et al. 2006) has been away from strictly empirical data collection toward fully integrated design and formative evaluation, such as participatory design. These methods tend to highlight issues related to the quality of life of the users, codetermination, involvement, and consensus building, and continuous reflection in design. Field-based research of any type is notoriously difficult to perform and requires considerable experience on the part of the participant-observer (Francis 2004; Kaikkonen et al. 2005; Mitropoulos-Rundus and Muszak 2001). Finally, numerous researchers advocate the use of multiple data-collection techniques when testing the usability of a system in development, including competitive evaluation, talk-aloud protocols, audio- or videotaping, pre- and postinterviews emphasizing demographic and user satisfaction evaluations, focus groups, walk-throughs, and where possible, more elaborate feedback approaches such as beta-testing, guided interaction, natural user observation, and user-log reports (Darnell and Halgren 2001; Mehlenbacher 1993; Norman and Panizzi 2006; Selber, Johnson-Eilola, and Mehlenbacher 1997).

6   A Framework for Everyday Instructional Situations

1. The word "everyday" is used in the title of numerous books across subject matters and disciplines (see, e.g., Bird 2003; Goffman 1959; Haddon 2004; Lave 1988; Nippert-Eng 1995; Norman 1990, 2003; Roskelly and Jolliffe 2004; Silverstone 1994). Often "everyday" serves as an adjective for "life" or "things" (a quick search for "everyday" books using Amazon.com returns approximately 422,000 items, for "everyday life" 193,000, for "everyday things" more than 21,000 items, and for "everyday learning" 6,370 items). "Everyday" is also attractive for juxtaposing itself against subjects that we tend not to think about in everyday ways, such as mathematics, cognitive psychology, statistics, history, economics, rhetoric, medical anthropology, and physics.

2. Shneiderman's (2003) *Leonardo's Laptop: Human Needs and the New Computing Technologies* describes four stages of human activities using a framework that is similar to that of Bruce and Levin (1997), emphasizing how we collect, relate, create, and donate (or disseminate) ideas, products, and processes (Shneiderman 2003, pp. 84–86).

3. Of course research on what it means to find something interesting or engaging complicates rather than simplifies the intuitive appeal of this instructional goal. For instance, Langer (2000) describes a study in which she and a colleague asked subjects to rank how humorous cartoons were. For half the subjects, the activity was described as *work* and for the other half it was described as *play*. Interestingly, subjects reported not enjoying and having a difficult time focusing on the "work" activity. Langer (2000) concludes that something as simple as instructing learners to describe *new* features of common phenomenon rather than asking them to learn about the same phenomenon tends to heighten their engagement.

4. Slaughter (2000) graphically represents a compelling image of the numerous agencies and issues that contribute to the social construction of physics curricula (pp. 276–277). At the heart of her conceptualization is a professor and a student and, in growing complexity and surround-

ing that ideal dialectic are, for example, the classroom, discipline, department and college curriculum committees, university curriculum committee, university administration, professional associations, journals, American society committees, umbrella science organizations, government mission agencies, legislative governing funding, defense contractors, foundations, accrediting and testing associations, bridge groups, and corporate associates. Readers interested in beginning to parameterize the sociocultural elements that contribute to the institutional construct that is our contemporary classroom are encouraged to review the chapter.

References

Abbott, A. (2002). The disciplines and the future. In S. Brint (ed.), *The Future of the City of Intellect: The Changing American University* (pp. 205–230). Stanford, CA: Stanford University Press.

Accalogoun, I. B., Sunal, D. W., and Nichols, S. (2006). Enhancing elementary teachers' understanding of inquiry: Teaching and learning using online scientific discourse. In V. H. Wright, C. S. Sunal, and E. K. Wilson (eds.), *Research on Enhancing the Interactivity of Online Learning* (pp. 127–147). Greenwich, CT: Information Age Publishing.

Achtenhagen, F. (2003). Curriculum-embedded mastery learning as a tool for fostering transfer. In T. Tuomi-Gröhn and Y. Engeström (eds.), *Between School and Work: New Perspectives on Transfer and Boundary-Crossing* (pp. 139–156). Kidlington, Oxford: Elsevier Science.

Adams-Spink, G. (2005). Blind student "hears in colour." *BBC News,* February 14. Available online: http://news.bbc.co.uk/2/hi/technology/4257961.stm.

Adler, A., Nash, J. C., and Noël, S. (2006). Evaluating and implementing a collaborative office document system. *Interacting with Computers, 18*(4), 665–682.

Adler, P. S., and Winograd, T. A. (eds.) (1992). *Usability: Turning Technologies into Tools.* New York: Oxford University Press.

Agarwal, R., and Venkatesh, V. (2002). Assessing a firm's Web presence: A heuristic evaluation procedure for the measurement of usability. *Information Systems Research, 13*(2), 168–186.

Alexander, P. M. (2002). Teamwork, time, trust, and information. In P. Kotzé, L. Venter, and J. Barrow (eds.), *Proceedings of the 2002 Annual Research Conference of the South African Institute of Computer Scientists and Information Technologists on Enablement through Technology (SAICSIT'02)* (pp. 65–74). New York: ACM Press.

Allen, B. L. (1996). *Information Tasks: Toward a User-Centered Approach to Information Systems.* San Diego, CA: Academic Press.

Allen, B. S., Otto, R. G., and Hoffman, B. (2004). Media as lived environments: The ecological psychology of educational technology. In D. H. Jonassen (ed.), *Handbook of Research on Educational Communications and Technology* (2nd ed., pp. 215–241). Mahwah, NJ: Lawrence Erlbaum.

Allen, I. E., and Seaman, J. (2008). *Staying the course: Online education in the United States, 2008.* Needham, MA: Sloan-C. Available online: http://www.sloan-c.org/publications/survey/pdf/staying_the_course.pdf.

Allen, M., Bourhis, J., Burrell, N., and Mabry, E. (2002). Comparing student satisfaction with distance education to traditional classrooms in higher education: A meta-analysis. *American Journal of Distance Education, 16*(2), 83–97.

Allen, W. (1989). *Getting Even: Without Feathers, Getting Even, Side Effects.* New York: Quality Paperback.

Álvarez, I., and Kilbourn, B. (2002). Mapping the information society literature: Topics, perspectives, and root metaphors. *First Monday, 7*(1) Available online: http://firstmonday.org/htbin/cgiwrap/bin/ojs/index.php/fm/article/view/922/844.

Ancona, D. G., Okhuysen, G. A., and Perlow, L. A. (2001). Taking time to integrate temporal research. *Academy of Management Review, 26*(4), 512–529.

Anderson, J. R. (1995). *Learning and Memory: An Integrated Approach.* New York: Wiley.

Anderson, J. R., Bothell, D., Byrne, M. D., Douglass, S., Lebiere, C., and Qin, Y. (2004). An integrated theory of the mind. *Psychological Science, 3*(4), 1036–1060.

Anderson, J. R., Greeno, J. G., Reder, L. M., and Simon, H. A. (2000). Perspectives on learning, thinking, and activity. *Educational Researcher, 29*(4), 11–13.

Anderson, L. W., and Krathwohl, D. R. (2001). *A Taxonomy for Learning, Teaching, and Assessing.* Boston: Allyn and Bacon.

Anderson, T. (2003a). Getting the mix right again: An updated and theoretical rationale for interaction. *International Review of Research in Open and Distance Learning, 4*(2). Available online: http://www.irrodl.org/index.php/irrodl/article/view/149/230.

Anderson, T. (2003b). Modes of interaction in distance education: Recent developments and research questions. In M. G. Moore and W. G. Anderson (eds.), *Handbook of Distance Education* (pp. 129–144). Mahwah, NJ: Lawrence Erlbaum.

Anderson, T. (2004). Toward a theory of online learning. In T. Anderson and F. Elloumi (eds.), *Theory and Practice of Online Learning* (pp. 33–60). Athabasca, Alberta: Athabasca University. Available online: http://cde.athabascau.ca/online_book/ch2.html.

Anderson, T., Rourke, L., Garrison, D. R., and Archer, W. (2001). Assessing teaching presence in a computer conferencing context. *Journal of Asynchronous Learning Networks, 5*(2), 1–17.

Andrews, C. (2006). *Slow Is Beautiful: New Visions of Community, Leisure, and Joie de vivre.* Gabriola Island, British Columbia: New Society Publishers.

Andrews, P. (1999). *How the Web Was Won: Microsoft from Windows to the Web: The Inside Story of How Bill Gates and His Band of Internet Idealists Transformed a Software Empire.* New York: Broadway.

Angervall, P., and Thång, P.-O. (2003). Learning in working life—from theory to practice. In T. Tuomi-Gröhn and Y. Engeström (eds.), *Between School and Work: New Perspectives on Transfer and Boundary-Crossing* (pp. 257–270). Kidlington, Oxford: Elsevier Science.

Anson, C. M. (1999). Distant voices: Teaching and writing in a culture of technology. *College English, 61*(3), 261–280.

Antonietti, A., Ignazi, S., and Perego, P. (2000). Metacognitive knowledge about problem-solving methods. *British Journal of Educational Psychology, 70*(1), 1–16.

Arbaugh, J. B. (2004). Learning to learn online: A study of perceptual changes between multiple online course experiences. *Internet and Higher Education, 7*(3), 169–182.

Arbaugh, J. B., and Hiltz, S. R. (2005). Improving quantitative research on ALN effectiveness. In S. R. Hiltz and R. Goldman (eds.), *Learning Together Online: Research on Asynchronous Learning Networks* (pp. 81–102). Mahwah, NJ: Lawrence Erlbaum.

Aristotle (1926). *"Art" of Rhetoric*. J. H. Freese (trans.). Loeb Classical Library. Cambridge, MA: Harvard University Press.

Arnold, P., and Smith, J. D. (2003). Adding connectivity and losing context with ICT: Contrasting learning situations from a community of practice perspective. In M. Huysman, E. Wenger, and V. Wulf (eds.), *Communities and Technologies* (pp. 465–484). Boston: Kluwer Academic Publishers.

Arrow, H., Poole, M. S., Henry, K. B., Wheelan, S., and Moreland, R. (2004). Time, change, and development: The temporal perspective on groups. *Small Group Research, 35*(1), 73–105.

Asaolu, O. S. (2006). On the emergence of new computer technologies. *Educational Technology and Society, 9*(1), 335–343.

Association of College and Research Libraries (ACRL). (2000). *Information Literacy Competency Standards for Higher Education*. Available online: http://www.ala.org/ala/mgrps/divs/acrl/standards/informationliteracycompetency.cfm.

Astin, A. W. (1998). The changing American college student: Thirty-year trends, 1966–1996. *Review of Higher Education, 21*(2), 115–135.

Astleitner, H., and Steinberg, R. (2005). Are there gender differences in Web-based learning? An integrated model and related effect sizes. *AACE Journal, 13*(1), 47–63.

Atkinson, R. K., Derry, S. J., Renkl, A., and Wortham, D. (2000). Learning from examples: Instructional principles from the worked examples research. *Review of Educational Research, 70*(2), 181–214.

Austin, A. E. (2003). Creating a bridge to the future: Preparing new faculty to face changing expectations in a shifting context. *Review of Higher Education, 26*(2), 119–144.

Avital, M. (2000). Dealing with time in social inquiry: A tension between method and lived experience. *Organization Science, 11*(6), 665–673.

Ayres, P., and Sweller, J. (2005). The split-attention principle in multimedia learning. In R. E. Mayer (ed.), *The Cambridge Handbook of Multimedia Learning* (pp. 135–146). Cambridge: Cambridge University Press.

Ba, H., Tally, W., and Tsikalas, K. (2002). Investigating children's emerging digital literacies. *Journal of Technology, Learning and Assessment,* 1(4), 4–48. Available online: http://escholarship .bc.edu/jtla/vol1/4/.

Babbie, E. R. (1973). *Survey Research Methods.* Belmont, CA: Wadsworth.

Babbie, E. R. (1975). *The Practice of Social Research.* Belmont, CA: Wadsworth.

babynamewizard.com. (2004–2005). *The Baby Name Wizard's NameVoyager.* Available online: http://www.babynamewizard.com/voyager

Bachelard, G. (1958). *The Poetics of Space.* M. Jolas (trans.). Boston: Beacon Press.

Backer, P. R., and Saltmarch, M. (2000). Getting on board with multimedia and Internet training. In P. Hoffman and D. Lemke (eds.), *Teaching and Learning in a Networked World* (pp. 1–6). Washington, D.C.: IOS Press.

Baecker, R., Booth, K., Jovicic, S., McGrenere, J., and Moore, G. (2000). Reducing the gap between what users know and what they need to know. In J. Thomas (ed.), *ACM Conference on Universal Usability* (pp. 17–23). New York: ACM Press.

Bahri, D., and Petraglia, J. (2003). Traveling among the realms: A tale of big rhetoric and growing ambitions. In J. Petraglia and D. Bahri (eds.), *The Realms of Rhetoric: The Prospects for Rhetoric Education* (pp. 1–10). New York: SUNY Press.

Bain, J. D., McNaught, C., Mills, C., and Lueckenhausen, G. (1998). Describing computer-facilitated learning environments in higher education. *Learning Environments Research,* 1(2), 163–180.

Bainbridge, L. (1999). Verbal reports as evidence of the process operator's knowledge. *International Journal of Human-Computer Studies,* 51(2), 213–238.

Baker, L., Scher, D., and Mackler, K. (1997). Home and family influences on motivations for reading. *Educational Psychologist,* 32(2), 69–82.

Ball, M. S., and Smith, G. W. H. (1992). *Analysing Visual Data.* London: Sage.

Banks, M. A. (2008). *On the Way to the Web: The Secret History of the Internet and Its Founders.* Berkeley, CA: Apress.

Barab, S. A., Evans, M. A., and Baek, E.-O. (2004). Activity theory as a lens for characterizing the participatory unit. In D. H. Jonassen (ed.), *Handbook of Research on Educational Communications and Technology* (2nd ed., pp. 199–214). Mahwah, NJ: Lawrence Erlbaum.

Barab, S. A., and Plucker, J. A. (2002). Smart people or smart contexts? Cognition, ability, and talent development in an age of situated approaches to knowing and learning. *Educational Psychologist,* 37(3), 165–182.

Barab, S. A., and Roth, W.-M. (2006). Curriculum-based ecosystems: Supporting knowing from an ecological perspective. *Educational Researcher, 35*(5), 3–13.

Barab, S. A., and Squire, K. (2004). Design-based research: Putting a stake in the ground. *Journal of the Learning Sciences, 13*(1), 1–14.

Barber, B. R. (1995). *Jihad vs. MacWorld.* New York: Random House.

Bargh, J. A., and Chartrand, T. L. (1999). The unbearable automaticity of being. *American Psychologist, 54*(7), 462–479.

Barker, T. T. (1998). *Writing Software Documentation: A Task-Oriented Approach.* Needham Heights, MA: Allyn and Bacon.

Barnett, M. (1998). Testing a digital library of technical manuals. *IEEE Transactions on Professional Communication, 41*(2), 116–122.

Barney, D., and Gordon, A. (2005). Education and citizenship in the digital age. *Techné: Research in Philosophy and Technology, 9*(1), 1–7.

Barron, A. (1998). Designing Web-based training. *British Journal of Educational Technology, 29*(4), 355–370.

Bartholomew, K. (2004). Computer literacy: Is the emperor still exposed after all these years? *Journal of Computing Sciences in Colleges, 20*(1), 323–331.

Bastiaens, T. J., and Martens, R. L. (2000). Conditions for Web-based learning with real events. In B. Abbey (ed.), *Instructional and Cognitive Impacts of Web-Based Education* (pp. 1–31). Hershey, PA: Idea Group Publishing.

Bates, A. W., and Poole, G. (2003). *Effective Teaching with Technology in Higher Education: Foundations for Success.* San Francisco, CA: Jossey-Bass.

Bazerman, C. (1988). *Shaping Written Knowledge: The Genre and Activity of the Experimental Article in Science.* Madison, WI: University of Wisconsin Press.

Bazerman, C., and Paradis, J. (eds.) (1991). *Textual Dynamics of the Professions: Historical and Contemporary Studies of Writing in Professional Communities.* Madison, WI: University of Wisconsin Press.

Beabes, M. A., and Flanders, A. (1995). Experiences with using contextual inquiry to design information. *Technical Communication, 42*(3), 409–420.

Beale, R. (2005). Information fragments for a pervasive world. In S. Tilley and R. M. Newman (eds.), *SIGDOC'05: Proceedings of the 23rd Annual International Conference on Design of Communication* (pp. 48–53). New York: ACM Press.

Bearman, M., Cesnik, B., and Liddell, M. (2001). Random comparison of "virtual patient" models in the context of teaching clinical communication skills. *Medical Education, 35*(9), 824–832.

Becker, G. S. (1965). A theory of the allocation of time. *Economic Journal, 75*(299), 493–517.

Begole, J., Tang, J. C., Smith, R. S., and Yankelovich, N. (2002). Work rhythms: Analyzing visualizations of awareness histories of distributed groups. In E. F. Churchill, J. McCarthy, C. Neuwirth, and T. Rodden (eds.), *CSCW'02: Proceedings of the 2002 ACM Conference on Computer Supported Cooperative Work* (pp. 334–343). New York: ACM Press.

Bell, P. (2000). Scientific arguments as learning artifacts: Designing for learning from the Web with KIE. *International Journal of Science Education, 22*(8), 797–817.

Benbunan-Fich, R., Hiltz, S. R., and Harasim, L. (2005). The online interaction learning model: An integrated theoretical framework for learning networks. In S. R. Hiltz and R. Goldman (eds.), *Learning Together Online: Research on Asynchronous Learning Networks* (pp. 19–37). Mahwah, NJ: Lawrence Erlbaum.

Benjamin, D. (2007). Ease-of-use crisis: Designers or "feature creeps"? *EETimes*, April 5. Available online: http://www.eetimes.com/news/latest/showArticle.jhtml;jsessionid =02XDVJB24WIKQQSNDLOSKHSCJUNN2JVN?articleID=198800518.

Bennett, R. E. (2002). Inexorable and inevitable: The continuing story of technology and assessment. *Journal of Technology, Learning, and Assessment, 1*(1), 1–23. Available online: http://escholarship.bc.edu/jtla/vol1/1/.

Benson, L., Elliot, D., Grant, M., Holschuh, D., Kim, B., Kim, H., Lauber, E., Loh, S., and Reeves, T. C. (2002). Usability and instructional design heuristics for e-learning evaluation. In P. Barker and S. A. Rebelsky (eds.), *ED-MEDIA 2002: Proceedings of the World Conference on Educational Multimedia, Hypermedia and Telecommunications*. Chesapeake, VA: Association for the Advancement of Computing in Education.

Benyon, D., Stone, D., and Woodroffe, M. (1997). Experience with developing multimedia courseware for the World Wide Web: The need for better tools and clear pedagogy. *International Journal of Human-Computer Studies, 47*(1), 197–218.

Benyon, D., Turner, P., and Turner, S. (2005). *Designing Interactive Systems: People, Activities, Contexts, Technologies*. Essex: Pearson Education.

Bereiter, C. (1994). Implications of postmodernism for science, or, science as progressive discourse. *Educational Psychologist, 29*(1), 3–12.

Bereiter, C. (2002). *Education and Mind in the Knowledge Age*. Mahwah, NJ: Lawrence Erlbaum.

Berge, Z. L. (2003). Planning and managing distance training and education in the corporate sector. In M. G. Moore and W. G. Anderson (eds.), *Handbook of Distance Education* (pp. 601–613). Mahwah, NJ: Lawrence Erlbaum.

Berge, Z. L., and Mrozowski, S. (2001). Review of research in distance education, 1990 to 1999. *American Journal of Distance Education, 15*(3), 5–19.

Berggren, A., Burgos, D., Fontana, J. M., Hinkelman, D., Hung, V., Hursh, A., and Tielemans, G. (2005). Practical and pedagogical issues for teacher adoption of IMS learning design standards in Moodle LMS. *Journal of Interactive Media in Education, 2*, 1–24. Available online: http://www-jime.open.ac.uk/2005/02/berggren-2005-02.pdf.

Berlin, J. (1987). *Rhetoric and Reality: Writing Instruction in American Colleges, 1900–1985*. Carbondale, IL: Southern Illinois University Press.

Bernard, R. M., Abrami, P. C., Lou, Y., and Borokhovski, E. (2004a). A methodological morass? How can we improve quantitative research in distance education. *Distance Education, 25*(2), 175–198.

Bernard, R. M., Abrami, P. C., Lou, Y., Borokhovski, E., Wade, A., Wozney, L., Wallet, P. A., Fiset, M., and Huang, B. (2004b). How does distance education compare with classroom instruction? A meta-analysis of the empirical literature. *Review of Educational Research, 74*(3), 379–439.

Bernhardt, S. A. (1993). The shape of text to come: The texture of print on screens. *College Composition and Communication, 44*(2), 151–175.

Bernhardt, S. A., Wojahn, P. G., and Edwards, P. R. (1990). Teaching college composition with computers: A time observation study. *Written Communication, 7*(3), 342–374.

Berninger, V. W., and Richards, T. L. (2002). *Brain Literacy for Educators and Psychologists*. San Diego, CA: Academic Press.

Bersin, J. (2004). *The Blended Learning Book: Best Practices, Proven Methodologies, and Lessons Learned*. San Francisco, CA: Pfeiffer.

Bersin, J. (2006). E-Learning evolves into mature training tool. *T+D*, April, 20.

Bess, J. L. (1998). Teaching well: Do you have to be schizophrenic? *Review of Higher Education, 22*(1), 1–15.

Betrancourt, M. (2005). The animation and interactivity principles in multimedia learning. In R. E. Mayer (ed.), *The Cambridge Handbook of Multimedia Learning* (pp. 287–296). Cambridge: Cambridge University Press.

Bevan, N. (1998). *Usability Issues in Web Site Design: Proceedings of Usability Professionals' Association*. Washington, D.C.: Usability Professionals' Association.

Bias, R. G., and Mayhew, D. J. (eds.) (1994). *Cost-Justifying Usability*. Boston: Academic Press.

Biggs, J. (1999). What the student does: Teaching for enhanced learning. *Higher Education Research and Development, 18*(1), 57–75.

Biggs, J. (2003). *Teaching for Quality Learning at University: What the Student Does*. Buckingham: Society for Research into Higher Education and Open University Press.

Biggs, J. B., and Collis, K. F. (1982). *Evaluating the Quality of Learning: The SOLO Taxonomy*. New York: Academic Press.

Biggs, J., Kember, D., and Leung, Y. P. (2001). The revised two-factor study process questionnaire: R-SPQ-2F. *British Journal of Educational Psychology, 71*(1), 133–149.

Bird, S. E. (2003). *The Audience in Everyday Life: Living in the Media World*. London: Taylor and Francis.

Birkerts, S. (1994). *The Gutenberg Elegies: The Fate of Reading in an Electronic Age*. Boston: Faber and Faber.

Bitzer, L. F. (1968). The rhetorical situation. *Philosophy and Rhetoric, 1*, 1–14.

Black, P., and William, D. (2006). Developing a theory of formative assessment. In J. Gardner (ed.), *Assessment and learning* (pp. 81–100). Thousand Oaks, CA: Sage.

Blair, J. A. (2004). The rhetoric of visual arguments. In C. A. Hill and M. Helmers (eds.), *Defining Visual Rhetorics* (pp. 41–61). Mahwah, NJ: Lawrence Erlbaum.

Bleich, D. (2003). The materiality of rhetoric, the subject of language use. In J. Petraglia and D. Bahri (eds.), *The Realms of Rhetoric: The Prospects for Rhetoric Education* (pp. 39–60). New York: SUNY Press.

Bloom, B. S. (ed.). (1956). *Taxonomy of Educational Objectives: Handbook 1. Cognitive Domain*. New York: McKay.

Bloom, B. S. (1976). *Human Characteristics and School Learning*. New York: McGraw-Hill.

Bluedorn, A. C. (2002). *The Human Organization of Time: Temporal Realities and Experience*. Stanford, CA: Stanford University Press.

Blythe, M. A., Overbeeke, K., Monk, A. F., and Wright, P. C. (2003). *Funology: From Usability to Enjoyment*. Boston: Kluwer Academic Publishers.

Bodemer, D., Ploetzner, R., Bruchmüller, K., and Hacker, S. (2005). Supporting learning with interactive multimedia through active integration of representations. *Instructional Science, 33*(1), 73–95.

Bødker, S. (1991). *Through the Interface: A Human Activity Approach to User Interface Design*. Hillsdale, NJ: Lawrence Erlbaum.

Bogin, B. (2001). *The Growth of Humanity*. New York: Wiley-Liss.

Boisvert, R. (2006). Publications board report. Association for Computing Machinery Special Interest Group Board Meeting. Chicago: ACM Press.

Bonk, C. J., and Cummings, J. A. (1998). A dozen recommendations for placing the student at the center of Web-based learning. *Educational Media International, 35*(2), 82–89.

Bonk, C. J., and Dennen, V. (2003). Frameworks for research, design, benchmarks, training, and pedagogy in Web-based distance education. In M. G. Moore and W. G. Anderson (eds.), *Handbook of Distance Education* (pp. 331–348). Mahwah, NJ: Lawrence Erlbaum.

Bonk, C. J., Wisher, R. A., and Champagne, M. V. (2007). Toward a comprehensive model of E-Learning evaluation: The components. In B. H. Khan (ed.), *Flexible Learning in an Information Society* (pp. 260–271). Hershey, PA: Idea Group.

Boote, D. N., and Beile, P. (2005). Scholars before researchers: On the centrality of dissertation literature review in research preparation. *Educational Researcher, 34*(6), 3–15.

Booth, W. C. (2003). Seriously considering rhetoric education. In J. Petraglia and D. Bahri (eds.), *The Realms of Rhetoric: The Prospects for Rhetoric Education* (pp. vii–ix). New York: SUNY Press.

Borgmann, A. (1995). The depth of design. In R. Buchanan and V. Margolin (eds.), *Discovering Design: Explorations in Design Studies* (pp. 13–22). Chicago: University of Chicago Press.

Borgmann, A. (2000). *Holding on to Reality: The Nature of Information at the Turn of the Millennium.* Chicago: University of Chicago Press.

Botkin, J., and Kaipa, P. (2004). Putting it all together: A business perspective on Web-based learning. In T. M. Duffy and J. R. Kirkley (eds.), *Learner-Centered Theory and Practice in Distance Education: Cases from Higher Education* (pp. 409–423). Mahwah, NJ: Lawrence Erlbaum.

Bousquet, M. (2008). *How the University Works: Higher Education and the Low-Wage Nation.* New York: NYU Press.

Bowden, S., and Offer, A. (1994). Household appliances and the use of time: The United States and Britain since the 1920s. *Economic History Review, 47*(4), 725–748.

Bowker, G. C., and Star, S. L. (1999). *Sorting Things Out: Classification and Its Consequences.* Cambridge, MA: MIT Press.

Boy, G. (1992). Computer integrated documentation. In E. Barrett (ed.), *Sociomedia* (pp. 507–532). Cambridge, MA: MIT Press.

Boyd, D. M., and Ellison, N. B. (2007). Social network sites: Definition, history, and scholarship. *Journal of Computer-Mediated Communication, 13*(1), article 11. Available online: http://jcmc .indiana.edu/vol13/issue1/boyd.ellison.html

Branaghan, R. (2001). From ease of use to experience design. In R. J. Branaghan (ed.), *Design by People for People: Essays on Usability* (pp. 35–39). Chicago: Usability Professionals' Association.

Brand, S. (1987). *The Media Lab: Inventing the Future at MIT.* New York: Viking.

Branden, N. (1994). *The Six Pillars of Self-Esteem.* New York: Bantam.

Brandt, D. (2005). Writing for a living: Literacy and the knowledge economy. *Written Communication, 22*(2), 166–197.

Bransford, J. D., Barron, B., Pea, R. D., Meltzoff, A., Kuhl, P., Bell, P., Stevens, R., Schwartz, D. L., Vye, N., Reeves, B., Roschelle, J., and Sabellie, N. H. (2006). Foundations and opportunities for an interdisciplinary science of learning. In R. K. Sawyer (ed.), *The Cambridge Handbook of the Learning Sciences* (pp. 19–34). Cambridge: Cambridge University Press.

Bransford, J., Brown, A. L., Cocking, R. R., and National Research Council (2000). *How People Learn: Brain, Mind, Experience, and School.* Washington, D.C.: National Academy Press.

Bransford, J., Vye, N., Bateman, H., Brophy, S., and Roselli, B. (2004). Vanderbilt's AMIGO project: Knowledge of how people learn enters cyberspace. In T. M. Duffy and J. R. Kirkley (eds.), *Learner-Centered Theory and Practice in Distance Education: Cases from Higher Education* (pp. 209–234). Mahwah, NJ: Lawrence Erlbaum.

Bredo, E. (1994). Reconstructing educational psychology: Situated cognition and Deweyian pragmatism. *Educational Psychologist, 29*(1), 23–35.

Brenner, M., Brown, J., and Canter, D. (eds.) (1985). *The Research Interview: Uses and Approaches.* New York: Academic Press.

Brewer, W. (1987). Schemas versus mental models in human memory. In I. P. Morris (ed.), *Modelling Cognition* (pp. 187–197). London: John Wiley.

Brewster, S. (2003). Nonspeech auditory output. In A. Sears and J. Jacko (eds.), *The Human–Computer Interaction Handbook: Fundamentals, Evolving Technologies and Emerging Applications* (pp. 220–239). Mahwah, NJ: Lawrence Erlbaum.

Broadfoot, P., and Black, P. (2004). Redefining assessment? The first ten years of *Assessment in Education. Assessment in Education: Principles, Policy, and Practice, 11*(1), 7–26.

Brockmann, R. J. (1990). The why, where, and how of minimalism. In J. R. Talburt (ed.), *SIGDOC'90: Proceedings of the 8th Annual International Conference on Systems Documentation* (pp. 111–119). New York: ACM Press.

Brockmann, R. J. (1998). *From Millwrights to Shipwrights to the Twenty-First Century: Explorations in a History of Technical Communication in the United States.* Cresskill, NJ: Hampton Press.

Brooks, D. (2001). Time to do everything except think. *Newsweek, 137*(18), April 30, 71.

Brown, A. L. (1992). Design experiments: Theoretical and methodological challenges in creating complex interventions in classroom settings. *Journal of the Learning Sciences, 2*(2), 141–178.

Brown, A. L., Ash, D., Rutherford, M., Nakagawa, K., Gordon, A., and Campione, J. C. (1993). Distributed expertise in the classroom. In G. Salomon (ed.), *Distributed Cognition: Psychological and Educational Considerations* (pp. 188–228). Cambridge: Cambridge University Press.

Brown, B. A. T., and Perry, M. (2000). Why don't telephones have off switches? Understanding the use of everyday technologies: A research note. *Interacting with Computers, 12*(6), 623–634.

Brown, G. (2000). Where do we go from here? *Technology Source,* January/February. Available online: http://technologysource.org/article/where_do_we_go_from_here/.

Brown, G., and Wack, M. (1999). The difference frenzy and matching buckshot with buckshot. *Technology Source,* May/June. Available online: http://technologysource.org/article/difference_frenzy_and_matching_buckshot_with_buckshot/.

Brown, J. S. (1999). Learning, working, and playing in the digital age. Paper delivered at the 1999 Conference on Higher Education of the American Association for Higher Education. Washington, D.C.: AAHE. Available online: http://serendip.brynmawr.edu/sci_edu/seelybrown/.

Brown, J. S. (2000). Look-closely-right-now. *Forbes,* October 2. Available online: http://www.forbes.com/asap/2000/1002/026.html.

Brown, J. S. (2002a). Growing up digital: How the Web changes work, education, and the ways people learn. *USDLA Journal*, *16*(2). Available online: http://www.usdla.org/html/journal/FEB02 _Issue/article01.html.

Brown, J. S. (2002b). The social life of learning: How can continuing education be reconfigured in the future? *Continuing Higher Education Review*, *66*, 50–69.

Brown, J. S., and Duguid, P. (2000). *The Social Life of Information*. Boston: Harvard Business Publishing.

Brown, J., and Canter, D. (1985). The uses of explanation in the research interview. In M. Brenner, J. Brown, and D. Canter (eds.), *The Research Interview: Uses and Approaches* (pp. 217–245). New York: Academic Press.

Brown, R. A. J., and Renshaw, P. D. (2000). Collective argumentation: A sociocultural approach to reframing classroom teaching and learning. In H. Cowie and G. M. van der Aalsvoort (eds.), *Social interaction in Learning and Instruction: The Meaning of Discourse for the Construction of Knowledge* (pp. 53–66). Kidlington, Oxford: Elsevier Science.

Bruce, B. C., and Levin, J. A. (1997). Educational technology: Media for inquiry, communication, construction, and expression. *Journal of Educational Computing Research*, *17*(1), 79–102.

Bruner, J. S. (1966). *Toward a Theory of Instruction*. Cambridge, MA: Harvard University Press.

Bruss, M., Albers, M. J., and McNamera, D. (2004). Changes in scientific articles over two hundred years: A Coh-metrix analysis. In S. Tilley and S. Huang (eds.), *SIGDOC'04: Proceedings of the 22nd Annual International Conference on Design of Communication* (pp. 104–109). New York: ACM Press, 104–109.

Bryant, S. M., Kahle, J. B., and Schafer, B. A. (2005). Distance education: A review of the contemporary literature. *Issues in Accounting Education*, *20*(3), 255–272.

Buchanan, R. (1992). Wicked problems in design thinking. *Design Issues*, *8*(2), 5–21.

Buchanan, R. (1995). Rhetoric, humanism, and design. In R. Buchanan and V. Margolin (eds.), *Discovering Design: Explorations in Design Studies* (pp. 23–66). Chicago: University of Chicago Press.

Buchanan, R. (2001). Design and the new rhetoric: Productive arts in the philosophy of culture. *Philosophy and Rhetoric*, *34*(3), 183–206.

Buchanan, R., and Margolin, V. (eds.) (1995). *Discovering Design: Explorations in Design Studies*. Chicago: University of Chicago Press.

Bugeja, M. J. (2007). Distractions in the wireless classroom. *Chronicle of Higher Education*, Chronicle Careers, January 26. Available online: http://chronicle.com/jobs/news/2007/01/ 2007012601c.htm.

Bull, G., Knezek, G., Roblyer, M. D., Schrum, L., and Thompson, A. (2005). A proactive approach to a research agenda for educational technology. *Journal of Research on Technology in Education*, *37*(3), 217–220.

Bullen, C. V., and Bennett, J. L. (1991). Groupware in practice: An interpretation of work experiences. In C. Dunlop and R. Kling (eds.), *Computerization and Controversy: Value Conflicts and Social Choices* (pp. 257–287). New York: Academic Press.

Burbules, N. C. (2004). Rethinking the virtual. *E-Learning, 1*(2), 162–183.

Bureau of Labor Statistics (2005). Computer and Internet use at work summary. *Economic News Release.* Washington, D.C.: U.S. Department of Labor. Available online: http://www.bls.gov/news .release/ciuaw.nr0.htm.

Bures, E. M., Abrami, P. C., and Amundsen, C. (2000). Student motivation to learn via computer conferencing. *Research in Higher Education, 41*(5), 593–621.

Burgelman, J. C. (2000). Traveling with communication technologies in space, time, and everyday life: An exploration of their impact. *First Monday, 5*(3). Available online: http://firstmonday .org/htbin/cgiwrap/bin/ojs/index.php/fm/article/view/733/642.

Burgess, L. A. (2003). WebCT as an e-learning tool: A study of technology students' perceptions. *Journal of Technology Education, 15*(1), 6–15.

Burke, K. (1941). *The Philosophy of Literary Form.* Berkeley, CA: University of California Press.

Burke, K. (1966). *Language as Symbolic Action.* Berkeley, CA: University of California Press.

Burke, K. (1969). *A Grammar of Motives.* Berkeley, CA: University of California Press.

Burkhardt, G., Monsour, M., Valdez, G., Gunn, C., Dawson, M., Lemke, C., Coughlin, E., Thadani, V., and Martin, C. (2003). *enGauge 21st Century Skills: Literacy in the Digital Age.* Naperville, IL: North Central Regional Educational Laboratory (NCREL) and the Metiri Group. Available online: http://www.grrec.ky.gov/SLC_grant/engauge21st_Century_Skills.pdf.

Burns, C. M., and Hajdukiewicz, J. R. (2004). *Ecological Interface Design.* Boca Raton, FL: CRC Press.

Burton, J. K., Moore, D. M., and Magliaro, S. G. (2004). Behaviorism and instructional technology. In D. H. Jonassen (ed.), *Handbook of Research on Educational Communications and Technology* (2nd ed., pp. 3–36). Mahwah, NJ: Lawrence Erlbaum.

Buscher, M., and Hughes, J. (2003). Screen scenery: Learning from architecture and people's practices of navigation in electronic environments. In K. Höök, D. Benyon, and A. J. Munro (eds.), *Designing Information Spaces: The Social Navigation Approach* (pp. 83–103). London: Springer.

Bush, V. (1945). As we may think. *Atlantic Monthly, 176*(1), 101–108. Available online: http:// www.theatlantic.com/doc/194507/bush.

Bussey, K., and Bandura, A. (1999). Social cognitive theory of gender development and differentiation. *Psychological Review, 106*(4), 676–713.

Butler, K. A. (1996). Usability engineering turns 10. *Interaction, 3*(1), 58–75.

Buzhardt, J., and Heitzman-Powell, L. (2005). Stop blaming the teachers: The role of usability testing in bridging the gap between educators and technology. *Electronic Journal for the Integration of Technology in Education*, 4(1), 13–29.

Campbell, C. S., and Maglio, P. P. (2003). Supporting notable information in office work. In G. Cockton and P. Korhonen (eds.), *Proceedings of ACM CHI 03 Conference Extended Abstracts on Human Factors in Computing Systems* (pp. 902–903). New York: ACM Press.

Campbell, D. J. (1988). Task complexity: A review and analysis. *Academy of Management Review*, 13(1), 40–52.

Cantelon, J. E. (1995). The evolution and advantages of distance education. In M. H. Rossman and M. E. Rossman (eds.), *Facilitating Distance Education* (pp. 3–10). New Directions for Adult and Continuing Education Series, number 67. San Francisco, CA: Jossey-Bass.

Capper, J. (2001). The emerging market for online learning: Insights from the corporate sector. *European Journal of Education*, 36(2), 237–245.

Carabajal, K., LaPointe, D., and Gunawardena, C. N. (2003). Group development in online learning communities. In M. G. Moore and W. G. Anderson (eds.), *Handbook of Distance Education* (pp. 217–234). Mahwah, NJ: Lawrence Erlbaum.

Carchidi, D. (2002). *The Virtual Delivery and Virtual Organization of Post-Secondary Education*. New York: Falmer Press.

Card, S. K., Moran, T. P., and Newell, A. (1983). *The Psychology of Human–Computer Interaction*. Hillsdale, NJ: Lawrence Erlbaum.

Carlson, S. (2005). The Net Generation goes to college. *Chronicle of Higher Education*, Information Technology, October 7. Available online: http://chronicle.com/free/v52/i07/07a03401.htm.

Carmean, C., and Haefner, J. (2002). Mind over matter: Transforming course management systems into effective learning environments. *EDUCAUSE Review*, November/December, 27–34.

Carr, N. (2008). Is Google making us stupid? *Atlantic Monthly*, July/August, 302(1), 56–63.

Carr-Chellman, A. A. (ed.) (2005). *Global Perspectives on E-Learning: Rhetoric and Reality*. Thousand Oaks, CA: Sage.

Carr-Chellman, A. A. (2006). Where do educational technologists really publish? An examination of successfully emerging scholars' publication outlets. *British Journal of Educational Technology*, 37(1), 5–15.

Carroll, J. M. (ed.) (1990). *The Nurnberg Funnel: Designing Minimalist Instruction for Practical Computer Skill*. Cambridge, MA: MIT Press.

Carroll, J. M. (ed.) (1998). *Minimalism beyond the Nurnberg Funnel*. Cambridge, MA: MIT Press.

Carroll, J. M., and Kellogg, W. A. (1989). Artifact as theory-nexus: Hermeneutics meets theory-based design. In K. Bice and C. Lewis (eds.), *Proceedings of ACM CHI 89 Conference on Human Factors in Computing Systems* (pp. 7–14). New York: ACM Press.

Carroll, J. M., Smith-Kerker, P. L., Ford, J. R., and Mazur-Rimetz, S. A. (1987). The minimal manual. *Human–Computer Interaction*, *3*(2), 123–153.

Caruso, J. B., and Kvavik, R. B. (2005). Students and information technology, 2005: Convenience, connection, control, and learning. *EDUCAUSE Center for Applied Research Report*. Boulder, CO: ECAR. Available online: http://www.educause.edu/ECAR/ECARStudyofStudentsandInformat/ 158586.

Casarotti, M., Filipponi, L., Pieti, L., and Sarton, R. (2002). Educational interaction in distance education: Analysis of a one-way video and two-way audio system. *PsychNology*, *1*(1), 28–38.

Castells, M. (1996). *The Rise of the Network Society* (vol. 1): *The Information Age: Economy, Society, and Culture*. Oxford Basil Blackwell.

Cazden, C. B. (1988). *Classroom Discourse: The Language of Teaching and Learning*. Portsmouth, NH: Heinemann.

Chandler, P., and Sweller, J. (1991). Cognitive load theory and the format of instruction. *Cognition and Instruction*, *8*(4), 293–332.

Chapman, D. (2005). Introduction to Learning Management Systems. In C. Howard, J. V. Boettcher, L. Justice, K. Schenk, P. L. Rogers, and G. A. Berg (eds.), *Encyclopedia of Distance Learning* (pp. 1149–1155). Hershey, PA: Idea Group Reference.

Charney, D. H., Reder, L. E., and Kusbit, G. W. (1991). Improving documentation with hands-on problem-solving. In *Proceedings of the First Conference on Quality in Documentation* (pp. 134–153). Waterloo, Ontario: University of Waterloo Press.

Chauvin, B. A. (2003). Visual or media literacy? *Journal of Visual Literacy*, *23*(2), 119–128.

Chen, C. J., Toh, S. C., and Ismail, W. M. F. W. (2005). Are learning styles relevant to virtual reality? *Journal of Research on Technology in Education*, *38*(2), 123–141.

Chen, J. (2007). Flow in games (and everything else). *Communications of the ACM*, *50*(4), 31–33.

Chenoweth, N. A., Hayes, J. R., Gripp, P., Littleton, E. B., Steinberg, E. R., and Van Every, D. A. (1999). Are our courses working? Measuring student learning. *Written Communication*, *16*(1), 29–50.

Chevalier, A., and Ivory, M. Y. (2003). Web site designs: Influences of designer's expertise and design constraints. *International Journal of Human–Computer Studies*, *58*(1), 57–87.

Chi, M. T., Feltovich, P. J., and Glaser, R. (1981). Categorization and representation of physics problems by experts and novices. *Cognitive Science*, *5*, 121–152.

Chi, M. T., Glaser, R., and Rees, E. (1982). Expertise in problem solving. In R. J. Sternberg (ed.), *Advances in the Psychology of Human Intelligence* (vol. 1, pp. 7–75). Hillsdale, NJ: Lawrence Erlbaum.

Chickering, A. W., and Ehrmann, S. C. (1998). Implementing the seven principles: Technology as lever. *AAHE Bulletin*. Available online: http://www.tltgroup.org/programs/seven.html.

Chickering, A. W., and Gamson, Z. F. (1987). Seven principles for good practice in undergraduate education. *AAHE Bulletin, 39*, 3–7.

Chickering, A. W., and Mentkowski, M. (2006). Assessing ineffable outcomes. In A. W. Chickering, J. C. Dalton, and L. Stamm (eds.), *Encouraging Authenticity and Spirituality in Higher Education* (pp. 220–242). San Francisco, CA: Jossey-Bass.

Churchman, C. W. (1967). Wicked problems. *Management Science, 14*(4), B-141–B-142.

Cicero (1949). *De inventione—de optimo genere oratorum—topica*. H. M. Hubbell (trans.). Loeb Classical Library. Cambridge, MA: Harvard University Press.

Cicero. (1970). *On Oratory and Orators*. J. S. Watson (trans.) and R. A. Micken (ed.), Carbondale: Southern Illinois University Press.

Clark, D., and Linn, M. C. (2003). Designing for knowledge integration: The impact of instructional time. *Journal of the Learning Sciences, 12*(4), 451–493.

Clark, R. C. (2005). Multimedia learning in e-Courses. In R. E. Mayer (ed.), *The Cambridge Handbook of Multimedia Learning* (pp. 589–616). Cambridge: Cambridge University Press.

Clark, R. C., and Mayer, R. E. (2003). *E-Learning and the Science of Instruction: Proven Guidelines for Consumers and Designers of Multimedia Learning*. San Francisco, CA: Pfeiffer.

Clark, R. E. (1983). Reconsidering research on learning from media. *Review of Educational Research, 53*(4), 445–459.

Clark, R. E. (1994). Media will never influence learning. *Educational Technology Research and Development, 42*(2), 21–29.

Clark, R. E., and Feldon, D. F. (2005). Five common but questionable principles of multimedia learning. In R. E. Mayer (ed.), *The Cambridge Handbook of Multimedia Learning* (pp. 97–115). Cambridge: Cambridge University Press.

Clarke, G. E. (1997). The arts and the scattered self: Reflections in the age of cyberspace. *Arts Education Policy Review, 98*(6), 2–7.

CNN.com. (2005). E-mails "hurt IQ more than pot." *CNN.com World Report*, April 22. Available online: http://www.cnn.com/2005/WORLD/europe/04/22/text.iq/index.html.

Coe, M. (1996). *Human Factors for Technical Communicators*. New York: John Wiley.

Cole, E., and Dehdashti, P. (1990). Interface design as a prosthesis for individuals with brain injuries. *SIGCHI Bulletin, 22*(1), 28–32.

Cole, M., and Derry, J. (2005). We have met technology and it is us. In R. J. Sternberg and D. D. Preiss (eds.), *Intelligence and Technology: The Impact of Tools on the Nature and Development of Human Abilities* (pp. 209–227). Mahwah, NJ: Lawrence Erlbaum.

Cole, M., and Engeström, Y. (1993). A cultural-historical approach to distributed cognition. In G. Salomon (ed.), *Distributed Cognition: Psychological and Educational Considerations* (pp. 1–46). Cambridge: Cambridge University Press.

Colella, V. (2000). Participatory simulations: Building collaborative understanding through immersive dynamic modeling. *Journal of the Learning Sciences, 9*(4), 471–500.

Collins, A. (1996). Design issues for learning environments. In S. Vosniadou, E. De Corte, R. Glaser, and H. Mandl (eds.), *International Perspectives on the Design of Technology-Supported Learning Environments* (pp. 347–361). Mahwah, NJ: Lawrence Erlbaum.

Collins, A., Joseph, D., and Bielaczye, K. (2004). Design research: Theoretical and methodological issues. *Journal of the Learning Sciences, 13*(1), 15–42.

Collins, M. P., and Berge, Z. L. (1995). Computer-communication and the online classroom in higher education. In Z. L. Berge and M. P. Collins (eds.), *Computer-Mediated Communication and the Online Classroom,* volume 2: *Higher Education* (pp. 1–10). Cresskill, NJ: Hampton Press.

Collins, R. (2002). Credential inflation and the future of universities. In S. Brint (ed.), *The Future of the City of Intellect: The Changing American University* (pp. 23–46). Stanford, CA: Stanford University Press.

Collis, B., and Moonen, J. (2001). *Flexible Learning in a Digital World: Experiences and Expectations.* London: Taylor and Francis.

Collis, D. J. (2002). New business models for higher education. In S. Brint (ed.), *The Future of the City of Intellect: The Changing American University* (pp. 181–202). Stanford, CA: Stanford University Press.

Collison, G., Elbaum, B., Haavind, S., and Tinker, R. (2000). *Facilitating Online Learning: Effective Strategies for Moderators.* Madison, WI: Atwood.

Colquitt, J. A., LePine, J. A., and Noe, R. A. (2000). Toward an integrative theory of training motivation: A meta-analytic path analysis of 20 years of research. *Journal of Applied Psychology, 85*(5), 678–707.

Cook, D. L. (1995). Community and computer-generated distance learning environments. In M. H. Rossman and M. E. Rossman (eds.), *Facilitating Distance Education* (pp. 33–39). New Directions for Adult and Continuing Education Series, number 67. San Francisco, CA: Jossey-Bass.

Cooke, L. (2005). Eye tracking: How it works and how it relates to usability. *Technical Communication, 52*(4), 456–463.

Cooper, C. L. (2005). The future of work: Careers, stress, and well-being. *Career Development International, 10*(5), 396–399.

Cooper, G., and Bowers, J. (1995). Representing the user: Notes on the disciplinary rhetoric of human-computer interaction. In P. J. Thomas (ed.), *The Social and Interactional Dimensions of Human–Computer Interfaces* (pp. 48–66). Cambridge: Cambridge University Press.

Cooper, J., and Weaver, K. D. (2003). *Gender and Computers: Understanding the Digital Divide.* Mahwah, NJ: Lawrence Erlbaum.

Cooper, M., and Holzman, M. (1983). Talking about protocols. *College Composition and Communication, 34*(3), 284–296.

Cooper, S. (2006). The posthuman challenge to Andrew Feenberg. In T. Veak (ed.), *Democratizing Technology: Andrew Feenberg's Critical Theory of Technology* (pp. 19–36). Albany, NY: SUNY Press.

Crawford, C. (2003). Web-enhancing university coursework: An innovative professional development model to support a step-by-step approach towards Web-enhancing courses and empowering instructors. *International Journal on E-Learning, 2*(1), 5–13.

Créplet, F., Dupouët, O., and Vaast, E. (2003). Episteme or practice? Differentiated communitarian structures in a biology laboratory. In M. Huysman, E. Wenger, and V. Wulf (eds.), *Communities and Technologies* (pp. 43–63). Boston: Kluwer Academic Publishers.

Crick, R. D., Broadfoot, P., and Claxton, G. (2004). Developing an effective lifelong learning inventory: The ELLI Project. *Assessment in Education: Principles, Policy, and Practice, 11*(3), 247–272.

Cross, N. (1995). Discovering design ability. In R. Buchanan and V. Margolin (eds.), *Discovering Design: Explorations in Design Studies* (pp. 105–120). Chicago: University of Chicago Press.

Csikszentmihalyi, M. (1990). *Flow: The Psychology of Optimal Experience.* New York: Basic.

Csikszentmihalyi, M. (1996). *Creativity: Flow and the Psychology of Discovery and Invention.* New York: HarperCollins.

Csikszentmihalyi, M. (1997). *Finding Flow: The Psychology of Engagement with Everyday Life.* New York: HarperCollins.

Csikszentmihalyi, M., and Rochberg-Halton, E. (1981). *The Meaning of Things: Domestic Symbols and the Self.* Cambridge: Cambridge University Press.

Cubitt, S. (1998). *Digital Aesthetics.* London: Sage.

Cummings, J. A., Bonk, C. J., and Jacobs, F. R. (2002). Twenty-first century college syllabi: Options for online communication and interactivity. *Internet and Higher Education, 5*(1), 1–19.

Curda, S. K., and Curda, L. K. (2003). Advanced distributed learning: A paradigm shift for military education. *Quarterly Review of Distance Education, 4*(1), 1–14.

Curran, C. (2001). The phenomenon of online learning. *European Journal of Education, 36*(2), 113–132.

Curzon, S. C. (2003). Scope, timeline, and budget. In E. A. Dupuis (ed.), *Developing Web-Based Instruction: Planning, Designing, Managing, and Evaluating for Results* (pp. 7–22). New York: Neal-Schuman.

Czubaroff, J. (1997). The public dimension of scientific controversies. *Argumentation*, *11*(1), 51–74.

Dabbagh, N. (2005). Pedagogical models for E-learning: A theory-based design framework. *International Journal of Technology in Teaching and Learning*, *1*(1), 25–44. Available online: http://ijttl .sicet.org/issue0501/DabbaghVol1.Iss1.pp25-44.pdf.

Dabbagh, N., and Bannan-Ritland, B. (2005). *Online Learning: Concepts, Strategies, and Application.* Upper Saddle River, NJ: Pearson.

Daniels, K. (2000). Measures of five aspects of affective well-being at work. *Human Relations*, *53*(2), 275–294.

D'Antoni, H. (2003, June 30). I.T. Professionals cash in on company training. *InformationWeek.* Available online: http://www.informationweek.com/news/global-cio/training/showArticle .jhtml?articleID=10801363.

Darnell, E., and Halgren, S. (2001). Usability throughout the product development cycle. In R. J. Branaghan (ed.), *Design by People for People: Essays on Usability* (pp. 79–86). Chicago: Usability Professionals' Association.

Darwin, T. J. (2003). Pathos, pedagogy, and the familiar: Cultivating rhetorical intelligence. In J. Petraglia and D. Bahri (eds.), *The Realms of Rhetoric: The Prospects for Rhetoric Education* (pp. 23–37). New York: SUNY Press.

Davenport, R. (2006). Editor's note: Picking at the bricks and mortar. *T+D*, April, 8.

Davenport, T. H., and Beck, J. C. (2001). The attention economy. *Ubiquity*, *2*(14), April 22–28. Available online: http://www.acm.org/ubiquity/book/t_davenport_2.html.

Davies, P. (1995). *About Time: Einstein's Unfinished Revolution.* New York: Simon and Schuster.

Davies, R. S. (2006). Learning intent and online learning. In V. H. Wright, C. S. Sunal, and E. K. Wilson (eds.), *Research on Enhancing the Interactivity of Online Learning* (pp. 5–26). Greenwich, CT: Information Age Publishing.

Davis, D. J. (2003). Developing text for Web-based instruction. In M. G. Moore and W. G. Anderson (eds.), *Handbook of Distance Education* (pp. 287–295). Mahwah, NJ: Lawrence Erlbaum.

De Alva, J. K. (1999/2000). Remaking the academy in the age of information. *Issues in Science and Technology*, *16*(2), 52–58.

DeBell, M., and Chapman, C. (2006). *Computer and Internet Use by Students in 2003 (NCES 2006-065).* U.S. Department of Education. Washington, D.C.: National Center for Education Statistics.

Dede, C. (2002). Vignettes about the future of learning technologies. In *2020 Visions: Transforming Education and Training through Advanced Technologies* (pp. 18–25). Washington, D.C.: Department of Education.

de Freitas, S. I. (2006). Using games and simulations for supporting learning. *Learning, Media and Technology*, *31*(4), 343–358.

de Jong, T., and van Joolingen, R. (1998). Scientific discovery learning with computer simulations of conceptual domains. *Review of Educational Research*, *68*(2), 179–201.

Deka, T. S., and McMurry, P. (2006). Student success in face-to-face and distance teleclass environments: A matter of contact? *International Review of Research in Open and Distance Learning*, *7*(1). Available online: http://www.irrodl.org/index.php/irrodl/article/view/251/468.

DeSanctis, G., and Monge, P. (1999). Introduction to the special issue: Communication processes for virtual organizations. *Organization Science*, *10*(6), 693–703.

de Souza, C. S. (2005). *The Semiotic Engineering of Human–Computer Interaction*. Cambridge, MA: MIT Press.

Deuze, M. (2006). Participation, remediation, bricolage: Considering principle components of a digital culture. *Information Society*, *22*(2), 63–75.

Dewey, J. (1943). *The Child and the Curriculum/The School and Society*. Chicago: University of Chicago Press.

Dewey, J. (1991). *How We Think*. Amherst, NY: Prometheus.

Dholakia, R. R. (2006). Gender and IT in the household: Evolving patterns of Internet use in the United States. *Information Society*, *22*(4), 231–240.

Diaz, D. P. (2000). Carving a new path for distance education research. *Technology Source*, March/April. Available online: http://technologysource.org/article/carving_a_new_path_for_distance_education_research/.

Dibiasc, D. (2000). Is distance education a Faustian bargain? *Journal of Geography in Higher Education*, *24*(1), 130–135.

Dickey, M. D. (2005). Engaging by design: How engagement strategies in popular computer and video games can inform instructional design. *Educational Technology Research and Development*, *53*(2), 67–83.

Dieberger, A. (2003). Social connotations of space in the design of virtual communities and social navigation. In K. Höök, D. Benyon, and A. J. Munro (eds.), *Designing Information Spaces: The Social Navigation Approach* (pp. 293–313). London: Springer.

Dietz, J. L. G. (2005). The deep structure of business processes. *Communications of the ACM*, *49*(5), 59–64.

Dillon, A. (1994). *Designing Usable Electronic Text: Ergonomic Aspects of Human Information Usage*. London: Taylor and Francis.

Dillon, A., and Gabbard, R. (1998). Hypermedia as an educational technology: A review of the quantitative research literature on learner comprehension, control, and style. *Review of Educational Research*, *68*(3), 322–349.

Dillon, C., and Greene, B. (2003). Learner differences in distance learning: Finding differences that matter. In M. G. Moore and W. G. Anderson (eds.), *Handbook of Distance Education* (pp. 235–244). Mahwah, NJ: Lawrence Erlbaum.

Doheny-Farina, S. (1996). *The Wired Neighborhood.* New Haven, CT: Yale University Press.

Doherty, E. P., Cockton, G., Bloor, C., Rizzo, J., Blondina, B., and Davis, B. (2002). Yes/no or maybe—Further evaluation of an interface for brain-injured individuals. *Interacting with Computers, 14*(4), 341–358.

Dordai, P., and Rizzo, J. (2006). Echo boom impact. *American School and University*, November, 300–303. Available online: http://asumag.com/DesignPlanning/university_echo_boom_impact/.

Downey, S., Wentling, R. M., Wentling, T., and Wadsworth, A. (2005). The relationship between national culture and the usability of an e-learning system. *Human Resource Development International, 8*(1), 47–64.

Draper, S. W. (1998). Practical problems and proposed solutions in designing action-centered documentation. In J. M. Carroll (ed.), *Minimalism beyond the Nurnberg Funnel* (pp. 349–374). Cambridge, MA: MIT Press.

Drucker, P. F. (1994). The age of social transformation. *Atlantic Monthly, 271*(5), 53–80.

Ducheneaut, N., and Bellotti, V. (2003). Ceci n'est pas un objet? Talking about objects in e-mail. *Human–Computer Interaction, 18*(1/2), 85–110.

Ducheneaut, N., and Watts, L. A. (2005). In search of coherence: A review of e-mail research. *Human–Computer Interaction, 20*(1/2), 11–48.

Duderstadt, J. J. (1999/2000). New roles for the 21st-century university. *Issues in Science and Technology, 16*(2), 37–44.

Duderstadt, J. J., Wulf, W. A., and Zemsky, R. (2005). Envisioning a transformed university. *Issues in Science and Technology, 22*(1), 35–42.

Duffy, T. M., and Kirkley, J. R. (2004a). Introduction: Theory and practice in distance education. In T. M. Duffy and J. R. Kirkley (eds.), *Learner-Centered Theory and Practice in Distance Education: Cases from Higher Education* (pp. 3–13). Mahwah, NJ: Lawrence Erlbaum.

Duffy, T. M., and Kirkley, J. R. (2004b). Learning theory and pedagogy applied in distance learning: The case of Cardean University. In T. M. Duffy and J. R. Kirkley (eds.), *Learner-Centered Theory and Practice in Distance Education: Cases from Higher Education* (pp. 107–141). Mahwah, NJ: Lawrence Erlbaum.

Duffy, T. M., Palmer, J. E., and Mehlenbacher, B. (1993). *Online Help: Design and Evaluation.* Norwood, NJ: Ablex.

Duin, A. H. (1993). Test drive—Techniques for evaluating the usability of documents. In C. M. Barnum and S. Carliner (eds.), *Techniques for Technical Communicators* (pp. 306–335). New York: Macmillan.

Dumas, J. S. (2001a). Usability testing methods: Subjective measures—measuring attitudes and opinions. In R. J. Branaghan (ed.), *Design by People for People: Essays on Usability* (pp. 107–117). Chicago: Usability Professionals' Association.

Dumas, J. S. (2001b). Usability testing methods: Think-aloud protocols. In R. J. Branaghan (ed.), *Design by People for People: Essays on Usability* (pp. 119–129). Chicago: Usability Professionals' Association.

Dumas, J. S. (2001c). How many participants in a usability test are enough? In R. J. Branaghan (ed.), *Design by People for People: Essays on Usability* (pp. 173–182). Chicago: Usability Professionals' Association.

Dumas, J. S. (2003). User-based evaluations. In A. Sears and J. Jacko (eds.), *The Human–Computer Interaction Handbook: Fundamentals, Evolving Technologies, and Emerging Applications* (pp. 1093–1117). Mahwah, NJ: Lawrence Erlbaum.

Dumas, J. S., and Redish, J. C. (1993). *A Practical Guide to Usability Testing.* Greenwich, CT: Ablex.

Dumont, R. A. (1996). Teaching and learning in cyberspace. *IEEE Transactions on Professional Communication*, *39*(4), 192–204.

Duran, R. L., Kelly, L., and Keaten, J. A. (2005). College faculty use and perceptions of electronic mail to communicate with students. *Communication Quarterly*, *53*(2), 159–176.

Durlach, D. (1997). Affectionate technology. In P. E. Agre and D. Schuler (eds.), *Reinventing Technology, Rediscovering Community: Critical Explorations of Computing as a Social Practice* (pp. 249–258). Greenwich, CT: Ablex.

Dziuban, C., Shea, P., and Arbaugh, J. B. (2005). Faculty roles and satisfaction in asynchronous learning networks. In S. R. Hiltz and R. Goldman (eds.), *Learning Together Online: Research on Asynchronous Learning Networks* (pp. 169–190). Mahwah, NJ: Lawrence Erlbaum.

Edelson, D. C. (2002). Design research: What we learn when we engage in design. *Journal of the Learning Sciences*, *11*(1), 105–121.

Ehn, P. (1988). *Work-Oriented Design of Computer Artifacts.* Hillsdale, NJ: Lawrence Erlbaum.

Ekman, R. H. (2000). Can libraries of digital materials last forever? *Change*, *32*(2), 23–29.

Eldred, J. C., and Hawisher, G. E. (1995). Researching electronic networks. *Written Communication*, *12*(3), 330–359.

Ellis, A. P. J., Bell, B. S., Ployhart, R. E., Hollenbeck, J. R., and Ilgen, D. R. (2005). An evaluation of generic teamwork skills training with action teams: Effects on cognitive and skill-based outcomes. *Personnel Psychology*, *58*(3), 641–672.

Ellström, P.-E. (2001). Integrating learning and work: Problems and prospects. *Human Resource Development Quarterly*, *12*(4), 421–435.

Emerson, L., and MacKay, B. R. (2006). Subjective cognitive workload, interactivity and feedback in a Web-based writing program. *Journal of University Teaching and Learning Practice, 3*(1), 1–14.

Engeström, Y. (1999). Activity theory and individual and social transformation. In Y. Engeström, R. Miettinen, and R. Punamäki (eds.), *Perspectives on Activity Theory* (pp. 19–38). Cambridge: Cambridge University Press.

Engeström, Y. (2000). Can people learn to master their future? *Journal of the Learning Sciences, 9*(4), 525–534.

Eraut, M. (2004). Informal learning in the workplace. *Studies in Continuing Education, 26*(2), 247–273.

Erickson, T., and Kellogg, W. A. (2003). Social translucence: Using minimalist visualisations of social activity to support collective interaction. In K. Höök, D. Benyon, and A. J. Munro (eds.), *Designing Information Spaces: The Social Navigation Approach* (pp. 17–41). London: Springer.

Ericsson, K. A., and Simon, H. A. (1984). *Protocol Analysis: Verbal Reports as Data.* Cambridge, MA: MIT Press.

Evans, V. (2004). *The Structure of Time: Language, Meaning, and Temporal Cognition.* Amsterdam: John Benjamins.

Fabos, B., and Young, M. D. (1999). Telecommunication in the classroom: Rhetoric versus reality. *Review of Educational Research, 69*(3), 217–259.

Fahnestock, J. (2005). Rhetoric in the age of cognitive science. In R. Graff, A. E. Walzer, and J. M. Atwill (eds.), *The Viability of the Rhetorical Tradition* (pp. 159–179). Albany, NY: SUNY Press.

Fahy, P. J. (2002). Use of linguistic qualifiers and intensifiers in a computer conference. *American Journal of Distance Education, 16*(1), 5–22.

Faigley, L., and Hansen, K. (1985). Learning to write in the social sciences. *College Composition and Communication, 36*(2), 140–149.

Fawcett, H., Ferdinand, S., and Rockley, A. (1993). The design draft—Organizing information. In C. M. Barnum and S. Carliner (eds.), *Techniques for Technical Communication* (pp. 43–78). New York: Macmillan.

Feenberg, A. (1999). *Questioning Technology.* London: Routledge.

Feinberg, S., Murphy, M., and Duda, J. (2003). Applying learning theory to the design of Web-based instruction. In M. J. Albers and B. Mazur (eds.), *Content and Complexity: Information Design in Technical Communication* (pp. 103–128). Mahwah, NJ: Lawrence Erlbaum.

Felder, R. M. (1993). Reaching the second tier: Learning and teaching styles in college science education. *Journal of College Science Teaching, 23*(5), 286–290.

Felder, R. M. (2006). A whole new mind for a flat world. *Chemical Engineering Education, 40*(2), 96–97.

Fenwick, T. (2006). Tidying the territory: Questioning terms and purposes in work-learning research. *Journal of Workplace Learning*, *18*(5), 265–278.

Fetherston, T. (2001). Pedagogical challenges for the World Wide Web. *AACE Journal*, *9*(1), 25–32.

Fischer, G. (2000). Lifelong learning—More than training. *Journal of Interactive Learning Research*, *11*(3/4), 265–294.

Fischer, G. (2006). Beyond binary choices: Understanding and exploiting trade-offs to enhance creativity. *First Monday*, *11*(4). Available online: http://firstmonday.org/htbin/cgiwrap/bin/ojs/index.php/fm/article/view/1323/1243.

Fischer, G., Greenbaum, J., and Nake, F. (2000). Return to the Garden of Eden? Learning, working, and living. *Journal of the Learning Sciences*, *9*(4), 505–513.

Fish, S. (2009). The last professor. *New York Times*, January 18. Available online: http://fish.blogs.nytimes.com/2009/01/18/the-last-professor/.

Fisher, W. R. (1984). Narration as human communication paradigm: The case of public moral argument. *Communication Monographs*, *51*(1), 1–22.

Fisher, W. R. (1987). *Human Communication as Narration: Toward a Philosophy of Reason, Value, and Action*. Columbia, SC: University of South Carolina Press.

Fleming, D. (2003). Becoming rhetorical: An education in the topics. In J. Petraglia and D. Bahri (eds.), *The Realms of Rhetoric: The Prospects for Rhetoric Education* (pp. 93–116). Albany, NY: SUNY Press.

Fletcher, J. D., Tobias, S., and Wisher, R. A. (2007). Learning anytime, anywhere: Advanced distributed learning and the changing face of education. *Educational Researcher*, *36*(2), 96–102.

Flowers, J. (2005). Usability testing in technology education. *Technology Teacher*, *64*(8), 17–19.

Foehr, U. G. (2006). *Media Multitasking among American Youth: Prevalence, Predictors, and Pairings*. Report of the Program for the Study of Entertainment Media and Health. Menlo Park, CA: Kaiser Family Foundation. Available online: http://www.kff.org/entmedia/entmedia121206pkg.cfm.

Foreman, J., Gee, J. P., Herz, J. C., Hinrichs, R., Prensky, M., and Sawyer, B. (2004). Game-based learning: How to delight and instruct in the 21st century. *EDUCAUSE Review*, *39*(5), 50–66.

Fowler, C. S. (2003). Audience and stakeholders. In E. A. Dupuis (ed.), *Developing Web-Based Instruction: Planning, Designing, Managing, and Evaluating for Results* (pp. 37–46). New York: Neal-Schuman.

Francis, D. (2004). Learning from participants in field based research. *Cambridge Journal of Education*, *34*(3), 265–277.

Fraser, B. J. (1998). The birth of a new journal: Editor's introduction. *Learning Environments Research*, *1*(1), 1–5.

Freed, K. (1999). A history of distance learning. *Media Issues: Imagining Options and Outcomes.* Available online: http://www.media-visions.com/ed-distlrn1.html.

Freese, J., Rivas, S., and Hargittai, E. (2006). Cognitive ability and Internet use among older adults. *Poetics, 34*(4–5), 236–249.

Friedlander, A. (2002). *Dimensions of Use of the Scholarly Information Environment: Introduction to a Data Set Assembled by the Digital Library Federation and Outsell, Inc.* Digital Library Federation and Council on Library and Information Resources Report. Washington, D.C.: Council on Library and Information Resources. Available online: http://www.clir.org/pubs/reports/pub110/contents .html.

Froke, M. D. (1995). Antecedents to distance education and continuing education: Time to fix them. In M. H. Rossman and M. E. Rossman (eds.), *Facilitating Distance Education* (pp. 61–70). New Directions for Adult and Continuing Education Series, number 67. San Francisco, CA: Jossey-Bass.

Frolov, S. (1998–2009). *Soviet Digital Electronics Museum.* Available online: http://rk86.com/frolov/ calcolle.htm.

Frost, S. H., Jean, P. M., Teodorescu, D., and Brown, A. B. (2004). Research at the crossroads: How intellectual initiatives across disciplines evolve. *Review of Higher Education, 27*(4), 461–479.

Fry, T. (1995). Sacred design I: A re-creational theory. In R. Buchanan and V. Margolin (eds.), *Discovering Design: Explorations in Design Studies* (pp. 190–218). Chicago: University of Chicago Press.

Furnas, G. W., Landauer, T. K., Gomez, L. M., and Dumais, S. T. (1987). The vocabulary problem in human–system communication. *Communications of the ACM, 30*(11), 964–971.

Furr, P. F., Ragsdale, R., and Horton, S. G. (2005). Technology's non-neutrality: Past lessons can help guide today's classrooms. *Education and Information Technologies, 10*(3), 277–287.

Garrison, D. R., Anderson, T., and Archer, W. (2000). Critical inquiry in a text based environment: Computer conferencing in higher education. *Internet and Higher Education, 2*(2–3), 87–105.

Garrison, R. (2000). Theoretical challenges for distance education in the 21st century: A shift from structural to transactional issues. *International Review of Research in Open and Distance Learning, 1*(1). Available online: http://www.irrodl.org/index.php/irrodl/article/view/2/333.

Garrison, R. (2003). Self-directed learning and distance education. In M. G. Moore and W. G. Anderson (eds.), *Handbook of Distance Education* (pp. 161–168). Mahwah, NJ: Lawrence Erlbaum.

Gates, B. (1995). *The Road Ahead.* New York: Viking/Penguin.

Gates, G. S. (2000). Teaching-related stress: The emotional management of faculty. *Review of Higher Education, 23*(4), 469–490.

Gay, G., and Hembrooke, H. (2004). *Activity-Centered Design: An Ecological Approach to Designing Smart Tools and Usable Systems*. Cambridge, MA: MIT Press.

Gayeski, D. M. (2007). Mobile learning technologies. In B. H. Khan (ed.), *Flexible Learning in an Information Society* (pp. 146–152). Hershey, PA: Idea Group.

Gazzaniga, M. S. (2008). *Human: The Science behind What Makes Us Unique*. New York: HarperCollins.

Gee, J. (1990). *Social Linguistics and Literacies: Ideology in Discourse*. New York: Falmer Press.

Gee, J. P. (2000). Communities of practice in the new capitalism. *Journal of the Learning Sciences*, *9*(4), 515–523.

Genov, A. (2005). Iterative usability testing as continuous feedback: A control systems perspective. *Journal of Usability Studies*, *1*(1), 18–27.

George, C. A. (2005). Usability testing and design of a library Website: An interactive approach. *OCLC Systems and Services*, *21*(3), 167–180.

Gery, G. (1991). *Electronic Performance Support Systems: How and Why to Remake the Workplace through the Strategic Application of Technology*. Boston: Wiengarten Publications.

Gibson, C. C. (2003). Learners and learning: The need for theory. In M. G. Moore and W. G. Anderson (eds.), *Handbook of Distance Education* (pp. 147–160). Mahwah, NJ: Lawrence Erlbaum.

Gibson, J. J. (1966). *The Senses Considered as Perceptual Systems*. Boston: Houghton-Mifflin.

Gieryn, T. F. (1983). Boundary-work and the demarcation of science from non-science: Strains and interests in professional ideologies of scientists. *American Sociological Review*, *48*(6), 781–795.

Gilbert, G. N., and Mulkay, M. (1984). *Opening Pandora's Box: A Sociological Analysis of Scientists' Discourse*. Cambridge: Cambridge University Press.

Gilbert, L., and Moore, D. R. (1998). Building interactivity into Web courses: Tools for social and instructional interaction. *Educational Technology*, May/Jun, 29–35.

Glass, R. L. (1998). Everything old is new again. *Communications of the ACM*, *41*(5), 17–20.

Glastra, F. J., Hake, B. J., and Schedler, P. E. (2004). Lifelong learning as transitional learning. *Adult Education Quarterly*, *54*(4), 291–307.

Gleick, J. (1999). *Faster: The Acceleration of Just About Everything*. New York: Pantheon Books.

Glyn, T. (2004). A typology of approaches to facilitator education. *Journal of Experiential Education*, *27*(2), 123–140.

Godshalk, V. M., Harvey, D. M., and Moller, L. (2004). The role of learning tasks on attitude change using cognitive flexibility hypertext systems. *Journal of the Learning Sciences*, *13*(4), 507–526.

Goffman, E. (1959). *The Presentation of Self in Everyday Life*. New York: Doubleday.

Gomez, L. M., Lochbaum, C. C., and Landauer, T. K. (1990). All the right words: Finding what you want as a function of richness of indexing vocabulary. *Journal of the American Society for Information Science, 41*(8), 547–559.

Goodall, S. D. (1991). Online help in the real world. In R. J. Brockmann and B. Mirel (eds.), *SIGDOC'91: Proceedings of the 9th Annual International Conference on Systems Documentation* (pp. 21–29). New York: ACM Press.

Goodman, L. (1990). *Time and Learning in the Special Education Classroom*. Albany, NY: SUNY Press.

Goodyear, P. (2006). Technology and the articulation of vocational and academic interests: Reflections on time, space and e-learning. *Studies in Continuing Education, 28*(2), 83–98.

Gorn, G. J., Chattopadhyay, A., Sengupta, J., and Tripathi, S. (2004). Waiting for the Web: How screen color affects time perception. *JMR, Journal of Marketing Research, 41*(2), 215–225.

Grabinger, S. (2004). Design lessons for social education. In T. M. Duffy and J. R. Kirkley (eds.), *Learner-Centered Theory and Practice in Distance Education: Cases from Higher Education* (pp. 49–60). Mahwah, NJ: Lawrence Erlbaum.

Grabinger, S., Aplin, C., and Ponnappa-Brenner, G. (2007). Instructional design for socio-cultural learning environments. *E-Journal of Instructional Science and Technology (e-JIST), 10*(1). Available online: http://www.usq.edu.au/electpub/e-jist/docs/vol10_no1/papers/full_papers/grabinger_aplin_ponnappabren.htm.

Graham, G. (2004). E-learning: A philosophical enquiry. *Education and Training, 46*(6/7), 308–314.

Gräsel, C., Fischer, F., and Mandi, H. (2000). The use of additional information in problem-oriented learning environments. *Learning Environments Research, 3*(3), 287–305.

Gray, J. (2001). Work in the coming age. *Ubiquity, 2*(10), April 24–30. Available online: http://www.acm.org/ubiquity/views/j_gray_1.html.

Green, W. S., and Jordan, W. (eds.) (2002). *Pleasure with Products: Beyond Usability*. London: Taylor and Francis.

Greenhow, C. (2008). Connecting informal and formal learning experiences in the age of participatory media: Commentary on Bull, et al. (2008). *Contemporary Issues in Technology and Teacher Education, 8*(3), 187–194.

Grice, R. (1989). Online information: What do people want? What do people need? In E. Barrett (ed.), *The Society of Text: Hypertext, Hypermedia, and the Social Construction of Information* (pp. 22–44). Cambridge, MA: MIT Press.

Grice, R., and Ridgway, L. (1993). Usability and hypermedia: Toward a set of usability criteria and measures. *Technical Communication, 40*(3), 429–437.

Grossen, M. (2000). Institutional framings in thinking, learning, and teaching. In H. Cowie and G. M. van der Aalsvoort (eds.), *Social Interaction in Learning and Instruction: The Meaning of Discourse for the Construction of Knowledge* (pp. 21–34). Kidlington, Oxford: Elsevier Science.

Gumport, P. J. (2002). Universities and knowledge: Restructuring the city of intellect. In S. Brint (ed.), *The Future of the City of Intellect: The Changing American University* (pp. 47–81). Stanford, CA: Stanford University Press.

Gunawardena, C. N., Lowe, C. A., and Anderson, T. (1997). Analysis of a global online debate and the development of an interaction analysis model for examining social construction of knowledge in computer conferencing. *Journal of Educational Computing Research*, *17*(4), 397–431.

Gunawardena, C. N., and McIsaac, M. S. (2004). Distance education. In D. H. Jonassen (ed.), *Handbook of Research on Educational Communications and Technology* (2nd ed., pp. 355–395). Mahwah, NJ: Lawrence Erlbaum.

Gunzenhauser, M. G., and Gerstl-Pepin, C. I. (2006). Engaging graduate education: A pedagogy for epistemological and theoretical diversity. *Review of Higher Education*, *29*(3), 319–346.

Guri-Rozenblit, S. (1988). The interrelations between diagrammatic representations and verbal explanations in learning from social science texts. *Instructional Science*, *17*(3), 219–234.

Guzdial, M., and Turns, J. (2000). Effective discussion through a computer-mediated anchored forum. *Journal of the Learning Sciences*, *9*(4), 437–469.

Haas, C. (1989). Seeing it on the screen isn't really seeing it: Computer writers' reading problems. In G. Hawisher and C. Selfe (eds.), *Critical Perspectives on Computers and Composition Instruction* (pp. 16–29). New York: Teacher's College Press.

Hackbarth, S. (1997). Web-based learning activities for children. In B. H. Khan (ed.), *Web-Based Instruction* (pp. 191–212). Englewood Cliffs, NJ: Educational Technology Publications.

Hackman, M. Z., and Walker, K. B. (1990). Instructional communication in the televised classroom: The effects of system design and teacher immediacy on student learning and satisfaction. *Communication Education*, *39*(3), 196–206.

Hackos, J. T., and Redish, J. C. (1998). *User and Task Analysis for Interface Design*. New York: John Wiley.

Haddon, L. (2004). *Information and Communication Technologies in Everyday Life: A Concise Introduction and Research Guide*. Oxford: Berg.

Haddon, L. (2006). The contribution of domestication research to in-home computing and media consumption. *Information Society*, *22*(4), 195–203.

Hafner, K. (2005). You there, at the computer: Pay attention. *New York Times*, February 10. Available online: http://www.nytimes.com/2005/02/10/technology/circuits/10info.html?_r =1andex=1156132800anden=2549daec886676c2andei=5070.

Hahn, T. B. (2003). Statistics and metrics. In E. A. Dupuis (ed.), *Developing Web-Based Instruction: Planning, Designing, Managing, and Evaluating for Results* (pp. 93–106). New York: Neal-Schuman.

Halasz, F. G. (1988). Reflections on NoteCards: Seven issues for the next generation of hypermedia systems. *Communications of the ACM, 31*(7), 836–852.

Hallowell, E. M. (1999). The human moment at work. *Harvard Business Review, 77*(1), 58–66.

Hamilton, D., Dahlgren, E., Hult, A., Roos, B., and Söderström, T. (2004). When performance is the product: Problems in the analysis of online distance education. *British Educational Research Journal, 30*(6), 841–854.

Hample, D. (2000). Cognitive editing of arguments and reasons for requests: Evidence from Think-aloud protocols. *Argumentation and Advocacy, 37*(2), 98–108.

Hampton, R. (1990). The rhetorical and metaphorical nature of graphics and visual schemata. *Rhetoric Society Quarterly, 20*(4), 345–356.

Hanna, D. E. (1998). Higher education in an era of digital competition: Emerging organizational models. *Journal of Asynchronous Learning, 2*(1), 66–95.

Hanna, D. E. (2003). Organizational models in higher education, past and future. In M. G. Moore and W. G. Anderson (eds.), *Handbook of Distance Education* (pp. 67–78). Mahwah, NJ: Lawrence Erlbaum.

Hannafin, M. J., and Kim, M. C. (2003). In search of a future: A critical analysis of research on Web-based teaching and learning. *Instructional Science, 31*(4/5), 347–351.

Hannafin, M. J., and Land, S. M. (1997). The foundations and assumptions of technology-enhanced student-centered learning environments. *Instructional Science, 25*(3), 167–202.

Hannafin, M., Oliver, K., Hill, J. R., Glazer, E., and Sharma, P. (2003). Cognitive and learning factors in Web-based distance learning environments. In M. G. Moore and W. G. Anderson (eds.), *Handbook of Distance Education* (pp. 245–260). Mahwah, NJ: Lawrence Erlbaum.

Hannafin, M. J., and Peck, K. L. (1988). *The Design, Development, and Evaluation of Instructional Software.* New York: Macmillan.

Hansell, S. (2005). More people turn to the Web to watch TV. *New York Times*, August 1. Available online: http://news.cnet.com/More%20people%20turn%20to%20the%20Web%20to%20watch%20TV/2100-1026_3-5813360.html.

Hara, N., and Kling, R. (2001). Student distress in Web-based distance education. *EDUCAUSE Quarterly, 24*(3), 68–69.

Harpine, W. D. (2004). Is modernism really modern? Uncovering a fallacy in postmodernism. *Argumentation, 18*(3), 349–358.

Hart-Davidson, W., Spinuzzi, C., and Zachry, M. (2006). Visualizing writing activity as knowledge work: Challenges and opportunities. In S. Huang, R. Pierce, and J. Stamey (eds.), *SIGDOC'06:*

Proceedings of the 24th Annual International Conference on Design of Communication (pp. 70–77). New York: ACM Press.

Hassani, S. N. (2006). Locating digital divides at home, work, and everywhere else. *Poetics, 34*(4–5), 250–272.

Hatch, T., and Gardner, H. (1993). Finding cognition in the classroom: An expanded view of human intelligence. In G. Salomon (ed.), *Distributed Cognition: Psychological and Educational Considerations* (pp. 164–187). Cambridge: Cambridge University Press.

Hauser, G. A. (2004). Teaching rhetoric: Or why rhetoric isn't just another kind of philosophy or literary criticism. *Rhetoric Society Quarterly, 34*(3), 39–53.

Hawthorn, D. (2000). Possible implications of aging for interface designers. *Interacting with Computers, 12*(5), 507–528.

Hayes, J. R. (1989). Writing research: The analysis of a very complex task. In D. Klahr and K. Kotovsky (eds.), *Complex Information Processing: The Impact of Herbert A. Simon* (pp. 209–234). Hillsdale, NJ: Lawrence Erlbaum.

Hayes, J. R., and Flower, L. S. (1983). Uncovering cognitive processes in writing: An introduction to protocol analysis. In P. Mosenthal, L. Tamor, and S. Walmsey (eds.), *Research in Writing: Principles and Methods* (pp. 207–220). New York: Longman.

Hayes, J. R., Waterman, D. A., and Robinson, C. S. (1977). Identifying the relevant aspects of a problem text. *Cognitive Science, 1*(3), 297–313.

Hayles, N. K. (1999). The condition of virtuality. In P. Lunenfeld (ed.), *The Digital Dialectic: New Essays on New Media* (pp. 69–94). Cambridge, MA: MIT Press.

Hede, T., and Hede, A. (2002). Multimedia effects on learning: Design implications of an integrated model. In S. McNamara and E. Stacey (eds.), *Untangling the Web: Establishing Learning Links*. Proceedings of the ASET Conference 2002. Melbourne, Australia. Available online: http://www.ascilite.org.au/aset-archives/confs/2002/hede-t.html.

Heidegger, M. (1968). *What Is Called Thinking?* J. G. Gray (trans.). New York: Harper and Row.

Heinström, J. (2003). Five personality dimensions and their influence on information behavior. *Information Research, 9*(1). Available online: http://informationr.net/ir/9-1/paper165.html.

Heller, A., and Parker, A. (2005). Experiment and theory have a new partner: Simulation. *Science and Technology*, January/February, 4–13.

Hendricks, J. A. (2004). The Netgeneration: The Internet as classroom and community. *Current Issues in Education, 7*(1). Available online: http://cie.asu.edu/volume7/number1/.

Henning, P. H. (2004). Everyday cognition and situated learning. In D. H. Jonassen (ed.), *Handbook of research on educational communications and technology* (2nd ed., pp. 143–168). Mahwah, NJ: Lawrence Erlbaum.

Henninger, S., Haynes, K., and Reith, M. W. (1995). A framework for developing experience-based usability guidelines. In G. M. Olson and S. Schuon (eds.), *DIS'95: Proceedings of the 1st Conference on Designing Interactive Systems: Processes, Practices, Methods, and Techniques* (pp. 43–53). New York: ACM Press.

Herrington, J., Oliver, R., and Herrington, A. (2007). Authentic learning on the Web: Guidelines for course design. In B. H. Khan (ed.), *Flexible Learning in an Information Society* (pp. 26–35). Hershey, PA: Idea Group.

Herrington, J., Oliver, R., and Reeves, T. C. (2003). Patterns of engagement in authentic online learning environments. *Australian Journal of Educational Technology*, *19*(1), 59–71.

Herron, J. F., and Wright, V. H. (2006). Assessment in online learning: Are students really learning? In V. H. Wright, C. S. Sunal, and E. K. Wilson (eds.), *Research on Enhancing the Interactivity of Online Learning* (pp. 45–64). Greenwich, CT: Information Age Publishing.

Hertzum, M., Andersen, H. H. K., Andersen, V., and Hansen, C. B. (2002). Trust in information sources: Seeking information from people, documents, and virtual agents. *Interacting with Computers*, *14*(5), 575–599.

Hestenes, D., Wells, M., and Swackhamer, G. (1992). Force concept inventory. *Physics Teacher*, *30*(3), 141–158.

Hickson, M., III, Bodon, J., and Turner, J. (2004). Research productivity in communication: An analysis, 1915–2001. *Communication Quarterly*, *52*(4), 323–333.

Hill, C. A. (2004). The psychology of rhetorical images. In C. A. Hill and M. Helmers (eds.), *Defining Visual Rhetorics* (pp. 25–40). Mahwah, NJ: Lawrence Erlbaum.

Hill, C. A., and Mehlenbacher, B. (1998). Transitional generations and World Wide Web reading and writing: Implications of a hypertextual interface for the masses. *TEXT Technology*, *8*(4), 29–47.

Hill, J. R., Wiley, D., Nelson, L. M., and Han, S. (2004). Computer-mediated communication. In D. H. Jonassen (ed.), *Handbook of Research on Educational Communications and Technology* (2nd ed., pp. 433–460). Mahwah, NJ: Lawrence Erlbaum.

Hilton, G. L. S. (2003). Using scenarios as a learning and teaching strategy with students. *European Journal of Teacher Education*, *26*(1), 143–153.

Hiltz, S. R., and Goldman, R. (2005). What are asynchronous learning networks? In S. R. Hiltz and R. Goldman (eds.), *Learning Together Online: Research on Asynchronous Learning Networks* (pp. 3–18). Mahwah, NJ: Lawrence Erlbaum.

Hiltz, S. R., and Shea, P. (2005). The student in the online classroom. In S. R. Hiltz and R. Goldman (eds.), *Learning Together Online: Research on Asynchronous Learning Networks* (pp. 145–168). Mahwah, NJ: Lawrence Erlbaum.

Hislop, G. W., and Ellis, H. J. C. (2004). A study of faculty effort in online teaching. *Internet and Higher Education*, *7*(1), 15–31.

Hitlin, P., and Rainie, L. (2005). *The Internet at School*. Report of the PEW Internet and American Life Project. Available online: http://www.pewinternet.org/Reports/2005/The-Internet-at-School.aspx.

Hobart, M. E., and Schiffman, Z. S. (1998). *Information Ages: Literacy, Numeracy, and the Computer Revolution*. Baltimore, MD: The Johns Hopkins University Press.

Hoc, J.-M. (2005). Cooperation between human cognition and technology in dynamic situations. In R. J. Sternberg and D. D. Preiss (eds.), *Intelligence and Technology: The Impact of Tools on the Nature and Development of Human Abilities* (pp. 135–157). Mahwah, NJ: Lawrence Erlbaum.

Hodes, C. L. (1998). Understanding visual literacy through visual information processing. *Journal of Visual Literacy, 18*(2), 131–136.

Hoey, J. J., Pettitt, J. M., and Brawner, C. E. (1997). Assessing Web-based courses at NC State. *Project 25 Information*. Available online: http://legacy.ncsu.edu/info/assessment.html.

Holley, L. C., and Steiner, S. (2005). Safe space: Student perspectives on classroom environment. *Journal of Social Work Education, 41*(1), 49–64.

Hollnagel, E. (2001). Extended cognition and the future of ergonomics. *Theoretical Issues in Ergonomics, 2*(3), 309–315.

Holmberg, B. (2003). A theory of distance education based on empathy. In M. G. Moore and W. G. Anderson (eds.), *Handbook of Distance Education* (pp. 79–86). Mahwah, NJ: Lawrence Erlbaum.

Honeycutt, L. (2001). Comparing E-mail and synchronous conferencing in online peer response. *Written Communication, 18*(1), 26–60.

Höök, K., Benyon, D., and Munro, A. J. (eds.) (2003). *Designing Information Spaces: The Social Navigation Approach*. London: Springer.

Hoover, J. N. (2007). The ultimate search engine. *InformationWeek*. Available online: http://www.informationweek.com/news/internet/search/showArticle.jhtml?articleID=201202986.

Horrigan, J., and Rainie, L. (2006). *The Internet's Growing Role in Life's Major Moments*. Report of the PEW Internet and American Life Project. Available online: http://www.pewinternet.org/Reports/2006/The-Internets-Growing-Role-in-Lifes-Major-Moments.aspx.

Hsu, Y.-C. (2006). The effects of metaphors on novice and expert learners' performance and mental-model development. *Interacting with Computers, 18*(4), 770–792.

Huart, J., Kolski, C., and Sagar, M. (2004). Evaluation of multimedia applications using inspection methods: The cognitive walkthrough case. *Interacting with Computers, 16*(2), 183–215.

Hull, G. A., and Nelson, M. E. (2005). Locating the semiotic power of multimodality. *Written Communication, 22*(2), 224–261.

Hutchins, E. (1995). *Cognition in the Wild*. Cambridge, MA: MIT Press.

Inaba, K., Parsons, S. O., and Smillie, R. (2004). *Guidelines for Developing Instructions*. Boca Raton, FL: CRC Press.

Ingraham, B., Watson, B., McDowell, L., Brockett, A., and Fitzpatrick, S. (2002). Evaluating and implementing learning environments: A United Kingdom experience. *AACE Journal, 10*(2), 28–51.

Internet Archive. (2001). *Prelinger Archives*. Available online: http://www.archive.org/details/prelinger.

Ivinson, G. (2000). The development of children's social representations of the primary school curriculum. In H. Cowie and G. M. van der Aalsvoort (eds.), *Social Interaction in Learning and instruction: The Meaning of Discourse for the Construction of Knowledge* (pp. 67–92). Kidlington, Oxford: Elsevier Science.

Ivory, M. Y., and Megraw, R. (2005). Evolution of Web site design patterns. *ACM Transactions on Information Systems, 23*(4), 463–497.

Iwata, H. (2003). Haptic interfaces. In A. Sears and J. Jacko (eds.), *The Human–Computer Interaction Handbook: Fundamentals, Evolving Technologies and Emerging Applications* (pp. 206–219). Mahwah, NJ: Lawrence Erlbaum.

Jablokow, K. W. (2005). The catalytic nature of science: Implications for scientific problem solving in the 21st century. *Technology in Society, 27*(4), 531–549.

Jackson, S. (1998). Disputation by design. *Argumentation, 12*(2), 183–198.

James, W. B., and Gardner, D. L. (1995). Learning styles: Implications for distance learning. In M. H. Rossman and M. E. Rossman (eds.), *Facilitating Distance Education* (pp. 19–31). New Directions for Adult and Continuing Education Series, number 67. San Francisco, CA: Jossey-Bass.

Jasinski, J. (2001). Introduction: On defining rhetoric as an object of intellectual inquiry. In J. Jasinski (ed.), *Sourcebook on Rhetoric: Key Concepts in Contemporary Rhetorical Studies* (pp. xiii–xxxv). Thousand Oaks, CA: Sage.

Jenkins, J. J. (1978). Four points to remember: A tetrahedral model of memory experiments. In L. S. Cermak and F. I. M. Craik (eds.), *Levels of Procession and Human Memory* (pp. 429–446). Hillsdale, NJ: Lawrence Erlbaum.

Jessop, M. (2005). In search of humanities computing in teaching, learning and research. *ACH/ALLC Conference 2005, Conference Abstracts:The 17th International Conference of the Association for Literary and Linguistic Computing*. Victoria, BC: University of Victoria. Available online: http://mustard.tapor.uvic.ca/cocoon/ach_abstracts/xq/pdf.xq?id=28.

John, B. E. (2005). The Human Computer Interaction Institute at Carnegie Mellon University. *Interaction, 12*(5), 28–29.

Johnson, K., and Magusin, E. (2005). *Exploring the Digital Library: A Guide for Online Teaching and Learning*. San Francisco, CA: Jossey-Bass.

Johnson-Eilola, J., Selber, S. A., and Selfe, C. L. (1999). Interfacing: Multiple visions of computer use in technical communication. In T. C. Kynell and M. G. Moran (eds.), *Three Keys to the Past: The History of Technical Communication* (pp. 197–226). Stamford, CT: Ablex.

Johnson-Laird, P. N. (1983). *Mental Models: Towards a Cognitive Science of Language, Inference, and Consciousness.* Cambridge, MA: Harvard University Press.

Johnston, S. (1996). Questioning the concept of "dissemination" in the process of university teaching innovation. *Teaching in Higher Education, 1*(3), 295–304.

Joint Information Systems Committee (2006). *Designing Spaces for Effective Learning: A Guide to 21st Century Learning Space Design.* Bristol: Higher Education Funding Council for England (HEFCE). Available online: http://www.jisc.ac.uk/media/documents/publications/learningspaces .pdf.

Jonassen, D. H. (1997). Instructional design models for well-structured and ill-structured problem-solving learning outcomes. *Educational Technology Research and Development, 45*(1), 65–94.

Jonassen, D. H., and Grabowski, B. L. (1993). *Handbook of Individual Differences, Learning, and Instruction.* Hillsdale, NJ: Lawrence Erlbaum.

Jonassen, D. H., Hannum, W. H., and Tessmer, M. (1989). *Handbook of Task Analysis Procedures.* Westport, CT: Greenwood Press.

Jonassen, D. H., Lee, C. B., Yang, C.-C., and Laffey, J. (2005). The collaboration principle in multimedia learning. In R. E. Mayer (ed.), *The Cambridge Handbook of Multimedia Learning* (pp. 247–270). Cambridge: Cambridge University Press.

Jones, D. (2004). The conceptualisation of e-learning: Lessons and implications. *Studies in Learning, Evaluation, Innovation, and Development, 1*(1), 47–55.

Jones, S. (2005). Fizz in the field: Toward a basis for an emergent Internet studies. *Information Society, 21*(4), 233–237.

Jones, S. G. (1995). Understanding community in the information age. In S. G. Jones (ed.), *Cybersociety: Computer-Mediated Communication and Community* (pp. 10–35). Thousand Oaks, CA: Sage.

Jones-Kavalier, B. R., and Flannigan, S. L. (2006). Connecting the digital dots: Literacy of the 21st century. *EDUCAUSE Quarterly, 29*(2), 8–10.

Jost, W. (2003). The *logos* of *techne* (or, by virtue of art). In J. Petraglia and D. Bahri (eds.), *The Realms of Rhetoric: The Prospects for Rhetoric Education* (pp. 13–21). Albany, NY: SUNY Press.

Journet, D. (1990). Writing, rhetoric, and the social construction of scientific knowledge. *IEEE Transactions on Professional Communication, 33*(4), 162–167.

Kaikkonen, A., Kekäläinen, A., Cankar, M., Kallio, T., and Kankainen, A. (2005). Usability testing of mobile applications: A comparison between laboratory and field testing. *Journal of Usability Studies, 1*(1), 4–17.

Kalantzis, M., and Cope, B. (2004). Designs for learning. *E-Learning*, *1*(1), 38–93.

Kalous, K. S. (2005). Win the e-learning challenge. *T+D, July*, 27–28.

Kantner, L. (2001a). Following a fast-moving target: Recording user behavior in Web usability testing. In R. J. Branaghan (ed.), *Design by People for People: Essays on Usability* (pp. 235–244). Chicago: Usability Professionals' Association.

Kantner, L. (2001b). Assessing Web site usability from server log files. In R. J. Branaghan (ed.), *Design by People for People: Essays on Usability* (pp. 245–261). Chicago: Usability Professionals' Association.

Kanuka, H., and Conrad, D. (2003). The name of the game: Why "Distance Education" says it all. *Quarterly Review of Distance Education*, *4*(4), 385–393.

Kaptelinin, V., Nardi, B., and Macaulay, C. (1999). The activity checklist: A tool for representing the "space" of context. *Interaction*, *6*(4), 27–39.

Kari, L., and Rozenberg, G. (2008). The many facets of natural computing. *Communications of the ACM*, *51*(10), 72–83.

Katz, L., and Rezaei, A. (1999). The potential of modern telelearning tools for collaborative learning. *Canadian Journal of Communication*, *24*(3). Available Online: http://www.cjc-online.ca/index.php/journal/article/view/1115/1021.

Kay, J., and Thomas, R. C. (1995). Studying long-term system use. *Communications of the ACM*, *38*(7), 61–69.

Kaye, J. J. (2004). Making scents: Aromatic output for HCI. *Interaction*, *11*(1), 48–61.

Kearsley, G. (1988). *Online Help Systems: Design and Implementation*. Norwood, NJ: Ablex.

Kearsley, G. (2000). *Online Education: Learning and Teaching in Cyberspace*. Belmont, CA: Wadsworth/Thomson Publishing.

Keeton, M. T. (2004). Best online instructional practices: Report of phase I of an ongoing study. *Journal of Asynchronous Learning Networks*, *8*(2), 75–100. Available online: http://www.aln.org/publications/jaln/v8n2/v8n2_keeton.asp.

Keller, G. (2001). The new demographics of higher education. *Review of Higher Education*, *24*(3), 219–235.

Kemp, W. C. (2002). Persistence of adult learners in distance education. *American Journal of Distance Education*, *16*(2), 65–81.

Kendon, A. (1990). *Conducting Interaction: Studies in the Behaviour of Social Interaction*. Cambridge: Cambridge University Press.

Kennedy, D., and Duffy, T. (2004). Collaboration—A key principle in distance education. *Open Learning*, *19*(2), 203–211.

Kenney, J., Hermens, A., and Clarke, T. (2004). The political economy of e-learning educational development: Strategies, standardisation, and scalability. *Education and Training*, *46*(6/7), 370–379.

Kerr, C. (2002). Shock wave II: An introduction to the Twenty-First Century. In S. Brint (ed.), *The Future of the City of Intellect: The Changing American University* (pp. 1–19). Stanford, CA: Stanford University Press.

Kerr, S. T. (2004). Toward a sociology of educational technology. In D. H. Jonassen (ed.), *Handbook of Research on Educational Communications and Technology* (2nd ed., pp. 113–142). Mahwah, NJ: Lawrence Erlbaum.

Keyes, E., Sykes, D., and Lewis, E. (1989). Technology + design = information design. In E. Barrett (ed.), *Text, Context, and HyperText* (pp. 251–264). Cambridge, MA: MIT Press.

Khan, B. H. (ed.). (1997). *Web-Based Instruction*. Englewood Cliffs, NJ: Educational Technology Publications.

Kiesler, S., and Cummings, J. (2002). What do we know about proximity in work groups? A legacy of research on physical distance. In P. Hinds and S. Kiesler (eds.), *Distributed Work* (pp. 57–80). Cambridge, MA: MIT Press.

Kincheloe, J. L., and Tobin, K. (2006). Doing educational research in a complex world. In K. Tobin and J. Kincheloe (eds.), *Doing Educational Research—A Handbook* (pp. 3–13). Rotterdam, Netherlands: Sense Publishers.

King, J. L., and Frost, R. L. (2002). Managing distance over time: The evolution of technologies of dis/ambiguation. In P. Hinds and S. Kiesler (eds.), *Distributed Work* (pp. 3–26). Cambridge, MA: MIT Press.

Kinneavy, J. L. (1971). *A Theory of Discourse: The Aims of Discourse*. Englewood Cliffs, NJ: Prentice-Hall.

Kintsch, E. (1990). Macroprocesses and microprocesses in the development of summarization skill. *Cognition and Instruction*, *7*(3), 161–195.

Kintsch, W. (1986). Learning from text. *Cognition and Instruction*, *3*(2), 87–108.

Kintsch, W., and Vipond, D. (1979). Reading comprehension and readability in educational practice and psychological theory. In L. G. Nilsson (ed.), *Perspectives on Memory Research: Essays in Honor of Uppsala University's 500th anniversary* (pp. 329–365). Hillsdale, NJ: Lawrence Erlbaum.

Kirkley, J., and Duffy, T. (2000). Expanding beyond a cognitivist framework: A commentary on Martinez's "Intentional learning in an intentional world." *ACM Journal of Computer Documentation*, *24*(1), 21–24.

Kirkley, S. E., Savery, J. R., and Grabner-Hagen, M. M. (1998). Electronic teaching: Extending classroom dialogue and assistance through e-mail communication. In C. J. Bonk and K. S. King (eds.), *Electronic Collaborators: Learner-Centered Technologies for Literacy, Apprenticeship, and Discourse* (pp. 209–232). Mahwah, NJ: Lawrence Erlbaum.

Kirkwood, A., and Price, L. (2006). Adaptation for a changing environment: Developing learning and teaching with information and communication technologies. *International Review of Research in Open and Distance Learning*, 7(2). Available online: http://www.irrodl.org/index.php/irrodl/article/view/294/614.

Kirsh, D. (2005). Metacognition, distributed cognition, and visual design. In P. Gårdenfors and P. Johansson (eds.), *Cognition, Education, and Communication Technology* (pp. 147–179). Mahwah, NJ: Lawrence Erlbaum.

Klein, G., and Miller, T. E. (1999). Distributed planning teams. *International Journal of Cognitive Ergonomics*, 3(3), 203–222.

Knezek, G., and Christensen, R. (2002). Impact of new information technologies on teachers and students. *Education and Information Technologies*, 7(4), 369–376.

Knight, W. (2005a). Augmented-reality machine works in real time. *NewScientist.com*, February 3. Available online: http://www.newscientist.com/article/dn6965.

Knight, W. (2005b). Mirror that reflects your future self. *NewScientist.com*, February 2. Available online: http://www.newscientist.com/article/mg18524856.200-mirror-that-reflects-your-future-self.html.

Koch, M. (2003). Community support in universities—The Drehscheibe project. In M. Huysman, E. Wenger, and V. Wulf (eds.), *Communities and Technologies* (pp. 445–463). Boston: Kluwer Academic Publishers.

Kolatch, E. (2000). Designing for users with cognitive disabilities. Department of Computer Science White Paper. College Park, MD: University of Maryland.

Kolb, D. A. (1984). *Experiential Learning: Experience as the Source of Learning and Development*. Englewood Cliffs, NJ: Prentice-Hall.

Kolodner, J. L. (1991). The *Journal of the Learning Sciences*: Effecting changes in education. *Journal of the Learning Sciences*, 1(1), 1–6.

Könings, K. D., Brand-Gruwel, S., and van Merriënboer, J. J. G. (2005). Towards more powerful learning environments though combining the perspectives of designers, teachers, and students. *British Journal of Educational Psychology*, 75(4), 645–660.

Konstan, J. A., and Riedl, J. (2003). Collaborative filtering: Supporting social navigation in large, crowed infospaces. In K. Höök, D. Benyon, and A. J. Munro (eds.), *Designing Information Spaces: The Social Navigation Approach* (pp. 43–82). London: Springer.

Koohang, A., and Durante, A. (2003). Learners' perceptions toward the Web-based distance learning activities/assignments portion of an undergraduate hybrid instructional model. *Journal of Information Technology Education*, 2(2), 105–113.

Koohang, A., and Weiss, E. (2003). Effect of prior experience with the Internet on graduate students' perception toward courseware usability and Web-based distance learning instruction: An exploratory study in a hybrid instruction environment. *Issues in Information Systems*, *4*(2), 535–542.

Koschmann, T., Kelson, A. C., Feltovich, P. J., and Barrows, H. S. (1996). Computer-supported problem-based learning: A principled approach to the use of computers in collaborative learning. In T. Koschmann (ed.), *CSCL: Theory and Practice of an Emerging Paradigm* (pp. 83–124). Mahwah, NJ: Lawrence Erlbaum.

Kostelnick, C. (2004). Melting-pot ideology, Modernist aesthetics, and the emergence of graphical conventions: The statistical Atlases of the United States, 1874–1925. In C. A. Hill and M. Helmers (eds.), *Defining Visual Rhetorics* (pp. 25–40). Mahwah, NJ: Lawrence Erlbaum.

Kostogriz, A. (2006). Putting "space" on the agenda of sociocultural research. *Mind, Culture, and Activity*, *13*(3), 176–190.

Kotovsky, K., Hayes, J. R., and Simon, H. A. (1985). Why are some problems hard? Evidence from Tower of Hanoi. *Cognitive Psychology*, *17*(2), 248–294.

Koumi, J. (2005). Pedagogic design guidelines for multimedia materials: A mismatch between intuitive practitioners and experimental researchers. *European Journal of Open, Distance and E-Learning*, II. Available online: http://www.eurodl.org/materials/contrib/2005/Jack_Koumi.htm.

Kozma, R. B. (1991). Learning with media. *Review of Educational Research*, *61*(2), 179–211.

Kozma, R., Chin, E., Russell, J., and Marx, N. (2000). The roles of representations and tools in the chemistry laboratory and their implications for chemistry learning. *Journal of the Learning Sciences*, *9*(2), 105–143.

Kramarae, C. (2003). Gender equity online, when there is no door to knock on. In M. G. Moore and W. G. Anderson (eds.), *Handbook of Distance Education* (pp. 261–272). Mahwah, NJ: Lawrence Erlbaum.

Kraut, R. E., Fussell, S. R., Brennan, S. E., and Siegel, J. (2002). Understanding effects of proximity on collaboration: Implications for technologies to support remote collaborative work. In P. Hinds and S. Kiesler (eds.), *Distributed Work* (pp. 137–162). Cambridge, MA: MIT Press.

Kreber, C., and Cranton, P. A. (2000). Exploring the scholarship of teaching. *Journal of Higher Education*, *71*(4), 476–495.

Kreitzberg, C. B., and Shneiderman, B. (2001). Making computer and Internet usability a priority. In R. J. Branaghan (ed.), *Design by People for People: Essays on Usability* (pp. 7–20). Chicago: Usability Professionals' Association.

Krendl, K. A., and Warren, R. (2004). Communication effects of noninteractive media: Learning in out-of-school contexts. In D. H. Jonassen (ed.), *Handbook of Research on Educational Communications and Technology* (2nd ed., pp. 59–78). Mahwah, NJ: Lawrence Erlbaum.

Kress, G., and van Leeuwen, T. (1996). *Reading Images: The Grammar of Visual Design*. New York: Routledge.

Krueger, C. W. (2006). New methods in software product line practice: Examining the benefits of next-generation SPL methods. *Communications of the ACM, 49*(12), 37–40.

Kuhn, K. (2000). Problems and benefits of requirements gathering with focus groups: A case study. *International Journal of Human-Computer Interaction, 12*(3/4), 309–325.

Kukla, C. D., Clemens, E. A., Morse, R. S., and Cash, D. (1992). Designing effective systems: A tool approach. In P. S. Adler and T. A. Winograd (eds.), *Usability: Turning Technologies into Tools* (pp. 41–65). New York: Oxford University Press.

Kutnick, P., and Kington, A. (2005). Children's friendships and learning in school: Cognitive enhancement through social interaction? *British Journal of Educational Psychology, 75*(4), 521–538.

Ladner, S. (2008). Laptops in the living room: Mobile technologies and the divide between work and private time among interactive agency workers. *Canadian Journal of Communication, 33*(3), 465–489.

Lakoff, G., and Johnson, M. (1980). *Metaphors We Live By*. Chicago: University of Chicago Press.

Landauer, T. K. (1997). *The Trouble with Computers: Usefulness, Usability, and Productivity*. Cambridge, MA: MIT Press.

Landauer, T., Egan, D., Remde, J., Lesk, M., Lochbaum, C., and Ketchum, D. (1993). The textbook of the future. In C. McKnight, A. Dillon, and J. Richardson (eds.), *Hypertext: A Psychological Perspective* (pp. 71–136). Chichester: Ellis Horwood.

Langer, E. J. (2000). Mindful learning. *Current Directions in Psychological Science, 9*(6), 220–223.

Lanham, R. A. (2002). The audit of virtuality: Universities in the attention economy. In S. Brint (ed.), *The Future of the City of Intellect: The Changing American University* (pp. 159–180). Stanford, CA: Stanford University Press.

Larreamendy-Joerns, J., and Leinhardt, G. (2006). Going the distance with online education. *Review of Educational Research, 76*(4), 567–605.

Larson, B. E. (2000). Classroom discussion: A method of instruction and a curriculum outcome. *Teaching and Teacher Education, 16*(5–6), 661–677.

Latour, B. (1988). *Science in Action*. Cambridge, MA: Harvard University Press.

Latour, B., and Woolgar, S. (1979). *Laboratory Life: The Social Construction of Scientific Facts*. London: Sage.

Laurillard, D. (2002). Rethinking teaching for the knowledge society. *Educause Review, 37*(1), 16–25. Available online: http://net.educause.edu/ir/library/pdf/erm0201.pdf.

Lave, J. (1988). *Cognition in Practice: Mind, Mathematics, and Culture in Everyday Life*. New York: Cambridge University Press.

Lave, J. (1996). Teaching, as learning, in practice. *Mind, Culture, and Activity, 3*(3), 149–164.

Lave, J., and Wenger, E. (1991). *Situated Learning: Legitimate Peripheral Participation*. New York: Cambridge University Press.

Lawless, K. A., and Brown, S. W. (2003). Introduction: From digital dirt road to educational expressway: Innovations in Web-based pedagogy. *Instructional Science, 31*(4/5), 227–230.

Lazar, J., Jones, A., Hackley, M., and Shneiderman, B. (2006). Severity and impact of computer user frustration: A comparison of student and workplace users. *Interacting with Computers, 18*(2), 187–207.

Lea, M. R. (2004). Academic literacies: A pedagogy for course design. *Studies in Higher Education, 29*(6), 739–756.

Ledbetter, J. (1986). The case of the disappearing author: Ractor, the poetic computer. *New Republic*, August 11 and 18, 39.

Lee, S. H. (1999). Usability testing for developing effective interactive multimedia software: Concepts, dimensions, and procedures. *Journal of Educational Technology and Society, 2*(2). Available online: http://www.ifets.info/journals/2_2/sung_heum_lee.html.

Lee, Y., Driscoll, M. P., and Nelson, D. W. (2004). The past, present, and future of research in distance education: Results from a content analysis. *American Journal of Distance Education, 18*(4), 225–241.

Leinhardt, G., and Steele, M. D. (2005). Seeing the complexity of standing to the side: Instructional dialogues. *Cognition and Instruction, 23*(1), 87–163.

Levin, D. S., Ben-Jacob, T. K., and Ben-Jacob, M. (2000). The learning environment of the 21st century. *ACCE Journal, 1*(13), 8–12.

Levine, G. (1997). Research without a theory: Working in academia. In E. A. Kaplan and G. Levine (eds.), *The Politics of Research* (pp. 34–45). New Brunswick, NJ: Rutgers University Press.

Levine, R. V., and Norenzayan, A. (1999). The pace of life in 31 countries. *Journal of Cross-Cultural Psychology, 30*(2), 178–205.

Lévy, P. (2001). *Cyberculture*. R. Bononno (trans.). Minneapolis: University of Minnesota Press.

Levy, P. (2003). A methodological framework for practice-based research in networked learning. *Instructional Science, 31*, 87–109.

Lewis, C., Perry, R., and Murata, A. (2006). How should research contribute to instructional improvement? The case of lesson study. *Educational Researcher, 35*(3), 3–14.

Lewis, L., Farris, E., Snow, K., and Levin, D. (1999). *Distance Education at Postsecondary Education Institutions: 1997–98*. U.S. Department of Education. Washington, D.C.: National Center for Education Statistics.

Lewis, T., Amini, F., and Lannon, R. (2000). *A General Theory of Love*. New York: Vintage.

Liao, Y.-K. C. (1999). Effects of hypermedia on students' achievement: A meta-analysis. *Journal of Educational Multimedia and Hypermedia, 8*(3), 255–277.

Libet, B. (2004). *Mind Time: The Temporal Factor in Consciousness*. Cambridge, MA: Harvard University Press.

Lin, H. X., and Salvendy, G. (1999). Instruction effect on human error reduction. *International Journal of Cognitive Ergonomics, 3*(2), 115–130.

Lindgaard, G. (1994). *Usability Testing and System Evaluation: A Guide for Designing Useful Computer Systems*. London: Chapman and Hall Computing.

Linn, M. C. (2000). Designing the knowledge integration environment. *International Journal of Science Education, 22*(8), 781–796.

Linn, M. C. (2006). The knowledge integration perspective on learning and instruction. In R. K. Sawyer (ed.), *The Cambridge Handbook of the Learning Sciences* (pp. 243–264). Cambridge: Cambridge University Press.

Lipponen, L. (2000). Towards knowledge building: From facts to explanations in primary students' computer mediated discourse. *Learning Environments Research, 3*(2), 179–199.

Lipson, H. (2007). Robots that are "self-aware." *TED Talks*, March. Available online: http://www.ted.com/index.php/talks/hod_lipson_builds_self_aware_robots.html.

Litchfield, R. E., Oakland, M. J., and Anderson, J. A. (2002). Relationships between intern characteristics, computer attitudes, and use of online instruction in a dietetic training program. *American Journal of Distance Education, 16*(1), 23–36.

Liu, Y., and Ginther, D. (1999). Cognitive styles and distance education. *Online Journal of Distance Learning Administration, 2*(3). Available online: http://www.westga.edu/~distance/liu23.html.

Lockee, B. B., Burton, J. K., and Cross, L. H. (1999). No comparison: Distance education finds a new use for "No significant difference." *Educational Technology Research and Development, 47*(3), 33–42.

Lockee, B. B., Moore, M., and Burton, J. K. (2001). Old concerns with new distance education research. *EDUCAUSE Quarterly, 24*(2), 60–62.

Lohr, S. (2007). Is information overload a $650 billion drag on the economy? *New York Times*, December 20. Available online: http://bits.blogs.nytimes.com/2007/12/20/is-information-overload-a-650-billion-drag-on-the-economy/?scp=1andsq=information+overload.

Loomis, J. M., and Lederman, S. J. (1986). Tactual perception. In K. R. Boff, L. Kaufman, and J. P. Thomas (eds.), *Handbook of Perception and Human Performance*, vol. II: *Cognitive Processes and Performance* (pp. 31.1–31.41). New York: John Wiley/Interscience.

Luczak, H., Roetting, M., and Oehme, O. (2003). Visual displays. In A. Sears and J. Jacko (eds.), *The Human–Computer Interaction Handbook: Fundamentals, Evolving Technologies and Emerging Applications* (pp. 187–205). Mahwah, NJ: Lawrence Erlbaum.

Lunenfeld, P. (1999). Introduction—Screen grabs: The digital dialectic and new media theory. In P. Lunenfeld (ed.), *The Digital Dialectic: New Essays on New Media* (pp. xiv–xxi). Cambridge, MA: MIT Press.

Lynch, M. (1991). Science in the age of mechanical reproduction: Moral and epistemic relations between diagrams and photographs. *Biology and Philosophy, 6*(2), 205–226.

Lynch, M. M. (1998). Facilitating knowledge construction and communication on the Internet. *Technology Source.* December. Available online: http://technologysource. org/article/facilitating _knowledge_construction_and_communication_on_the_internet/.

Lyotard, J.-F. (1979, 1984). *The Postmodern Condition: A Report on Knowledge.* G. Bennington and B. Massumi (trans.). Theory and History of Literature, vol. 10. Minneapolis: University of Minnesota Press.

MacDonald, C. J., Breithaupt, K., Stodel, E. J., Farres, L. G., and Gabriel, M. A. (2002). Evaluation of Web-based educational programs via the demand-driven learning model: A measure of Web-based learning. *International Journal of Testing, 2*(1), 35–61.

MacDonald, C. J., and Gabriel, M. A. (1998). Toward a partnership model for Web-based learning. *Internet and Higher Education, 1*(3), 203–216.

MacDonald, C. J., Stodel, E. J., Farres, L. G., Breithaupt, K., and Gabriel, M. A. (2001). The demand-driven learning model: A framework for Web-based learning. *Internet and Higher Education, 4*(1), 9–30.

MacDonald, C. J., and Thompson, T. L. (2005). Structure, content, delivery, service, and outcomes: Quality e-learning in higher education. *International Review of Research in Open and Distance Learning, 6*(2). Available online: http://www.irrodl.org/index.php/irrodl/article/view/237/321.

Mack, R. L., and Nielsen, J. (1994). Executive summary. In J. Nielsen and R. L. Mack (eds.), *Usability Inspection Methods* (pp. 1–23). New York: John Wiley.

MacPherson, K. (2006). Experts concerned about children's creative thinking. *Post-Gazette,* July 3. Available online: http://www.post-gazette.com/pg/04228/361969.stm.

Madden, M. (2003). *America's Online Pursuits: The Changing Picture of Who's Online and What They Do.* Report of the PEW Internet and American Life Project. Available online: http://www .pewinternet.org/Reports/2003/Americas-Online-Pursuits.aspx.

Madej, K. (2003). Towards digital narrative for children: From education to entertainment: A historical perspective. *ACM Computers in Education, 1*(1), 1–17.

Maehr, M. L., and Meyer, H. A. (1997). Understanding motivation and schooling: Where we've been, where we are, and where we need to go. *Educational Psychology Review, 9*(4), 371–409.

Mahapatra, R., and Lai, V. S. (2005). Evaluating end-user training programs. *Communications of the ACM, 48*(1), 66–70.

Mann, D. (1996). Serious play. *Teachers College Record, 97*(3), 446–469.

Manzini, E. (1995). Prometheus of the everyday: The ecology of the artificial and the designer's responsibility. In R. Buchanan and V. Margolin (eds.), *Discovering Design: Explorations in Design Studies* (pp. 219–243). Chicago: University of Chicago Press.

March, J. G., and Simon, H. A. (1958). *Organizations*. New York: John Wiley.

Marchese, T. J. (1998, 2002). The new conversations about learning: Insights from neuroscience and anthropology, cognitive science, and workplace studies. *New Horizons for Learning*. Available online: http://www.newhorizons.org/lifelong/higher_ed/marchese.htm.

Margolin, V. (1995). The product milieu and social action. In R. Buchanan and V. Margolin (eds.), *Discovering Design: Explorations in Design Studies* (pp. 121–145). Chicago: University of Chicago Press.

Margolis, N. H. (ed.) (2004). LITRE: Learning in a technology-rich environment: A quality enhancement plan for North Carolina State University. Raleigh, NC: North Carolina State University. Available online: http://litre.ncsu.edu/pdf/litre_qep.pdf.

Marshall, C., Nelson, C., and Gardiner, M. M. (1987). Design guidelines. In M. M. Gardiner and B. Christie (eds.), *Applying Cognitive Psychology to User-Interface Design* (pp. 221–278). New York: John Wiley.

Marshall, G. (1999). Exploring assessment. *Education and Information Technologies, 4*(3), 313–329.

Mattelart, A. (1996). *The Invention of Communication*. S. Emanuel (trans.). Minneapolis: University of Minnesota Press.

Mattelart, A. (2000). *Networking the World, 1794–2000*. L. Carey-Libbrecht and J. A. Cohen (trans.). Minneapolis: University of Minnesota Press.

Maughan, P. D. (2003). Focus groups. In E. A. Dupuis (ed.), *Developing Web-Based Instruction: Planning, Designing, Managing, and Evaluating for Results* (pp. 107–127). New York: Neal-Schuman.

Mayer, R. E. (2001). *Multimedia Learning*. New York: Cambridge University Press.

Mayer, R. E. (2005). Cognitive theory in multimedia learning. In R. E. Mayer (ed.), *The Cambridge Handbook of Multimedia Learning* (pp. 31–48). Cambridge: Cambridge University Press.

Mayer, R. E., and Moreno, R. (2003). Nine ways to reduce cognitive load in multimedia learning. *Educational Psychologist, 38*(1), 43–52.

Mayhew, D. J. (1999). *The Usability Engineering Lifecycle: A Practitioner's Handbook for User Interface Design*. San Francisco, CA: Morgan Kaufmann.

Maynard, A. E., Subrahmanyam, K., and Greenfield, P. M. (2005). Technology and the development of intelligence: From the loom to the computer. In R. J. Sternberg and D. D. Preiss (eds.), *Intelligence and Technology: The Impact of Tools on the Nature and Development of Human Abilities* (pp. 29–53). Mahwah, NJ: Lawrence Erlbaum.

Maznevski, M. L., and Chudoba, K. M. (2000). Bridging space over time: Global virtual team dynamics and effectiveness. *Organization Science, 11*(5), 473–492.

McCormack, C., and Jones, D. (1998). *Building a Web-Based Education System*. New York: John Wiley.

McCracken, M., and Wallace, M. (2000). Exploring strategic maturity in HRD—Rhetoric, aspiration, or reality? *Journal of European Industrial Training, 24*(8), 425–426.

McGrath, A., and Munro, A. (2003). Footsteps from the garden: Arcadian knowledge spaces. In K. Höök, D. Benyon, and A. J. Munro (eds.), *Designing Information Spaces: The Social Navigation Approach* (pp. 175–200). London: Springer.

McIsaac, M. S., and Blocher, J. M. (1998). How research in distance education can affect practice. *Educational Media International, 35*(1), 43–47.

McKenzie, B. K., Mims, N. G., Bennett, E., and Waugh, M. (2000). Needs, concerns, and practices of online instructors. *Online Journal of Distance Learning Education, 3*(3). Available online: http://www.westga.edu/~distance/ojdla/fall33/mckenzie33.html.

McLuhan, M. (1964). *Understanding Media: The Extensions of Man*. New York: McGraw-Hill.

Medsker, K. L., and Holdsworth, K. M. (eds.) (2001). *Models and Strategies for Training Design*. Silver Spring, MD: International Society for Performance Improvement.

Mehlenbacher, B. (1992). Navigating online information: A characterization of extralinguistic factors that influence user behavior. In R. MacLean (ed.), *SIGDOC'92: Proceedings of the 10th Annual International Conference on Systems Documentation* (pp. 35–46). New York: ACM Press.

Mehlenbacher, B. (1993). Software usability: Choosing appropriate methods for evaluating online systems and documentation. In P. Beam (ed.), *SIGDOC'93: Proceedings of the 11th Annual International Conference on Systems Documentation* (pp. 209–222). New York: ACM Press.

Mehlenbacher, B. (1997). Technologies and tensions: Designing online environments for teaching technical communication. In S. A. Selber (ed.), *Computers and Technical Communication: Pedagogical and Programmatic Perspectives* (pp. 219–238). Greenwich, CT: Ablex.

Mehlenbacher, B. (1998). Web-based writing instruction: Assisting teaching, assessing learning. Presentation at the 3rd Annual NC State Information Technology Expo. Raleigh, NC: North Carolina State University.

Mehlenbacher, B. (2002). Assessing the usability of online instructional materials. In R. S. Anderson, J. F. Bauer, and B. W. Speck (eds.), *Assessment Strategies for the On-line Class: From Theory to Practice* (pp. 91–98). New Directions for Teaching and Learning Series, number 91. San Francisco, CA: Jossey-Bass.

Mehlenbacher, B. (2003). Documentation: Not yet implemented but coming soon! In A. Sears and J. Jacko (eds.), *The Human–Computer Interaction Handbook: Fundamentals, Evolving Technologies, and Emerging Applications* (pp. 527–543). Mahwah, NJ: Lawrence Erlbaum.

Mehlenbacher, B. (2007a). The accelerated academy: Research-based strategies for managing e-mail. Learning Technology Seminar. Raleigh, NC: North Carolina State University. Available online: http://www4.ncsu.edu/~brad_m/research/accelerated07.html.

Mehlenbacher, B. (2007b). Mapping the research literatures related to distance teaching and learning. In *Proceedings of the Annual Conference on Distance Teaching and Learning 2007* (pp. 64–69). Madison, WI: Board of Regents of the University of Wisconsin System.

Mehlenbacher, B. (2008). Me, MySpace, and the changing face of higher education. Guest Lecture for the Finance and Business Senior Leadership Team Fall Retreat. Raleigh, NC: North Carolina State University. Available online: http://www4.ncsu.edu/~brad_m/socialinstruction.html.

Mehlenbacher, B., Bennett, L., Bird, T., Ivey, M., Lucas, J., Morton, J., and Whiteman, L. (2005). Usable e-learning: A conceptual model for evaluation and design. In *Proceedings of HCI International 2005: 11th International Conference on Human-Computer Interaction*, volume 4: *Theories, Models, and Processes in HCI* (pp. 1–10). Las Vegas, NV: Mira Digital Press.

Mehlenbacher, B., Hardin, B., Barrett, C., and Clagett, J. (1994). Multi-User Domains and virtual campuses: Implications for computer-mediated collaboration and technical communication. In N. Wishbow (ed.), *SIGDOC'94: Proceedings of the 12th Annual International Conference on Systems Documentation* (pp. 213–219). New York: ACM Press.

Mehlenbacher, B., Miller, C. R., Covington, D., and Larsen, J. (2000). Active and interactive learning online: A comparison of Web-based and conventional writing classes. *IEEE Transactions on Professional Communication, 43*(2), 166–184.

Mehlenbacher, B., Wogalter, M. S., and Laughery, K. R. (2002). On the reading of product owner's manuals: Perceptions and product complexity. In *Proceedings of the HFES 2002 Conference* (pp. 1–5). Baltimore, MD: HFES.

Merrill, M. D. (2002). First principles of instruction. *Educational Technology Research and Development, 50*(3), 43–59.

Mesher, D. (1999). Designing interactivities for Internet learning. *Syllabus, 12*(7), 16–20.

Messick, S. (1996). Bridging cognition and personality in education: The role of style in performance and development. *European Journal of Personality, 10*(5), 353–376.

Metcalf, H. (2003). Increasing inequality in higher education: The role of term-time working. *Oxford Review of Education, 29*(3), 315–329.

Meyer, D. E., and Kieras, D. E. (1997). A computational theory of executive cognitive processes and multiple-task performance. 1. Basic mechanisms. *Psychological Review, 104*(1), 3–65.

Meyer, K. A. (2002). *Quality in Distance Education: Focus on On-line Learning*. San Francisco, CA: Jossey-Bass.

Miah, A. (2000). Virtually nothing: Re-evaluating the significance of cyberspace. *Leisure Studies, 19* (3), 211–225.

Miller, C. R. (1979). A humanistic rationale for technical writing. *College English*, *40*(6), 610–617.

Miller, C. R. (1985). Invention in technical and scientific discourse: A prospective survey. In M. G. Moran and D. Journet (eds.), *Research in Technical Communication: A Bibliographic Sourcebook* (pp. 117–162). Westport, CT: Greenwood.

Miller, C. R. (1994a). Opportunity, opportunism, and progress: Kairos in the rhetoric of technology. *Argumentation*, *8*, 81–96.

Miller, C. R. (1994b). The cultural basis of genre. In A. Freedman and P. Medway (eds.), *Genre and the New Rhetoric* (pp. 67–78). London: Taylor and Francis.

Miller, C. R., Carter, M., and Gallagher, V. (2003). Integrated approaches to teaching rhetoric: Unifying a divided house. In J. Petraglia and D. Bahri (eds.), *The Realms of Rhetoric: The Prospects for Rhetoric Education* (pp. 209–228). Albany, NY: SUNY Press.

Miller, C. S., Lehman, J. F., and Koedinger, K. R. (1999). Goals and learning in microworlds. *Cognitive Science*, *23*(3), 305–336.

Miller, T. P. (2005). How rhetorical are English and communications majors? *Rhetoric Society Quarterly*, *35*(1), 91–113.

Minielli, M. C., and Ferris, S. P. (2005). Electronic courseware in higher education. *First Monday*, *10*(9). Available online: http://firstmonday.org/htbin/cgiwrap/bin/ojs/index.php/fm/article/view/1279/1199.

Minogue, J., and Jones, M. G. (2006). Haptics in education: Exploring an untapped sensory modality. *Review of Educational Research*, *76*(3), 317–348.

Mirel, B. (1998). Minimalism for complex tasks. In J. M. Carroll (ed.), *Minimalism beyond the Nurnberg Funnel* (pp. 179–218). Cambridge, MA: MIT Press.

Mirel, B. (1999). Complex queries in information visualizations: Distributing instruction across documentation and interfaces. In J. Johnson-Eilola and S. A. Selber (eds.), *SIGDOC'99: Proceedings of the 17th Annual International Conference on Computer Documentation* (pp. 1–8). New York: ACM Press.

Mitchell, W. J. (1999). Replacing place. In P. Lunenfeld (ed.), *The Digital Dialectic: New Essays on New Media* (pp. 113–128). Cambridge, MA: MIT Press.

Mitropoulos-Rundus, D., and Muszak, J. (2001b). Consumer "in-home" usability testing. In R. J. Branaghan (ed.), *Design by People for People: Essays on Usability* (pp. 131–151). Chicago: Usability Professionals' Association.

MLA (2007). *Report of the MLA Task Force on Evaluating Scholarship for Tenure and Promotion*. New York: MLA. Available online: http://www.mla.org/tenure_promotion.

Moldow, B. D. (1985). Computers and communication. In D. P. Donnelly (ed.), *The Computer Culture: A Symposium to Explore the Computer's Impact on Society* (pp. 106–117). Cranbury, NJ: Associated University Presses.

Moll, L. C., Tapia, J., and Whitmore, K. F. (1993). Living knowledge: The social distribution of cultural resources for thinking. In G. Salomon (ed.), *Distributed Cognition: Psychological and Educational Considerations* (pp. 139–163). Cambridge: Cambridge University Press.

Montalvo, F. T., and Torres, M. C. G. (2004). Self-regulated learning: Current and future directions. *Electronic Journal of Research in Educational Psychology*, *2*(1). 1–34. Available online: http://www.investigacion-psicopedagogica.org/revista/articulos/3/english/Art_3_27.pdf.

Montgomery, H., Sharafi, P., and Hedman, L. R. (2004). Engaging in activities involving information technology: Dimensions, modes, and flow. *Human Factors*, *46*(2), 334–348.

Moore, M. G. (1992). Distance education theory. *American Journal of Distance Education*, *5*(3), 1–6.

Moore, M. G. (2004). Research worth publishing. *American Journal of Distance Education*, *18*(3), 127–130.

Moore, M. G., and Kearsley, G. (1996). *Distance Education: A Systems View*. Belmont, CA: Wadsworth Publishing.

Moran, T. P., Cozzi, A., and Farrell, S. P. (2005). Unified activity management: Supporting people in e-business. *Communications of the ACM*, *48*(12), 67–70.

Morello, A. (1995). Discovering design means [re-]discovering users and projects. In R. Buchanan and V. Margolin (eds.), *Discovering Design: Explorations in Design Studies* (pp. 69–76). Chicago: University of Chicago Press.

Morris, W. T. (1967). On the art of modeling. *Management Science*, *13*(12), B-707–B-717.

Mortimore, P. (2000). Does educational research matter? *British Educational Research Journal*, *26*(1), 5–24.

Mountford, R. (2001). On gender and rhetorical space. *Rhetoric Society Quarterly*, *30*(1), 41–71.

Movshovitz-Hadar, N., and Hazzan, O. (2004). How to present it? On the rhetoric of an outstanding lecturer. *International Journal of Mathematical Education in Science and Technology*, *35*(6), 813–827.

Moyle, M., and Cockburn, A. (2005). A flick in the right direction: A case study of gestural input. *Behaviour and Information Technology*, *24*(4), 275–288.

Mulder, I., de Poot, H., Verwijs, C., Janssen, R., and Bijlsma, M. (2006). An information overload study: Using design methods for understanding. In T. Robertson, J. Kjeldskov, and J. Paay (eds.), *OzCHI'06: Proceedings of the 18th Australia Conference on Computer-Human Interaction: Design: Activities, Artefacts and Environments* (pp. 245–252). New York: ACM Press.

Mumford, L. (1934). *Technics and Civilization*. San Diego, CA: Harcourt Brace.

Murphy, D. A. (2003). Teams and partners. In E. A. Dupuis (ed.), *Developing Web-Based Instruction: Planning, Designing, Managing, and Evaluating for Results* (pp. 23–36). New York: Neal-Schuman.

Murphy, E., and Ciszewska-Carr, J. (2006). Landscape without bearings: Instructors' first experiences in Web-based synchronous environments. *First Monday, 11*(3). Available online: http://firstmonday.org/htbin/cgiwrap/bin/ojs/index.php/fm/article/view/1317/1237.

Murphy, P. K., and Woods, B. S. (1996). Situating knowledge in learning and instruction: Unanswered questions and future directions. *Educational Psychologist, 31*(2), 141–145.

Murray, D. E., and McPherson, P. (2006). Scaffolding instruction for reading the Web. *Language Teaching Research, 10*(2), 131–156.

Murray, J. (2006). Cybernetic circularity in teaching and learning. *International Journal of Teaching and Learning in Higher Education, 18*(3), 215–221.

Myers, G. (1990). *Writing Biology: Texts in the Social Construction of Scientific Knowledge.* Madison, WI: University of Wisconsin Press.

Mynatt, E. D. (1997). Transforming graphical interfaces into auditory interfaces for blind users multimodal interfaces. *Human–Computer Interaction, 12*(1/2), 7–45.

Naidu, S. (2003). Designing instruction for e-Learning environments. In M. G. Moore and W. G. Anderson (eds.), *Handbook of Distance Education* (pp. 349–365). Mahwah, NJ: Lawrence Erlbaum.

Najjar, L. J. (1998). Principles of educational multimedia user interface design. *Human Factors, 40*(2), 311–323.

Nardi, B. A., and Engeström, Y. (1999). A Web on the wind: The structure of invisible work. A special issue of CSCW. *Computer Supported Cooperative Work, 8*(1), 1–8.

Nardi, B. A. (2005). Beyond bandwidth: Dimensions of connection in interpersonal communication. *Computer Supported Cooperative Work, 14*(2), 91–130.

Nardi, B. A., and O'Day, V. (1999). *Information Ecologies: Using Technologies with Heart.* Cambridge, MA: MIT Press.

Nardi, B. A., and Whittaker, S. (2002). The place of face-to-face communication in distributed work. In P. Hinds and S. Kiesler (eds.), *Distributed Work* (pp. 83–110). Cambridge, MA: MIT Press.

Nardi, B. A., Whittaker, S., and Schwarz, H. (2000). It's not what you know, it's who you know: Work in the information age. *First Monday, 5*(5). Available online: http://firstmonday.org/htbin/cgiwrap/bin/ojs/index.php/fm/article/view/741/650.

National School Boards Association. (2007). *Creating and Connecting: Research and Guidelines on Online Social—and Educational—Networking.* Alexandra, VA. Available online: http://www.nsba.org/site/docs/41400/41340.pdf.

National Science Foundation (2007). *Women, Minorities, and Persons with Disabilities in Science and Engineering.* Division of Science Resources Statistics Report. Available online: http://www.nsf.gov/statistics/wmpd/.

Needleman, J. (2003). *Time and the Soul: Where Has All the Meaningful Time Gone—and Can We Get It Back?* San Francisco, CA: Berrett-Koehler.

Negroponte, N. (1979, 1996). Books without pages. *ACM Journal of Computer Documentation, 20*(3), 2–8.

Negroponte, N. (1995). *Being Digital.* New York: Vintage.

Nelkin, D. (1978). Threats and promises: Negotiating the control of research. *Daedalus, 107,* 191–209.

Nerur, S., and Balijepally, V. (2007). Theoretical reflections on agile development methodologies. *Communications of the ACM, 50*(3), 79–83.

Neuhauser, C. (2002). Learning style and effectiveness of online and face-to-face instruction. *American Journal of Distance Education, 16*(2), 99–113.

Newell, A., and Simon, H. A. (1972). *Human Problem Solving.* Englewood Cliffs, NJ: Prentice-Hall.

Newman, R. (2008). The 10 worst assumptions of 2008. *USNews.com and World Report,* December 15. Available online: http://www.usnews.com/blogs/flowchart/2008/12/15/the-10 -worst-assumptions-of-2008.html.

Nichols, M. (2003). A theory for e-learning. *Journal of Educational Technology and Society, 6*(2), 1–10.

Nickerson, R. S. (2005). Technology and cognition amplification. In R. J. Sternberg and D. D. Preiss (eds.), *Intelligence and Technology: The Impact of Tools on the Nature and Development of Human Abilities* (pp. 7–27). Mahwah, NJ: Lawrence Erlbaum.

Nielsen, J. (1994). Heuristic evaluation. In J. Nielsen and R. L. Mack (eds.), *Usability Inspection Methods* (pp. 25–62). New York: John Wiley.

Nielsen, J. (1997). Usability engineering. In A. B. Tucker, Jr. (ed.), *The Computer Science and Engineering Handbook* (pp. 1440–1460). Boca Raton, FL: CRC Press.

Nielsen, J. (1999). *Designing Web Usability: The Practice of Simplicity.* Indianapolis, IN: New Riders Publishing.

Nielsen, J., and Mack, R. L. (eds.) (1994). *Usability Inspection Methods.* New York: John Wiley.

Niesten, R., and Sussex, R. (2006). Lucidity and negotiated meaning in Internet chat. In L. van Waes, M. Leijten, and C. M. Neuwirth (eds.), *Writing and Digital Media* (pp. 65–75). Amsterdam: Elsevier.

Nikitina, S. (2005). Pathways of interdisciplinary cognition. *Cognition and Instruction, 23*(3), 389–425.

Nippert-Eng, C. E. (1995). *Home and Work: Negotiating Boundaries through Everyday Life.* Chicago: University of Chicago Press.

Noam, E. M. (1995). Electronics and the dim future of the university. *Science, 270*(5234), 247–249.

Noble, D. F. (1998). Digital diploma mills: The automation of higher education. *First Monday, 3*(1). Available online: http://firstmonday.org/htbin/cgiwrap/bin/ojs/index.php/fm/article/view/569/490.

Norlin, G. (trans. and ed.) (1928, 1954). *The Works of Isocrates*, volumes 1–3. Cambridge, MA: Harvard University Press.

Norman, D. A. (1990). *The Design of Everyday Things*. New York: Basic.

Norman, D. A. (1993). *Things That Make Us Smart: Defending Human Attributes in the Age of the Machine*. Reading, MA: Addison-Wesley.

Norman, D. A. (2003). *Emotional Design: Why We Love (or Hate) Everyday Things*. New York: Basic.

Norman, D. A., and Spohrer, J. C. (1996). Learner-centered education. *Communications of the ACM, 39*(4), 24–27.

Norman, K. L., and Panizzi, E. (2006). Levels of automation and user participation in usability testing. *Interacting with Computers, 18*(2), 246–264.

Nova, N. (2005). A review of how space affords socio-cognitive processes during collaboration. *PsychNology, 3*(2), 118–148.

Novick, D. G., and Ward, K. (2006). Why don't people read the manual? In S. Huang, R. Pierce, and J. Stamey (eds.), *SIGDOC'06: Proceedings of the 24th Annual International Conference on Design of Communication* (pp. 11–18). New York: ACM Press.

Oblinger, D. G., and Oblinger, J. L. (2005). *Educating the Net Generation*. Boulder, CO: EDUCAUSE. Available online: http://www.educause.edu/5989andbhcp=1.

Odell, L., Goswami, D., and Herrington, A. (1983). The discourse-based interview: A procedure for exploring tacit knowledge of writers in nonacademic settings. In P. Mosenthal, L. Tamor, and S. Walmsley (eds.), *Research on Writing: Principles and Methods* (pp. 221–235). New York: Longman.

Odescalchi, E. K. (1986). Productivity gain attained by task oriented information. In *33rd International Technical Communication Conference Proceedings* (pp. 359–362). Washington, D.C.: Society for Technical Communication.

O'Hagan, R. G., Zelinsky, A., and Rougeaux, S. (2002). Visual gesture interfaces for virtual environments. *Interacting with Computers, 14*(3), 231–250.

O'Leary, M., Orlikowski, W., and Yates, J. (2002). Distributed work over the centuries: Trust and control in the Hudson's Bay Company, 1670–1826. In P. Hinds and S. Kiesler (eds.), *Distributed Work* (pp. 27–54). Cambridge, MA: MIT Press.

Olson, D. R. (1974). Introduction. In D. R. Olson (ed.), *Media and Symbols: The Forms of Expression, Communication, and Education* (pp. 1–24). Chicago: University of Chicago Press.

Olson, D. R. (2005). Technology and intelligence in a literate society. In R. J. Sternberg and D. D. Preiss (eds.), *Intelligence and Technology: The Impact of Tools on the Nature and Development of Human Abilities* (pp. 55–67). Mahwah, NJ: Lawrence Erlbaum.

Olson, J. S., Teasley, S., Covi, L., and Olson, G. (2002). The (currently) unique advantages of collocated work. In P. Hinds and S. Kiesler (eds.), *Distributed Work* (pp. 114–135). Cambridge, MA: MIT Press.

Ong, W. J. (1982). *Orality and Literacy: The Technologizing of the Word*. New York: Methuen.

Onwuegbuzie, A. J., and Leech, N. L. (2005). A Typology of errors and myths perpetuated in educational research textbooks. *Current Issues in Education, 8*(7). Available online: http://cie.asu .edu/volume8/number7/.

Oppenheimer, T. (1997). The computer delusion. *Atlantic Monthly, 280*(1), 45–62. Available online: http://www.theatlantic.com/issues/97jul/computer.htm.

Orel, T. (1995). Designing self-diagnostic, self-cure, self-enhancing, and self-fashioning devices. In R. Buchanan and V. Margolin (eds.), *Discovering Design: Explorations in Design Studies* (pp. 77–104). Chicago: University of Chicago Press.

Orrill, C. H., Hannafin, M. J., and Glazer, E. M. (2004). Disciplined inquiry and the study of emerging technology. In D. H. Jonassen (ed.), *Handbook of Research on Educational Communications and Technology* (2nd ed., pp. 335–353). Mahwah, NJ: Lawrence Erlbaum.

Østerlund, C., and Carlile, P. (2003). How practice matters: A relational view of knowledge sharing. In M. Huysman, E. Wenger, and V. Wulf (eds.), *Communities and Technologies* (pp. 1–22). Boston: Kluwer Academic Publishers.

Outreach Communication (2005). A century of commitment to distance education. Penn State Online: World Campus History. Available online: http://www.worldcampus.psu.edu/AboutUs _History.shtml.

Pascarella, E. T., and Terenzini, P. T. (1998). Studying college students in the 21st Century: Meeting new challenges. *Review of Higher Education, 21*(2), 151–165.

Pasmore, W. A. (1994). *Creating Strategic Change: Designing the Flexible, High-Performing Organization*. New York: John Wiley.

Pea, R. D. (1993). Practices of distributed intelligence and designs for education. In G. Salomon (ed.), *Distributed Cognition: Psychological and Educational Considerations* (pp. 47–87). Cambridge: Cambridge University Press.

Penzias, A. (1989). *Ideas and Information: Managing in a High-Tech World*. New York: Simon and Schuster.

Perkins, D. N. (1993). Person-plus: A distributed view of thinking and learning. In G. Salomon (ed.), *Distributed Cognition: Psychological and Educational Considerations* (pp. 88–110). Cambridge: Cambridge University Press.

Perkins, D. N. (2008). Beyond understanding. In R. Land, J. H. F. Meyer, and J. Smith (eds.), *Threshold Concepts within the Disciplines* (pp. 3–19). Rotterdam, Netherlands: Sense Publishers.

Perkins, R. (2001). Remote usability evaluation over the Internet. In R. J. Branaghan (ed.), *Design by People for People: Essays on Usability* (pp. 153–162). Chicago: Usability Professionals' Association.

Perlow, L. A. (1999). The time famine: Toward a sociology of work time. *Administrative Science Quarterly, 44*(1), 57–81.

Pesce, M. (2000). *The Playful World: How Technology Is Transforming Our Imagination.* New York: Ballantine Books.

Peters, J. D. (2001). *Speaking into the Air: A History of the Idea of Communication.* Chicago: University of Chicago Press.

Peters, J. D. (2003). Space, time, and communication theory. *Canadian Journal of Communication, 28*(4), 397–411.

Peters, O. (2003). Learning with new media in distance education. In M. G. Moore and W. G. Anderson (eds.), *Handbook of Distance Education* (pp. 87–112). Mahwah, NJ: Lawrence Erlbaum.

Petherbridge, D., and Mehlenbacher, B. (2007). Addressing the concerns of faculty adopting Learning Management Systems (LMSs). In *Proceedings of the Society for Applied Learning Technology (SALT) 2007 Washington Interactive Technologies Conference* (pp. 1–14). Arlington, VA: SALT.

Petraglia, J. (1998). *Reality by Design: The Rhetoric and Technology of Authenticity in Education.* Mahwah, NJ: Lawrence Erlbaum.

Petraglia, J. (2003). Identity crisis: Rhetoric as a pedagogic and an epistemic discipline. In J. Petraglia and D. Bahri (eds.), *The Realms of Rhetoric: The Prospects for Rhetoric Education* (pp. 151–170). Albany, NY: SUNY Press.

Petroski, H. (1982). *To Engineer Is Human: The Role of Failure in Successful Design.* New York: St. Martin's Press.

Petroski, H. (1989). *The Pencil: A History of Design and Circumstance.* New York: Knopf.

Petroski, H. (2003). *Small Things Considered: Why There Is No Perfect Design.* New York: Knopf.

Pfeffer, J. (1993). Barriers to the advance of organizational science: Paradigm development as a dependent variable. *Academy of Management Review, 18*(4), 599–620.

Phillips, R. (2005). Challenging the primacy of lectures: The dissonance between theory and practice in university teaching. *Journal of University Teaching and Learning Practice, 2*(1), 1–12.

Phipps, R., and Merisotis, J. (1999). *What's the Difference? A Review of Contemporary Research on the Effectiveness of Distance Learning in Higher Education.* Institute for Higher Education Policy. Available online: http://www.ihep.org/assets/files/publications/s-z/WhatDifference.pdf.

Pierskalla, C. D., and Lee, M. E. (1998). An ecological perception model of leisure affordances. *Leisure Sciences, 20*(1), 67–79.

Pittman, V. V. (2003). Correspondence study in the American university: A second historiographic perspective. In M. G. Moore and W. G. Anderson (eds.), *Handbook of Distance Education* (pp. 21–35). Mahwah, NJ: Lawrence Erlbaum.

Plaisant, C., Clamage, A., Hutchinson, H. B., Bederson, B. B., and Druin, A. (2006). Shared family calendars: Promoting symmetry and accessibility. *ACM Transactions on Computer-Human Interaction, 13*(3), 313–346.

Plowman, L. (2005). Getting the story straight: The role of narrative in teaching and learning with interactive media. In P. Gärdenfors and P. Johansson (eds.), *Cognition, Education, and Communication Technology* (pp. 55–76). Mahwah, NJ: Lawrence Erlbaum.

Polin, L. (2004). Learning with dialogue with a practicing community. In T. M. Duffy and J. R. Kirkley (eds.), *Learner-Centered Theory and Practice in Distance Education: Cases from Higher Education* (pp. 17–48). Mahwah, NJ: Lawrence Erlbaum.

Popper, K. (1972). *Objective Knowledge: An Evolutionary Approach.* Cambridge: Oxford University Press.

Popper, K. (1992). *In Search of a Better World: Lectures and Essays from Thirty Years.* L. J. Bennett (trans.). London: Routledge.

Powell, W. W., and Owen-Smith, J. (2002). The new world of knowledge production in the life sciences. In S. Brint (ed.), *The Future of the City of Intellect: The Changing American University* (pp. 107–130). Stanford, CA: Stanford University Press.

Pratt, J. A. (1998). Where is the instruction in online help systems? *Technical Communication, 45*(1), 33–37.

Preece, J. (2001). Sociability and usability in online communities: Determining and measuring success. *Behaviour and Information Technology, 20*(5), 347–356.

Prelli, L. J. (1989). *A Rhetoric of Science: Inventing Scientific Discourse.* Columbia, SC: University of South Carolina Press.

Pruitt, S., and Barrett, T. (1991). Corporate virtual workspace. In M. Benedikt (ed.), *Cyberspace: First Steps* (pp. 383–409). Cambridge, MA: MIT Press.

Putnam, R. D. (2000). *Bowling Alone: The Collapse and Revival of American Community.* New York: Simon and Schuster.

Quan-Haase, A., and Cothrel, J. (2003). Uses of information sources in an Internet-era firm: Online and offline. In M. Huysman, E. Wenger, and V. Wulf (eds.), *Communities and Technologies* (pp. 143–162). Boston: Kluwer Academic Publishers.

Quellmalz, E. S., and Kozma, R. (2003). Designing assessments of learning with technology. *Assessment in Education: Principles, Policy, and Practice, 10*(3), 389–408.

Quesenbery, W. (2003). The five dimensions of usability. In M. J. Albers and B. Mazur (eds.), *Content and Complexity: Information Design in Technical Communication* (pp. 81–102). Mahwah, NJ: Lawrence Erlbaum.

Quinn, C. N., and Wild, M. (1998). Supporting cognitive design: Lessons form human-computer interaction and computer-mediated learning. *Education and Information Technologies, 3*, 175–185.

Quintana, C., Shin, N., Norris, C., and Soloway, E. (2006). Learner-centered design. In R. K. Sawyer (ed.), *The Cambridge Handbook of the Learning Sciences* (pp. 119–134). Cambridge: Cambridge University Press.

Rafaeli, S., and Sudweeks, F. (1997). Networked interactivity. *Journal of Computer-Mediated Communication, 2*(4). Available online: http://jcmc.indiana.edu/vol2/issue4/rafaeli.sudweeks.html.

Rainie, L., and Horrigan, J. (2005). Internet: The mainstreaming of online life. In L. Rainie and J. Horrigan, *How the Internet Has Woven Itself into American Life* (pp. 56–69). Washington, D.C.: Pew Internet and American Life Project. Available online: http://www.pewinternet.org/~/media//Files/Reports/2005/Internet_Status_2005.pdf.pdf.

Ramsden, P. (2003). *Learning to Teach in Higher Education*. London: Routledge.

Rappin, N., Guzdial, M., Realff, M., and Ludovice, P. (1997). Balancing usability and learning in an interface. In S. Pemberton (ed.), *Proceedings of ACM CHI 97 Conference on Human Factors in Computing Systems* (pp. 479–486). New York: ACM Press.

Rau, P.-L. P., and Hsu, J.-W. (2005). Interaction devices and Web design for novice older users. *Educational Gerontology, 31*(1), 19–40.

Raubenheimer, D., Spurlin, J., Martin, S. N., and Mehlenbacher, B. (2007). Faculty in technology-rich contexts: Connecting teaching, learning and assessment in the classroom. In *2007 UNC Teaching and Learning with Technology Conference*. Raleigh, NC: University of North Carolina. Available at http://conference.unctlt.org/proceedings/2007Proceedings.htm.

Ravenscroft, A. (2001). Designing e-learning interactions in the 21st century: Revisiting and rethinking the role of theory. *European Journal of Education, 36*(2), 133–156.

Ravetz, J. R. (1996). The microcybernetic revolution and the dialectics of ignorance. In Z. Sardar and J. R. Ravetz (eds.), *Cyberfutures: Culture and Politics on the Information Superhighway* (pp. 42–60). New York: NYU Press.

Readings, B. (1997). Theory after theory: Institutional questions. In E. A. Kaplan and G. Levine (eds.), *The Politics of Research* (pp. 21–33). New Brunswick, NJ: Rutgers University Press.

Redfern, S., and Naughton, N. (2002). Collaborative virtual environments to support communication and community in Internet-based distance education. *Journal of Information Technology Education, 1*(3), 201–211.

Redish, J. C. (1988). Reading to learn to do. *Technical Writing Teacher, 15*(3), 224–233.

Redish, J. C. (1993). Understanding readers. In C. M. Barnum and C. Carliner (eds.), *Techniques for Technical Communication* (pp. 14–41). New York: Macmillan.

Reed, S. K., and Saavedra, N. C. (1986). A comparison of computation, discovery, and graph procedures for improving students' conception of average speed. *Cognition and Instruction, 3*(1), 31–62.

Reeves, T. C., and Reeves, P. M. (1997). Effective dimensions of interactive learning on the World Wide Web. In B. H. Khan (ed.), *Web-Based Instruction* (pp. 59–66). Englewood Cliffs, NJ: Educational Technology Publications.

Reeves, T. C., Herrington, J., and Oliver, R. (2004). A development research agenda for online collaborative learning. *Educational Technology Research and Development, 52*(4), 53–65.

Reid, A., and Petocz, P. (2004). Learning domains and the process of creativity. *Australian Educational Researcher, 31*(2), 45–62.

Reigeluth, C. M. (1999). What is instructional-design theory and how is it changing? In C. M. Reigeluth (ed.), *Instructional-Design Theories and Models*, volume 2: *A New Paradigm of Instructional Theory* (pp. 5–29). Mahwah, NJ: Lawrence Erlbaum.

Relan, A., and Gillani, B. B. (1997). Web-based instruction and the traditional classroom: Similarities and differences. In B. H. Khan (ed.), *Web-Based Instruction* (pp. 41–46). Englewood Cliffs, NJ: Educational Technology Publications.

Renkl, A. (2005). The worked-out examples principle in multimedia learning. In R. E. Mayer (ed.), *The Cambridge Handbook of Multimedia Learning* (pp. 229–245). Cambridge: Cambridge University Press.

Repenning, A., Ioannidou, A., and Ambach, J. (1998). Learn to communicate and communicate to learn. *Journal of Interactive Media in Education, 98*(7), 1–50. Available online: http://www-jime.open.ac.uk/98/7/.

Resnick, L. B., Lesgold, A., and Hall, M. W. (2005). Technology and the new culture of learning: Tools for education professionals. In P. Gårdenfors and P. Johansson (eds.), *Cognition, Education, and Communication Technology* (pp. 77–107). Mahwah, NJ: Lawrence Erlbaum.

Rettig, M. (1991). Nobody reads documentation. *Communications of the ACM, 34*(7), 19–24.

Rheinfrank, J. J., Hartman, W. R., and Wasserman, A. (1992). Design for usability: Crafting a strategy for the design of a new generation of Xerox copiers. In P. S. Adler and T. A. Winograd (eds.), *Usability: Turning Technologies into Tools* (pp. 15–40). New York: Oxford University Press.

Rice, M., Huston, A., and Wright, J. (1982). The forms of television effects on children's attention, comprehension, and social behavior. In D. Pearl, L. Bouthilet, and J. Lazar (eds.), *Television and Behavior: Ten Years of Scientific Inquiry and Implications for the Eighties*, volume 2: *Technical Review* (pp. 24–38). Washington, D.C.: U.S. Government Printing Office.

Rice, R. E., and Gattiker, U. E. (2005). New media and organizational structuring. In F. M. Jablin and L. L. Putnam (eds.), *The New Handbook of Organizational Communication: Advances in Theory, Research, and Methods* (pp. 544–570). London: Sage.

Rice, R. E., Hiltz, S. R., and Spencer, D. H. (2005). Media mixes and learning networks. In S. R. Hiltz and R. Goldman (eds.), *Learning Together Online: Research on Asynchronous Learning Networks* (pp. 215–237). Mahwah, NJ: Lawrence Erlbaum.

Richards, C. (2006). Towards an integrated framework for designing effective ICT-supported learning environments: The challenge to better link technology and pedagogy. *Technology, Pedagogy and Education, 15*(2), 239–255.

Richardson, J. T. E. (2004). Methodological issues in questionnaire-based research on student learning in higher education. *Educational Psychology Review, 16*(4), 347–358.

Rickman, J., and Grudzinski, M. (2000). Student expectations of information technology use in the classroom. *EDUCAUSE Quarterly, 23*(1), 24–30.

Rickman, J., Todd, K., Verbick, T., and Miller, M. (2003). The evolution of the electronic campus: From a communication system to an educational delivery system. In *Proceedings of ACM SIGUCCS 03 Conference* (pp. 65–69). New York: ACM Press.

Rittel, H. (1972). On the planning crisis: Systems analysis of the "first and second generations." *Bedrifts Ojonomen, 8*, 390–396.

Rittle-Johnson, B., and Koedinger, K. R. (2005). Designing knowledge scaffolds to support mathematical problem solving. *Cognition and Instruction, 23*(3), 313–349.

Roberts, G. (2003). Teaching using the Web: Conceptions and approaches from a phenomenographic perspective. *Instructional Science, 31*(1–2), 127–150.

Roberts, M. M. (2006). Lessons for the future Internet: Learning from the past. *Educause Review, 41*(4), 16–25. Available online: http://www.educause.edu/EDUCAUSE+Review/EDUCAUSEReviewMagazineVolume41/LessonsfortheFutureInternetLea/158065.

Roberts, T. G., Irani, T. A., Telg, R. W., and Lundy, L. K. (2005). The development of an instrument to evaluate distance education courses using student attitudes. *American Journal of Distance Education, 19*(1), 51–64.

Roblyer, M. D., and Knezek, G. A. (2003). New millennium research for educational technology: A call for a national research agenda. *Journal of Research on Technology in Education, 36*(1), 60–71.

Roblyer, M. D., and Wiencke, W. R. (2003). Design and use of a rubric to assess and encourage interactive qualities in distance courses. *American Journal of Distance Education, 17*(2), 77–98.

Rodriquez, F. G., and Nash, S. S. (2004). Technology and the adult degree program: The human element. *New Directions for Adult and Continuing Education, 103*, 73–79.

Rogers, D. L. (2000). A paradigm shift: Technology integration for higher education in the new millennium. *AACE Journal, 1*(13), 19–33.

Romiszowski, A., and Mason, R. (2004). Computer-mediated communications. In D. H. Jonassen (ed.), *Handbook of Research on Educational Communications and Technology* (2nd ed., pp. 397–431). Mahwah, NJ: Lawrence Erlbaum.

Rose, E. (1999). Deconstructing interactivity in educational computing. *Educational Technology,* Jan./Feb., 43–49.

Rosenblueth, A., and Wiener, N. (1945). The role of models in science. *Philosophy of Science, 12*(4), 316–321.

Roskelly, H. C., and Jolliffe, D. A. (2004). *Everyday Use: Rhetoric at Work in Reading and Writing.* New York: Longman.

Rosner, M. (2001). Theories of visual rhetoric: Looking at the human genome. *Journal of Technical Writing and Communication, 31*(4), 391–413.

Ross, S. M., and Morrison, G. R. (2004). Experimental research methods. In D. H. Jonassen (ed.), *Handbook of Research on Educational Communications and Technology* (2nd ed., pp. 1021–1043). Mahwah, NJ: Lawrence Erlbaum.

Roth, W.-M., McGinn, M. K., Woszczyna, C., and Boutonné, S. (1999). Differential participation during science conversations: The interaction of focal artifacts, social configurations, and physical arrangements. *Journal of the Learning Sciences, 8*(3/4), 293–347.

Rouet, J.-F., and Potelle, H. (2005). Navigational principles in multimedia learning. In R. E. Mayer (ed.), *The Cambridge Handbook of Multimedia Learning* (pp. 297–312). Cambridge: Cambridge University Press.

Rovai, A. P., and Jordan, H. M. (2004). Blended learning and sense of community: A comparative analysis with traditional and fully online graduate courses. *International Review of Research in Open and Distance Learning, 5*(2). Available online: http://www.irrodl.org/index.php/irrodl/article/view/192/274.

Rowe, A. L., and Cooke, N. J. (1995). Measuring mental models: Choosing the right tools for the job. *Human Resource Development Quarterly, 6*(3), 243–255.

Rowland, G. (2004). Shall we dance? A design epistemology for organizational learning and performance. *Educational Technology Research and Development, 52*(1), 33–48.

Roy, A. (ed.). (1993). *Artists' Pigments: A Handbook of Their History and Characteristics* (vol. 2). Cambridge: Oxford University Press.

Royce, W. W. (1970). Managing the development of large software systems. *Proceedings of IEEE WESCON, 26*(August), 1–9.

Ruban, L. M., and McCoach, D. B. (2005). Gender differences in explaining grades using structural equation modeling. *Review of Higher Education, 28*(4), 475–502.

Rubin, J. (1994). *Handbook of Usability Testing: How to Plan, Design, and Conduct Effective Tests.* New York: John Wiley.

Ruhleder, K. (2004). Interaction and engagement in LEEP: Undistancing "distance" education at the graduate level. In T. M. Duffy and J. R. Kirkley (eds.), *Learner-Centered Theory and Practice in Distance Education: Cases from Higher Education* (pp. 71–89). Mahwah, NJ: Lawrence Erlbaum.

Russell, T. L. (1999). *The No Significant Difference Phenomenon.* Montgomery, AL: IDECC. Available online: http://www.nosignificantdifference.org/.

Ryan, M.-L. (1994). Immersion vs. interactivity: Virtual Reality and literary theory. *Postmodern Culture*, *5*(1). Available online: http://jefferson.village.virginia.edu/pmc/text-only/issue.994/ryan.994.

Rymer, J. (1988). Scientific composing processes: How eminent scientists write journal articles. In D. A. Jolliffe (ed.), *Writing in Academic Disciplines: Advances in Writing Research* (vol. 2, pp. 211–250). Norwood, NJ: Ablex.

Saba, F. (2000). Research in distance education: A status report. *International Review of Research in Open and Distance Learning*, *1*(1). Available online: http://www.irrodl.org/index.php/irrodl/article/view/4/337.

Saba, F. (2003). Distance education theory, methodology, and epistemology: A pragmatic paradigm. In M. G. Moore and W. G. Anderson (eds.), *Handbook of Distance Education* (pp. 3–20). Mahwah, NJ: Lawrence Erlbaum.

Sadler-Smith, E., and Riding, R. (1999). Cognitive style and instruction preferences. *Instructional Science*, *27*(5), 355–371.

Salaway, G., and Katz, R. N. (2006). *The ECAR Study of Undergraduate Students and Information Technology, 2006.* Research Study from EDUCAUSE Center for Applied Research. Boulder, CO: ECAR. Available online: http://www.educause.edu/12479andbhcp=1.

Säljö, R. (2003). Epilogue: From transfer to boundary-crossing. In T. Tuomi-Gröhn and Y. Engeström (eds.), *Between School and Work: New Perspectives on Transfer and Boundary-Crossing* (pp. 311–321). Kidlington, Oxford: Elsevier Science.

Salomon, G. (1993). No distribution without individuals' cognition: A dynamic interactional view. In G. Salomon (ed.), *Distributed Cognition: Psychological and Educational Considerations* (pp. 111–138). Cambridge: Cambridge University Press.

Sambrook, S. (2003). E-learning in small organisations. *Education + Training*, *45*(8/9), 506–516.

Sandoval, W. A., and Millwood, K. A. (2005). The quality of students' use of evidence in written scientific explanations. *Cognition and Instruction*, *23*(1), 23–55.

Savery, J. R. (1998). Fostering ownership for learning with computer-supported collaborative writing in an undergraduate business communication course. In C. J. Bonk and K. S. King (eds.), *Electronic Collaborators: Learner-Centered Technologies for Literacy, Apprenticeship, and Discourse* (pp. 103–127). Mahwah, NJ: Lawrence Erlbaum.

Savery, J. R., and Duffy, T. M. (1995). Problem-based learning: An instructional model and its constructivist framework. *Educational Technology*, *35*(5), 31–38.

Savery, J. R., and Duffy, T. M. (1996). Problem-based learning: An instructional model and its constructivist framework. In B. G. Wilson (ed.), *Constructivist Learning Environments: Case Studies in Instructional Design* (pp. 135–148). Englewood Cliffs, NJ: Educational Technology Publications.

Sawyer, R. K. (2006). Introduction: The new science of learning. In R. K. Sawyer (ed.), *The Cambridge Handbook of the Learning Sciences* (pp. 1–16). Cambridge: Cambridge University Press.

Scenters-Zapico, J. T., and Cos, G. C. (2003). A new canon for a new rhetoric education. In J. Petraglia and D. Bahri (eds.), *The Realms of Rhetoric: The Prospects for Rhetoric Education* (pp. 61–71). Albany, NY: SUNY Press.

Schank, R. C. (2005). *Lessons in Learning, E-Learning, and Training*. San Francisco, CA: Pfeiffer.

Schank, R. C., and Menachem, Y. J. (1991). Empowering the student: New perspectives on the design of teaching systems. *Journal of the Learning Sciences*, *1*(1), 7–35.

Schell, D. A. (1986). Testing online and print user documentation. *IEEE Transactions on Professional Communication*, *29*(4), 87–92.

Schmeck, R. R. (ed.). (1988). *Learning Strategies and Learning Styles*. New York: Plenum.

Schnotz, W. (2005). An integrated model of text and picture comprehension. In R. E. Mayer (ed.), *The Cambridge Handbook of Multimedia Learning* (pp. 49–69). Cambridge: Cambridge University Press.

Schön, D. A. (1983). *The Reflective Practitioner: How Professionals Think in Action*. New York: Basic.

Schön, D. A. (1987). *Educating the Reflective Practitioner*. San Francisco, CA: Jossey-Bass.

Schrepp, M., Held, T., and Laugwitz, B. (2006). The influence of hedonic quality on the attractiveness of user interfaces of business management software. *Interacting with Computers*, *18*(5), 1055–1069.

Schriver, K. A. (1989a). Document design from 1980 to 1989: Challenges that remain. *Technical Communication*, *36*(4), 316–331.

Schriver, K. A. (1989b). Evaluating text quality: The continuum from text-focused to reader-focused methods. *IEEE Transactions on Professional Communication*, *32*(4), 238–255.

Schriver, K. A. (1997). *Dynamics in Document Design: Creating Texts for Readers*. New York: John Wiley.

Schwartz, D. L., and Bransford, J. D. (1998). A time for telling. *Cognition and Instruction*, *16*(4), 475–522.

Schwartz, D. L., Martin, T., and Nasir, N. (2005). Designs for knowledge evolution: Towards a prescriptive theory for integrating first- and second-hand knowledge. In P. Gärdenfors and

P. Johansson (eds.), *Cognition, Education, and Communication Technology* (pp. 21–54). Mahwah, NJ: Lawrence Erlbaum.

Schwier, R., and Balbar, S. (2002). The interplay of content and community in synchronous and asynchronous communication: Virtual communication in a graduate seminar. *Canadian Journal of Learning and Technology, 28*(2). Available online: http://www.cjlt.ca/index.php/cjlt/article/view/81/74.

Seels, B., Fullerton, K., Berry, L., and Horn, L. J. (2004). Research on learning from television. In D. H. Jonassen (ed.), *Handbook of Research on Educational Communications and Technology* (2nd ed., pp. 249–334). Mahwah, NJ: Lawrence Erlbaum.

Selber, S. A. (2004a). Technological dramas: A meta-discourse heuristic for critical literacy. *Computers and Composition, 21*(2), 171–196.

Selber, S. A. (2004b). *Multiliteracies for a Digital Age.* Carbondale: Southern Illinois University Press.

Selber, S. A., Johnson-Eilola, J., and Mehlenbacher, B. (1997). Online support systems: Tutorials, documentation, and help. In A. B. Tucker, Jr. (ed.), *The Computer Science and Engineering Handbook* (pp. 1619–1643). Boca Raton, FL: CRC Press.

Selfe, C. L., and Hawisher, G. (2006). Literacies and the complexities of the global digital divide. In L. van Waes, M. Leijten, and C. M. Neuwirth (eds.), *Writing and Digital Media* (pp. 253–285). Amsterdam: Elsevier.

Selfe, C. L., and Meyers, P. R. (1991). Testing claims for online conferences. *Written Communication, 8*(2), 163–192.

Sener, J. (2005). Escaping the comparison trap: Evaluating online learning on its own terms. *Innovate: Journal of Online Education, 1*(2). Available online: http://www.innovateonline.info/index.php?view=articleandid=11andaction=article.

Serdiukov, P. (2001). Models of distance higher education: Fully automated or partially human? *AACE Journal, 9*(1), 15–25.

Servage, L. (2005). Strategizing for workplace e-learning: Some critical considerations. *Journal of Workplace Learning, 17*(5/6), 304–317.

Shaffer, S. C. (2005). System dynamics in distance education and a call to develop a standard model. *International Review of Research in Open and Distance Learning, 6*(3). Available online: http://www.irrodl.org/index.php/irrodl/article/view/268/813.

Shale, D. (2003). Does "distance education" really say it all—or does it say enough? A Commentary on the article by Kanuka and Conrad. *Quarterly Review of Distance Education, 4*(4), 395–399.

Shank, P. (2004). When to use instructional technology. *T+D*, September, 31–37.

Shannon, C. (1949). *The Mathematical Theory of Communication.* Urbana: University of Illinois Press.

Shea, P. J., Pickett, A. M., and Li, C. S. (2005). Increasing access to higher education: A study of the diffusion of online teaching among 913 college faculty. *International Review of Research in Open and Distance Learning*, *6*(2). Available online: http://www.irrodl.org/index.php/irrodl/article/view/238/851.

Shea, P. J., Pickett, A. M., and Pelz, W. E. (2003). A follow-up investigation of "teaching presence" in the SUNY learning network. *Journal of Asynchronous Learning Networks*, *7*(2), 61–80.

Shearer, R. (2003). Instructional design in distance education: An overview. In M. G. Moore and W. G. Anderson (eds.), *Handbook of Distance Education* (pp. 275–286). Mahwah, NJ: Lawrence Erlbaum.

Shen, S.-T., Woolley, M., and Prior, S. (2006). Towards culture-centred design. *Interacting with Computers*, *18*(4), 820–852.

Shneiderman, B. (1987). *Designing the User Interface: Strategies for Effective Human–Computer Interaction*. Reading, MA: Addison-Wesley.

Shneiderman, B. (2001). CUU: Bridging the digital divide with universal usability. *Interaction*, *8*(2), 11–15.

Shneiderman, B. (2003). *Leonardo's Laptop: Human Needs and the New Computing Technologies*. Cambridge, MA: MIT Press.

Siedlaczek, K. (2004). Perceptions about teaching online versus in a classroom environment. *College Quarterly*, *7*(3). Available online: http://www.senecac.on.ca/quarterly/2004-vol07-num03-summer/siedlaczek.html.

Silverstone, R. (1994). *Television and Everyday Life*. London: Routledge.

Simon, H. A. (1969, 1981). *The Sciences of the Artificial*. Cambridge, MA: MIT Press.

Simon, H. A. (1979). *Models of Thought*. New Haven, CT: Yale University Press.

Simons, H. W. (ed.) (1989). *Rhetoric in the Human Sciences*. London: Sage.

Singh, G., O'Donoghue, J., and Worton, H. (2005). A study into the effects of eLearning on higher education. *Journal of University Teaching and Learning Practice*, *2*(1), 13–24.

Sitzmann, T. M., Wisher, R., Stewart, D., and Kraiger, K. (2005). The effectiveness of Web-Based Training compared to classroom instruction: A meta-analysis. In S. Carliner and B. Sugrue (eds.), *ASTD 2005 Research-to-Practice Conference Proceedings* (pp. 196–202). Alexandria, VA: American Society for Training and Development.

Skelton, T. M. (1992). Testing the usability of usability testing. *Technical Communication*, *39*(3), 343–359.

Slack, F., Beer, M., Armitt, G., and Green, S. (2003). Assessment and learning outcomes: The evaluation of deep learning in an online course. *Journal of Information Technology Education*, *2*, 305–317.

Slaughter, S. (2002). The political economy of curriculum-making in American universities. In S. Brint (ed.), *The Future of the City of Intellect: The Changing American University* (pp. 260–289). Stanford, CA: Stanford University Press.

Slaughter, S., and Rhoades, G. (2004). *Academic Capitalism and the New Economy: Markets, State, and Higher Education*. Baltimore, MD: Johns Hopkins University Press.

Smart, K. L. (2003). Contextual inquiry as a method of information design. In M. J. Albers and B. Mazur (eds.), *Content and Complexity: Information Design in Technical Communication* (pp. 205–232). Mahwah, NJ: Lawrence Erlbaum.

Smith, A., Dunckley, L., French, T., Minocha, S., and Chang, Y. (2004). A process model for developing usable cross-cultural Websites. *Interacting with Computers, 16*(1), 63–91.

Smith, A., and Smith, E. (2006). Learning for success: Distance education students' use of their learning materials. *Journal of University Teaching and Learning Practice, 3*(1), 34–48.

Smith, G. G. (2001). Interaction evokes reflection: Learning efficiency in spatial visualization. *Interactive Multimedia Electronic Journal of Computer-Enhanced Learning, 3*(2). Available online: http://imej.wfu.edu/articles/2001/2/05/index.asp.

Smith, K. A., Sheppard, S. D., Johnson, D. W., and Johnson, R. T. (2005). Pedagogies of engagement: Classroom-based practices. *Journal of Engineering Education, 94*(1), 87–102.

Smith, P. A., Newman, I. A., and Parks, L. M. (1997). Virtual hierarchies and virtual networks: Some lessons from hypermedia usability research applied to the World Wide Web. *International Journal of Human-Computer Studies, 47*(1), 67–95.

Smith, P. J., Murphy, K. L., and Mahoney, S. E. (2003). Towards identifying factors underlying readiness for online learning: An exploratory study. *Distance Education, 24*(1), 57–67.

Smith, S. L., and Mosier, J. N. (1984). *Design Guidelines for User-System Interface Software*. Technical Report ESD-TR-84-190, NTIS AD A154 907. Hansom Air Force Base, MA: USAF Electronic Systems Division.

Snyder, I. (2002). Introduction. In I. Snyder (ed.), *Silicon Literacies: Communication, Innovation, and Education in the Electronic Age* (pp. 3–12). New York: Routledge.

Solomon, M. (2001). Is *isn't* the thought that counts. *Argumentation, 15*(1), 67–75.

Solomon, N., Boud, D., and Rooney, D. (2006). The in-between: Exposing everyday learning at work. *International Journal of Lifelong Education, 25*(1), 3–13.

Soloway, E., Jackson, S. L., Klein, J., Quintana, C., Reed, J., Spitulnik, J., Stratford, S. J., Studer, S., Jul, S., Eng, J., and Scala, N. (1996). Learning theory in practice: Case studies of learner-centered design. In B. Nardi, G. C. van der Veer, and M. J. Tauber (eds.), *CHI'96: Proceedings of SIGCHI Conference on Human Factors in Computing Systems: Common Ground* (pp. 189–196). New York: ACM Press.

Song, H.-D. (2003). Development of a systematic assessment framework for analyzing interaction in online environments. *Quarterly Review of Distance Education, 4*(4), 437–444.

Southern Association of Colleges and Schools Commission on Colleges (2003). *Distance Education Policy Statement*. Available online: http://www.sacscoc.org/pdf/081705/distance%20education .pdf.

Spinuzzi, C. (2002). Modeling genre ecologies. In K. Haramundanis and M. Priestley (eds.), *SIGDOC'02: Proceedings of the 20th Annual International Conference on Design of Communication* (pp. 200–207). New York: ACM Press.

Spinuzzi, C. (2003). *Tracing Genres through Organizations: A Sociocultural Approach to Information Design*. Cambridge, MA: MIT Press.

Spinuzzi, C. (2005). The methodology of participatory design. *Technical Communication, 52*(2), 163–174.

Spinuzzi, C. (2006). What do we need to teach about knowledge work? Computer Writing and Research Lab White Paper Series: 060925-1. Austin, TX: University of Texas at Austin. Available online: http://www.cwrl.utexas.edu/node/962.

Spinuzzi, C. (2007). Introduction to TCQ Special Issue: Technical communication in the age of distributed work. *Technical Communication Quarterly, 16*(3), 265–277.

Spiro, R. J., Collins, B. P., and Ramchandran, A. R. (2007). Modes of openness and flexibility in cognitive flexibility hypertext learning environments. In B. H. Khan (ed.), *Flexible Learning in an Information Society* (pp. 18–25). Hershey, PA: Idea Group.

Spiro, R. J., Feltovich, P. J., Jacobson, M., and Coulson, R. L. (1992). Cognitive flexibility, constructivism, and hypertext: Random access instruction for advanced knowledge acquisition in ill-structured domains. In T. M. Duffy and D. H. Jonassen (eds.), *Constructivism and the Technology of Instruction: A Conversation* (pp. 57–75). Hillsdale, NJ: Lawrence Erlbaum.

Spiro, R. J., Vispoel, W. P., Schmitz, J. G., Samarapungavan, A., and Boerger, A. E. (1987). Knowledge acquisition for application: Cognitive flexibility and transfer in complex content domains. In B. K. Britton and S. M. Glynn (eds.), *Executive Control Processes in Reading* (pp. 177–199). Hillsdale, NJ: Lawrence Erlbaum.

Squire, K. (2006). From content to context: Videogames as designed experience. *Educational Researcher, 35*(8), 19–29.

Squires, D. (1999). Usability and educational software design: Special Issue of Interacting with Computers. *Interacting with Computers, 11*(5), 463–466.

Squires, D., and Preece, J. (1999). Predicting quality in educational software: Evaluating for learning, usability and the synergy between them. *Interacting with Computers, 11*(5), 467–483.

Stacey, E. (2005). The history of distance education in Australia. *Quarterly Review of Distance Education, 6*(3), 253–259.

Steinkuehler, C. A. (2006). Massively multiplayer online video gaming as participation in a discourse. *Mind, Culture, and Activity, 13*(1), 38–52.

Stelzer, M., and Vogelzangs, I. (1995). Isolation and motivation in online and distance learning courses. Available online: http://projects.edte.utwente.nl/ism/Online95/Campus/library/online94/chap8/chap8.htm.

Stemler, L. K. (1997). Educational characteristics of multimedia: A literature review. *Journal of Educational Multimedia and Hypermedia, 6*(3/4), 339–359.

Stevens, R. R. (2000). Divisions of labor in school and in the workplace: Comparing computer and paper-supported activities across settings. *Journal of the Learning Sciences, 9*(4), 373–401.

Stewart, B. L. (2004). Online learning: A strategy for social responsibility in educational access. *Internet and Higher Education, 7*(4), 299–310.

Stewart, I., Hong, E., and Strudler, N. (2004). Development and validation of an instrument for student evaluation of the quality of Web-based instruction. *American Journal of Distance Education, 18*(3), 131–150.

Stinson, J. (2004). A continuing learning community for graduates of an MBA program: The experiment at Ohio University. In T. M. Duffy and J. R. Kirkley (eds.), *Learner-Centered Theory and Practice in Distance Education: Cases from Higher Education* (pp. 167–182). Mahwah, NJ: Lawrence Erlbaum.

Stone, R. J. (2001). Haptic feedback: A brief history form telepresence to virtual reality. In S. Brewster and R. Murray-Smith (eds.), *Haptic Human–Computer Interaction* (pp. 1–16). New York: Springer-Verlag.

Strange, C. C., and Banning, J. H. (2001). *Educating by Design: Creating Campus Learning Environments That Work*. San Francisco, CA: Jossey-Bass.

Stromquist, N. P. (2007). Introduction: The academic profession in the face of changing societal and institutional expectations. In N. P. Stromquist (ed.), *The Professoriate in the Age of Globalization* (pp. 1–27). Rotterdam: Sense Publishers.

Suchman, L. A. (1983). Office procedures as practical action: Models of work and system design. *ACM Transactions on Information Systems, 1*(4), 320–328.

Suchman, L. A. (1987). *Plans and Situated actions: The Problem of Human Machine Communication*. Cambridge: Cambridge University Press.

Sugrue, B., and Rivera, R. J. (2005). *2005 State of the Industry: ASTD's Annual Review of Trends in Workplace Learning and Performance*. Alexandria, VA: American Society for Training and Development.

Sugumaran, V., Park, S., and Kang, K. C. (2006). Software product line engineering. *Communications of the ACM, 49*(12), 29–32.

Sullivan, K. P. H., and Lindgren, E. (2006). Digital tools for the recording, the logging and the analysis of writing processes. In L. van Waes, M. Leijten, and C. M. Neuwirth (eds.), *Writing and Digital Media* (pp. 153–157). Amsterdam: Elsevier.

Sullivan, P., and Flower, L. (1986). How do users read computer manuals? Some protocol contributions to writers' knowledge. In B. T. Petersen (ed.), *Convergences: Transactions in Reading and Writing* (pp. 163–178). Urbana, IL: National Council of Teachers of English (NCTE).

Sutcliffe, A., Fickas, S., Sohlberg, M. M., and Ehlhardt, L. A. (2003). Investigating the usability of assistive user interfaces. *Interacting with Computers, 15*(4), 577–602.

Sutherland, R., Armstrong, V., Barnes, S., Brawn, R., Breeze, N., Gall, M., Matthewman, S., Olivero, F., Taylor, A., Triggs, P., Wishart, J., and John, P. (2004). Transforming teaching and learning: Embedding ICT into everyday classroom practices. *Journal of Computer Assisted Learning, 20*(6), 413–425.

Sutherland, R., Robertson, S., and John, P. (2004). Interactive education: Teaching and learning in the information age. *Journal of Computer Assisted Learning, 20*(6), 410–412.

Svensson, M., and Höök, K. (2003). Social navigation of food recipes: Designing Kalas. In K. Höök, D. Benyon, and A. J. Munro (eds.), *Designing Information Spaces: The Social Navigation Approach* (pp. 201–222). London: Springer.

Swarts, H., Flower, L. S., and Hayes, J. R. (1984). Designing protocol studies of the writing process: An introduction. In R. Beach and L. S. Bridwell (eds.), *New Directions in Composition Research* (pp. 53–71). London: Guilford.

Sweller, J. (2005). Implications for cognitive load theory for multimedia learning. In R. E. Mayer (ed.), *The Cambridge Handbook of Multimedia learning* (pp. 19–30). Cambridge: Cambridge University Press.

Sweller, J., van Merriënboer, J. J. G., and Paas, F. G. W. C. (1998). Cognitive architecture and instructional design. *Educational Psychology Review, 10*(3), 251–296.

Taboada, M. (2004). The genre structure of bulletin board messages. *TEXT Technology, 13*(2), 55–82.

Tabs, E. D. (2003). *Distance Education at Degree-Granting Postsecondary Institutions: 2000–2001.* Washington, D.C.: National Center for Education Statistics.

Tallent-Runnels, M. K., Thomas, J. A., Lan, W. Y., Cooper, S., Ahern, T. C., Shaw, S. M., and Liu, X. (2006). Teaching courses online: A review of the research. *Review of Educational Research, 76*(1), 93–135.

Tancer, B. (2008). *Click: What Millions of People Are Doing Online and Why It Matters.* New York: Hyperion.

Tapscott, D. (1997). *The Digital Economy.* New York: McGraw-Hill.

Taylor, M. (2006). Generation NeXt comes to college: 2006 updates and emerging issues. In *A Collection of Papers on Self-Study and Institutional Improvement*, vol. 2 (pp. 48–55). Chicago: The Higher Learning Commission. Available online: http://www.taylorprograms.org/images/Gen_NeXt_article_HLC_06.pdf.

Taylor, P. J., and Blum, A. S. (1991). Ecosystems as circuits: Diagrams and the limits of physical analogies. *Biology and Philosophy, 6*(2), 275–294.

Thelwall, M. (2004). Digital libraries and multi-disciplinary research skills. *LIBRES: Library and Information Science Research Electronic Journal, 14*(2). Available online: http://libres.curtin.edu.au/libres14n2/index.htm.

Theofanos, M., and Quesenbery, W. (2005). Towards the design of effective formative test reports. *Journal of Usability Studies, 1*(1), 28–46.

Thimbleby, H. (2000). Calculators are needlessly bad. *International Journal of Human–Computer Studies, 52*(6), 1031–1069.

Thirunarayanan, M. O. (2006). Thoughteracy for all. *Ubiquity, 7*(5). Available online: http://www.acm.org/ubiquity/views/v7i05_thoughteracy.html.

Thomson, J. R., Greer, J., and Cooke, J. (2001). Automatic generation of instructional hypermedia with APHID. *Interacting with Computers, 13*(6), 631–654.

Tilson, R., Dong, J., Martin, S., and Kieke, E. (1998). Factors and principles affecting the usability of four E-commerce cites. In *Proceedings of the 4th Conference on Human Factors and the Web.* Basking Ridge, NJ: AT&T Labs. Available online: http://zing.ncsl.nist.gov/hfweb/att4/proceedings/tilson/index.html.

Tolmie, A., and Boyle, J. (2000). Factors influencing the success of computer mediated communication (CMC) environments in university teaching: A review and case study. *Computers and Education, 34*(2), 119–140.

Tomasello, M. (1995). Language is not an instinct. *Cognitive Development, 10*(1), 131–156.

Tomasi, M. D., and Mehlenbacher, B. (1999). Re-engineering online documentation: Designing examples-based online support systems. *Technical Communication, 46*(1), 55–66.

Tomlinson-Keasey, C. (2002). Becoming digital: The challenge of weaving technology throughout higher education. In S. Brint (ed.), *The Future of the City of Intellect: The Changing American University* (pp. 133–158). Stanford, CA: Stanford University Press.

Torraco, R. J. (1999). Integrating learning with working: A reconception of the role of workplace learning. *Human Resource Development Quarterly, 10*(3), 249–270.

Toulmin, S. (1958). *The Uses of Argument.* Cambridge: Cambridge University Press.

Tractinsky, N., Katz, A. S., and Ikar, D. (2000). What is beautiful is usable. *Interacting with Computers, 13*(2), 127–145.

Trenner, L., and Bawa, J. (eds.) (1998). *The Politics of Usability: A Practical Guide to Designing Usable Systems in Industry.* Berlin: Springer-Verlag.

Trouche, L. (2003). From artifact to instrument: Mathematics teaching mediated by symbolic calculators. *Interacting with Computers, 15*(6), 783–800.

Tu, C.-H., and Corry, M. (2003). Design, management tactics, and strategies in asynchronous learning discussions. *Quarterly Review of Distance Education, 4*(3), 303–315.

Tucker, A., and Wegner, P. (eds.) (1996). ACM 50th-anniversary symposium: Perspectives in computer science. *ACM Computing Surveys, 28*(1), 169–200.

Tufte, E. (1983). *The Visual Display of Quantitative Information*. Cheshire, CT: Graphics Press.

Tufte, E. (1990). *Envisioning Information*. Cheshire, CT: Graphics Press.

Tuomi-Gröhn, T., and Engeström, Y. (eds.) (2003a). *Between School and Work: New Perspectives on Transfer and Boundary-Crossing*. Kidlington, Oxford: Elsevier Science.

Tuomi-Gröhn, T., and Engeström, Y. (2003b). Conceptualizing transfer: From standard notions to developmental perspectives. In T. Tuomi-Gröhn and Y. Engeström (eds.), *Between School and Work: New Perspectives on Transfer and Boundary-Crossing* (pp. 19–38). Kidlington, Oxford: Elsevier Science.

Turkle, S. (1984). *The Second Self: Computers and the Human Spirit*. New York: Simon and Schuster.

Turkle, S. (1997). Seeing through computers: Education in a culture of simulation. *American Prospect, 8*(31). Available online: http://www.prospect.org/cs/articles?article=seeing_through _computers_3197.

Turkle, S. (1998). Cyborg babies and cy-dough-plasm: Ideas about life in the culture of simulation. In R. Davis-Floyd and J. Dumit (eds.), *Cyborg Babies: From Technosex to Technotots*. New York: Routledge.

Turkle, S. (1999). What are we thinking about when we are thinking about computers? In M. Biagioli (ed.), *The Science Studies Reader* (pp. 543–552). New York: Routledge.

Turner, J. W., and Reinsch, N. L., Jr. (2007). The business communicator as presence allocator: Multicommunicating, equivocality, and status at work. *Journal of Business Communication, 44*(1), 36–58.

Tyack, D. B. (1974). *The One Best System: A History of American Urban Education*. Cambridge, MA: Harvard University Press.

Tynjälä, P., and Häkkinen, P. (2005). E-learning at work: Theoretical underpinnings and pedagogical challenges. *Journal of Workplace Learning, 17*(5/6), 318–336.

Ubiquitous Conversations. (2005). *Ubiquity, 6*(45), December 7–13. Available online: http://www .acm.org/ubiquity/views/v6i48_ubcon.html.

Ummelen, N. (1997). *Procedural and Declarative Information in Software Manuals: Effects on Information Use, Task Performance, and Knowledge*. Amsterdam: Rodopi.

Unsworth, J. (1997). Documenting the reinvention of text: The importance of failure. *Journal of Electronic Publishing, 3*(2). Available online: http://quod.lib.umich.edu/cgi/t/text/text-idx?c =jep;view=text;rgn=main;idno=3336451.0003.201.

Unsworth, J. (2000). Scholarly primitives: What methods do humanities researchers have in common, and how might our tools reflect this? Talk given at Humanities Computing Symposium: Formal Methods, Experimental Practice. London: King's College. Available online: http://www.iath.virginia.edu/~jmu2m/Kings.5-00/primitives.html.

U.S. Department of Commerce (2001). Age: 2000. *U.S. Census 2000 Brief.* Available online: http://www.census.gov/prod/2001pubs/c2kbr01-12.pdf.

U.S. Department of Commerce (2004). *A Nation Online: Entering the Broadband Age.* National Telecommunications and Information Administration (NTIA) Report. Available online: http://www.ntia.doc.gov/reports/anol/index.html.

U.S. Department of Labor (2006). *American Time Use Survey: Leisure and Sports Activities.* Bureau of Labor Statistics Report. Available online: http://www.bls.gov/tus/charts/leisure.htm.

Vaezi-Nejad, S. M., and Olabiran, Y. (2005). Telematics education II: Teaching, learning and assessment at foundation level. *International Journal of Electrical Engineering Education, 42*(2), 147–163.

van Dam, A. (1987). Keynote address. In S. Weiss and M. Schwartz (eds.), *Proceedings of ACM Hypertext '87 Conference.* New York: ACM Press. Available online: http://www.cs.brown.edu/memex/HT_87_Keynote_Address.html.

van den Hooff, B., Elving, W., Meeuwsen, J. M., and Dumoulin, C. (2003). Knowledge sharing in knowledge communities. In M. Huysman, E. Wenger, and V. Wulf (eds.), *Communities and Technologies* (pp. 119–141). Boston: Kluwer Academic Publishers.

van der Aalsvoort, G. M., and Harinck, F. J. H. (2000). Studying social interaction in instruction and learning: Methodological approaches and problems. In H. Cowie and G. M. van der Aalsvoort (eds.), *Social Interaction in Learning and Instruction: The Meaning of Discourse for the Construction of Knowledge* (pp. 5–20). Kidlington, Oxford: Elsevier Science.

van der Meij, H., and Carroll, J. M. (1995). Principles and heuristics for designing minimalist instruction. *Technical Communication, 42*(2), 243–262.

van Eijl, P. J., Pilot, A., and de Voogd, P. (2005). Effects of collaborative and individual learning in a blended learning environment. *Education and Information Technologies, 10*(1/2), 49–63.

van Merriënboer, J. J. G., and Kester, L. (2005). The four-component instructional design model: Multimedia principles in environments for complex learning. In R. E. Mayer (ed.), *The Cambridge Handbook of Multimedia Learning* (pp. 71–93). Cambridge: Cambridge University Press.

van Merriënboer, J. J. G., and Sweller, J. (2005). Cognitive load theory and complex learning: Recent developments and future directions. *Educational Psychology Review, 17*(2), 147–177.

Vanderheiden, G., and Zimmerman, G. (2002). State of the science: Access to information technologies. In J. M. Winters, C. Robinson, R. Simpson, and G. Vanderheiden (eds.), *Emerging and Accessible Telecommunications, Information, and Healthcare Technologies* (pp. 152–184). Arlington, VA: RESNA Press. Available online: http://trace.wisc.edu/docs/2002SOS-Report-IT/index.htm.

Veldof, J. R. (2003). Usability tests. In E. A. Dupuis (ed.), *Developing Web-Based Instruction: Planning, Designing, Managing, and Evaluating for Results* (pp. 129–146). New York: Neal-Schuman.

Venkatesh, V., and Speier, C. (2000). Creating an effective training environment for enhancing telework. *International Journal of Human-Computer Studies, 52*(6), 991–1005.

Vera, A. H., and Simon, H. A. (1993). Situated action: A symbolic interpretation. *Cognitive Science, 17*(1), 7–48.

Verbeek, P.-P. (2005). *What Things Do: Philosophical Reflections on Technology, Agency, and Design.* University Park, PA: Penn State University Press.

Voithofer, R. (2005). Designing new media education research: The materiality of data, representation, and dissemination. *Educational Researcher, 34*(9), 3–14.

von Hippel, E., and von Krogh, G. (2003). Open source software and the "private-collective" innovation model: Issues for organizational science. *Organization Science, 14*(2), 209–223.

Vosniadou, S. (1996). Towards a revised cognitive psychology for new advances in learning and instruction. *Learning and Instruction, 6*(2), 95–109.

Vosniadou, S., De Corte, E., Glaser, R., and Mandl, H. (1996). *International Perspectives on the Design of Technology-Supported Learning Environments.* Mahwah, NJ: Lawrence Erlbaum.

Voss, J. F., Greene, T. R., Post, T. R., and Penner, B. C. (1983). Problem solving skill in the social sciences. In G. H. Bower (ed.), *The Psychology of Learning and Motivation: Advances in Research Theory* (vol. 17, pp. 165–213). New York: Academic Press.

Vygotsky, L. S. (1978). *Mind in Society: The Development of Higher Psychological Processes.* Cambridge, MA: Harvard University Press.

W3C (2006). *Web Content Accessibility Guidelines 2.0.* Available online: http://www.w3.org/TR/WCAG20/.

Wachter, C. J., and Kelly, J. R. (1998). Exploring VCR use as a leisure activity. *Leisure Sciences, 20*(3), 213–227.

Wagner, E. D. (2006). On designing interaction experiences for the next generation of blended learning. In C. J. Bonk and C. R. Graham (eds.), *The Handbook of Blended Learning: Global Perspectives, Local Designs* (pp. 41–55). San Francisco, CA: Pfeiffer.

Wajcman, J. (1991). *Feminism Confronts Technology.* University Park, PA: Penn State University Press.

Waldstein, M. (2005). The politics of the Web: The case of one newsgroup. *Media Culture and Society, 27*(5), 739–763.

Wallace, D. R., and Weiner, S. T. (1998). How might classroom time be used given WWW-based lectures? *Journal of Engineering Education, 87*(3), 237–248.

Wallace, R. M. (2003). Online learning in higher education: A review of research on interactions among teachers and students. *Education Communication and Information*, *3*(2), 241–280.

Walther, J. B., and Bunz, U. (2005). The rules of virtual groups: Trust, liking, and performance in computer-mediated communication. *Journal of Communication*, *55*(4), 828–846.

Walton, D. (1999). The appeal to ignorance, or *Argumentum Ad Ignorantiam*. *Argumentation*, *13*(4), 367–377.

Wang, H., and Gearhart, D. L. (2006). *Designing and Developing Web-Based Instruction*. Upper Saddle River, NJ: Pearson Education.

Wang, S.-K., and Yang, C. (2005). The interface design and the usability testing of a fossilization Web-based learning environment. *Journal of Science Education and Technology*, *14*(3), 305–313.

Wang, Y.-M., and Artero, M. (2005). Caught in the Web: University student use of Web resources. *Educational Media International*, *42*(1), 71–82.

Ward, G., and Maylor, E. A. (2005). Age-related deficits in free recall: The role of rehearsal. *Quarterly Journal of Experimental Psychology*, *58A*(1), 98–119.

Ward, M., and Sweller, J. (1990). Structuring effective worked examples. *Cognition and Instruction*, *7*(1), 1–39.

Ware, C. (1997). Output devices and techniques. In A. B. Tucker, Jr. (ed.), *The Computer Science and Engineering Handbook* (pp. 1512–1530). Boca Raton, FL: CRC Press.

Warschauer, M. (2002). Reconceptualizing the Digital Divide. *First Monday*, *7*(7). Available online: http://firstmonday.org/htbin/cgiwrap/bin/ojs/index.php/fm/article/view/967/888.

Web-Based Education Commission (2000). *The Power of the Internet for Learning: Moving from Promise to Practice*. Report of the Web-Based Education Commission to the President and the Congress of the United States. Washington, DC. Available online: http://www.ed.gov/offices/AC/WBEC/FinalReport/index.html.

Weber, S. (2003). Boundary-crossing in the context of intercultural learning. In T. Tuomi-Gröhn and Y. Engeström (eds.), *Between School and Work: New Perspectives on Transfer and Boundary-Crossing* (pp. 157–177). Kidlington, Oxford: Elsevier Science.

Webster, J., and Ho, H. (1997). Audience engagement in multimedia presentations. *ACM SIGMIS Database*, *28*(2), 63–77.

Weeks, L. (2007). The eye generation prefers not to read all about it. *Washingtonpost.com*, July 6, C02. Available online: http://www.washingtonpost.com/wp-dyn/content/article/2007/07/05/AR2007070502055.html.

Weinberger, D. (2007). *Everything Is Miscellaneous: The Power of the New Digital Disorder*. New York: Time.

Weiss, R. M. (2000). Taking science out of organization science: How would postmodernism reconstruct the analysis of organizations? *Organization Science, 11*(6), 709–731.

Wenger, M. S., and Ferguson, C. (2006). A learning ecology model for blended learning from Sun Microsystems. In C. J. Bonk and C. R. Graham (eds.), *The Handbook of Blended Learning: Global Perspectives, Local Designs* (pp. 76–91). San Francisco, CA: Pfeiffer.

Wenzel, G. (1998–2009). *Museum of Pocket Calculating Devices.* Available online: http://www.calculators.de/.

Westamp, M. (2004). *Newsmap.* Available online: http://marumushi.com/apps/newsmap/newsmap.cfm.

Whitburn, M. D. (2000). *Rhetorical Scope and Performance: The Example of Technical Communication.* Stamford, CT: Ablex.

Wiens, G., and Gunter, G. A. (1998). Delivering effective instruction via the Web. *Educational Media International, 35*(2), 95–99.

Wiggins, G. P., and McTighe, J. (1997). *Understanding by Design.* Alexandria, VA: Association for Supervision and Curriculum Development.

Wilder, H., and Ferris, S. P. (2006). Communication technology and the evolution of knowledge. *Journal of Electronic Publishing, 9*(2). Available online: http://quod.lib.umich.edu/cgi/t/text/text-idx?c=jep;view=text;rgn=main;idno=3336451.0009.201.

Williams, J. R. (2004). *Developing Performance Support for Computer Systems: A Strategy for Maximizing Usability and Learnability.* Boca Raton, FL: CRC Press.

Williams, R. (1981). Communications technologies and social institutions. In R. Williams (ed.), *Contact: Human Communication* (pp. 225–238). Cambridge: Thames and Hudson.

Wilson, M. R., and Krapfl, C. M. (1994). The impact of graphics calculators on students' understanding of function. *Journal of Computers in Mathematics and Science Teaching, 13*(3), 252–260.

Winiecki, D. J. (2003). Instructional discussions in online education: Practical and research-oriented perspectives. In M. G. Moore and W. G. Anderson (eds.), *Handbook of Distance Education* (pp. 193–215). Mahwah, NJ: Lawrence Erlbaum.

Winn, W. (2003). Learning in artificial environments: Embodiment, embeddedness, and dynamic adaptation. *Technology, Instruction, Cognition, and Learning, 1*(1), 87–114.

Winn, W. (2004). Cognitive perspectives in psychology. In D. H. Jonassen (ed.), *Handbook of Research on Educational Communications and Technology* (2nd ed., pp. 79–112). Mahwah, NJ: Lawrence Erlbaum.

Winner, L. (1995). Political ergonomics. In R. Buchanan and V. Margolin (eds.), *Discovering Design: Explorations in Design Studies* (pp. 146–170). Chicago: University of Chicago Press.

Winograd, T. A. (2006). Designing a new foundation for design. *Communications of the ACM,* *49*(5), 71–73.

Winograd, T. A., and Flores, F. (1986). *Understanding Computers and Cognition: A New Foundation for Design.* Norwood, NJ: Ablex.

Wisher, R. A., and Curnow, C. K. (2003). Video-based instruction in distance learning: From motion pictures to the Internet. In M. G. Moore and W. G. Anderson (eds.), *Handbook of Distance Education* (pp. 315–330). Mahwah, NJ: Lawrence Erlbaum.

Witmer, B. G., Jerome, C. J., and Singer, M. J. (2005). The factor structure of the presence questionnaire. *Presence, 14*(3), 298–312.

Wizemann, T. M., and Pardue, M.-L. (eds.) (2001). *Exploring the Biological Contributions to Human Health: Does Sex Matter?* Washington, D.C.: National Academy Press.

Wolfe, J, (2000). Gender, ethnicity, and classroom discourse. *Written Communication, 17*(4), 491–519.

Woodall, J. (2004). The rhetoric of new technology and instructional design. *Human Resource Development International, 7*(3), 291–294.

Woods, R. H., Jr., and Baker, J. D. (2004). Interaction and immediacy in online learning. *International Review of Research in Open and Distance Learning, 5*(2). Available online: http://www.irrodl .org/index.php/irrodl/article/view/186/268.

Wooley, B. (1992). *Virtual Worlds: A Journey in Hype and Hyperreality.* New York: Penguin.

Yang, Y., and Cornelious, L. F. (2005). Preparing instructors for quality online instruction. *Online Journal of Distance Learning Administration, 8*(1). Available online: http://www.westga.edu/ %7Edistance/ojdla/spring81/yang81.htm.

Younglove-Webb, J., Gray, B., Abdalla, C. W., and Thurow, A. P. (1999). The dynamics of multidisciplinary research teams in academia. *Review of Higher Education, 22*(4), 425–440.

Zaccai, G. (1995). Art and technology: Aesthetics redefined. In R. Buchanan and V. Margolin (eds.), *Discovering Design: Explorations in Design Studies* (pp. 3–12). Chicago: University of Chicago Press.

Zaharias, P. (2004a). A usability evaluation method for e-learning courses. Unpublished dissertation. Athens, Greece: Athens University of Economics and Business.

Zaharias, P. (2004b). Usability and e-learning: The road towards integration. *ACM eLearn, 2004* (6), 4.

Zane, T., and Frazier, C. G. (1992). The extent to which software developers validate their claims. *Journal of Research on Computing in Education, 24*(3), 410–419.

Zeven, P. (2006). Do people need the gizmos we're selling? *c|net NEWS.com,* December 18. Available online: http://news.cnet.com/Do%20people%20need%20the%20gizmos%20were%20selling/ 2010-1041_3-6144335.html.

Zhu, X., and Simon, H. A. (1987). Learning mathematics from examples and by doing. *Cognition and Instruction, 4*(3), 137–166.

Ziefle, M., and Bay, S. (2005). How older adults meet complexity: Aging effects on the usability of different mobile phones. *Behaviour and Information Technology, 24*(5), 375–389.

Zimbardo, P., and Boyd, J. (2008). *The Time Paradox: The New Psychology of Time That Will Change Your Life.* New York: Free Press.

Zimmerman, B. J. (2002). Becoming a self-regulated learner: An overview. *Theory into Practice, 41*(2), 64–70.

Ziv, A., Ben-David, S., and Ziv, M. (2005). Simulation based medical education: An opportunity to learn from errors. *Medical Teacher, 27*(3), 193–199.

Author Index

Subject Index